INDIAN PREHISTORIC ARCHAEOLOGICAL ANTHROPOLOGY

By the same author

- ★ Sampreshanatmak Manavashastra
- ★ Chikitsatmak Manavashastra
- ★ Bharatiya Pragaitihasik Puratatvik Manavashastra
- ★ Neo Anthropological Theory
- ★ Bio-Cultural Evolution
- ★ Jaivik-Sanskritik Udvikasa
- ★ Social-Cultural Anthropology
- ★ Developmental Anthropology
- ★ Anthropological Research Methodology

About the Author

Gaya Pandey (*b.* 1954) is one of Senior faculties in the Department of Anthropology, Ranchi University, Ranchi, Jharkhand. After getting a First class M.Sc. degree in Anthropology, Ranchi University, Ranchi, he joined as a Doctoral Research Fellow in A.N. Sinha Institute of Social Study, Patna, Bihar. As a Doctoral Fellow he wrote a field based doctoral dissertation on Bonded Labour System of Palamau. He was awarded doctoral degree by Ranchi University. After getting doctoral degree he joined in the Department of Anthropology in February 1985. Since then he is actively engaged in teaching and research programme of the Department. He has to his credit 3 dozen articles in journals and edited books of national and international repute. He has participated in two and half dozen seminars and has been in one and half dozen organizing committees of national and international seminar. He has published 25 books in Hindi and English version on different branches of Anthropology.

INDIAN PREHISTORIC ARCHAEOLOGICAL ANTHROPOLOGY

Gaya Pandey

CONCEPT PUBLISHING COMPANY PVT. LTD.
NEW DELHI - 110 059

ISBN-13 : 978-93-86682-34-5 (H.B.)
ISBN-13 : 978-93-86682-35-2 (P.B.)

First Published 2020

Published and Printed by

Concept Since 1974

Concept Publishing Company Pvt. Ltd.
A/15-16, Commercial Block, Mohan Garden
New Delhi-110059 (India)
T: 25351460, 25351794, *F*: 091-11-25357109
E: publishing@conceptpub.com, W: www.conceptpub.com

Cataloging in Publication Data--Courtesy: D.K. Agencies (P) Ltd. <docinfo@dkagencies.com>

Pandey, Gaya, 1954- **author.**
Indian prehistoric archaeological anthropology / Gaya Pandey.
pages cm
Includes bibliographical references and index.
ISBN 9789386682345 (HB)
ISBN 9789386682352 (PB)

1. Anthropology, Prehistoric--India. 2. Antiquities, Prehistoric--India. 3. Stone age--India. 4. Prehistoric people--India. I. Title.

LCC DS425.P36 2018 | DDC 934 23

Dedicated to

Mother: Smt. Ansuiya Devi, Wife: Smt. Indu Devi, Daughters: Sudha, Suman, Sarita and Anu, Son: Shekhar and Grandsons: Kushagra and Harshit, with all regards, respects, love and gratitude who have been always with me in completion of the book.

PREFACE

This book *Indian Prehistoric Archaeological Anthropology* is an academic attempt to bring all materials dealing with Indian Prehistoric Archaeological Cultures under one cover to extend help to students, scholars, teachers, and aspirants of competitive examinations in Indian expressions. This subject is taught at undergraduate and post-graduate level courses in Anthropology in different Universities of India. The aspirants who opt Anthropology in competitive examinations also have to study this subject. There are a number of books in English medium on this subject, but they do not provide informations as per the syllabus. Therefore, students of Anthropology have to face a great problem. Keeping this problem in mind an attempt has been made to present cultures of our those ancestors who were hunters, gatherers, cave dwellers, shifting cultivators, agriculturists and leading their lifestyle with the help of stone tools. But after neolithic revolution, they had started permanent village life. With the discovery of copper, bronze and iron, they laid the foundation of civilization in Indus Valley. Thus, Indian Prehistoric Archaeological Anthropology is very interesting branch of Anthropology dealing with cultures of our preliterate ancestors and describing them with the help of stone tools, copper tools, bronze tools, iron tools and potteries.

The author does not claim any new contribution in the field of Indian Prehistoric Archaeological Anthropology. Rather, informations provided in this book are based on books and papers written by great masters of Indian Prehistoric Archaeological Anthropology. Thus, the purpose of the book has been purely textual. Sometimes and somewhere the contributions of the great masters have been presented *in toto* to make description meaningful and authentic. All these have been done to extend help to readers by presenting all informations under one cover through simple English language and Indian expression.

This book achieved its success by help and cooperation extended by different persons at different levels and time. Hence, as author it is my pious duty to express some words to show respect and gratitude towards each person individually and collectively.

First of all I extend my sincere gratitude towards those great masters of Indian Prehistoric Archaeological Anthropology whose contributions in the form of books and articles have been proved as a boon in completion of the book.

I extend my thanks to all my colleagues of the Department of Anthropology who helped me much through their discussions and encouragement to accomplish this task as early as possible.

I am thankful to all U.G.C. Junior Research Fellows, Senior Research Fellows, Rajiv Gandhi fellows and M.Phil. and Ph.D. Research Scholars who made me aware of the problems they face on this subject as a reader. Their suggestions have proved beneficial for me in accomplishing this task.

I extend my thanks to Librarian of the Department of Anthropology who helped me much in providing valuable books and journals from the library of the Department.

My family members, mother Smt. Ansuiya Devi, wife Smt. Indu Devi, Daughters — Sudha, Suman, Sarita and Anu, Son — Shekhar and Grandsons — Kushagra Divyansh and Harshit Vatsa deserve special thanks who have extended every kind of help in completion of this book.

In am thankful to Sri Ashok Kumar Mittal, Managing Director, Concept Publishing Co. (P.) Ltd., New Delhi and his team members who took all care to print the hand written manuscript with meticulous care.

Gaya Pandey
Department of Anthropology
Ranchi University, Ranchi, Jharkhand

CONTENTS

List of Tables

List of Diagrams Showing River Site Sections

List of Maps Showing Cultural Sites

List of Figures of Tools, Potteries, House Types and Urban Centres

1

Indian Prehistoric Archaeological Anthropology: An Introduction

Indian Prehistoric Anchaeological Anthropology is that branch of anthropology which deals with the study of Indian prehistoric sites, prehistoric industries, prehistoric traditions and prehistoric culture chronologically and systematically. India is such a country which has yielded evidences of glacial and interglacial periods like Europe and America and at the same time evidences of pluvial and interpluvial periods like Africa. It is clear that both types of prehistoric environments were available in our country during those prehistoric period of pleistocene.

From the researches of prehistoric sites of India, it is clear that Northern India had witnessed Ice ages and Inter-Ice ages like prehistoric Europe and America. But researches done till date also make it clear that in our country human beings left their evidences of habitation belonging to first and second Interglacial periods. These evidences are lower Palaeolithic pebble tools of Soan culture. The name Soan culture has been done on the basis of a small River Soan situated in the State of Punjab. The pebble tools of Soan culture look like tools of entire old world (Africa, Europe and China) in shape and size. But no human remains have been found along with these tools in India. Elsewhere in the world, the credit of establishing these industries goes to primitive anthropoid types. For example, Jinjanthropus and Homohabilis of Africa, Pithecanthropus erectus of Jawa and Sinanthropus of Peking.

In Southern lower Palaeolithic India, an another prehistoric stone industry was flourishing which was probably contemporary to Soan industry. The man of this culture had built core tool. They used to make core tools by taking out flakes from the core in beautiful manner. The man of this culture had more control over technique of tool production than man of Soan culture. This culture is known as Madrasian culture and the industry is known as Madras industry. The core tools of Madras culture show similarity with tools of Africa, Western Europe and England. Elsewhere in the world such core tools have been reported with more Advanced human type known as *Homo sapiens*.

The Ganga Valley is one of the newest geological layers. Geologists believe that during those days when Soan and Madras industries were flourishing, Ganga Valley was like a shallow sea. But there were contacts between both industries through Rajasthan. The tools of one industry have been found in more number in the areas of another industry. The mankind who used tools of these lower Palaeolithic culture would have lived in India for lakhs of year. But who were they and what happened to them, nothing can be said with certainty. But there is no doubt that their blood is following generation after generation even today. If the builders of Soan culture would have been proto-anthropoid type, they would have become extinct like Java Man, Peking man, and Neauderthal man. The existence of *Homo sapiens* continued. The evolution of *Homo sapiens* in India would have occurred in late part of upper-palaeolithic period like other places of the world. The descendants of *Homo sapiens* would have developed their technological knowledge and fashioned microlithic tools from microliths. The evidences of microliths have been reported from every part of India. In Deccan area microlithic tools have been found along with polished stone axes. The researches done in this area bear testimony that use of microlithic tools was replaced by iron tools during Christian era.

Palaeolithic and microlithic men was hunter and gatherer. They lived in caves nearby water sources. Thev lived in small bands. They had discovered fire. They used to hide their body with skin and leaves. In this way, like other parts of the globe man lived in India for lakhs of year.

During geological holocene period around 8,000 B.C. – 6,000 B.C., a drastic change in the life of mankind tool place. The hunters began to domesticate animals. The gatherers became agriculturist. The cave dwellers became house dwellers. The band dwellers became village dwellers. The mankind invented pottery, clothes and megalithic culture. They polished their stone tools. Thus, mankind gave birth to revolution during neolithic period. That is why neolithic period is known as revolution.

The tools fashioned by neolithic man was certainly superior to palaeolithic and mesolithic man in technology and efficiency. Neolithic tools have been reported from all parts of India. But majority of tools have been reported from east-west and Deccan areas. Thus, neolithic culture flourished in India from thousands of years.

Evidences of settled village life and developed agriculture have been reported from 7th millennium B.C. in middle-east. In India evidences of settled village life have been reported from Baluchistan in the form of small agricultural villages belonging to 4th millennium B.C.

According to classical writers, when the Alexander, the Great had crossed Indus river (320 B.C.), the climate of Western India was very favourable for production. The river valley was very much fertile and the nearby forests were quite green. But, the climate of the area during 3000 years B.C. was quite different. The entire area was full of forests during those times. There were numerous elephants and rhinoceros in the forests. Fuel woods were available in plenty for making fire bricks. The elephants and rhinoceros used to get food and water in plenty from the forest. Baluchistan was full of rivers during those days. That is why a number of villages came in to existence in those days in Baluchistan. The agriculturists had made their villages in the valley of Baluchistan, Makran and lower Indus nearby fertile land.

In the early part of 3rd millennium B.C., Government in the form of organised system over a big area came into existence. With this development, civilization appeared in the Valley of Nyle, Euphratus and Indus. We have sufficient evidence about civilization of Mesopotamia and Egypt. The builders of those civilizations have left written evidences. But the writings of Indus Valley Civilization have not been deciphered satisfactorily till date. That is why Indus Valley Civilization is known as Protohistoric Civilization. Indus Valley Civilization was a mixture of stone age and metal age. Along with stone tools remains of copper and bronze tools have also been reported.

The advent of iron age brought technological and economic development in the history of mankind. The remains of Iron age have been reported from Baluchistan, north-west India, the plains between the rivers Ganga and Yamuna. According to prehistoric evidences, the Iron age came into existence in India in 1100 B.C.

From the above given accounts, it is quite clear that like other parts of the globe, Indian Prehistoric Archaeological culture has evolved through different stone ages and metal ages. They are as follows:

- Palaeolithic age — 1 million year – 10,000 B.C.
- Mesolithic age — 10,000 B.C. – 2,000 B.C.
- Neolithic age — 4,000 B.C. – 1,000 B.C.
- Pre-Harappa age — 2,700 B.C. – 2,400 B.C.
- Harappa age — 2,350 B.C. – 1,750 B.C.
- Copper age — 1,750 B.C. – 1,000 B.C.
- Iron age — 1,100 B.C. – 600 B.C.

Palaeolithic age is again divided into three:

- Lower Palaeolithic age — 1 million year – 50,000 B.C.
- Middle Palaeolithic age — 50,000 B.C. – 20,000 B.C.
- Upper Palaeolithic age — 20,000 B.C. – 10,000 B.C.

Tradition of Indian Prehistoric Archaeological Researches

European scholars were interested in researches of Indian prehistoric archaeological anthropology since 18th century. But prehistoric archaeological researches got recognition only after achievements of stone tools from the gravel of Somme Valley by Boucher-de-Perthes in 1874. He is regarded as founder of European prehistoric archaeological anthropology. The collection of stone tools from the gravel deposit of Somme Valley brought a revolutionary thought among the scholars to know more and more about the culture of prehistoric ancestors of mankind.

In India, it was Meadows Taylor who had discovered a neolithic tool from Ling Sugur in 1842 for the first time. An another scholar Le-Mesurier had obtained a polished stone tool in 1860. But credit of establishing Indian prehistoric archaeological anthropology goes to Robert Bruce Foote. He was a geologist of Geological Survey of India. He had discovered a true Palaeolithic tool from laterite gravel of a place Pallavaram of Tamil Nadu in 1865. He started his work in 1863 and stayed in India for 40 years. He surveyed the different parts of the country and made a huge collection of stone tools. His collections have been preserved in Madras Museum even today. He is regarded as founder of Indian prehistoric archaeological anthropology. Robert Bruce Foote along with his associate Willium King had obtained Palaeolithic tools in Attirampakkam from gravel layer of Kortalayer Valley and Narnavaram near Chennai (Tamil Nadu).

An another scholar Wynne had obtained an agate flake in Hyderabad near Pathan on the bank of river Godavari. In 1873, a scholar named Hacket had obtained a quartzite hand-axe associated with fossilized mammal.

When Robert Bruce Foote was busy in collection of prehistoric tools in Chennai (Tamil Nadu), Karnataka, Andhra Pradesh and Gujarat, a scholar named Ball was engaged in collection of tools in Orissa. An another scholar Cockburn was busy in collection of stone tools from southern Uttar Pradesh.

He had done work in Singrauli basin and Kon block. He had also surveyed Banda and Khasi hill areas of Assam. The credit of discovering an ideal site of Singrauli basin goes to Cockburn. He had obtained stone tools from gravel deposit on Talchir rocks. He had named these tools as Axe head, Celt or Rude flake. By these names he meant the same what we mean today as Hand axe. He had also obtained fossils from the village Gaharwar nearby Singrauli basin. He had also discovered rock painting with the help of a scholar Karlayal.

Like Sir John Evance, Robert Bruce Foote had also imagined about a Hiatus. He had attempted to understand this Hiatus (the end of Palaeolithic period and beginning of Neolithic period) on

Sabarmati river on the basis of geological sections. There was a great change in the layers of Palaeolithic and Neolithic tools. He had obtained microlithic tools along with neolithic tools. Karlayal had also reported about the existence of microlithic tools from Mirzapur and Rewan on Vindhya hills in open space and rockshelters.

After Robert Bruce Foote and his contemporary scholars, significant contributions in Indian prehistoric archaeological anthropology were made by Cammiade and Richards. In true sense, they have revitalised Indian prehistoric archaeological anthropology after a long gap. They had made a huge collection of palaeolithic tools from Andhra Pradesh and Tamil Nadu. Their entire collection was studied by M.C. Burkilt. Burkilt had published an essay in this regard with the help of Cammiade. Burkilt and Cammiade had divided all palaeolithic tools into four series:

- In series I, they had placed hand axe and cleaver.
- In series II, they had put flakes and developed hand axe.
- In series III, they had placed blades, burin and scrapers.
- In series IV, they had placed microlithic tools.

All series of tools were related to different strata. They had attempted to correlate the environmental change during pleistocene in India with environmental change of Africa through pluvial and interpluvial periods. It was an important step in Indian prehistoric archaeological anthropology. In order to examine the conclusion of Burkitt and Cammiade, Cammiade and Richards haa recollected tools from the Madras region. On the basis of their new collection of tools, they had published an essay in 1932 to confirm the conclusion of first essay.

The year 1932 brought a definite status in the study of Indian prehistoric archaeological anthropology. In this year, all previous resistances related to study were not only ended, but the study in Indian prehistoric archaeological anthropology was started with new energy. In the year 1932, DeTerra had collected stone tools from Himalayan region. DeTerra had also examined the collection of Todd and Wadia, scholars of Geological Survey of India. On the basis of his examination, he had opined that the pluvial and interpluvial periods of South India can be correlated with glacial and interglacial periods of North India. In order to test his hypothesis, he had planned a full developed expedition which was named as Cambridge-Yale expedition. DeTerra was director of this expedition. The other members of the expedition were Tilhard de Chardin and T.D. Paterson. These three scholars had made a survey of Kashmir Valley, from Punchh to Kashmir and Salt hill areas situated in middle of Jhelum to understand the pleistocene stratigraphy in Indian context. It was really a great achievement for Indian prehistoric archaeological anthropology. DeTerra had also made survey in Narmada Valley.

DeTerra and his associates had made micro-study of different strata of pleistocene. They had correlated the deposits of nearest hills and plains with pleistocene deposits. Different glacial periods had influenced the Himalayas and its neighbouring areas. Where glacial periods were not in existence, their effects were studied in the form of river terraces because river terraces were the habitation sites of mankind. DeTerra and his associates had chosen Siwalik ranges because stone tools were available from these areas.

Yale-Cambridge expedition had made a detailed study of pleistocene deposits of northern India. But there was still lack in all-India level knowledge in this regard. It was because this expedition team had not made any study of pluvial and interpluvial periods of south India. Therefore, an all-India knowledge regarding pleistocene was incomplete. It was also necessary to correlate the pleistocene deposits of north India with pleistocene deposits of south India. In order to remove these weaknesses, the Yale-Cambridge expedition made a study of Narmada Valley in central India. Stone tools and fossils were reported from the Narmada Valley. That is why this area was also very much important from the point of view of Indian prehistoric archaeological anthropology.

DeTerra and Paterson had obtained prehistoric tools from three deposits of Narmada Valley. From the basal gravel of lower group, DeTerra had obtained tools like pre Soan industry such as big flakes, Abbevillian and Acheulian hand axe, cleaver, core and flakes. Taking these tools as evidence, DeTerra had correlated the gravel of lower group with first Terrace T_1. The deposit of Pink concretionary clay over lower group gravel was correlated with the Terrace T_2. The gravel of upper group was correlated with the Terrace T_3. The clay deposit over it was correlated with Terrace T_4. The Regur or Cotton soil deposit over the pleistocene deposit of upper group was correlated with the Terrace T_5. From the gravel and sand deposit, DeTerra and Tilhard had obtained tools of microlithic in which there were plenty of small blades and scrapers.

DeTerra and Tilhard had also worked in Kortalayer Valley of south India. Here, they had obtained Abbevillian to advanced Acheulian tools from three terraces.

By the year 1935-36, the outline of Indian lower palaeolithic culture was clearly framed. From the continuous efforts of DeTerra and his associates, this fact came to light that during lower Palaeolithic period two distinct types of cultures were flourishing. They were Soanian culture in north India and Madrasian culture in south India. In Soanian culture there was prevalence of pebble choper-choping tool tradition and in Madrasian culture there was prevalence of core hand axe-clever tradition. The spread of Soan culture was in north-west India and the spread of Madrasian culture was in south India. In central India, there was prevalence of both types of tool traditions.

In the year 1940-41, a new personality emerged in the study of prehistoric archaeological anthropology in India. His name was H.D. Sankalia. Under his dedication and commitment Deccan College, Pune became the chief centre of prehistoric archaeological anthropology. Sankalia had started his work of prehistoric archaeological interests in the area of Gujarat and Kathiawad. He had obtained microlithic tools from a place Nanded Madhameshwar on the bank of river Godavari. Following Robert Bruce Foote, he had made a survey of Sabarmati Valley.

At the same time, N.K. Bose and Dharni Sen of Calcutta University worked in the Burha Balang river valley of Mayurbhanj in Orissa. They had also done excavation in Kuliyana.

By the middle of 20th century, a good number of prehistoric sites were studied and their cultures were explored. As a result, a huge collection of prehistoric tools were made. But till now our knowledge in geo-chronology and environmental archaeology was quite insufficient. In order to bridge-up this gap of knowledge, an eminent professor of geo-chronology and environmental archaeology of London University, Professor Zeuner was invited by Archaeological Survey of India and Deccan College of Poona. During his stay in India Zeuner made a survey of Sabarmati, Mahi and Arsang rivers in Gujarat, Godavari river valley in Maharashtra, river Balia in Southern Uttar Pradesh, Mayurbhanj in Orissa, Malprabha Valley in Karnataka, Giddasur in Karnool and Teri in Tamil Nadu. Professor Zeuner had analysed geo-chronological deposits at all places. This survey under the leadership of Professor Zeuner led the publication of a number of research papers dealing with Indian prehistoric archaeological anthropology.

Professor G.R. Sharma of Allahabad University had made a survey of Singrauli Basin under the guidance of Professor Zeuner. Krishna Swamy of Archaeological Survey of India had also taken part in this survey of Balia river in Singrauli basin. In this survey, the site reported by Cockburn was re-examined. Prehistoric tools were also collected. They had obtained tools of both styles —Soanian and Madrasian from the Balia river of Singrauli basin. The prehistoric anthropological culture of this area was published by Krishna Swamy and Soundar Rajan in their papers.

Although, Giddalur site was explored and its prehistoric culture was studied by Burkitt and Cammiade for the first time. They had also established its geo-chronology with pluvial and interpluvial periods. Zeuner with the help of Krishna Swamy did survey of this area again. They had confirmed the conclusion of Burkitt and Cammiade. From Giddalur I, they had obtained tools belonging to series I and II. In their collection pebble tool and Clactonian flake were also found along with Acheulian-Abbevillian bifacial industry. Abbevillian and Acheulian industry was also found from Giddalur II, but their sizes were comparatively small. Tools were influenced by Levalloisean technique. Some burinate flakes and blade tools were also obtained. The entire collection seemed to be of upper-palaeolithic. These tools may be placed under series II and III of Cammiade and Burkitt. From Giddalur-II a number of microlithic tools were also found, which is known as Epi-palaeolithic-microlithic industries. In fact, Giddalur is one of the important sites of Indian palaeolithic culture. Here all cultures of different palaeolithic and mesolithic periods were found.

Professor Zeuner had done significant work in Teri site. He had done micro-study of eleven microlithic sites in Tuticorin and Tiruchenur Talukas. In order to know the scientific forms of these microlithic sites, he had made a modern geological study of seashore. After study he came to the conclusion that microlithic industry sites were more older than ancient weathering. They were related to higher level of present sea level. 20 to 30 feet high sea level was related to late monestrian or epimonestrian or post-glacial periods. According to him, in post-glacial Atlantic times or nearly 4,000 B.C., there would have been more Eustatic effect. His conclusion was that the dating of Teri site could be brought under pleistocene period. But this experiment ended with Zeuner.

In the later half of 20th century, the constructive period of Indian prehistoric archaeological anthropology has begun. Dr. Sankalia himself led a number of students to do researches on prehistoric cultures in different areas. Such type of step was initiated by Subba Roy in 1948, who under the guidance of Dr. Sankalia had studied the Palaeolithic culture of Bellary. Like Bellary, Malprabha Valley, Malwa, Orissa, Karnool, Rajasthan, Northern Bundelkhand, Son, Karuna, Nalgonda, Chithor, Kudappa, Middle Narmada Valley, and Mulamuchha valley Palaeolithic culture were studied scientifically.

By 1955-56, the clear knowledge about lower palaeolithic culture was brought to the light with the support of DeTerra, Paterson, Sankalia and his students. But besides hand axe, cleaver and scraper tools, an another industry was coming into light which showed the clear-cut impact of Levalloisean technique. Such types of tools were collected by Burkitt and Commiade in Karnool, Todd in Khandivli and Bombay, DeTerra and Paterson in Punjab and from cotton soil in Narmada valley. This industry was based on flakes. The chief tools of this industry were scraper, point, and blades. For making tools, good quality of stones were used. A clear-cut knowledge about this stratum and associated culture came after research done by Sankalia at Nevasa. Sankalia had obtained three stone industries in stratified deposits of Pravara river valley. He had divided these industries into three series — I, II and III. The tools of series I — hand axe, cleaver-scraper — were correlated with Ist aggradational period. The tools of series II — blade-flake-scraper — were correlated to IInd aggradational period. On the basis of this, Sankalia designated them as Middle palaeolithic, Banerjee as Nevasian, Subba Roy as Middle Stone Age and Mallick as blade-flake-scraper type.

After the exploration of Nevasa culture, the middle palaeolithic culture was recognised in Indian prehistoric archaeological anthropology.

An another scholar B.B. Lal had done survey and excavation of a site in Birbhanpur village located in Burdwan district of West Bengal. He had also done survey in Vyas and Banganga valleys in Punjab. He had obtained prepottery non-geometric microlithic industry. Such an independent microlithic industry site was not found elsewhere in our country. He had placed this industry in holocene period on the basis of chemical analysis of strata. In Vyas and Banganga valley he had obtained the blade tools of Soan styles.

Professor G.R. Sharma of Department of Ancient History, Allahabad University had worked with Zeuner in Singrauli basin of Mirzapur district in southern Uttar Pradesh. Professor Sharma had discovered a number of rockshelter paintings in Mirzapur. He had also discovered microlithic stone industry in Mirzapur. Radha Kant Verma had done his researches on palaeolithic culture of Mirzapur and submitted his thesis under the guidance of Professor G.R. Sharma. The survey of Mirzapur had explored a number of microlithic industries and rockshelter paintings. In order to solve the problem of paintings and microlithic industries, Verma had done excavation at two rockshelters. One at Morahana hill near Bhainsor village and another at Bagahikhor. His this excavation was very much important from the point of view of microlithic culture of Indian prehistoric archaeological anthropology. His excavations revealed that microlithic industries had evolved through four stages. The Ist stage was termed as prepottery non-geometric tool. The IInd stage was designated as geometric tool without pottery. The IIIrd stage was called as geometric tool with pottery and the IVth stage was known as microlithic tools. Such type of evolutionary sequence was not reported from anywhere in India. From the Bagahikhor rockshelter a human skeleton was also found along with tools.

B.D. Mishra had done excavation of an another rockshelter named Lekhahiya Sarai near Bhainsor village. This excavation had revealed materials belonging to eight chronological periods. Seventeen skeletons were discovered from this site. The excavations of both these rockshelter sites brought a clear understanding of mesolithic industry in India. Professor Sharma and his associates had done significant researches in Sidhi and Rewa district of Madhya Pradesh, Banda, Allahabad, Mirzapur and Banaras districts of Uttar Pradesh on palaeolithic culture.

In the period between 1965 to 1970, the most important research was done in Belan valley in Allahabad district. The research of Belan valley had yielded chronological evoluation of palaeolithic culture from lower palaeolithic period to mesolithic period. The chronological sequences of different cultural periods were established on the basis of stratified deposits in Belan valley. Such type of chronological cultural evidences have not been found in India till date.

Before the study of Belan valley our knowledge about Indian prehistoric culture was confined only to lower Palaeolithic culture and middle palaeolithic culture. The concept of Upper palaeolithic was not known. Scholars were of view that evolution of microlithic industry would have taken place from Levalloisean industry. In an international conference organised at Delhi in 1961 on Archaeology of Asia, it was resolved that Indian prehistoric culture has evolved like African prehistoric culture following prehistoric ages like Early stone age, Middle stone age and Late stone age. Later on, some scholars began to criticize it on the basis of evidences of upper palaeolithic culture.

In an International Seminar organised by Tata Institute of Fundamental Researches on "Radiocorbon and Indian Archaeology in 1971", the existence of Upper Palaeolithic culture was unanimously accepted. It was also unanimously resolved that Indian prehistoric culture can be studied through lower palaeolithic, middle palaeolithic, upper palaeolithic, mesolithic, neolithic, chalcolithic, bronze age and iron age periods.

Subject Matter of Indian Prehistoric Archaeological Anthropology

The subject matter of Indian Prehistoric Archaeological Anthropology are as follows:

- Physical Background of Prehistoric archaeological India.
- Pleistocene, Ice Age and Pluvial Age in India.
- Indian Lower Palaeolithic Culture.
- Indian Middle Palaeolithic Culture.
- Indian Upper Palaeolithic Culture.
- Indian Mesolithic Culture.
- Indian Neolithic Culture.
- Indian Megalithic and Burial Culture.
- Indian Prehistoric Art Culture.
- Pre-Harappa Culture.
- Harappa Culture (Indus Valley Civilization).
- Indian Chalcolithic Culture.
- Indian Iron Age Culture.

2

Physical Background of Prehistoric Archaeological India

In order to know prehistory, prehistoric mankinds and the culture of a country, it is essential to have knowledge of physical background. It is because physical condition has been controlling the culture and civilization of a region. There is no doubt that the climate has been influencing man in all periods. It has influenced man in past. It is influencing today and it will continue to influence in future. It is also true that with victory of man over natural forces, his dependency on nature has become less and less. But he has not become fully independent of natural forces. He is still dependent on nature and will continue to depend on it in future. During prehistoric ages — from lower palaeolithic period to mesolithic period, mankind was fully dependent on nature. He was not producer, rather he was consumer and parasite on nature. In these prehistoric ages of instability, nature controlled his life. Changes in nature had destroyed, transformed and decorated the life of mankind, during prehistoric period. That is why for the study of prehistoric culture knowledge about the then climate, environment and geographical condition is very pertinent.

Indian prehistoric archaeological anthropology deals with cultures of those societies who were illiterate. There is complete lack of written materials about culture and society of those mankind. Besides, the time spread of prehistory is so vast that it cannot be explained in solar years. It can be divided and explained only by geological era. The knowledge of geology makes us aware of not only chronology of culture and civilization, but also about geographical and climatic conditions. Indian prehistoric culture has been influenced by climate and physical condition in the same way as cultures of other places have been influenced by climate and geographical conditions.

India was such a place where was no one type of climate in prehistoric time. North-western India was influenced by glacial and interglacial environments, whereas South and Peninsular India was influenced by pluvial and interpluvial periods. The geological strata formed during glacial periods were different from geological strata formed during pluvial period. Thus, the knowledge of prehistoric archaeological anthropology is half without the knowledge of geological deposits. That is why it is the fitness of the thing to present here physical background of prehistoric archaeological India.

Physical Background of Prehistoric Archaeological India

India is located in the middle of 8° and 37° Northern latitude and 61° and 97° Eastern longitude. It is bounded by mountain King Himalayas in North, Hind Mahasagar in South, Bay of Bengal in East and Arabian Sea in West. From north to south its spread is 3200 km. This area is full of physical and climatic diversities. On the basis of physical form, stratigraphy and structure, entire India can be divided into three divisions, which are as follows:

- Peninsular India.
- Indo-Gangetic plain.
- Extra Peninsular India.

Peninsular India

The description of peninsular India can be presented as follows:

Mountain Hill Range

Mountain range is the oldest land mass of India. They are bounded by Vindhyan series in north, Hind Mahasagar in south, Bay of Bengal in east and Arabian Sea in west. Leaving coastal areas, mountains of these areas are of hard and permanent nature.

The chief mountain ranges of India are Eastern Ghat, Western Ghat, Satpura hill range and Vindhyan hill range.

Western Ghats

The hill ranges of Western Ghats are situated on Western ghat from Kanyakumari to Tapti Valley. At different places its height is 2,000 to 6,000 feet. The ranges of Western ghat and Eastern ghat meet in the south of Mysore. Here they are known as Nilgiri. Among peninsular Indian hill ranges, Nilgiri is the highest hill range. The maximum height of its top Doddabeta is 8,640 feet. Hill valley are slope. The ghats of Mysore and south Mumbai is known as Sahyadris.

Eastern Ghat

The hill ranges of Eastern ghat are different from the hill ranges of Western ghat. They are in separate ranges from Balasor to Nellor. Their spread is from Arcot and Salem to Nilgiri. The average height of these hills are 2,000 feet.

Satpura Hill Ranges

Satpura hill ranges are in the form of several parallel hill ranges in between rivers Narmada and Tapti. These hill ranges are extended from Rajpipala of Mumbai, Central India, northern Madhya Pradesh to south of Ganges in Bihar. Their chief hill ranges are Mahadev hills of Panchamarhi-Gondwana, Mechal hill range of Amarkantak and hills of Surguja, Ranchi, Hazaribagh and Monghyr which are archaean. Mahadev is the highest among all these hill ranges. Their height is 4,000 feet.

Vindhyan Hill Ranges

Vindhyan hill ranges are extended from north of Narmada valley to Indore, Bhopal and Satna in Madhya Pradesh, Banda, Allahabad, Mirzapur and Banaras in Utter Pradesh and south-eastern part of Bihar. The average height of Vindhya is 2,000 to 4,000 feet.

Arawali Hill Ranges

Arawali hill ranges extend from plain of Gujarat to Delhi in north-east direction. They cross the entire Rajputana.

Rivers

The chief rivers of Peninsular India are Mahanadi, Godavari, Krishna, Kaveri, Penner, Narmada and Tapti. In the northern part of peninsular chief rivers are Chambal, Betwa and Son. These rivers are flowing continuously since ancient times and they have formed their ghats. Majority of rivers have wide and shallow valleys. Narmada and Tapti flow from east to west, while other rivers flow from west to east. Narmada flows from rocky basin of pleistocene to alluvial deposit of holocene. Previously, it flew in south-west direction in Khandesh and met with the river Tapti. Later on, Narmada and Tapti made their own routes. The direction of flow of rivers Chambal, Betwa and Son is towards north.

Indo-Gangetic Plain

The Indo-Gangetic plain is situated in north of peninsular India. This part is different from other parts of India. It is wide and plain. The entire land mass is formed by alluvium deposits of rivers. The alluvium deposits consist of sand, silt and biological debris in the form of strata. Geologically, they belong to pleistocene and holocene. Ganga valley was formed due to rise of Himalayas. Due to rise of Himalayas, a deep gap was created in between Vindhya and Himalayas. The river Ganges and others rising from Himalayas had filled-up this deep gap by debris brought by them. They had provided it the present form. The important rivers of Indo-Gangetic plain are Ganga, Yamuna, Brahmaputra and Sindhu. Other rivers are their tributary.

Extra Peninsular India

It is the northern most part of Indo-Gangetic plain. The present form of this area has come into existence due to geological disturbances. Although old rocks are found in this area, but mountains belonging to Cambrian to early tertiary period are found in folded and faulted conditions due to tectonic movements. They are very thick. They are formed by stratified rocks. The southern most part of this area is formed by fresh water and saturnine deposits. It seems that they were formed during middle miocene and pliocene.

Hill Ranges

The land mass of extra peninsular India is still unstable. The tectonic movements are still continuously going on. Hills formed due to tictonic movements have not come into existence at the same time. But they all look semi-circular in north of Indo-Gangetic plain.

Different hill ranges of Himalayas can be divided into four main parts:

- Trans Himalayas.
- Great Himalayas.
- Middle Himalayas.
- Siwalik ranges.

Trans-Himalayas

These are the northern most hill ranges of Himalayas. Their width is 25 miles. They include valleys of those rivers which flow from north of Himalayas.

Great Himalayas

They are hill ranges of original Himalayas. They are always covered with ice. They are situated 128 km to 144 km north from the Indo-Gangetic plain. The original part of this hill range is very old and does not contain any animal remains. Its upper part is formed of stratified rocks.

Middle Himalayas

During miocene period second rise of Himalayas took place. Due to this, the great Himalayas went more up and middle Himalayas was formed. The hill ranges of this series are known as Little Himalayas. Their width is 64-80 km. They are situated at an average height of 10,000 feet. They have ice in some months of winter, but in other months they do not have ice.

This hill range consists of different types of stones of different periods. The core or original part of this hill range are formed of stones similar to peninsular India. Due to second rise of Himalayas and formation of little Himalayas, a narrow gap has been created between it and peninsular India. Over little Himalayas, a number of water currents flowing towards south meet and form a great river. This great river falls in Indus Valley crossing through Assam, Nainital, Shimla and Punjab. This great river gave rise to rivers Ganges, Brahmaputra and Sindhu. This great river was named as Siwalik river by a scholar Pilgrim.

Siwalik Ranges

The hill ranges between south of little Himalayas and north of Indus-Ganges are known as Siwalik ranges. This hill ranges extend from the plain of Bannu in west to Brahmaputra valley in east. This is known as exterior Himalayas. Its width is 8 to 48 km. Its average height is 3000 feet. There is no any rainfall over it. They are full of deep forest. They are folded, faulted and overthrust. These series are formed by debris, aelion, clay, soil and boulders. It is assumed that they were formed by materials established by great river Siwalik.

The different hill ranges of Himalayas in their present forms came in to existence during early middle pleistocene period. They were not so high previously. They were surrounded by forests and Siwalik was full of animals. The animal remains have been found in plenty. In the early middle pleistocene period, the third rise of Himalayas took place. As a result Siwalik valley was vanished. The Siwalik river got divided in the three — Ganga, Brahmaputra and Indus and the present forms of these rivers came into existence.

The extension of Siwalik hill ranges is from the north of Ganga-Indus valley to Brahmaputra valley. Hill ranges situated between below Rawalpindi and Jhelum rivers are known as Salt ranges. They form the southern boundary of Potwar plateau. Their direction is east-west. It is formed by different stones in different periods. Its highest top is 5010 feet. Above salt ranges, there are a number of *Jheels* whose water is sweet. The water of entire Potwar plateau fall in river Wahi. The rest water of this area falls in Soan river which meets Indus little above Kalabagh. The river Indus flows near Kalabagh cutting the salt ranges.

Potwar plateau is situated between Hajara ranges and Salt ranges. Its length is 240 km. and width is 96 km. Its average height is 1500 feet. This plateau is formed due to folded Siwalik deposits. The water of this area gets discharged in Indus, Soan and Jhelum rivers. The Potwar plateau gets narrowed at Kohat. There is alluvium deposit over it in plain of Bannu.

Structural Base

Prehistoric archaeological anthropology deals with origin and evolution of culture of prehistoric mankind. On the basis of geological evidences available to us, we cannot trace the origin of man not before quarternary period. For prehistoric anthropologists layers after tertiary period are more important. From this point of view, Siwalik occupies significant place. Prehistoric anthropological researches were done more in the area. Eminent geologist and archaeologist DeTerra, Tilhard de Chardin and T.T. Paterson had studied entire Siwalik deposits and archaeological materials scientifically.

Siwalik

The name Siwalik has been given after a hill named Siwalik near Haridwar. Siwalik is formed of sand stone, grit, boulder, pseudoboulder, clay and salt. Siwalik deposits are 15,000 feet to 17,000 feet thick. These deposits were influenced by folding and fault. Some early scholars believed that the deposit of Siwalik had taken place in different basins. But scholars like E.H. Pasci and G.E. Pilgrim were of view that the entire deposit was of a huge river which was known as Siwalik and which flew from Assam towards Siwalik hills. The study of Siwalik deposits provided us evidences about the then climatic conditions. The deposit of thick particles was done by river during pluvial periods. The deposit of thin particles was done by air during interpluvial period. According to this law, the deposits of lower Siwalik and middle Siwalik belonged to pluvial period. The deposit of Dhokpathan belonged to interpluvial period. The deposit of upper Siwalik was of pluvial period. In the last period, the climate began to be cooled which indicates that glaciation was to come in near future.

The Siwalik deposits have yielded a number of fossils belonging to plants and animals. Salt ranges and Potwar plateau were more significant from this point of view. The study of fossil remains suggest that during the periods of deposits, more plants and animals were in existence and they used to wander in different areas. The study also revels facts about origin, evolution and migration of animals. The deposits yielded 30 types of elephant, but now we have only one type of elephant. On the basis of study of fossils, the Siwalik deposits have been classified into different parts. Each part has its own characteristics. They are as follows:

- Upper Siwalik
- Middle Siwalik
- Lower Siwalik

Upper Siwalik

This deposit is 6,000 to 8,000 feet. For the purpose of study this deposit is again divided into three sub-parts. They are as follows:

- Boulder Conglomerate
- Pinjor Stage
- Tatrot Stage

Boulder Conglomerate

This is the upper most deposit of Upper Siwalik. It is formed of boulder conglomerate. Nothing can be said about the period of their formation. But DeTerra and Patterson had placed them in early middle pleistocene. They were formed during 2nd glacial period.

Pinjor Stage

This stage was named after a place Pinjor near Kalka. From this layer a number of fossils of animals have been discovered who were near ancestors of present-day animals. The fossils of Bos and

Equus have also been obtained which have been placed under Villafranchian animal group in Europe. According to DeTerra and Patterson, this layer belonged to lower pleistocene.

Tatrot Stage

This stage has been named after Tatrot. This layer is formed of soft sandstone and small pebbles. The fossils of Villafranchian animal groups have also been found from this layer. DeTerra and Patterson had placed this layer under lower pleistocene.

Middle Siwalik

This deposit is 6,000 to 8,000 ft. thick. It is divided into two main classes which are as follows:

- Dhokpathan
- Nagari

Dhokpathan Stage

This stage has been named after a place Dhokpathan situated on the bank of river Soan. This layer is formed by sandstone, orange colour silt and gravel. The layer has yielded the most number of fossils. DeTerra had placed it under upper pliocene.

Nagari Stage

This stage is formed of hard sandstone, soil stone and soil. This layer has yielded a good number of fossil remains of primates, Brahmapithecus, Sugrivapithecus and Shivapithecus. DeTerra and Patterson had placed this layer under middle miocene period.

Lower Siwalik

Lower Siwalik is also divided into three parts. They are as follows:

- Chinje
- Camlial
- Muree

Chinje Zone

This deposit is nearly 3,000 feet thick. It is made-up of light grey sandstone and red soil stones. A number of primate fossils have also been discovered from this layer. They are Dryopithecus, Brahmapithecus and Shivapithecus fossils. DeTerra has placed them in lower pliocene period.

Camlial Zone

This layer is formed by soil mixed hard red sandstones and gravel. DeTerra has placed it under upper miocene period.

Murre Zone

At many places Muree deposit was mixed with Camlial deposit in such a way that it is very difficult to isolate them. It has been placed under upper miocene period.

3

Pleistocene, Ice Age and Pluvial Age in India

The Cenozoic era has been divided into two geological periods. They are Tertiary and Quarternary. The geological period tertiary is again divided into Palaeocene, Eocene, Oligocene, Miocene and Pliocene. Each division has a number of sub-divisions. But we are not concerned with them. Because they deal with pre-human stages of man. Their evidences have been found in these deposits.

The Quarternary is the last of eras of life on the earth. It is divided into two epochs — Pleistocene and Holocene. As man has originated in Pleistocene period, so, it can be said that prehistory also began in Pleistocene. The environment of Pleistocene is closely related to cultural equipment and way of life of man. Pleistocene period began about 3-4 million years ago anywhere in the world and continued till 10,000 B.C., when Holocene epoch began and is continuing till date.

The beginning of Pleistocene epoch is marked by a drastic change in the environment. The homogenous warm climatic conditions characteristics of pre-Pleistocene epoch were no more seen in Pleistocene epoch. Pleistocene epoch was marked by Arctic ice region, temperate Europe and warmth Africa. During Pleistocene climatic change from warmth to cold and *vice versa* were noticed. Due to this climatic variation, Pleistocene period is known as ice age.

During pleistocene epoch two kinds of climatic changes were occurring in the world. Arctic region, Europe and America were witnessing the ice ages, while Africa was witnessing the pluvial ages. In between ice ages, there were interglacial periods. Similarly in between pluvial periods, there were interpluvial periods. The glacial and pluvial periods have been correlated. Similarly, interglacial and interpluvial periods have also been correlated. The first, second, third and fourth glacial periods have been correlated to first, second, third and fourth pluvial periods respectively. In the same way, first, second and third interglacial periods have been correlated to first, second, third and interpluvial periods.

On the basis of stratigraphical arrangements of rocks in Alps mountains, four main advances of glaciations have been recognized by two scientists A. Penck and E. Bruckner. The four main advances of glaciations recognized by Penck and Bruckner are known as ice ages. They have been named as Gunj, Mindel, Riss and Wurm. These are widely adopted as ice ages of Pleistocene. These four ice ages were intervened by three periods of normal conditions. They were termed as interglacial periods. They were named as Gunj-Mindel, Mindel-Riss and Riss-Wurm.

In the beginning Pleistocene was stratified as lower Pleistocene, middle Pleistocene and upper Pleistocene. It was believed that Pleistocene began in Gunj glacial period. The pre-Gunj Villafranchian strata were believed to have belonged to Donau period. But on the basis of pollengrain evidences from southern Alps, it was felt that the climate was cold. So, the Donau period can be counted as beginning of Pleistocene. The inclusion of Donau period in Pleistocene brought five glacial periods — Donau, Gunj, Mindel, Riss and Wurm and four interglacial periods — Donau-Gunj,

Gunj-Mindel, Mindel-Riss and Riss-Wurm. Now, the concept of basal Pleistocene stratum was also developed.

When Europe and America were witnessing the periods of glaciations and interglaciations, Africa was witnessing the periods of pluviations and interpluviations. During Pleistocene, there was intense spread of ice sheets and cold in temperate zones. But in the tropical zones of Africa, there were heavy rain fall as indicated by heavy rains. On the basis of study of river terraces and evidences found in them, four pluvial and three interpluvial periods were recognized. The four pluvial periods are Kageran, Kamasian, Kanjeran and Gamblian. The three interglacial periods are — Kageran-Kamasian, Kamasian-Kanjeran and Kanjeran-Gamblian.

But when Donau was included in Pleistocene, five pluvial and four interpluvial periods were recognized. The five pluvial periods are: Donau, Kageran, Kamasian, Kanjeran and Gamblian. The four interpluvial periods are: Donau-Kageran, Kageran-Kamasian, Kamasian-Kanjeran and Kanjeran-Gamblian.

Table 3.1 shows Pleistocene Chronology of Europe and Africa.

Table 3.1: Pleistocene Chronology Ice Age and Pluvial Age

Epoch	*Division of Epoch*	*Glacial Period*	*Interglacial Period*	*Pluvial Period*	*Interpluvial Period*	*Fauna*	*Time in B.P.*
Pleistocene	Upper Pleistocene	Wurm	Riss-Wurm	Gamblian	Kanjeran-Gamblian	Eemian	1,00,000
	Middle Pleistocene	Riss	Mindel-Riss	Kanjeran	Kamasian-Kanjeran	Hoxian	2,00,000
	Lower Pleistocene	Mindel	Gunj-Mindel	Kamasian	Kageran-Kamasian	Cromerian	4,00,000
	Basal Pleistocene	Gunj	Donau-Gunj	Kageran	Donau-Kageran	Tiglian	6,00,000
		Donau		Donau		Villafran-chain	30,00,000

Source: H.D. Sankalia, 1974, *Prehistory and Protohistory of India and Pakistan.*

Pleistocene Epoch in India

India was witnessing both types of climatic conditions during Pleistocene. During Pleistocene, north-west India was witnessing the climatic variations of glacial and interglacial periods. But Peninsular India and coastal areas were witnessing the climatic changes of pluvial and interpluvial periods. Thus, both types of climate variations prevalent in world were existing in India during Pleistocene epoch.

During Pleistocene period neighbouring areas of Himalayas had witnessed the situation of extensive glaciations. As a result ice ages came into existence in these areas. The huge deposits of late moraine can be seen in the entire area of several places. They reveal evidences of ice ages before us. Besides faceted boulders and notched stones have been found at a height of 5,000 feet in Kashmir, Garhwal and other places also tell us the same story. Eminent natural scientist Alfred Russel Wallace has opined that the sudden disappearance of Siwalik animals indicates that by the end of pliocene period, the environment was so changed that Siwalik animals could not stay their and they moved towards suitable places. In some areas of kangaro, glaciers had reached up to the height of 3,000 feet.

DeTerra had made a study of development and contraction of glacier in Kashmir valley. He had correlated the moraines of glacial periods with different layers of Punjab-Siwalik areas.

Pleistocene and Ice Age in Kashmir Valley

In different areas of Kashmir one finds glacial deposits belonging to Pleistocene epoch in plenty. Among glacial deposits of Kashmir valley, Karewa deposit occupies the prominent place. They are present in majority of parts in Jhelum valley. In between Srinagar and Gulmarg and northern slope of Pirpanjal series their preserved sections can be seen. In fact Karewa deposit was fluviatile, lacustrine and glacial deposit. This deposit consists of sand, clay, loam and gravel in mixed form. Sometimes varve deposits are also found.

In Kashmir, Karewa has a spread of 80 km in north-west and south-east direction. It covers an area of 4,800 kms. In northern area of Pirpanjal this deposit is nearly 5,000 sq.ft. thick. The deposit below it is more thin.

The entire Karewa deposit can be divided into two parts. They are: Upper Karewa and lower Karewa. Their thickness together is more than 700 feet. The scholars are of opinion that this area of Himalayas would have witnessed glaciations not less than four times. Evidences of glacial periods are clearly visible in river terraces.

In Kashmir valley below lower Karewa one finds late moraines of first glacial period. Karewa deposits had witnessed tectonic movements in the form of folding and fault. All these geological processes were completed before second interglacial period. Above lower Karewa deposits, stratified deposits of silt and sand is found like loess. This loess like deposit is known as upper Karewa. They indicate towards the end of second glacial period and beginning of second interglacial period. The last evolution of Pirpanjal series had taken place in this period. Due to rise of this series, the water of Karewa Jheel was flown. As a result of this Jhelum valley and first terrace of upper Karewa were created. These processes would have been completed before third glacial period. Although the second terrace is not very clear, but at several places it can be correlated with late moraine of third glacial period. The third terrace is very clear and wide. This would have been formed in third interglacial period. The fourth glacial period of Kashmir valley was comparatively less intensive. Its deposit is also very thin. The fourth terrace is located at a height of 40-50 feet above water level.

Besides the above four terraces, one more terrace has also been found. It was formed due to erosion of fourth terrace. This terrace would have been formed after fourth glaciation.

It was a scholar named Daniel who had thrown light on four ice ages in India for the first time. He was of opinion that the first glacial period of India was contemporary to the second interglacial period of Europe. But DeTerra and Paterson did not accept it. According to them all four glacial periods were contemporary to all four glacial periods of Europe. Thus, the ice ages of India and Europe were contemporary.

Table 3.2 shows Pleistocene Chronology of Siwalik Valley.

Table 3.2: Siwalik Stratigraphy and Ice Age in Kashmir Valley

Siwalik stratigraphy	*Sub-division*	*Ice Age*
Upper Siwalik	8. Boulder conglomerate	2nd Himalayan Glacial Period
	7. Pinjor	1st Himalayan Interglacial Period
	6. Tatrot	1st Himalayan Glacial Period
Middle Siwalik	5. Dhokpathan	Upper Pleistocene
	4. Nagari	Middle Pleistocene

(*Contd.*)

TABLE 3.2 (*Contd.*)

Siwalik stratigraphy	*Sub-division*	*Ice Age*
Lower Siwalik	3. Chinje	Lower Pleistocene
	2. Camlial	Upper Pleistocene
	1. Muree	Upper Pleistocene

Source: H.D. Sankalia, 1974, *Prehistory and Protohistory of India and Pakistan.*

Pleistocene and Ice Age in Potwar Siwalik

Potwar Siwalik has also revealed the evidences of Ice age and Pleistocene. In this area Pleistocene appears from the Tatrot zone. On the basis of study of fossils and geological and chemical analysis of soil, the Tatrot zone of upper Siwalik has been correlated to 1st glacial period. In comparison to other layers, this layer of Siwalik has yielded less number of animal fossils. The Pinjor zone of Potwar has been correlated to 1st Interglacial period. On the basis of only animal remains, Pinjor zone can be separated from Tatrot zone. But on the basis of analysis of deposits, a clear-cut distinction can be made between Tatrot and Pinjor zones. The gravels of Tatrot are brown in colour, whereas the Pinjor deposit is formed of Pink silt and sand. The change in colour of deposits reveals change in climatic condition. Such type of change has also taken place in Kashmir area. The loess deposit found in Pinjor indicates that it was a deposit of interglacial period.

Second glacial period and last evolution of Siwalik-boulder conglomerate were contemporary. Extensive erosion had taken place in this period. Due to erosion bolder conglomerates were deposited in plain and plateaus. This extensive deposit symbolizes heavy rainfall and is known as boulder conglomerate of Siwalik. This deposit has been correlated to second glacial period. It gets mixed-up with late moraine of second glacial period. On this basis chronology of Terraces of Soan has been established. From this layer, the remains of Elephas Namadicus have been obtained. They are like remains obtained from Narmada and Godavari of same period.

During second interglacial period, the first terrace of Soan (T_1) was formed due to erosion of boulder conglomerate. In Soan valley this terrace is at a height of 220 feet from water level. But in Indus valley it is 410 feet high from the water level. This terrace has been formed due to redeposition of boulder conglomerate. No fossils have been reported in the Potwar area from this layer. Its dating is based on archaeological materials. From Narmada area animal remains of buffalo, elephant and horse belonging to middle pleistocene have been found like here.

The second terrace (T_2) was formed due to depositional activity. This has two layers — Basal gravel and yellow loessic silt. It is also known as Potwar loess. The second terrace was formed during third glacial period. This is situated at a height of 120 feet in Soan valley. The second terrace of Soan has been correlated with second terrace of Kashmir formed during third glacial period.

The terrace third (T_3) has been formed due to erosional activity. It was formed during third interglacial period. It is situated at a height of 80 feet from water level. In Kashmir, Punchh and Jammu, this terrace was formed due to erosional activity.

The fourth terrace (T_4) was formed due to depositional activity during 4th glacial period.

This terrace is formed by Pinkish loam, sand and gravel deposit. In Soan valley its height is 40 feet from the water level. But in Indus valley its height is 90 feet. The Pleistocene ends in Potwar area with the formation of fourth terrace.

Besides, the above four terraces, there was also a terrace — fifth terrace in Soan valley. It was formed due to depositional activity after Pleistocene in Holocene period. According to DeTerra, it was like 5th terrace in mountainous regions. From water level its height was 20 feet.

Pleistocene in Indo-Gangetic Plain

In Indo-Gangetic plain very few researches have been done. Here the alluvial deposit of river Indus and Ganges have covered almost all old deposits. That is why here study is not easy and simple. In this area deposit began with last rise of Himalayas and is still going on. The area now known as plain of Indus-Ganges, was a deep valley. But after the last rise of Himalayas, the rivers Indus and Ganges have filled up the deep valley and formed the plain. Some scholars have termed it as Fore Deep. This entire area extends over 3,00,000 sq. miles. Sindh, Northern Rajasthan, Punjab, Bihar, Bengal, and half of Assam come under this area. Its width is 144 km to 4800 km. Its depth is 1300 feet below the modern land level. This depth is not same at all places. In Saharanpur, Ambala, and Ludhiana areas the maximum height from the sea level is nearly 900 feet. This elevation has controlled the flow of rivers of east and west. Their flows were not like of today. For example, Yamuna and Saraswati were falling in Arabian Sea through Punjab and Rajasthan. But in due course their flow turned towards east. The river Saraswati is now not in existence. Yamuna meets Ganges in Allahabad. The flow route of other rivers were also changed.

The entire alluvial deposits of Ganga and Yamuna can be divided into following geological layers:

- Old alluvial deposit — Bhangar of Ganga valley
- New alluvial deposit — Khadar of Punjab
- Delta deposit of Indus-Ganges — Holocene

Old Alluvial Deposit

The Bhangar of Ganga valley is an example of this deposit. It belongs to middle pleistocene. They are found in small plateaus at the highest places. The remains of Elephas, Antiquus, Aquas, Namadicus, Manis Gigantia and extinct species of Rhinoceros have been found.

New Alluvial Deposit

The Khadar of Punjab is example of this deposit.

Delta Deposit of Ganga-Yamuna

It was formed during Holocene period.

Desert of Rajasthan

Rajasthan spreads up to Indus valley in west and from Sutlej valley to 25' latitude. The extensive sand field is characteristics of this area. This deposit is too late from alluvial deposits of Indus-Ganga. This area has very little rainfall. In majority of parts south-western wind blows. They bring sand from sea coast and valley of Kuchh continuously. As a result, desert of Rajasthan has been formed. The entire Rajasthan is not Registan. A number of places have water and plants and trees. In the north of Kuchh and south of Punjab, population in good number resides there some time before today.

Pleistocene in South India and Middle India

The pleistocene deposits in south India and middle India is similar. Therefore, here pleistocene deposits of Narmada valley is being described in detail as an example of pleistocene deposits of central India and south India.

DeTerra and his associates had made a survey of pleistocene deposits of Narmada valley. His study was limited to Hoshangabad and Narsinghpur areas, but it was proved to be very significant archaeologically and geologically.

Although in the main valley of Narmada river, evidences of terraces are not available clearly. But in its tributaries DeTerra discovered evidences of four clear terraces nearby Harpur. He had observed three circles of destruction in main and tributaries of Narmada valley. In each circle, gravel, sand and silt were found. They were divided into three:

- Lower group
- Upper group
- Cotton group or Regur group.

In Narmada valley in between Hoshangabad and Narshingpur, these deposits look like terraces. Below these deposits, there is a deposit of laterite. Including laterite four strata have been found. Between these deposits evidences of three unconformity have been found. These evidences lead towards erosional periods.

In Narmada valley, in both lower and upper group above basal gravel, there is a deposit of pink or orange concretionary clay and silt. The faunal group does not indicate any change. These both deposits belong to middle pleistocene period.

Lower Group

The lower group has been dated to first and second terraces. Its basal conglomerate is more thick and cemented. The clay is also more deep in colour and concretionary. The laterisation of conglomerate has not taken place. From the lower layer of lower group, stone tools and animal fossils have been found. They are of *Bos namadicus, Elephas namadicus, Hexa protodons* and *Bubalus*. There is no difference in faunal groups, but their archaeological materials are important. DeTerra had obtained a tool like of pre-Soan industry from basal gravel. He had also obtained Abbevillian and Acheulian tools like early Soan industry from here.

From the deposit of red concretionary clay and silt, an advance Acheulian bifaceal tool and a number of fresh flakes have been found. From lower group a number of unrolled Acheulian tools have been found. Along with some rolled Acheulian tools, flakes of early Soan have also been found. This indicates that Acheulian industry was contemporary to basal conglomerate. Such types of tools have also been found from first and second terraces of Soan. On this basis basal gravel of Narmada has been correlated with first terrace and pink silt with second terrace.

Upper Group

This group of Narmada valley is contemporary to 3rd and 4th terraces of Soan valley. The basal gravel of this group is less cemented and thick. It has a thick layer of clay, but it is light red. It is also less concretionary. From the neighbouring area of Narsinghpur both layers of upper group have yielded the remains of same faunal groups belonging to middle pleistocene. Both layers have revealed tools of two different industries. They were evolved from the industry of lower groups. One is of Acheulian industry which seems rolled and deposited. The tools of other industry are fresh and unrolled. They are contemporary to late Soan industry.

New Alluvial Deposit

The dating of cotton soil group or Rigur group is contemporary to 5th terrace of Soan. In the pleistocene deposits above upper group, there is a discontinuity. Above upper group there is a new deposit of sands and gravels. This is known as new alluvial deposit. They are known as Grey clay or Rigur group or Cotton soil (black soil). They are contemporary to 5th terrace of Soan valley. They belong to holocene period.

Below basal gravel deposit and Rigur deposit, DeTerra and Tilhard had obtained remains of flake industry. They were small blades and scrapers. They were placed under microlithic tool.

Narmada valley pleistocene chronology and Potwar (Kashmir) pleistocene chronology have been presented in Table 3.3.

Table 3.3: Pleistocene Chronology of Potwar and Narmada

Geological Epoch	*Potwar (Kashmir)*	*Narmada*
Holocene	T_5	Cotton soil
Upper Pleistocene	T_4 T_3	Gravel of Rigur group Orange silt
Middle Pleistocene	T_2 T_1	Sandy gravel Pink silt
Lower Pleistocene	Boulder conglomerate Pinjor Tatrot	Basal gravel Pluvial laterite Non-existence of river

Source: H.D. Sankalia, 1974, *Prehistory and Protohistory of India and Pakistan.*

Coastal Alluvial Deposit

On the eastern coast right from the delta of Ganges up to southern coast a wide band of alluvial deposit is found. This deposit belongs to tertiary or post-tertiary periods. The tertiary period deposits have been placed under Kuddilur series. Post-tertiary period deposits have been found in limited areas of eastern and western coasts. These deposits consist of remains of sea shells and animals. On the bank of Malabar towards south, this band is very narrow. But in north it becomes wide nearby Gujarat. On the seashore of Kathiawad an another type of deposit has been found which is known as Porbandar stone or milidite. It is an air deposit.

Table 3.4: Pleistocene Chronology of Kashmir and Alpine

Geological Epoch	*Deposits and River Terraces in Kashmir*	*Climatic Change in Kashmir*	*Alpine Equivalent*
Holocene	Terrace-V (Deposition)	Mesolithic and Neolithic sites of Burzahome and number of Proto-neolithic pre-pottery stage of Sambur and Pampur	Post-glaciation
Upper Pleistocene	Terrace-IV (Deposition) Terrace-III (Erosion) Terrace-II (Deposition)	IV Glacial period III Interglacial III Glacial	Wurm glacial Riss-Wurm interglacial Riss glacial
Middle Pleistocene	Terrace-I Upper Karewa Bed Karewa Gravel	II Interglacial II Glacial	Mindel-Riss interglacial Mindel glacial
Lower Pleistocene	Lower Karewa Jheel layer Malshahikag Boulder conglomerate	I Interglacial I Glacial	Ganj-Mindel interglacial Gunj glacial

Source: H.D. Sankalia, 1974, *Prehistory and Protohistory of India and Pakistan.*

Sand Dunes

Sand dunes occupy significant place in the structure of western coast of India. Sand dunes are also found on the bank of Orissa. Sand dunes are also found in the valleys of Krishna and Godavari inside the peninsular India. They are found in plenty in Kuchh region. The stone mountain found on the coast of Tinnevelli is known by the name Teri.

Cave Deposit

In France and Italy cave deposits belonging to pleistocene periods have been found. But in India pleistocene cave deposits are negligible. In Karnool region some pleistocene cave deposits have been found which lie in neighbouring areas of Bangan valley. They are of limestone and are found in hills of Karnool series. In 25-30 feet thick basal cave deposit of staglemite, a number of animal remains have been found. They have been dated to Holocene period. Such types of cave deposits may be found more in number. So, a systematic survey of cave deposits needs in future.

Laterite

In order to understand the geological layers and archaeological materials of south India and central India, the knowledge about the date of laterite formation is very essential. Laterite is strange iron mixed material. Laterites have been formed in tropical climatic conditions where there are existence of pluvial-interpluvial, pluvial-interpluvial periods alternatively. Due to climatic variations in cycle of pluvial-interpluvial, pluvial-interpluvial periods some special types of rocks get broken. The breaking of such special rocks gives rise to laterite formation. Such special types of rocks contain gneiss, granite and basalt. They are porous clay soil rocks. They are of red, yellow and grey colour. They have linsonite layer in upper part. At the time of opening they are soft. They can be cut with any sharp tool. But when left open for some time, they become hard.

Laterite can be formed by different types of rocks. But in their formation hydroxide of iron, alumina and manganese make contribution. Other materials come out as chemical solution. The laterites having ferric salt are known as ferruginous laterite. The laterites having manganese ore termed as manganiferrous laterites and the laterites having alumina are called as alluminous laterites. The colour of ferruginous laterites red to grey. The colour of alluminous laterite is creamier grey and the colour of manganiferrous laterite is deep gray to black.

For the formation of laterites, pluvial-interpluvial, pluvial-interpluvial, alternating climatic conditions are must. For its formation storage of water is also essential. That is why laterites are not formed in sloping places.

On the basis of place of occurrence, laterites can be divided into two parts: upper layer laterite and lower layer laterite. Deposits of laterite are found generally on hills of 2000 to 5000 feet high. Lower layer laterites are known as secondary laterites. Protolaterite deposits are found at original place, local, but secondary laterites are found on other places away from original place.

In India laterites are found in wide area. They are found in south India, central India, south Utter Pradesh, Bihar, Jharkhand on hills in plenty. In Mumbai, Madhya Pradesh and Orissa they belong to Tertiary period to Pleistocene period. DeTerra had found laterite layer below lower group. There is unconformity between basal gravel and laterite of lower group. This shows that laterite formation had taken place in independent period. According to DeTerra, laterite formation in Narmada valley belongs to Pleistocene period.

In Uttar Pradesh laterites are found in hills and valley of Vindhyan. On hills and in valley, a thick deposit of laterite can be seen. The situation of laterite formation in Narmada valley and Vindhyan valley is same. Hence, the dating of Narmada valley and Vindhyan valley is same.

Pleistocene in Peninsular India

The Pleistocene climate of peninsular India — Orissa, Andhra Pradesh, Maharashtra and Gujarat was similar. In these states alternate periods of pluvial-interpluvial, pluvial-interpluvial had occurred. According to Commiade and Burkitt, seven evidences of climatic changes had come into existence. The 7th evidence was of Holocene period, while remaining evidences belong to Pleistocene period. In peninsular India, the chronology of climatic changes were as described in Table 3.5.

Table 3.5: Pleistocene Chronology of Peninsular India

Geological Epoch	*Climatic Change*
Upper Pleistocene	Third pluvial and third interpluvial periods
Middle Pleistocene	Second pluvial and second interpluvial periods
Lower Pleistocene	First pluvial and first interpluvial periods

Source: H.D. Sankalia, 1974, *Prehistory and Protohistory of India and Pakistan.*

4

Indian Lower Palaeolithic Culture (1 MY – 50,000 B.C.)

Indian Lower Palaeolithic culture has been explored from the study of sites, industries, traditions and culture of that periods. From recent researches, it has been established that lower Palaeolithic period in India began nearly 1 million year ago in north-west India and continued till 50,000 years B.C. in peninsular India. Lower Palaeolithic tools have been reported from every part of India. But for the purpose of proper understanding, we can study Indian Palaeolithic culture by dividing it into following groups:

- Lower Palaeolithic Culture of Northern India
- Lower Palaeolithic Culture of Western India
- Lower Palaeolithic Culture of Central India
- Lower Palaeolithic Culture of Eastern India
- Lower Palaeolithic Culture of Peninsular India

Lower Palaeolithic Culture of Northern India

Under lower Palaeolithic culture of northern India, lower Palaeolithic cultures of Punjab and Uttar Pradesh states are being discussed.

Lower Palaeolithic Culture of Punjab

From the point of view of lower Palaeolithic culture, the state of Punjab occupies the most significant place. It is because its north-western part — Potwar and Siwalik area has rivers like Soan, Jhelum and Indus. The terraces of these rivers were surveyed by different scholars. The Cambridge-Yale expedition had also made survey of this region. DeTerra, the director of this expedition had observed and explored the quarternary geological deposits of this area. The geological layers of this region had yielded Palaeolithic tools. DeTerra and his associates had made a special survey and study of the Kashmir valley to salt-hill ranges in between rivers Indus and Jhelum. First of all glacial periods of Kashmir were studied. Then glacial periods of Kashmir were correlated with different deposits of Siwalik which had yielded Palaeolithic tools.

In the state of Punjab, Siwalik deposit is 20,000 feet thick, which were divided into three parts. These three parts are Lower Siwalik, Middle Siwalik and Upper Siwalik. The deposits of Lower and Middle Siwalik had taken place during Tertiary periods. The deposits of Upper Siwalik belonged to Quarternary periods. The Upper Siwalik is again divided into three parts: (1) Tatrot, (2) Pinjor, and (3) Boulder conglomerate. The Tatrot part was formed during lower pleistocene and the Pinjor part was formed during middle pleistocene. In other words, we can say that Tatrot part was formed during first Himalayan glacial periods and the Pinjor part was formed during first

Himalayan interglacial period. The boulder conglomerate was formed in second Himalayan glacial period. On this basis, the different terraces of Soan river were correlated to different Himalayan glacial periods. DeTerra and Paterson showed that Tertiary period animal remains ended with Dhok Pathan. In Pinjor Villafranchian animals remains came into existence. This was related to the first Himalayan glaciation. This can be understood in better way by Table 4.1.

Table 4.1: Siwalik Chronology and Himalayan Glaciation

Siwalik Chronology	*Siwalik Parts*	*Himalayan Glaciation*
Upper Siwalik	7. Pinjor	1st Himalayan interglacial period
	6. Tatrot	1st Himalayan glacial period
Middle Siwalik	5. Dhok Pathan	Upper pliocene
	4. Nagari	Middle pliocene
Lower Siwalik	3. Chinji	Lower pliocene
	2. Kamlial	Upper miocene
	1. Muree	Upper miocene

Source: H.D. Sankalia, 1974, *Prehistory and Protohistory of India and Pakistan.*

DeTerra and Paterson made study of terraces of river Soan. They termed the early bed as T_D which was formed by boulder conglomerate. From this incidence, till the formation of present layer, they termed the five terraces of Soan as T_1, T_2, T_3, T_4 and T_5. These terraces were correlated with climatic change of pleistocene. This can be understood in better way as shown in Table 4.2.

Table 4.2: Soan Terraces and Pleistocene Climate

Geological Epoch	*Soan Terrace*	*Pleistocene Climate*
Holocene	T_5	New soil
Upper Pleistocene	T_4	4th Glacial period
	T_3	3rd Interglacial period
Middle Pleistocene	T_2	3rd Glacial period
	T_1	2nd Interglacial period
	T_D	2nd Glacial period
Lower Pleistocene	Pinjor	1st Interglacial period
	Tatrot	1st Glacial period

Source: H.D. Sankalia, 1974, *Prehistory and Protohistory of India and Pakistan.*

The region T_D was formed by boulder conglomerate. The faunal group found associated with this deposit has been termed as Narmada faunal group. This deposit belonged to second glacial period.

The region T_1 was formed due to erosion. Hence, it was an erosional deposit. It is situated at a height of 220 feet from the water level of Soan and at 410 feet from the water level of river Indus. In this region previous materials have been shown as redeposition. It has been correlated with second interglacial period.

The region T_2 is result of depositional activity. It has been correlated with third glacial period. This deposit is located at a height of 120 feet from the water level of present Soan river. This deposit has been classified into two groups — Basal gravel and Potwar loess. From the Potwar loess layer animal remains of horse, bison, camel and wolf have been found. These faunal remains indicate that climate was dry during this period.

The region T_3 was formed during third interglacial period due to erosional activity. It is situated at a height of 80 feet from the water level of river Soan. It was a result of long period of erosion. It shows redeposition abovc previous materials. This terrace is related to third interglacial period.

During fourth glacial period, terrace T_4 of Soan river was formed due to depositional activity. This terrace was formed by pink silt, sand and pebbles. It is situated at a height of 40 feet in Soan valley and 90 feet in Indus valley. This terrace shows the end of glacial period and pleistocene epoch in Soan valley.

The terrace T_5 of Soan valley was formed during Holocene period. This terrace is also a result of depositional activity. It is at a height of 20 feet from the water level of Soan river. This terrace is related to 5th glacial period of hill areas. It was formed by silt.

From the above account of study of river terraces in Kashmir valley, it is clear that terraces of river Soan present chronological layers of climatic changes during Pleistocene epoch. They present clearly a chronology of climatic change. DeTerra and Paterson had discovered a number of Palaeolithic tools fashioned and used by prehistoric man living in Soan, Kashmir and Himalayan areas during pleistocene epoch. Tools found from different terraces and industry sites have been classified into three groups by DeTerra and Paterson. They are as follows:

- Pre Soan
- Early Soan
- Late Soan

Pre Soan

All tools gathered from the T_D terrace of Soan river have been placed under a group to show a cultural stage. This cultural stage is known as Pre Soan. DeTerra and Paterson had named them Pre Soan in the same way as the term Prechallean was proposed in the context of Somme valley in France by Gaivriel de Mortelet.

From the upper parts of boulder conglomerate layer of second glacial period, DeTerra and Paterson had discovered crude unfashioned tools made up of quartzite. They constitute the earliest Palaeolithic culture of India. They are large flakes made from crude split pebbles. They all are rolled. The upper surface is generally unworked, except for occasional scars. The under surface shows primary flaked surface with flat bulbs, but well developed cones. The striking platforms are simple unfaceted. There is no secondary working. But edges are worn out by nature or use. Such tools were found near the top of boulder conglomerate at Malakpur, Adial, Chauntra, Kallar, Chaomukh and Jammu in Potwar, south-east of Rawalpindi. A number of scholars treat them as pseudo artifact. But scholars like Movius (1944) and Fair Service (1971) treat them as pre-stage of early Soan. If these tools are pre-stage of early Soan, then pre Soan culture will emerge as the oldest prehistoric culture of the world.

Early Soan

The early Soan industry consists a large number of tools made on split pebbles (pebble halves) and comparatively small number of flakes, the material comprising variety of fine grained quartzite as well as smooth greenish grey Punjab trap. Patination and the state of wear divide these tools into three groups. These groups are as follows:

- Group A

- Group B
- Group C

Although there is no stratigraphic evidence to support this classification, but it seems that group 'A' is heavily painted and much rolled and is the earliest. Group 'B' is deeply painted, but is unworn. The group 'C' is less painted and fairly fresh.

Among all these groups there are pebble tools, scrapers, cores and flakes and few proto hand axes. But the first one predominates. The characteristic method of flaking them is generally underside up and not on both faces or sides of the pebble. Thus, it makes early Soan a pebble tool industry.

Choppers

All pebble tools have been divided into two — flat based and rounded by Paterson. But Movius proposed the name choppers for both types of tool — flat based or rounded. In flat based pebble tool, the flakes have been struck upward in such a way as to form a thick, sleep cutting. The edge is convex, straight or rarely pointed, but never concave. It is further marked by secondary retouch, either on one side or both sides, so that we have single or double sided choppers.

The rounded pebble tools differ from the others not only in shape but in method of flaking. The flakes have been struck from the original surface of pebble and not from the flat undersurface. The cutting edge is made from one side only. Thus, both types of pebble tools — flat based and rounded are choppers. They are unifacial.

Chopping Tools

The pebble tools having rounded back and a jagged wavy or W shaped edge worked from both sides by alternate flaking are called as *chopping tools* by Movius. These are in a sense *bifacial tools*.

Flake Tools and Cores

There are no flakes in group 'A'. In group 'B', there are flakes which in many cases retain the cortex on the upper surface and the platform is not prepared. The angle with flake surface is comparatively high. The group 'C' exhibits flakes which show extensive primary flaking and even simple faceted striking platform. Both these techniques are suggestive of a proto-Levalloisean or prepared core and faceted platform technique. Corresponding to both these types of flakes are Clacton-like and tortoise type cores. The former are roughly discoidal or elongated in shape and flaked almost all over.

Late Soan Industry

The late Soan industry is stratigraphically and typologically divisible into two types. They are as follows:

- Late Soan A
- Late Soan B

Late Soan A

The tools of this industry have been found in the basal gravel of Soan terrace T_2. This terrace belongs to third glacial period. Majority of tools comprise pebble tools and clactone like flakes which characterise the early Soan. But we also find a small number of flakes and cores. The flakes are skillfully flaked on upper surface, implying a clear preparation of the core. A few parallel sided blades and elongated flakes also appear, which strengthen the impression that Late Soan A is definitely Levalloisean in character and falls into middle Palaeolithic period in early part of upper pleistocene.

Late Soan B

This industry was found at the bottom of thick Potwar loessic silt of third interglacial or glacial. Here, the Levalloisean tradition noticed in Late Soan A continued. Nearly 50 per cent of the flakes show faceted platform and their upper surfaces are carefully trimmed. Although no retouch specimens are found, but the flakes and cores barring pebble tools, remained one of the Late Levalloisean of Western Europe.

The Late Soan culture was very widespread in the Punjab as it has been recorded from a no less than 21 sites.

Evolved Soan Industry

The evolved Soan name was given to the assemblage of tools from Dhok Pathan by Movius. It was a site near Pindi Gheb, which belonged probably to fourth glacial period. The tools are not different from early and Late Soan, though they are smaller. One new type of tool has been found which is a kind of awl made on a small oval pebble flaked on both surfaces at one end to form a sharp point. Since this recalls a typical tool of Series II or middle Palaeolithic age of peninsular India, it is reproduced here.

The Handaxe Industry

As mentioned earlier that few tools — handaxes or bifaces are found in heavily rolled conditions at four sites in Soan valley. These sites are as follows:

- A site near Rawalpindi in the gravels of second interglacial periods (T_1).
- A site named Chauntra in deposits of third glacial (T_2).
- A site Balwa near Chakri in the gravels of third glacial (T_2).
- A site Gariala, near Attock in Indus valley in the gravels of third glacial (T_2).

Stratigraphically, the tools of the first site are the earliest and here alone they are found unmixed with those of Soan culture. At Chauntra, Balwa and Adial, bifaces are found in association with early and Late Soan tools. At Gariala a very rolled cleaver was found. From these evidences, it seems that handaxe culture had independent existence in Punjab. Since then it is found in similar dated deposits. It is very difficult to say which one is earlier — the handaxe of Soan excluding the earliest pre-Soan flake industry.

As far as tools — handaxes, cleavers, and flakes — are concerned, it is important to note that both primitive looking handaxes and pebble butted recalling Middle Acheulian technique are found in the earliest deposits. Hence, distinction between handaxes into Abbevillian and Acheulian is only typological and has no basis in stratigraphy. It is also possible that beautiful ovates and heart shaped handaxes from Chauntra are indeed later.

Age and Culture Couple

Besides these handaxes and occasional cleavers, there do occur a few cores, discoided cores and crudely retouched flakes. Some are with plain striking platform. These form a normal complement of handaxe culture in India and Africa and in Western Europe, too. Thus, the Punjab handaxe culture is stratigraphically of Middle Pleistocene and typologically to the great Lower Palaeolithic handaxe culture.

It together with Soan culture seems to have survived all through the Third Glacial Period and later climatic phase in the region with some improvement in technique and form, which unfortunately are not well documented stratigraphically as in Late Soan.

Lower Palaeolithic Culture of Uttar Pradesh

The state of Uttar Pradesh occupies significant place in India so far as Palaeolithic culture is concerned. Allahabad and Mirzapur districts of Uttar Pradesh occupy significant place from the point of view of lower Palaeolithic culture. It was Cockburn who had reported Palaeolithic tool from the Singrauli basin of Mirzapur. In 1935, DeTerra had also paid attention towards the special Palaeolithic status of Mirzapur. Being located in between glacial-interglacial periods of north India and pluvial-interpluvial periods of south India, Mirzapur had attracted the attention of scholars working in prehistoric cultures of India. All India Archaeological Survey organised under the leadership of Professor Zeuner (1949) had also chosen Mirzapur for archaeological and pre-historic cultural researches. This expedition team had researched the pre-historic sites and its culture already researched by Cockburn on the river Balia opposite of Hitauni. R.K. Verma of Allahabad University had made a resurvey of Mirzapur for his doctoral dissertation. The central and south parts of Mirzapur are most significant from the point of view of Lower Palaeolithic period. The main river of central Mirzapur is Belan. The river Belan rises from east of Vijaygarh and falls in the river Tones in Allahabad. The river Tones itself is a tributary of the river Ganges. The three significant valleys of this area are Kon valley, Duddhi valley and Singrauli basin. The most important rivers of this area are Son and Rihand. Besides these rivers, Kanhar and Malia rivers are found in Duddhi area, Pandu river in Kon area and Balia river in Singrauli basin.

Besides the Lower Palaeolithic tools reported by Cockburn, a number of Palaeolithic industries belonging to Lower Palaeolithic culture have been collected from Rihand river of Singrauli basin and from the village Gaharwar in Singrauli basin, on the Rihand river. Thema and Malia rivers in Duddhi valley and near Chopan on Son river. In the deposits of all these rivers of this area, two or three gravels are found. The first gravel has been correlated to the first aggradational phase of the river. From this layer Lower Palaeolithic tools have been found. The first gravel has been formed by big pebbles, thick sand and stones. They are in cemented and uncemented conditions. Where gravels are not cemented, tools have been found in river valley scattered here and there. The second gravel has been formed by comparatively small stones and thin sands. From the first layer of this gravel different types of tools have been found. The Lower Palaeolithic culture of Mirzapur represents a mixed industry. From here pebble tools of Soan tradition and handaxe tool of Madrasian tradition both types have been found. In comparison to handaxe cleaver tradition, the number of pebble tool is negligible. Both advanced and non-advanced types of tool have been found. The quartzite has been used more and more in making tools. Besides, sand stones, chist and dolerite have also been used for making tool. These stones are easily available in Mirzapur. The use of cores and flakes has been done for making stone tools. But flake tools are more in number than the core tools. The flakes are of different sizes. The bulb of percussion was elevated. The angle was increasing or decreasing between 100° to 125°. They have been placed under Clactonian type. The lower Palaeolithic people of Mirzapur were not aware of Levalloisean technique. Flake scars of Acheulian type of handaxe show that they were formed by soft hammer technique.

Lower Palaeolithic Culture of Singrauli Basin

After the creation of Rihand dam, the major part of Singrauli basin has become drowned. In Singrauli basin it was Cockburn who for the first time had discovered lower palaeolithic industry site at Hinauli on southern bank of river Balia. The river Balia demarcates the boundary between Mirzapur and Riwan.

Below humus soil a 5 feet thick deposit of pink silt and stone pieces has been found. Below this deposit, a 3 feet thick deposit of stone pieces and pebble was found. Palaeolithic tools were found from this deposit. Again below this a 3 feet thick deposit of sand and stone pieces was found which was based on Talchir. Some tools were collected from the pebble deposit of river *in situ*. But majority of tools were gathered from scattered gravel near the boundary of Riwan. Only three tools were on veinquartz, others were made up of quartzite. Forty two per cent tools were of handaxe and cleaver type. Only 15 per cent tools belonged to Soan type. A good number of cores and flakes were also found. Eighteen per cent flakes were of proto-Levalloisean type. Seven per cent flakes were of Levalloisean type. According to Krishna Swamy and his associates, though Singrauli basin lower Palaeolithic culture was influenced by Soan industry, but it is proper to place it under bifacial tradition of Madrasian culture. On this ground, the hypothesis of DeTerra and his associates was rejected that Mirzapur was a meeting place of Soan and Madras culture. According to Krishna Swamy and Soundar Rajan, Singrauli stone industry represents Abbevillian-Acheulian bifacial tradition. But it was influenced by flaking technique of Soan. Singrauli industry can be placed under Middle Pleistocene. Because such types of industry in Narmada has been correlated with Middle Pleistocene.

Lower Palaeolithic Culture of Belan Valley

Belan valley is located in between southern Allahabad and western Mirzapur. From the point of view of Palaeolithic industry, the survey of Belan valley occupies significant place. It is because the survey of Belan valley brought to the light the chronological development of Palaeolithic culture in India. Belan river enters in Allahabad near Meja Tehsil. After flowing through 40 km in Allahabad, Belan river meets with Tons river. The Tons river is a tributary of river Ganges. The plateau area of Mirzapur extends over southern Allahabad. In Allahabad area plateau and central part of Kaimur are 16 km to 24 km wide. Like Mirzapur, the water of this plateau of Allahabad is taken out by Belan river. The middle part of Allahabad plateau and Kaimur hills are like a shallow valley. In this valley, the Belan river flows. Here cemented gravel deposits are found in wide areas. These deposits were formed by river Belan and its tributary Sewati and drainage. It seems that these deposits were made during pleistocene by an another wide river. From a place Daiyo, situated at a distance of 6 km east of Khajari village, to Deoghat, a 18 metre high section of the river is visible. In this paleolithic tools belonging to lower Palaeolithic to mesolithic cultures have been found in chronological sequence. Towards south of Belan river Vindhyan hills of less heights meet with Kaimur hills. All these hills located on southern bank of river Belan, were the chief habitat of prehistoric man during pleistocene period. Murali, Mahugarh, Chaudutari, Ramgarh, Belrahi, Karaundia hills, there have been a number of industry sites of prehistoric man. From those industry sites, tools of different stages have been found. All industry sites are located on plain and slope of hills and on land just below the hills. Palaeolithic man of Belan valley had used quartzite at all sites to fashion stone tools. At some places, sand stones were also used. Majority of tools were collected in unfinished condition. Among them cores and flakes occupy prominent place. Pebble tools have not been found from here. In tools, Abbevillian handaxe, cleaver and scrapers have been placed.

Middle Palaeolithic industry sites were found on middle layer of slopes of hills. The upper palaeolithic tools have been found at places where hill slopes meet with land.

Due to erosion of Belan river, a chronological sequence from pleistocene deposits to holocene deposits comes into existence clearly. The sequence of deposits of Belan valley from down to top are as follows:

10. The rock bed on the lowest layer, has a deposit of decomposed rock. The average thickness of this layer is 1.52 metre. No tools have been found from this deposit.
9. Upon decomposed rock, there is a deposit of *first gravel*. This deposit is formed of different stones of different sizes: stone pieces and small balls of laterite. From all layers of the deposit small and big stones have been found which indicate that deposit had occurred hastily and materials were not brought from distant places. From this deposit tools of lower palaeolithic period have been found. A number of faunal remains have also been found.
8. Above the first gravel deposit, there is a deposit of silt. This has been termed as *First Silt*. Small pieces of stones were formed due to leaching of calcium. No tools have been found from this deposit. Nor any stones have been found from this deposit. The deposit had taken place probably in stable water. The average thickness of deposit was 3.5 metre.
7. Over the first silt deposit, a deposit of gravel is again found. This is known as *second gravel*. The average thickness of second gravel deposit is 2.74 metre. This deposit is quite different from the deposit of first gravel. Here, there are no stone slabs. Gravels are of very small size and the quantity of laterite is very much. At several places, this deposit bears evidences of three clear-cut sub-divisions, which have been designated as A, B and C from top to bottom. In between each sub-division, a thin layer of soil is found. From the sub-division A, lower palaeolithic tools like cleaver and scrapers have been found. The palaeolithic tools of this layer have been made in majority on flakes. In making tools quartzite has been used.
6. No palaeolithic tools have been found from the sub-division B. From this layer only tools of middle palaeolithic culture have been found. The use of quartzite is comparatively less. The tools obtained from sub-division C are more small and in beautiful shape. In construction of the tool, the use of quartzite has been made less.
5. Above the deposit of second gravel, there is again a deposit of silt whose colour is reddish. This deposit consists of lime carbonate, laterite balls, and chips of stone. The average thickness of this deposit is 1.25 metre. The tools of middle palaeolithic have been found from this deposit. Scrapers occupy significant place in tools of this deposit. The tools have been made on churt.
4. Above reddish soil deposit, a deposit of yellow silt is found. The average thickness of this deposit is 1.52 metre. From this deposit different types of scrapers and blade tools have been found. This deposit indicates a transition from middle palaeolithic culture to upper palaeolithic culture.

3. Upon yellow silt deposit, a deposit of gravel is found again. This is known as third gravel deposit. Its average thickness is 1.21 metre. The third gavel deposit has more quantity of sand than the second gravel deposit. The third deposit is not so hard. It is not cemented at all places. The pieces of stone found from this deposit are comparatively small, rolled and rounded. From this deposit blade tools have been found. They belong to upper palaeolithic culture. All tools have been made on churt.
2. Above the third gravel deposit, there is a deposit of muddy black soil in which calcium carbonate and stone chips have been found. The average thickness of this deposit is 1.82 metre. This deposit has revealed blade tool and non-geometric microlithic tools related to pottery.
1. Above black muddy soil deposit, a deposit of black soil is found there which contains small pieces and chips of stone. The average thickness of this deposit is 2.4 metre. From this deposit geometric microlithic tools related to pottery have been found.

From the above stratigraphical account, it is clear that the Belan valley was a habitation site of prehistoric man right from lower palaeolithic period to mesolithic period. It is because the different geological layers of Belan valley have yielded evidences of all prehistoric cultural stages in chronological sequence. That is why Belan valley occupies significant place among all prehistoric industry sites.

In Belan valley, lower palaeolithic tools have been collected from the first gravel deposit. This layer has given us developed and undeveloped tools of pebble and handaxe-scraper traditions. In pebble tool traditions both chopper and chopping have been found. Majority of pebble tools show heavy patination. All tools are made of quartzite. Among all tools, 10 per cent are pebbles and 53 per cent are handaxe. Handaxes are of big size. They are of harsh Abbevillian to developed Acheulian type. They have been made on chunk or stone slabs. The working edge has been developed by alternate flaking technique. There is cortex on other parts of the tool. Scrapers and cleavers represent 30 per cent of all tools. They have been divided into U/V and straight sided. Majority of cleavers are made on flakes and their average length is 13-14 cm. Like handaxe and cleaver, scrapers are also of developed and undeveloped types. But they are made on cores.

Some tools obtained from Belan valley may be placed under mixed category. They are handaxe, scraper or cleaver scraper.

The lower palaeolithic tools of Belan valley have revealed evidences of hafting. Such type of evidence has not been found from any other lower palaeolithic sites of India. The prehistoric men of Belan valley were technologically so skillful that they increased the efficiency of the tools by hafting for different purposes.

Lower Palaeolithic Culture of Western India

Under lower Palaeolithic culture of Western India, we are going to discuss the following cultures:

- Lower Palaeolithic Culture of Maharashtra
- Lower Palaeolithic Culture of Gujarat
- Lower Palaeolithic Culture of Rajasthan

Lower Palaeolithic Culture of Maharashtra

The state of Maharashtra is bound by Gujarat and Madhya Pradesh in north, Andhra Pradesh in south-east, Mysore in south and Arabian Sea in north. The western coastal area of the state, Konkan and eastern part is known as Deccan Plateau. From north to south in coastal area, there are hill ranges of Western Ghat or Sahyadri hill ranges. This part is covered with dense forests. In eastern part, forest is comparatively less. The rivers of this state can be divided into two: (i) The rivers which fall into Arabian Sea; and (ii) The rivers which fall in Bay of Bengal. The rivers falling in Arabian Sea are small, but rivers falling in Bay of Bengal are long.

Narmada, Tapti, Bhima, Godavari and Krishna are chief rivers of the state Maharashtra. Narmada and Tapti are towards north. They flow from east to west and fall in Arabian Sea. Godavari and Bhima are towards middle. They flow from western to eastern side and fall into Bay of Bengal. Robert Bruce Foote was of opinion that southern plateau having height of 2,000 to 2,600 feet were full of thick forests. That is why it was not suitable for the stay of lower palaeolithic man. But Dr. H.D. Sankalia on the basis of his researches has made it clear that valley of Godavari and its tributaries were also so important for lower palaeolithic man as areas of south India. The evidences of lower palaeolithic cultures have been found from Nasik, Akola and Nevasa.

Lower Palaeolithic Culture of Godavari and Pravara Valley

Dr. H.D. Sankalia and his associates had made an extensive and intensive survey of Godavari valley and its tributary Pravara valley. The survey was made at places like Gangapur, Tapodhan, Tamaswadi, Nandur and Maghmeshwar in Godavari valley and at Bitte, Mahenduri, Induri, Nevasa in Pravara valley. The deposit of Godavari river and its tributary Pravara river is full of its local speciality. At all places two terraces were found. From the first terrace, lower Palaeolithic tools were found, but from the second terrace, middle palaeolithic tools were found. The tools obtained from the first terrace and second terrace were termed as Series-I and II. The sequence of deposit at all places was as follows:

Terrace	*Composition*	*Industry*
I	Thick deposit of pebble gravels and silt	Lower palaeolithic hand axe-cleaver
II	Cemented gravel	Middle palaeolithic point-scraper
Gravel extension	Stone pieces and sandy gravel	Microlithic tools

From cemented gravel deposit (Series-II), remains of middle pleistocene animals have been found. At all places, flakes tool occupied significant place. There were no pebble tools in these rivers. Among tools, the number of cleaver was more. Besides cleaver, there were handaxe, scraper and some round tools.

Lower Palaeolithic Culture of Nevasa

Nevasa site is located at Pravara river of the state of Maharashtra. The river Pravara is a tributary of Godavari. Nevasa is a significant lower palaeolithic site in India. The geological chronology sequence of Nevasa is same as described in the table presented just above. In the site nos. I, IV, and V of Nevasa, the sequence of prehistoric cultures from top to down are as follows:

8. Cotton soil (black soil) — Base of Chalcolithic culture
7. Yellow or grey silt
6. Thin gravel
5. Yellow or thin gravel

4. Comparatively scattered and small gravels, tools of Series-II and remains of *Bos namadicus* Falconer.
3. Erosional silt deposit
2. Cemented gravel — Series-I and fossil of *Bos namadicus*
1. Base rock

All tools obtained from Nevasa can be divided into following classes:

1. Handaxe
2. Cleaver
3. Flake
4. Core
5. Hammer stone or chopping tool
6. Chopper or side scraper

Besides Pravara river, tools collected from Mula, Bhima and Tapti rivers also reveal the same types of tools.

Lower Palaeolithic Culture of Chiraki (Nevasa)

The Chiraki industry site is lccated on the confluence of Chiraki-Nevasa. It is at a distance of 3 km from Nevasa towards the flow of Pravara. It was an Acheulian industry site. The credit of exploring this site goes to Gudran Karvinus who had done excavation here form 1966 to 1969. The lower Palaeolithic tools in Chiraki area were found from the surface. They seem to come out from alluvial deposit. Upon base rock, a deposit of 8 metre thick was found. In this gravel deposit middle palaeolithic tools have been found from all layers.

The prehistoric man would have come to live here, when the river would have started filling up the valley, the man would have been living in the plain area on the bank of river valley. He would have used the boulders made terraces as industry site. Upon boulders made gravel deposit, there is an alluvial gravel deposit. This deposit has yielded Nevasian or middle palaeolithic tools. Tools were made on chalcedony and jasper. Carvinus was of opinion that Nevasian would have developed from Acheulian. In entire Acheulian industry, there were 2050 tools. Among them 1511 were complete. The number of core tool was 95 and the waste flakes were 444. All tools have been divided into two classes — pebble and flake. The tools of pebble class were chopper, chopping, hammer stone, blunt chopper, multipurpose tool, and core. The tools of flake class were handaxe, cleaver, scraper, retouched flake and waste flakes. Few bone remains were also found. They were of teeth and horns of bos and elephus.

Lower Palaeolithic Culture of Mumbai Area

In Indian prehistory Mumbai area was brought in to light by a scholar named Todd who had made a survey of this region. He had published his essay in 1939. He had declared about the existence of stone industry from geological layers of Borivlli and Khandivli. In Khandivli, the sequence of geological layers were as follows:

- There is a 3" to 50" thick deposit over base rock or foundation stone. This deposit nas been named as lower clay. Tools of Clactonian or Soanian types were found from this deposit.
- Over lower clay deposit, a 1 to 6 feet thick deposit of red mixed grey gravel has been found. This deposit is known as lower gravel deposit. From the lower part of this deposit,

Abbevillian and Acheulian types of tools were found. They were made on churt and shale. From the upper part of the deposit, fresh Clactonian and Acheulian types of tool were found.

- Over the deposit of lower clay, a deposit of middle clay was found. From this deposit, cores, scraper, blade and small sized handaxe were found.
- Upon middle clay deposit, a 3 feet thick deposit of upper gravel was found. From this upper gravel deposit layer, blade and burin tools were found.
- Over upper gravel deposit, a 18 feet thick deposit of brown clay has been found. From this deposit tools of developed blade and burin industry have been found. From upper surface microlithic tools were found.

With the help of Mohpatra and Mishra, Sankalia re-examined and surveyed the entire area surveyed by Todd. But he did not find such sequence as reported by Todd anywhere. On the advice of Sankalia, Subba Roy and Zeuner also made survey of this area. But they, too, did not find the sequence of industry as reported by Todd. In this situation, the description of Todd seems to be doubtful.

Lower Palaeolithic Culture of Konkan

The credit of exploring the lower palaeolithic culture of Konkan area goes to Kumari Gajdhar. She explored a number of lower palaeolithic sites from Ratnagiri district of South Konkan. All industry sites were located at laterite plateau. Only one site is located in the flow area of the river Chod. The stone tool industry belongs to flake industry. Only one handaxe was found. Cleavers have been found in limited number. Churt has been used for making tools. Step flaking technique was used for the purpose of flaking.

Lower Palaeolithic Culture of Gujarat

Gujarat is the most western part of India. It is bounded by Arabian Sea in west, Madhya Pradesh in east, Rajasthan in north and Maharashtra in south. Entire Gujarat is nearly plain. In this state Sahyadri, Satpura and Arawali hill ranges are located on the boundaries. Northern Gujarat is full of sand dunes which are 20 feet to 100 feet high. Mahi and Narmada are main rivers of central Gujarat. They meet in Arabian in Kuchh gulf. The neighbouring areas of Barodara are also like northern part. But sand dunes are of small sizes. Towards the south of Tapti, a number of rivers arise from Sahyadri hill ranges and fall into Arabian Sea. That is why coastal area are swamp.

Lower Palaeolithic Culture of Sabarmati, Mahi and Arsang Valley

Sabarmati, Mahi, Narmada and Tapti are chief rivers of Gujarat state. Among them, Sabarmati valley had attracted the attention of scholars for exploration of prehistoric culture. The credit of exploring the lower palaeolithic culture in Sabarmati valley goes to Robert Bruce Foote. Following Robert Bruce Foote, Sankalia had organised a survey of Sabarmati, Arsang and Karjan river valley under his supervision in between 1941 to 1949. As a result, a number of industry sites were explored.

From the point of view of section, Hadol, Pedhamali and Virpur occupies significant place. The sequence of deposit in Hadol was as follows:

- Yellow sandy silt 20 feet
- Red silt 10 feet

- Gravel conglomerate 12 feet
- Granite 15 feet

There was slight difference in deposit sequence of Pedhamali and Virpur. Here a laterite layer is found below cemented gravel on sand stones shale foundation. Pebble tools have been found from these places. Handaxe, cleavers, and flakes have been found in Hadol. In Pedhamali, tools have been found from red silt. Some tools have also been found from upper deposit. The tools of this layer are of developed type. Undeveloped Abbevillian and developed Acheulian tools have been found from all layers in mixed condition.

In Sabarmati tool community, there are big cores, handaxe, cleaver, flake and small discoid cores. Tools have been prepared from stone hammer technique and cylinder hammer technique. The angles of majority of tools are not right angle, but angles of some tools are right angle. There is lack of true Levalloisean flake or core.

The tools obtained from Mahi, Arsang and Karjan are not different from Sabarmati. In Arsang valley tools have been found in mixed form. Long blades made by Levalloisean technique and Acheulian handaxe have been found. This type of developed tools have also been found in Karjan valley. The tools include long handaxe, different types of cleaver, discoid and pebble handaxe. From the point of view of tool, Mahi, Arsang and Karjan valleys do not occupy significant place. But they are significant because they are such rivers of Peninsular India where systematic study of pleistocene deposits have been made by Zeuner. Zeuner had obtained evidences of lower palaeolithic climate.

Lower Palaeolithic Culture of Bhadar Valley

The western part of Gujarat is known as Saurashtra. This area was famous for Indus valley civilization till recently. No more palaeolithic tools were reported from this area. But on the basis of later researches it appears that the area was famous for middle palaeolithic, mesolithic, neolithic and chalcolithic cultures. Robert Bruce Foote had obtained a tool made of jaspar and churt. He had correlated the tool with neolithic culture. With the effort of Sankalia other stone industries belonging to different cultural periods came into existence. Bhadar is the biggest river of Saurashtra. Its flow area is nearly 192 kms. The sequence of deposit of Bhadar is same as that of Maharashtra. The sequence of deposits of Bhadar river is as follows:

Above basal trap, there is a deposit of pebble gravel. During dry phase, the river brought small stone pieces mixed red soil and deposited them.

After the above deposit, the another circle began with erosion. In this period, river carried away the previous deposits up to rock base. Thereafter, the river made a gravel deposit again at all places. But this gravel deposit was comparatively thick and fine. The river made again a thick deposit of grey silt.

Dr. Sankalia had obtained lower Palaeolithic tools from the First gravel and middle palaeolithic tool from the Second gravel.

In Saurashtra area, lower palaeolithic tools were found in three conditions: (i) harsh, (ii) from upper gravel and redeposited root, and (iii) on surface.

In making tools, red churt of good quality were used. The tool community included handaxe, clever, scraper, chopping and different types of flakes. Besides Bhadar valley, lower palaeolithic and middle Palaeolithic tools were found from Dokamarde drain, Sherdi river, Junagarh and near Somnath. Some neolithic tools have also been found from Kuchh.

Lower Palaeolithic Culture of Rajasthan

The state of Rajasthan is located in south of Punjab. Arawali hill ranges divide this state into two parts. The western part of Rajasthan is known as Mewar. Majority of land of this part is full of desert. Here rainfall has been reported less than 10". This part does not contain any river which has water round the year. The main river of this area is Luni which rises from Annasagar of Ajmer and falls into desert near Kuchh valley after flowing the entire Mewar area. A number of small rivers rising from Arawali hills meet in the river Luni. These rivers flow towards east-north and west-south. The south-east part of Arawali is called Mewar. This part is comparatively green. The lands of this part are irrigated by Banas, Berach, Gambhiri and other small rivers. The water of these rivers fall in Chambal river. Chambal river is itself a tributary of river Yamuna. The river Yamuna meets in Ganges and the river Ganges falls in Bay of Bengal. Thus, the water of this entire area falls ultimately in Bay of Bengal through the river Ganges.

Today Mewar of Rajasthan is deserted. But in ancient time the area was full of fertile land and river valleys. There were a number of Indus valley sites here up to nearly 2000 B.C. They were located on the bank of extinct river Saraswati. In prehistoric period, the area would have been habitation sites of prehistoric man. This area would have been significant from the point of view of communication between north and south India. But due to continuous climatic changes, the area was converted into desert. Mankind left this place to settle at another places. Their habitation sites were covered by sand. In Luni and its tributary a number of middle palaeolithic sites have been found. But evidences of lower palaeolithic periods have not been found. There is a need to make more research in this regard. The south-east part of Rajasthan is significant from the point of view of lower palaeolithic period. Chambal, Berach, Gambhiri valleys occupy significant place in this regard. It was S.S. Rao who had initiated the study of lower palaeolithic culture in this area in 1953-54. With his efforts, tools of both Soan and Madras industries came into existence in mixed form. He had done limited excavation at Sonita and Bhensarorgarh in Chambal valley.

At Sonita, there was a 4 feet thick deposit of conglomerate. Over this conglomerate deposit, there was a deposit of gravel. From conglomerate layer, 19 tools were found. Among 19 tools, there were 3 choppers, 4 cleavers, 8 scrapers, one oval and 3 unclear tools. From gravel deposit, different types of scrapers were found along with Levalloisean and Clactonian flakes.

In Bhensarorgarh, tools were obtained from two places. At both places, the lower layer was formed by a thick deposit of boulder conglomerate. Over this deposit, there was a thin deposit of gravel and metamorphised shale. The conglomerate deposit was based on decomposed shale. A total of 27 tools were found from Bhensarorgarh. Among 27 tools, there were 4 choppers, 7 handaxes, 5 cleavers, 9 scrapers, and 2 disc scrapers.

Besides above palaeolithic tools, some middle palaeolithic tools were also found in which there were 4 flake tools. There were plenty of bifacial tools belonging to Madras tradition. The tools of Soan tradition — choppers were less in number. This seems that Soan tradition was meeting an end here.

Above the layer of conglomerate, a handaxe of Acheulian tradition, a cleaver and a scraper were found. By reaching this layer, this industry was also ending. The tools of Series-II, i.e., middle palaeolithic culture, were taking place. Besides Rao, A.P. Khatri and V.N. Mishra had done micro and extensive study of Chambal valley.

Lower Palaeolithic Culture of Berach Valley

The river Berach rises from Arawali hills and flows towards north of Udaypur. Its slope over hill is more. The deposit of pebble and boulder can be seen nearby Udaypur. The bottom of the river Berach is almost shallow. Bagan, Gambhiri and Kadamali are tributaries of the river Berach. Bagan river rises from Arawali hill near Sadari and meets with Berach river at Hajiakheri. Gambhiri river meets with Berach river near Sridih. Kadamali rises from hills near Sadari and meets with Gambhiri river. The section of Berach river from down to top was as follows:

- A deposit of mud soil over base rock was found. Its thickness was 4.5 metre. This deposit was formed due to decomposition of foundation or base rock. No tool was found from this deposit.
- Above mud soil deposit, there was a deposit of gravel with boulder or pebble with cemented gravel. The thickness of this deposit was 0.3 metre to 5 metre. Lower Palaeolithic tools were found from this deposit.
- There is a deposit of silt over cemented gravel deposit whose thickness was 0.3 metre to 5 metre. No tools were found from this deposit.

On the bank of river Gambhiri such types of deposits were also found. In Bagan and Kadamali rivers, two more deposits were found besides these three deposits. They were as follows:

- Over mud soil, a thin deposit of sand and gravel were found. Its thickness was 1.50 metre. From this deposit tools of lower Palaeolithic and middle Palaeolithic were found.
- Over this deposit, a deposit of red silt is found whose average thickness is 2 metre. Except Kadmali river, tools of Berach, Gambhiri, and Bagan rivers shows similarity in tool community. The tools community of these three rivers show handaxe in more number. But in Kadmali tool community, the number of core and chopper/scraper are more. There is lack of Levalloisean type flake, blade and discoid. The tool community of Berach, Bagan and Gambhiri has been divided in to following classes: 1. Core, 2. Flake or blade, 3. Core chopper/scraper, 4. Discoid, 5. Handaxe, and 6. Cleaver.

Lower Palaeolithic Culture of Central India

In this heading, we are going to discuss the lower palaeolithic culture of Central India only. For this purpose, the lower Palaeolithic culture of following areas belonging to central India are being discussed:

- Lower Palaeolithic Culture of Narmada valley.
- Lower Palaeolithic Culture of Son valley.
- Lower Palaeolithic Culture of Maihar.
- Lower Palaeolithic Culture of Damoh area.
- Lower Palaeolithic Culture of Gwalior area.
- Lower Palaeolithic Culture of Bhimbetka.

But before dealing with Palaeolithic cultures of above areas of central India, let us have a description of the state of Madhya Pradesh in brief. Madhya Pradesh has been bifurcated into Chhattisgarh and Madhya Pradesh in the year 2000.

It is central most state of India. It is bounded in north-west by Rajasthan, in north by Uttar Pradesh, in east by Chhattisgarh, Jharkhand and Bihar and Odisha, in south by Andhra Pradesh and Maharashtra, and in west by Gujarat. The equator passes through its centre parallel to Narmada. Here Vindhya and Satpura hill ranges are situated centrally parallel to each other from west to east direction. Chambal, Betwa, Son, Narmada, Tapti, Mahanadi and Chandrawati are chief rivers of this state. This state is full of climatic, land and cultural diversities. Nearly all types of minerals are available here. It was a scholar named Hacket who for the first time had found a handaxe related to fossilised mammals in 1873 near Bhutra from the bank of Narmada river. That is why Narmada valley occupies significant place.

Lower Palaeolithic Culture of Narmada Valley

The river Narmada rises from Amarkantak in Machal hill of Shahdol district. It covers a flow route of nearly 1280 km in Madhya Pradesh and Gujarat. It falls in Arabian Sea in Kuchh valley. Passing through hilly areas, the river Narmada has a good number of visiting places on its bank. Nearly at a distance of 8 km from the rising place, the river Narmada falls from a height of 150 feet and forms a beautiful fall. The river Narmada looks very beautiful when it flows through Marble mountain near Bheraghat. From the point of view of Palaeolithic culture, the central part of Narsinghapur and Hoshangabad occupies important place. From this part, a good number of palaeolithic tools and fossils have been collected. This place was also chosen by Cambridge Yale expedition for survey and research. That is why this place has attracted the attraction of prehistorians and archaeologists.

DeTerra and his associates had found three circles of deposit in Narmada valley near Hoshangabad and Narsinghpur. In each circle there were deposits of gravel, sand and silt. They have been divided into three groups: (i) lower group, (ii) upper group, and (iii) cotton soil or Regur group. The deposit of these three groups are found in the form of river terrace up to a depth of 150 feet near Hoshangabad and Narsinghpur. At other places their depth is up to 500 feet. Bedrock was not found even up to a depth of 500 feet. In Hoshangabad, a laterite deposit was found below it. After each deposit circle, evidences of unconformity were found. Evidences of three erosional period related to three unconformities were found. These three deposits have been correlated to the deposits of Potwar (Kashmir). In each deposit circle of Narmada, two layers were found. The lower layer was of gravel and the upper layer was of pink silt or orange silt mixed with pieces of stone. There was no difference in animal remains of both group. The faunal group of both groups was related to middle pleistocene. DeTerra and Paterson had presented the deposit sequence of Narmada valley in following ways:

Deposit	Group	Period
1. Black soil 2. Fine Gravel	Holocene	
3. Pink Silt 4. Gravel comparatively loose	Upper group	Middle pleistocene
5. Pink-Reddish silt 6. Cemented Gravel 7. Laterite bed rock	Lower group	

According to DeTerra and Paterson, the lower group of Narmada was contemporary to terraces — T_1 and T_2. Fossils and lower Palaeolithic tools have been found from the basal gravel. In Umaria and Hoshangabad basal layer separates lower and upper groups near unconformity. From here fossils of *Bos namadicus, Elephus namadicus* and *Hexa protodon* and *Babulus* were found. The faunal remains of both groups — lower and upper, did not exhibit any difference, but there was difference in their archaeological material. From basal gravel of lower group, a big flake like pre-Soan type was obtained. Abbevillian and Acheulian handaxe, cleaver, core and flake were also found. Thus, Acheulian industry was considered contemporary to basal conglomerate. This industry determines the upper limit of Acheulian industry.

The upper group of Narmada valley has yielded faunal remains of middle pleistocene. From the deposit of upper group two different types of industries were found. These industries were more developed than the industries of lower group. One industry is bifacial rolled Acheulian, which seems to be redeposited from the gravel of lower group. The tools of another industry are fresh. These tools seem to be contemporary of upper group. These tools include flake, discoid core and pebble. They seem to be of late Soan type. They have been considered as contemporary to terrace T_3 and terrace T_4 of Soan river valley. Here gravel has been correlated to T_3 and pink silt has been correlated to T_4. Over the pleistocene deposit of upper group, a disturbance has come into existence. Due to this disturbance, a new cycle of deposits has appeared. Sand and gravel together have formed the lowest terrace of the river Narmada. A flake industry was discovered by DeTerra and Tilhard below the sand and gravel deposit. Blades and scrapers were the chief tools of this industry. This industry was considered contemporary to mesolithic period. The tools of this industry were made on flint, chalcedony and jaspar. DeTerra had given the name Proto-neolithic to these tools.

The deposits of Narmada and their correlation with terraces of Soan river valley has been presented below:

Narmada Deposits and Terraces of Soan River Valley

Narmada valley deposit	Soan valley Terrace	
Lower basal gravel	First Terrace (T_1)	Lower group
Pink silt with stone pieces	Second Terrace (T_2)	
Upper gravel	Third Terrace (T_3)	Upper group
Pink silt	Fourth Terrace (T_4)	
Cotton soil/Regur group	Fifth Terrace (T_5)	

A.P. Khatri had also made study of Narmada valley in 1966. He had brought to the light the deposits of Narmada valley different from DeTerra and Paterson. According to him, the lowest deposit of Mahadeo Piparia, Murga Khera, Burman Ghat, Sandia and Ajhera is of red clay. The first gravel was based over it. According to Khatri, the sequence of deposits in Narmada valley is as follows:

6. Yellow silt and modern soil
5. Breccla deposit
4. Yellow cross bedded sand
3. Cemented sandy gravel
2. Boulder conglomerate gravel
1. Red clay.

The evolutionary sequence of handaxe industry in Narmada valley, according to A.P. Khatri, is as follows:

1. Chopper-Chopping Tool Layer (Mahadevian) — Found from red clay and first gravel.
2. Late Acheulian — Early Acheulian layer found from Gravel II and Burman Ghat.
3. Middle Acheulian — Found from Adamgarh hill laterite.
4. Late Acheulian — Yellow cross bedded sand.

H.D. Sankalia had also made a survey of Narmada valley. He like Khatri did not find the deposits of Narmada from one place as reported by DeTerra and Paterson.

S.G. Supekar had reconstructed the sequence of deposits of Narmada valley in the following words:

- The lowest deposit was of conglomerate in the form of gravel. Its thickness was 3 feet to 11 feet. It was based on Vindhya sand stone. No laterite deposit has been found below it at any place. But laterite deposit would have been there because they were found in bore hole. From the boulder conglomerate layer remains of *Elephus, Equus, Bos* and other were found. This layer had also yielded lower palaeolithic tools from different places. From the excavation of this deposit at Mahadeo Piparia, remains of *Bos namadicus* were found which belonged to middle pleistocene.
- Above the boulder conglomerate deposit, a deposit of red clay 9 to 15 feet thick was found. This deposit was not significant from the point of view of cultural materials.
- Red brown stone pieces mixed silt and sandy gravel deposit seems equal at Murga Khera and Deva Kachhar. But on the basis of excavation at Mahadeo Piparia and bore hole, the unequal structure seems local.
- In middle Narmada valley, there is a sandy pebble gravel deposit of 30 to 40 feet thick. This layer had yielded remains of *Bos, Equus*, and *Elephus*. At Deva Kachhar, they were found with middle palaeolithic tools. The tools collected did not exhibit technological and typological difference. The animals remains found from both gravels also did not show any difference.
- Sandy pebble gravels gradually met with yellow-brown sandy silt. Some animal remains were found from this deposit. But over surface of this deposit, microlithic tools were found.

Tools collected from middle Narmada valley included chopper-chopping flake, Acheulian hand axe and cleaver. Tools were made on big flakes and cores. From middle palaeolithic layer, scraper, point, borers, flake and core were found. Some burin, small hand axe and chopper were also found. This industry was mainly a flake industry. Supekar was of opinion that people of different cultures would have lived here in different periods or they would have lived together in the same period.

Sankalia along with his associates had made a survey of deposits near Maheshwar. According to him, there was no difference in the deposits of Maheshwar, Hoshangabad and Narsinghpur.

Lower Palaeolithic Culture of Son Valley

The survey of Son valley was made by Professor Sharma and his associates of Department of Ancient History, Allahabad University. This micro survey was done from the confluence of Son-Gopad to Narkuhi in Sindhi district. This survey revealed that Son valley had threes clear terraces. The first terrace was formed during pleistocene period. Other terraces were formed later on. In this area the river Son flows on shale rock. The river had made its flow route by cutting the base rock. From the study of geological layers, it appears that the river Son was flowing at more height from the present status since the prehistoric past. Big boulder conglomerate brought and deposited on both banks of the river bears testimony in this regard. At places, its height is 30 metre or even more. The entire deposits of Son from top to bottom can be presented in the following sequence.

Cemented Gravel

This is the lowest layer of the deposit at bedrock. The average thickness of this layer was 1 metre. This layer has yielded lower palaeolithic tools from places like Nakhjhar Khurda, Nakjhar Kalan, Pawansiya, and Burwasa.

Red Silt Deposit or Sand Deposit

Over the cemented Gravel-I, a deposit of red silt was found. At some places, a deposit of sand in place of red silt was found. The thickness of this deposit was 3 to 6 metre. Its upper surface was undulating. This shows that after deposition, the upper surface was eroded.

Cemented Gravel-II or Coarse Sand

Upon undulating red silt deposit, a deposit of cemented gravel is found again. This is known as cemented Gravel-II. At some places, coarse sand is found in place of cemented Gravel-II. Sometimes both deposits are found alternatively. Its maximum thickness was 5 metre. From this layer, tools of middle palaeolithic periods were found from the places like Baghor, Dhobanahi, Patpara and Baliyaa.

Coarse Sand

Above cemented gravel deposit, there is a deposit of coarse sand whose maximum average thickness was 15 metre.

Lime Concretion

There is a deposit of lime concretion above coarse sand. Its maximum thickness was 6.25 metre to 0.50 metre.

Yellow Silt

Above lime concretion, a deposit of yellow silt was found. Its average thickness was 3 metre.

Lime Concretion

Above yellow silt, there was a deposit of second lime concretion. Its maximum thickness was 5 metre.

Yellow Silt

Above second lime concretion, again a yellow deposit was found. Its maximum thickness was 6 metre.

Lime Concretion

Above second yellow silt, third lime concretion was found whose maximum thickness was 3 metre.

Yellow Silt

Above third lime concretion, there was a deposit of third yellow silt whose maximum thickness was 3 metre.

Black Soil

The top most layer was of black soil. This deposit has iron nodules. Its thickness was 1.75 metre to 0.75 metre.

Thus, the entire deposits of Son valley revealed layers in sequence from top to down. In Son valley lower palaeolithic tools were found from first gravel deposit. Altogether 57 industries were found. All industry sites were located in Son valley and middle hills of Kaimur. Typologically and technologically, tools obtained from Son valley can be placed under middle and developed Acheulian. Abbevillian types and pebble tools were not found. Majority of tools were fresh and flaked completely in a shape. Besides, hand axes, cleaver and scraper, picks were found in good number. Tools were made on churt and quartzite. Soft or cylinder hammer technique and step flaking technique was known to them. Some tools were influenced by Levalloisean technique.

The middle Palaeolithic tools were found from 84 sites in Son valley. Among 84 sites, 23 are industry sites. They were obtained from the slope of medial ridge. The tools included point, borer, blade and scrapers. They were made on churt and flint.

In Son valley, 78 sites of upper palaeolithic tool were found in which 39 were industry sites. They include different types of scrapers, elongated, blunted and side blades, big lunate, point, borer and burin. The number of blade was more than other tools.

The significant achievement of Son valley is existence of animal remains. More than 5,000 animals remains were collected from there. They were collected from the places like Ramnagar, Murawa, Pawaria, Baghor and Lauwar. Fossils were found more in tributaries of Son. Majority of fossils were found from second gravel deposit. The fossil includes *Bos, bison, bubalas, hippopotamus, aquus, sus, Ghawialis, antelope, elephus* and others. They are of upper pleistocene to holocene period.

Lower Palaeolithic Culture of Maihar

Maihar is located at a distance of 66 km from Riwan on Jabalpur-Riwan road. The water of this area is flown by the river Lilji. The river Lilji is a tributary of Tons river. In the south-west of Maihar Devi hills, Vindhyan hills are situated in semi circular manner. The river Lilji flows in south of the temple. There is a drain in the north of the temple which is a tributary of Lilji. The river flows at present over shale. Here, the deposit sequence from down to top was as follows:

- Over shale an undulating deposit of boulder conglomerate was found. Its average thickness was 1 metre.
- Over this boulder conglomerate deposit, there was a 1.5 metre thick deposit of deep grey silt.
- Over the deep grey deposit, there was a deposit of yellow silt whose average thickness was 2.5 metre.
- Above yellow silt, there was a 2 metre thick deposit of black soil.
- The top most deposit was of red silt with stone pieces.

Only lower Palaeolithic and middle Palaeolithic tools were found from Maihar. The lower Palaeolithic tools have been found from those places where deposit over shale was flown away. Majority of tools were fresh and their transfer had not taken place. Here altogether 430 tools were found. The tools included core, flake, waste flake, handaxe, broken handaxe, cleaver, broken cleaver and scrapers. The tools were made by block on block and hammer stone technique.

Lower Paleolithic Culture of Damoh

R.P. Joshi has made a survey of Damoh area to know the palaeolithic culture. He had surveyed the river Sonar-Kopara and Berwa river valleys. Both these rivers are tributaries of river Kane. The river Kane is itself a tributary of the river Yamuna. In Rehali, Ghaghara and Harat of Sonar valley, there is a deposit of gravel conglomerate on bed rock whose thickness is 4-10 feet. This is a deposit of quartzite pebble, sandstone and shale.

Over this deposit, there is a deposit of 10-15 feet thick silt. Again over this silt deposit, there is a deposit of modern clay. From this valley, 114 tools were collected. The tools included handaxe, ovate, cleaver, scraper, flake, core and core chopper. The tools were made on quartzite. Typologically, tools gathered from gravel deposit may be placed under middle Acheulian. But tools collected from the surface may be placed under Abbevillian to Acheulian layer.

Lower Palaeolithic Culture of Gwalior Area

B.K. Lal and K.P. Nautiyal had made a survey of Gwalior area to find out culture of prehistoric man in this area. They had found a number of sites and industries of prehistoric man who had lived in this area. The most important site is Gupteshwar which is located at a distance of 3 km from the Gwalior town. In the way of Gupteshwar Tigra dam there is a hill. From here lower Palaeolithic tools were gathered from the surface of earth. An excavation work was also done by Lal and his associates. The excavation was made at layer 1st, layer 2nd and layer 3rd. The first layer is located on the top plain of Amara hill. Its height is 1011 to 1045 feet. The 2nd layer is 150 feet below the 1st layer. The 3rd layer is below 100 feet from the 2nd layer. For the purpose of excavation 160 metre long trench was taken from 2nd layer to 3rd layer which was divided into 16 equal parts. The excavation work had revealed sequence of deposits from all layers.

More than 1000 tools were obtained from all three layers. The tools revealed reciprocal relation in typology. All tools were made of quartzite. Besides, core, handaxe, cleaver, scraper and blade, waste flakes were obtained abundantly. Waste flakes were indicating towards the existence of industry site.

The tools of 1st layer were heavily patinated. Only scraper was found in *in situ* condition. The size of scraper was comparatively small. The scrapers were of four types — side, end, round and straight.

The tools of 2nd layer were also made on quartzite. They were less rolled and they had more patination. Handaxes are less in number here. Cleavers are more in number. Majority of them are on end flake. One cleaver is made on Levalloisean flake. It seems to be of late Acheulian.

Long blades of sandstone have also been found. They are related to lower Palaeolithic period. Such types of blades were also found from Late Soan and Chauntra. Some handaxes of small size have also been found. They have been termed as toy type. The tools found from Gupteshwar included 53 handaxes, 332 scraper, 107 cleavers, 145 core and 38 blades.

The excavationists were of view that the prehistoric man of Gupteshwar were forest dwellers. They survived on gathering and hunting.

Lower Palaeolithic Culture of Bhimbetka

The lower Palaeolithic culture of Madhya Pradesh cannot be completed without description of Bhimbetka. It is a name of a hill which is 1 km long in east-west and 1/2 km wide in north-south. It is 100 metre longer than the neighbouring plains. This hill has many hundred caves. Several caves are painted. Bhimbetka hill in Vindhya valley is 45 km south of Bhopal. It is 2 km south-west of Miyanpur village in Raisen. It is 30 km north of Hoshangabad. It is located in between Ubaidullahganj and Barkhera. Both these towns have railway station of Delhi-Mumbai branch of Central railway.

The credit of highlighting this cave groups of Bhimbetka goes to Professor V.S. Wakankar of Vikram University, Ujjain. He along with his associates had made an excavation of a cave in 1972 for the first time. In this excavation he had attained Acheulian layer. In 1973, V.N. Mishra of Pune University did an excavation work there. Under his guidance, a number of scholars, researchers, students and teachers came here each year and did researches on Bhimbetka.

The term 'Bhimbetka' is corrupt form of the Hindi term '*Bhimbaithaka*'. Probably this was a seat of Bhim, one of five *Pandavas* during the period of unknown stay. This hill would have been, probably, a proper place for unknown stay. There is also a neighbouring tribal village Bhiyapur, which seems corrupt form of the term 'Bhimpur'. The remains of Pandopur village have also been found in neighbour area. There is a waterfall named *Vanganga* which was created by Arjuna by his arrow.

While standing on Bhimbetka hill, it appears like a series of long and huge rocks. During geological time, it was a huge rock. But in course of time, it got broken into rocks due to weathering effect. From a distance, these rocks look like Mughal fort. Caves and rock shelters have been found in the bed of rocks or slope or hills. Caves and rock shelters were created due to breaking of soft sandstones in lacs of years. Altogether, there are more than 100 caves and rock shelters which spread over an area of 10 km long from east to west.

Bhimbetka hill is full of perennial flora. Although forest cover has decreased due to felling of trees on large scale, but this valley still has thick forest. The area records 100 cm rainfall per year. That is why the area looks green round the year. The forest of this area has wild animals. For example leopard, hyena, fox, jackal, deer, antelope, *nilgay*, sambhar, bear and several birds. Thus, the area was full of floral and faunal food for prehistoric man. The basic needs of prehistoric man such as food, water, shelter and skinhide were fulfilled here. That is why prehistoric man lived here for lakhs and thousands of years.

Classification and Numbering of Caves

For the purpose of study, the Bhimbetka cave from Karitalai village in east to Godas village in west has been divided into 8 groups or areas. Those groups were given numbers from I to VIII. These groups have been divided again into cluster shelter and they have been given names as ABC.... In each group number of sub-group is changing. The individual habitation sites of each cluster has been provided 1, 2, 3, ... number. Thus, caves have been classified by three layer system, *e.g.*, III R23. On the under wall of each habitation site, the number has been written by Indian ink. The work of classification and numbering was done by Dr. V.S. Wakankar and his associates and students. Yashodhar Math Pal had provided number to caves left by Professor Wakankar.

History of Researches of Bhimbetka

The site name Bhimbetka was discovered by Professor Dr. V.S. Wakankar of Vikram University, Ujjain in 1957. After its discovery in 1957, no further researches were done here for 15 years. In the year 1971, Professor Dr. K.D. Vajpayee and Dr. S.K. Pandey had made limited excavation of two habitation sites. In the year 1972, Professor Wakankar restarted the excavation work here along with his associates. He worked here for 6 years and excavated 8 excavation sites. Teachers and students of Department of Archaeology, Pune University under the supervision of Professor V.N.

Mishra stayed and worked here continuously from 1973 onwards each year. Their work was chiefly concerned with cave III F-23, but they had also done excavation of cave III F-13 and II B-33.

Maximum deposit of habitation site was found from cave No. III B-23. The team of Pune University had excavated this habitation site from 1973 to 1976. The thickness of deposit in cave was found as 4 metre. This deposit had inside it the prehistory of lower Palaeolithic to middle Palaeolithic. The excavation work of this habitation site revealed a sequence of prehistoric cultures, which is as follows:

Lower Palaeolithic Culture (Chopper-Chopping Culture before 10,00,000 years)

Evidences of the earliest culture came in to light from the excavation of two caves by Professor Wakankar. Below Acheulian deposit of cave no. III F-24, chopper-chopping tools were found. They were separated by a non-living layer from the Acheulian deposit. The number of tools were very less. The tools were more weathered due to storage of water at cave bed. From an another cave no. III A-29, these tools were found below mesolithic deposit, but they were again separated by a non-living layer. Tools were made on round pebble. They were also made on some small boulder by minimum flaking. They were made on metamorphis and stones which were available in plenty in neighbouring hills. The researches done so far has yielded a very thin layer of this culture. The number of tool was also less and shapeless. Therefore, in order to establish an independent cultural stage of this culture, more and more researches and evidences are required.

Lower Palaeolithic Culture (Acheulian Culture 10,00,000–40,000 B.C.)

This stage of Palaeolithic culture at Bhimbetka is quite clear. The best evidence of this culture has been obtained from the cave no. III F-23. The total habitational deposit of this site was 3.90 metre which was divided into 8 layers. Layers 1-3 are related to mesolithic period. Layer 4 is related to upper Palaeolithic period. Layer 5 related to middle Palaeolithic period. The layer 6-8 are related to lower Palaeolithic period. In this cave, the deposit of Acheulian culture is 2.50 metre. This is more than the deposit found in any rock shelter. Materials related to Acheulian culture have also been found from the cave no. III F-24 and III A-30.

The sequence of layer and Bhimbetka cultures is being presented below.

Layer 1

The thickness of this layer is 5-10 cm. It has been formed by light yellow-brown sandy clay. Some angular stones have also been found. This layer had yielded evidences of geometric microlithic tools of chalcedony, flake and blade of quartzite, milestone, muller, stone beads related to light-brown or red pottery.

Layer 2

The thickness of this layer is 10-25 cm. It is yellow-brown clay deposit. Leaving stone beads and potsherds, the cultural materials of this layer exhibited similarity with cultural materials of layer 1. This deposit has evidences of more industry.

Layer 3

The thickness of this layer is 10-20 cm. It is a deposit of brown clay mixed with pieces of red stones. Its colour becomes light in the rock shelter. Stone pieces also become less. The number of microliths is also reduced.

Layer 4

The thickness of this layer is 15-20 cm. It is made of light brown clay mixed with pieces of big stones. This deposit had revealed flake, blade, side scraper, end scraper and burin of quartzite stone.

Layer 5

Its thickness is 40-50 cm. It is formed of light red-brown clay. This layer has given us evidences of different types of scrapers, Levalloisean flakes, blades, cleavers and handaxe from the deposit below 10 cm. These tools have been correlated to middle Palaeolithic Mousterian culture.

Layer 6

Its thickness is 80-90 cm. This deposit is like the deposit of layer 5. But it is more solid and red. This layer has given evidences of late Acheulian industry.

Layer 7

Its thickness is 90-100 cm. It is a glittering red-brown colour deposit. This layer has also revealed evidences of late Acheulian industry. Tools are reddish.

Layer 8

Its thickness is 80 to 90 cm. The colour of this deposit is orange. It is comparatively solid. This deposit has shown tools of late Acheulian.

From the researches done in cave no. III F-23, it appears that Acheulian man had arranged boulders and stone slabs outside cave to get entrance inside the cave. They had prepared floor in the cave nos. III F-23 and III C-24 with boulders and slabs. The floors have revealed several hundred tools in construction and used conditions scattered over the floor. The lowest layer tools seems more withered. Their sharp edges were no more. Some were broken in to sand powder.

Acheulian tools include handaxe, cleaver, different types of cleavers, serrated knife, notch, waste flakes, blade and flakes. The handaxes are elongated and pointed. They were made by flaking from both sides. They were used for digging, cutting, and scraping. Cleavers were four cornered tools like rectangles, square and triangles. Their cutting edges are flat and sharp. It would have been used for cutting meat and wood. In the Acheulian industry of Bhimbetka, the ratio of cleaver and handaxe was 3 : 1. Majority of tools were of small size and made of flakes. Chopper and chopping tools are not found in Acheulian industry.

Majority of flakes were made by Levalloisean technique. Small discoidal core to core of 40 kg. weight have been found. The tools were prepared inside the cave. Several broken and damaged tools indicate that they were used inside the cave.

Tools were made on local quartzite metamorphic sand stones. For handaxes and cleavers, hard deep blue stones were used. These tools used to resist withering effect and they look fresh even today. Majority of flake tools were made of soft yellow stone. The flake tools found from upper layer were more fresh than the tools found from lower layer. The lower layer tools were more withered.

Middle Palaeolithic Culture (40,000–20,000 Years)

The middle Palaeolithic culture of Bhimbetka has evolved from the Acheulian culture. In fact, it reveals readoption of Acheulian culture. In this culture handaxes and cleavers gradually get vanished and the shape of tools start becoming small comparatively. Tool types remain almost same. One significant change appears that the tools are not made on flakes, but on natural stone slabs. The number of blades start increasing.

Upper Palaeolithic Culture (20,000–10,000 Years)

The upper Palaeolithic culture of Bhimbetka is not very clear. Its revolution has taken place due to development of local mesolithic culture. Increase in number of blades and small thin sized blades are characteristics of this culture. Some micro-blades have also appeared. This deposit has yielded more end scrapper. Some burins have also been found.

Mesolithic Culture (10,000–2500 B.C.)

After Acheulian culture, mesolithic culture of Bhimbetaka is more clear. In this period, majority of caves and rock shelters were occupied by man. The population of Bhimbetka had gone up suddenly in this period. This became possible due to change in environment, technology and increase in food material. Our knowledge about Bhimbetka mesolithic period is rich because remains of animals in the form of carbonic materials have been found. Human burial sites have also been found in the caves. The one part of painting of caves may be correlated with this practice. From the drawing and painting of caves, contemporary life and environment can be understood. Contact between palaeolithic Bhimbetka dwellers and peasant communities can also be explained.

The Bhimbetka Palaeolithic man had acquired knowledge and skill of technology and types of tools of this period. They had acquired the technique of microlithic blade production by cylinder core and pressure technique. Their one or more ends were made blunted. The microlithic tools includes blunted blades, obliquedy truncated blades, points, lunates, crescent, triangle, trapeze, arrow head. These tools were fitted in handle of bone and wood and were used as knife, spear, arrow, and sickles. Besides these tools, side scraper, end scraper, borer, burin, damaged flakes and other flakes and cores were found. Geometric microlithic tools were less in number. Points made of horns, teeth and bones were also used.

Chert and chalcedony used for tool making were not available in neighbouring hills of Bhimbetka. Such materials are found in veins of Deccan Lava. The nearest source of these materials for Bhimbetka man was Barkhera, located at a distance of 6 km towards south. The mesolithic man of Bhimbetka used to bring these materials from there. The existence of Muller and Rubber indicates that these tools were used for drawing and painting.

The mesolithic man of Bhimbetka used to bury their deads in the cave with all regards. The dead body was kept either in bending or extending position. Head was kept in east. Sometimes head was kept in west. Muller, rubber, horns, bonepins, pieces of hematites were kept with dead body in burial.

The mesolithic man used fire regularly. The evidences of burnt ash, coal, bone indicate in this regard. Bones, teeth and horns of animals were broken and burnt. Bones and horns were cut with sharp weapons.

The Bhimbetka mesolithic man used to prepare floor with stone slabs and boulders. One of the walls of cave no. III F-23 is 6 metre long and 1 metre wide.

From the middle layer of Bhimbetka deposit, chalcolithic tools and painted and non-painted potteries were found. This indicates that tool gatherers and hunters of Bhimbetka had relation with peasants of the neighbouring plain.

From the top most layer iron age ceramic, iron tools and punch coin were found. It seems that the Bhimbetka cave dwellers would have left hunting and gathering when they came in contact with local plain dwellers practising agriculture. They gradually adopted the occupation of cultivation and came to settle in plain areas as peasants.

Lower Palaeolithic Culture of Eastern India

Here we are going to discuss the lower Palaeolithic culture of following states:

- Bihar
- Jharkhand
- West Bengal
- Meghalaya
- Orissa

Lower Palaeolithic Culture of Bihar

The state of Bihar is the most eastern state of India. It is bounded by Nepal in north, Bangladesh in east, Jharkhand in south and Uttar Pradesh and Chhattisgarh in west. In fact Bihar is the central and lower part of Ganga valley. This state is in between *Bhangar* (dry doab) and *Khadar* (pluvial doab). The river Ganges flows in its northern part from west to east and divides the state into two parts — north Bihar and south Bihar. This part is also known as the plain area of Ganga. The Kaimur hills from Mirzapur of Uttar Pradesh to the Rohtas district of south Bihar extend over an area of 800 square miles. In Bihar its highest range is 1472 feet. The rivers may also be divided in to two parts — First is Ganga and its tributaries which come from north and south both directions to meet it. The second one is the biggest river Son. But Son is also a tributary of Ganga.

Historically, the state of Bihar (Magadha) has played significant role in shaping the history of India. In fact the history of ancient India has been written by Magadha. But we have very little knowledge about the prehistory of Bihar. It is due to lack of sufficient researches. The another reason is that Bihar is geologically newest formation of Ganga valley. Hence, evidences of lower palaeolithic period are difficult to get.

The most significant reported prehistoric site of Bihar is Bhimbandh of Monghyr (Munger). Joshi and Singh had made a survey of this site. They had obtained rolled handaxes from bank of Ranjana river. Tools made of quartzite, scrapers, flakes and cores were also found. These tools were of developed Acheulian type. No cleaver was found. A little away from Bhimbandh on the left bank of river Ranjana, Acheulian tools of quartzite were found on the hills.

N.K. Bose and his associates had obtained lower palaeolithic tools on 830 feet high hill, 7 km away from Bhimbandh.

Lower Palaeolithic Culture of Jharkhand

The state of Jharkhand came into existence on 15th of November, 2000 by bifurcation of the state of Bihar. It is bounded by Bihar in north, Bengal in east, Orissa in south and Uttar Pradesh and Chhattisgarh in west. In the south hills of Ganga in Bihar, Chhotanagpur and Santhal pargana of Jharkhand came into existence. The region of Chhotanagpur is based on plateau and archean gneiss. The northern part of Damodar and Pane plane part of Hazaribagh are at a height of 1300 feet from sea level. In its north there is Damodar valley and in its south there is plateau area of Ranchi.

They are at a height of 2000 feet and 2500 feet from the sea level. Nearby the river Swarnarekha its height decreases gradually. Towards the delta, plateau area meets in plain area.

The Singhbhum district is most significant from the point of view of prehistoric archaeological anthropology. The most of prehistoric survey was done in the district of Singhbhum. The district of Singhbhum lies in south-east part at 21°58' and 23°36' north latitude 86°54' east longitude. The three important rivers of this district are Swarnarekha, Baitarni and Brahmani. Among all three river, Swarnarekha is the biggest river. Sanjai and Kharwai rivers are tributaries of Swarnarekha. In Kharwai several small rivers meet. Important among them are Gamuagara and Roro.

The prehistoric survey of Roro valley was done by Dharni Sen and A.K. Ghosh in 1960. They had obtained palaeolithic tools from the Roro river valley of Singhbhum district. Tools were made on quartzite and jaspar. They were found in the form of pebbles in the valley.

Sen and Ghosh had discovered three terraces in the Roro valley situated at a height of 60, 40 and 20 feet. These terraces were local.

Near Timildah they had discovered three alluvial terraces. They were formed due to local agradation. Over first terrace gravel was found which is covered with yellow clay at places. Below gravel, a deposit of moram was found. The second terrace is very fast and gravel is also found over it. The tools were found from the first gravel. Some tools were also found from second and third terraces. They were brought from the first terrace by water current.

The excavation of chain has revealed the sequence of local deposit. Here at the lowest layer, there is a deposit of steatite. Over this deposit, there is 20 feet thick deposit of boulder conglomerate. Over this, there is a 15 feet thick deposit of gravel. Over this, there is a deposit of red clay and yellow sandy clay. The thickness of reddish clay is 5 feet and yellow sandy clay is 1-2 feet. The base of first deposit is laterite.

Dharni Sen and Ashok Kumar Ghosh had divided all tools in three categories: (i) pebble tool, (ii) core tool, and (iii) flake tool. Only one pebble blade handaxe was found. The core tool included bifacial chopping, Abbevillian-Acheulian handaxe and cleaver. The flake tools included chopper and scrapers.

Altogether 35 tools were discovered from here. Among all 35 tools, there were 26 handaxe, 2 chopper-chopping, 3 cleaver and 4 scrapers. 21 tools were of jaspar and other were of sand stone, churt, quartzite and basalt. They seem to be of Madrasian hand axe-cleaver tradition.

A.K. Ghosh in his unpublished Ph.D. thesis *Palaeolithic Culture of Singhbhum* (1964) has described systematically the sequence of geological deposits. According to him, the sequence of pleistocene and holocene deposit was as follows:

- Over bedrock of quartzite, there was a deposit of pebble laterite.
- Over pebble laterite deposit, there was a deposit of mottled clay.
- Over mottled clay deposit, there was a deposit of gravel conglomerate. An unconformity was found between the two deposits.
- Over gravel conglomerate deposit, there was a deposit of silt clay.
- Over silt clay deposit, there was a deposit of gravel. There was an unconformity between the two deposits.
- At some places, in place of deposits of gravel conglomerate, silt clay and gravel stones, secondary gravels have taken place. This is known as secondary laterite. It is a very thick deposit.
- The pleistocene ended with deep grey silt along with late basal gravel.
- The top most deposit is modern deposit.

The secondary laterite deposit has been correlated with pleistocene. They were formed during pluvial periods. Over this mottled clay deposit was of interpluvial period. No tools were found from these two deposits. These deposits are not significant from the point of view of prehistoric archaeology. The prehistoric cultures began to appear from the third or boulder conglomerate deposit. It is also known as lower gravel.

The lower Palaeolithic industry of Chaibasa reveals two elements. They were (i) Chopper, and (ii) bifacial tools or chopping. All tools were divided into Abbevillian and Acheulian types. The tools were made by cyclinder hammer technique. The tool community had chopper, handadze, handaxe, cleaver and scraper. They were formed on cores and flakes. Some flakes were also found. Fabricator core retouched flakes were also found from here. Handadzes have been reported only from here in India. Handadzes have been made on core and pebble both. The number of handaxe was more. Bifacial cleaver were also found.

The upper gravel layer of Chaibasa has revealed flake tools. The flake tools have Levalloisean elements. The chief tool of this period was scraper. Points and borers were also parts of industries of this period.

The last part of tool community is flake-blade. An another type of stone has been used for the purpose of tool making. Small sized choppers, scraper, knife, point, borer and burin have also been found.

Thus, the palaeolithic culture of Chaibasa has revealed tool communities belonging to lower Palaeolithic, middle Palaeolithic and upper Palaeolithic cultures in chronological sequence.

Lower Palaeolithic Culture of West Bengal

The state of West Bengal lies in the lower valley of Ganges. Jharkhand and Bihar states are in its west, Bangladesh in east, Himalayas in north, Bay of Bengal in south and Orissa in south-west. The major part of this state is irrigated by Ganges and its tributaries. Jalpaigudi, Darjeeling and Cooch Behar of north Midnapur, Bankura and Purulia districts of west-south are not irrigated by the river Ganges. The south-east part of this region is Coastal delta plain.

It was a scholar B.B. Lal who had discovered a handaxe from Bankura district in 1865 for the first time. After a long gap with the efforts of Calcutta University and State Archaeological Survey a number of habitation sites of prehistoric man were explored in 1959-60 from Bankura, Purulia and Midnapur districts. Scholars like Krishna Swamy, Sen, Ghosh and Das Gupta explored a number of lower Palaeolithic sites in Bankura district. The most important river of this area is Dwarkeshwar. Gandheshwari, Damodar, Kumari and Kasai rivers also flow in this area. Sena and Ghosh had made a prehistoric survey in the valleys of Dwarkeshwar, Kasai and Kumari rivers near Bankura. The prehistoric tools were found from gravel mixed laterite deposits. This deposit is based on rock bed at several places.

Among all industry sites, Hathikhera site occupies special significance. A good number of handaxe, chopper-chopping and scraper were found from this site. The colour of tools was grey-red. All tools discovered from Bankura were placed in the three groups — (i) Chopper, (ii) Scraper, and (iii) Handaxe.

Choppers were made on pebble as well as core. They were made of quartzite stone. Handaxes were made on core. They were pear shaped or ovate. Only one cleaver was found from here. The industries of Bankura and Singhbum seem to be contemporary stratigraphically and technologically. The chopper tools were showing similarity with Soan pebble made choppers. But unlike Soan tradition, flakes were not found from Bankura.

Besides Bankura, Archaeological Department had also made a prehistoric survey of Susunia hill neighbouring river valleys. Das Gupta of Archaeology Department had discovered 35 industry sites from river banks and their valleys. He had discovered a huge number of lower Palaeolithic tools and established a stone culture in this regard. In tool community developed Acheulian handaxe and cleaver were found. They were made by employing alternate flaking technique. Das Gupta was of opinion that handaxe tool producing and using prehistoric man would have come to settle first on sand stone. Thereafter, pluvial period would have started. In pluvial period, gravels were carried and deposited on banks and valleys. Majority of tools were found from gravel deposit. Near Susunia, the average height of gravel deposit was nearly 1 metre. There were quartz, quartzite, laterite balls, and mud in this deposit. Due to change in flow route, redeposited gravel deposits were found at several places. In cemented gravel, yellow to light red colour sand stone deposit was found. From this deposit tools of middle Palaeolithic period were found. A good number of fossils were also found from here. On the basis of fossil evidence, it has been correlated to upper pleistocene period. A deposit of light yellow sand stone was found over it which contained laterite balls. This deposit was correlated to holocene period. The environment at that time would have been pluvial. This deposit was correlated to microlithic blade, flake and neolithic tools. Tools were found from secondary laterite deposits.

Kangaruwati valley of Purulia district was also an important site of lower palaeolithic industry. Das Gupta had made a survey of Kangs valley. Near Kankardara, he had obtained 100 clearly developed Acheulian handaxe and cleaver.

The Midnapur district of West Bengal was also an important site of prehistoric man. Here heights of hills at several places are 1,000 feet and on the earth laterite deposit is found. From Gopalpur, Begunadih, Hathibara, Muransol, Chakdoa, Ganganirmath and Kansawati of Midnapur district, Palaeolithic tools were reported. At all places chopper, handaxe and scraper were found from secondary laterite deposit.

Das Gupta and his associates had also obtained lower palaeolithic cultural tools from Bokankati in Jaya valley from erosional laterite and gravel deposit.

Lower Palaeolithic Culture of Meghalaya

Meghalaya is the easternmost state of India. Previously, it was known as Assam. But later on, Assam was divided into Nagaland, Meghalaya, Arunachal Pradesh, Mizoram, Manipur and Assam. Dr. T.C. Sharma of Gauhati University had brought Meghalaya on the map of prehistoric India. Professor Sharma and his associates had made a prehistoric survey of Garo hills and discovered a number of palaeolithic sites. Garo hill is a town of Meghalaya. Here members of Garo tribe reside in hilly areas. That is why the hill was named as Garo hills. Here, hill ranges are located in between two alluvial areas — Brahmaputra valley in north and Sumi valley in south. These hill ranges have a maximum height of 4000 feet. The chief rivers of this district are Someshwari, Ganol, Rongram and Jinziram. Geologically Garo hill ranges are archaen extension of peninsular India. In between them, there is dyke of dolerite which was used by prehistoric man for making the tools.

In the year 1974, Rongram, Waram, Simsang, Selbal and Didami valleys were also surveyed and palaeolithic tools were collected from the upper part of river. Altogether 9 sites were discovered. Among 9 sites, 4 sites namely, Rongram-Algiri, Chhivragiri, Waramathebrogiri and Romgiri were stratified site. From this deposit chopper and handaxe were found. The complete sequence of pleistocene deposits was not found at any place in Garo hills. From Waramthebrogiri site several flake tool, handaxe and cleaver were found. This site is a terrace of Waram valley. These tools were found from yellow silt and boulder conglomerate stratified deposits. This deposit was correlated with early pleistocene period. Prehistoric man had lived here continuously from lower palaeolithic period to mesolithic period. Because blade-flake and microlithic tools were also found here.

Professor T.C. Sharma had established the sequence of stone stool traditions from down to top as follows:

- Pebble and chopper tool tradition.
- Core and handaxe cleaver tradition.
- Flake tool tradition.
- Microlithic tool tradition.

Lower Palaeolithic Culture of Orissa

Orissa is the easternmost part of India. It lies in the south of Bengal. It is bound in north by Midnapur of West Bengal and Singhbhum of Jharkhand, in north-west by Simdega of Jharkhand, in west by Raigarh and Raipur of Chhattisgarh, in south-west by Bastar district of Chhattisgarh and in south by Srikakulam, Vishakhapatnam and east Godavari district and in east by Bay of Bengal. Geologically and geographically entire Orissa may be divided into two parts:

1. Plains formed by deltaic deposits of rivers.
2. Plateau or hill areas.

The first part is situated between Bay of Bengal in east and plateau areas in west. In forming this part of land, rivers have made significant contributions. Swarnarekha, Burhawalang, Vaitarni, Brahmani and Mahanadi are chief rivers of this area. Mahanadi rises from Chhattisgarh and Suwarnarekha rises from Jharkhand. The river Brahmani has been created by meeting the two rivers — Shankh and Koel of Jharkhand. Vaitarni and Burhawalang rise from Keonjhar and Mayurbhanj hills. The second part of Orissa is an extension of hills of Jharkhand and Chhattisgarh.

It was a scholar Ball who for the first time had discovered four stone tools from different places in 1875. But before 1939, no systematic prehistoric survey was made in Orissa. In 1939 Warman and Acharya had made collection of some tools from Mayurbhanj. Dr. D. Banerjee had also made a similar type of collection. In the same year, N.K. Bose and Dharni Sen of Calcutta University made a systematic survey of prehistoric tools and deposits at a site Kuliyana. They continued their work till 1942. Their work was extended from Kuliana to 10-11 miles pillar on Baripad-Bangriposi route in north-west of Baripad. From neighbouring sites of Kuliana, tools were gathered from laterite gravel pits. They are termed as Gurhikhadans in local language. Some tools were also gathered from gravels of Burhawalang river.

All neighbouring sites of Kuliana had similar types of deposits. But deepest survey was made only at Kuliana. Twenty feet below the upper surface, there was a deposit of mud soil. Over this deposit, there was a deposit of primary laterite. But in Khadanic of Kuliana, boulder conglomerate made cemented gravel deposit was found. This deposit was formed by a tributary of Burhawalang. Over primary laterite a deposit of secondary laterite was found. Tools were found from all sites of deposit. The tools possessed following characteristics:

- Choppers were the oldest tool. Their working edges were straight or convex. Their flaking was done unifacial, irregular and alternating. The other end was thick and used as butt end. Working edges were untouched. Stepflaking scars were found.
- In this group irregular bifacial tools and flakes with natural striking platform were included. Here, flakes were made from core and flakes were flaked again to form a core.

- In this group retouched bifacial tools and cleavers were included. Only one cleaver had beautiful shape.

Bose and Sen were of opinion that Kuliana industry was basically a core industry. Pebbles and flakes were also found from this industry. But handaxes and cleavers were more in number than other tools. Handaxes were ovate and oblong — Rastroid handaxe and knife were also found in tool community. Only Clactonian falkes were found but their number was very less. Levalloisean flake was not found. Kuliana industry had come into existence when flaking technique was not developed. But prehistoric people were gradually acquiring the technique of flaking.

N.K. Bose and his associates had made a resurvey of Burhawalang river at Karampol and other places in 1950-57. According to Bose, the stratigraphical sequence of Mayurbhanj was as follows:

- The lowest deposit of grey blue clay.
- Over this deposit, there was a deposit of boulder conglomerate.
- Over boulder conglomerate deposit, there was an alluvial deposit. From lower layer of deposit, early to developed bifacial tool, cleaver and flakes were found.

In between 1957-59, Mohpatra had made a prehistoric archaeological survey of Mahanadi and discovered Palaeolithic sites like Dheknal, Sundargarh, Sambalpur, Koenjhar and Mayurbhanj. Mohpatra was of opinion that like Peninsular India, Orissa had also witnessed pluvial and interpluvial periods. In first pluvial period, the primary laterite deposit was formed over rock bed. The deposits of Narmada Valley and south-east coast would have taken place in similar climate like Orissa. No evidences of human presence were found. After Ist pluvial period, Ist interpluvial period would have come. In this period, an alluvial deposit over primary laterite deposit had taken place. No tools have been found in this period. During second pluvial period, gravel deposit would have taken place. This deposit was 10 to 12 feet thick. The secondary laterite deposit had taken place in this period. Prehistoric man had left their evidences of stay in this period. The first gravel layer of Orissa seemed to be contemporary of lower gravel deposit of Narmada. Over gravel deposit, there was a deposit of red silt which had become sometimes 40 feet thick. No tools were found from this deposit.

During third pluvial period, a thin gravel deposit was formed over red silt. This deposit was 2-6 feet thick. Middle Palaeolithic tools were found from this deposit. After third pluvial period, third interpluvial period started. In third interpluvial period red silt was deposited. No tools were found from this period. The upper clay deposit of Narmada was contemporary to red silt deposit of Orissa. During holocene Orissa, rivers were depositing in plain areas and erosion of plateau area was taking place. Mohpatra had divided all tools into three stages on the basis of technology. They are as follows:

Phase 1: Under this phase, handaxe, irregularly flaked bifacial tool, flake, irregularly flaked pebble tools were included.

Phase 2: Under this phase, handaxe, cleaver, scraper, core, flake and irregularly flaked pebbles were kept.

Phase 3: Under this phase handaxe, cleaver, scrapers, point, flake, core and irregularly flaked tools were kept.

According to G.C. Mohpatra, the lower Palaeolithic culture of Orissa was mainly bifacial tool tradition. In this tradition, both cores and flakes were used. Soan like pebble, chopper and chopping were not found. The number of handaxe was more. From phase 2, cleavers were found, but their number was less. Scrapers are of small size. Point, flake and core were also found in good number. The lower Palaeolithic culture of Orissa may be placed under Abbevillian-Acheulian type.

Lower Palaeolithic Culture of Peninsular India

Under lower Palaeolithic culture of peninsular India, we are going to discuss the lower Palaeolithic culture of following states:

- Lower Palaeolithic Culture of Andhra Pradesh
- Lower Palaeolithic Culture of Tamil Nadu
- Lower Palaeolithic Culture of Kerala
- Lower Palaeolithic Culture of Karnataka.

Lower Palaeolithic Culture of Andhra Pradesh

The state of Andhra Pradesh is bounded by Orissa, Chhattisgarh and Maharashtra in north, Mysore in west, Madras in south and Bay of Bengal in east. This state occupies significant place so far as Palaeolithic culture of India is concerned. Geologically, this part is the oldest landmass of earth. Red land, shallow rivers and hills tell us about the antiquity of this part of India. Godavari, Krishna and Pennar are the chief rivers of this state. They irrigate northern, central and southern parts of the state respectively. Nallamalai and Arramalai hill ranges of eastern ghat are spread south-west to north-east directions centrally in this state. In south there is Palkonda hill ranges.

Scholars like Cammiade and Burkitt had made their significant study in Chittur area of Andhra Pradesh. They made collection of palaeolithic tools from this area. They had also correlated the tools with geological layers and pleistocene period. Commiade had collected tools from the sites nearby Gundala Brahameshwar and Giddalur. They had divided tools on the basis of stratigraphy, typology and condition into following four classes:

- Handaxe of oldest industry made on quartzite.
- Tools of flake industry and beautifully fashioned handaxes made of quartzite sand stone and chalcedony.
- Blunted side blade, burin and end scraper made on flint.
- Microlithic tools made on Agate.

In this area, prehistoric man would have come after laterite deposit. In this area, there would have been seven climatic changes in prehistoric time. They were as follows:

- Extensive pluvial period in which laterite was formed. No tools were found in this period.
- Extensive interpluvial period in which forest and plains were formed. In this period prehistoric men with hand axe culture came to settle.
- Fast pluvial period in which second layers were formed and handaxe culture ended.
- Interpluvial period in which expansion of new culture took place over erosional laterite deposit. Tools of flake and other category were used.
- Pluvial period in which alluvial deposit in place of laterite deposit took place. In this period tools of second series were used.
- In 6th period, decrease in pluviation took place and tools of third series were used.
- In 7th period modern climate came into existence and tools of fourth series were used.

After Cammiade and Burkitt, Krishnaswamy and Soundar Rajan under the chairmanship of Zeuner made a prehistoric survey of Giddalur areas again in 1949 and a good number of stone tools were collected. These scholars had obtained the tools of Series-I and Series-II from Giddalur-I and tools of Series-III and series-IV from Giddalur-II. From Kanjipalle and Talpalle, tools of first series were obtained which were influenced by middle palaeolithic period. In their collection, Rastrocarinate and Victoria west occupied significant and special position. The shape of these tools are big. One facial and bifacial tools were also found. According to Soundar Rajan, tools of Giddalur-I were irregular and made of pebble. They were similar to Kafuan and Oldowan pebble tool of Africa. The tools of Giddalr-II was made on broken pebbles. They were like Soan pebble tools. Two different traditions of pebble tools of Abbevillian-Acheulian tradition of south India were found. Decrease in pebble tools and increase in cleavers indicated that pebble tool tradition was an integral part of core tool tradition of south India. Here pebble element can be considered as local. Abbevillian and Acheulian tools were found in abundant. Besides these, cleavers were also found. They were made by bifacial flaking. They were made by single Vaal technique or double Vaal technique. In Giddalur-I, there were no Levalloisean flakes, while in Giddalur-II there were no Rastrocarinate and Victoria west type tools.

Lower palaeolithic tools were also found from Talpalle and Kanjilipalle. Mixed form of lower Palaeolithic tools and middle Palaeolithic tools were found from there.

Lower Palaeolithic Culture of Nagarjuna Konda

Nagarjuna Konda site is located at Krishna valley in Guntur district of Andhra Pradesh. At a distance of 2-3 km from Nagarjuna Konda hill ranges, a scholar named Soundar Rajan had discovered Palaeolithic tools from 6 localities which he termed Locality-A, Locality-B, Locality-C, Locality-D, Locality-E and Locality-F. From these localities, from 1st series to fourth series of Burkitt and Cammiade, all Palaeolithic cultures were found. This reveals clearly that prehistoric men had lived here from lower palaeolithic period to neolithic period.

The description of localities and tool types were as follows:

Locality-A : Abbevillian-Acheulian hand axe, cleaver, and some pebble tools found from stony land. No flake tool was found.

Locality-B : The locality was in south-east from the locality-A. Flakes and flake tools were found from here. Flakes were influenced by Levalloisean technique. Bifacial tools were not found from this locality.

Locality-C : A deposit of basal gravel over rock bed was found from this locality.

Locality-D : Only pebble tools and big flakes were found from this locality.

From a drain in south-east of Lambadiguddem, big flakes and angular flakes were found which were of Abbevillian style. Pebble tool was not found from this site. Probably there were two traditions of prehistoric culture in this valley. The prehistoric people living nearby Krishna river (Locality A-D) were getting pebbles easily. Therefore, they were making pebble tools. But those people who crossed drain to settle in hill area, they began to fashion core tools and Clactonian tools. Acheulian tools were developed later on. Blade-flake-burin fashioning upper Palaeolithic men used to select high sites. Because plenty of stones were available for fashioning tools. For preparing lower and middle Palaeolithic tools, quartzite were chosen. For preparing upper Palaeolithic tools, churt stones were chosen.

Lower Palaeolithic Culture of Karempudi

The Karempudi site is located at a distance of 40 km south-east from Nagarjuna Konda on Naguleru river. Nearby Karempudi, 4 sites-II, III, IV and V are located on Naguleru river. But site-I is located on tributary of Naguleru. From the site-I, Oldowan of Africa like pebble tools were found. But from sites-II, III, IV and V Abbevillian, Acheulian, Clactonian and proto Levalloisean tools were found. There was complete lack of pebble tool. It seems that prehistoric man lived first of all at site-I. But he gradually moved towards chief river Naguleru. Here he stopped for making pebble tools. Now, he began to make flake tools and cleaver. From sites II to V, flake tools and cleavers were found.

Lower Palaeolithic Culture of Chittur

Chittur of Andhra Pradesh is an important lower Palaeolithic cultural area. The chief river of this area is Suwarnamukhi. Except the Rallakalawa river, all other rivers of the area are depositing in their valleys. In Rallakalawa river, old river deposits were still preserved. Lower palaeolithic tools were found from Chandragiri, Tirupati and Vedullacheruvu.

Vedullacheruvu is located at a distance of 4 km in north-west from Renigunta. Here the best section of river is preserved. From here three clear cycles of deposits were found. The lowest deposit was of well connected pebbles and gravels whose thickness was 4 to 6 feet. It was covered with red silt whose thickness was 15 feet. From this deposit lower palaeolithic tools were found. The second deposit was of unconnected pebbles and gravels. It was covered with yellow silt. From this deposit, tools of middle Palaeolithic culture were found. The uppermost deposit was of modern soil. From this deposit tools of upper Palaeolithic period were found.

M.L.K. Murray had divided all tools obtained from Rallakalawa into 5 classes: A, B, C, D and E. From all classes, sequence of technological development was found. The classes A, B and C were related to lower Palaeolithic tools. From class D middle palaeolithic tools and from the class E upper-palaeolithic tools were found. The pebble tool, bifacial core, and flake were made by flaking techniques. The bifacial cores were more in number. From Rallakalawa B and C cleavers and discoid scrapers were found. The pebble tools of Rallakalawa were like Soan pebble tools and handaxe cleaver tools were like Madras handaxe-cleaver type.

Lower Palaeolithic Culture of Tamil Nadu

Tamil Nadu is the southernmost state of our country India. It is bounded in north by Andhra Pradesh, east by Bay of Bengal, in south by Indian ocean, and in west by plateau part of Karnataka and Kerala. Tamil Nadu state occupies a significant place in Indian prehistoric archaeological anthropology. It is because it was the state from where Robert Bruce Foote had started the researches of Indian prehistoric archaeological anthropology by reporting the existence of Palaeolithic tools in 1863. His this discovery made him known as father of Indian prehistoric archaeological anthropology. This state also occupies special significance because from here a separate tool tradition of lower Palaeolithic culture was found. This is known as handaxe-cleaver tradition and the lower Palaeolithic culture is known as Madrasian culture. The tool tradition of Madrasian culture was quite different from the tool tradition of Soanian culture. In Soanian culture there was existence of pebble-chopper-chopping traditions, but in Madrasian culture there was existence of core hand axe-cleaver tradition. Thus, in two different geographical and environmental regions of India two different tool traditions of lower palaeolithic culture were in existence. They were of pebble made chopper-chopping traditions of Punjab in north India and core made handaxe cleaver tradition of Tamil Nadu in south in India. The prehistoric environment of Punjab was of glacial and interglacial, but the prehistoric environment of Tamil Nadu was of pluvial and interpluvial.

On 30th May of 1863, Robert Bruce Foote had discovered a palaeolithic tool from a gravel pit. This gravel pit was located at a distance of 100 yards from Pallawaram Cantonment. This discovery had made him founder of Indian prehistoric anthropology. After this achievement, an associate of Robert Bruce Foote, King had obtained two beautifully fashioned ovate from a drain Attiram Pakkam. Robert Bruce Foote and his associate King had obtained a good number of quartzite made tools from the laterite deposit on plantshale. Besides these places, Robert Bruce Foote had also obtained tools from laterite conglomerate layer at several places. But in fact they were of after laterite deposit.

Robert Bruce Foote had divided all tools into three groups, which are as follows:

Group I	:	The tools of this group were pointed or wedged shaped and their ends were blunted.
Group II	:	Under this group one end pointed, both ends pointed, ovate and discoid tools were included.
Group III	:	Under this group only flakes were included.

After Bruce Foote and King, a scholar named B.D. Krishna Swamy had made a survey of plain of Pallar near Madras. He had obtained a quarternary deposit of boulder conglomerate over tertiary deposits. At places, he had also obtained erosional deposit of laterite.

After Krishna Swamy, DeTerra and Paterson had discovered four terraces belonging to Pleistocene near Madras. At a place Erumaivettiplaiyam near red hill, Peneplane area of laterite terraces were found. They were made by Kortalayer river. The Cambridge Yale expedition had attempted to correlate geological layers with archaeological materials. Their sequence was as follows:

- First of all erosional laterite deposit was made over a white boulder conglomerate.
- Then this deposit was cut by the river Kortalayer and three terraces were formed in Kortalayer valley.
- The terraces were termed as 1st, 2nd, and 3rd.
- These terraces are located at Kortalayer valley at heights of 60, 20 and 8 feet respectively.
- The 1st terrace was erosional and the 2nd terrace was depositional. This is very clear at a site Attirampakkam. No fossils were found from here. But lower Palaeolithic tools were found. All tools were made on quartzite.
- The most significant evidence from a site Vadmadurai was found from the boulder conglomerate layer. All tools obtained from Vadmadurai sites were divided into three groups on the basis of typology and chemical colouring.

Early Group

The tools of this group were heavy and of cream colour. They were contemporary to boulder conglomerate layer. The tools of this group were divided again into two series — early and late on the basis of chemical colouring and typology.

Under early series tools of white chemical colouring, Abbevillian type handaxe and core were placed which were irregular and harsh.

Under late series those tools were include which showed less chemical colouring. The core tools are of developed types. The handaxe was regular like early Acheulian.

Second Group

The tools of this group were found on laterite above conglomerate. They had become red due to contact with laterite. Handaxes were flat and beautifully fashioned like middle Acheulian type. Tools were ovate and pear shaped. Tools were made by step flaking technique. Discoid cores were also found.

Third Group

The tools of this group did not possess laterite colour. Flaking on handaxe have been done by soft hammer technique. They were like upper Acheulian type. Handaxes were ovate, elongated and pointed. The number of cleaver was less. Flakes were thin and some retouched.

In Kortalayar valley, Attirampakkam site occupies significant place after Vadmadurai so far as lower Palaeolithic culture is concerned. The terraces of Attirampakkam have shown evolutional sequence of Palaeolithic culture. From the basal laterite deposit of 1st terrace to the loam deposit of red terrace of Attirampakkam, a number of Palaeolithic tools were found. They showed evolutional sequence. From laterite gravel, the tools of early and 2nd group were found. They were rolled, unrolled and fresh. These tools were contemporary to third group of Vadmadurai. The handaxe obtained from Attirampakkam were like late Acheulian type of Europe and Africa. They were also influenced by micoquian type of France. They were elongated, flat and thin and made on flakes. Cleavers were more in number. They were like cleavers made by Vaal technique of South Africa. Along with bifacial tools, Soan type flake and tools were also found. From loam deposit Levalloisean type flakes were also found.

Krishna Swamy had correlated the dating of laterite deposit near Madras to 1st and 2nd terrace of Potwar area. According to him, bolder conglomerate of Potwar was contemporary to boulder conglomerate of Vadmadurai. But in cultural materials, they showed differences. From the boulder conglomerate of Potwar pre-Soan type tools were found, but from the boulder conglomerate of Vadmadurai remains of Abbevillian-Acheulian industry were found.

After Krishna Swamy, Dr. D.K. Banerjee and R.V. Joshi of Archaeological Survey of India had done prehistoric survey in Tamil Nadu. In north Arcot and Chingleput districts of Tamil Nadu a survey was done by them. As a result of survey, a good number of Palaeolithic tools were collected from the prehistoric sites of these districts. Banerjee and his associates had done limited excavation in a cave named Gudium and its neighbouring area in 1962-64. Gudium cave is located in Chingleput district.

In the excavation of Gudium-I, tools were found from old floor layer to upper silt layer. From the lower pebble gravel layer tools of late Acheulian were found. Among tools, one half fashioned handaxe was also included. From upper layer, middle Palaeolithic tools were found.

From the excavation of GDM-II, two layers were found. From lower layer flake tools were found in majority. From upper layer mixed tools were found. Among tools of this layer scraper, point, borer, handaxe, cleaver and blades were included.

In GDM-III near Krishnapuram, a laterite mixed pebble deposit was found whose thickness was 60 cm. Below this deposit, there was a deposit of laterite up to 1.25 metre. This deposit had turned yellow due to contact with shale up to 30 cm. From this deposit late Acheulian type tools were found. No tool was found from lower shale.

In North Arcot district, lower Palaeolithic tools were found from Kallar river gravel. Banerjee had attempted to correlate the stone industry with laterite on the right bank of Budiamenu Banku in Attirampakkam. He had also made excavation for this purpose. He had found the sequence from down to top in following ways:

- From the upper part of Sriparambadur shale, Acheulian hand axe and cleaver were found.
- There was a grey silt deposit over erosional laterite in which no tools were found.
- From the top layer, microlithic tools were found.

From the excavation of Banerjee, it appears that laterite gravels are not Acheulian layer and silt cannot be said as late Acheulian flake industry layer.

Lower Palaeolithic Culture of Kerala

Kerala is the most south-western State of India. It is bounded by Arabian sea in west, Indian ocean in south, Tamil Nadu in east and Karnataka in north. But unfortunately Palaeolithic culture of this state has not been explored as yet. There is a need to enitiate Palaeolithic survey and researches in this regard.

Lower Palaeolithic Culture of Karnataka

The state of Karnataka lies in north of Kerala and west of Andhra Pradesh. The entire state is a plateau region. In its west there is Arabian Sea and in north there is Andhra Pradesh. In western part of the state there is heavy rainfall. The eastern part receives low rainfall. Krishna, Kaveri and Tungabhadra are chief rivers of this state. These rivers flow in west to east direction. Krishna flows in northern, Kaveri in south and Tungabhadra in central part. There are a number of small rivers too. For example Pennar, Pallar, Malprabha, Ghat Prabha etc. From the point of view of lower Palaeolithic culture Karnataka is not so important as Maharashtra and Andhra Pradesh. In Karnataka, it was Robert Bruce Foote who had obtained Palaeolithic tool in Shimoga district. After Bruce Foote, the scholars like Joshi worked on Palaeolithic culture of Karnataka in Malprabha river and its tributary. He had discovered 20 industry sites from Malprabha valley. He had also attempted to study the geochronology and pleistocene environment of Malprabha river valley. He had also correlated human made tools with deposits during Pleistocene period. Malprabha and Ghat Prabha rise from eastern hills. These both rivers are tributary of Krishna river. These both rivers flow parallel to each other — Ghat Prabha in north and Malprabha in south. At all sites of Malprabha valley cotton soil or black soil and red or grey silt are found over earth surface. The black soil is found generally in southern part of river and grey silt in northern part of the river. The deposit of black soil is more old and was formed during more pluvial environment. On the bank of river, there is a deposit of grey silt below upper soil. In Malprabha valley this deposit is almost at every site. Robert Bruce Foote had termed it as laterite sub-soil.

A scholar named Sheshadri had worked at a site Kibbanhalli in Tumkur district. Here early and developed Acheulian tools were found in mixed form. The tools included handaxe, different types of cleavers, scraper, chopper and chopping. Some beaked tools were also found.

Below sandy soil, there was a deposit of gravel conglomerate. Tools were found from this deposit. At Hiremulangi site, this deposit over water is 1 to 10 feet thick. Pebbles of quartzite were found in it. Some pebbles of sand stone, granite, cyst, pegmetite and dyke were also found. All developed and undeveloped tools were found from this deposit.

Nearby at every site gravel conglomerate deposit is based on mottled soil or clay. Its colour is different at different sites. The present bed of river is on shale group. The river had attained this status by erosing mottled soil or black soil. The majority of tools found from this deposit were flake tools. The tools made of pebbles and cores were less. All tools were fresh and recently fashioned. All tools were divided into three classes — Abbevillian, Acheulian and Levalloisean. In all tools handaxes occupied significant place. They were made of pebble, core, side flakes, end flakes. Some pseudo-burins were also found. Cleavers were made on flakes. Besides handaxe and cleaver chopper, core-scraper and discoid were also found. The tools of Malprabha valley may be placed under developed Acheulian type. From Ghat Prabha valley lower palaeolithic tools were obtained from several sites. The tools included were Acheulian handaxe, cleaver and discoid.

From Sherapur Doab, a scholar named Paddaiya had made collection of lower palaeolithic tools. The tools collected were handaxe, cleaver, unifacial and bifacial pebble tool, core and flake. These tools can be placed under Acheulian type.

Lower Palaeolithic Culture of Tungabhadra Valley

The Tungabhadra valley of Karnataka occupies significant place from the point of view of lower palaeolithic culture. The river Tungabhadra rises from Gangamulain Western Ghat and ends in river Krishna at Karnool. On the right bank of Tungabhadra nearly 3.5 miles towards west of Tekkalkota, there is a village named Nittur in Bellary district. This village was an industry site during prehistoric period. From this site, a scholar named J.D. Ansari had obtained Soan type unifacial pebble tool. Fossils were also found along with tools. The remains of *Bos namadicus* were in plenty. Unifacial pebble tools were found only in Soan industry. In the area of handaxe-cleaver industry of south India, finding of unifacial pebble industry like of Soan in north India had thrown light on prehistoric connection between south India and north India. It is also a thinkable question that can we divide prehistoric India into two great regions — north and south?

The section of Tungabhadra river near Nittur village was 4.50 metre thick. In this 35 cm thick deposit is of pebble gravels. The stones of pebble gravels are rolled. From this gravel deposit, middle palaeolithic tools were found. In between section and water current pieces of bolder gravels are scattered. They were probably gathered due to resistance of rocks. They were breaking on their real place. In Nittur pebble industry self-broken pebbles were fashioned into tools by minimum flaking. Flakes were removed generally from one side, but sometimes they were removed from both sides. Thus, pebble chopper-chopping tradition was prevalent. Majority of tools were choppers. From Nittur, a total of 31 tools were collected, in which unifacial chopper were 11, bifacial chopper were 13 and 2 were flakes and others were 5.

Characteristics of Indian Lower Palaeolithic Culture

Chief characteristics of Indian Palaeolithic culture can be described as follows:

- The lower Palaeolithic industries were prevalent in all parts of India — northern, western, eastern, central and peninsular regions. This indicates clearly that lower Palaeolithic Indians were living in all chief regions.
- The scholars who had worked in this field have divided Indian lower Palaeolithic culture into three main parts:
    - North-western Indian lower Palaeolithic culture.

- South Indian lower Palaeolithic culture.
- Central Indian lower Palaeolithic culture.

- The north-western lower Palaeolithic culture is known as Soan culture or Sohan culture. The chief centre of this culture was terraces of Soan river.
- The south Indian culture is known as Madrasian culture. The chief centre of this culture was terraces of Attirampakkam and Vadmadurai in Kortalayer valley.
- The extension of Soan culture was in entire north-western India, but extension of Madrasian culture was in entire peninsular India.
- The Soan culture was marked by pebble chopper-chopping industry. The Madrasian culture was marked by hand axe-cleaver industry.
- The tool community of Soan culture included pebble tool, pebble core and flake. The tool community of Madrasian culture included — hand axe, cleaver, core and flakes.
- In lower Palaeolithic India, Soanian and Madrasian culture developed independently from each other. But they had reached in the area of each other.
- Soan culture has been placed under Levalloisean-Clactonian tradition. But Madras culture has been placed under Abbevillian-Acheulian tradition.
- In Narmada and Sabarmati axis, the chopper-chopping traditions of north-western lower Palaeolithic cultures and handaxe-cleaver tradition of south Indian lower Palaeolithic culture would have probably met with each other.

Almost all scholars working into Palaeolithic culture of India have accepted this opinion. But such conclusions had also raised some problems. These questions are as follows:

- Whether Madrasian and Soanian cultures were quite different from each other?
- Whether these two traditions had same source of origin?
- Whether these two traditions were indigenous?

Builders of Indian Lower Palaeolithic Culture

One pertinent question is considerable here as to who were the builders of lower Palaeolithic Indian culture?

According to existing concepts till date, Soan and Madras industries are treated quite differently. If this is true then one more question appears before us, whether the builders of these two lower Palaeolithic industries in India were of two different races.

According to Movius, one of renowned scholars of prehistoric anthropology, the builders of chopper-chopping tools were *Homo erectus — Pithecanthropus erectus* and *Sinanthropus pekinensis*. It was because, chopper-chopping tools were found in association with skull remain of Java man and Peking man. So, the builders of chopper-chopping tools would have been descendants of *Homo erectus* — Java man and Peking man. But Movius was also of opinion that the builder of Madras lower Palaeolithic culture would have been older than the builder of Soan lower Palaeolithic culture. But opinion based on such racial differences is based on assumption and cannot be taken as completely true.

On the basis of available evidences, scholars have treated handaxe-cleaver tradition more old than the chopper-chopping tradition. The main base behind the view was non-existence of any pebble tool from boulder conglomerate deposit of Punjab. But from the boulder conglomerate deposit of Madras and Mayurbhanj in Orissa, which was contemporary to Soan, pebble tools were found along with biface core tool. The south Indian pebble industry was quite different from pebble industry of north India. Although from all sites pebble tools were found from lower layers, but their techniques of manufacturing was similar to some extent. On the basis of similarity in technique of production, it can be assumed that both traditions were related to one. From the pebble tools of north India biface tools were not found. The pebble tools of north India were related to Clactonian and Levalloisean technique. But pebble tools of south India were related to Abbevillian-Acheulian tradition. On this very ground, scholars have considered them separately. All scholars have correlated Soan industry with pebble-flake industry and Madras industry as core-handaxe-cleaver industry.

According to a renowned scholar of Prehistoric Anthropology Graham Clark, handaxe tradition would have spread to south-west Europe, from north-west Africa. In Asia, this tradition would have reached through Egypt. Through Faras valley, this tradition came to India from north coastal areas of Arabian Sea. This tradition spread mainly in south of Narmada. Already existing chopper-chopping tradition of Soan region could not influence it. But this concept of Graham Clark cannot be accepted because the tools of early Soan and the oldest tools of Madras were contemporary. Another considerable point is that if handaxe-cleaver tradition would have come to India from Africa through Egypt and northern coastal regions of Arabian Sea, then it would have taken more time. In this situation, tools found from prehandaxe layers of India and other places should not be found. From all places developed tools should have been obtained from the lower layer. But primitive tools were obtained at all places from the lower layer.

After reviewing all facts and evidences, we can come to the conclusion that original source of both — Soan and Madras traditions would have been one. These both traditions were indigenous. But in course of time, in different environment they appeared with their separate identity.

In India, a full human calvarium have been obtained from Narmada valley. It has been dated to middle Pleistocene. It has been named as Narmada man. This evidence reveals that towards the end of lower Pleistocene or beginning of middle Pleistocene, the tradition of producing tool would have come to the existence independently. First all pebble tool — chopper and chopping — would have come into existence. But towards the end of middle Pleistocene or beginning of upper Pleistocene, undeveloped and developed Abbevillian and Acheulian types came into existence at all lower Palaeolithic sites. They are found mixed with each other at all sites.

Probably migration of prehistoric man would have taken at large scale during middle of middle Pleistocene. It seems possible that developed handaxe-cleaver tradition came to India from Africa through Egypt and north coast of Arabian Sea. Since the environments of Africa and south India were similar, prehistoric man would have migrated towards south. Now, hand axe tradition of India would have come in contact with developed handaxe tradition of Africa. As a result, the local hand axe tradition would have become dynamic. But the climate of north-west India was quite different. That is why lower Palaeolithic culture developed slowly in this region. The prehistoric man who had brought developed handaxe-cleaver tradition in India, they would not have reached in north-west India due to climatic reasons. The lower Palaeolithic north India was more cold than the lower Palaeolithic south India. But in course of time, this climatic difference could not become a barrier for spread of one culture in the area of another and *vice versa*. The handaxe tradition could not flourish in revolutionary way in north India. This tradition had to face the situation of isolation in north India. In north India, before the full development of this tradition, an another tradition took the place of Soan tradition. This new or another tradition was blade-flake-scraper tradition. This tradition is known as Late Soan, Nevasian, Series-II or middle Palaeolithic tradition.

Life and Culture of Indian Lower Palaeolithic Man

Who were the builder of Indian lower Palaeolithic culture? Where they went and what happened to them?, the answers of these complex questions are still to be solved and nothing could be said with certainty. But two different types of tool traditions were existing in India. They were Soan tool tradition and Madras tool tradition. The Soan tool tradition shows similarity with tools of Java man and Peking man. But Madras tool tradition have shown similarity with tool traditions of Prehistoric man of Africa. It seems quite probable that the builders of Indian lower Palaeolithic tool traditions were proto-anthropoid type, they would have vanished quite early.

Period: The period of Indian lower Palaeolithic culture has been dated between 10,00,000 B.C. to 50,000 B.C.

Habitat: The habitat of Indian lower Palaeolithic man would have been caves, rock shelters, trees and below trees.

Clothing: Indian Palaeolithic man was using barks, and leaves to cover his body or he was bound to remain naked.

Food: The food of Indian lower Palaeolithic man was leaves, root, shoot, bark, flower, fruits, seeds and animals killed and left by tiger, lion, wolf, leopard.

Economy: Indian lower Palaeolithic man was not producer. He was a consumer only. He was dependent completely on nature. He was leading a parasitic mode of life on nature. His economy was hunting and gathering. He used to survive also on animals killed and left by lion, tiger, wolf, leopard etc.

Water Source: The Indian lower Palaeolithic man used to live nearby water sources particularly river, fountain, water fall, lakes, sea etc. He used to stay also nearby the forest.

Society: Nothing could be said with certainty, but it can be said that he used to live in group.

Language: There is no evidence about the language of Indian lower Palaeolithic man. But he was a speaking animal. It was a minimum condition for living in group. Probably, they used both kinds of languages — verbal and non-verbal.

Use of Fire: The Indian lower Palaeolithic man was aware of fire because his contemporary in other parts of the world was well acquainted with fire.

Industry: Indian lower Palaeolithic man had given birth to stone industries at several sites in the country. The industries can be divided mainly into two groups: pebble chopper-chopping tradition and core handaxe-cleaver tradition.

5

Indian Middle Palaeolithic Culture (50,000 B.C. – 20,000 B.C.)

From the point of view of stratigraphy middle Palaeolithic period is a stage after lower Palaeolithic period and before upper Palaeolithic period. Till 1954, nothing was known about middle Palaeolithic period in India. Although scholars working in Indian Prehistoric Archaeological Anthropology were getting tools related to a particular industry. The tools of this special industry were obtained by DeTerra and Paterson from Punjab and cotton soil of Narmada valley, by Burkitt and Cammiade in Karnool, and by Todd in Bombay and Khandivli. But these scholars had provided different names for those tools of special industry. The tools of this special industry were made on flakes. The tool community of this special industry included scraper, point, borer and blade. Burkitt and Cammiade had given the name to tools of this special industry as *Series-II*, DeTerra and Paterson had called the tools of this special industry as *Late Soan* in Punjab and *Protoneolithic* in cotton soil of Narmada valley. Besides these sites, a number of other sites in India were furnishing evidences of tools of this special industry continuously. But a clear-cut knowledge about the tools and tool community of this special industry came before us after the study of stratigraphy and tools of Nevasa site by H.D. Sankalia. Sankalia had obtained three stone industries from stratified deposits of Pravara valley. He had termed them as Series-I, Series-II and Series-III. From Series-I, tools of hand axe-cleaver tradition were found. It was related to the first aggradational phase or Ist gravel deposit of Pravara river. From the second gravel deposit of river, different types of tools were obtained. Sankalia had placed them under *Series-II*. They were definitely related to second aggradational phase or second gravel of Pravara river. From the top layer, microlithic tools were obtained. Sankalia had termed them as Series-III. Dr. Banerjee had given the term Nevasian to Series-II tools of Sankalia. He had placed those tools under middle Palaeolithic. Mallick had provided them a name of flake-blade-scraper industry.

The scholars of Prehistoric Archaeological Anthropology were confused over the term to be given to tools obtained from second aggradational phase or second gravel deposit of river valleys situated in different parts of India. They were not deciding as to which terminology they should follow and whether they should follow African terminology like early stone age, middle stone age and late stone age or European terminology like lower Palaeolithic, middle Palaeolithic, upper Palaeolithic, mesolithic and neolithic periods. Since India has a tropical regions, and tools of upper Palaeolithic periods were not reported from India, therefore, scholars began to think that African terminology should be applied for Indian Prehistoric Anthropology. On this very ground Subba Rao, in First Asian Archaeological Congress organised in Delhi in 1961, suggested to follow African Prehistoric terminology for Indian prehistory. His opinion was accepted by the scholars working in this field. But upper Palaeolithic tools began to appear from the layers between middle stone age and mesolithic age. Besides this, microlithic industries were developed from upper Palaeolithic industries. In this situation, the proposal of Subba Rao began to be rejected related to

African terminologies for Indian Prehistoric Anthropology. In the year 1972, an International Symposium on Radio Carbon and Indian Archaeology was organised by Tata Institute. In this International Symposium, it was unanimously accepted to use European terminologies for Indian prehistoric Anthropology. Thus, middle Palaeolithic period began to be used in Indian Prehistoric Archaeological Anthropology in place of middle stone age.

In India, middle Palaeolithic industries were found from the second aggradational phase of river valleys. It was also known as second gravel deposit. Besides river valleys and gravel deposits, middle Palaeolithic tools were found from river terraces, and on middle of hill slope. On the top of hills, lower Palaeolithic tools were found. In the middle of slope, middle Palaeolithic tools were found on the meeting place of hill slope with ground, upper Palaeolithic tools were found. Probably due to decrease in pluviation this would have happened.

The middle Palaeolithic tools had their own speciality. In this period, the lower Palaeolithic industry of handaxe cleaver tradition began to end and industry of a new tradition began to appear. This new tradition was known as blade-flake-scraper tradition. The scraper is the characteristic tool of this period. Although scrapers had made their appearance during lower Palaeolithic period, but the scrapers of middle Palaeolithic period were quite different and they were in developed form. The scrapers of both periods were different in shape, size and technique. Flake element had started appearing in lower Palaeolithic period, but in middle Palaeolithic period they become visible clearly. Blade element had also started attracting the attention. Due to significance of blade, flake and scrapper, the middle Palaeolithic industry was placed under blade-flake-scraper tradition. The blades of middle Palaeolithic period and upper Palaeolithic period were quite different. In fact, the proper term for them was blade flake.

In middle Palaeolithic period, blades were made from common core or Levalloisean core. The use of Levalloisean technique occupies significant place in this period. Now, core with faceted platform or tortoise core and flaked or retouched flake began to appear in plenty.

The technique of retouch brought special changes in tools of this period. For the purpose of retouch nipid technique began to be used. The retouchings of several tools were so micro that it was not possible by direct and indirect percussion technique.

In shape and size, the tools of middle Palaeolithic period were also changed. They became beautiful in shape and smaller in size. Their efficiency was also increased.

The selection of stone for tool making was also changed. The quartzite used in this period was of good quality. Besides quartzite, basalt, jaspar, churt, flint were also used for making tools of middle Palaeolithic period. The selection of stone for tool making was dependent on local availability.

How a change occurred in the tools and techniques of middle Palaeolithic culture and what was reason behind it? Probably this change would have occurred due to change in environment and emergence of new human species. Till now no full skeleton of man has been found of Palaeolithic man in India. From Narmada valley, a full calvarium of man was found which was termed as Narmada man. It was dated to middle Pleistocene. But in absence of skeletal remains, nothing can be said with certainty about the mankind. It is also very difficult to conclude as to why such changes had taken place and from where for the first time such changes occurred. How they spread to all parts of India? How new human species would have appeared and how they developed efficiency in making new tools? Migration and movement cannot be rejected in this regard. But in order to know them we need more evidences which are not available to us. So, we will have to depend on changes in climatic conditions for explaining such tool typological and technological changes. In new changed climatic condition, new tools were made to adapt with changed environment. For making new tools, new techniques were evolved. With the help of new techniques, smaller and beautiful tools were made. Now, the tools were beautiful, small and more useful. In place of multipurpose tools, special tools were made in this period.

Indian Middle Palaeolithic Culture

For the purpose of study, we can deal with Indian middle Palaeolithic culture by dividing it into following parts:

- Middle Palaeolithic Culture of Uttar Pradesh.
- Middle Palaeolithic Culture of Jharkhand.
- Middle Palaeolithic Culture of Orissa.
- Middle Palaeolithic Culture of Andhra Pradesh.
- Middle Palaeolithic Culture of Karnataka.
- Middle Palaeolithic Culture of Maharashtra.
- Middle Palaeolithic Culture of Madhya Pradesh.
- Middle Palaeolithic Culture of Rajasthan.

Middle Palaeolithic Culture of Uttar Pradesh

In Uttar Pradesh, Belan valley and its neighbouring areas are significant from the point of view of middle Palaeolithic culture. It was the first site in India from where significant informations regarding the origin and evolution of middle Palaeolithic tools were obtained. Here each phase of origin of tool has been correlated to geological layers. The speciality of Belan valley is that the same type of geological layer is found in very extensive area.

From the first gravel of Belan valley lower palaeolithic tools were found. The middle Palaeolithic tools were found from the second gravel. The maximum thickness of second gravel deposit was found as 5 metre. In this deposit an average 2 to 4 cm long pebbles were found. On the basis of structure, the entire gravel deposit was divided into three parts and were termed as A, B and C from top to down. From B part clear-cut cross-bedding was found. At some places a thin silt deposit was seen between parts. This deposit was very much clear in Sewati river, a tributary of Belan river.

Tools found from the three parts of second gravel deposit revealed an evolutionary sequence of Palaeolithic tools. The part 'C' of second gravel deposit revealed a change from lower Palaeolithic period to middle Palaeolithic tool. The tools found from this deposit were made of flakes. No handaxe was found. Cleavers were less in number and scraper were more in number. The tools were comparatively small. Evidences of retouch were found on some tools. Leaving two tools, all tools were made of quartzite. The remains of *Bos namadicus* were found from this deposit.

From part 'B' of second gravel deposit of Belan valley, tools belonging to flake-blade-scraper tradition were found. They were same as tools found from part 'C'. 73 per cent tools were scraper, 57 per cent tools were made on quartzite. Remains of *Bos* and *Elephas* were in majority.

From part 'A' of second gravel deposit, tools same as of part 'B' were found. The only difference was in size. The tools were now more small than before. Their average length-breadth was 4 × 3 cms. Now, churt and similar stones were used more for making tools.

Upon second gravel deposit, there was a deposit of reddish silt. This deposit was formed of lime carbonate, laterites balls and stone chips. This deposit had also yielded middle Palaeolithic tools. The representation of scraper was found 89 per cent and of blade was only 15 per cent. The tools were mainly made on churt.

Above the middle Palaeolithic layers of Belan valley, evidences related to changes from middle Palaeolithic to upper Palaeolithic culture were found. In this deposit the number of blades was increased. Stone of good quality was now used for making tools. All these evidences were indicating the arrival of upper Palaeolithic culture.

From the neighbouring areas of Belan valley, a good number of middle Palaeolithic tools were found from sites like Bataubir and Khutabir. Nearly all tools were made of quartzite. But the quality of quartzite was definitely better than previous quartzite of middle Palaeolithic culture. The iron content in quartzite was now more. Churt was not used for tool making. From small rock slabs flakes were detached. Among tools scrapers were more in number. Among scrapers, discoid or circular scrapes were more in number. Flaking on scraper was done from periphery to centre. Regular flaking technique was used in making the tools. Evidences of retouch or secondary work was also found. Percussion technique was not used, but soft or cylinder hammer technique was used for flaking.

Middle Palaeolithic Culture of Orissa

A Prehistoric Archaeological Anthropologist, G.C. Mohpatra had done significant work on middle Palaeolithic culture of Orissa. According to him, tools of middle Palaeolicthic culture were obtained from second or fine gravel deposit which was based on silt. The silt deposit had separated the lowest gravel deposit from the fine gravel or second gravel deposit. Thus, stratigraphically it could be said that tools obtained from fine or second gravel deposit were later than tools found from first gravel deposit. In Orissa, microlithic tools were always found from the surface or river valley. So, it could be said that middle Palaeolithic tools were of early period than tools of microlithic period. In making middle Palaeolithic tools good stones like churt, jaspar, and opale were used. Soft or cylinder hammer technique was used for flaking. Tortoise cores were not used for making tools. Retouch technique was applied in limited manner. Majority of tools were fresh. Scraper, borer, burin, point and scraper point occupied significant place in tool community. A number of flake, blade and core were also found. Tools made on wide blade were also found. They were used as side scraper. The blades of this period were earlier than mesolithic blades.

Mohpatra had made a collection of total 404 tools and flakes in which there were 151 scraper, 46 point, 4 borer, 4 burin, and 5 craper borer. When Mohpatra had made collection of tools, the status of upper Palaeolithic tool was not known. That is why he had placed burin and blade in middle Palaeolithic period. But in fact they belonged to upper Palaeolithic culture.

Middle Palaeolithic Culture of Andhra Pradesh

The credit of highlighting series of Palaeolithic cultures in Andhra Pradesh goes to Cammiade and Burkitt. In this series, middle Palaeolithic culture was also included. These tools were of flake industries which were made on quartzite. Sand stone and chalcedony were also used for making tools. Along with flake tools, some beautifully made hand axe were also found. The flake industry was of quarternary period when climate has become dry. On this time, origin and diffusion of new culture tooks place on erosional laterite.

The scholar like Soundar Rajan had also obtained tools of middle Palaeolithic culture from Giddalur-II and Talpatte. On 'C' locality of Nagarjuna Konda, three gravel deposits were found from the same site. This type of deposit was also found in Belan valley of Uttar Pradesh. The study of these deposits had thrown light on lower, middle and upper Palaeolithic cultures.

Not only stones for making tools of middle Palaeolithic culture were different, but technique of making them was also different. The tools of middle Palaeolithic culture were indicating the use of developed Levalloisean technique and retouch technique. For retouch percussion technique was used. Soft or cylinder hammer technique was used. The scrapers were of various types. Such as side scraper, end scraper, hallow scraper, disc scraper. Besides these tools, awe, point and planning tools were also found. Some blade and burin tools were also found which were related to upper Palaeolithic culture. The flake-blade industry of here had three tendencies:

- Mousterian impact on flake.
- Blade and burin tool.
- Use of retouch and percussion technique.

In first group tools, flakes and points were more in number. Some hand axe like bifacial tool of smaller size were found. Incipient Tang were also found.

In second group tool, blades were more in number. They were of different size. Blades were thin and in good shape.

The third group tool included, scrapers of different types and sizes. They were similar to middle Palaeolithic scrapers.

Among all the three groups, only first group represented the middle Palaeolithic culture.

Rao had made a survey of Nalgonda district and discovered a number of sites related to middle Palaeolithic culture. He had collected middle Palaeolithic tools from slope of hills and river valleys. Middle Palaeolithic tools were obtained from five gravel deposit over grey silt. On the bank of Krishna river, there was an important middle Palaeolithic site named Shamtirthampaye. This site is located at a distance of 8 km from Cheleshwaram. In its neighbouring 10 areas, 600 tools were collected. All tools were divided into two groups:

- Tools made on flake and blade.
- Tools made on flakes detached from artificial core.

In first group big flakes were kept which were prepared by soft/cylinder hammer technique. In second group tools made from thin and small flakes were kept. They were triangular or ovate. Their striking platform was not prepared. Blade taken out by fluted core were also found.

On the basis of working edge, tools were divided into two groups:

(A) In this group only those tools were kept which possessed only one working end.

(B) In this group those tools were included which possessed more than one working edge. They are known as multiple tool.

All tools were placed under scraper, borer and point type.

M.L.K. Murray had discovered middle Palaeolithic tool from second gravel or reddish silt. He had also obtained middle Palaeolithic tool from Rallakalawa-D. Along with middle Palaeolithic tools, beautifully made hand axes were also found. Here also scrapers were more in number. Some flakes with faceted plat form were also found. Besides flakes, point-awl, flake-blade, flake and core were also found.

In Kuduppo and Nellor, middle Palaeolithic industry sites were also discovered. But detailed study about them is not available.

Middle Palaeolithic Culture of Karnataka

In the state of Karnataka, middle Palaeolithic sites and tools were reported from Belgaon, Bijapur, Gulbarga and Dharwad. K.D. Banerjee had termed the middle Palaeolithic industry as Karnataka-Nevasian. There were importance of point in this industry. Scraper-borer were also integral part of this industry. At the time of Banerjee, clear-cut division of Indian Palaeolithic culture was not in existence. But later on, a systematic study of Sherapur Doabs and Krishna valley was made.

Paddayya had obtained 8 sites related to middle Palaeolithic industry in Sherapur Doab. Middle Palaeolithic tools were obtained from river valley gravel and upper land gravel. In the rivers of Sherapur Doab, three depositional terraces were found. The first terrace was located at 45 feet, second terrace was located at 25 feet and third terrace was located at a height of 5 feet. The first terrace was formed by old alluvial deposit. Second gravel was formed by beach grey silt. The third gravel was formed by sand-pebble-gravel.

On the bank of Bhima river, Hagargudagi is an important middle Palaeolithic site. From this site, 181 tools were gathered. Among tools, 43 tools were found *in situ*. Majority of tools were made of chalcedeny. In tools, there were borer, flake-blade, and blade. Along with tools, remains of *Bos*, *elephas* and *cervidae* were found.

On the basis of shape and working edge, Paddeya had classified all tools into three groups:

- Edge tool.
- Non-edge tool.
- Multiple tool.

Different types of scraper, point and borer tools were included in these groups.

Krishna valley is an important site from the point of view of middle Palaeolithic culture in Karnataka. The credit of highlighting middle Palaeolithic sites in Krishna valley goes to R.S. Pappu. He had discovered 3311 tools from 20 sites in this valley. Of 20 industry sites, 14 were located in Krishna valley and 6 on the bank of river Malprabha. Among all these sites, Kaldagi area is most significant. In this area, Kowalli and Angawadi sites occupied special significance. Kowalli site is located on the left bank of Ghatprabha. Here churts are found in plenty. Majority of tools were made of flakes. They were of 20 mm to 125 mm. Big flakes were taken out by stone hammer technique. Small flakes were taken out by soft or cylinder hammer technique.

Retouch or secondary work was also done.

The representation of tools were like different types of scrappers 80 per cent, borer 11 per cent and point 7 per cent.

Middle Palaeolithic Culture of Maharashtra

Middle Palaeolithic culture related industry and tools were reported from nearly all areas of Maharashtra. First of all Todd had obtained a series of Palaeolithic industries from Khandivli near Mumbai. After him, Sankalia and his associates made resurvey of the area. He had obtained two cycles of deposition and erosion. The 1st gravel deposit was old and original gravel deposit. The first deposit was of pluvial period and deposit after that was of interpluvial period. In this period, a thick deposit of pebble gravel and silt had taken place. This was resulted in the formation of 1st terrace. In the second pluvial period, the erosion of first terrace had taken place. As a result of which an angular gravel was formed. In the interpluvial period, a thin deposit of silt had taken place. From entire deposits Sankalia had collected 85 tools. thirty tools were found from basal gravel. There were no technological difference between tools obtained from different deposits. The tool community included core, different types of scrapers, Rastrocarinate, point, borer, nodules with working edge.

The most important middle Palaeolithic site in Maharashtra was reported from the banks of Pravara and Godavari in Ahamadnagar district. The most significant site is Nevasa. Here middle Palaeolithic tools were found for the first time from stratified deposit. Such types of tools were also found from Belpandhari, Suregaon and Kalegaon. In the beginning Sankalia believed that these tools of all sites belonged to lower gravel deposit. It was because earlier than this deposit, no evidence of deposit was found at those sites. But when he discovered an another tool of earlier period from earlier deposit, his concept was changed completely. The second gravel deposit was quite different from first gravel deposit and third gravel deposit.

Tools obtained from Belpandhari, Kalegaon, Nevasa and Nandur Maghmeshwar were divided in to four groups:

- Point
- Scraper
- Borer
- Scraper-*cum*-borer.

The representation of these tools were 15.7, 57.5, 24.9 and 2.2 per cent respectively. Tang points were found which were unishouldered or bishouldered.

On Tapti and its tributary Rakalava in between Kumbhra and Ubhaj middle Palaeolithic tools were also found.

Middle Palaeolithic Culture of Madhya Pradesh

A scholar named Rameshwar Singh had made a survey of Ghasan and Betwa rivers in Madhya Pradesh. On Ghasan river near Sihora and on Betwa river near Gonchi, he had discovered middle Palaeolithic industry sites. He had termed them as late Palaeolithic. According to him, the early stone age had come to an end here before the beginning of late stone age. From the second gravel deposit hand axe of smaller sizes, long flake, and flake-blade were found. Here the builders of tools would have followed the types of tools already existing. For example subtriangular ovate hand axe and U-shaped cleaver. In course of time, the ovate tools become more small. As a result small sub-triangular point and borer were made. Scraper also changed into nail scraper.

In Sihora 321 and in Gonchi 230 tools were found. Churt was used for the construction of tools. Chert was available there. In tool community there were hand axe, cleaver, point, awl, scraper and core. In Sihora, the ratio of scraper was more than Gonchi.

From the point of view of tool and stratigraphy, the area between Jogdahabride and Gopal confluence were of great significance. Here a research team under the supervision of Professor G.R. Sharma of Allahabad University had made survey and discovered a number of sites. The team had also attempted to correlate the geological layers with stone industries. The research of this area had become significant from different point of view.

The stratigraphical sequence of Son river has been described in the chapter *Indian Lower Palaeolithic Culture*. Therefore, it is not being repeated here. The middle Palaeolithic industry related to Son valley was completely developed. The use of Levalloisean technique was started. Flakes were removed by indirect percussion technique and cylinder or soft hammer technique. Lower Palaeolithic tools were not found from the middle Palaeolithic layer. Only one cleaver was found which was beautiful and smaller. But it had no industrial significance in middle Palaeolithic industry.

The tool community of Son valley included scraper, wide and long flake-blade, blade, borer and point. Retouching on tools were found. Retouching was done by direct percussion technique and cylinder or soft hammer technique. Stones of fine particles was used for making tool. Animal remains of *elephas*, *bos*, *equus*, *sus*, *Ghaviyalis*, *chelonia* etc. were found in abundance.

From the layer-5 of Bhimbetka in Madhya Pradesh middle Palaeolithic tools were discovered.

Middle Palaeolithic Culture of Rajasthan

From the point of view of middle Palaeolithic culture, Luni valley of Rajasthan is very significant. Here Professor V.N. Mishra had worked to explore palaeolithic culture. According to him, the sequence of deposits in Luni valley was as follows:

- White clay
- Cemented gravel
- Silt and sand.

Mishra had termed the tools obtained from gravel deposit as palaeolithic. But on the basis of typological similarity of tools, it can be correlated with second aggradational phase and middle Palaeolithic culture of south India. In western Rajasthan, stones used for making tools may be divided into two groups. In one group, quartzite, sand stone, churt, flint, chalcedony, and jaspar were kept. In another group, Leolite found from valcano was included. The tools were fresh and made on flakes. Soft or cylinder hammer technique was used. Levalloisean technique was also used. Blades were detached by indirect percussion technique. On Acheulian handaxe, shallow flakes were taken out by step flaking technique.

In the tool community of western Rajasthan, scraper, flake and blade were important tools. Majority of tools were found in river valley. Some tools were found *in situ*. Tools found in valley were stitched to gravel. They had come out of gravel deposit. No tool was found from white clay silt or sand deposit.

In western Rajasthan, tools were gathered from 21 sites and 7 river valleys. Handaxes were found from 4 sites. They were divided into two groups — developed and undeveloped. Handaxes were of different size such as pear shaped, chordate, ovate, pomegranate etc. Cleavers were also there in limited number. From only two sites, 7 cleavers were found. Cleavers were inseparable part of middle Palaeolithic industries.

Scrapers were divided into two groups — A and B. The group A scrapers possessed a working edge at side or at end. They were made of flake or pebble. The other type of group A scrapers possessed thick working edge or blunt edge. The tools having working edge at side were thin and long. But the tools having working edge at end are ovate in shape. The tools of group B were same but they were undeveloped. All borers were made on flake. They were made by making notch near the end. Borer-scraper was a compound tool which was used as both borer and scraper. All tools of point group had pointed end. They are unifaical or bifacial both. Flake knife was also an important tool. Its working edge was straight. The opposite side of working edge is blunt and thick. They are made on flakes and are 5 to 9 cm long. Besides these tools, blades and flakes were also found. Some flakes were common and some were Levalloisean type.

From the Bagan and Kadmali river valley middle Palaeolithic tools were found from southern Rajasthan. 217 tools were found from 4 sites in Bagan valley in which 24 tools were found *in situ*.

14 tools were found from first gravel and 10 from other gravels. According to Mishra, 14 tools from gravel first, 1 tool from gravel second and 7 from gravel third were found. The status of 2 tools was not clear.

Bagan valley had 3 gravel deposits and from all 3 gravels middle Palaeolithic tools were found. This has brought confusion among the scholars working in this area. Either three gravels were not in existence or tools found from there were not of middle Palaeolithic culture. In order to solve these questions more micro-level researches are required.

From Kadamally valley 65 tools were found. Among these 65 tools, 33 from second gravel, 3 from mottled clay and 29 from river valleys were found. The tools were mainly made of quartzite. The tool community included flake, blade and scraper. But some lower Palaeolithic handaxes and cleavers were found. But they were very few in number.

Chief Characteristics of Indian Middle Palaeolithic Culture

The chief characteristics of Indian middle Palaeolithic culture can be described in following ways:

Period: The period of Indian middle Palaeolithic culture has been dated as 50,000 B.C. – 20,000 B.C.

Industry Site: Middle Palaeolithic sites have been reported from almost every part of the country. At a number of places correlation between tools of industry and geological layers has been done. The chief middle Palaeolithic sites are Belan, Luni, Son, Nevasa, Sherapur Doab and Nagarjuna Konda. Middle Palaeolithic tools have been obtained from second gravel deposit.

Tools: The characteristic tool of this period was scraper made on flakes. The scrapers were of different types such as side scraper, end scraper, hollow scraper, concave scraper, convex scraper, disc scraper. Besides scraper, borer and point were also found. They are inseparable part of Indian middle Palaeolithic industry. Some beautiful handaxe, flake and core were also present in the industry site.

Technique of Manufacturing Tools

Indian middle Palaeolithic man had made tools from the flakes by employing technique like direct and indirect percussion technique, soft or cylinder hammer technique and retouch technique. Step flaking technique and fluting technique were also employed in some cases.

Function of Tools: Scraping and cutting skin and meat of animal, bark of tree, plants, and so on.

Human Species: Who were the builder of Indian middle Palaeolithic culture? Nothing could be said with certainty. It is because we do not have sufficient evidence. Elsewhere the credit of establishing this culture is associated with Neanderthal man. But we do not have such evidence in Indian context. So far as our knowledge till date is concerned, we can say that the descendants of lower Palaeolithic man would have built this culture in our country under changed environment and circumstances. Indian lower Palaeolithic man had acquired the knowledge of taking out flakes by direct or indirect percussion technique. They were also skilled in making flake by Levalloisean, Clactonian and Micoquian technique. It is believed that the descendants of lower Palaeolithic man in India gave rise to flake-blade tradition. They began to make smaller tools on flakes.

Habitat: The habitat of middle Palaeolithic man was cave and rock shelters. They lived on hills and hill slopes near the source of water and forest.

Food: The food of Indian middle Palaeolithic man was root, shoot, Stem, tuber, bulbs, leaves, flowers, fruits, seeds and meat of animal hunted. Along with tools of middle Palaeolithic culture, remains of *bos, elephas, equus, carnivor, bison, sus, chetonia* were found.

Cloth: The middle Palaeolithic man used to wear skin of animals, bark of trees and leaves of trees and plants.

Economy: Indian middle Palaeolithic man was not producer. He was consumer of things produced by nature. He was a parasite on nature.

Society: The middle Palaeolithic men lived in group. Nothing could be said about the form of society. But the form of social organisation would have been band. Due to sexual communism or proximity, the child would have been known by mother. This practice would have given the birth of matriarchal form of society.

Political Life: Nothing could be said about the political organisation of middle Palaeolithic man living in India. But if they were living in band, there would have been a leader to guide and control the band members.

Magical Belief: Some form of magical belief would have been there in the society. But nothing could be said with certainty.

Use of Fire: The middle Palaeolithic man of India was using fire as a weapon to save himself from wild animals and to get light during night. He would have been roasting meat, bulbs and fruits to eat.

6

Indian Upper Palaeolithic Culture (20,000 B.C. – 10,000 B.C.)

The upper Palaeolithic period is a period after middle Palaeolithic period and before mesolithic or microlithic period. In the beginning the status of upper Palaeolithic period in India was doubtful. Although from the very beginning of prehistoric researches in India, tools of such industry were coming into existence from such layer which was termed as upper Palaeolithic later on. Cammiade and Burkitt were the first scholar who had declared the existence of those industries from south-east coast of India in 1930. These scholars had placed their tools of Series-III under blade and burin industry. These industries were found from above Series-II and below Series-IV. Issac and Saundarajan had also collected such types of tools. Todd had also declared the existence of such industry from Mumbai. But the status of upper Palaeolithic culture became clear after 1964. Now, such surface sites and stratified deposits began to appear which removed all doubts related to upper Palaeolithic culture. Scholars like G.R. Sharma of Allahabad University reported the existence of upper Palaeolithic culture from Madhya Pradesh and Uttar Pradesh, Murthy from south-eastern coastal areas, Paddeya from Sherapur Doab, Salee from Maharashtra and Alchian and Gudia from Gujarat. From the rockshelter of Bhimbetka in Madhya Pradesh, the existence of such industry was also reported.

When the same type of tools of same industry and of same layer began to appear clearly, the scholars working in the field of Indian Prehistoric Anthropology were fully convinced by the separate existence of upper Paleolithic culture. In an international symposium organised by Tata Institute of Fundamental Research, Mumbai on C^{14} and Indian Archaeology, the existence of upper Palaeolithic culture was unanimously accepted by the participants in 1972. Again in a national seminar on "Prehistory 1974" organised by Deccan College, Pune, the upper Palaeolithic culture of India got proper place unanimously. Since then scholars working in this field brought to light the existence of upper Palaeolithic culture in India from almost all parts.

For proper understanding of Indian upper Palaeolithic culture, we can divide it into following groups for the purpose of description and explanation:

- Upper Palaeolithic Culture of Uttar Pradesh
- Upper Palaeolithic Culture of Andhra Pradesh
- Upper Palaeolithic Culture of Karnataka
- Upper Palaeolithic Culture of Maharashtra
- Upper Palaeolithic Culture of Madhya Pradesh

Upper Palaeolithic Culture of Uttar Pradesh

The Belan valley of Uttar Pradesh occupies the most significant place from the point of view of upper Palaeolithic culture. This site of Uttar Pradesh had gained all-India recognition for the existence of upper Palaeolithic culture. It is because such type of stratified geo-chronology was not found elsewhere in the country. The sequence of deposits of Belan valley has been presented in the chapter on *Indian Lower Palaeolithic Culture.* Hence, the sequence of deposit is not being presented again.

The observation of stratified deposits and tools found from them reveals clearly that blades and tools made on them began to appear first of all from cemented gravel-II. But they were placed under flake-blade series. From this deposit, middle palaeolithic tools were reported. In sixth deposit, blade elements were more in number. In fifth deposit, blades occupied significant place. The number of flakes was reduced in this deposit. Thus, the stratigraphical evidence of Belan valley indicates clearly that upper palaeolithic industries developed from middle palaeolithic industries.

The fifth deposit of Belan valley reveals a transition from middle Palaeolithic period to upper Palaeolithic period. The third gravel deposit over it was really related to upper Palaeolithic period.

From fourth deposit over it, blade and blade tools were found. But they revealed a transition from upper Palaeolithic to mesolithic period. From third deposit, microlithic tools were found.

In the neighbouring areas of Belan valley, a number of surface sites were found. Majority of them were located on hills and meeting place of hill slope and ground. These all sites were divided into several groups. In 1st group those sites were included which were revealing a transition from middle Palaeolithic period to upper Palaeolithic period. In second group only those tools were included which belonged to upper Palaeolithic period. In third group those tools were included which showed a transition from upper Palaeolithic period to mesolithic period.

In first group flake-blades were more in number than blades. Flake-blades were taken out from Levalloisean cores. The bulb of percussion of flake-blade was developed type. Some true blades had begun to appear. Although true cylindrical or fluted cores were not developed, but attempt to make them had begun. In order to take out blades, one end of core began to be touched. Blunted side blades were negligible. Lunates were not found. Scrapers were same as before. But notch scrapers were more in number. In order to make scraper flake-blades were used.

The tools of second group were related to upper Palaeolithic period. The upper Palaeolithic tool community had tools like different types of blade-burin, borer, point, scraper and lunate. Although the production of blade had begun in middle Palaeolithic period, but there was a great difference between blades of middle Palaeolithic culture and upper Palaeolithic culture. The middle Palaeolithic tools were taken out from common cores or Levalloisean cores. But upper Palaeolithic blades were taken out from cylindrical cores or fluted cores. The blades detached from cores were of parallel sided. The width of middle Palaeolithic blade was more than the length. Irregular flake scars were found on their upper surface. But the length of upper Palaeolithic blade was more than width. As we move from upper Palaeolithic to mesolithic, the width and length both of blade get reduced. But in this situation, too, the width was less than the length. The width of upper Palaeolithic blades was generally 15 mm, but mesolithic blades were more narrow. Besides parallel sided blades, baked blades were also found. For baking the blades, they were retouched in such a way so that the cutting edge would become functionless.

Blade-knife was also an important tool of upper Palaeolithic period. They were made by bifacial retouching of one side of parallel sided blades or stone slabs.

After blade an another important tool of upper palaeolithic period was burin. No burin was found from any site of middle Palaeolithic period. Burins were found only from upper Palaeolithic period. Burins were made from the flakes taken out from the residual cores. They were not made on thin flakes. Burins were of different types depending on working edge.

Borers were also reported from the upper Palaeolithic sites. Some borers were made on long thin blades. They had middle ridge. Their working edge was long. They were retouched from both sides. Some other types of borers were made on wide flakes. In such type of borer, the working edge was formed by making a notch at one end.

After blade, scrapers were more in number. Scrapers were of different types such as side scraper, end scraper, disc scraper, concave scraper and notch scraper. Notch scraper is a special tool of upper Palaeolithic period. Notch scraper was not found in middle Palaeolithic period.

In the upper Palaeolithic tool community of Belan area, lunate also occupied a significant place. In fact lunates are mesolithic tools. But the upper Palaeolithic lunates are quite different from mesolithic lunate. The upper Palaeolithic lunates were big and wide. The biggest lunate found from this area was 43 × 26 mm. The width of lunate was more than half of length of lunate. But in mesolithic lunate width was less than half length of lunate.

Only one bone tool was found from the Murwa. It is not significant statistically. But it is significant because it indicated towards the use of bone tools.

The Art of Belan Valley

The most significant discovery of upper Palaeolithic period in Belan valley was bone made image of mother Goddess. It was found from Lohanda drain from third gravel deposit. No such image has been reported from any upper palaeolithic sites in India. Thus, from the point of view of palaeolithic art in India, Belan valley occupies a very important place.

Upper Palaeolithic Culture of Andhra Pradesh

The state of Andhra Pradesh occupies its special importance so far upper Palaeolithic culture is concerned. From here upper Palaeolithic sites like Renigunta, Yeregond Plem, and Muchchhatala Chintamanugavi were reported. Renigunta is located in Chittur district on Madras-Mumbai route. The water of this area flows through the river Rallakalawa which is a tributary of the river Swarnamukhi. On the river Rallakalawa two aggradational terraces were found. They were formed by gravel and silt. These terraces had yielded tools of lower, middle and upper Palaeolithic cultures.

From Timaiyyagunta, Benkmanayanipalli and Chundi, upper Palaeolithic blade-burin industries were obtained. From Vedulcherubu and Nallagundalu blade-burin industry and mesolithic tools were found together. They were separated on the basis of shape and size of stones and tools. Blade and burins were made of thin particle stone. Mesolithic tools were made on milky quartz.

In Nallagundalu an area of 12 square feet was divided into four squares of 4 square feet. They were eroded. The erosion revealed the concentration of blade-burin industry below 8 inch from the surface. Some of them were found on surface along with mesolithic tools. On this ground, it was concluded that blade-burin industry had come into existence before the existence of mesolithic industry. The tools of two industries belonging to Palaeolithic periods from the same surface would have been due to erosion.

The chief characteristics of Renigunta industry was blade and blade made tools. The blade tools were made by taking out blades from fluted core, scrapers and choppers were made on simple core. But blade tools were made on fluted core. The blades were beautiful, long, parallel sides or irregular sides. One or more ridge were also found on it. Their cross-section was generally trapezoidal and sectoral. Blades were made by soft-hammer or cylinder hammer technique by indirect percussion. From fluted cores, blades were detached by alternate flaking technique of both ends. When flakes were taken out from alround, the remaining part of core was used for making burin. The blades were retouched to get point, knife, lunate etc.

The number of total tools collected was 5,993 in which 1,279 tools were obtained from 8 inch below the surface in excavation. The representation of complete tool was 13.2 per cent. Among tools, the representation of blades was 19.3 per cent and of others 67.5 per cent. 14.40 per cent blades were of 36 to 40 mm. Among tool community, the representation of tools was chopper-27, scraper-63, burin-131, blunt side-532, awl-30 and point-16.

The burins obtained from here were classified in six groups — central-30, bevel-44, right angle-44, concave-6, convex-2, and incomplete-2.

Besides burin, different types of blunted side tools were also found. They were knife, point, awl, lunate, triangle and trapeze. No crested blades were found from here.

Muchchhatala Chintamanugavi Upper Palaeolithic Culture

The upper Palaeolithic culture of Andhra Pradesh cannot be completed without mentioning the Muchchhatala Chintamanugavi site. It was a rockshelter situated in Karnool district. It is located at a distance of 5 km towards south-west from Betmachalan at the end of a small hill. This cave was excavated by Murray after the excavation of Renigunta site. This site was situated in structure of old group limestone. There are three ways to reach the cave. Leaving the months of February to June, the cave remains in darkness for rest of the months. The excavation of this site had yielded three layers. They were termed as 1, 2 and 3. The thickness of first layer was 15 cm and its colour was brown. A deep bowl was found from this layer which had a hole in the bottom. Besides bowls, stone and bone tools were also found from here.

The thickness of second layer was 70 cm. It was a deposit of grey clay. From this layer stone tools, bone tools, teeth of animals and a hammer stone were found.

The thickness of third layer was 45 cm and it was made up of chocolate grey colour. This was the lowest deposit based on bedrock. It is properly cemented and stony. There were pieces of stones and limestones. Besides bones and stone tools, remains of teeth and bones were found from here.

From the point of view of culture, this site presents remains of upper Palaeolithic and Neolithic culture. Only one stone hammer was found which was related to neolithic period. All other tools were related to upper Palaeolithic period. No typological difference was found in tools from all three deposits. There was difference only in their condition. In all upper Palaeolithic tools there were 223 stone tools and 200 bone tools.

In stone tool community, there were flake, blade, core, chips and hammer stone. Retouch was not found in tools. Tools were made from common cores by stone hammer technique. Nearly all tools were regular and visible parallel ridge indicated that they were taken out from fluted cores.

Muchchhatala Chintamanugavi was mainly a bone tool industry. Altogether 2003 bone tools were found from this site in which 151 were finished. All finished tools were divided into following classes:

• Scraper	11
• Perforator	61
• Chisel	12
• Scoop	14
• Tang point	27
• Barb	18
• Spatula	08
	151

Bone tools were made from long bones. Bone tools were made in three phases. In first phase, epiphysis of long bones were cut obliquely. In second phase, bones were cut from the length side or vertically. In third phase, flakes were removed from the sides. According to Sankalia, Indian upper Palaeolithic man used to make bone tools in the same way as Western European upper Palaeolithic man. Perhaps burins were used to cut bones vertically. Scrapers were generally made on thick and wide bones.

The faunal remains found from here in association with tools indicated that there would have been a thick forest and plain of long grass. According to Murthy, this cave site was not a permanent hunting habitation site of upper Palaeolithic man. Rather upper Palaeolithic man used to stay here temporarily in course of their journey. Thus, it was a temporary habitation site.

Upper Palaeolithic Culture of Karnataka

The credit of providing upper Palaeolithic cultural identity to the state of Karnataka goes to a site named Sherapur Doab. It is situated in the district of Gulbarga. This site was formed due to confluence of rivers Krishna and Bhima. Here upper Palaeolithic site spread over 2 acres of land 22 km away from Sherapur taluka in western direction. Paddeya had discovered a similar site in Meralbhavi nearly 2 km south of Sherapur taluka. It was spread in 7-8 acres. Here middle Palaeolithic and upper Palaeolithic tools were found in mixed condition. 196 tools belonged to middle Palaeolithic industry and 446 tools were of blade industry. As they were found from surface, so they were of no value.

Paddayya had made an excavation of this site measuring 4 × 4 feet. But no conclusion was found.

From Gulhal, Benhatti, and Hunsangi, blade tools were found from the same surface. At all sites these tools were found from the black grey silt with pebble and gravel. Fortunately, Paddeya had obtained following sequence of deposit in Hunsangi drain which is situated in eastern part of Meralbhavi hill:

6. Surface.
5. Black-brown silt with pebble-gravel.
4. Yellow-grey silt.
3. Pebble-gravel.
2. Thick boulder conglomerate.
1. Rock bed.

From the second deposit of this sequence, middle palaeolithic tools were obtained. From the fifth deposit, the deposit of black-grey silt with pebble-gravel, tools of blade-burin industry were found. Microlithic tools were found from the surface. According to Paddeya, these three industries should be taken as of three different chronology.

The tools of blade-burin industries were made on churt which were found in sand stones abundantly. Churts were reddish to grey colour. Some were red, yellow and blue. The tools were fresh. Pieces of long cylindrical stones were flaked to convert into fluted cores. Flakes were taken out by direct and indirect technique. On the basis of working edge, Paddeya had classified the tools into following groups:

- Edge tool
- Non-edge tool
- Multiple tool

In edge tools, different types of blade and burin were included. Paddeya had divided them into eleven types. In non-edge tool, different types of borers or perforators were included. In multiple tool group, different types of burin were included. They were divided in 5 types such as single blow burin, bed-de-flute burin, polyhedral burin, angular burin and beaked burin.

Upper Palaeolithic Culture of Maharashtra

Although upper Palaeolithic sites were reported from a number of areas in Maharashtra, but the Patne site occupied special significance among them. The Patne site is located in the district of Jalgaon 13 km south of Chalisgaon railway station nearby Adadrain. The water of this area flows in the river Tittur which is a tributary of the river Tapti. In the south of Patne village at a distance of half km, a sequence of Palaeolithic culture was discovered. From here right from middle Palaeolithic culture to mesolithic culture, an evolutionary sequence was obtained, which was as follows:

Layer-1	It was a deep grey gravel deposit. Its thickness was 20 cm. It was termed as III-C. It was related to late mesolithic period.
Layer-2	It was a grey loess silt deposit. Its thickness was 1.40 metre. It was termed as III-B.
Layer-3	It was a fossil soil deposit. Its thickness was 40 cm. It was termed as III-A. It was related to early mesolithic period.
Layer-4	It was a sandy fine gravel deposit of 1 metre.
Layer-5	It was a yellow gravel silt deposit. Its thickness was 1.50 metre. It was related to upper palaeolithic culture.
Layer-6	It was a fine gravel, pebble and boulder conglomerate deposit. Its thickness was 30 cm.
Layer-7	It was a grey soil deposit. It was termed as II-D. Its thickness was 20 cm.
Layer-8	It was a fine soil deposit. It was termed as II-C. Its thickness was 90 cm.
Layer-9	It was a sandy fine gravel deposit. Its thickness was 30 cm.
Layer-10	It was a grey silt deposit. Its thickness was 70 cm.
Layer-11	It was an angular powder gravel deposit. Its thickness was 30 cm. It was termed as II-B. It was related to early upper Palaeolithic period.
Layer-12	It was a powder silt deposit. Its thickness was 1.30 cm. It was termed as II-A.
Layer-13	It was a reddish sandy fine gravel deposit. Its thickness was 1.5 metre.
Layer-14	It was formed by waste basalt.

From the study of geological layers of Patne, it appears that the entire archaeological remains can be divided into following cultural periods:

- Developed middle Palaeolithic period
- Upper Palaeolithic period
- Mesolithic period

Developed Middle Palaeolithic Period

The Layer-13, which was formed of reddish sandy fine gravel deposit, had yielded tools of middle Palaeolithic. The tool community included scraper, point, borer and wide retouched blade-flake. Jaspar was used for making tools.

Upper Palaeolithic Period

From the deposits of Patne Layer-12 to 4, upper Palaeolithic tools were found. It was really a true upper Palaeolithic layer. S.A. Sali, had divided all tools of upper Palaeolithic period into two parts:

- Early upper Palaeolithic tool
- Late upper Palaeolithic tool

These were again divided into five sub-parts. These five sub-parts were termed as A, B, C, D, E. From A and B sub-parts early upper Palaeolithic tools were found and from C, D and E sub-parts late upper Palaeolithic tools were found. There were difference in material, shape and type of tools in all sub-parts.

Patne II-A: From this sub-group tools made mainly of Jaspar were found. This layer had yielded blunt side knife, scraper, point and burin. Blades were more in number. According to Sankalia, this layer represented the construction period of upper Palaeolithic period.

Patne II-B: It was the 1st layer related to the upper Palaeolithic period. Tools made of blade and burin were more in number. The blades were long, wide and thick. Besides these tools, baked side blade, retouched blade, end scraper, scraper and some fluted core were found. The tools were made-up of jaspar.

Patne II-C: The tools of this layer were made-up of chalcedony. The tools were smaller in size. Blade and burin tools were more in number. In blades these were tang blade, pen knife blade, blunt side blade and beautifully retouched blades. Blades, flakes and cores were used for making tools. Some tang points were also obtained. Disc bead was also obtained. It was made on eggs of ostrich.

Patne II-D: The tools obtained from this layer were comparatively much smaller. Real burin was found from here first of all.

Patne II-E: The tools of this group show similarity with tools of II-D. But some geometric tools like triangles and trapezoids were also found. The number of lunate, perforator and point was increased. This layer indicates the end of upper Palaeolithic culture and beginning of mesolithic culture. Besides stone tools, pieces of ostrich eggs, beads, shells and bones were also obtained. Among these three — II-D and II-E — criss-cross between two parallel lines were engraved. Besides these, two incomplete bead of ostrich eggs and one shell beads from II-D and II-E were found.

Upper Palaeolithic Culture of Gujarat

In the state of Gujarat, a site named Visadi occupied special position so far as the upper Palaeolithic culture of Gujarat is concerned. This site is located nearby the Pawgarh. Here some stone tools were found some inch below the surface of the a field. It seems that when sand dunes were being formed, the upper Palaeolithic man had used this site as industry. The tools of Visadi industry showed more developed bulb of percussion than middle Palaeolithic man. They were more thick in ratio of length and breath. They were detached by direct percussion technique. The size and thickness of blades are such that lunate and triangles could not be made from them. Blade cores and blade-flake cores were of various types. No tortoise core was found.

Blades were of various types. There were only 4 scrapers — one end scraper, one concave scraper and two awl like concave scraper. Burin was also found. Majority of them showed experiment sign. Total 21 burins were found. Quartzites were used for making tools.

Upper Palaeolithic Culture of Madhya Pradesh

In Madhya Pradesh Son valley occupied very special place so far as upper Palaeolithic culture is concerned. Son valley is situated in Sidhi district of Madhya Pradesh. First of all scholars like Radhakant Verma and Brij Bihari Mishra had explored upper palaeolithic site in Son valley near Jagdaha bridge. Later on, a micro survey of the entire area was done as a result of which the correlation of upper Palaeolithic tools with geological layer was established. A number of upper Palaeolithic sites were discovered.

In Son valley upper Palaeolithic tools had started appearing from thick sand deposit over second gravel. But its real layer was lime gravel deposit. Besides river valleys, upper Palaeolithic tools were discovered from a number of other sites. These sites were discovered on the northern bank of Son river parallel to medial ridge or foothills of Kaimur abundantly. The condition of these sites are similar to Belan valley. But Son industry was more developed than Belan industry. From Son industry, blades were found more in number. Besides blades, burin, blade-flake, blade-knife, scraper, point, perforator were also found. Blades were 10-12 cm long. They were 2 cm wide and of parallel sides. Some blades were more wide. They were placed under blade-flake. Medial ridge was found over blades. Fluted cores were developed. Both ends of core were flaked one after other. Point was also an important tool. They were triangular or cordate form. They were made by retouching both sides. Blade-knife was also an important tool. In scrapers, concave scrapers were more in number. Scrapers were made on blade-flake. All tools possessed evidence of retouching. For retouching pressure technique was employed. Tools were made on churt, flint, jasper.

From the Banjer valley and Bhimbetka rock shelter III F-23, upper Palaeolithic tools were also found.

Characteristics of Indian Upper Palaeolithic Culture

The chief characteristics of Indian upper Palaeolithic culture can be discussed in the following ways:

Period: The period of Indian Palaeolithic period has been established as 20,000 B.C. – 10,000 B.C.

Sites: Upper Palaeolithic sites have been reported from all parts of India.

Industry: The upper Palaeolithic industries have been termed as blade-burin industry. Bone industries were also in existence.

Tools: The chief tools of this period were different types of blade and burins. Bone tools were also found.

Technique: Pressure and fluting technique and grove and splinter technique were employed.

Habitat: Upper Palaeolithic people were living in caves or rock shelters near water resources and forests.

Food: The food of Indian upper Palaeolithic man was root, shool, stems, bark, leaf, flower, fruit and seed. Their food was also hunted animals or hunted animals left by carnivorous animals.

Fire: The upper Palaeolithic man was well acquainted by the use of fire. They used to preserve fire in rock shelter. They used fire as weapon and also for roasting food.

Cloth: The upper Palaeolithic man used to cover their body by animal skin, bark of trees and leaves. The cloth was not invented.

Social Life: The upper Palaeolithic man lived in band. The form of society was matrilineal. Children were known by their mothers. It is probable that each band possessed a leader who had full command over females and men of the group. Some kind of division of labour based on age and sex would have started. Females were assigned the duty of rearing and caring children and collecting food materials nearby the habitat. The male members under the guidance of band leader used to do hunting. When they had time they used to prepare tools. Each band had its own tools and population. Each band was self-sufficient.

Political Life: Nothing could be said about the political life of upper Palaeolithic man. But as they lived in band and each band possessed a leader, therefore, the leader possessed leadership quality. He was representative of his band. He had control over band members. He represented his band in band meeting.

Magical-religious Belief: Nothing could be said with certainty about the magical-religious belief of upper Palaeolithic man. But it seems possible that the leader of the group would have been practising magical-religious belief for the success of hunting. The leader of the band would have become the magician of the group. After success in hunting, it was believed by band members that the leader had some super human power under his control. Thus, he would have become magician.

From the Belan valley, the image of mother Goddess was found. It seems that the upper Palaeolithic people of India had belief in mother Goddess and the form of society was matriarchal.

Art: Upper Palaeolithic people were fond of arts. They had shown their artistic behaviour on stone and bone tools. They had established blade-burin industry and bone industry. The tools were smaller in size and beautiful in shape. Burins of bones and stones indicate that upper Palaeolithic man was aware of drawing and painting. Images of mother God, shell beads, stone beads, criss-cross on ostrich eggs, ostrich egg beads, small and beautiful size of tools all furnish evidences towards the artistic behaviour of upper Palaeolithic man in India.

Builder of Upper Palaeolithic Culture in India

Who were the builders of upper Palaeolithic culture in India? There is no clear cut evidence about it. But elsewhere in the world the credit of establishing this special prehistoric culture goes to true *homo sapiens* — Cromagnon man, Chalcelade man and Grimaldi man. These *homo sapiens* or true *Homo sapiens* are regarded as builders of upper Palaeolithic culture. It is also possible that the descendants of middle Palaeolithic culture would have evolved into full or true *homo sapiens* in our country. They would have established blade-burin industry and bone industry in our country. Descendants of these upper Palaeolithic man would have given rise to mesolithic culture, neolithic culture, Harappa culture, Chalcolithic culture and Iron age culture in India.

7

Indian Mesolithic Culture (10,000 B.C. – 2,000 B.C.)

From the point of view of stratigraphy mesolithic is a prehistoric condition after upper Palaeolithic and before neolithic. Due to lack of knowledge in the beginning, the existence of this prehistoric condition was doubtful. The founder of Indian prehistory, Robert Bruce Foote had obtained only two types of tools which he had termed as Palaeolithic tool and Neolithic tool. In between these two prehistoric periods he had propounded the theory of *Hiatus*. When Robert Bruce Foote was working in India, outline of European prehistory was not clear. There also prevailed an assumption of *Hiatus* between two prehistoric periods — Palaeolithic and Neolithic. No scholars were knowing till that time as to how mesolithic period began and in which shape. But this problem was solved quickly in Europe. There mesolithic industries were found from middle layer. The layers before and after it were termed as upper Palaeolithic industry and neolithic industry respectively. This became possible due to excavation of a site in France named Masd 'Azil. The industry found from the middle layer was termed as meeting of two periods — upper palaeolithic and neolithic. It was also termed as transitional period or phase between upper Palaeolithic period and neolithic period. But as researches in this direction progressed, the facts came before researchers that mesolithic industries had developed from upper Palaeolithic industries. It was Hodder Westrop who had used the term mesolithic for these transitional industries in 1866.

In fact mesolithic period is not only meeting period of Palaeolithic period and neolithic period, but this period reveals transition phase. As we have discussed in earlier chapter that the environment of Palaeolithic period was unstable. In pleistocene epoch, the world was witnessing two kinds of environments (1) glacial and interglacial, and (2) pluvial and interpluvial. The environment of earth was restless. But on the commencement of holocene epoch, a change in environment began at universal level. The parts of world having ice sheet began to become narrow. The parts having excessive pluvial periods began to face dry condition. The places having ice sheet turned into the field of grass or turned into green grass land. The places having pluvial period began to turn into thick green forest. Such changes during holocene period influenced not only mankind but also animals of the earth. Reindeers and mammoths found in glacial environment began to become extinct or a change in their shape and size started occurring. Now, small animals surviving on grass began to appear. For example deer, goat, sheep, cow etc.

The end of extreme environment and beginning of tropical environment began to increase the fertility power of earth. New species of grass, plants and trees began to cover the earth surface. Many of these grasses were ancestors of modern day grains. The origin of new species of grasses influenced man and animals both equally. Both were attracted towards these environmental transition due to which agriculture and animal husbandry were established in later prehistoric period called neolithic. Due to such changes, a revolutionary change in economy of mankind had taken place. The hunters and gatherers began to domesticate plants and animals.

Any human society in any period has to make adaptation with changed condition. New conditions give rise to new needs. In order to satisfy new needs, man develops new technology. The mesolithic man also had to make adaptation with changed environment. He had made changes in technology and tools. The change in tools and technology had brought changes in lifestyle of mankind. Towards the end of upper Paleolithic period, these changes had started appearing. The tools made had become more small. Blade and blade made tools were increased in number. The blades and blade made tools of mesolithic period had become more and more small in size. They were made from small, narrow and thin blades. Now, they were termed as microlithic tools. The industries associated with microlithic tool production were termed as microlithic industries. In the beginning, it was believed that microlithic industries were indicative of decadent society. But when researched deeply it was found that they were indicator of mental power and progress. These tools were small in looking, but they were more useful, efficient and lethal. They could be used from a distance.

As facility of life increases, population also increases in the same ratio. Increase in population increases the number of industry sites and habitation sites. Increase in population and facilities encourage human society for migration and movements. Due to these reasons, people of different areas would have come in contact. This contact would have given a number of problems. In order to solve problems, new needs and aspirations would have taken birth. In order to solve these problems mesolithic man had started living in small band.

Microlithic Industry or Mesolithic Industry

Mesolithic industry is known as microlithic tool industry. Microlithic tools have been found right from upper Palaeolithic period to Chalcolithic period. The blades found in Chalcolithic period were termed as short blade industry. The tools of Chalcolithic industries were crested ridge blade, serrated blade and Ribbon flake-blade. But these blades were not found from any mesolithic sites in India.

In the beginning, the origin and evolution of mesolithic tools were doubtful, because there was lack of clear cut knowledge in this regard. When upper Palaeolithic tools were treated as doubtful, then scholars were of opinion that they would have evolved from middle Palaeolithic Levalloisean industry. But when the status of upper Palaeolithic period was established clearly, it was accepted unanimously that microlithic industries were developed from upper Palaeolithic industries. Evidences gathered through researches in Belan valley had thrown proper light on microlithic tool industry.

Microlithic tools were divided into two categories:

- Non-geometrical microlithic tool.
- Geometrical microlithic tool.

Under non-geometrical microlithic tools, parallel sided blades, blunt side blade, point, lunate, scraper, borer and burin were included.

Under geometrical microlithic tools, triangles and trapezoids were included.

Stratified evidences of microlithic industries were found from the excavations of Morahana Pahar and Baghahikhor for the first time. Its existence was also obtained from the excavation of Lekhahiya. From the excavations of different mesolithic or microlithic sites, it became clear that microlithic industries were evolved through at least four stages. These were as follows:

- Non-geometric pre-pottery stage.

- Geometric pre-pottery stage.
- Geometric pottery stage.
- Diminutive geometric stage.

Characteristics of Mesolithic Period

Bow and arrow is regarded as characteristic tool of mesolithic period.

For the purpose of proper understanding, we can divide Indian mesolithic culture into four areas, which are as follows:

- Western India region.
- Central India region.
- Eastern India region.
- Southern India region.

Mesolithic Culture of Western India Region

The mesolithic culture of western India region can be described well with the help of following microlithic industry sites:

- Tilwara industry site.
- Bagor industry site.
- Langhnaj industry site.

Tilwara Industry Site

This microlithic industry site is located in the most western part of western Rajasthan. It is situated in Barmer district on the bank of desert. This site was excavated by V.N. Mishra. He obtained two stages of this industry. In the first stage, evidences of mesolithic habitation site were obtained. He had obtained pieces of iron, glass, beads, and wheel made pottery. On the floor, circular decorated stones were presenting evidences about human habitation. From this microlithic industry site, Mishra had obtained trapezoids, lunate, point, parallel end flakes and fluted cores.

Bagor Industry Site

Bagor is the most important mesolithic industry site in Rajasthan. This industry site is in a famous village in Mewar area of Bhilwara district. This is located on the left bank of Kothari river at a distance of 25 km from the district headquarters Bhilwara. Kothari river is a tributory of Van river. This prehistoric site is located at sand dunes. Such type of sand dunes are found rarely on the bank of river. This sand dune is quite different from sand dunes found in western Rajasthan. Professor V.N. Mishra of Pune University had worked here in between 1968 to 1970 along with his associates. The dune of Bagor is 7 metre high from the neighbouring land. The dune was formed by sands brought by wind. In all deposits of sand microlithic tools were found. From this it appears that when dune was being formed, the spread of mesolithic culture had taken place.

Cultural Periods of Bagor

On the basis of excavation the entire deposit of Bagor (1.50 metre to 1.75 metre) was divided into three cultural periods. Right from early to late period, no evidence of discontinuity was found. The development of microlithic industry had taken place along with use of new material respectively.

1st Cultural Period (5,000 B.C. – 2,800 B.C.)

The entire thickness of this period is 50 to 80 cm. This layer had yielded microlithic tools and animal remains more in number. The study of tools reveals that they were hunters and gatherers. They had built floor with stones for habitation purpose. They used to make huts, too. They used to bury their dead in extending position in east-west direction. This industry of this period was placed under pre-pottery geometric tools.

2nd Cultural Period (2800 B.C. – 600 B.C.)

The thickness of this period was 30 to 50 cm. Pottery and copper tools had entered in this period. The use of microlithic tool was continued. But their number was reduced. Earthern pots were made with the help of hands. They were engraved and decorated. Deads were buried in east-west direction in extended position. Some materials were also placed in grave along with dead. Probably, they were agriculturists and animal rearers.

3rd Cultural Period (600 B.C. – 200 B.C.)

The entire thickness of this cultural period was 35 cm to 75 cm. But it was limited only up to middle part of the dune. The number of microlithic tools and animal remains was decreased. The use of iron tools was started. Potteries were obtained in more number. Deads were buried in north-south direction.

Tool Industry

In the excavation of Bagor, the most number was of microlithic tools. Although these tools were found from all cultural periods, but in the first cultural period their number was the most. Microlithic tools were made on churts and quartzite. The small size blades were retouched to make microlithic tools. Scraper made on flake and burin made on core were rare. The tool community included retouched blade, cross-cut-blade, different types of triangle, trapezes and trapezoids, lunate and point. Some scraper made on flake and some burin made on core were also there. Serrated flakes were not found, though they were present in other mesolithic industries. Majority of tools were 15-20 mm long. Some tools were 5-10 mm long.

Animal Remains

From the study of bones and teeth remains of animals, it appears that 80 per cent animals were domestic such as sheep, goat, pig, deer, antelope, fox and hare. Some water animals remains like tortoise and fish were also found.

Copper Tools

From the layer of second cultural period, 5 copper tools were found. These tools were found from two graves. In these, one was needle or awl which was 10-15 cm long. It was folded at one end to make a hole. Another tool was spear head whose lower part was broken. The other three tools were triangular points. Such types of tools were also found from Harappa cultural sites.

Iron Tool

They were available only from the layer of 3rd period.

Pottery

The Bagor site has yielded evidences of pottery from second cultural period. In first cultural period, some pot sherds had began to appear. But they would have reached here from other medium. The real layer of pottery is from second cultural period. Majority of pottery was made by hand. The pottery industry of Bagor shows similarity with pottery industry of Ahar and Kayatha. The pottery of third period was different from second period.

House Construction

In the beginning of first cultural period, the evidence of house was found. But after some time, remains of stone floor were found. The floor was constructed by small and big stone slabs and round or circular stones. The bones of meat left after eating and stone tools were found in plenty. Besides, circle of 3-5 metre of stones were also found. These were probably remains of circular huts. They used to build huts with the help of reed, plants and trees. A safe floor was also obtained from the 3rd cultural period. In this period, the use of brick was started.

Death Ritual

In the mesolithic culture of Bagor evidences about death rituals were found. The remains of 5 burials were found from all three cultural periods. In the first cultural period one, in the second cultural period three and in the third period one burials were found. All burials were found from the habitation site. This indicates that mesolithic people of Bagor used to bury their deads in their habitation sites. The dead skeletal remains of dead body in burial of first cultural period was in extended position. The head was in west direction. The left hand was kept on stomach. Some bones were also found from the burials. Probably, they were kept as grave materials.

The study of burials of second period reveals that dead body was placed in grave by folding both feet. Two dead bodies were placed in south-east and north-west position. The third dead body was kept in east-west direction. Food materials, tool and pottery were placed in grave as grave materials.

The dead body in third cultural period was placed in north-south direction.

Ornaments

From the mesolithic culture of Bagor evidences of agate beads and carnelian beads were found. The mesolithic people of Bagor used them as ornament. In the neck of one skeleton, a couple bead was found.

Other Stone Objects

In the mesolithic culture of Bagor, stone hammer, mace head, muller, rubber, pestle, slab and stone beads were also found. These tools were found more in the context of neolithic and chalcolithic.

Mesolithic Culture of Langhnaj

Langhnaj is the most significant mesolithic site of northern Gujarat. It is situated at a distance of

59 km north of Ahmedabad. It is located on the bank of river Sabarmati in the Mehsana district of Gujarat. This area had attracted attention of scholars like Subba Rao to Sankalia. This area was excavated six times. The excavations revealed that the site was used for both habitation and burial. In excavations 16 human skeleton were found. Their dead bodies were buried.

Cultural Stage

Three cultural stages were identified from Langhnaj site. These stages were termed as first, second and third.

First Cultural Stage: From this cultural stage microlithic tools, graves, animal remains and sun baked pottery were found.

Second Cultural Stage: This cultural stage had yielded microlithic tools, polished stone axes, and a stone ring.

Third Cultural Stage: From this cultural stage microlithic tools, potteries, iron tanged axe, one spear head and stone mill were found.

Tool Community

In the tool community of Langhnaj flakes were in majority. Parallel sided flakes occupied second position. The number of blunt side blade and lunate were next in number. Triangle and right angles were very less in number. The number of burin was negligible.

The microlithic tools found from different layers of Langhnaj do not exhibit typological difference. Chert, chalcedony and quartzite were used for making tools. Sometimes carnelian and lydianite were used for making tools.

Two polished stone axes were also found. They were made of dolerite cyst. These stones were not available there. So, they were brought from the river Jhelam.

Along with microlithic tools rubbed red ochre and wedge (snake hood) like pieces of sand stone were found. They were used for crushing grains and making tools.

Along with human skeleton quartzite pebbles were also found. Pieces of red ochre were used for getting red colour. Colour was applied over body in living or dead stage.

House

No clear cut evidence of houses appears in the excavation of Langhnaj site. But broken, cut and half burnt bones bear testimony regarding the existence of habitation site.

Use of Fire

No remains of hearth, ash and coal were found in the excavation of Lunghraj site. But burnt bones present evidence that mesolithic people of Langhnaj were aware of use of fire.

Pottery

In Langhnaj, the layer from 3 to 5 feet presents the influence of pottery. The potteries of Langhnaj have been divided into five groups which are as follows:

- Burnished red ware
- Burnished red and black ware
- Incised coarse red ware
- Rusticated ware.

Majority of potteries were made by hand. But some potteries were also of wheel made.

Animal Remains

The excavation of Langhnaj has yielded the remains of several animals. Majority of animals were of domestic type. Some were also of wild type. Cow, buffalo, pig, goat, and sheep were domestic animals. Rhinoceros, deer, *sambhar, nilgay* etc. were wild animal.

Death Ritual

Mesolithic people of Langhnaj knew to perform rituals related to dead. They used to bury their deads in grave nearby their habitation site. 14 skeletal remains were discovered in the excavation of Langhnaj. 13 skeletons were in bend position and one skeleton was in extended position. The parts of heads of all skeletons were broken. It seems that they were a cannibal. But it also seems that the heads were broken by natural causes. Probably they were buried after a war. No grave goods were found in the burial along with skeletal remains. The heads of 13 skeletons were in east direction and feet were in west direction. The head of only one skeleton was in west and feet in east. Their feet were bent and placed laterally. It seems that they were buried twice.

Builder of Langhnaj Culture

The builders of Langhnaj culture were of mixed race. The maximum length of male was 174 cm and the maximum length of female was 158 cm. It appears that they possessed mediterranean and Vedic elements.

Mesolithic Culture of Central India

The mesolithic culture of central India can be discussed with the help of following mesolithic sites of this region:

- Bhimbetka
- Adamgarh Rockshelter
- Sarai Nahar Rai
- Belan valley
- Chopani Mandi
- Lekhahiya Rockshelter
- Baghahi Khor Rockshelter
- Morahana Rockshelter.

Bhimbetka Mesolithic Culture

This mesolithic site is situated in Raisen district of Madhya Pradesh. From this site evidences of cave dwelling, rockshelter and cavern dwelling were found.

Period

The mesolithic period of Bhimbetka has been established as 10,000 B.C. – 2500 B.C.

Culture

In the mesolithic culture of Bhimbetka, one finds the supremacy of technological change, increase in population and use of new materials. It also reveals the better use of plants and animals as food material, death rituals and drawing art.

Industry

The mesolithic people of Bhimbetka had used new technology and materials for making tools. The Bhimbetka mesolithic industry was basically a microlithic industry. Microlithic tools were made on thin micro-blades. Thin micro-blades were separated from fluted or cylindrical cores by applying pressure technique. One or more sides of thin micro-blade were made blunted. The tool community of Bhimbetka mesolithic culture, included blunt side blade, obliquely truncated blade, point, crescent, triangle, rectangle, and arrow. These microlithic tools were fitted in a bone or wooden handle and used for various purposes. They were used as arrow, knife, sickle and spear head. Besides these microlithic tools, side scraper, end scraper, borer, burin, waste flake and core tools were also found. The tools were made on chert and chalcedony. The mesolithic Bhimbetka man used bones, horns and teeth for tool making. Chert and chalcedony were not found on Bhimbetka hills. They had brought them from a place Barkhera situated at a distance of 6 km from Bhimbetka in south direction.

Economy

Mesolithic Bhimbetka man was gatherer and hunter. They were successful in preparing bow, arrow, spearhead, knife, sickle and pellet bow. With the help of these tools, they were able to hunt fast running animals and flying or sitting birds. They had started collecting wild grains from wild plants and also root, shoot, stem, leaves, flowers, fruits and seeds of plants and trees to use as food materials in a better way.

Habitat

The mesolithic man of Bhimbetka had made floor of his habitat with stone slabs, boulders and pieces of stones. From the cave no. III F-23, a stone slab and boulder made wall measuring 6 metre long and 1 metre wide was found. The wall would have been erected to divide caves into different parts.

Use of Fire

The inhabitants of mesolithic Bhimbetka were fully aware of use of fire. They used fire for roasting or cooking food materials, to get light during night, to protect themselves from wild animals and severe cold. In the light of fire they used to make tools. From their habitats ash, coal and burnt bones, teeth and horns were found. Horns, bones and teeth were of antelopes, deer, buffalo and wild pigs. Horns and bones were cut by sharp weapon.

Death Rituals

The inhabitants of mesolithic Bhimbetka used to bury their deads with respect and rituals. They used to bury their deads in the caves located nearby their residence. The dead bodies were placed either in bent or in extended position. The heads of dead bodies were placed in east direction. But sometimes, the head was placed in west direction too. Stone muller, slab, pestle, arrow head, stone tools and bolls of ochre were placed in the grave as grave materials. Skeletons were found in broken state.

Drawing and Painting

The inhabitants of mesolithic Bhimbetka used to make drawing and painting on their dwelling sites. They used to decorate their habitation, rockshelters, caves, stones slabs and their tools by painting and drawings. Entrance, floor, walls, ceiling, stone slabs of caves and rockshelters were painted with different colours and pictures of hunting animals were made. This shows the interest of Bhimbetka mesolithic man in drawing and painting. The Bhimbetka mesolithic artists had attempted to paint and draw pictures even in those narrow sites of caves, rockshelter and cavern where it was very difficult to go and stand-up. They would have painted and drawn pictures at those sites only in sleeping position. Again they have also painted the ceiling situated at very height. They would have faced great difficulty in reaching there. But this indicates their dedication and love towards drawing and painting. The work of artists would have been done only by those individuals of society who were spared from the work of gathering and hunting. These individuals would have become magician and priest of the band. They would have started controlling the behaviour of members of the society by their intelligence. They would have started welfare works for the society as magician and priest. Thus, they would have become respected and leader of the society.

Mesolithic Culture of Adamgarh Rockshelter

Adamgarh rockshelter is located in the state of Madhya Pradesh near Hoshangabad. From here microlithic tools were found from rockshelters and outside areas in good number. This rockshelter was excavated by Joshi and Khare of Archaeological Survey of India. Altogether excavation was done in 18 Trenches. Among them ADG-1 and ADG-2 were the most representative trench.

The trench ADG-1 was located near rockshelter no. 12. Its ceiling was extended outwardly to a distance. But it had fallen down later on. The excavation was made outside the rockshelter. There was a surface deposit of 2-3 cm. This deposit was made of grey powder soil. Only one or two microlithic tools were found from this deposit. Below this layer, there was a 4-5 cm thick deposit of stone pieces and stone powder. Below this deposit, there was 50-150 cm thick deposit of black viscous soil. This deposit had yielded microlithic tools. In its lowest layer, some palaeolithic tools were found. They were there before the arrival of mesolithic man. The stratification of entire deposit was not made.

The ADG-2 was a trench inside the rockshelter. In front of mouth of rockshelter, there was a shell thalus deposit. A long trench was made from inside rockshelter to outside thalus deposit of shale. Inside rockshelter, there was a 1-5 cm surface deposit. Outside the rockshelter below the surface deposit, there was a deposit of deep grey. The microlithic tools were found from this deposit. The laterite deposit was the lowest deposit, but no tools were found from this deposit.

The black soil deposit found here was made by air. When this deposit was taking place, it would have been a dry phase. Evidences of such dry phases were found from Teri site, Birbhanpur site and Langhnaj site.

The tool community of mesolithic Adamgarh culture included core blade and point more in number. Scraper and triangle were less in number. Right angles and borer were negligible in number. Joshi had called the Adamgarh industry as point and blade industry.

Besides stone tools, bone remains of animals were found in abundance. Among animals 50 per cent were domestic and other 50 per cent wild. The domestic animals were buffalo, ox, sheep, pig and goat. The wild animals were deer, elephant, rhinoceros, *sambhar* and horse.

It is worth mentioning here that evidences about domestication of animals were found only from here in India. This indicates that mesolithic inhabitants of Adamgarh were moving fastly towards neolithic period.

Mesolithic Culture of Sarai Nahar Rai

A number of mesolithic sites have been reported from the valley of the river Ganges. Among them Rajapur, Harahi Bhatuli, Patepur and Sarai Nahar Rai in Pratapur district; Kurdha, Bichhia, Bhikhanpur and Mahrudih in Allahabad and Gahwa in Varanasi are important sites. From all these sites, mesolithic culture has yielded two stages. They are as follows:

- Non-geometric prepottery stage.
- Geometric prepottery stage.

Non-geometric Prepottery Stage

The tool community of this stage included thick wide blade, retouched or unretouched big size lunate, scraper, blunt side blade, thin and narrow blade and point. Majority of tools were free from chemical colouring. They were made on chert. The mesolithic tools of this stage were found from Garhawa, Kurdha, Bhikhanpur, Maharudih, Harahi Bhatuli and Patepur.

Geometric Prepottery Stage

The tools of this stage were found from Sarai Nahar Rai and Bichhia. The tool community included point, lunate, blunt side blade, scraper, and triangles. They were made of agate, chalcedony and carnelian. In Sarai Nahar Rai no rectangles were found.

Sarai Nahar Rai Site's Mesolithic Culture

The site Sarai Nahar Rai occupied the most significant place among all mesolithic sites reported from the river valley of Ganges. This site is located in south direction from Pratapur at a distance of 15 km nearby Mandhata. Here excavation work was done by Allahabad University in 1970-71 and 1972-73. The mesolithic site of Sarai Nahar Rai was extended over an area of 1800 square metre. In the entire area microlithic tools were found scattered here and there. This site has been placed under geometric prepottery stage. The study of this site reveals that it was used by mesolithic man as habitation and burial site. Burials were confined only in north-east parts. From south-western parts, evidences of floor and hearth were found. Here excavation of 11 burials and 8 hearths was made.

Period

Radio carbon dating of Sarai Nahar Rai is available. It has been dated as 10,345 ± 110 B.P.

Industry

The industry of mesolithic Sarai Nahar Rai has been placed under geometric prepottery stage.

Habitat

The mesolithic man of Sarai Nahar Rai used to make floor with stone, gravels and sand. An evidence of circular floor was found. Probably they used to erect huts.

Economy

The mesolithic inhabitants of Sarai Nahar Rai were gatherers and hunters. They lived in small bands. They led wandering lifestyle. They used to do collective hunting and gathering.

Food

Besides gathering edible materials from plants and trees, they did hunting of wild animals. They used to trap fishes, small snail and turtles for eating purpose. They used to roast meat and fish in the hearth.

Hearth and Fire

The mesolithic people of Sarai Nahar Rai used to make hearth. The hearths were round, oval and irregular in shape. Their mouths were wide and bottoms were narrow. The measurement of mouth was 1.49 metre to 0.72 metre. The measurement of bottom was 1.02 metre to 0.45 metre. Its depth was 0.25 metre to 0.10 metre. Horns or dry woods were used to dig hearths. Remains of coal and ash were found. They used to roast their vegetarian and non-vegetarian food materials in the fire of hearth.

Social Life

The mesolithic inhabitants of Sarai Nahar Rai were living in small band. Each band had a leader. He used to command respect by all members. He was the controlling authority of the band. The nature of band was wandering. The members had strong feeling for the band. They had strong we feeling. The form of society would have been matrilineal. The band was collective hunter.

Death Ritual

The excavations of burials in Sarai Nahar Rai site has presented before us beliefs and rituals associated with death of individuals. Sarai Nahar Rai mesolithic man used to bury their deads. In burials all dead bodies were kept in extended position. Shallow, long or circular pits were dug as grave or burial. All dead bodies were buried in west-east direction, head towards west and feet towards east. Before placing dead body in burial, a 3-4 cm thick layer of soil was prepared in the grave. Microlithic tools and nails were put in the grave as grave materials. The graves were filled with ash and burnt soil of hearth. Hands of deads were kept on stomach crossing each other. The method of digging grave, placing dead body in grave, putting grave materials with dead body and filling-up the grave reveals that the mesolithic inhabitants of Sarai Nahar Rai had developed death rituals in respect and regard of their deads. Among all burials, grave No. VII was of special significant. In this grave four dead bodies were buried together. There were two layers in which dead bodies were placed. In each layer, there were a male and a female. Females were in left side and males were in right side in both layers. Probably, they were of same family and were husband and wife.

Age and Length

The age of all deads was between 16 years to 30 years. The average length of males was 1.80 metre and the average length of females was slightly less.

Morahana Hill Rockshelter Mesolithic Culture

Morahana hill rockshelter is at a distance of 5 km from road south of Bhainsor village. Here excavation was done inside and outside rockshelter No. 1. At both sites a trench was made.

Excavation Outside the Morahana Hill Rockshelter

The excavation outside the Morahana hill rockshelter was made at a distance of 10 yard east of rockshelter No. 1. As a result of excavation 3 feet thick deposit was found. This deposit was divided into 6 layers. A brief description of these layers are being presented here.

Layer-5A: This was the lowest layer of the Morahana rockshelter's outside deposit. Its average thickness was less than an inch. This deposit was based on bedrock. It was made of melted or destroyed sandstone. No archaeological materials were found from this layer.

Layer-5: This deposit is made of gravel, sand and pieces of sandstones. Its colour is reddish and thickness is 9 inch. The deposition of this layer had taken place in pluvial period. First of all microlithic tools were found from this layer. They were of non-geometric type. They were not related to pottery. The tools were deeply coloured. The tool community included blunt side blades, lunate, point, and retouched and used flakes in more number.

Layer-4: This layer was similar to layer-5, but it was formed by small gravels and pieces of sandstones. Geometric and non-geometric both types of tools were found from this layer. The number of geometric tools were negligible. They represented only one per cent. In other kinds of tool, there were parallel side blade, blunt side blade, lunate, point and borer. Some flakes and cores were also found. Potsherds were also found from here along with microlithic tools. They were breakable. They had more quantity of ochre.

Layer-3: It was made of fine gravel. No sandstones were found. The quantity of sand was very much. It was greyish layer. Its average thickness was 6-5 inch. This layer had yielded the largest number of microlithic tools. The tool community included parallel side blade, blunt side blade, lunate, point, triangle, flake and core. The potsherds were also found, but they were similar to potsherds of layer-4.

Layer-2: It was a deposit of fine sand brought by air. Its average thickness was 7 inch. This layer had more geometric tool. The other tools included parallel side blade, blunt side blade, lunate, point, flake and core. From this layer more pieces of potteries were found.

Layer-1: This was a very fine sand deposit. Its average thickness was 5 inch. From the lowest layer of this deposit, parallel side blade, point and triangles were found. This deposit had taken place during dry phase. From this layer pieces of pottery were found in plenty. They represented nearly 50 per cent of the total collection. One inch below the surface, a rectangular arrow head of iron was found. Pottery pieces were of jar.

Excavation Inside Morahana Rockshelter

Morahana hill is located in great Deccan route. It is situated at a distance of 5 km from Hanumana (Madhya Pradesh) nearby Bhainsor village in west direction. Its rockshelter No. 4 is located near the Bhainsor village in west direction. In this rockshelter an excavation of 6 × 4 sq.ft. was made up to a depth of 1 feet 10 inch. The excavation of this deposit had brought four layers into light. A brief description about these layers from down to top is as follows:

Layer-4: The maximum thickness of this layer is 3 inches. Its colour was reddish mixed with yellowish. From this layer, geometric and non-geometric microlithic tools were found. The tool community included tools like parallel blade, blunt side blade, lunate, point, borer, burin, core, triangle and parallelogram. The representation of geometric tools was 8 per cent. Potsherds were also found. They were ochre reddish, half baked, used, and brown section. The pieces of potteries were 14 in number, whereas microlithic tools were 4107 in number.

Layer-3: The average thickness of this deposit was 1.5 inch. This layer was formed by fragile burnt soil. Its colour was reddish-yellowish-blackish. Altogether 8255 microlithic tools were collected from this layer. The tool community included tools like parallel blade, blunt side blade, lunate, point, core, triangles and right angles. The pieces of potteries were same as that of layer-4, but they were more in number.

Layer-2: The average thickness of this layer was 2 inch. It was made-up of hard yellow soil which had pieces of potteries and pebbles. In the tool communities, there were tools like parallel side blade, blunt side blade, lunate, point, scraper, burin, triangle, right angles and cores. Potteries did not exhibit any difference. They represented 10 per cent of the total tool collection.

Layer-1: It was a light red colour deposit brought by air. Its thickness was 1/4 inch to 1 inch. No microlithic tools were found from this layer. But a closed pit was found from here. Potteries were similar to the potteries of previous layers. From the surface of upper layer an iron made arrow head was found.

At both sites of Morahana rockshelter, chert, chalcedony, quartz, crystal, agate and carnelian stones were used for making tools.

Mesolithic Culture of Baghahi Khor Rockshelter No. 1

Baghahi Khor rockshelter is located at a distance of 1 km east from Morahana rockshelter. Here in the rock shelter no. 1, an excavation was made through a trench of 12 × 6 feet. The trench was dug up to a depth of 1 feet and 10 inch. This excavation had brought to the light 5 layers. A brief description about those five layers is as follows:

Layer-4: The average thickness of this layer was 3.5 inch. It was formed by stone chips, ash and ash mixed soil. From this layer only non-geometric microlithic tools were found. The tool community included tools like parallel side blade, blunt side blade, point, lunate and core.

Layer-3: This layer was made-up of fine sandy soil. Its average thickness was 3 inch. Its colour was reddish mixed yellowish. A burial was made cutting the rock through layer 2A, 3 and 4. This layer had also revealed only non-geometric type microlithic tools. The tool community had tools like parallel side blade, blunt side blade, lunate, point and core. Pieces of pottery were also obtained from this layer.

Layer-2A: Its average thickness was an inch. It was formed by ash mixed soil and stone chips.

Layer-2: It was similar to layer-2A. But it was formed by more melted or destroyed soil. A human skeleton was found covered with this layer. From layer-2A and 2, good number of microlithic tools were found. The tool community had tool like parallel side blade, blunt side blade, lunate, point, core, triangle, and right angle. The pottery pieces were similar to previous layers. But their representation has gone up to 4 per cent.

Layer-1: The average thickness of this layer was an inch. It was a regular hard deep colour deposit. The tool community had tools like parallel side blade, blunt side blade, lunate, point, triangle and rectangle, core and flake. Chert, chalcedony, agate and carnelian were used for making tools.

Pieces of Potteries

Pieces of pottery were found from layer-3. They were divided into two categories — decorated and undecorated. Pieces of potteries were also found from layers-2A, 2 and 1. From the upper most surface 2 arrow heads and an iron piece were found.

Extended Human Burial

From the excavation of Baghahi Khor rockshelter, an evidence of extended human burial was found below layer 2 at a depth of 12 inch from the surface. The burial pit was made by cutting layers 2A, 3 and 4. The bedrock was also cut in such a way that the head and feet of dead body should remain at high and the rest part of body should remain on the burial surface. The head of the skeleton was towards east and feet towards west. Good number of microlithic tools were found along with skeleton. These microlithic tools were placed as grave materials. The entire skeleton was covered with stone chips. The pelvic region of the skeleton was broken due damage caused by later pits. This skeleton was of a female whose age would have been of 21 years.

Chief Facts Related to Baghahi Khor Excavation

The chief facts obtained in excavation of Baghahi Khor rockshelter were as follows:

1st Stage	Development of non-geometric tool.
2nd Stage	Development of geometric tool in limited number.
3rd Stage	Development of handmade pottery.
4th Stage	Development of smaller tools in shape and size.

Mesolithic Culture of Lekhahiya Rockshelter

Lekhahiya rockshelter is situated at a distance of 3 km from Bhainsor village in east direction. In order to verify the results obtained from Morahana hill and Baghahi Khor rockshelters, south Lekhahiya rockshelter nos. 1 and 2 were excavated.

Excavation Outside the Rockshelter

Outside rockshelter towards south two trenches of maximum depth 3 feet was dug. Each trench was 20 feet long and 10 feet wide. The entire deposit obtained in excavation was divided into 9 layers. Their description from down to top are as follows:

Layer-9: This layer was formed due to destruction of bedrock. It had balls of laterite. But no archaeological materials were found.

Layer-8: This layer was formed by laterite balls and rolled boulders. It was yellowish in colour.

Layer-7: This layer was made-up of loose yellow soil, laterite balls and pieces of stones.

Layer-6: It was a deposit of loose yellow soil. The pieces of stone were negligible and there was no laterite ball.

Layer-5: Its colour was yellowish brown. There was no laterite balls and stone pieces.

Layer-4 to 1: The layer 4 to 1 deposit was of deep yellowish colour. Its deposition had taken place due to dissolved chemical materials. It had more quantity of fine objects and soil.

From layers 7 and 8 non-geometric microlithic tools were obtained. The tool community had tools like parallel side blade, blunt side blade, point, lunate, scraper and core. Waste flakes and broken flakes were also found. In the layers 6 and 5, besides the tools of layers 8 and 7, triangles were also found. No rectangle or right angle was found. Remains of pottery were also not available.

It seems that the use of triangle would have started before the use of right angles. The use of pottery would have appeared after the use of geometric tools.

Excavation Inside Lekhahiya Rockshelter No. 1

Inside Lekhahiya rockshelter a 17 × 8 feet trench having a maximum depth of 1 feet was excavated. This excavation revealed the evidences of 17 skeleton. They have given us witness of extended burials. Along with skeleton, a good number of microlithic tools were found. On the basis of stratification, 14 skeletons were divided into 8 time periods. Leaving skeleton nos. XI and XII, heads of all 15 skeletons were in west and feet in east. The head of skeleton XII was in north and feet in south.

The status of geometric and non-geometric tools related to skeletons was as follows:

Period	*Skeleton Nos.*	*Geometric tools*	*Non-geometric tools (%)*
I	II	56	44
II	III	57	43
III	IV	73	27
IV	V, VIII, IX, XI	75	25
V	X, XII, XIV	79	21
VI	XIII, XV	90	10
VII	XVI	81	19
VIII	XVII	99	1

Use of Colour

The mesolithic man of Lekhahiya rockshelter knew to use colour. It is because ochre and crushed laterite globules found along with microlithic tools bear testimony in this regard. They were used probably for making dyes.

Carbon Dating

From Lekhahiya rockshelters two carbon dating were found which are as follows:

1.	TF	419	2410 ± 115 B.C.
2.	TF	417	1710 ± 910 B.C.

Mesolithic Culture of Chopanimando

Chopanimando mesolithic site is located at a distance of 3 km towards east from Deoghat on the left bank of the river Belan. Deoghat is located at a distance of 8 km south of Koraon in Meja Tehsil of Allahabad. This site is located in the river valley of Belan. Here two trenches were dug up of 3.05 × 1.52 metre each with a maximum depth of 1.82 metre. The entire deposit was divided into 11 layers on the basis of archaeological material. A brief description about them is as follows:

Layer-11: This is a deep grey weak deposit. It was formed by broken rocks and laterite balls. No archaeological material was found from here.

Layers-10, 9, and 8: These layers were formed by compact light deep grey soil. These show the 1st cultural stage of microlithic culture.

Layer-7: It was formed by compact deep grey soil. This layer shows a transition of lower and upper layers.

Layers-6, 5, 4, and 3: These layers were formed by deep black colour soil which had stone chips. They were like solidified mud.

Layers-2 and 1: These layers are loose or weak in comparison to other layers. It had more quantity of sand. Stone chips were very less.

Tools

From layers-10, 9 and 8 non-geometric type microlithic tools were found, but no remain of pottery was obtained. From layer-10 some upper palaeolithic long blades were obtained. They were revealing the first cultural period of mesolithic. Layer-7 was revealing second cultural period. From this layer geometric tool triangles were found. Some remains of pottery were also found. They were not baked properly. They were of ochre and yellowish grey in colour. Layers-6 to 1 revealed third cultural period. From them pottery related geometric and non-geometric microlithic tools were found. Right angles and rectangles were found from layer-4 and afterwards. For making tools in first cultural period, chert and flints were used. But in later cultural period, chalcedony, agate and carnelian were used for making tools. Potteries were partly breakable and partly rubbed. They do not resemble any shape.

Chopanimando excavation had revealed the following facts:

- In first stage non-geometric tools were developed, but no development towards pottery had taken place.
- In second stage, geometric tools were developed but no development of pottery had occurred.
- In the third stage, development of pottery had taken place.
- In fourth stage, tools were similar to previous stages. They had become smaller in shape and size. They were beautifully rubbed.

Mesolithic Culture of Belan Valley

The study of geological layers of Belan valley, reveals the development of mesolithic tools. The description of Belan valley layers has already been presented in the Chapter, *Indian Lower Palaeolithic Culture*. Hence, it is not being repeated. On the third gravel deposit of Belan valley a 2 to 3 metres thick deposit of cotton soil or black soil was found. This deposit reveals the existence of thick flora cover when the formation of deposit was taking place. The climate at that time was more pluvial than before. It was a meeting period of pleistocene and holocene. Along with upper palaeolithic tools, non-geometric microlithic tools were also found from this layer. Thus, this layer revealed meeting of upper palaeolithic culture and mesolithic culture. Two layers above this deposit are 4 metre thick. It was formed by air. They had yielded non-geometric and geometric tools respectively. The tool, geological layer and cultural sequence of third gravel were as follows:

Climates	*Structure*	*Industry*	C^{14} *dating*
Dry	Deposited by air	Pottery related geometric microlithic tool	
Dry	Deposited by air	Pottery unrelated geometric microlithic tools	
Pluvial	Humus soil (end of Pleistocene)	Non-geometric microlithic tools and upper Palaeolithic tools	
Meeting of dry and Pluvial period	Cemented gravel-III	Upper Palaeolithic blade and burin industry	19715 ± 340

Mesolithic Culture of Eastern India: Region

Under eastern Indian region, states of Bihar, Jharkhand, West Bengal and Orissa come. In this region some sites were studied extensively. These sites were Kuchai and Birbhanpur. Hence, we are going to describe only Kuchai and Birbhanpur.

The Mesolithic Culture of Kuchai

Kuchai is a Mesolithic industry site located in the state of Orissa. Here mesolithic layer was found below the neolithic culture. Here non-geometric microlithic tools were found, but geometric tools were not found. The tool community had revealed tools like blunt side blade, lunate, borer, burin, side scraper, end scraper, fluted core and flake.

Mesolithic Culture of Birbhanpur

This mesolithic site is located on the bank of river Damodar near Durgapur in Burdhaman district of West Bengal state. In this region two terraces of Damodar river are seen clearly. They have been given name as T_n and T_{n1}. The newest terrace T_n did not yield any tool. On T_{n1}, two trenches — BBP-2 ad BBP-1 were dug at height of 264 feet and 230 feet respectively from sea level. BBP-1 was 24 × 8 feet with a maximum average depth of 7.5 feet. In the middle of them again a 5 × 4 feet trench was dug from the upper surface up to a depth of 12 feet. The excavation of BBP-1 revealed 5 layers, which were as follows in a sequence from down to top:

Layer-5: It was a sandstone deposit of thick pebbles. Its colour was white but sometimes black lines were also seen.

Layer-4: It was a mottled silt deposit whose thickness was from 1.5 feet to 2 feet. Red spots were found in its middle.

Layer-3: It was formed by laterite gravel and stone chips. The layer after it was wavy. It was a land surface where mesolithic man lived.

Layer-2: It was formed by ochre pieces and quartzites. Its thickness was 9 inch to 1 feet. 6 to 8 inch. Below it, good number of microlithic tools were found. But no evidence of pottery was found there.

Layer-1: It was the top most deposit of sandy soil. Its average thickness was 2.5 feet. It was formed during half dry period.

Excavation of BBP-2

At a distance of 2 km north of BBP-1, a trench of 12 × 7 feet was dug. It was divided into two parts by providing a 2.5 feet partition. The eastern part (6 × 3 feet) was dug up to depth of 12.5 feet from the surface. But bedrock was not found even at the depth. This excavation had also revealed 5 layers, a brief description about them is being presented below:

Layer-5: This layer was formed by mottled clay, silt and sand. It also had laterite pills. Two feet above this layer some microlithic tools were found. But micro-study revealed that microlithic tools would have reached here through some gaps. This layer was earlier than mesolithic layer. On its wavy surface mesolithic man used to live.

Layer-4: It was a sandy silt deposit mixed with laterite pills. Its thickness was 9 inch to 1 feet 4 inch. Microlithic tools were not found up to upper 4-5 inches. Below 4 feet 5 inch of surface, a stone piece measuring 6 inch long, 4 inch wide and 2 inch thick was found. Probably this was used as an anvil.

Layer-3: This layer was formed by thick sand whose thickness was 5 to 9 inch. It had laterite balls, too.

Layers-2 and 1: These both layers were made-up of some sandy clay. Both have been separated on the basis of colour. The compound thickness of these layers was 2.5 feet. No microlithic tools were found from layers 3, 2 and 1.

Besides excavations, tools were also collected from terrace T_{n-1}. The places where surface sandy soil was carried away by water, red silt was eroded. Those sites had yielded microlithic tools. Microlithic tools were collected from 5 such sites. They seemed as industry site. Waste flakes and cores were found there.

Birbhanpur Industry

Birbhanpur industry was basically prepottery non-geometric microlithic industry. Quartzite was mainly used for making tool. Some brown colour pottery was found from open sky site, but they were not found in excavation. That is why they were not related to microlithic tools.

Out of 400 tools collected, only one triangle and one right angle were found. Hence, it was a non-geometric industry. For the construction of tools, quartzite, chert, chalcedony, crystal, basalt and fossil wood were used. There were different types of core, flakes, blades, lunate, borer, burin, scraper, a triangle and a right angle.

There were no triangles in Birbhanpur industry. This industry was also not related to pottery. They do not have crested ridge. They were obtained from geological layers. Typologically, they seem close to tools of Singrauli basin and Giddalur Naudinama. They were termed as early mesolithic or epi palaeolithic-microlithic. On this ground, the Birbhanpur industry may be considered as of early holocene. On the basis of Teri industry, it may be dated as atleast 4000 B.C.

Mesolithic Culture of Southern Region

The most important site of southern region is the Teri industry site. It is situated in Tinevelly district of Tamil Nadu state. This industry was situated on sand dune. Sand dune is termed as Teri in local language. That is why the mesolithic industry of here is termed as Teri industry. This industry site is located in Tutikorin and Tiruchendur near sea shore. Tutikorin and Tiruchendur are situated towards south of Tamraparni river. The formation of northern and southern parts of mouth of river had taken place during Pleistocene or early holocene. Here scholars like Alchin and Zeuner had studied 11 mesolithic sites in the north and south of Tamraparni river.

This area occupies special significance because scholars like Zeuner had attempted to study the background of site formation and sea water bottom and air change. According to Zeuner when dune was being formed that period would have been of air action. After formation of dunes, through chemical processes dunes occupied the form of fossil dunes in second period. Thereafter, the period of air action had taken place again. This period was just before modern period. At that time, the sea bottom would have been 20-30 feet high than the present-day sea bottom. He had expressed three probabilities when sea bottom was high and the first air action had taken place. These probabilities were as follows:

- This would have been the last ice age.
- This period would have been interstadial of the last ice age.
- It would have been after glacial period nearly 4000 B.C.

Among all these three probabilities, Zeuner had accepted the last one as most accurate.

Zeuner and Alchin had made study of 11 mesolithic sites. Among them Meghanapuram was the most ancient one. In this industry site there were no blade, point and geometric tools. Unifacial and bifacial disc tools were found.

From other 10 sites blade, blunt blade, concave scraper, lunate, different types of point, triangle and chopping tools were found. Among all tools, lunate were more in number. Triangles were found only from Kullutur.

Characteristics of Indian Mesolithic Culture

The chief characteristics of Indian mesolithic period can be discussed as follows:

Dating of Indian Mesolithic Culture

Attempts have been made to date the mesolithic culture of India. But there is no unanimity among the scholars over this issue. But majority of scholars are of opinion that the date of mesolithic period is 10,000 B.C. – 6,000 B.C. But in some areas this date may be taken up to 2100 B.C.

Cultural Sites

Mesolithic cultural sites have been reported from western region, eastern region, central region, and southern region. Thus, mesolithic culture was in existence in all parts of our country.

Industry

Mesolithic inhabitants of India had following types of mesolithic or microlithic industries:

- Non-geometric industry.
- Geometric industry.
- Pottery type industry.

Tools

The tools produced in microlithic industries were of two types:

- Non-geometric tools.
- Geometric tools.

Non-geometric tools community had tools like parallel side blade, blunt-side blade, point, lunate, borer, scraper, flake and core.

The geometric tool communities had tools like triangle, trapezes and trapezoids.

Pottery

The mesolithic inhabitants of India had acquired the knowledge of making potteries. In the beginning, they used to make potteries with hands and bake them in sun. But later on they had started baking the handmade potteries in fire. They were breakable. The pieces of potteries did not yield any shape. Only at one site, a shape of Jar appeared with the help of 6 pieces of pottery. They were perishable. Their colour was ochre. Some were painted too. We can say that Indian mesolithic man had acquired the knowledge of making pottery with hands and had started baking them in fire. Thus, the initial stage of pottery was developed in this period.

Habitat

The habitat of Indian mesolithic man was situated in caves, rock shelters and caverns. They had also chosen to stay on sand dunes. Probably they had also acquired the knowledge of erecting huts. They used to erect floor too.

Cloth

The mesolithic inhabitants of India used to cover their body with animal skin, bark and leaves. They used to sew skin and leaves for using as cloth.

Food

The food materials of mesolithic Indians were root, shoot, stem, flower, leaves, fruits, seeds, bulbs, and wild grains. They used to kill animals with arrow and bow and also with spearhead. Thus, they were both vegetarian and non-vegetarian.

Fire and Hearth

The mesolithic inhabitants of India were full aware of use of hearth and fire. They used to make hearth in the habitation site to cook food. They used to roast vegetarian and non-vegetarian food materials in the fire with the help of hearth. They used to preserve fire in the hearth. Fire used to protect them during cold season and also from the wild animals. They also used fire during night to get light.

Animal Remains

From the habitat of mesolithic man, remains of domestic and wild animals were obtained. Cow, buffalo, goat, pig, sheep, dog were domestic animal. Elephant, deer, antelope, bear, *chital* and *sambhar* were wild animal.

Ornament

The mesolithic inhabitants of India were well acquainted with the art of decorating their body. They used to decorate their neck with garland of carnelian and agate beads. They used to decorate their bodies with colour. It is also possible that they used to colour the dead body. They used to make garland from shells.

Economy

The economy of Indian mesolithic period was gathering and hunting. They used to do gathering of root, shoot, stem, leaves, flower, fruits, seeds, seeds of wild grains and varieties of bulbs available in and around forest. They used to hunt deer, antelope, *chital, sambhar* and bore. Thus, mesolithic man in India was leading a parasitic life on nature. He was consumer of things provided by nature. He had not become producer of grains.

Social Life

The mesolithic Indians lived in a small band. It was the form of social organisation during mesolithic period. The society was matrilineal. Children were known by their mother. All males of the group were husbands of all females of the group. Marriage by exchange of girls between two bands would have started. Thus, band exogamy rule would have started. Each band had a totem as its originator. Hunting of totem was a taboo. On the occasion of collective hunting, the meeting of different bands would have taken place. On this special joyous occasion, the custom of wife hospitality would have started between bands. This reveals towards a limited promiscuity.

The division of labour in society would have taken place. Females were assigned the duty of rearing children and gathering food materials from the neighbouring environment. Men were assigned duty of hunting and bring stones for making tools. Aged were assigned duty of looking after kids.

Political Life

Each band had a leader who was powerful and skillful. He was respected and obeyed by all members. He used to provide leadership at the time of hunting. He used to protect the members of the band during war from another band. He was offered special part of animals or birds hunted as gift for his special work for the band society.

Magical and Religious Life

The mesolithic inhabitants of India had faith in magic and religion. Pictures drawn and painted in caves reveal that the captain of the band used to perform different kinds of magic for the success of group in hunting expedition. He used to choose the lonely place in cave for this purpose. He used to make attack on the picture of animals to be hunted with the help of arrow heads and spearhead. The lonely place in cave was probably also a place of worship for him. Here he used to worship his ancestors and all superhuman powers. He would have been performing some special rituals to please and keep superhuman power under his control. Thus, the captain of the band would have been the first magician and priest of the band.

Art and Artifacts

From the study of Bhimbetka, Bagor and other mesolithic sites, evidences about mesolithic art and artistic behaviour have come into existence. The inhabitants of mesolithic Bhimbetka used to decorate the entrance, walls, floors, and ceilings of caves, rockshelters and caverns. They used to decorate their tools. They used to provide beautiful shape and size to their tools by pressure flaking and retouch techniques. With the help of burins they used to engrave pictures on walls and tools. They used to prepare *pucca* floor with stone slabs. They used to erect walls to prevent air and animals. They painted walls of rockshelters with pictures of wild animals. They used to make garland of agate and carnelian beads. They also used to make garlands of shells. They used to paint and decorate their potteries, too.

Death Ritual

The mesolithic inhabitants of India used to perform death rituals through burial culture. They used to dig burial in or around their habitat. The burials were long or oval. The dead bodies were buried in extended position. The heads of majority of dead bodies were towards west and feet towards east. In some cases, the direction of heads and feet were in opposite direction. Only in one case, the head was towards north and the feet towards south. One hand of dead was kept over stomach crossing one side to another. In case of male, right hand was kept on stomach, but in case of female left hand was put on stomach. Husband and wife were buried together. Wife was buried left to husband. After digging burial, a cover of 4 inch thick soil was made on the bottom of burial. Over this soil cover dead body was placed. Stone tools, potteries, bones, and shells were put in burial along with dead body as grave materials. After performing these rituals, the burial was filled-up with ash, coal, soil and soil of hearths. Thus, mesolithic man of India had full faith in death rituals.

Builders of the Mesolithic Culture

The builders of Indian mesolithic culture were certainly descendants of *Homo sapiens*. The descendants of *Homo sapiens* developed microlithic culture, bow-arrow culture, band culture, rockshelter culture and pottery culture. With these developments, they laid the foundation of mesolithic culture in India.

8

Indian Neolithic Culture (4,000 B.C. – 1,000 B.C.)

Neolithic period is the last stage of Palaeolithic period. It is a period after mesolithic period and before Chalcolithic period. After neolithic period, metal age was started. But even in metal age, the use of stone tools continued. That is why the period after neolithic is known as chalcolithic.

In previous chapter, it has been referred in brief that drastic change in environment had taken place during holocene age. Those drastic changes in environment had brought a drastic change in the lifestyle of man. Due to change in environment and lifestyle, a new culture came into existence. This new culture was termed as neolithic culture. Neolithic culture was different from mesolithic culture. This difference was limited not only to periods and tool types, but also in their economies. These changes were as follows:

- Cave dwellers become house dwellers.
- Wandering lifestyle was replaced by settled village life.
- Food gatherers become food producers by adopting agriculture.
- Hunters became animal rearers.
- Leaves, skin and bark wearing man become cloth wearing man.
- Sun baked pottery was replaced by fire baked pottery.
- Megalithic culture was developed.
- Polished and grinded tools were made.

In this way, a great change in the lifestyle of neolithic man took place. That is why neolithic period is known as revolution. Peasantisation of edible flora, animal husbandry, polished and grinded tools, co-existence with modern creatures, development of ceramic art, invention of cloth and megalithic culture are taken as chief characteristics of neolithic culture. But it is also true that except polished and grinding tools, other traits had started appearing during mesolithic period. No evidence of peasantisation was collected from any mesolithic sites in India. But stone slab and pestle were obtained from mesolithic sites. It is possible that mesolithic men were aware of edible property of some wild plant seeds. Probably, they were ancestors of present-day grains. Mesolithic man used to gather them and crush them through muller and pestle for the purpose of food. It is possible that wild grains were collected and crushed by megalithic man for the purpose of food. So far as evidence of animal husbandry is concerned, remains of domestic animals were obtained from Langhnaj site of Gujarat. They were of cow, buffalo, sheep, goat and pig. The Adamgarh mesolithic site of Madhya Pradesh has also revealed evidences of domestic animal remains.

It is true that full development of ceramic art had taken place in neolithic period. But ceramic art was not inseparable part of neolithic culture. Jorden valley, Queta valley, Kile Ghul Mohammad, Ghali Gai and Sarai Khob sites do not reveal ceramic in early period. Thus, in conclusion we can say that the traits of animal husbandry, agricultural ceramic arts, which had brought revolutionary changes in neolithic period, but their seeds had germinated in mesolithic period.

In Indian context no such site has been explored till date which could show reciprocal relation between mesolithic period and neolithic period.

In Sangan Kalu site situated in Bellary district of Karnataka below the surface of neolithic period is the surface of mesolithic period. But here prepottery microlithic tools were of chemical colouring. They were found with sandstone blades. In Kuchai site of Odisha, above prepottery non-geometric mesolithic layer, neolithic layer was found. But reciprocal relation between surface of both cultures was not established. In Nagarjuna Konda of Andhra Pradesh, neolithic surface is above geometric microlithic tool surface. Neolithic blades seem to be influenced by mesolithic blades. But here, too, reciprocal relation was not established. The excavations of Lekhahiya, Morahana hill and Chopanmandi sites had revealed a deposit having stratigraphical layers of microlithic tools development in a sequence. Potteries were obtained from 3rd and 4th phases. But no deposit was found over them. Therefore, reciprocal relation between mesolithic culture and neolithic culture was not established.

From all parts of India neolithic industry sites were reported. The scholars working in this field have divided them into different geographical regions. They are as follows:

Sl.No.	*Neolithic Cultural Area*	*Geographical Area*	*Main Habitation Sites*
1.	Northern culture	Kashmir	Burzahome
2.	North-western culture	Baluchistan, Swat and Upper Indus valley in Pakistan	Kile Ghul Mohammad, Ghali Gai, Sarai Khob and Mehargarh
3.	Central culture	Vindhya region in south of Ganges valley	Koldihwa, Mahagarha, Panchoh and Kanjhum
4.	Central eastern culture	Saran district of Bihar	Chirand
5.	Eastern culture	Chotanagpur plateau, eastern districts of U.P., Orissa, Jharkhand, and West Bengal	Kuchai and Barudih
6.	North-eastern culture	Assam, Chittagaon, Sub-Himalayan and Darjeeling	Dao Jali Heding, Sarutaru and Marakdoha
7.	Southern culture	Peninsular India	Brahmagiri, Sangan Kallu, Maski, Piklihal, Uttanur, Nagarjuna Konda, T. Narsipur, Hemmige, Paiyyam Palli, Tekkel Kota, Terdalhalur, Pelway, Kupgal, Singah Palli, Takakodekkal

Northern Neolithic Culture

The evidences of northern neolithic culture was obtained from Burzahome and Bhartanda near Srinagar on second terrace of river Jhelam. The Burzahome site was excavated several times. The Burzahome culture presented a mixture of mesolithic food gathering economy and neolithic food producing economy. Thus, it was an example of meeting period of two different prehistoric cultures — mesolithic and neolithic.

Tools

From the phase I of Burzahome bone tools were obtained in abundance. Among bone tools, there were arrow, awl, point, harpoon, scrapers and needles. Among stone tools, there were axe, edge, wedge and digging stick. These tools were made by polishing and grinding technique.

Pit Dwelling

The excavation of Burzahome yielded evidences of 16 pit dwellings. The majority of pit dwellings had round or oval mouth. The floor of the pit dwelling was square or rectangular. The diameter of mouth of the biggest pit dwelling was 2-7 metre. At the base its extension was 4 metre. Steps were made to reach at the surface by cutting soils. On the external border of the pit dwelling, witness of postholes were found. There were niches and steps in the walls of the pit. Ash was found on the floor of the pit dwelling. The inhabitants of Burzahome used to thatch the mouth of pit with wood and bushes. These evidences prove that pits were used for stay.

Pottery

Potteries found from Burzahome were handmade. At the bottom of potteries mat impression was found. The potteries were not baked properly. A 26 inch long jar with lid was found. The neck of jar was cylindrical and the bottom was round.

Economy

It is true that the inhabitants of Burzahome used to live in pits of soft kareva surface. They used to make round or oval mouthed pits by digging the soft kareva surface. But the base of their livelihood was animal husbandry or agriculture. There is no clear cut evidence in this regard. Muller, pestle and stone slabs were not found. No microlithic tool was found from Burzahome. But a hunting scene was engraved on a stone slab. So, it can be said that people were aware of use of bow and arrow. They used to hunt deer and fish. They used bone made points as arrow for the purpose of hunting.

From the second phase of Burzahome, it began to appear that neolithic inhabitants had started erecting walls of mud or mud made bricks on the surface. The walls were plastered with mud and painted with ochre. From here tools like mace head, harvestor, knife, pick axe and hoe were obtained. These tools were indicating towards primitive form of agriculture. In this period wheel made black burnished potteries were invented. Polished stone axes and number of bone tools were indicating towards hunting economy of Burzahome inhabitants. At the end of this period, a copper arrow head was found. This indicates towards contact with metals to Burzahome inhabitants.

Burial Culture

Among the inhabitants of Burzahome, primary and secondary burials of man and animals were found. In primary burials, dead bodies were buried after applying colour particularly ochre. In secondary burials some special selected bones were buried. From a burial of animals, 5 wild dogs, horn of deer and bones of wolves were found. Human burials had revealed the evidence of head breaking. They performed death rituals by different methods. In some burials, skeletons were bent. In some burials skeleton were placed horizontally on the surface. Some burials had exhibited evidence of primary and secondary burials.

C^{-14} Dating

Attempts were made to make dating of Burzahome site by C^{-14} method. On the basis of TF 128 and TF 15, the dating of 1st phase of Burzahome was calculated as between 2400 B.C. – 1500 B.C.

North-Western Neolithic Culture

There were three important sites related to north-western neolithic culture. They were as follows:

- Kile Ghul Mohammad.
- Damb Sadat.
- Mehargarh.

Neolithic Culture of Kile Ghul Mohammad

It was a small mound situated nearby Queta town. Its area was 500 sq.metre. This site was excavated to a depth of 11 metre. Three different cultural stages were identified from here. Five metre depth from below was related to first stage.

From the first stage, a hut of unbaked bricks, wood and bushes was found. From here a number of microlithic blades and bone tools were found. Arrow head, harpoon, point, awl, scraper and needles were found. Blades of chert, jasper and chalcedony were found. Pecked and ground stone tools and broken muller were also found. No evidence of grains was found. But the presence of sickle blades reveals that neolithic people of Kile Ghul Mohammad used to gather grains available in the form of wild seeds of grasses and plants. This habitation site had yielded remains of buffaloes, sheep, goat, and cow in plenty. This indicates that neolithic people of Kile Ghul Mohammad were aware of animal husbandry. This site would have been probably seasonal habitation site of animal rearers. Towards the end of this period, inhabitants of Kile Ghul Mohammad had started making houses with mud brick and hard prepared mixed mud.

From the second phase of Kile Ghul Mohammad, harsh handmade pottery with basket impression were found, besides cultural remains of first phase. From here evidences of stone seat, ring stone, stone wheel, and axes were found.

Neolithic Culture of Damb Sadat

It was an another mound. It was located at a distance of 12 km towards south of Kile Ghul Mohammad. This site had shown continuity and regularity of cultural materials found from Kile Ghul Mohammad.

Mehargarh

Reporting about this north-western neolithic site was made by a French research team in 1977. It was situated nearby Belan in Baluchistan. This area was excavated by the scholars like Jaringer and Wallier. Here an excavation of 11 metre long occupational deposit was made. The excavation had yielded 7 archaeological phases. The phases 1 to 3 were placed under neolithic period. Its dating was done as 5,100 B.C. by Radio Carbon method or C^{-14} method. Mehargarh was regarded as the oldest neolithic site of this area. From here evidences of a rectangular house made-up of unbaked bricks were found. From the lower level, microlithic blades were found. The tool community had lunate, crescent, triangle, right angle and untouched blades. Some microliths were attached with the help of bitumen.

The second phase of Mehargarh had yielded a shaw made-up with the help of 10 microliths attached with bitumen. No pottery was found.

Central Neolithic Culture

The expansion of central neolithic culture was up to Vindhya valley in south of Ganges valley. From this region pointed triangular celt of southern neolithic culture and round celt of eastern neolithic culture were found abundantly. This area was explored and excavated by Allahabad University. As a result of which its archaeological surface was brought to the light.

Koldihwa and Panchoh were excavated sites of this region. All these sites are situated in Belan valley, Vindhya region near Devas. The excavation of these sites had yielded round celt, microlithic tools, stone slab, muller, pestle, stone balls, and stone sharpner. Garland of shells were also found from here.

From Mahagarha remains of round huts were found. On the floor of huts bones of cow, ox, deer, fish, turtle were found. From here muller, pestle, stone slab, bone made point, pecked and ground stone tools, mud beads, symbol of bamboo or wood poles and burnt soils were found.

Evidences of paddy cultivation were found from here. In handmade potteries, husk of paddy was used as degraissant. From Koldihwa two carbon dates were available. These dates were 5440 ± 240 B.C. and 4530 ± 185 B.C. This is the most ancient date of paddy cultivation in the world.

All potteries found from Koldihwa were handmade. They were divided into corded ware, rusticated ware, burnished red ware and burnished black ware. In the preparation of pottery no prepared soil was used. Iron and calcium pills were mixed in the soil. Floral means like husk of paddy were used as degraissant. Potteries were made by beating the prepared soil with turtle shell. Thus, by this technique corded wares were made.

From Kanjhanu, a site in the Sidhi district of Madhya Pradesh on right bank of river Son tools similar to Belan valley were found. From here, mace head, round celt, microlithic tools were found. Corded ware, bamboo and wood poles sign were also found.

From Bundelkhand and Baghelkhand of Vindhya region pointed triangular neolithic celt was found.

From the Koldihwa site, evidences of cattle shed were found. Poles sign were towards periphery and footprint signs of cattle were in the middle.

The dating of this neolithic culture was established as last stage of 2000 B.C.

Central-Eastern Neolithic Culture

The expansion area of this neolithic culture was old Saran region of Bihar state. Only one habitation site of neolithic culture was discovered from here in the valleys of river Ganges. This only habitation site was termed as Chirand. From here ground round celt were found. Balls in few number were also found. But tools made from bones and horns of antelopes were found in good number. The bone tools included needles, points, borer, pins, tanged and socketed arrow heads, scrapers and pedants. In stone tools, there were parallel side blades, lunates and points like microlithic tools were obtained. Celt, muller and pestles were polished and pecked.

The first phase of Chirand was free from metal. Here neolithic occupation would have been established nearly in 2000 B.C. This was a rich bone tool industry. From the first and second phase, 4 ground and polished stone axes were found. Blade, burin and borer tools were also found.

House Construction

The excavation of Chirand revealed that neolithic Chirand inhabitants used to erect house for their stay. In the beginning they used to live in pits dug for the purpose of stay. Later on, they had started making houses with the help of bamboo, wooden poles, soil and bushes. The shape of house was round. The diametre of house was 2 metres. The houses were in the shape of huts. From a hut, a group of several hearths was found.

Artifacts

Neolithic inhabitants of Chirand had deep interest in art and decoration. They used to make garland or beads and pendants of sub gems, bangles of terracotta and bones, images of animals, birds and snakes. These were the artifacts and decorative materials of neolithic inhabitants of Chirand.

Pottery

The excavation of Chirand had revealed remains of handmade potteries. Potteries were baked in fire. They were decorated by red ochre, applique and drawing. Potteries obtained form here have been placed under groups like red, grey, black and redware cup, lid, plate, and spouted pots were made.

Agriculture

The excavation of Chirand had revealed burnt husk in pieces of soil. On the basis of these evidences, it can be said that the inhabitants of neolithic Chirand were agriculturist. They were aware of agricultural works. Evidences of wheat and kidney bean were also found.

Tools

Besides stone tools, this place was a rich industry of bone tools. Bone made pick, axe, scraper, eyed needle, were also found from Chirand.

Eastern Neolithic Culture

Chotanagpur plateau of Jharkhand, eastern districts of Uttar Pradesh, Bihar, Orissa and West Bengal states have been included under eastern neolithic culture. The representative sites of this area are Kuchai and Barudih.

The excavation of Kuchai was done on the basis of neolithic traits found from Kuchai. An attempt was made to show the neolithic culture of entire eastern region.

Kuchai is a neolithic site situated on the bank of the river Burhabalong. This site was excavated by B.K. Thapar. As a result of excavation, the Kuchai site exhibited the following neolithic characteristics:

Tool

The excavation of Kuchai site had revealed neolithic tools like round ground butt axe, faceted hoe, chisels, mace head, pounder and grinding stone. The existence of these tools clearly reveals that Kuchai was a neolithic site.

Pottery

Remains of pottery were obtained in the excavation of Kuchai site. Potteries were handmade but baked in fire. The potteries were thick and sandy. Their colour was grey and orange.

Agriculture

No clear-cut evidence about agriculture was found from here. But mace head, pounder, and grinding stone like tools were found. The existence of these tools indirectly hint towards agriculture.

Period

The period of eastern neolithic culture has been established as around 2000 B.C.

North-Eastern Neolithic Culture

Under this neolithic culture, areas like Assam, Chittagoan, sub-Himalayan and Darjeeling were included. From habitation sites of these areas corded ware, shouldered and round flat butt axe, muller, and pestle were found. No clear evidence of agriculture and animal husbandry was found. But *jhum* cultivation is existing in this area probably since neolithic period.

Southern Neolithic Culture

The southern neolithic culture was studied extensively by the scholars working in this field. In this area an excavation was made for the first time by Martimer Wheeler. He had excavated Brahmagiri site (Karnataka). Thereafter, a number of sites were explored and excavated.

Uttanur and Nagarjuna Konda in the northernmost neolithic sites and Paiyam Palli in the southernmost sites occupied special significance. Besides these sites, Sangaur Kallu, Hallur, Pikhalihal and Tekkal Kota are some Neolithic sites from where tools and industries were explored. All neolithic sites of southern region had yielded flat based axe, pottery and microlithic tools. The neolithic cultures of all these southern region sites, exhibit similarity with Tekkal Kota site. Hence, a description of Tekkal Kota neolithic culture is being presented here.

Tekkal Kota is a neolithic site located in the state of Karnataka. On the basis of remains of pottery found in excavation, the neolithic culture was divided into two phases—first phase and second phase.

In the first phase, neolithic man used to live on Granite hills, their flat terraces and plain land between two hills.

In the first phase, neolithic man used to make pottery with the help of hand and bake them in fire. After baking, bands were made on grey pottery with the help of red or yellow ochre colour.

The neolithic man of first phase of Tekkal Kota used to make polished and ground tools, microlithic tools, bone tools and muller and pestles. They used these tools for satisfaction of their various needs.

Evidences of cow, sheep, goat and ox rearing were found. Ash mound was also found from here.

From the second phase of neolithic culture of Tekkal Kota, evidences of round huts erected with the help of wooden poles and bushes were found. The floor of huts were made of soil. Majority of huts were erected with the support of wooden poles. Some huts were also erected from the support of walls. Rocks and pebbles found on the surface bear testimony that walls were erected for the purpose of huts.

Burnished grey wares were the chief pottery of this phase. On the red surface of potteries, grey blue colour linear design were made.

The chief tools were beads of steatite, and blades. Other tools were axe, adze, wedge, chisel, picks, grinding or rubing stone and pounder.

The neolithic man of southern India had well developed burial culture. They used to perform death rituals through graves or burials. They used to make various kinds of burials. For example extended burial, pot burial and partial burial. The extended burial was made in such a way that dead body could be put in extended position. There was custom of putting grave materials in the grave. As grave materials, tools, ornaments, animal sacrifice, shell, snail etc. were put. They used to make burial below the floor of the huts.

The neolithic inhabitants of Tekkal Kota were lovers of art. On a pottery lid of Tekkal Kota, a picture of bull was pierced with the help of needle. They had also engraved the picture of two antelopes and a snake with the help of bone needle. They used to do this artistic work before baking in the sun and fire.

The excavation of Tekkal Kota had revealed remains of domestic animals. They used to domesticate cow, ox, buffalo, sheep, goat and dog.

Dating

With the help of Radio Carbon method of dating, the dating of first phase was established as 2300 B.C. – 2045 B.C. and the dating of second phase was done as 1800 B.C. – 1600 B.C.

Characteristics of Indian Neolithic Culture

After describing the regional features of neolithic sites and cultures of India, we can present the characteristics of Indian neolithic culture as a whole. The chief characteristics of Indian neolithic culture are as follows:

Dating

The Indian neolithic period has been established as 4000 B.C. – 1000 B.C.

Neolithic Sites

Neolithic sites were reported from every part of our country such as north, south, east, west and central Indian regions. This indicates clearly that in every region of India, neolithic man had made his stay and developed neolithic culture. They left evidences of their stay as remains of house, tools, potteries, ornaments, arts and animal remains whom he used to domesticate. Their neolithic culture traits were found buried in the earth which were explored, excavated and studied by scholars working in this field.

Regional Neolithic Culture

Excavations and study of regional neolithic sites had yielded some common and some regional features of neolithic culture in India. Although polished and ground stone axes, adze, chisel, picks, mace head, ring stone, grinder and pounder were obtained from every regional neolithic culture, but there were some differences, too. Handmade potteries were also found from everywhere.

Northern neolithic culture was characterised by pit dwelling and pointed butt celt.

Eastern neolithic culture was characterised by different types of shouldered celts.

Central and western neolithic culture was characterised by microlithic tools and pottery pieces. They were more in number than celts.

Southern neolithic culture was characterised by flat butt celt.

Tools and Techniques

In neolithic period, new tools were prepared by new techniques. The preparation of new tools by new technique had given rise to neolithic culture. There was supremacy of different types of celts. The celt family included axe, adze, and chisel. Besides these stone tools of the celt family, wedge, picks, pins, macehead, rubber stone, mill stone, ring stone, hammer stone, flakes, flake-blades were also included in new tools. Microlithic tools were also included in the tool community. They have become more thin and small than mesolithic period. They had become more beautiful too. Besides stone tools, bone industries were also prevalent in neolithic period. Bone tools were awl, point, pins, harpoons, scraper, needles. Probably points were used as arrow head.

New stone and bone tools were made by new technique. The new technique of making tool of this period was known as grinding and polishing technique. In this technique, tools were rubbed against another stone for polishing and sharpening the edge. For rubbing the tools against a stone, water and sands were added before grinding. Animal fats were also used. By grinding and polishing technique, the efficiency of tools was increased. The edges of tools were made sharp. They become beautiful in look. It was not necessary to grind and polish all parts of the tools. In grinding and polishing the utility of tools was taken into consideration. Sometimes only working edge was polished, while sometimes, the entire surface of the tool was polished.

Neolithic Economy

From the evidences gathered from the neolithic habitation sites and industry sites, it appears that the economy of neolithic Indians was based on agriculture and animal husbandry. This cannot be concluded that hunting and gathering economy was totally replaced because they are continuing even today. Collection of wild edible materials were done and hunting of wild animals was continued even after invention of agriculture and domestication of animals. Fishing was also continued. But it is true that for the first time evidences related to agriculture and domestication of animals were introduced during neolithic period. In this period man had become producer in place of parasite on nature.

The economy of Burzahome inhabitants was dependent on hunting of deer and fishes. The neolithic inhabitants of Kile Ghul Mohammad were cattle rearer. Their habitation sites had yielded bones of cow, buffalo, sheep, and goat in excavation. From here sickle blades and broken muller were found. This reveals that neolithic inhabitants of Kile Ghul Mohammad were aware of collecting seeds of wild grains and using them as food materials. The inhabitants of Dambsadat were cattle rearer. The inhabitants of Mehargarh were aware of animal husbandry.

The neolithic inhabitants of Koldihwa were aware of agriculture. Here the husk of paddy was used as degraissant in making pottery with the help of hands. Muller and pestle were also obtained from here.

The neolithic inhabitants of Chirand (Saran, Bihar) were aware of agriculture. From here evidences of wheat and kidney bean were obtained.

The neolithic inhabitants of Kuchai used to make mace head, mill stone and grinder stone, These tools were related to agriculture.

From the neolithic sites of Assam, Chittagong, and Darjeeling no evidence of agriculture was found in excavation. But it is probable that *Jhum* cultivation was started in this period in these areas.

The neolithic inhabitants of Tekkal Kota were cattle rearer. Evidence of burnt ash mound was found from here. Grinder stone was also found from here. Thus, from the excavations of neolithic habitation sites and industry sites, it is quite clear that neolithic Indians were aware of agriculture and animal husbandry.

Pottery

The excavations of neolithic habitation sites and industry sites reveal that neolithic Indians were aware of art of making potteries. Probably, the production of grains would have brought the problem of storage. This problem would have forced them to invent pottery. They would have seen red and black burnt soil of hearths. This observation would have prepared the ground for the invention of pottery. They would have brought wet soil from the river bank and have prepared soil in such a way so that it could be converted into a shape of pottery with the help of hand. In the beginning, the handmade potteries were baked only in sun. But they were easily breakable. They lost their identity in water. But soon they began to bake potteries in fire. This practice increased the hardness of potteries. In the beginning potteries were made by ring and band methods. In this method, first of all rings of different shapes and sizes were made by wet prepared soil. Then they were placed one above the other and integrated with the help of wet soil. The invention of potteries solved the problem of storage of grains. This also helped in cooking food and storing water. Now neolithic people could live slightly away from the water sources.

When wheel was invented, neolithic man began to make wheel made pottery. Now, potteries were made in various beautiful sizes and they were decorated by drawing pictures with inserting bone pins in wet potteries. Then they were baked in sun. By this method they used to engrave pictures of birds and animals. Potteries were painted too with the help of ochre.

All potteries found from Burzahome were handmade. Mat impression was found below the bottom of the potteries. They were not fire baked properly. A 26 inch high jar with lid was found from here. The neck of jar was cylindrical and bottom was round.

From Kile Ghul Mohammad, Dambsadat, and Mehargarh, relics of handmade potteries were found. The soil for making pottery was prepared by adding husk of paddy.

The pottery remains of Koldihwa were divided into corded ware, rusticated ware, burnished ware, and red ware. Earthen cup, lid, plate and sprout pots were found in the excavation of Koldihwa neolithic site.

The Kuchai neolithic site had also shown evidences of potteries but they were thick and mixed with sand. Here orange and brown colour pottery were made.

The Tekkalkota neolithic site had also revealed remains of potteries made by hand. Here yellow-grey or sometimes black-grey potteries were made. The potteries were painted with red ochre colour.

From the above account, it is quite clear that pottery industry had come into existence during neolithic period in India.

House

The neolithic Indians were quite aware of art of erecting huts. From Burzahome neolithic site, evidence of pit dwelling was found. The neolithic inhabitants of Burzahome used to make pit in the soft Karewa deposit for the purpose of living. The excavation of this site has revealed evidences of 16 pit dwellings. All these pit dwellings were obtained from the first phase. The mouth of majority of pit dwellings was round or oval. The diametre of mouth of the biggest pit dwelling was 2.7 metre. Near the base its expansion was 4 metre. Nitches and stake were made by cutting the walls to reach the floor surface of pit dwelling. Ash was found on the floor surface. There were hearths nearby the entrance gate. The neolithic inhabitants of Burzahome pit dwelling used to thatch the mouth of pit with the help of wood and bushes.

The neolithic inhabitants of Kile Ghul Mohammad used to erect house with the help of sun baked bricks and wood and bushes. The neolithic inhabitants of Mehargarh used to erect square shaped house with the help of sun baked bricks, wood and bushes.

The inhabitants of neolithic Koldihwa used to erect cattle shed with wood, and bushes.

The inhabitants of neolithic Chirand were pit dwellers in the beginning. But later on, they had started erecting house with the help of wet soil, wood, bamboo and bushes. The diametre of the hut was 2 metre. Several remains of hearths have been found from a hut of Chirand.

From the neolithic site Tekkal Kota, relics of round house were obtained. Floor was made of soil. Walls were made of wet soil, bamboo and wood. The houses were thatched with wood and bushes.

Village

The inhabitants of neolithic period had laid the foundation of settled village life in India. They had erected houses and started agriculture and domestication of animals. From the neolithic habitation sites of Burzahome, evidences of 16 pit dwellings were found. The existence of 16 pit dwellings on the same place reveals clearly that the development of villages had taken place. From Chirand, Koldihwa and Tekkalkota evidences of separate houses at the same place were found. Thus, the concept of village and village organisation had taken place.

Social Life

Evidences collected from neolithic sites of India revealed that a number of families lived together as inhabitants of a village. In a neolithic village, 15 to 20 families lived together. Probably in a village descendants of same ancestors used to live. The concept of lineage and clan would have come into existence. Probably inhabitants followed exogamy rule in marriage. Each village had a headman. He used to represent his village in inter-village meeting. In village level decision, he used to play significant role. Agriculture and domestication of animals was done at collective level. The head of the village used to distribute the produce of agriculture and domestication of animal among all families of the village. The concept of common village property had come into existence. The concept of individual property was not known. The village head was not only the social head, but he was also religious and magical head of the village.

The form of society was perhaps patrilineal. For running society property, simple division of labour had taken place. The basis of division of labour was age and sex. Cooking, bringing and storing water, rearing and caring children, collection of edible food materials from the neighbouring environment were done by women. Men used to do agriculture, hunting and domestication of animals, bringing stones and bones for fashioning different kinds of tools, watching cattle and agricultural fields.

The girls used to cooperate their mothers and boys used to cooperate their fathers. The aged used to look after kids and cattle. In the erection of houses and construction of tools all men and women cooperate each other. Women were not allowed to do heavy works. Special cares were taken for lactating and expectant women.

Magical-Religious Life

From the excavations of neolithic habitation sites, no images of Gods and Goddesses were found.

But from excavations of burials and megalithic burials, some knowledge about their magical and religious life was obtained. They have full faith in soul of ancestors. They believed and performed rituals related to burials and megaliths. They believed that burials and megaliths were the abode of their ancestors. Their relationship with their dead persons as ancestors was maintained. The tools used and ornaments worn by them were put in burials or megaliths along with dead bodies as grave materials. Bones, horns, shells, stone pieces were also placed in grave as grave materials. For the peace of soul of dead, animal sacrifice was also made. It is also possible that animals were also buried along with dead bodies. From the megaliths and burials, bone remains of animals were also found. In order to perform these rituals some magician or priest would have come into existence. In the beginning, the head of village used to do the work of magician and priest. But later on, he would have been only secular head and other individuals would have become magician and priest. These magical and religious personnel would have been performing their magical and religious rituals during illness, flood and starvation.

Death Rituals

From the excavation of neolithic sites located in different parts of India, evidences of burials have come into existence. The study of burials and megaliths reveals that neolithic inhabitants of India used to dig a burial for performing death rituals. Burials were the site where death rituals were performed. The burials were of rectangular or oval in shape. Their sizes were such as the dead body could be put in extended or bent position properly. The excavation of Burzahome revealed the existence of burials. This shows that neolithic inhabitants of Burzahome used to perform death rituals in graves or burials. They used to dig different burials for man and animals. They used to apply ochre colour before burying the dead body. Probably, this ritual was related to rebirth. It was because ochre colour symbolized the blood which was associated with belief in rebirth. The Burzahome site had yielded evidences of both primary and secondary burials. In primary burial, entire dead body was buried. But in secondary burials only heads and ribs were buried. From a burial of animals, bone remains of 5 dogs, horns of antelope, wolf, and cocks were found. Human burials had presented the evidence of head breaking. This was probably related to their religious belief. Probably, they believed that soul resided in head and without breaking of head, the soul would remain inside the head and would not assume another form of life.

The Tekkalkota neolithic site of south India had also yielded evidences of burial rituals. The inhabitants of neolithic Tekkalkota had full belief in burial death rituals. They used to dig different types of burials. For example extended burials, Jar burials, partial burials. They used to dig burials below habitation site or nearby the habitation site. Grave materials were put in burials along with dead bodies. Stone pieces, stone tools, shells, bones, ornaments, and earthern pots were put in the burial as grave materials. Animals were also sacrified in burials for the peace of departed soul.

Expression of Arts

The neolithic inhabitants of India had great affection for art. They had attempted to express their artistic behaviours on stone and bone tools and on potteries. They not only provided different beautiful sizes of potteries, but they used to beautify them with painting. They used to decorate potteries with dot lines, dot pictures and painting. They used to engrave dot lines or dot pictures with bone needles when potteries were not baked in sun. They used to beautify their stone tools and bone tools with the help of grinding and painting. From Tekkalkota habitation site, granite pebbles were found. On earthern lids, dot pictures of snake, bull, two antelopes were carved. They used to make microlithic tools. They used to polish their tools made of stones or bones. They used to make floor and erect rectangular or square shaped houses. All these artistic behaviours indicate that neolithic inhabitants were lovers of arts.

Builders of Indian Neolithic Culture

The builders of Indian neolithic culture were definitely descendants of true *Homo sapiens*. They were *Homo sapiens*. They had assumed *Homo sapien* state during upper palaeolithic period. Their descendants laid the foundation of mesolithic and then neolithic cultures.

9

Indian Prehistoric Art Culture

The prehistoric inhabitants of India had left their relics of art culture in their rockshelters, cave dwellings, cavern dwellings, stone tools, bone tools and potteries which they had made and used. The study of these material objects left by our prehistoric ancestors give us evidences regarding their art culture. Our prehistoric ancestors had attempted to paint and draw pictures on entrance, floor, walls, ceiling, narrow spaces of caves, caverns and rockshelters. They had decorated their tools of stones, bones and potteries with piercing, polishing and painting. They would have felt that their dwelling places should look beautiful. Not only dwelling places, but tools and potteries should also be decorated. Body parts should also be decorated with the help of colour, garlands and ornaments. In order to express their hidden feeling, they started painting and drawing. For polishing stone and bone tools, they had used pecking and grinding technique. For decorating potteries, they used to draw dot lines, dot pictures, draw square, rectangles and circles. These artistic behaviour of our prehistoric ancestors laid the foundation of prehistoric art culture in India.

Now, the description about the development of prehistoric art culture in India is being presented here in chronological order.

Art Culture of Upper Palaeolithic Period

The credit of providing an evidence of art culture of upper palaeolithic period in India goes to Belan valley of Uttar Pradesh state. The Belan valley site gave us an evidence of beautifully bone made image of mother Goddess. This is regarded as the most significant contribution of upper palaeolithic Indians in the context of prehistoric art culture.

From the Muchchhatala Chintamanugawi site of Andhra Pradesh beautiful and decorated bone tools were found. From this upper palaeolithic site, a bone made burin was also found which naturally attracted our attention towards the art culture of upper palaeolithic Indians.

From the Patne upper Palaeolithic site of Maharashtra, a criss-cross symbol on ostrich eggs and beads of shells were found.

From all above-mentioned facts found in excavation of upper Palaeolithic sites from different parts of India it becomes clear that upper Palaeolithic Indians had started their steps towards art culture slowly. They had started sewing skins for using as cloth too.

Art Culture of Mesolithic Period

Bhimbetka, Bagor and Birbhanpur sites of mesolithic period have yielded good evidences of mesolithic art cultures of Indians. From the samples found from the excavations of above mesolithic sites, it becomes clear that mesolithic Indians used to decorate their place of residences such as rockshelters, caves and caverns. They used to decorate and beautify the entrance, floor, walls, ceilings, narrow spaces of caves, caverns and rockshelters by painting and drawing pictures. They used to provide beautiful looks to their tools by the technique of retouch and pressure flaking. With the help of burins they used to beautify their residences and tools. They used to make beautiful floors with the help of pebbles, stones and shells. They used to erect walls to prevent air. They decorated walls of caves by drawing pictures of animals and carving hunting scenes. The picture art obtained from Bhimbetka is regarded as the most significant example of mesolithic art of India.

From the excavations of Bagor and Birbhanpur mesolithic sites, evidences of garlands and beads of agate and carnelian stones were found. Turtle shell signs on pottery also presents an excellent example of mesolithic art culture.

Neolithic Art Culture of India

Neolithic Indians had also made significant contributions in the field of art. They had given birth to polishing and grinding art, house construction art, cloth weaving art and pottery art. Neolithic inhabitants of India used to express their arts in different ways. They used to make beautiful stone and bone tools by polishing and grinding technique. This technique was also used to make sharp edge of the tools. By painting and picture drawing techniques they used to decorate and beautify their potteries. They used to erect square or rectangular shaped houses. Expressions of such artistic behaviour reveal the prehistoric art culture of neolithic period.

Prehistoric Art Culture of Bhimbetka

In Bhimbetka evidences of prehistoric arts are as rich as human habitation. Although some engraved artistic designs can be seen on bone tools found from here, but chief evidences regarding art culture are available from drawing and paintings. The Bhimbetka site presents a concentration of painted prehistoric habitation in India. It is not only in India, but the largest prehistoric habitation site of the world.

From the Bhimbetka complex remains of paintings and picture writings were available nearly in 500 caves and rockshelters. The theme and style of painting show very much differences, but they are related to an extensive time period.

Place of Painting

The prehistoric man of Bhimbetka had made paintings on walls, lower portion of ceiling, entrance points, floor, vacant places and notches. Sometimes, flat surfaces were left unpainted, whereas unflat surfaces were made painted. Sometimes, paintings were made at such a height where the artists would have to face great difficulty in reaching there. The artists would have taken artificial support to reach at those heights for paintings. Sometimes, faulty paintings were found in caves used for dwellings. Sometimes, more evidences of paintings were available in the caves which were never used for living purposes. Sometimes, the later artists had made paintings over the paintings of former artists. The artists of two time periods had made painting on the same surface which influenced negatively in looking. All these behavioural evidences reveal that the prehistoric inhabitants of Bhimbetka used to decorate and beautify their places of residence.

Background of Painting and Colour

Majority of pictures were drawn with the help of white and red colour. But sometimes blue, green or yellow colour were also used for drawing pictures. Some shadows of red, ochre, light red, yellow and deep chocolate colour were also seen. Paintings were made by natural mineral colour. Red hematite was used as a chief colour. It was because this colour was widely available in geological layers of the soil in neighbouring areas. Countless boulders of hematite were available from the excavation of mesolithic deposits in more than 20 colours. The powder of these boulders were mixed with water, ghee or animal fats to make paints of different colours. With these paints natural surfaces of rocks were painted.

Preservation of Paintings

The preservation of paintings in Bhimbetka was found in different stages. The preservation stage was dependent on antiquity and location of the paintings. The new paintings were more preserved than the old ones. The paintings found in open skey were less preserved than paintings found inside caves or rockshelters. A number of paintings were totally damaged and some were partially damaged. Some were damaged in such a way that nothing appeared after wetting the painting.

Painting over Paintings

As referred to earlier that later artists had made paintings over the painting of former artists. The new drawings had covered fully or partially the old drawings. This behaviour was against artistic creation. But these behaviours have been proved boon for the archaeologists. Because on the basis of covered drawings relative chronology can be established. Sometimes four layers of paintings were found.

By comparing the drawings of one cave with another caves 16 layers of figures were established. All figures were not of same time and same culture. In fact, those paintings were made in the period of 10,000 years. That is why there were differences in themes and styles of drawings. It was because prehistoric inhabitants of Bhimbetka were witnessing changes in their lifestyle.

On the basis of covering drawings, theme and styles, Bhimbetka drawings were divided in to 9 (nine) periods. The drawings of periods I to IV were placed under mesolithic culture, while the drawings of periods V and VI were related to animal husbandry. This was related to neolithic culture. The figures of periods VII to IX were placed under historical age.

Technique of Drawing

The prehistoric inhabitants of Bhimbetka used feathers of birds or green thin stem made brush for the purpose of drawings. In the beginning for drawing animal or human bodies outlines were drawn. But sometimes entire body was filled with colour. In later stages, the figures of animals or men were made by dot lines or wavy lines geometrically. Even in technique of earlier drawings one finds expertise. No stoppage was found in the drawing of figures. Lines were meeting each other freely. Outlines of men and animals were presented through figures. They do not appear correct scientifically, but they seem reliable in look. Human figures were presented in stick form. Animal figures were presented in natural way. It seems that animals had attracted the mind of artists. It would have been possible due to environment in which inhabitants of prehistoric Bhimbetka lived.

Theme of Paintings

In mesolithic painting, the common themes were wild animals. Position of men came later. Animals were shown standing, running, walking, grazing and hunting. They were shown individually or collectively. Sometimes animals were shown 50 in number. In Zoo park a big flat ceiling

(8 metre long and 5 metre wide was shown full of animals. All species of animals were included here. Among animal figures, buffalo, tiger, leopard, bear, bore, black buck, deer, fox, jackal and monkey were drawn. Antelopes had established its prominence due to its beautiful horns. The size of animals in figures was from some cm to full life time. Some figures were more than 4 cm long. Small figure of deer's children, neck figures of deer, grazing in pleasant mood deer, attacking by spears on deer by hunters present very beautiful and natural scene. These prehistoric paintings present natural courage and correct information of animal body. Prehistoric artists believed in natural and realistic drawings.

In many cases drawing of figures is not simple. They are not limited to animal world and their different stages. They tell us mythological and religious tales. For example, the figure of famous bull rock. Here such a big animal figure is drawn whose mouth is like bore, horns are like bull. and hairs were rising on back. It has been shown as attacking on a man. Before running man, there is a big figure of crab. This figure seems related to mythological stories. Big bore appears like God. Same type of drawings were also found from other two rock shelters.

The paintings of Bhimbetka, throw light on life of Bhimbetka cave dwellers. They supplement fully the knowledge obtained from excavations. In cave III C-21, a group of *chitals* falling in fountain has been shown. It was a hunting technique of prehistoric man. In this technique, grazing animals were forced to go towards water falls. Then they were compelled to make a jump in the fountain. Thus, they were killed in group. In a number of rockshelters, hunters are shown attacking with spear, bow and arrow on animals bands.

In several figures, men and women climbed upon trees have been shown. They were shown plucking fruits, flowers, leaves, seeds and honey in baskets. The figure of trapping wild animals and birds and also fishing were shown. Our knowledge about basket net and fishing during mesolithic period has been gained from the drawings of Bhimbetka cave dwellings.

In a figure, a man has been shown drinking with the help of a jar. In a figure, a sorrowful scene expressing big group members on the death of a child has been shown. In some figures, man carrying hunted animal with bamboo or wood support were shown. Some figures shows men engaged in grazing animals. In some figures men dancing and running with fear have been shown. In hunting figures, men have been shown wearing mask and carrying spear, bow and arrow. They were wearing special hunting dresses. The figure of pregnant women were also made.

In the early Bhimbetka figures, one finds informations related to naturalism, hunting gathering lifestyle, nearness to nature and predominance of nature. There are some drawings before this period, but they have become invisible completely or they are still to be explored. These figures provide us not only informations about antiquity of prehistoric art in India, but also about environment and human life of several thousand years back.

In the painting of Stage VI, one finds Chalcolithic pottery designs. This would have been possible due to contact of Bhimbetka cave dwellers with agriculturists of plain area. Bodies of animals were decorated with pierced lines, wavy lines and zig-zag lines. Domestic animals also appear in this stage. Men have been shown controlling the grazing animals.

The paintings of Stages VII-IX belong to historic period. They were related to the establishment of towns in plain areas. These drawings were made on prehistoric drawings. These figures reveal royal procession, war figures, decorated horse and elephant with warriors, metal spear, sword, arrow, war dance and war musical instruments. Animals and men figures were far away from realist form. The body of animals was not shown in proportion. They were shown in broken stage. Neck of horses were shown long like ziraffe. In later stage, the figure of horses has become rude style. In the last stage horses were shown through adding head and feet in half circle. This shows downfall of drawing technique. This art was not related to the life of artist. By this artists had left living in caves. Their descendants were living in valleys. But they had maintained the tradition of art culture established by their ancestors. The last activities related to art culture of Bhimbetka was of 6th or 7th century. It was related to Shaulah or Conch Shell spirit.

Dating of Bhimbetka Painting

This curiosity among readers is quite natural that Bhimbetka painting is how much old and how its dating could be established. The paintings of the Stages VII to IX were related to 1st millennium B.C. Some of them also belong to late stage. Decorated horses, metal made arrow, spear, sword, war scene and royal procession belong to the period when urban life was established in plain area and the use of iron was made for common man. According to archaeologists, such type of life pattern would not have become possible before the middle of 2nd millennium B.C. The paintings of Stage VI show influence of Chalcolithic. It was related to 2nd millennium and early 1st millennium B.C.

The paintings of I to V stages were related to 2nd millennium B.C. The earliest one among them would have been of more than 10,000 years ago. Their themes were related to gathering and hunting lifestyle. They did not reveal any evidence of domestication of animals and agriculture. Their character was definitely prehistoric. The presence of numerous pieces of rolled hematites of mesolithic layers showed that painting was done in this period. According to Radio carbon dating, the earliest painting belonged to 5000 B.C. Some deposits are older, while some other deposits are contemporary.

10

Indian Megalithic Culture

The remains of megalithic culture in India have been discovered and reported from different regions. Although the development of megalithic culture had taken place during neolithic period, but this culture remained continuing in later periods. Megalithic culture was related to respect and regards of deads. It was also related to great social organisation. For the purpose of megalithic death rituals, big stone boulders or slabs were chosen and flaked in desired shapes. They were brought to the burial sites. In order to carry them up to burial site, more man power was required. Without village and intervillage organisation, this work was impossible. The village organisation appeared for the first time in neolithic period. During Chalcolithic period, the size and population of the village was increased more. Interdependence of villages also appeared during Chalcolithic period. Village level organisation and intervillage level organisation ultimately gave rise to megalithic culture and maintained this culture for a long period.

During Neolithic and Chalcolithic periods, the full development of transportation had not taken place. For the practice of megalithic culture rocks were chosen nearby the hills. They were flaked in a definite size such as square, rectangular, polo, round, semi-round or even zig-zag shapes. All villagers and neighbouring relatives and friend brought megaliths from hills to burial sites by rolling them through bamboo and wooden poles. The megaliths were erected or placed horizontally over on or before the burial in respect of dead persons buried in that grave.

Even today, the practice of megalithic culture is continued in tribes living nearby the hills. But its shapes and sizes have become smaller. This culture in Jharkhand tribes is locally known as *Hargari* (burying bone) or *pathargari* (inserting stones). The place where this ritual is performed is known as *sasan* or *masan* in local terms. This ritual is performed on 9 (nine) days or 11 (eleven) days after the death and burial ritual. On the day of placing stone or inserting stones in memory of dead person, sacrifice of cocks are also made. Every village has a *sasan* or *masan*. But in a multiclan village, there are as many *sasan* as the number of clans in the village.

Some megaliths are 20 feet long, 5 feet wide and 7 feet thick or even more than these measurements. Now-a-days, megaliths of small sizes are prepared. They are brought by tractors, bullock cart, rickshaw and even on bicycle. The megaliths were the early form of an epitaph or *Samadhi* in the memory of a dead person. Now-a-days, an epitaph is prepared with the help of cement, bricks, marble and sands with an image of the dead person having record of birthday and death day.

The remains of megalithic culture began to appear since 1872. But they were explored systematically in 1944. Since then nearly thousands of megalithic sites have been explored. Majority of burials made of megaliths were obtained from south India. Burials made of megaliths have also been reported from other parts of India, but their number is less.

Megalithic burials of same type were found in Chingleput district, Akhor district and Chittur district in Tamil Nadu of south India.

In Chingleput district alone nearly 200 megalithic memorials and burials were obtained. In Chingleput district, 5 types of megalithic burials were found. They were as follows:

- Stones placed encircling a burial in erect position.
- Stone placed above jar burials.
- Stone placed over rubbed stones as an umbrella.
- In the middle of burial a big stone and small stones encircling it.
- *Thela* cart shaped burial.

Except *thela* cart shaped burial, in all burials, megaliths were found in circular shape.

Upward standing megaliths were found on rocky and upward land. Round megaliths were found on slopes. In jar burials, more than one jar were found. In upward jar burials, several footed terracotta potteries were found. These burials were like pomegranate in shape. In these jars, potteries were also found.

Memorial symbols of Kuchai area in east were made-up of high jars. There was a big hole in the jar. The dead body was buried putting in jars.

From Kochin, a number of megalithic memorial symbols were found. Some were like elevated jars, while some others were like rubbed stone memorial. These megalithic memorials were semi-round from the upper and were inserted in the land. They were in more than one round circle.

In several places of India umbrella shaped megalithic memorial symbols were found.

In north India long stone slabs inserted in land were found as symbols of megalithic memorial stones. In prehistoric archaeological terms, they are known as menhir.

In Jharkhand majority of megalithic memorial stones were found lying flat on the ground. In prehistoric archaeological term, they are called as *Dolmen*. Some menhirs were also found in Jharkhand. At several places square shaped, round, rectangular or zig-zag stone shape were found symbolising megalithic memorial signs. Probably, the size and shape of megalithic memorial stones depended on social status of the dead. For village head, intervillage head, priest and other village functionaries, big stones were used as megalithic memorial symbols. But for common man, stone slabs of small sizes were used as memorial stones.

In some places of Kochin underground caves were found. The excavation of those caves had yielded potteries and metal tools along with skeletal remains. The size of memorial site was round. Below this round memorial site, there was a four cornerned place from where skeletal remains, potteries and metal tools were found.

Megalithic memorial stone symbols were found from not only in south India, but also from Bihar, Jharkhand, Madhya Pradesh, Uttar Pradesh, Delhi and Almora.

From Indian megalithic cultural sites, skeletal remains were found in very less number. It was because megaliths were placed as memorial symbols of deads.

11

Pre-Harappa Culture (2,700 B.C. – 2,400 B.C.)

The Indian prehistoric culture which was in existence before Harappa culture or sometimes with Harappa culture is known as pre-Harappa culture. The characteristic of this culture is such that it presents some such cultural traits which can be taken as beginning of urbanisation. The other traits of this culture are fortified walls, house, pottery and other objects. Since this culture came into existence before Harappa culture, therefore, it is regarded as precursor of Harappa culture. From the point of view of stratification, small layers of this culture were found below Harappa culture.

Geographical Extent of Pre-Harappa Culture

From the point of view of geographical regions, the area of pre-Harappa culture is very wide. It can be broadly divided into two regions:

- Indo-Iranian boundary area.
- Indian boundary area.

From the hills situated in the Indo-Iranian boundary of Baluchistan and Afghanistan, a separate village culture remains were found. Although its basic features show similarity, but some of villages were developed as urban centres.

The chief pre-Harappa cultural sites in Indian boundary were found from Sindh, Punjab, Gujarat and northern Rajasthan. In the valleys of Indus and its tributaries, a rain brought wide area is found. This area was full of agricultural efficiency. Enriched agricultural efficiency had given birth to rich urban centres in this area. This culture was influenced by Iran and western Asia. Pre-Harappan people would have migrated here through Baluchistan and Afghanistan.

Sources of Study Materials

The study of pre-Harappa culture were obtained from two chief sources:

- Vacated habitation sites.
- Excavated sites.

The chief excavated sites were as follows:

- Mundigak of Afghanistan.
- Kile Ghul Mohammad, Damb Sadat, Periyano, Ghundai, Anjira, Siah, Damb, Nal, Nundara, Shahi tump and Killimeki in Baluchistan.
- Amari, Kotdiji, Mohenjodaro and Gumla in Sindh.
- Harappa in Punjab.

- Kalibanga in north Rajasthan.
- Lothal in Gujarat.

Materials found from these sites have been proved valuable for the study of pre-Harappa culture. These sites have yielded some common features of pre-Harappa culture, but they also reveal some differences. Mohammad Rafiq Mughal has termed pre-Harappa culture as *Early Harappa* Culture.

Dating of Pre-Harappa Culture

In order to know the significance of pre-Harappa culture, it is essential to understand the background of Pre-Harappa sites. The study of pre-Harappa sites indicate that the datings of sites of pre-Harappa culture cannot be established in chronological order on the basis of absolute dating. But attempts have been made to date this culture.

On the basis of archaeological evidences found from — Kotdiji-I, Mundigak-IV, Damb Sadat-II, Kulli-II, and Amnari-II, the dating of pre-Harappa culture has been done as 2,700 B.C. – 2,400 B.C. The Radio Carbon dating of Kotdiji was made which revealed it as 2,600 B.C. – 2,200 B.C. The Radio Carbon dating of Kalibanga is 2,400 B.C.

Background of Pre-Harappa Culture

In order to know the importance of pre-Harappa culture, it is necessary to know the background of pre-Harappa sites. In Baluchistan near Quetta, four cultural stages of a site named Kile Ghul Mohammad were found. The lowest layer of these cultural stages, i.e., Stage-I had revealed evidences of pre-pottery stage. The carbon date of this stage was 3,712 B.C. – 3,688 B.C. This stage has revealed evidences of sheep, goat, and ox rearing. Their tools included blades of chert, chalcedony and jaspar, broken polished and ground stones. No metal made tools were found. Awls and needles made of bones were found. No evidence of pottery was found.

After this stage people started migrating from the west. This migration of people gave rise to individual pottery industries in mountain valley of Baluchistan. The development of pottery industry led the establishment of a cultural stage. In the beginning potteries were made with hands. The people of Rana Ghundai-I, Surangjal-I, Mundigak-I, and other Quetta and Jhob sites used handmade potteries. But among 12 potteries obtained from here, only two were handmade, while other 10 were wheel made.

It appears clearly that wheel made potteries had started appearing gradually. The pottery revealed figure of dot lines, triangles and star as motiff. Decorated bands also appeared on pottery. The surface of pottery were decorated. Some potteries revealed signs of basket. Some baskets were soft. The colour designs of some potteries were like Kile Ghul Mohammad-II and Anjira-I. Needles of bones, alabaster, jar, stone blades, shells, and flint garlands had started appearing in this period. From Kile Ghul Mohammad-II and III, 22 potteries were obtained in which 17 were wheel made and 5 were handmade. Mundigak-I and Kile Ghul Mohammad-II had revealed evidences of use of copper.

From Kile Ghul Mohammad, Anjira, Siah, Damb and Rana Ghundai habitational sites, no evidence of house structure was found. This revealed that people were leading a wandering life style. These remains showed relationship with Siyalak and Hissar and belonged to 3300 B.C. – 3000 B.C.

Evidences obtained from a number of permanent habitation sites revealed that people would have started leading a settled village life after 3000 B.C. Towards the end of Stage-I, the inhabitants of Kile Ghul Mohammad had started erecting houses with sun baked bricks. Some houses were also erected with hard prepared soil. The Mundigak site had revealed beautifully erected houses. The houses of this stage were thickly erected. From the Damb Sadat, evidences of soil hearths and furnace were obtained. The inhabitants of Mundigak used sun baked bricks for erecting houses. No evidence of construction was found from Amnari, but the evidence of Jar burial was found. For the burials of dead, Jar was prepared with the help of hands and baked in sun.

In Amnari, houses were erected by stones and sun backed bricks. In Gumla a round pit was found whose edge was covered with mud soil. Probably, it was a community furnace with the help of which foods were cooked for community members. Animal bone remains and microliths were also found from here.

From Kulli, Mehi, Nundara and other sites square shaped structure was prepared with the help of untouched stones. From Damb Sadat, a house model of ceramic was found. The model of these houses reads informations regarding houses erected in nearly 3000 B.C.

The occupation of animal husbandry and agriculture was continued. Due to this occupation development of settled life and villages continued. The inhabitants of these periods did animal husbandry of sheep, goat and ox. The existence of bull throws light on agriculture and transportation. The evidence of mill stone, muller and pestle from Damb Sadat reveals facts about grain production and agriculture.

From local industries, the inhabitants of villages used to get employment. This was also helpful in development of village. Due to invention of wheel, ceramic industries had gained popularity very much. Different sites had their own speciality of potteries. The pottery of Kile Ghul Mohammad revealed band of black over red. They were known as black-on-red ware. From the Kagibeg site black-on-Buff ware were found. Similarly, Quetta ware and painted ware were also found.

Multi-colour decoration was limited to upper land, whereas bicolour decoration had extension from below southern hills to Indus plain. But ceramics of both types had some similarity in size and nature. In Mundigak, multi-colour and bicolour traditions were existing together. But they were separated later on. The inhabitants of Nal had started mixed agriculture and animal husbandry along with multi-colour decoration. But inhabitants of below hills whose extension was up to Indus plain had given birth to Indus valley civilisation following bicolour tradition.

The pottery of Baluchistan was an example of Jhob culture. They were included under red ware culture. The Buff ware culture was limited to south only. But a mixed form was created later on.

The advent of iron was an important event in the history of mankind. Due to invention of metal more hard and sharp tools in comparison to stones, bones and wood came into existence. Metal tools were used for agriculture and clearing forest and bushes for agriculture. The development of civilisation became possible due to invention of metals. From the Mashej valley of Iran, a site named Tal-e-Ibis was found. It was one of centres of metal tools. From Iran, the technique of copper tool making had reached to Baluchistan and Afghanistan. From Mundigak in Afghanistan, a full sequence of metal work was available. Copper remains were also obtained from Damb Sadat. From Kulli, a mirror, pin and axe were found. From Nandara only bangles were found. Good number of metal tools were obtained from the Nal site. In tool community, knife, blade, bangle and axe were included.

Fortified Settlement of Town

Evidences obtained from the excavations of pre-Harappa sites, had revealed transformation of villages as fortified settlement of town after 2700 B.C. Evidences of big protective walls, square shaped fort made-up of sun baked bricks were found from the Mundigak site. Symbols of palace and temples were obtained from here. Symbol of rampart was available from Amnari. From Tharo and Kohatras Butti evidence of Pre-Harappa fortified habitation was obtained. From Kotdiji evidences of two fort and external town were available. The pre-Harappa habitation sites may be termed as beginning of towns. It is because they had revealed evidences of fortified walls, protective walls, wide road, beautifully erected houses with sun baked bricks. Foundation of houses were made of stone slabs and boulders and above foundation walls were made of sun baked bricks and mud paste or mortal. From the point of view of protection, forts were erected at regular intervals over walls. At some places, the height of the wall was 12 to 14 feet. The maximum length of wall was 108 feet. Houses were separated by street.

Pottery

The pottery of pre-Harappa culture were quite different from the pottery of Harappa culture. The pottery of pre-Harappa culture were thin, pink colour, but not made beautifully. In type and structure, pre-Harappa pottery show close resemblance with early Baluchistani and Iranian pottery. Such type of multi-colour painted pottery were available in entire Baluchistan and up to Indus. Now, pierced and stone grey ware had become universal. In place of geometric gesture, significance of natural gesture was increased. Now, bull had become chief gesture. Besides these common features of pre-Harappa culture pottery, some sites had their own regional speciality. Pre-Harappa pottery of Kalibanga were made by wheel. They were light, thin and pink. They were painted with black and white colour. Neck and shoulder of pottery were painted. The design of pottery was of natural as well as geometric both. The lower parts of pottery were not touched.

After the downfall of Afghanistan and Baluchistan cultures in plain Indus region, a group of cultures had come into existence. These cultures were divided on the basis of decoration style and structure of pottery. They were as follows:

Quetta Ware

The pottery coming under this science were cream colour, buff and thick black. Decorations were done in the form of squares, waves and steps. The pottery of last phase had flower motif.

Jhob Ware

The potteries of this typology were made by slipping technique. They showed a different red soil layer in the outside. They were decorated with black colour same as Quetta ware. The decorative art of pottery revealed animal, bird and man as motif.

Amri-Nal Ware

In this typology, potteries of two groups — Amri and Nal were included. Since these two groups belonged to two different regions, but were of same period, that is why they were placed together under Amri-Nal ware. Amri culture was related mainly to plain area, whereas Nal culture was related mainly to hill area. But these two cultures had some common traits. The structure of pottery of both culture was thin and beautiful. Both had cream colour band. The painting design was generally geometric, although animal motifs were also in plenty. Pictures of fishes, scorpion and hunch backed bull were found. The decorative art of Amri revealed two colour, whereas decorative art of

Nal revealed multi-colour. In Amri decorative art only red and black colours were found. But in Nal decorative art multi-colours — black, grey, yellow, red, green and blue — were found.

Kuli Ware

Under this typology potteries of round bottle shape and pierced jars were included. The structure of potteries showed buff-pink with white or yellow-red band. Decorative art revealed pictures of animals and environment. Geometric designs were found in the form of dots and lines.

Kotdiji Ware

The pottery of this culture was similar to Amri culture. From here 16 habitational sites were found in excavation. Majority of them were earlier than Harappa culture.

Kalibangan

The above mentioned all sites now are located in Pakistan. But Kalibanga site is located in India on the bank of the river Ghaghara. Here, excavations have been done by Archaeological Survey of India since 1959. Here, below the layer of Harappa fort, potteries of non-Harappa period were found. They showed close relation with Amri and Kotdiji. Potteries were made by wheel. They were light and thin and of pink to red colour. Decoration revealed painting of black and red sand. Decoration was shown on neck and shoulder. The decoration was done in geometric design like line, square and triangle.

Use of Metal

The inhabitants of pre-Harappa sites were aware of use of metal. From Mundigak, Nal and Mahi some metal objects were found. The Nal site alone had yielded 18 copper artifacts which included axe, chisel and saw. From Damb Sadat, a dagger and some pieces of copper were found. From Kotdiji, a copper bangle was obtained. The Kalibanga site had yielded three copper objects. Seals were also made from copper.

Stone Tool

From the pre-Harappa sites blades and points made of chalcedony and jaspar were found. With the help of these blades and needles, the inhabitants of pre-Harappa used to do hunting, fishing and harvesting. Other stone tools were mill stone, pestle, muller, polished bell and pellet-bow. Cake and core of baked soil were also made. Shar-e-Shokhta Seistan was a significant production centre of stone jars. There was also a local centre of manufacturing stone garlands. Stone garlanders used to make stone garlands.

Dress and Ornaments

From the Kotdiji site a baked soil spindle wheel was found which revealed that the inhabitants of pre-Harappa sites used to prepare cotton threads and weave clothes. Inhabitants used cotton clothes. Bangles and garlands were used as ornaments. Beads or garlands were made by chalk, shell, carnelian, baked soil, and copper. Bangles, and hand ring were made by baked soil, shell and copper. Some ornaments were painted too. The excavation of Nal and Seistan had yielded evidences of garland industry.

Agriculture and Food Production

The Kalibanga site had yielded evidence of ploughed field which showed that pre-Harappa inhabitants used to do agriculture. Wheat and oats were produced. Domestication of animals was also continued. Fishing and hunting of wild animal was also continuing.

Trade and Commerce

Availability of raw materials and things produced in plenty gave rise to trade and commerce. Artisans came to settle in new towns. Cake and ball of baked soil were used as weight and measure. Different types of seals were used for exchanging goods. Terracotta bullockart revealed evidences of transportation and means of communication.

Terracotta Figures and Religion

From pre-Harappa sites, a number of Terracotta figures and small images of mother Goddess were found. This shows that there was predominance of mother Goddess cult in pre-Harappa culture. The worship of snake God was also prevalent. Some deities were shown with horns.

Script

Signs left over potteries reveal evidences of writing of pre-Harappa inhabitants. But as script, writing was not developed earlier than Harappa culture.

Disposal of Dead

From the excavations of burials of pre-Harappa sites, it appears that the inhabitants of pre-Harappa sites used to bury their deads. They followed following methods for buring their deads:

- Inside house but putting in jar burial.
- After decay of body putting in jar inside house burial.
- After cremation putting burnt ashes of dead body in a jar in a burial.

In burials grave materials were also put inside. The grave materials included pottery, round earthen plate, copper tools and ornaments, mirror of copper and bronze.

End of Pre-Harappa Culture

The end of pre-Harappa culture at some sites were done by inhabitants of Harappa sites. At some sites, the pre-Harappa culture came to an end due to incident of great fire. At some places this culture met an end due to flood and war. Still some other places, this culture was replaced peacefully by the spread of Harappa culture.

12

Harappa Culture (Indus Valley Civilization) (2,350 B.C. – 1,750 B.C.)

Harappa culture has been named after a site near Montegomery now in Pakistan. From this site specific characteristic of this culture had come into existence for the first time. In this culture, there was cultural similarity for centuries over a large area. This culture occupies special significance in Indian prehistory and protohistory due to its special achievement. Due to affluence of raw materials and things produced from them, urban centres were built. Its builders are known as prehistoric or protohistoric town planners. Their drainage system was very superior to any other thing of that time. Script was also invented by them. But the script has not been deciphered till date properly. At the same time, their culture witnessed rise of metal. Different types of copper and bronze artifacts were discovered in the excavation of Indus valley sites. The development of trade and commerce also took place at the same time. For the first time system of weight and measure came into existence in this culture.

For a long period historians were of opinion that the history of civilization in India began after the arrival of Aryan. But excavations of Mohenjodaro and Harappa sites in Indus valley revealed a good number of remains of civilization. The study of those remains found in excavation established the existence of a superior civilization in India centuries before *Rigvedic* period in the valley of the river Indus. This civilization was contemporary to the civilization of Mesopotamia and Egypt. It was a metal age civilization. This is also known as chalcolithic civilization.

Geographical Extent

Archaeological discoveries and excavations of Indus valley sites have brought before us a very wide geographical extent of Indus valley civilization. This civilization had equal extension in Punjab and Sindh or Indus. This civilization had its extent in valleys of Ganges, Yamuna, Tapti and Narmada rivers. This civilization had its extent up to Kathiawad in east to Makran in west. The remains of this civilization have been found in Kalibanga site of Rajasthan and Lothal site of Gujarat. From the Surkotada of Kachh remains of this civilization were found. The remains of this civilization were also obtained from Alamgirpur, Bhagat Rao and Bahawalpur. Evidences of Harappa culture were also obtained from Haryana. Banwali, Mitathal and Rakhigarhi are important Harappa cultural sites of Haryana. Till now the number of Indus valley civilization sites has gone up to 350.

Great Site

The great sites of Indus valley civilization or Harappa culture are as follows:

Harappa	On left bank of the river Ravi now in Pakistan.
Mohenjodaro	On right bank of Indus river at a distance of 725 km from Harappa.
Kalibanga	On the bank of now invisible river Saraswati in the district of Ganganagar in Rajasthan.
Chanhudaro	Nearly 125 km south of Mohenjodaro now in Pakistan.
Kotdiji	On the left bank of Indus river opposite to Mohenjodaro, now in Pakistan.
Lothal	Near Sabarmati delta in Gujarat.

Dating of Harappa Culture

The early scholars had attempted to date Harappa culture as 3250 B.C. – 2750 B.C. Some other scholars had attempted to date this culture as 2500 B.C. – 1500 B.C. The world famous scholar V. Gordon Childe had dated the beginning of this culture as 3000 B.C. But according to C^{-14} method of dating, the dating of Indus valley civilization was done as 2350 B.C. – 1750 B.C.

Builders of Indus Valley Civilization

From the excavations of different sites, the form which has appeared before us was really a form of evolved culture. About its 1st phase and systematic development we do not have definite knowledge. Therefore, it is still a matter of debate who were the builders of this civilization.

Some scholars are of opinion that the motivator of Harappa culture was Mesopotamia culture. According to them, Harappa culture was a colonial branch of Mesopotamia culture. This culture was brought in the regions of Indus by the Sumerians. In order to show correlation between Indus and Mesopotamian civilizations those scholars have presented the examples of use of wooden beams in the construction of south-east fort. The royal granary, fort, and building of sun-baked bricks were also taken as examples of Mesopotamian influence. Since these types of construction processes were very much popular in Mesopotamia, therefore, the inhabitants of Mesopotania may be the builder of Indus valley civilization.

The world famous scholar V. Gordon Childe was of opinion that inhabitants of Mesopotamia came to Indus through sea route. They cultivated the developed traits of their civilization in new situation and gave rise to a new culture.

Some other scholars are not ready to accept the view that inhabitants of Mesopotamia civilization were creator of Indus valley civilization. According to them, there were a number of differences in these two civilizations. For example, the remains of temples were available from Mesopotamia, but no relic of temple was obtained form Indus. No grand burials like Mesopotamia were available from Indus. The physical traits of both civilizations also presented dissimilarity. For examples war weapons, stone images, potteries, terracotta images and seals. It is true that the objects of Mesopotamia were found in Indus and the objects of Indus were found in Mesopotamia, but they show only reciprocal exchange, trade and commerce. There were also differences in town planning and weights and measures of both civilizations.

Still some other scholars consider the Baluchistani and Irani cultures as originator of Harappa culture. According to them, Indianization of Baluchistanian and Iranian cultures had taken place in the region of Indus valley. As a result Indus valley civilization had come into existence. The inhabitants of hilly areas of Baluchistan and Iran had come to settle in plain fertile areas of Indus valley. They would have been attracted towards fertile land and sufficient water resources in Punjab and Indus. Always availability of water in rivers for transportation and irrigation, sufficient fishes for food in rivers and fertile land of Indus become helpful in development of civilization in this valley.

Some scholars are of opinion that the development of Indus valley civilization was made by Indian themselves not by foreigners. They had developed beautiful town planning. They had developed towns in planned way. They developed trade relationship with Mesopotamia for economic prosperity. They did standardization of different regions. They maintained the economic structure of agricultural community and tradition of ceramic industries. Besides these traditional traits of rural community, they adopted some new traits too. The excavation works done in Baluchistan, Indus and Punjab have revealed that the civilized life began in Indus valley on regional basis.

Some scholars have recognized Indus valley civilization as non-Aryan civilization. They have attempted to provide a racist opinion of Indus valley civilization. They have termed it as Dravidian civilization.

On the basis of above discussions on builders of Indus valley civilization, it can be concluded with certainty that Indus valley civilization had come into existence before Vedic civilization. Its creators were not Vedic Aryans.

There is no doubt that south India was residence of Dravidians. They alone were not builder of this great civilization.

Earthen pots and stone pots of Dravidians and inhabitants of Indus valley showed resemblance to a great extent. Inhabitants of both regions had similar ornaments. But study of skeletons and image heads obtained in excavations of different sites reveals that inhabitants of Indus valley civilization were of mixed castes. This opinion regarding the creators of Indus valley civilization seems more suitable.

Form of Indus Valley Civilization

The remains available from excavation of different sites of Indus valley civilization throw light on the form which Indus valley civilization possessed at the time of its existence. Relics obtained in excavation reveals that this civilization was a mixture of stone and metal age. Because excavation of its sites have yielded remains of metal as well as stones, no evidence of war, army organization, and imperialism was found in the excavation. Names of Kings, arms and ammunition were completely absent in remains of excavation. Therefore, it can be guessed that Indus valley civilization was a peaceful civilization. This civilization was urban and trade-oriented. The inhabitants of this culture used to lead urban life. They used to see each object from the point of view of utility. Big towns were established. Relationships with foreign civilizations were established. Great building and great bath were erected. They were related to collective life of the inhabitants. On this ground some scholars believed that Indus valley civilization was a democratic civilization. The existence of king had not been established in this civilization. The peaceful and unchanging behaviour of inhabitants of Indus valley civilization reveals that politics was influenced by religion.

Characteristics of Indus Valley Civilization

The chief characteristics of Indus valley civilization are as follows:

Chalcolithic Civilization

Indus valley civilization is known as Chalcolithic civilization. In excavation of sites, copper tools and ornaments were found along with stone tools and ornaments. That is why this civilization is termed as Chalcolithic civilization.

Bronze Age Civilization

The inhabitants of Indus valley knew to make bronze by adding tin in copper. Bronze made tools were found in good number in excavation. Due to predominance of Bronze, Indus valley civilization is also known as Bronze Age Civilization.

Urban Civilization

The excavation of sites have revealed evidence of great building, great bath, beautiful and wide state highway, well planned roads, streets and drainage system and organized rule. These evidences produce sufficient clue that Indus valley civilization was an urban civilization.

Civil Civilization

The excavation of sites of Harappa culture have revealed that it was a civil civilization. Here civil amenities were provided by the administration. Inhabitants enjoyed good and wide roads, wide streets and well drainage system through an organized rule. This is why we can say that it was a civil civilization.

Commercial Civilization

Evidences obtained in excavation of sites of Harappa culture indicate that the economic life of inhabitants was dependent on trade and commerce. Each trader used to do only one type of trade or business. People engaged in same type of trade used to live in the same colony. The commercial relation of this civilization was up to foreign countries. Thus, it was a trade-oriented civilization.

Industrial Civilization

The economic life of inhabitants of Indus valley civilization was based on industries. Here, a number of industries were established. The economic life was based on industrialization and localization. The division of labour and organization of labour were also present here. An individual used to do only one business. The people engaged in same trade were living in the same colony.

Democratic Civilization

This civilization was a democratic civilization. No evidence of king, Royal palace and Royal treasury was found. There were two centres of ruling — Mohenjodaro and Harappa. Harrapa was the centre of rule of southern part and Mohenjodaro was centre of rule of northern part. Great assembly and great bath were indicative of collective life of inhabitants of Indus valley civilization.

Peaceful Civilization

The Indus valley civilization was a peaceful civilization. One does not find the existence of war weapons. The existence of spear, trident, bow and arrow were not related to their intention of war but they were associated with protective intention. They were used for self-defence, not for the purpose of war.

Town Planning

The Indus valley civilization was termed as Harappa culture by the archaeologists. The town planning of this civilization was well planned and systematized. Such type of town planning was in existence in the then Iran, Egypt or West Asia. The town structures available from Harappa, Mohenjodaro, Kalibanga, Kotdiji, Lothal, Rangpur, Sutkajenger and Surkotada sites reveals clearly that they were erected following maps. Maps of town planning were well designed. The remains of great-assembly and great-bath were found. Beautiful, clean and wide state highway, wide street, well administration of sanitation, long and wide drains, great public bath, wells for drinking water, and houses with big windows show clearly that township was developed in well planned way. The town planning of each sites showed similarity. That is why towns, buildings, roads, streets, structures, size of bricks and drainages all exhibit similarity. This similarity was brought perhaps by centralization of production and efficient administration. Among all towns Mohenjodaro and Harappa had attained the status of metropolitan.

Characteristics of Town Planning

The chief characteristics of town planning in Indus valley civilization were as follows:

- Fortified cities
- Streets and lanes
- Drainage system
- Buildings
- Labour colony
- Public building
- Granary
- Dockyard
- Materials used in building construction
- Great bath.

Now, let us discuss about each feature of Indus valley civilization one by one.

Fortified Cities

The excavation of Indus valley civilization sites have presented before us evidences of fortified cities. The towns were planned in rectangular manner. This was the feature of the then township. From the point of view of safety, strong boundary walls were erected covering the outer area of the town. In town planning emphasis was placed on construction of town fort and lower towns. Forts were erected on a wide base of a soil. The walls of forts were high. There was a gate to enter in the town. From the point of view of protection, pits were dug outside around the fort. There were towers at regular intervals in the walls of town. The fort of Harappa was rectangular in shape. The wall of fort was 40 feet wide and 36 feet high. Inside town walls, buildings were erected on an earthern platform or a platform of sun baked bricks. The buildings were protected properly by fortified walls. The fortified walls had *minars* (towar) at regular intervals. There were entrance gates in north and west direction.

Street and Lanes

The excavation of Indus valley civilization sites reveals that there were planned drainage system in the towns. A town had a number of wide roads. The roads crossed from north to south and east to west. They cut each other at right angles. They divided towns into several groups of rectangular buildings. The roads were related to streets. In each street, there was a public well. The streets were 3 to 7 feet wide and the roads were 9 feet to 34 feet wide. There was no encroachment of public road and street by buildings. The roads were *kuchcha* not metalled. Attempts were made to provide *pucca* form of roads at some places by fire baked potteries. On roads and streets wooden poles were erected to prevent the loss of building by bullockcart. There was arrangement of light through wooden poles.

The town Lothal was divided into six groups of buildings. Each building group was erected on a high platform whose heights differed. In excavation, evidences of 4 roads and 2 streets were found. Two roads run in north to south and two in east to west. From two sides, there were street. Buildings were erected on one side of the road. In onc row there were 12 houses. There were small houses on both sides of other roads. Probably, they were shops. The shops were of 2-3 rooms.

Drainage System

In the excavation of Harappa culture sites, evidences of extended drainage system were found. No such drainage system like Indus valley was present in other countries except Nosas, the Capital of Creat. These drainages are witness that inhabitants of Indus valley were well aware of the importance of sanitation in their healthy life. Their town planning was scientific and they knew the science of sanitation. The drainages were 18 inches deep. In the roads and street of Harappa and Mohenjodaro, evidences of stone made and brick made drainages were found. The drainage of each house were connected to the main drainage of the street and finally to the road. Ditches were made at regular intervals to prevent garbages in the drainages. Garbages were made at several places to put waste materials. The drainages of kitchen, bathroom and latrine of a house met in big drainage. The drainages of different houses met with a big public drainage. Drainages were covered with stones and bricks. For the flow of dirty water from the multi-storey building fire baked earthern pipes were used. Such type of *pucca* earthern pipes were found from the excavation of Mohenjodaro and Chanhudaro sites. Evidences of wooden drainage pipe were obtained from Kalibanga site. This shows that the inhabitants of Indus valley civilization were attached with great significance to cleanliness and sanitation. This system also hints towards a regular administrative rule system in this civilization. In each house, there was a well. Besides personal wells, there were public wells too. The width of wells were 2 to 7 feet.

Buildings

Mohenjodaro, Lothal and Ropar sites have yielded evidences of erection of buildings on raised platform or base. The buildings wcrc of two types:

- Residential Buildings.
- Public Buildings.

Residential Buildings

The evidences of residential buildings obtained in excavations revealed diversity. The residential buildings were small as well as big both. In the construction of building special emphasis was placed on simplicity and utility. The inhabitants did not attach significance to decorations in construction of the buildings. Buildings were erected in planned way. On both sides of road big buildings were erected in rows. When inhabitants of Egypt were not aware of fire baked brick technology, inhabitants of Indus valley were using this technology at that time. The inhabitants of

Indus valley used *pucca* bricks for a number of construction works. The bricks were of small and big sizes. The houses were of several stories. Steps were made from outside to reach different upper storeis of the building. Each house had a kitchen, bathroom, latrine, courtyard, well and drainages. For the protection of town, boundary walls were erected from all sides. In Harappa culture zigzag arch were made. From the lower lawns of Mohenjodaro, evidences of latrine were found. In a house there were two rooms and a courtyard. At some places evidences of step drainage were found. The rich had big houses and the poor had small houses. Sun baked bricks were also used in the erection of small houses. The house possessed two rooms and a courtyard. Such houses were of 50 × 30 feet.

The rich had double storey buildings. The foundations of these buildings were very deep. The width of wall was also more. The ceiling was made with wood and soil. The walls were plastered with wet soil and lime. For watchman and servants, there were separate rooms in the building.

Labour Colony

Evidences of some such houses were obtained which indicate them as colony of labourers. In Mohenjodaro 16 such houses and in Harappa 14 such houses were found. Each house was 20 × 12 feet. In these colony such labourers used to live who had to work as slaves. From the Lothal site, remains of house of artisans were found. Probably, they were bronzesmiths and gardeners.

Public Buildings

From Mohenjodaro relics of public buildings were obtained in excavation on the *stupa* mound. A very thick walled great building structure was found near the *stupa*. It was termed as great collegiate building. Its length and breath were 230 feet and 78 feet respectively. Probably, some high officials used to live in this public building. Here, the chief religious functionary and his associates also used to stay. Public meetings were held here. It was probably a centre of social, religious and political life of inhabitants. From Mohenjodaro, remains of public restaurants were also found by the side of road at several places. In great public buildings, there were tables in several rows.

Granary

The remains of granary were obtained from the Harappa sites. The length and breath of granary were 50 feet and 20 feet respectively. This granary was divided into two rows. Each row had six *kuchcha* earthern stores prepared for this special purpose. In order to store grains there were big stores. The traders were very rich here. They had trade relation to distant foreign countries. The traders used to fulfil the needs of inhabitants through the market. The remains of market and shops were found by the side of roads.

Dockyard

The remains of Dockyard from the Lothal site is an excellent example of great public building. It was built by *pucca* bricks. Its shape was like a trapezoid. Its length was 710 feet and breath was 124 feet. Its present height was 14 feet but its height would have been more. There were entrance and exit gates. It was used for loading and unloading the ship. It was related to the ancient water level of Sabarmati. Some scholars are not ready to accept it as dockyard. According to them, it was probably a pond for the purpose of drinking water and irrigating fields. It was not a dockyard, but a village.

Materials Used in Erection of Buildings

Generally, *pucca* bricks were used in the construction of walls of town, floor, bathroom, lavatory, drainage and wells. *Kuchcha* bricks were used for preparing the foundation or base of the buildings. They were also used for filling the terraces. The remains of brick furnace was obtained from Mohenjodaro. Mortar was prepared to erect houses for joining the bricks. Lime and *pucca* brick powder paste were used in the construction of drainages. Soil, reed and wood were used in the erection of the house. On hills walls of stone boulders were made. In outer walls tower like structures were made.

Great Bath

Among all remains of buildings, the remains of great bath found from the fort of Mohenjodaro occupies significant place. It was a square shape pound. It was 30 feet long, 23 feet wide and 8 feet deep. Its floor was made up of *pucca* bricks. There were steps to go below in pond. There were drainages for inlet and outlet of the water of pond. Perhaps this pond was used for performing rituals. Water was filled in this great bath from the neighbouring wells. There was also arrangement of hot water. It was constructed in beautiful manner.

Social Life of Indus Valley Civilization

The social life of inhabitants of Indus valley civilization can be discussed under the following sub-headings:

- Class
- Food
- Pottery
- Dress
- Ornament
- Decorative items
- Means of entertainment
- Medicine
- Arms and weapons
- Animal
- Population
- Status of women
- Death rituals
- Script and language

Class

The inhabitants of Indus valley were divided into classes. There were four main classes. They were learned man, warrior, trader and labourers. The smallest unit of society was family. The form of society was matriarchal. The people of different occupations lived together. For example priest, state workers, astrologer, magician, *vaidya*, trader, potters, carpenters, goldsmith, bronze smith, copper smith, and garlanders.

Food

The food remains available from the excavations of Indus valley sites reveal clearly that inhabitants were vegetarian and non-vegetarian both. They ate wheat, rice, oat, vegetables, fruits, and milk as vegetarian food. They used to eat meat of ship, pig, cow and other animals. They ate eggs, too. They used to crush wheat, rice and oat with saddle and quern, mill stone, pestle and muller. They had stone implements for cutting meat into pieces.

Pottery

Potters used to make potteries with the help of wheel. Copper smith and bronze smiths used to make copper and bronze tools. Bowls, plates, tumbler and jar were made from earth, copper and bronze tools were made by the artisans. Wooden cots were used for sleeping purpose. In chief room they had wooden tables and chairs. Lamps of earthen were used for getting light. Baskets were made from bamboo and canes. Mats were prepared from grasses and bamboo.

Dress

We have obtained knowledge about dresses of inhabitants of Indus valley civilization from the symbols carved on seals and images found in excavation of Indus valley sites. There was similarity in dresses of males and females to some extent. Different types of dresses were used in different seasons. Some images were naked. It shows that probably tradition of living naked was prevalent. Woollen and cotton clothes were prepared. A good number of reels for whirling yarn were found in excavation. The rich had costly reels and poor had cheap reels. The reels were made-up of earthern or bones. A number of needles were found from Mohenjodaro. Inhabitants of Indus valley used to stitch clothes for the purpose of wearing. A piece of cotton cloth adhered to a silver jar was found. The cloth shows similarity with modern hand woven clothes. A long shawl was found over the body of a male image. The left shoulder and right arm were covered with shawl. Some female images have been shown with turban on heads. Male figures were found in naked condition. Both males and females used to wear caps. Some images were covered with skirts. Gods and heroes were shown wearing a special dress. Some images were shown with scarf. Probably, they were some officials or religious authority. The women used cloth in such a manner that they looked as downwards cloth. Women used to wear waist band. They used a special kind of fan dress on their heads. The fan dress was raised from back side.

Ornament

The inhabitants of Indus valley civilization were fond of ornaments. Ornaments were made-up of gold, silver, elephant tooth, valuable stone, gems, copper, snail and earthen. Ornaments were made from diamond, emerald, coral and ruby. In ornaments, chain, finger ring, bangle, bracelet and hand ring were worn by both males and females. There was diversity in chains. In chain, there were 17, 20, 48 and 53 beads. From Harappa, a chain of six string of pearls was found. Ear ring, earflower, waist band were worn only by woman. The rich used to wear ornaments of gold, silver, elephant teeth and valuable stones. The poor used to wear ornaments of copper, bronze, bone, shell, snail and earthen. Comb of elephant tooth, lip stick, and bronze mirror were found in excavation. Bangles of shell, earthern and chalk were also found. Woman used to wear several bangles.

In image of copper made dancing girl, left hand was shown having a number of bangles. Gold made bangles were found from Harappa and gold silver made bangles were found from Mohenjodaro. Women used to wear foot ornaments and a chain around waist.

Decoration

The inhabitants of Indus valley civilization were very fond of decoration. They used to decorate their hairs with combs and mirrors. The men used to have long hairs, beard and mustache. Sometimes they used to shave their hairs, beard and mustache. Usually, males used to do combing from the middle of the head. Razors and blades of copper and bronze were found. The females used to cleave hair from the middle. They used to make crest of hairs after tonsure. They used black ointment, powder, vermilion, oil, lip stick, and colour for decoration.

Means of Entertainment

Music, dance, play, animal fight, football, stone ball, chess, and a die were chief means of entertainment for inhabitants of Indus valley. Stone and earthen dies were found in abundance. Die of elephant teeth was also found. Some images present sign of music and dance. On seals, signs of drum, lyre, trumpet and dancer were found.

Hunting birds and animals was also a game for the inhabitants of Indus valley. On two amulets, hunting of deer and wild goat was presented. Trapping fishes was also a game of entertainment. Cock fight and bull fight were also their means of entertainment. Birds were domesticated too.

For children earthen birds, animals, bullockcart, whistle and rattles were made.

Medicine

In excavation a black matter was found which used to turn into almond colour after dissolving in water. Scholars were of opinion that it was probably mineral pitch (*shilajit*). It was used probably as medicine. The horns of rhinoceros and deer were used as medicine. Coral and margosa (*nim*) were also used as medicine. The foam of sea was also used as medicine.

Arms and Weapons

From the excavations of Mohenjodaro and Harappa sites, evidences of arms and weapons were found. They were made-up of brass and copper. They were used for war as well as hunting. Mace, spear, arrow, axe and bow were found. Pellet bows were also used during war. Swords were in use but they were not used in war. Their working edge was blunted. Spear, lance, chisel, axe, and saw were used for the work of blacksmithy and carpentry.

Animal

The study of bone remains, potteries and terracotta images indicate the existence of wild and domestic animals. The domesticated animals were sheep, goat, cat, dog, bull, cow, pig, buffalo, elephant and camel. The wild animals were tiger, lion, monkey, leopard, bear, deer and rhinoceros. Parrot, peacock, squirrel and goose were also found. The remains of wild ass were found but no evidence of regular use of horse was found.

Population

From archaeological sources, it is quite clear that the population of Indus valley was urban. Mohenjodaro and Harappa were metropolitan centres, whereas Lothal, Kalibangan, Chanhudaro and Rangpur were urban centres. The presence of rivers was boon for the production of grains in the Indus valley. More and more grains were produced due to irrigation of lands by the rivers. The rivers were also used as water routes for trade and business. Due to trade those metropolises and towns were established in Indus valley. Siwell and Guha had made a study of skeletal remains of Indus valley. According to them, they were related to four ethnic groups:

- Proto-australoid
- Mediterranean
- Mongoloid
- Alpine

According to them, the population of Indus valley presented an example of mixed metropolitan character. On the basis of study of Cephallic index, Sarkar had attempted to show that the inhabitants of Mohenjodaro were similar to the inhabitants of present day Sindh. The inhabitants of Harappa were like the present day inhabitants of Punjab. The inhabitants of Lothal were same as that of present day Gujarat.

Status of Women

The smallest unit of society in Indus valley was family. Each family had a separate house. The family was matriarchal. The mother was authority of family. Goddess worship was prevalent in Indus valley. These facts reveal that the status of women in Indus valley society was good and high. Women as mother were respected and revered. There was no *purdah pratha* in the society. Males and females used to take part equally in social and religious ceremonies.

Death Rituals

The inhabitants of Indus valley had full faith in death rituals. The excavation of Indus valley sites reveals that the inhabitants of Indus valley used to perform death rituals in three ways:

- Full burial
- Half burial
- Cremation.

In full burial rituals, the entire body of a dead was placed inside a burial. No change was made in the horizontal position of dead body.

In half burial ritual, the dead body was left for food of birds and animals. The skeleton remains were buried in a burial.

In cremation death ritual, the fire rituals were performed and the dead body was cremated. After cremation, bone and ash remains were buried in earth burial.

In burials grave materials were also placed. The grave materials included ornaments, arms, weapons, tools, food materials and potteries.

Script and Language

Social organization in the form of towns and metropolises gave rise to script and language. From Mohenjodaro and Harappa a good number of seals were found. These seals contained some kind of writing. The seals were of two types: square shaped and rectangular shaped. Essays were written only on rectangular seals. The number of symbols in Harappa script was nearly 400. Some scholars place the Indus valley script under the category of pictorial script. It is because the images of fishes, birds, animals and man were made in good number of seals. Some scholars have attempted to correlate Indus valley script with unlettered script.

Some other scholars have attempted to correlate the Indus valley script with Dravidian script. While some still other scholars have attempted to correlate Indus valley script with Santhali script. Some another scholars have tried to correlate Indus valley script with Brahmi script. But their claims have not been accepted as truth. The traders of Indus valley had relation with the traders of Sumer and Elam. Indus valley seals were discovered from those regions. Bilingual seals discovered from Irac draw our attention towards some truth. There is a need to explore properly the relation between Brahmi script and Harappa script. In conclusion, we can say that till date, we have not been able to decipher the Harappa script properly. There is a need to explore more and more facts to decipher the Indus valley script.

Economic Life

The economic life of inhabitants of Indus valley can be discussed under the following sub-headings:

- Agriculture
- Animal husbandry
- Cottage industries
- Trade.

Agriculture

The economic condition of inhabitants of Indus valley civilization was satisfactory. Its excavation had yielded evidences of prosperous villages, towns and metropolises. Mohenjodaro and Harappa were metropolises. They possessed thick population. In order to feed the thick population plenty of food materials were available. The valley of the river Indus was fertile. Prosperity and proper system of the towns and metropolises revealed clearly that inhabitants were economically rich. Town dwellers and metropolis dwellers were dependent on villages. The peasants of the villages used to cultivate wheat, oat, mustard, pea and sesamum. No evidence of paddy cultivation was obtained. From the potteries and ceramics obtained from Lothal and Rangpur in excavation particles of grains and bran chaff were found stiched. In Saurashtra millet were cultivated. The inhabitants of Lothal were aware of cultivation of pomegranate besides grains. Coconut, banana, watermelon and palmyrapan were grown. Cotton was also cultivated. There was mill stone, saddle and quern, muller and pestle to crush the grains. No evidence of plough was obtained. Their agriculture was dependent on hoe. For the purpose of harvesting stone sickles were used. There was no system of canal here like that of Mesopotamia. The fields were irrigated by flood water of rivers.

Animal Husbandry

The inhabitants of Indus valley had occupation of animal husbandry besides agriculture. They used to domesticate animals like ox, cow, buffalo, goat, sheep, and pigs. Ass and camel were reared for carrying load. Cat and dog were also domesticated. The inhabitants were aware of elephant. Perhaps they were not aware of horse. Goose, duck, hare, parrot, monkey, deer, cocks and hens were domesticated. Duck and peacock were engraved on earthen, brass, copper or bronze utensils. The images of wild animals like lion, tiger, bear, rhinoceros were engraved on toys and seals.

Cottage Industry

Besides the occupation of agriculture and animal husbandry, evidences of craftmanship and artisan activities were obtained. The inhabitants used to prepare stone tools and used them for various purposes. They used to prepare tools from copper, bronze and tin. Besides copper smith, bronze smith and brass smith, tin smiths were also there. Copper made axes, chisels, knives, arrow head and saw were found. Bronze made tools and utensils were also found. Gold smiths used to prepare ornaments of gold and precious stones. Copper made harpoons were also found. Turtles were also trapped.

The inhabitants of Indus valley were also versed in making tools and weapons from shells bones, horns and teeth. Beads and garlands were made from gold, silver, stone, shells, and smooth clay. The inhabitants were also aware of making canon and boat.

The cloth industry was in developed stage. Cotton was cultivated. Spinning wheel (*Charkha*) and bobbin of cotton (*Takali*) were obtained. These instruments were used for making thread and cloth. Potter, carpenter, and mason were also existing. Pottery industry, seal industry, toy industry, and industry related to house construction were also in existence.

Trade

The Harappa and the Mohenjodaro were a great centre of trade. The inhabitants used to do trade through river route, sea route and surface route. They had trade relation with Creat, Sumer, Elam, and Egypt. The dockyard of Lothal was a famous place in this regard. Boat, camel and bullockcart were the chief means of transportation. Evidences of bullock carts were obtained from Lothal, Harappa and Chanhudaro. Evidences of boats were obtained from Lothal and Harappa. Five models of boat were available. Shops were held on both sides of the road. Export and import of goods used to take place. Barter exchange system was prevalent in trade. In exchange of earthen, and other objects prepared by themselves and agricultural produce, they used to get metals from foreign countries.

Copper was brought from Rajputana and Baluchistan. Tin, gold and silver from Afghanistan and Iran, wood from Kashmir, stones from Mysore, coral, gems and metals from Nilgiri, glass from Afghanistan and Rajasthan, marble slab and jaspar from Rajasthan, *Shilajit* and *Deodar* from Himalaya and shells from Iran. Cotton cloths and potteries were sent outside. Traders had their own seals. The seals were of different sizes. But majority of seals were square shaped.

Weights and measures were used for weighing and measuring things. Credit system was also prevalent. Probably, the state had control over export and import.

Political Organization

Evidences available till date do not provide us a definite information about the political organization of Indus valley inhabitants. Archaeologist Sir Martimer Wheeler, like Sumer Indus region was also governed by the priest. This opinion was not accepted to all. Like Sumer, there were no evidence of temples or temple like building structure. Therefore, it cannot be accepted that Indus valley was ruled by the *purohit* or there was a *purohit raj*. Evidences of fire worship was obtained from the Lothal site, but no evidence of temple was available.

Some scholars were of opinion that the inhabitants of Indus valley were more interested in trade than war. Therefore, the Indus valley was probably ruled by trader class.

Some another scholars were of opinion that there was Federal government in Indus valley. Urban system was probably run properly by parliamentarians.

Still some other scholars were of opinion that the Indus valley was ruled by the Mayor. From the point of view of administration, town was divided into different parts. Each part had a separate ward member. Whatever the facts would have been, but nothing could be said with certainty about the ruling of the Indus valley. It might be monarchy, democracy or priestocracy. But one thing is clear that decentralization of power authority had taken place. On behalf of central authority, a number of administrative authorities used to rule the town. The inhabitants used to cooperate fully the authorities. The governance was so beautiful that there were no impact on the design of town.

Evidences of town planning indicate that there was municipality for urban administration. Cleanliness of town, drainage system, rows of houses, airy windows in house, safety system, construction of roads and public buildings, labour value, weight and measure system, all these facts are witness that there was governance of municipality in Indus valley towns. The theory of municipality would have been established. Otherwise, it would have been difficult to design such a beautiful town planning.

Some scholars are of opinion that the extent of Indus valley was over 400 miles. Lack of sufficient means of transportation would have forced the inhabitants for the governance of municipality. It was not possible to govern the entire area from one place. That is why two capitals were made — Mohenjodaro and Harappa. Harappa was capital of northern empire and Mohenjodaro was capital of southern empire. Evidences of one-one fort were obtained from Mohenjodaro and Harappa. Forts were erected on high mound. In forts, higher authorities of capital used to live.

Religious Life

No evidence of temples was found in the excavation of Indus valley sites. Therefore, our knowledge abut Indus valley religion is based on seals, amulets and terracotta figures. The figures engraved on seals, amulets and terracotta tell us about the religious life of Indus valley inhabitants.

The inhabitants of Indus valley were believer of polytheism. They were worshipper of nature and power. The religious life of inhabitants of Indus valley can be discussed under the following sub-headings:

- Mother Goddess worship
- Shiva worship
- Phallic (*Linga*) worship
- Tree worship
- Animal worship
- Snake (*Naga*) worship
- River worship
- Sun (*Surya*) worship
- Fire (*Agni*) worship
- Blind faith
- Priest.

Mother Goddess Worship

The inhabitants of Indus valley used to worship mother Goddess. From the excavations of Mohenjodaro, Harappa and Chanhudaro sites, a number of earthen women images were found.

These evidences reveal that the inhabitants of Indus valley were worshipper of mother Goddess. In the contemporary civilization of Elam, Creat, Mesopotamia, Asia Minor, Syria, Philistine and Egypt, the worship of mother Goddess was prevalent. Perhaps, the worship of mother Goddess would have emerged from the worship of mother earth. All women figures were related to mother nature. On a coin Raving inscription obtained from Harappa. A woman was standing on head. From her organ a plant was growing. The scholars were of opinion that it was a symbol of earth Goddess. It was related to origin and development of flora. In some figures, pregnancies were shown. This figure was accepted as fertility Goddess. In an another, a woman was shown in sitting position surrounded by priests and leaves of *Pipal* tree on head. It appears that these symbols gave the rise to mother worship.

Goddess worship, and energy worship became famous later on. The importance of mother Goddess was also established from the Vedic period. Even today, mother Goddess is worshipped by different names in different parts of rural and urban India. Even today each Hindu family has a *Kula devi* (stock Goddess). The Hindu worship Kali, Durga, Bhagwati, Gauri, Parvati, Chandi, Matadi, and Sherawali.

Shiva Worship

In the excavations of Indus valley sites, an image of male God was found on a seal along with images of female Goddess. This image was shown in *Yoga* pose. There were an elephant, a tiger, a rhinoceros and a hebuffalo around the male God. Below the seat of male God, there were two deers. This image has been considered as an early form of Lord Shiva. Some scholars regard it as an image of *Pashupati Mahadeo*. On some images, dancing Shiva has been shown. On an another coin, two cobra on both sides of Shiva and two cobra in front side of Shiva were shown. This image has been accepted as *Nagdhari* (holding cobra) Shiva. This also indicates that inhabitants of Indus valley used to worship Lord Shiva. Perhaps *Shaivite* religion was the most ancient form of religion in the world.

Phallic (Linga) Worship

In the excavation of Indus valley sites, a number of Phallic like structure were found. These phallics were made of stone, earth and shells. Some phallics were small and some were long in size. Probably different types of phallics were related to different sects. Later on, phallic worship had become the common worship of Hindus. Even today, stones are worshipped in the form of *Shaligram*, *Lingam* and *Yoni*. As *Shaligram*, the stone symbolizes Lord Vishnu, as *Lingam* stone symbolizes Lord Shiva and as *Yoni* (organ of generation) the stone symbolizes Goddess fertility. Thus, fertility cult was prevalent in Indus valley civilization.

Tree Worship

Among the tradition of Indus valley civilization, tree worship was prevalent. The tree of *Pipal* was regarded as most pious. The tree and leaves of *pipal* were found engraved on a number of seals. Even today *pipal* tree is regarded as most-religious tree among Hindus. It is believed that Lord Brahma resides in *pipal* tree. All other deities reside on its leaves. On some seals leaves of *Nim* and *Babul* were carved. On some other seals scene of worship of tree God or tree Goddess was engraved.

Animal Worship

On the seals of Indus valley civilization, images of a number of animals were found carved on them. Those images reveal the religious importance of animals. It also indicates that animal worship was prevalent in the tradition of Indus valley civilization. Ox, bull, hebuffalo, tiger, elephant and rhinoceros occupied prominent religious place. Some animals were regarded as vehicle (*vahan*) of God and Goddesses. Even today, birds and animals are regarded as vehicle of deities. For example, ox or bull of Lord Shiva, elephant of Lord Indra, tiger of Goddess Durga, sheep of Brahma, crocodile of Goddess Ganges, hebuffalo of Lord Yama, Dog of Lord Bhairava, Swan of Goddess Saraswati, eagle of Lord Vishnu, awl of Goddess Lakshmi, Peacock of Lord Kartikeya and mouse of Lord Ganesha.

Snake/Cobra (Naga) Worship

The inhabitants of Indus valley used to worship cobra. On earthern pots, images of cobra were carved. On a seal, cobra was shown both sides of a God. A figure of an individual worshpiping a snake was also shown on a seal. On a seal, cobra was shown on a platform. An image of *Nagdhari* (holding snake) Shiva was also found.

River Worship

The inhabitants of Indus valley used to worship the rivers. The rivers were helpful in transportation and irrigation. They were also used for drinking, washing and cleaning purposes. The water of rivers were regarded as life. Even today, the worship of rivers is performed by us.

Sun (Surya) Worship

Sun worship was also prevalent among inhabitants of Indus valley. On some seals images of *Swastika* and a wheel were found carved. These evidences indicate that sun worship was prevalent among the inhabitants of Indus valley.

Fire (Agni) Worship

The inhabitants of Indus valley were worshipper of fire. Evidences of fire tank and fire house were also found.

Blind Faith

Some blind faiths were also prevalent among the inhabitants of Indus valley civilization. They believed in magic, fetishism, *jharphuk*, *totaka* and *Bhuta-Preta* or evil spirits. They used to perform protective magic for their protection.

Priest

The prevalence of amulets, images of Gods, Goddesses, sacred animals and birds and the existence of writing reveal clearly that like Sumerian civilization, there was existence of powerful literate priestly class in Indus valley civilization. The religion and society of Indus valley civilization was influenced by the priestly class. In Harappa, heaps of bones of ox and sheep were found which indicate that perhaps sacrifice was also prevalent in Indus valley civilization.

Art of Indus Valley Civilization

The inhabitants of Indus valley occupied special position for their artistic behaviour. Their artistic behaviour can be discussed under the following sub-headings:

- The art of erecting building
- The art of making image
- The art of making seal
- The art of music and dance
- The art of writing
- The art of drawing and painting
- The art of making pots
- The art of making copper tools
- The art of spinning and dyeing
- The art of extracting metal and making metal tools.

The Art of Erecting Building

The inhabitants of Indus valley were excellent in the art of erecting building. Although there was lack of beautification and decoration, but the art of erecting building was very much developed. The buildings were erected in planned way. In the erection of building emphasis was placed on utility of the building. Two storey *pucca* building with steps was an excellent example of creation of that time. The knowledge of engineering was well developed.

The Art of Image Making

The art of making images was well developed among inhabitants of Indus valley. Images of stone, copper, bronze, earthen and slabs were carved. The images were in natural, living, attractive and strong poses. These were chief characteristics of image art of this period. Bronze made dancer image was full of its naturality and emotionality. The image of *Yogi* (an ascetic) in pose of devotion was also an excellent example of art of this period. A brass made goat toy kept in bronze made jar was also seeing worth. Plate of glass and human head of oyster were also important from the point of view of art. Dolls were made-up of gold, silver, stone, elephant teeth and snail.

The artists of this period were well versed in the art of flaking and cutting stones. Stone made images were also found. An image of ox was also found.

Earthen images were in a good number. They were of cow, ox, bull, sheep, dog, birds and monkeys. The images of males and females were also found. Terracotta images of dancers, *deva-dasi* (maid servants of God) and worshippers were obtained.

The Art of Making Seal

The artists of Indus valley were expert in seal making. They used to make seals of earthen, copper and bronze. Seals were found in a good number. They have prepared a frame for making seals. The shape of seal was rectangular and square shaped. Images were carved on seals. Seals were made-up of metals, elephant teeth and earthen. Images of ox, bull, elephant, rhinoceros and antelope were carved on seals.

Art of Music and Dance

The inhabitants of Indus valley were fond of music and dance. Metal made image of dancing girl reveals clearly the existence of dancing art in this period. A number of musical instruments were also found. On a seal an image of drum has been carved. Bronze made dancing girl image and slate stone made image in dancing pose are really a great contribution in the art of dance and music by the inhabitants of Indus valley.

Art of Writing

The inhabitants of Indus valley were expert in the art of writing. Their script was pictorial. In this script each figure was indicative of some sound, thing or view. The writing of the script was from right to left. Some scholars are of opinion that its script was same as the script used by the inhabitants of Egypt, Mesopotamia and Western Asia. But a number of scholars do not agree with this view.

The Art of Drawing and Painting

The drawing art of Indus valley was also developed. On potsherds pictures of animals and birds were drawn. The drawing on seals was also prevalent. The artists had the knowledge of colour like red, yellow and green. On seals, figures of bulls and hebuffaloes were drawn. The figures were full of life and beauty.

The Art of Making Pots

The inhabitants of Indus valley were expert in art of making pots from earthen and stone. They used to make small and big bowls, plates, cups, jar, and vessels. These pots were of various shapes and design.

The Art of Copper Plate Making

The inhabitants of Indus valley civilization used to make rectangular and square shaped copper plates for inscription. On one side, figures of animals and man was carved and on the other side inscriptions were written.

The Art of Weaving and Dyeing

The inhabitants were aware of the art of making threads from cotton and wool and weaving threads into clothes. Weaving and thread making instruments were obtained in good number. The thread making was done at family level. Cotton and silk clothes were prepared. clothes were coloured too. Colouring materials were found in abundance.

Metal Art

The metal art of this period was also well developed. The artists used to prepare beautiful images of metals. Gold, silver, brass, copper, bronze and glass were used for making ornaments. Besides various kinds of ornaments, decorative objects were also prepared from the metal. Hunch backed oxen of brass was also found. Brass made duck was also found. Bronze made dancing girl, and toy goat put in a jar of copper was also found. Ornaments of gold and silver were also found. In ornaments, necklace, bangle, arm ring, finger ring occupied prominent place. Ornament and dolls were prepared from earthen, stone, elephant teeth and snails.

Boon of Indus Valley Civilization

Indus valley civilization was in existence nearly 5,000 years ago. This civilization ended nearly 3,800 years ago. But this civilization has left deep imprint on our society and culture. Aryan civilization and Hindu civilization was greatly influenced by Indus valley civilization. Its influences on our society and culture are taken as its boon given to us. Its boon can be discussed under the following sub-headings:

- Impact on artisans
- Impact on dress
- Impact on ornaments
- Impact on means of entertainment
- Impact on costumes
- Impact on religion
- Impact on art.

Impact on Artisans

Even today potters make pottery with wheels and carpenters make wooden articles in the same way as that of potters and carpenters of Indus valley period.

Impact on Dress

Even today males and females wear the same kind of dresses as were worn by the inhabitants of Indus valley civilization.

Impact on Ornament

Even today males and females are wearing the same kind of ornaments as were worn by inhabitants of Indus valley.

Impact on Entertainment

Even today same types of games and plays are held as were held in Indus valley civilization. Chess and die are played even today.

Impact on Religion

The religion of Indus valley civilization has influenced our today's religion to a great extent. Even today Phallic worship, Lord Shiva worship, bull worship, tiger worship, swan worship, eagle worship, snake worship, river worship, sun worship, fire worship, mother Goddess worship, *pipal* tree worship etc. are continuing. These worships were introduced during Indus valley period.

Impact on Art

The Indus valley civilization had influenced our art to great extent. Even today image art, dance art and music art are continuing as were established during period of Indus valley civilization.

End of Indus Valley Civilization

Archaeological evidences reveal that Indus valley civilization came to an end nearly 1750 B.C. There were several causes for the downfall of Indus valley civilization. Chief causes responsible for the downfall of Indus valley civilization were as follows:

- Change in route of rivers
- Tectonic movement
- Flood and earthquake
- Great incidence of fire
- Epidemic
- Foreign attack
- Economic instability.

Change in Route of Rivers

Some scholars are of opinion that a great shift in water current of rivers Indus and Ravi had taken place. As a result, the routes of rivers were changed. The change in river route brought the situation of famine in Indus valley. The great famine resulted in the end of Indus valley civilization.

Tectonic Movement

Some scholars are of opinion that the tectonic movement had caused a great rise in water level of sea. The entire Indus region was overflooded. This situation caused the downfall of Indus valley civilization.

Flood and Earthquake

Some other scholars are of opinion that the downfall of Indus valley civilization had taken place due to frequent floods and earthquakes.

Great Incidence of Fire

Some scholars are of opinion that this civilization would have come to an end due to great incidence of fire.

Epidemic

Some scholars are of opinion that this Indus valley civilization would have come to an end due to epidemic like malaria and plague.

Foreign Attack

Some scholars are of view that Indus valley civilization met an end due to foreign attack. In Mohenjodaro heap of bones was found. There were skeletal remains of women and children too. Skeletons were wearing ornaments. Sign of attack by lethal weapons was also found. Some skeletons were found on steps. Evidences reveal clearly that the inhabitants of Indus valley were killed brutally by foreigners. They have included Aryans as invaders. They argue that Indra was the most powerful God of Aryans. He was termed as *Purandar* (Destructor of fort). Probably, Indus valley was a powerful fort of enemy of Indra.

Economic Instability

Some scholars are of opinion that Indus valley civilization met an end due to economic instability. The economy of Indus valley civilization was based on trade. The traders of Indus had trade relation with Egypt and Mesopotamia. The Egypt and Mesopotamia were facing the situation of instability. An instability was also caused in Indus valley civilization. The economic instability caused downfall of Indus valley civilization.

Besides above discussed causes of downfall of Indus valley civilization, some other causes were also responsible for the downfall of Indus valley civilization. These causes were increase in population, decrease in fertility of land and lack of natural resources. Thus, the downfall of Indus valley civilization took place due to a number of causes.

13

Indian Chalcolithic Culture (1,750 B.C. – 1,000 B.C.)

After the downfall of Harappa culture or Indus valley civilization, the rise of chalcolithic culture took place in India. The urban traditions of Harappa culture met an end and in place of urban traditions, traditions related to rural economy came into existence. During Chalcolithic period, people lived in villages in houses erected with prepared mixed soil. The main occupation was agriculture and animal husbandry. The excavations of chalcolithic sites has revealed the evidences related to copper made objects along with pottery. Although, the copper made objects were very few in number. These few copper objects were prepared by the people themselves or they were brought from outside, nothing can be said with certainty. But it is not important here whether they were made by the local people or brought from the outside, important here is beginning of the use of copper by the people. The beginning of use of copper objects laid the foundation of chalcolithic culture in India. The use of stone objects continued even after the beginning of use of copper objects. That is why archaeological anthropologists have termed this culture as chalcolithic culture. In this culture, the use of copper was in little amount and there was also lack of urban traditions. Probably, the people of this culture were not in a position to produce more grains to meet expenditure on copper smithy. Although the chalcolithic culture shared a common characteristic in food economy and technological development, but different regions were indicating differences in their chalcolithic culture. Each region had its own characteristics of ceramic tradition. They were related to local traditions. The dating of chalcolithic culture in India has been established between 1,750 B.C. – 1,000 B.C.

In the river valleys of India, a number of chalcolithic sites were discovered. This indicates that this culture had an extent over a large area. On chalcolithic site related mounds, people were living in community. Somewhere, they had left the mound to settle somewhere else and were cultivating the mounds at somewhere.

For the purpose of study, the chalcolithic culture of India can be divided into six local groups. They are as follows:

- Ahar-Banas chalcolithic culture
- Central region chalcolithic culture
- Northern Deccan chalcolithic culture
- Deccan neolithic-chalcolithic culture
- Ganga Doab chalcolithic culture
- Eastern chalcolithic culture.

The excavated sites of all above mentioned local chalcolithic cultural groups were as follows:

- Ahar, Bagar, and Gilund (Ahar-Banas culture)
- Kayatha, Maheshwar, Navdatoli, Nagada, Awara, Manoti and Eran (Central region culture)

- Piklihal, Brahmagiri and Maski (Deccan culture)
- Prakash, Bahal, Chandoli, Jarwe, Nevasa, Inamgaon and Nasik (North Deccan culture)
- Bahadarabad, Ambakhori, Hastinapur, Ataranjikhera (Ganga Doab culture)
- Chirand and Pandurajardhibi (Eastern culture)

All above mentioned local groups had reciprocal contact and communication.

Now, let us discuss about the each local chalcolithic culture one by one.

Ahar-Banas Culture

The chalcolithic culture of south-eastern Rajasthan is known as Ahar culture. It was named after a famous site Ahar near a small town of Udaypur. At this site, a big mound named Dhulcot was excavated. The length of the mound was 500 metre, breadth was 275 metre and height was 12.8 metre. On the basis of stratification and culture, it was divided into two periods — I and II. Each period was divided into three phases — A, B and C. The chief pottery types of this culture were black ware and red ware. There was complete absence of microlithic tools in this period. That is why this culture was known as chalcolithic culture.

This culture is also known as Banas culture. It was because a number of sites of this culture were discovered from the bank of river Banas and its tributaries. All these sites are located in Udaipur, Chittor and Bhilwara districts. The Ahar or Banas culture was established around 2,000 B.C.

A common trait which establishes correlation of Bagor microlithic culture with Ahar culture is different types of pottery. They were red, grey and black with white printing. This trait had come into existence in microlithic culture nearly 4,500 B.C. But this trait was in existence till the beginning of Ahar-Banas culture.

Why people had chosen this valley site for habitation? It had a number of causes. Perhaps, this valley site was chosen from the point of view of safety. Because this river valley was full of mountains. The valley had good rainfall. There was no dearth of drinking water and food materials. Good rainfall brought good harvest. The existence of forest was also in abundance. Hunting animals were available in the forest. The forest used to fulfil a number of needs of life. The stone having copper was available here. The copper was extracted from the copper ores by melting process. Stones were also available for erecting houses. The chief cultural features of Ahar-Banas culture were as follows:

House Construction

The excavation of Ahar culture has yielded evidences of erecting house with the help of stones and wet soil. They knew well the art of erecting foundation and walls of the houses. Foundation walls were made by stones. Over foundation, walls were made by wet soil mixed with small pebbles. Some walls over the foundation were of *kuchcha* bricks. Wood pillars and beams were used in houses. Roofs were made up of bamboo and bushes. The roofs were kept slope. Some big houses were of 30 ft. × 15 ft., 22 ft. × 17 ft. and 10 ft. × 9 ft. For making floor, two methods were employed. They were made either of pebbles mixed in wet soil or of hard burnt soil.

From the Gilund site, two important structures had come into existence. One structure was of parallel walls of *kuchcha* bricks whose length-breadth were 100 ft. × 80 feet. Another structure was made of *pucca* bricks whose size was 14 × 6 × 5 inches. Such a structure made-up of *pucca* bricks was not found from any other chalcolithic cultural sites of India. Such types of structures were found from Indus valley civilization. The walls of Gilund and other sites were made-up of bricks because stones were not available easily on those sites.

In the houses of Ahar culture, there were hearths for cooking food. The size of some hearths was very big. This shows that the size of some families was very big. There two or three types of food were cooked in big earthen pots. Probably, they were used on festive occasions when a number of people used to gather together. In a house, 6 hearths were found in a row. Probably, copper was melted there. They were also used for some other industrial purposes. Along with hearths, saddlequern, muller, pestle and earthen plates were also found. It seems that grains were crashed to get flour for making bread.

Grains

Regarding the grain it could be said with certainty that rice was included in their food. From the 1st phase of period-I, signs of rice along with potteries were found in abundance. The inhabitants were also aware of wheat. Nothing could be said with certainty about the other grains. The inhabitants were non-vegetarian, too. From the kitchen room of houses, bones of fish, turtle, cow, buffalo, hens, oxen, sheep, goats, pigs and deer were found.

Pottery

The inhabitants of Banas and Ahar used different types of potteries. But they have been placed under two important groups — Black ware and Red ware. The potteries included different kinds and sizes of plates, bowls and jars. The surface of these pots were soft and sometimes shining. There were red, grey, chocolate and orange colour shades. They were made by a good quality of wet soil prepared for this purpose. They were thin and thick. They had metallic rings. Their form was obtained from Harappa culture. The Ahar culture showed contacts with contemporary cultures like Saurashtra and Malwa. It was because from all excavated sites black wares and red wares were found. Red and black wares had reached in Deccan region very late. Their contact was also with Baluchistani culture. This reveals that in those early days Rajasthan and Baluchistan had contacts. Black wares and red wares were not available to common man, but red wares were more in use. But different types of wares were used for cooking, serving and drinking purposes. That is why they were termed as table wares. For storage purposes, red wares were used. These wares had lower part untouched. Their mouth, neck and shoulder were retouched. The jars were dug in earth.

Some other potteries were painted with black colour. Some were painted in grey, red and multi-colour. While some others were kept plain. In phase B of period-I, the use of stone pots was continued. Perhaps stone made pots were brought from outside. The light yellow and cream colour pots of this site were related to Amari and Nal sites. Such types of pots were also found from Gilund site. But in Navdatoli site on a cream colour pot dancing figures and dotted figures of animals were found engraved. Such types of pots were also available from periods-I and II of Gilund. The ceramic industries of Gilund and Navdatoli had reciprocal contacts.

Copper Tools and Weapons

Absence of stone tools and weapons completely reveals clearly that the inhabitants of Ahar-Banas were dependent fully on copper and mixed metal. Copper and its mixed metals were available in abundance nearby Ahar. There were several hearths for melting copper. This indicates that the economy of Ahar was dependent on copper industry. Probably this would have been reason which had attached the early colonial inhabitants towards Ahar and Banas valley. They would have stayed here for several years. In the excavation five axes, one knife blade, a sheet, a bangle and two finger rings of copper were found. These copper tools were probably used for flaking stones, cutting fish and bones, taking out skin and domestic works. They were also used for agricultural works. They also used copper made ornaments. The inhabitants of Ahar were fully dependent on copper, while the inhabitants of Gilund and other sites were dependent on copper partially.

It is worth mentioning here that not only in Ahar, but also in a neighbouring site named Khurshid, a colony of copper was found. This site is located in the middle of desert in Parbaster Tehsil of Nagpur district. There was no fountain in its neighbourhood. The copper tools included flat axe, square shaped chisels, thin edged Indian axe and a full bowl.

One of important cultural traits of Ahar culture was beads made-up of fire baked soil. On blades, animal and geometric motiff were found. Spinning disc found from here was not discovered from any chalcolithic sites. Terracotta images of bulls with clear evidence of horns were also found. From Gilund players with different heads were also found. From these evidences, it appears that bull cult was in existence in the chalcolithic culture.

Central Region Chalcolithic Culture

In central region, a number of chalcolithic sites were discovered in the river valleys of Chambal, Narmada and others.

From the excavations of Kayatha, Maheshwar, Nagda, Navdatoli, Awara, Manoti, Eran, Ajadnagar and Besanagarh sites, stratified chalcolithic layers were found. Although each chalcolithic site has its own characteristics, but they present a common picture of chalcolithic culture of Madhya Pradesh. From all chalcolithic sites of Madhya Pradesh painted potteries in different colours were found essentially. But among them black on red wares occupied prominent place. This black on red wares were not limited only to Madhya Pradesh, but its extent was up to Khandesh across the boundary and up to middle of Maharashtra. Besides different types of potteries, stone tools like parallel sided blades, copper made objects, beads, grains and terracotta images, were attached to this chalcolithic culture. Among all chalcolithic sites, Kayatha site is the most ancient one which had come into existence in 2,000 B.C.

Habitation

From the excavation of some chalcolithic sites, it appears that chalcolithic sites were established over black soil. Habitat was established in the form of huts of soil thatched with bushes and grasses. From the Manoti site, a structure of fire baked bricks had come into existence, but from the Nagda site a structure of sun baked bricks was found. From Manoti, a high square shaped structure was found which was made-up of fire baked bricks of various types. With the help of this structure, an attempt was made to protect the habitation site from the flood of Banas river. The inhabitants had also erected a great wall with the help of same types of bricks. Its width was 11 feet and height was 10 to 12 feet. Within wall several structures of bricks were situated. At Nagda site, a great structure of mortar and bricks was found. It was used for the purpose of living. There was a rampart fort within the structure.

From the Eran site protective walls were discovered. It was made-up of black and yellow earth. This wall was erected towards south of Awara site. From other sites rivers used to protect this site. The basal width of protective wall was 30.50 metres. The maximum height was 6.41 metre. A pit was dug after protective wall.

House Planning

There was no fixed house planning in chalcolithic culture of Madhya Pradesh. But Maheshwar and Navdatoli sites have yielded evidences of house planning. On these sites, houses were erected adhered to each other. After a row of four-five houses, there was a narrow street. The houses were erected with the help of thick wooden pillars. The wooden pillars were covered with bamboo cover. The bamboo cover was plastered with mortar from outside and inside. The size of houses were of different types. For example round, square, rectangular. The areas of these houses were also different. The diameter of a round room was 3 to 4 feet. It is doubtful whether it was used for living? Perhaps such small huts were prepared for storing grains. The size of rectangular houses were 20 feet × 40 feet. Generally, the size of a house was 10 feet × 8 feet. More than four persons could not live in these houses.

The floor of these houses was made with wet soil and cow dung. It was made smooth, strong and insect free. For this purposes powder of lime was spread over black or yellow soil. The pits were filled-up with black deposits. The Awara and Eran sites have yielded evidences of pebble mixed yellow soil floor. Sometimes floor was made-up of burnt soil mass. The floor was also made with pieces of burnt charcoals. Houses were erected by inserting wood pillars, bamboo pillars or both in the earth serially adhered to each other from one end to another. Bamboo pillars or wood pillars were covered with mortar from both sides. By this method walls of houses were erected. The two surfaces were separated by bamboo band. When walls were burnt due to some reason, the signs of pillars and bands remained in burnt plaster with mortar and lime. The walls were white washed with lime. The roof were made with reed, bamboo and bushes. But there was no evidence in this regard.

There were hearths for cooking food in these houses. In the houses of Navdatoli one mouthed or two mouthed hearths were found. One mouthed or two mouthed hearths revealed the status of owners of the house. On two mouthed hearth, two kinds of food was cooked at the same time. But on one mouthed hearth only one kind of food was cooked at a time. One mouthed hearths indicate the poor background of the family. One mouthed hearths needed less fuel for cooking. These hearths had small mouth and thin wall. From the Eman Saran of Navdatoli, an evidence of three mouthed hearth was found, two on the sides and one in the middle. Here three kinds of food were cooked at the same time. From Ajadnagar site near Indore, a child burial was unearthed from a house. The child was buried in north-south direction. The head was towards north.

Pottery

In chalcolithic houses small or big potteries were found essentially. Earthen pots were for cooking, serving food, serving water, drinking water and storing water and grains. All earthen pots were made on wheel. The storage jar were big, thick, and strong. Their necks were decorated. Cup, disc, and bowls were important pots.

Ceramics

The ceramic art of chalcolithic Madhya Pradesh can be divided into following types on the basis of sites for the purpose of study.

Kayatha Ware

The name Kayatha ware was given on the basis of a site named Kayatha situated at a distance of

25 km east of Ujjain. This site has been dated as 2,000 B.C. to 1,800 B.C. This chalcolithic site was the earliest site of this region. It has been correlated with pre-Harappa site Sothi. From the site three ceramic industries were discovered. Sturdy ware was the chief ceramic industry. On the potteries, a thick chocolate slip was found from lip to neck region. Sometimes, blue painting was done up to base. The jars were round and mouth was flat. The boarder of bowls was bent inside and thick. The majority of jars had ring like base. Very few jars were having cup like base.

Buff ware was second ceramic industry. The wares of this industry were made beautifully with mixed wet soil.

The third industry was known as combed ware. The wares of this industry were of simple red colour. No thin painting was found on the pots. Engraved pattern was present. Only birds and food were represented on potteries.

Black and Red Ware

The black and red wares would have been brought here from the Ahar site. Its dating has been done as 1,800 B.C. – 1,200 B.C. They were made by inverted firing technique. In Kayatha, the people using this ware had come to settle in between 1,800 B.C. – 1,200 B.C. Since Awara and Manoti sites were not very far from the Ahar site, this was found from the lowest layer in plenty.

In Navdatoli it was related to cup and bowls. But it was limited only to period-I. Such types of wares were also found from Nagada and Eran site. Near Besnagar three types of potteries were found on the basis of painting. They are known as red, black and red and grey and red wares.

Malwa Ware

The most common pottery of Malwa ware were red pottery painted with black design. Since this type of potteries were found from every part of Malwa region, they are termed as Malwa ware. This type of ware was in existence from the earliest chalcolithic site to the newest site Navdatoli. In the initial phase some designs and size came into existence. But later on they had become quite different. The most important pottery was bowl with tunnel. On the outer ends of bowl, there were designs all around. One figure of man was also engraved who was having hair like a warrior. He has taken a spear in his hand and his waist was tight. Such types of wares were also available from the lowest layer of Nagada and Eran. Kayatha, Manoti and Awara had also shown such types of pots.

White Stripped Fabric

Another important potteries were white stripped fabric. They were related to two early periods of Navdatoli. But they had become extinct later on. They were found in less number. White stripped was a common characteristic, but the size of potteries was not same. They had more diversities in size than the black and red ware. Cup, bowls, small bowls and small pots were found.

Jorwe Ware

From the phase-III of Navdatoli site, a new type of pottery structure was found which is known as Jorwe ware. The Jorwe site is located in Deccan. It is known grey black ware. It was in existence along with red ware. In these wares, designs and types were found in limited number. From example bent surface bowls, spouted pots and narrow high neck pots. Geometric designs and figures were carved on these pots. Kettle size bowls were probably used for sacrifice. A copper or bronze made jar was also found. Its size and type were same as that of earthen jars. Such types of potteries were also found from Parbastar site.

Other Types of Pottery

Red and black ware pieces were found from entire Malwa region. Although, these potteries were limited in number, but they were essentially used in chalcolithic culture. The storage jars were decorated by piercing. Piercing decoration was found even on small pots. These pots were in use in the Awara site till last two periods. Grey wares were used in Maheshwar, Navdatoli and Awara in very less number.

Grey Ware

During chalcolithic period, along with black painted, red and white painted, black and red painted potteries, grey wares were also found. Grey wares were found in abundance at Eran site. It was in use between 1,750 B.C. – 700 B.C. The thin pieces of these wares present a very beautiful decoration. These wares were different from painted grey ware of Ganges valley. They do not show any relation with south Indian painted neolithic grey wares. Some pieces of grey wares were collected from Bhind district. The structure of grey wares showed resemblance with grey ware of chalcolithic Eran site. The grey wares included jars and bowls. These wares were painted like black and red wares. These wares were like Malwa ware. Over black and red ware some figures of animals and birds were pierced. Spouted bowls were found here.

Painted grey ware potsherds were found from Ujjain fort too. These types of ware would have reached here later on.

Designs Over Pottery

Different types of beautiful designs were found on potteries and wares of chalcolithic period of Madhya Pradesh. These potteries and wares express artistic behaviour of chalcolithic people. From all painted wares of India, the painted wares of Navdatoli had shown designs more in number. Potteries and wares were decorated with designs from outside. The designs were made on neck, shoulder and sides. Some pots had designs made from inside on the edge. The ornamental designs are mainly geometric. The geometric designs were simple band, net, square, right angles, triangle, parallelogram, step, round, point, circle, circle upon circle, and rays. The figures of plants, birds and animals were also painted. For example, lion, tiger, leopard, deer, swan, peacock, cat, dog, fish and turtle. Some pictures of rising and setting sun were painted. Some leaves, flowers and fruits were also painted.

Socio-economic Condition

From the study of shape, size, design and diversity of potteries and wares, some indications about the socio-economic condition of chalcolithic people of Madhya Pradesh have come into existence. They are as follows:

Cultivation of Different Types of Grains

The chalcolithic people of Madhya Pradesh used to do cultivation of different types of grains. They were not nomadic or semi-nomadic. Rather they were settled agriculturists. No sites other than

Navdatoli present before us evidences of cultivation of grains, oil seeds, pot, flowers, and fruits. The chalcolithic people had started cultivating wheat and barley as appeared from the excavation of Navdatoli and Kayatha. The cultivation of paddy was not possible till the phase-I. But it had come into existence from II to IV stages. These people had started cultivating pulses of five types. They were lentil, kidney bean, pea and horse bean. The foods were cooked in linseeds. In fruits remains of plum and *amla* were found. Some fruits were not recongised. The cultivation of kidney bean, wheat and linseeds were started in early period. This indicates that they had contacts with western Asia. But cultivation of paddy was indigenous.

Method of Cultivation

Cultivation of wheat was done with the help of plough. The cultivation was done by digging earth with digging instruments. Stone sickles, stone slabs and pestles were found in abundance.

Food

The chalcolithic inhabitants of Madhya Pradesh cooked their food on hearths. The debris of houses have revealed evidences of hearths. Remains of oxen, horses, bulls, pigs, sheep, goats and deers were also found. This indicates that animals were domesticated for getting meat. They had started producing grains sufficiently, so, they were less dependent on animal meat for food. They were agriculturists. But they used to do hunting and fishing. Probably they were beef eaters. They used to eat meat of pigs and deers.

Use of Metal and Stone Tools

The inhabitants of chalcolithic Madhya Pradesh were aware of copper and bronze, but they used them as miser. Available copper and bronze objects indicate towards reform in metallurgy. From the Kayatha site two thick copper made axes and one chisel were found. The copper axes occupied prominent place in their coppersmithy. From the site Awara, a bronze axe was obtained. Some handleless axe, harpoons for fishing, pins and rings were also obtained from Maheshwar and Navdatoli sites. From the later phase sword and dagger were found.

After the emergence of all copper tools, the significance of stone blades was still maintained in this period. Stone blades were used in their day-to-day life. They used to cut vegetables, leafy vegetables and meat with stone blades. Stone blades were also used for scraping animal skin and punching stones. The stone blades were made with agate and chalcedony stone which were available abundantly in their environment. They were made from long parallel sided flakes. These tools were made with special technique. Bone or wood handle was fitted with the tool to increase the efficiency.

Ornament

The chalcolithic inhabitants of Madhya Pradesh were very fond of ornaments. They had started making ornaments of copper in this period. The copper bangles occupied prominent place among all copper ornaments. From the excavation of only one house, 29 copper bangles were found. These copper bangles were kept in an earthen pot. This indicates that the inhabitants of Kayatha were as prosperous as the inhabitants of Harappa. Copper and earthen bangles and rings were also found from the Maheshwar and Navdatoli sites. These inhabitants used them as ornaments. The ornaments of ear found from Navdatoli are plain and simple. From the Erom site, a disc of gold was found whose weight was 20 gm. But nothing could be said about its use. Several earthen beads were found. Some beads were of konch, shell, chalk, agate, jaspar, carnelian, and other stones. Garland and beads industry was prevalent at local level. Beads were of different types and size. For example small, medium, big, round, square, tubular, cylindrical, bicoincal and betel nut. Necklaces were made with the help of beads. Bangles, ring, necklaces, lids, amulets and other broken objects were found from Navdatoli and Maheshwar. This indicates that these objects had local industries.

Terracotta

The chalcolithic inhabitants of Madhya Pradesh used to prepare terracotta images as appeared from the excavation of different chalcolithic sites. The chalcolithic inhabitants used to decorate their habitat with terracotta. From the Kayatha sites, a number of strange bull images on terracotta had appeared. They were either natural or stylic. In stylic form hunched neck bull was shown. Its base was round. From Navdatoli an interesting image of small bull was found which had a tail, too. It was made by *Gota-Pota* method From Awara and Eran terracotta bulls were found. From Navdatoli terracotta birds were found. They had beaks and flat base.

From Awara, Navdatoli and Eran terracotta discs were found in abundance. Perhaps, they were used for weight and measure. Some of them were also used for rubbing the skin. Some stone balls were also found. They could be placed one above the other. Probably, they were used for measuring on earthen balance. The skin rubbing band was used by the people. They were pieces like tube.

Fire baked wheel was also obtained. Two wheel specimens were found from Navdatoli. One was biconcave. This shows a condition between one navel and two navel wheel. A toy cart was also found from Eran site. From this site with navel and without navel wheels were found. The most significant achievement of this site was a pierced sheet. Over it six stalks were painted in red colour. Such type of wheel was not available from any other chalcolithic site. No wooden wheel was found. The fire baked wheels throw light towards the transportation system.

In other terracotta objects small images of man and animal were included. Beak, seals and lids were also obtained. From Navdatoli site, a bone disc was found. Probably, it would have been spinning wheel. The seals of potters and weavers were found from Awara. They were used at the time of colouring.

Religion

The study of terracotta images reveals that chalcolithic inhabitants of Madhya Pradesh believed in bull worship. They worshipped mother Goddess and Swan too. In worship potteries were used. In worship sacrifice was made.

Northern Deccan Chalcolithic Culture

From the excavation of Jorwe, Nevasa, Daimabad, Chandoli, Songaon, Inamgaon, Prakash and Bahal sites, one gets knowledge about northern Deccan chalcolithic culture. Geographically, this regions is meeting place of Madhya Pradesh and Deccan areas. That is why one gets a mixture of Madhya Pradesh and Deccan chalcolithic cultures. In comparison to Madhya Pradesh chalcolithic cultures, we find here predominance of Deccan neolithic culture. The potteries and houses of here show a difference.

Habitat

The habitat of this chalcolithic culture was bank of river. These habitats were located in between Pravara and Godawari rivers and Ghod and Mahalangi rivers. These residences were built on black soil. This soil was formed due to seasonal weathering. In these river valleys chalcolithic people had come to settle. At that time, the area was full of forests. Sometimes, residences were erected in semidry region. Sometimes some houses were built over early remains. These residences may be termed as colony because the people who came to settle here were well aware of art and craft. No evidence of indigenous development was found from here.

House

No evidence of house structure has been found in excavation. But from Nevasa and Inamgaon sites, evidences of pit houses were found. Among pit houses, the diametre of a pit house was 8 ft. or 3 metre. Pole holes were found around the pit house. In excavation potsherds of Malwa wares were found. The people who had erected houses here would have been coming to live here in early time. But later on, they started erecting rectangular houses. Among all 8 houses from Inamgaon site, the length of the biggest house was 8.5 m (30 feet) and width was 3.30 m (12 feet). Evidences of big houses were also obtained from Nevasa. The measurement of a house was 45 × 20 feet, while the measurement of other house was 8 × 7 feet. The walls were small and the corners were round. The roof had support of wooden pillars and beams. The roof was flat. Some houses had good courtyards. There was a good system of outlet for the flow of rainwater. The floors of houses of Chandoli and Songaon were built with lime. There were 4 feet wide streets between two houses. The Inamgaon has yielded such type of evidences.

The chalcolithic inhabitants of Inamgaon used to erect fort with the help of mortar and untouched boulders. They used to construct dam on river for the storage of water. They had a well developed furnace for firing bricks. The furnace had a fire chamber and a tube for outlet of hot air. The inhabitants of here can be isolated from other places. Because they prepared different kind of pottery. They did not bury their deads inside house.

The people who came later to settle at Inamgaon site lived in a round house. Its size varied between 2 metre to 4.30 metre. The diametre of a well structured round house was 3 metre. The width of its wall was 40 cm. There were signs of 9 holes in the wall. The distance between two poles was 50 to 55 cm. A pole was inserted with the help of stone pieces. Inside house two groups of 4 wide stones and a hearth were found. The floor was made with black soil. The walls were plastered with mortar. The roof was conical. There were all-round 16 poles in the biggest house. Altogether evidences of 38 houses including big and small were found. The houses were erected nearby each other. The houses located in western sides were of artisans, craftman, potters, lime makers and gold smith.

Pottery

In excavation all houses yielded pottery in plenty. The potteries were related to eating or serving food, drinking water, cooking food, storing grains and water and burials. The pottery available from Prakash and Nevasa indicated that they were of yellow and grey ware painted with white design. There were different types of bowls, small pots and jars. From Prakash, Diamabad, Chandoli, Songaon and Inamgaon different types and sizes of Malwa ware were obtained. There were round circleless jars in majority. Some had tubular mouth. Straight edge bowls, concave edge bowls, beaked bowls, and small pots were included in the pottery. All potteries were painted with red and black paint. Painting designs were geometric and natural. In natural painting animals were painted in different poses. On a round pitcher of Daimabad forest and religious figures were made. This is an excellent example of natural scenes painted on pottery. The upper portion of the picture had a figure of male warrior and two deers. The peacock was in between two deers. The lower part of jar had a figure of tiger. The phase-I revealed the condition of early inhabitants of Dambsadat. Their potteries were placed under Sawalada ware. Along with them painted grey wares were also found.

Among the dominant wares of this region, the name of Jorwe ware comes first. This ware was named after a site named Jorwe. It was made by a well mixed and prepared wet soil. It had a metal ring. Above mat like surface black paint was done. From Nevasa different types and sizes of bowls, cups, disc, and spouted bowls were found. Different types and sizes of small pots were also found. Spouted bowls showed speciality of Nevasa site. There was no evidence of plate in the pottery obtained from the excavations. Decorations were natural in majority. The picture of a dog and deer reveals realistic feature. Although Chandoli and Inamgaon sites have contributed significantly, but Inamgaon site had made a new contribution. It showed a change in basic Jorwe type and construction. Bowls with *swastik* designs are wonderful contribution. A cylindrical jar was very long. On a big jar pictures of two hunched neck bulls drawing a cart were found. On tubular pottery, there were pictures of boats. A narrow necked jar was also found. Upon jar natural and geometric pictures were pierced. On back side there was a dog. From Inamgaon site big jar like Tekkalkota burial jar were found.

The pieces of Jorwe jars were sharpen to use as a tool. Its real use was not known. Probably, they were used as skin rubber or for burnishing potteries. Other types of pots were very few in number. From Prakash and Daimabad pierced pots were found.

Dress and Ornaments

From the excavation of Nevasa, Chandoli and Inamgaon sites, it appears that the chalcolithic men used to cultivate cotton, silk and flax. They made threads and finally clothes from them. These threads were used in copper beads too. The Nevasan and Chandoli sites have presented before us such evidences. No cloth specimen was available.

The ornaments included neck chain, earring, fingerring, and bangles. For making necklaces semi-gem stones like agate, jaspar, carnelian, terracotta conch, shells, chalk and steatite were used.

Sometimes chains were made with more copper and less gold beads. From the Nevasa site, a full copper beads made chain was found in the neck of a child's dead body. Bangles were made of copper and fired soils. Elephant teeth and bones were also used for making bangles.

Tools and Weapons

From the chalcolithic sites very few copper made objects were found. From the Chandoli site two copper chisels, an axe, three harpoons, and a copper rod were found. A dagger with antenna was found from Chandoli site. It was compared to sword of Fatehgarh of Uttar Pradesh.

From the Nevasa site, a chisel, a plate, a rod and a pot were found. From the Navdatoli, a triangular axe was found whose upper portion was broken. From the Jorwe site, six flat axes were reported. Besides copper tools, stone tools were also found. For example anvil, stone slab and pestle, stone hammer, polished axe, adze and chisels were found from the Nevasa, Chandoli and other sites. The copper was very loving object. It was used less in number. Stone tools were used more in number. Stone sickles were made. They were filled in a wooden or bone handle for performing domestic works. They were used for cutting fruits, vegetables, wood, and bone. Mullers were made in boat shape. Grains were crushed over ground stone or muller with pestle. Stone axes were polished.

Food

The chalcolithic village inhabitants used to eat meat of cow and deer. They used to eat meat of buffalo, goat, sheep and pigs. Fishes were also included in their foods. They were aware of cat, dog, cocks, hens and ducks. They knew well about dangerous wild animals like tiger, lion, leopard, wolf etc.

The chalcolithic villagers used to cultivate wheat, barley, millet, *masoor*, and *mung*. They used these grains as food materials. From the Inamgaon site evidences of barley, wheat, *masoor*, *mung*, green gram, horse gram, common pea, grass pea, Indian plum, and wild dates were obtained.

Terracotta

From chalcolithic sites, a number of terracotta images were obtained. From the Nevasa site, a terracotta image of a big women was obtained whose head was small and conical, but face of image was not seen. Her arms were small and extended, breasts were small. Her lower part did not show any speciality. Her size was concave by which it was kept on ground. The same type of a small terracotta image of woman was also obtained. The Inamgaon has also yielded a number of terracotta woman images. Some images were naked, some had heads, while some other did not possess head. The images without heads were seated on bull. An earthen box was also obtained whose length was 6 inch and width was 2 inch in the centre. An image of naked Goddess was found in it. An another earthen woman image without head was found seated on a bull. Some terracotta male images were also obtained in excavation. From the Nevasa and Chandoli sites an animal face jar was obtained in excavation. In fact, it was an image of a bull, but in place of face and head, there was a bottle size hole. The other part of the body show hunch-backed and a small tail. In place of four feet, there were four discs. The body of bull was painted and covered with clothes.

The study of terracotta images reveals that the worship of God, Goddess and bull was prevalent among chalcolithic inhabitants. From this region two tanks were also obtained. Probably, they were used for rituals. They were oval or rectangular in shape. Such types of tanks were obtained from Kalibanga, Amari and Navdatoli.

Copper Objects

Besides terracotta images, four bronze made strange objects were found. They included one elephant, one rhinoceros, one buffalo and a chariot driven by man. The chariot was drawn by two bulls.

Burial

From the Nevasa chalcolithic sites, evidences of 131 burials were found. Some remains of burials were also obtained from Bahal, Chandoli, Daimabad, and Songaon. The Inamgaon site had yielded evidences of 50 burials. The study of burials reveals that the dead bodies were buried below the floor of houses. The dead bodies were kept outside the house to be eaten by insects, birds and animals. When only skeletal remains were left, they were buried inside the floor of houses by keeping in jars. The bones of children were placed in two jars before burial rituals. The bones of adults and aged were put in 3, 4 or 5 jars before burial rituals. All burial jars were buried inside floor by digging burial. All skeletal remains were placed in extended position. But only one was placed in a special position. Skeletons were placed in north-south direction. From Nevasa 126, Chandoli 23, Songaon 4, Daimabad 3 and Inamgaon 50 children burials were found. The existence of children burial in such number reveals clearly that child mortality rate was very high in chalcolithic period. It seems probable that chalcolithic inhabitant of this region had acquired burial culture from southern neolithic culture.

Grave materials were also kept in burials. Potteries, tools, beads, and other materials used by dead were kept inside burials as grave materials. Some children's dead bodies were buried along with copper chains. This indicates that their economic condition was good. Cow dung and oil were applied as pastle over the dead body of a child.

South Indian Neolithic-Chalcolithic Culture

From the excavations of south Indian sites like Brahmagiri, Maski, Snagan Kallu, Hallur, Uttanur, Kupagal and T. Narsipur, knowledge about neolithic culture has come into existence. After Neolithic culture this region witnessed the emergence of chalcolithic culture around 1800 B.C. That is why this culture is termed as Neolithic-chalcolithic culture. Copper objects were obtained from the upper surface of Brahmagiri, Piklihal and Tekkalkota sites. This would have happened due to contact of neolithic people with the inhabitants of northern Deccan chalcolithic culture. On these sites chalcolithic culture had maintained its originality. The inhabitants of these sites used more neolithic polished stone tools. This was contrary to north Indian chalcolithic culture where polished stone tools were used in less number. That is why the neolithic and chalcolithic cultures of south India are discussed together.

House

From the excavation of different sites, knowledge about house pattern and house planning has appeared before us. From the excavation of Tekkalkota, Sangalkallu and Hallur sites, remains of a round house have come before us as evidence. Its foundation was of earth and was deep. The walls of house were covered with torn bamboo, reed and creepers. The roof of these houses was sloping one side. The roof was conical. The floor was plastered with lime, but walls were not plastered. From the Tekkalkota and Sangalkallu sites laterite made floor was obtained. A hearth made with three stones was obtained from Sangalkallu site. Storage jars were also obtained from these houses. Attention was paid towards cleanliness of the house. Bones were buried in pits after sharing meat as food. Ash and pottery pieces were also buried in the pit.

Pottery

From the excavation of houses special type and artistic potteries were obtained. Polished grey ware were special feature of neolithic-chalcolithic cultures. The wares were also influenced by north Indian elements. Black and red ware or red black wares were also obtained. These wares were painted with white colour. Only cup and lids were found. These two kinds of pottery were associated with death rituals. They were found in burials. Black on red painted potteries were also found from all sites.

In common pottery, cup, lid, small plate, small pot, jars and storage jars occupied important place. Tube, small jar, lamp were taken from Jorwey and other northern chalcolithic culture.

Stone Tools and Blade

A number of sites have yielded polished and ground tools. Among polished and ground tools, the most significant tool was axe. The other stone tools were adze, chisel, scraper, borer, pin, point, pointed axe, ground, pestle, mace, ring stone and pellet bow. Stone blades were made from chert and chalcedony.

Metal Objects

Along with stone tools, metal objects were also found. But here the number of metal objects is less than stone tools. Very less copper made objects were found from Tekkalkota, Brahmagiri, Mashi, Pikalihal, and Hallur. In Tekkalkota bronze made axe was found from the phase-I. A copper coil, a wire, a ring, a nail and pieces of copper were found from the phase-II. From Brahmagiri, a chisel and a rod were found. From Phase-II, copper chisel and a small boll edge were obtained. From the phase-I of Hallur, three copper objects were found. A harpoon and two uncommon objects were obtained. A small two edge axe was obtained. It was very small and thin. That is why it could be termed as sect object. An another object was small flat axe. Its cutting edge was flat. The surface specimen found from Brahmagiri was triangular. Its butt end was small and narrow. It was like a skin cutter of present day shoemaker.

The chalcolithic man used to wear chain made of copper beads. From Brahmagiri gold and copper ornaments were obtained. From T. Narsipur, a discoidal gold bead and a biconcave copper bead were found. They were used as ear ornament. Their weights were 7.49 gm and 5.37 gm respectively. It is clear that gold ornaments had made their appearance in this region nearly 2000 B.C.

Head Rest and Edge Ground

In excavation of chalcolithic sites some such objects were found whose use or importance is not well known till now. From Hallur, a piece of head rest and edge ground painted pottery was found. It had no edge and base. From T. Narsipur, Robbert Bruce Foote had obtained a head rest. Head rest was a decorative material of Egypt burial. This material highlights a cultural contact between ancient Egypt and Protohistoric Deccan. From Inamgaon such objects were found from a furnace. From Tekkalkota, Hallur, and Maski edge ground pieces of pottery were obtained. They were termed as skin rubber band.

Art

The chalcolithic inhabitants had developed some artistic expressions. They were probably the early rock painters. They had expressed their emotions by painting rocks of their habitat. They used to decorate their pottery by piercing technique. From Tekkalkota, an attractive bull image was obtained. Three types of drawing were found. They were: (i) Black colour drawing, (ii) White colour drawing, and (iii) Red colour drawing. The images of bull, deer, rhinoceros, goat, horse, man and trident were carved. Sometimes, figures of trees, animals, birds were made. From the phase-I of Tekkalkota, a figures of two deer, a peacock and a snake were made over a lid of grey ware. Images of animals drawn on potteries showed similarity with animals drawn on rocks. Some drawings were similar to Neolithic-chalcolithic paintings.

Religion

Knowledge about chalcolithic religion of this area was obtained from pottery, terracotta images and rock drawings. Ox, cow, bull were worshipped. From Uttanur and Kupagal heap of cow dung was obtained. Cow dung was burnt on the occasion of festivals and rituals. From Hallur site, a strange precious bowl was obtained. It had a hole in the bottom. This bowl was decorated from inside by thick dots. This bowl was probably of religious importance.

Agriculture and Animal Husbandry

It appears that south Indian neolithic-chalcolithic people were agriculturists and cattle rearers. They were cattle herders too. They were fully aware of domestication of cow, sheep and goat. They had big group of cattle. They used to herd them. Cow dung and ash mound available nearly their residences revealed these facts of cattle herding. Domesticated animals played significant role in their life. They used to cultivate *Ragi* and *Hulgi*. *Hulgi* was indigenous, but *Ragi* was brought from Africa. This area had contact through sea route.

Burial

Tekkalkota, Hallur, Piklihall, and other sites have shown evidences of burials. The study of burials reveals that adult dead individuals were buried in a special burial dug for this purpose. The dead body was kept in extended position in north-south direction. Some dead bodies were buried in east-west direction. Some grave materials were also placed in burials. They included lid, cup, plate, and stone blades. The potteries were coloured in ochre colour. Latter on, the tradition of burying adult in several jars had come into existence. All burial jars were of black and red colour. Children were buried just below the floor of house. Adults were buried away from residence. Children were buried in one or two jars. The jars were placed horizontally to each other. But in Brahmagiri and Nevasa jars were placed one above the other in vertical position.

Chalcolithic Culture of Ganges Doab

The Ganges valley was fertile and full of forests due to heavy rains in these areas. Bahadarabad, Wadgaon, Ambakheri, Ahichhatra, Ataranjikhera, Alam, Girpur, Hastinapur and Noh sites, one gets knowledge about chalcolithic culture of Ganges Doab. The characteristic features of this culture were ochre wares which were the earliest ware of chalcolithic period. Copper hoarding was an integral part of ochre ware.

Habitat

From the excavation of sites located in Ganges Doab, ochre colour pottery have come into existence. But no habitational surface has appeared. From Ambakheri evidences of a brick furnace and a hearth were obtained. The antiquity of the region reveals that these regions remained flooded and water remained stored for a long period. That is why this culture met to an end here. Thereafter, inhabitants of black and red ware and grey ware came and settled there. A number of evidences of floor surfaces and postholes were obtained. These evidences tell us about the type of houses in which the chalcolithic people used to live. The houses were round, square shaped and triangular shaped. The floors of houses were made. The roofs of the houses were supported with wooden poles, beams and bamboos. The houses were divided into two rooms with bamboo band. One room acted as kitchen.

Pottery

The excavation of chalcolithic sites located in Ganges Doab had brought before us three types of wares: (i) Ochre colour ware, (ii) black and red ware, and (iii) painted grey colour ware.

The name ochre colour ware was given accidentally to those potteries which had remained in water and showed a band. In fact they were red colour pottery. These wares were obtained for the first time by B.B. Lal from Bisauli site in Bandayu district and Rajpur site in Bijnaur district. This was also obtained from the lower layer of Hastinapur. Such potteries were also obtained from Bahadarabad site along with copper holding. Ambakheri and Badgaon of Saharanpur district, Ataranjikhera of Etawa district, Ahichhatrapur of Bardi district and Noh near Bharatpur had also revealed such types of potteries. The region ochre colour ware had an extent of Bahadarabad to Noh, i.e., 300 km from north to south and from Katpalan near Jalandhar to Ahichhatra, i.e. 450 km west to east.

Ochre colour wares were individualistic in type and design. They included bowl, jars, cup on handle and stand and lid with haft. Pierced triangular, notch, wavy lines, rectangular lines were found in parallel lines of pottery. The types and designs of these pots showed contact with pots of Harappa culture. No such design was found from any other pierced sites of ochre ware. The pots of Atranjikhera also had presented pierced design. From the Nal site ochre ware like piece of a pot was found which had revealed pierced decoration.

It is believed that the people with ochre ware were the originator of copper hoard culture in Ganges Doab. No definite and positive evidence was found from the point of view of stratification. From the Bisauli and Rajpur Parsa copper hoard culture site, no copper object was found along with ochre grey ware. In a controlled excavation near Badgaon evidences showing relation between copper hoard and ochre ware was found. But no such evidential relation was found from Bahadarabad site. A copper ring was found from Badgaon. Saipai site has also yielded relation between copper culture and grey ware culture. Copper harpoon was found from here. From Chaksu site in Jaipur district of Rajasthan existence of 6 copper axes was found.

The Problem of Copper Hoard

The scholars interested in the study of copper hoard culture are still in confusion as to who were the creator of copper hoard culture in this region. It was because the copper hoard was unstratified and copper objects did not show any relation between other objects. Besides Uttar Pradesh, copper hoard was found from Bihar, Madhya Pradesh, Orissa and Rajasthan. The copper objects from these places may be divided into following 8 types: broad axe, shouldered axe, sharp edge axe, ring, harpoon, spear head, antenna sword and human image.

From the northern plateau area of Bihar simple type broad axe and sharp edge axe were found from the copper hoard culture. From the Ganges Doab of Uttar Pradesh, three copper objects were found. They were harpoon, human figure, sword with antena. Thus, the regional classification of copper hold seems justified.

Black and Red Ware

Besides grey ware, black and red wares were also obtained. Black and red wares were found from

Ataranjikhera, Noh and Alamgirpur sites. Such types of wares were also obtained from eastern Uttar Pradesh. These sites were Kosambi, Sravasti, Prahladpur, Raighat, Masao, and Sohgaura. Limited wares were obtained from these sites, but they revealed permanent settled life in these region. The chalcolithic ware culture of western Uttar Pradesh showed relation with Ahar ware culture in type and structure. From Noh and Ataranjikhera sites, these wares were obtained from a different cultural layer. Here, they were obtained between ochre colour ware and painted black and red ware. The potteries related were thick black and red ware, black painted ware, and red ware. For example bowl, jars, plate, small pots and pitcher.

Eastern Chalcolithic Culture

The important sites related to eastern chalcolithic culture are Chirand, Sonpur, Vaishali, Maner, and Orium (in Bihar), Pandurajardhibi, Mahisdal, Narur, Haraipur and Thusirpur (West Bengal). The excavations of these sites have revealed significant informations regarding chalcolithic culture of eastern India. The chief feature of eastern chalcolithic culture is black and red ware.

House

The excavations of Chirand, Sonpur and Pandurajardhibi have yielded the evidences of floor, but not walls made of earth or bricks. This indicates that inhabitants of eastern chalcolithic culture used to erect houses with such materials which were decayed easily. They used to erect walls with torn bamboos and reed. They used to plaster reed and torn bamboo made walls with wet soil or mortar. The floors were made by mixing silt with soil. They also used to make floor with pebbles and stone pieces of the river. At last, the floor was plastered with lime to protect the house from insects. Nothing could be said with certainty about the roof. But it was certain that roof was made with the support of wood or bamboo poles. The house was divided into many rooms. One of rooms was kitchen. From all sites evidences of hearths were found essentially.

Pottery

The chief pottery of eastern chalcolithic culture were black and red ware. The early ceramic of Chirand was dated as 1700 B.C. by C^{-14} method. Such type of ceramic industries were also found from Sonpur, Vaishali, Maner and Antichak in Bihar. These wares were in existence for a very long period. Long neck pitcher, jars, bowls, small bowls, cup, disc, plate, lid and basin were the chief pots of this ceramic industry. Pieces of these wares were also found. These were the features of Bihar chalcolithic culture.

The inhabitants of chalcolithic Bengal used three types of pottery. They were known as black and red ware, bright red ware and chocolate band ware. These wares were painted in cream, white, grey and black colour. No animal or human design was made on pots. The various types of pots were bowls, small bowls, cup, plate, tubular bowls, stand, storage jars and lids.

Agriculture

From the study of excavations of all sties of this region, it appears that eastern chalcolithic culture inhabitants used to do cultivation. Agriculture was main means of their stay. On pots there were signs of paddy husk. These signs on pots reveal that agriculture was practiced by chalcolithic people. Along with paddy wheat was also cultivated. Along with hunting and gathering tools, good number of animal and fish bones were found. This reveals that people were non-vegetarian. They used copper, bronze and stone implements for hunting purposes. They used to do fishing too. Bone harpoons were found in good number. Some bronze harpoons were also found.

Ornaments

The inhabitants of chalcolithic people of this area were very fond of ornaments. Ornaments of semi-precious stones were obtained from all sites. Ornaments were prepared from carnelian, agate, chalcedony, quartz and crystal made beads, Stealite, fence and copper beads were scarce. Different types of chains were prepared from the beads. Rings were made from copper wire. In Mahisadal combs of bone were made. Some copper made individual tools were also obtained. For example, eye colouring pencil. Some terracotta beads were used as spinning wheel. This shows that people knew preparing clothes. The number of copper tools was less and the number of stone tools were more and more. Copper bangles and rings were also found.

Terracotta Images

Terracotta images obtained from all sites were divided into two categories — Human image and animal image. One dancing male image was found from Pandurajardhibi. A female image was also obtained whose breast was clear. Among animal images, hunch-backed bull images were very much popular. Animals were domesticated.

Tools

In chalcolithic eastern India, inhabitants knew to smelt copper from copper ore. They knew also to prepare tools from melted copper. Copper industries were in existence. From copper sheet, axe, tools, weapons, beads were made. Along with copper implements, stone tools were also used.

Trade

The inhabitants of eastern chalcolithic culture had trade relationship with inhabitants of contemporary chalcolithic cultures. Bullockcarts were used to carry man and goods. Terracotta made bullockcarts were found. The use of copper without trade was not possible. Four sided objects were also found. These objects hinted towards weights and measures. Probably, there was a system of barter exchange. Inhabitants used to buy copper objects, steatite and fiance from their surplus production of grains.

Religion

The inhabitants of chalcolithic culture used to believe in some kind of religion. After cremation ritual, bones and ash were buried in grave. Besides, big jars having bone pieces were also obtained. Such type of cremation site and burial site were obtained from Sonpur site. Primary and secondary death rituals were prevalent. The inhabitants with red and black wares used to cremate dead bodies. Grave materials were kept in graves along with dead persons. At the time of cremation, some materials were also kept along with dead. The grave materials included pots, weapons and food materials. This reveals that chalcolithic people believed in rebirth. Bulls were regarded as religious animal. Bulls were worshipped. Mother Goddess worship was also prevalent. Phallic worship was also in practice. They were associated with fertility cult. Figures painted on pots might be related to magical practices. Tubular bowls and three legged bowls indicated towards scme special rituals.

Chalcolithic Culture of Saurashtra

Pottery

The excavations of Lothal, Rangpur, Prabhaspatan, Somnath, Amra, Desalpar, and Rojade chalcolithic sites of Saurashtra reveal that inhabitants of chalcolithic culture had started making fire baked bricks in place of sun baked bricks. New kind of wares had also come into existence. They were bright red ware, black and red ware with white painting, and Prabhas ware. Three types of jars were found under bright red ware. They were (i) big bowls, (ii) small bowl, cup-plate, and (iii) pitcher. The walls of these wares were thin, and sizes were comparatively small. The bottom of bowls was ring based and body was semi-round. The edge of plate was tubular. Such types of bowls and plates occupied significant place. Some jars had high neck and edge was outwards. Besides, thick red wares and thick grey wares were also obtained. In these two types of wares, there were bowls, cups, plates, lamps, and jars. From Rangpur site pieces of pots with graffiti were found.

Agriculture and Animal Husbandry

The inhabitants of chalcolithic Saurashtra were agriculturists and cattle herder. Grains were crushed on stone ground with pestle. These stone implements were found in each house. They used to cultivate paddy, millet, wheat and cotton. They made threads and finally clothes from cotton. Spinning wheels of terracotta were found.

Harpoons and fish bones indicated that fishing was practiced in chalcolithic Saurashtra. Cow, ox, pig, sheep and goat were domesticated. Their bone remains and terracotta images were found. Probably, they used to domesticate ass, horse and elephant. People were aware of deer, tiger, leopard, lion and rhiroceros. They were also aware of duck.

Tools and Weapons

The chalcolithic inhabitants of Saurashtra used to make tools and weapons with copper, bronze and stone. Metal made axes, pins, blades and knife were found from almost all chalcolithic sites of Saurashtra. In stone tools, chert made long parallel sided blades and knife were found from everywhere.

Ornament

The chalcolithic inhabitants of Saurashtra used to make beads of copper terracotta and semi-precious stones. From beads, they used to make different kinds of chains. They used to make ornaments of gold too. Ornaments were worn in ear, neck and hands. The goldsmiths used to do the work of embroidery.

Art

The chalcolithic inhabitants were well versed in the art of terracotta images, painting, drawing and ornament making. They were expert in decorating pottery and making ornaments of various types. They used to decorate their houses with natural, pictorial and geometric designs.

Religion

In a round circle plastered with mortar or lime, pieces of pots and ash were found. This hints towards a family fire worship.

Graffiti Signs

In pieces of 20 pots found from excavation of Rangpur graffiti signs were found. Graffiti sings reveal man, animal, bird signs, linear sign and combination of several linear signs.

Origin of Chalcolithic Culture in India

How chalcolithic culture originated in India? Who were builders of this culture in India? The answer of these questions has not been given satisfactorily till date. There is no written evidence available to us in this regard. In building this culture some special elements have emerged. Some foreign elements are clearly visible. These foreign elements were adapted with local elements. The adaptation of foreign elements with local elements gave rise to different types of local chalcolithic cultures in different regions. Different prehistoric archaeological anthropologists have propounded different theories for the origin of chalcolithic culture in India. These theories are as follows:

- Influence of western Asia theory
- Pottery types and designs theory
- Blade industry theory
- Copper objects theory
- Beads theory
- Grain production theory
- Harappa culture theory
- Aryan theory
- Pre-Aryan theory
- Ancestors of primitive tribe theory
- Anthropological evidence theory.

Influence of Western Asia Theory

Some scholars are of opinion that Indian chalcolithic culture was influenced by western Asia. In the first quarter of second millennium B.C. attack of Indo-European tribes had taken place. Due to this attack Western Asian civilization was broken. As a result, folk revolution had taken place. As a result of folk revolution people migrated towards east. Culturally, the chalcolithic culture of Iran and Western Asia was very rich. It was also ancient and extensive. In this period, new types of tool, weapon and wares had come into existence. These development show clearly that Indian chalcolithic culture was influenced by Iranian and Western Asia chalcolithic culture.

Pottery Types and Designs Theory

Some scholars are of opinion that Indian ceramic industry was influenced by Iranian ceramic industry. Indian ceramic industries show impact of Iranian ceramic industries in colour, type, designs, structure and graffiti. From this, it can be concluded that Indian chalcolithic culture had contacts with Iranian and Egyptian chalcolithic culture.

Blade Industry Theory

Some scholars are of opinion that Indian chalcolithic stone blade industries were also influenced by Iranian chalcolithic blade industries. This technique would have reached to India from western Asia *via* Iran.

Copper Objects Theory

From Indian chalcolithic sites very few copper objects were found. For India copper was a scarce object. The scarcity of copper in northern India plain shows that copper industries would have not been indigenous.

Beads Theory

Beads available from excavations of different chalcolithic sites in India also show relation with Western Asia and Indus valley civilization. Terracotta beads and spinning wheels are also influenced by Western Asia and Iran.

Grain Cultivation Theory

Grains cultivated during Indian chalcolithic period also show influence of Western Asia. Wheat, *moong*, *masur* and *tisi* reveal Western Asia contact. But paddy-rice indicates indigenous impact. The south Indian inhabitants used to cultivate *ragi*, which was brought to India from Africa through sea route.

Above propounded all theories have been subjected to criticism. Some scholars are of opinion that Indian chalcolithic culture had emerged independently. It was not influenced by Iran and Western Asia.

Origin from Harappa Culture

Some scholars are of opinion that chalcolithic culture emerged in India from Harappa culture. After downfall of Indus valley civilization people would have migrated to Ganga-Yamuna Doab, Saurashtra, Malwa and Banas valley. They would have erected their houses on the bank of river. The ceramic industry of Harappa culture and ceramic industries of chalcolithic culture shows similarity to a great extent in type, construction, colour and design. But no evidence dealing with direct relation between Harappa culture and chalcolithic culture was obtained. Harappa culture was urban, but chalcolithic culture was rural.

Aryan Theory

Indian chalcolithic culture is limited to only 1750 B.C. – 1000 B.C. Some scholars are of opinion that Aryans came to India in two streams. One in 1750 B.C. and another in 1000 B.C. Thus, chalcolithic culture was influenced by the emergence of Aryans.

Pre-Aryan Theory

Some scholars are of opinion that if chalcolithic culture in India was not related to Aryan, this was certainly related to pre-Aryans.

Ancestors of Some Primitive Tribes

Some scholars are of opinion that originator of chalcolithic culture in India were ancestors of primitive tribes whose descendants are still found in hilly and forested area.

Anthropological Evidence

On the basis of anthropological evidences obtained from Nevasa, it can be said that in Indian chalcolithic culture indigenous traits were present. The study of limited skeletons reveals that there was preponderance of indigenous australoid traits in chalcolithic culture of India.

Above presented all theories regarding the builders of Indian chalcolithic cultures are based on only assumptions. Nothing could be concluded with certainty.

14

Indian Iron Age Culture (1,100 B.C. – 600 B.C.)

The production of iron and expertise in iron tool making was really a significant stage in history of technological development of mankind. After achieving expertise in fashioning copper and bronze tools, mankind moved towards the expertise of making iron tools. When mankind began to extract iron from iron ore and started making iron tools, Iron age began in the history of mankind. Indian Iron age culture has been dated as 1,100 B.C. – 600 B.C. The role of iron was not same everywhere.

In India Iron age was related to Painted grey ware culture, black and red ware culture and megalithic culture. Hence, here Indian iron age culture is being described under three sub-headings which are as follows:

- Painted Grey ware culture related Iron age.
- Black and Red ware culture related Iron age.
- Megalithic Culture related Iron age.

Painted Grey Ware Culture Related Iron Age

In the excavations of northern Indian sites, iron objects were found with painted grey wares. The most significant site in this regard is Ataranjikhera. From this site, the earliest date of iron objects along with painted grey ware was available as 1025 ± 1100 B.C. From this site, iron tools were found from every layers. This bears testimony that the use of iron tool was started along with painted grey wares. From this site iron tools like adze, dagger, spade, arrow head, spearhead, harpoon and forceps were found.

The excavation of Noh site has also revealed a comparable sequence like Ataranjikhera. Iron objects along with painted grey ware were found from early layers here. The iron tools were arrow head, spearhead, and leaf size point with shocket. The size of iron tools obtained from Ataranjikhera was medium. Their shape was like iron tools found from Vairat. From Vairat iron metal filth was found in good amount. This shows that iron industry was in existence here.

Hastinapur, Alamgirpur, Kaushambi and Ujjain site have also yielded iron tools along with painted grey wares. The remains of iron filth was also obtained from Hastinapur. This indicates towards the existence of iron industry at Hastinapur. From Alamgirpur site, iron tools were found from upper layer of the painted grey ware. The iron tools obtained were spearhead, arrowhead, nail, and pin. From Kaushambi site small shapeless iron objects were found. From the Ujjain site, spearhead, arrowhead, and knife like iron tools were found.

Black and Red Ware Related Iron Age

The sites like Eran, Prakash, Bahal and Nagada have revealed iron objects along with black and red ware. Altogether 59 iron objects were found related to black and red ware culture. Among those iron objects there were two edge daggers, gradually tapering pins, wide edge axes, a ring, arrowhead, a point, spearheads, knife blades and sickles. The existence of these iron tools reveals clearly that the use of iron objects was established here.

Iron made objects were also obtained from a site Prakash in Maharashtra. The iron objects were pointed arrow head, axe, knife, blade, piece of sickle, nail, and clamp. The Bakal site has also revealed the same kind of iron tools. The Eran site in Sagar district of Madhya Pradesh has also presented iron tools along with black and while ware.

Besides above mentioned sites, sites like Nagpal in Baroch district of Gujarat, Chirand in the then Saran district of Bihar, Mahishdal in Birbhum district of West Bengal, Sohagaura in Gorakhpur district of Uttar Pradesh and Rajghat in Varanasi district of Uttar Pradesh have revealed iron tools along with black and red ware culture.

The site Kaushambi has revealed painted grey ware culture and black and red ware culture together. In Mahishdal chalcolithic culture was isolated with white painted black and red ware. Here iron tools appeared in different forms such as arrowhead, spearhead, chisel, nail, iron ore and iron filth. The Chirand site of Bihar has revealed socketed spade, with black and red ware. The deposit was found here from the three upper layers. The Sonepur site in Gaya district of Bihar, iron filth remains were obtained from the upper surface of black and red ware culture. The Rajghat site of Varanasi has also revealed iron objects with black and red ware culture.

Iron Age Related to Megalithic Culture

Before the advent of Megalithic culture in south India, the use of iron was started. In the Hallur site iron age was started in 1105 B.C. The scholars are of opinion that here the use of iron was initiated through sea route. Again the use of iron was introduced in north India through south India. It is also possible that iron objects came to north India for the first time and from north India they spread to south India. At Hallur site it was related to black and red ware. From here, horse bones associated with iron objects were found soon after the layer of chalcolithic culture. Such type of remains were also found from Madurai site.

The full development of early iron age culture is closely related to burial complex. This reminds us towards our ancestors. It has religious value. South Indian megalithic culture presents before us various complex form. This includes circle of stone, and ash jar burial in the middle of stone circle, legged earthen coffin, stone burial with an arched gateway, serially arranged stone burial and burial cut in rock. Iron objects were found as grave material of every sites. Iron objects related to burial materials were wide axe, sickle, spade, chisel, nail, knife, tripod, lamp, pendant, horse materials, dagger and sword. With these iron objects needs related to war, hunting, agriculture, and domestic uses were fulfilled. These objects show uniformity in cultural life. This type of cultural life was followed by the organized community making iron tools. With these objects they had served the pastoral and agricultural community.

Among the famous Megalithic sites of south India, sites like Brahmagiri in Chitaldurg district of Karnataka, Nagarjuna Konda in Guntur district of Andhra Pradesh, Maski under Raipur district, Yelleswaram in Nalkonda district, Pochampad near Adilabad district, T. Narsipur in Mysore district of Karnataka, Hallur in Dharwad district, Sangankallu in Bellary district, Chingleput in Kannatur district in Tamil Nadu, Paiyampalli in North Arcot district occupy prominent place.

Megalithic Culture of South India

In south India after primitive neolithic and chalcolithic culture, megalithic culture had come into existence. This culture showed a quite different stage. The author of primitive neolithic and chalcolithic cultures were related to proto-australid race, whereas the author of megalithic culture belonged to Brachycephalic race. The megalithic people used Dravidian language. The inhabitants with this culture had full knowledge related to iron and iron tool making. They used to get iron from rich iron mines of Mysore, Hyderabad and Chennai. They used to make different kinds of iron tools. The iron tools made by them were spearhead, trident, arrowhead, axe, and chisel. In this culture, there was existence of iron industries. Besides iron, they used gold, silver, copper and bronze at small level.

In megalithic culture, big size stone slabs were used for making a grave. It also throws light on technological development. Stone slabs available in neighbouring surroundings were used frequently, but rocks were shaped according to a desire with the help of chisel and hammer. The services of stone cutters were hired for this purpose. The big stone slabs were brought to the grave site. For this purpose social organization was needed. This was possible only by organized effort. The stone slabs were brought up to grave side by rolling method employing wooden pillars and bamboo.

In this culture houses were erected with wooden pillars and beams. That is why they had made iron tools like axe, adze, and chisel.

The megalithic people were agriculturists and cattle herders. They used to make grave away from their house and agricultural fields. Rice was their main food. They used to domesticate sheep, goat and hens. They used to hunt tiger and hyena to protect their domestic animals. They used to domesticate ox for tilling land and cow for getting milk and calves. They used to domesticate horses for transportation and vehicle.

The another significant industry of megalithic culture was pottery. Black and red ware were characteristic features of this culture. Pottery were of different types and sizes. Pots were decorated, too. For burial jars and ash jars, big thick and undecorated pitchers were made. They were red like sand. The lids were prepared of the same size. Earthen coffins were also made. It was divided into two parts — the lower part and upper part. The lower part was main pot and the upper part was lid. Ash jars or burial jars or earthen coffins were made with the help of hand. Good number of earthen jars along with megalithic culture were found. It appears that food and drink were offered in the name of souls of dead persons so that the soul could make its endless journey. In ash jars, burial jars, or earthen coffins, a hole was found in east direction. The appearance of hole in east direction of these jars was significant religiously. This hole was made probably to allow the soul to come out of burial or grave. It was also related to another birth of a soul. Being located in east direction, it was probably related to sun worship.

APPENDICES

Appendix A: **Diagrams Showing River Site Sections**

Appendix B: **Maps Showing Cultural Sties**

Appendix C: **Figures of Tools, Potteries, House Types and Urban Centres**

Diagrams Showing River Site Sections

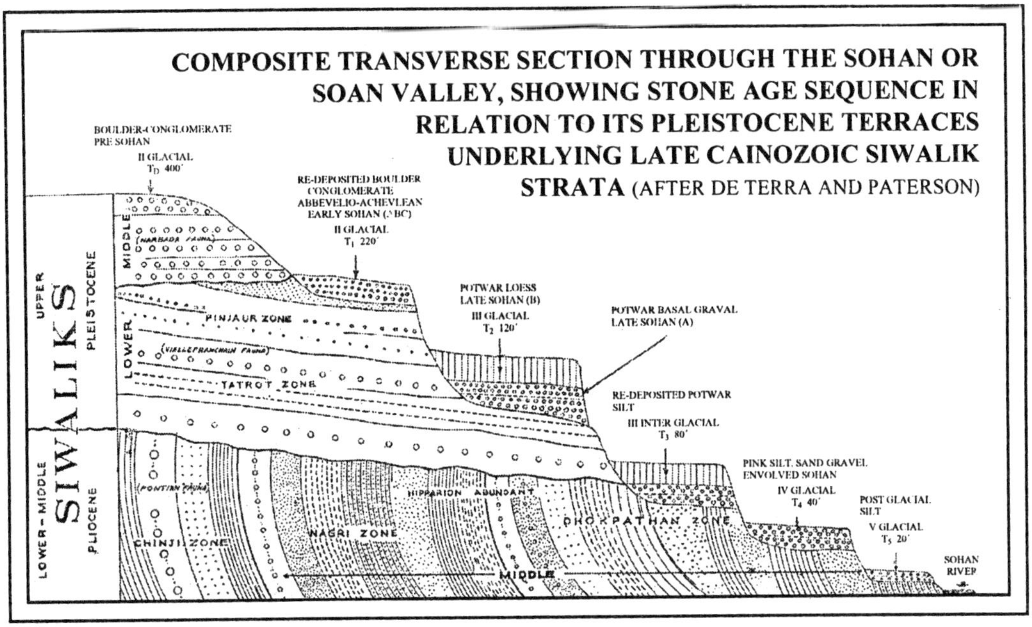

Source: H.D. Sankalia, 1974, *Prehistory and Protohistory of India and Pakistan.*

DIAGRAM 1: Transverse Section of Sohan/Soan Valley

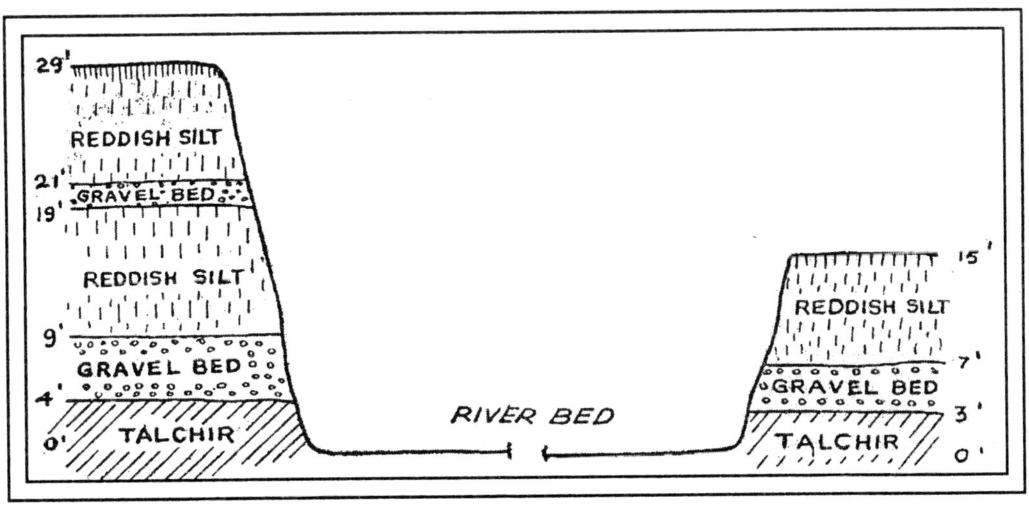

Source: H.D. Sankalia, 1974, *Prehistory and Protohistory of India and Pakistan.*

DIAGRAM 2: Section of Rihand River Midway between Kota and Pipri

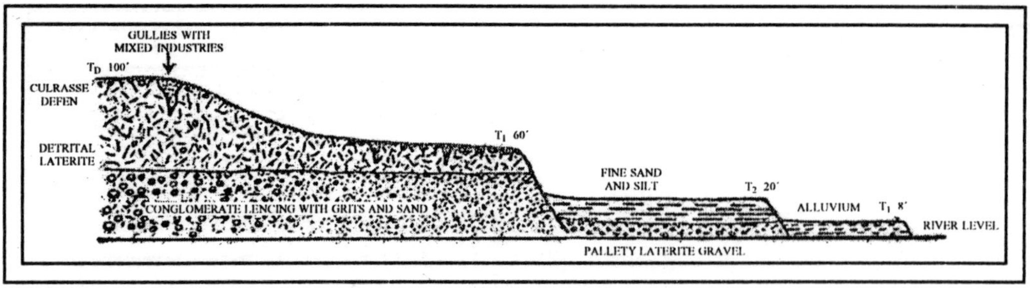

Source: H.D. Sankalia, 1974, *Prehistory and Protohistory of India and Pakistan.*

DIAGRAM 3: Terrace Sequence on the Kortalayer River, Near Madras

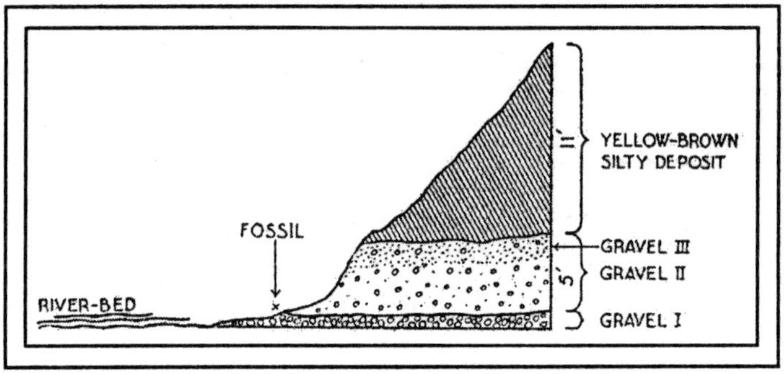

Source: H.D. Sankalia, 1974, *Prehistory and Protohistory of India and Pakistan.*

DIAGRAM 4: Section Along the Right Bank of Pravara Facing North

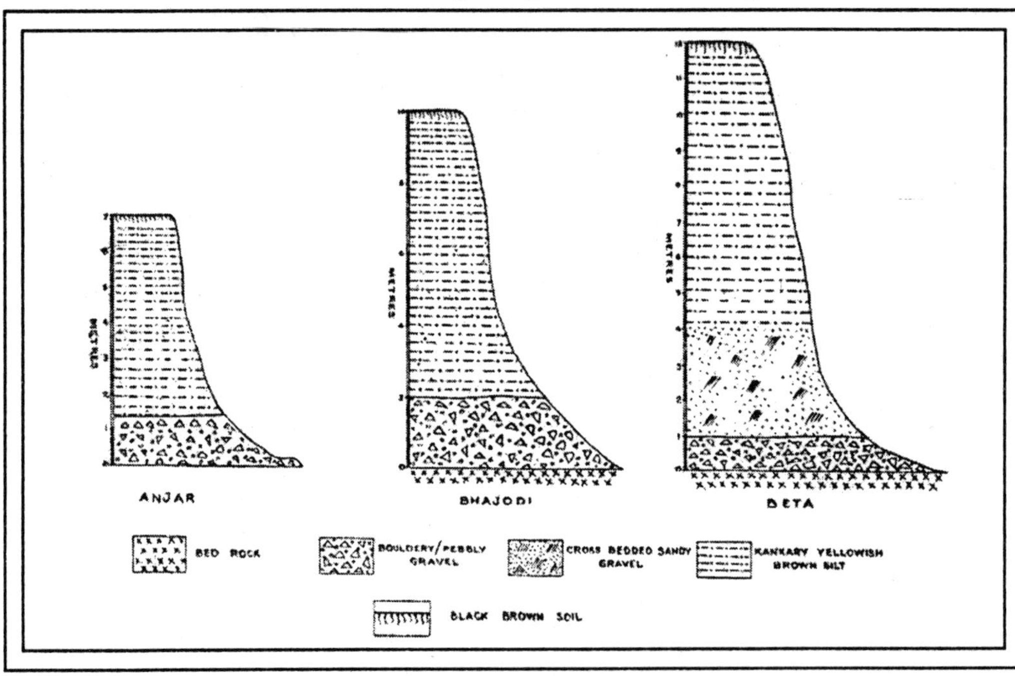

Source: H.D. Sankalia, 1974, *Prehistory and Protohistory of India and Pakistan.*

DIAGRAM 5: River Section from Kutch (Gujarat)

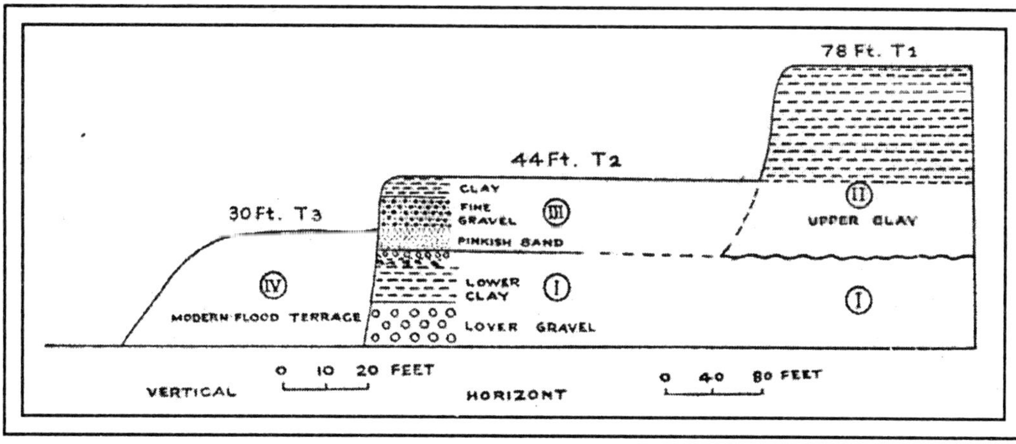

Source: H.D. Sankalia, 1974, *Prehistory and Protohistory of India and Pakistan.*

DIAGRAM 6: Section Across the River Narmada Opposite Sahasradhara

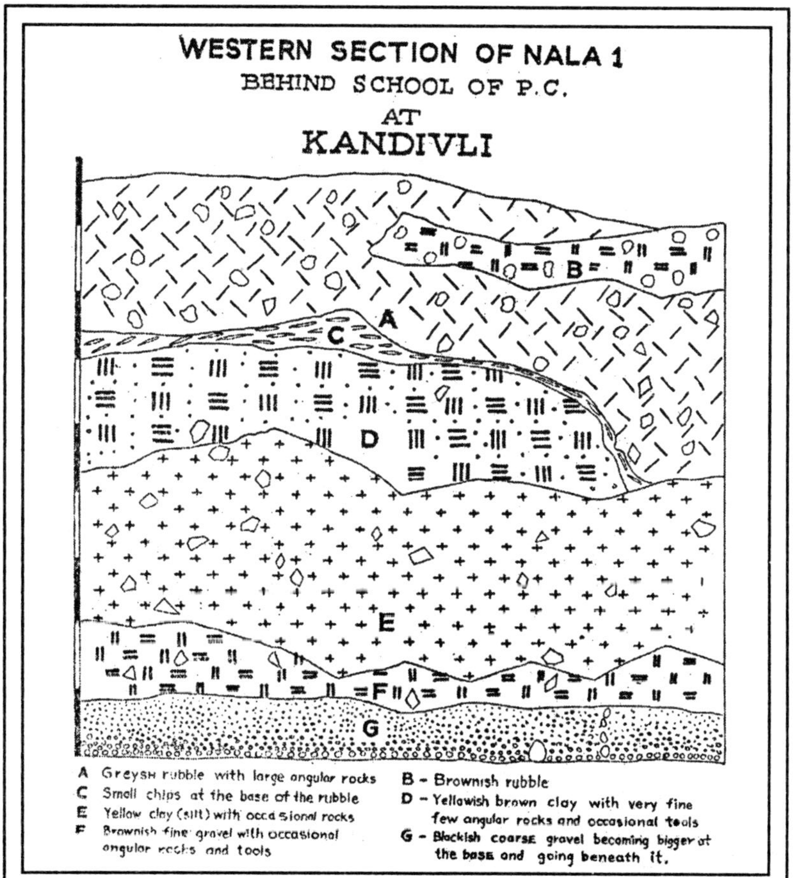

Source: H.D. Sankalia, 1974, *Prehistory and Protohistory of India and Pakistan.*

DIAGRAM 7: Western Section of Nala-1 Behind School of P.C. at Kandivli

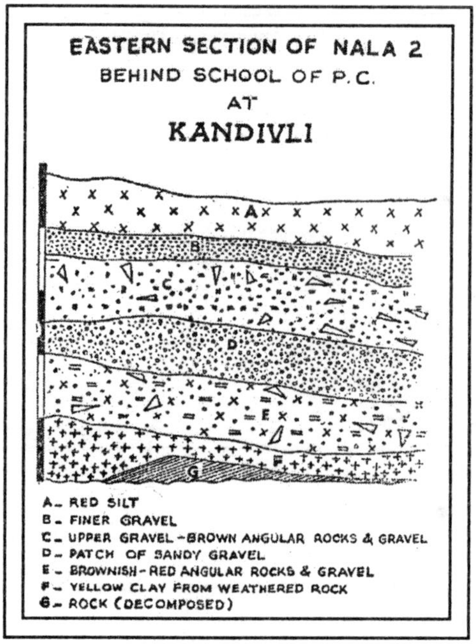

Source: H.D. Sankalia, 1974, *Prehistory and Protohistory of India and Pakistan.*

DIAGRAM 8: Eastern Section of Nala-2 Behind School of P.C. at Kandivli

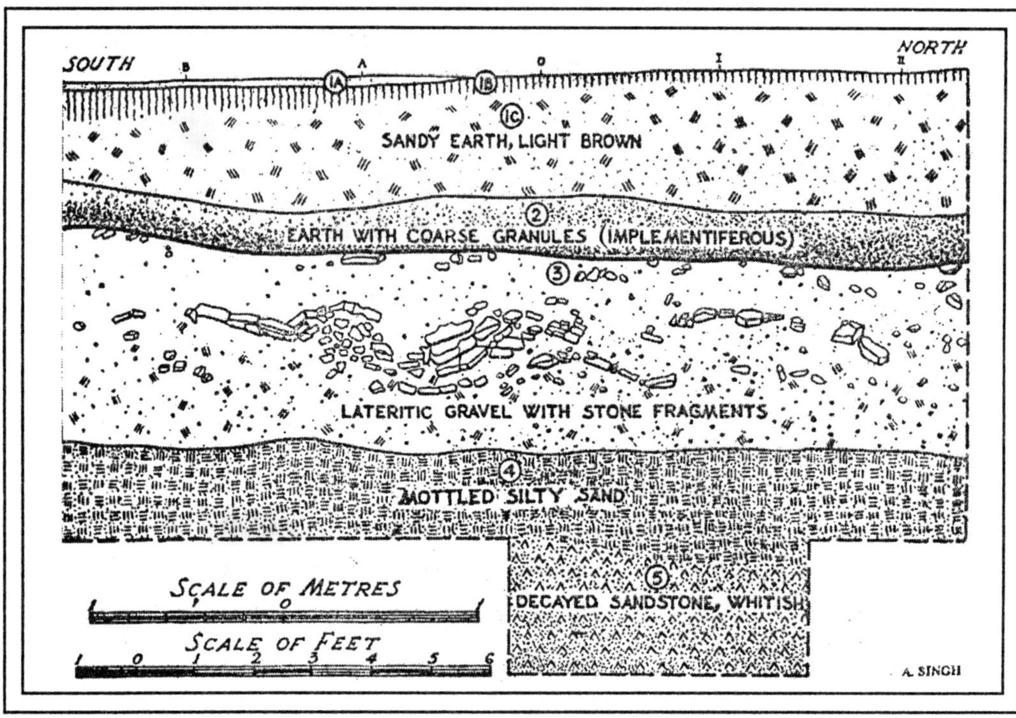

Source: H.D. Sankalia, 1974, *Prehistory and Protohistory of India and Pakistan.*

DIAGRAM 9: Section of Trench BBP-1, Birbhanpur, 1957

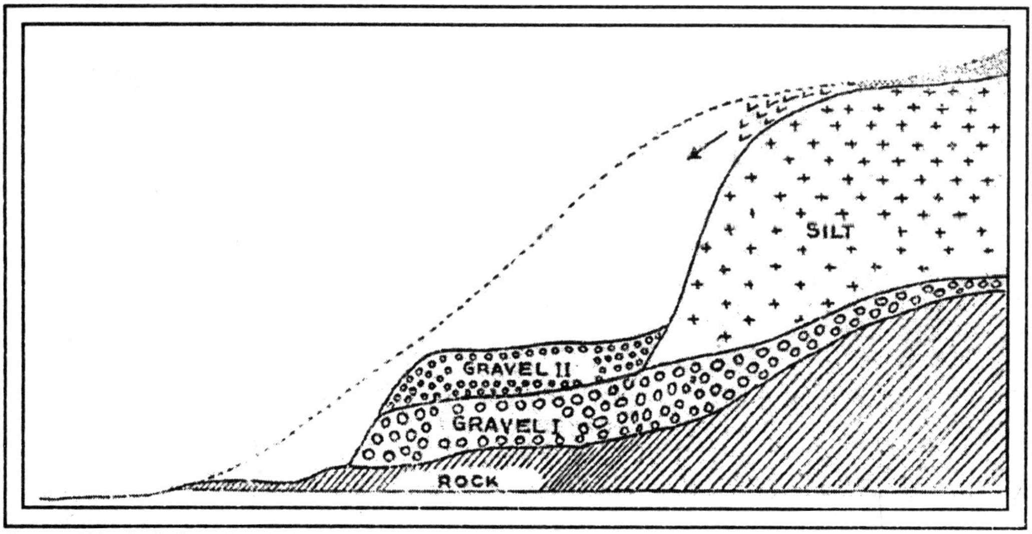

Source: H.D. Sankalia, 1974, *Prehistory and Protohistory of India and Pakistan.*

DIAGRAM 10: Section on the Pravara at Hathi Well Site, Near Nevasa, Maharashtra (suggested reconstruction)

Maps Showing Cultural Sites

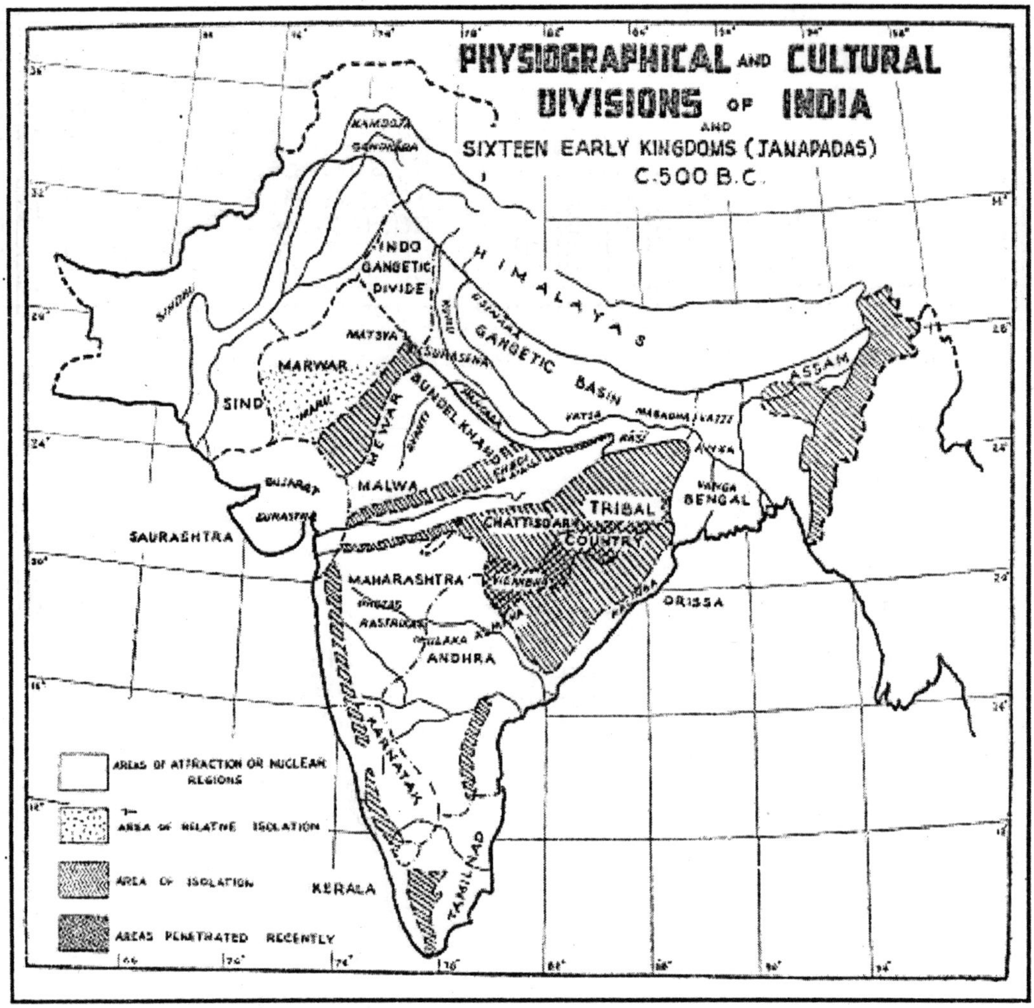

Source: H.D. Sankalia, 1974, *Prehistory and Protohistory of India and Pakistan.*

MAP 1: Early Historical Centres of Civilization and Physiographical and Cultural Divisions of India and Sixteen Early Kingdoms (Janapadas)

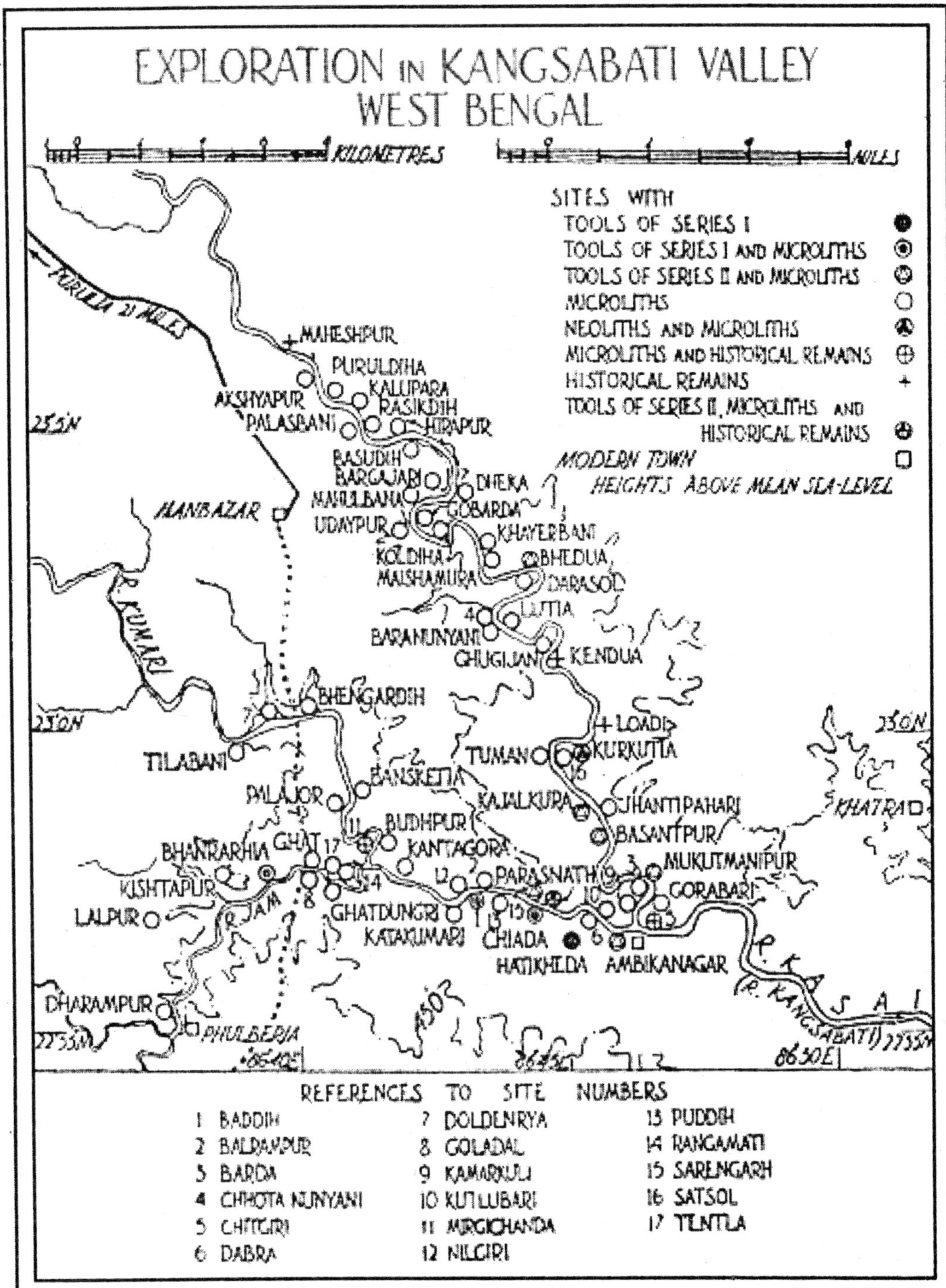

Source: H.D. Sankalia, 1974, *Prehistory and Protohistory of India and Pakistan.*

MAP 2: Exploration in Kangsabati Valley, West Bengal

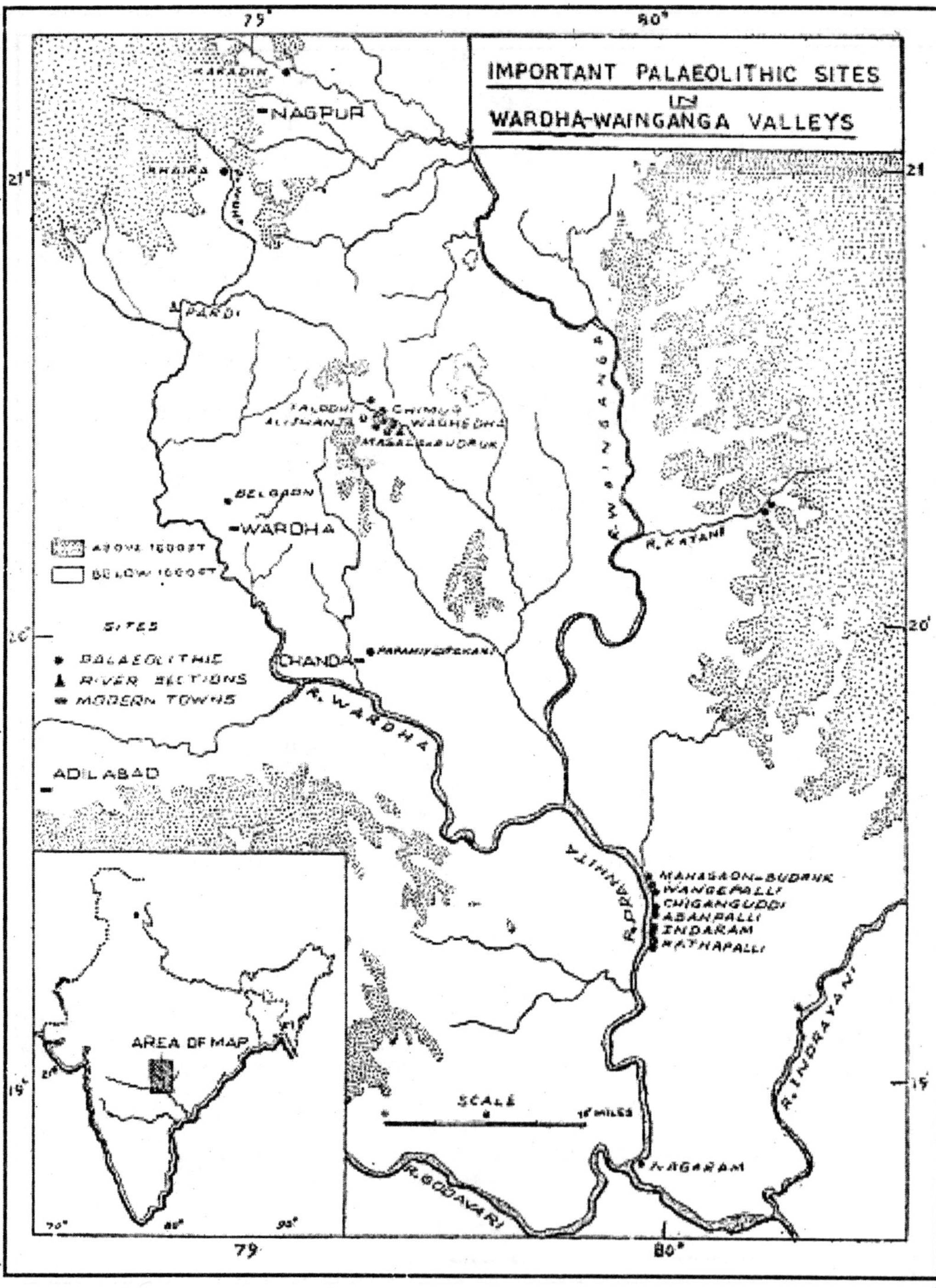

Source: H.D. Sankalia, 1974, *Prehistory and Protohistory of India and Pakistan.*

MAP 3: Palaeolithic Sites in Wardha-Wainganga Valleys

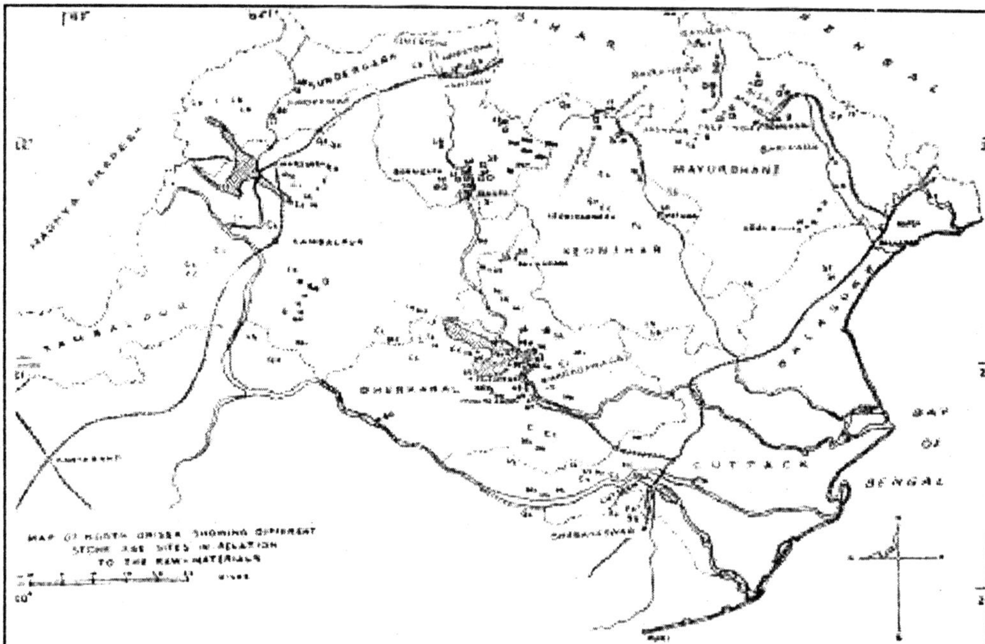

IMPORTANT MINERAL
& RAW MATERIAL INDEX

B	BERYL
C_C	CHINA CLAYS
F_C	FIRE CLAYS
P_S	POTTERY CLAYS
	COAL FIELDS
C_P	COPPER
F	FELSPAR (MICA BELT)
G_L	GLASS SAND
I_R	IRON ORE
L_S	LIME STONE
M_I	MICA
M_n	MANGANESE
M_P	MINERAL PIGMENTS
Q_S	ORNAMENTAL STONE
Q_Z	QUARTZITE
Q	QUARTZ CRYSTALS
R_Q	ROSE QUARTZ
S_L	SLATE
S_S	SAND STONE
S_T	STEALITE

SITE INDEX

SITES WITH EARLIER STONE AGE TOOLS
SITES WITH MIDDLE STONE AGE TOOLS
SITES WITH LATER STONE AGE TOOLS
SITES WITH POLISHED STONE CELTS

1.	BANALDA	18.	RAMLA	35.	SAMAL
2.	RAIRANCPUR	19.	UDAIPUR	36.	WARCHANDANPUR
3.	DADRA	20.	PATNA	37.	BHIMKAND
4.	DIJATAL	21.	JNIRPANI	38.	CHAKRASIL
5.	DISAI	22.	DISRA	39.	KANKILI
6.	MANDA	23.	BURHADI	40.	KULEI
7.	DORAIKA	24.	SATKUTA	41.	BHALITUNDI
8.	BARASOL	25.	BHANJGARH	42.	TALCHER
9.	DOMUMAN	26.	TUMKELAGHAT	43.	KHARAGPRASAD
10.	SIRSA	27.	BONAIGAR H.C.Q.	44.	MERAMANDALI Rly. Stn.
11.	RAHULIA	28.	BONAIGAR H.M.C.Q.	45.	KALIAKATA
12.	PRATAPPUR	29.	KHUNTAGAON	46.	PARANG
13.	CHANTASILA	30.	BHALUDUNORI	47.	HINDOL ROAD
14.	BANSPAL	31.	JAKORA	48.	JAGANNATHPUR
15.	MERDHAKHAI	32.	PALLANARA	49.	BISHALSURY
16.	OAGANNATHPOSH	33.	PALLAHARA (NETA)	50.	TIKARPARA
17.	CHAMPUA	34.	MUGNURICARIA		

Source: H.D. Sankalia, 1974, *Prehistory and Protohistory of India and Pakistan.*

MAP 4: Different Stone Age Sites in North Orissa in Relation to Raw Materials

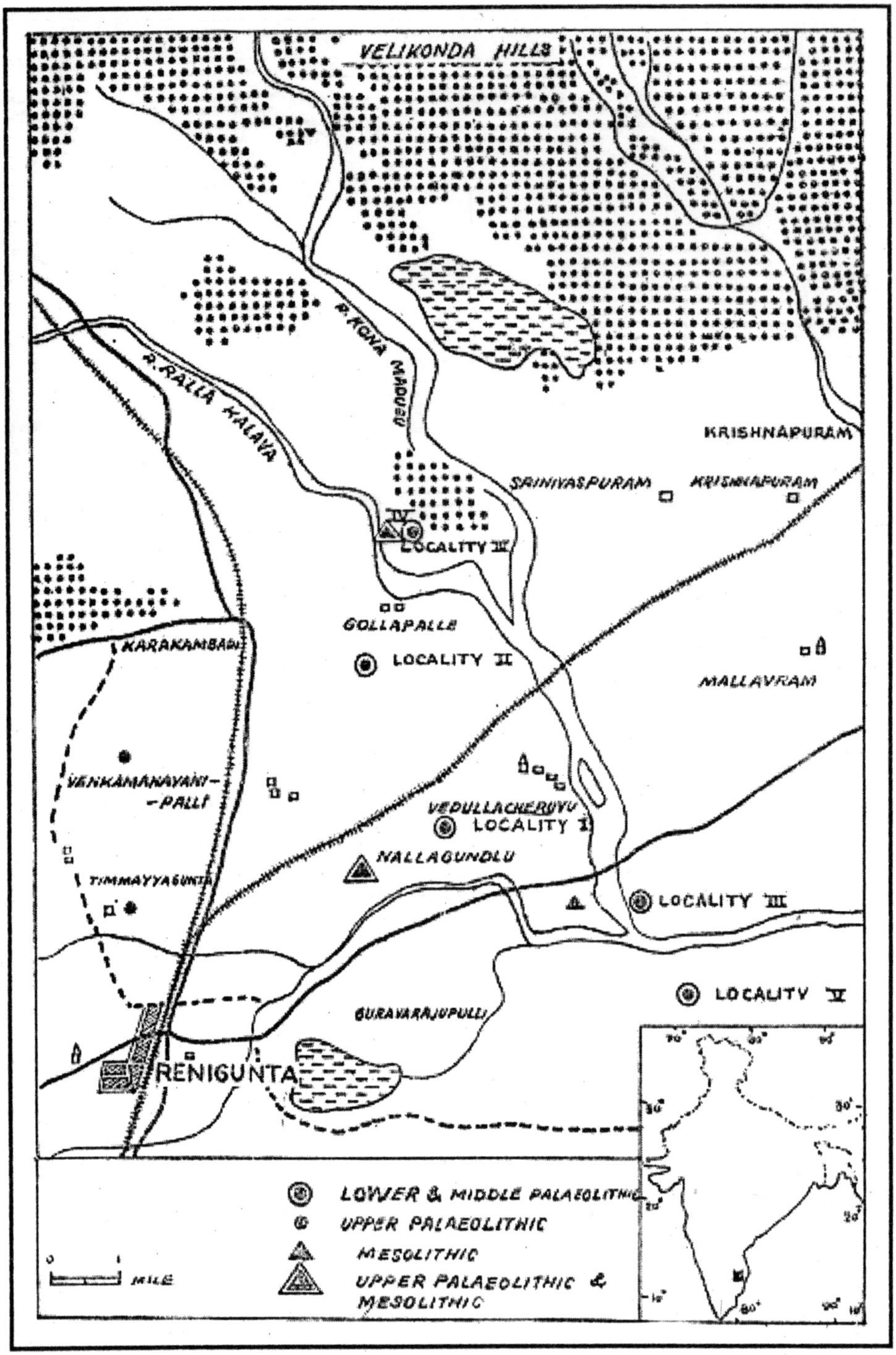

Source: H.D. Sankalia, 1974, *Prehistory and Protohistory of India and Pakistan*.

MAP 5: Tool Bearing Localities on the River Ralla Kalava Near Renigunta (District Chittoor, Andhra Pradesh)

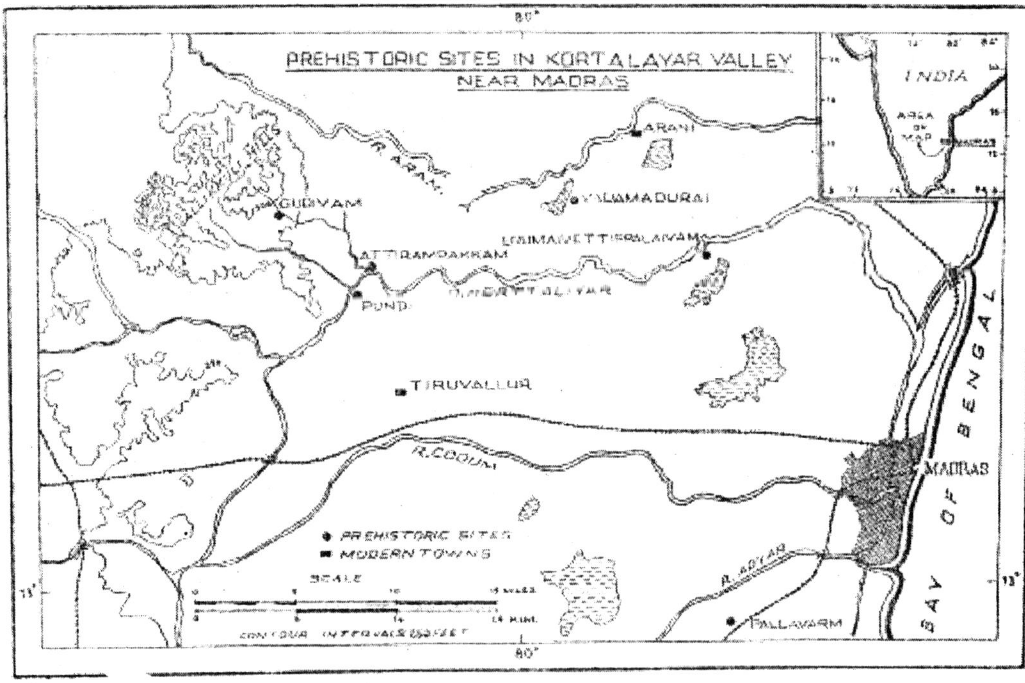

Source: H.D. Sankalia, 1974, *Prehistory and Protohistory of India and Pakistan.*

MAP 6: Prehistoric Sites in Kortalayer Valley Near Madras (Tamil Nadu)

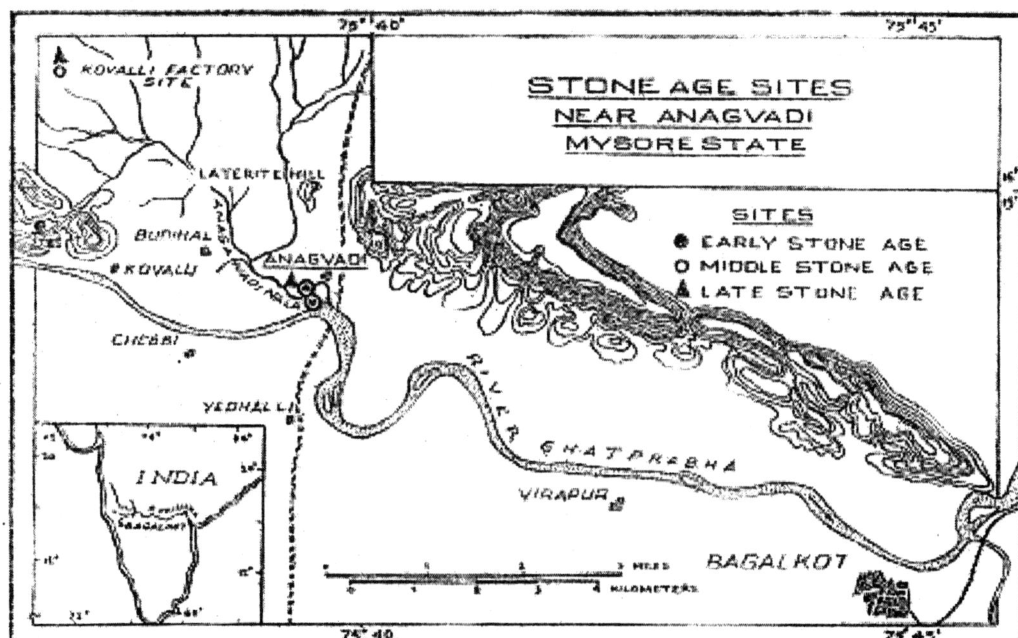

Source: H.D. Sankalia, 1974, *Prehistory and Protohistory of India and Pakistan.*

MAP 7: Stone Age Sites Near Anagvadi, Mysore (Karnataka)

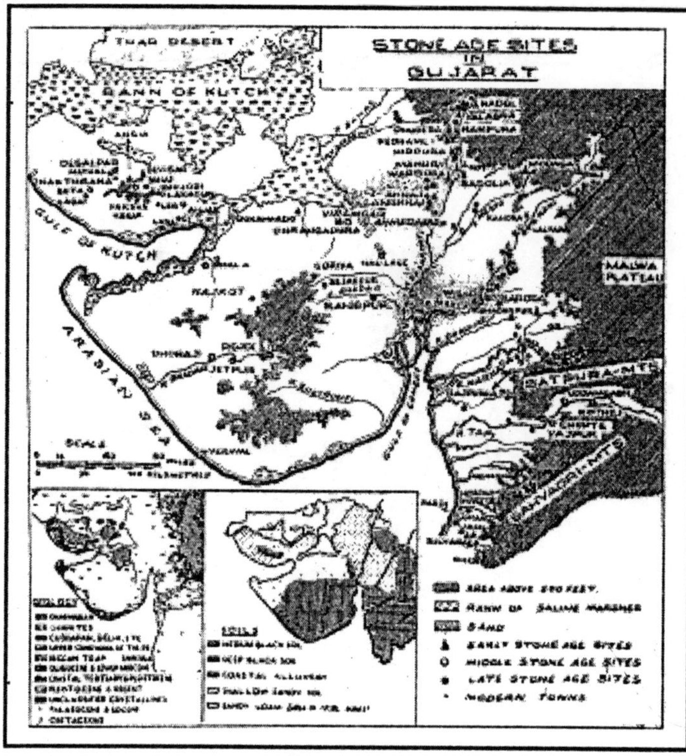

Source: H.D. Sankalia, 1974, *Prehistory and Protohistory of India and Pakistan.*

MAP 8: Stone Age Sites in Gujarat

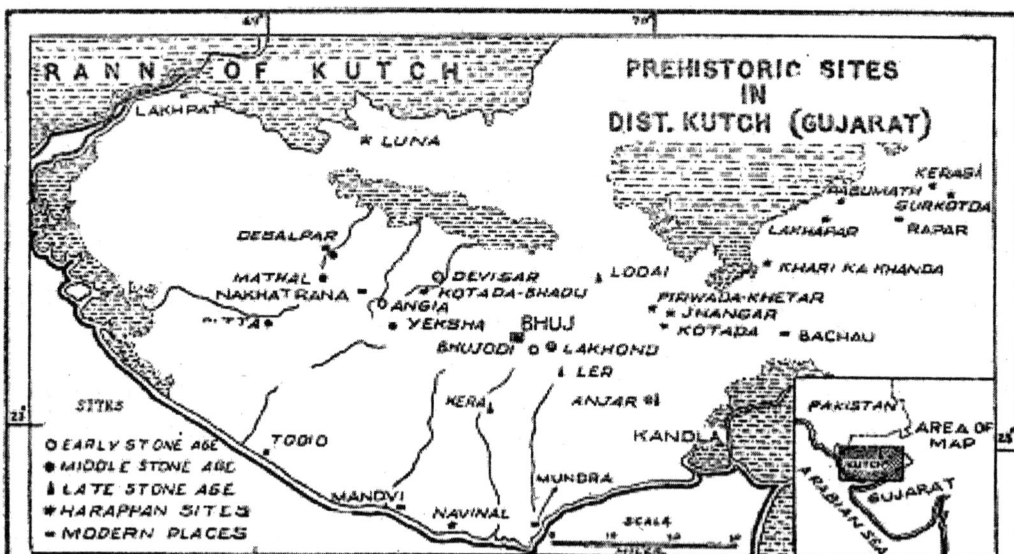

Source: H.D. Sankalia, 1974, *Prehistory and Protohistory of India and Pakistan.*

MAP 9: Prehistoric Sites in District Kutch (Gujarat)

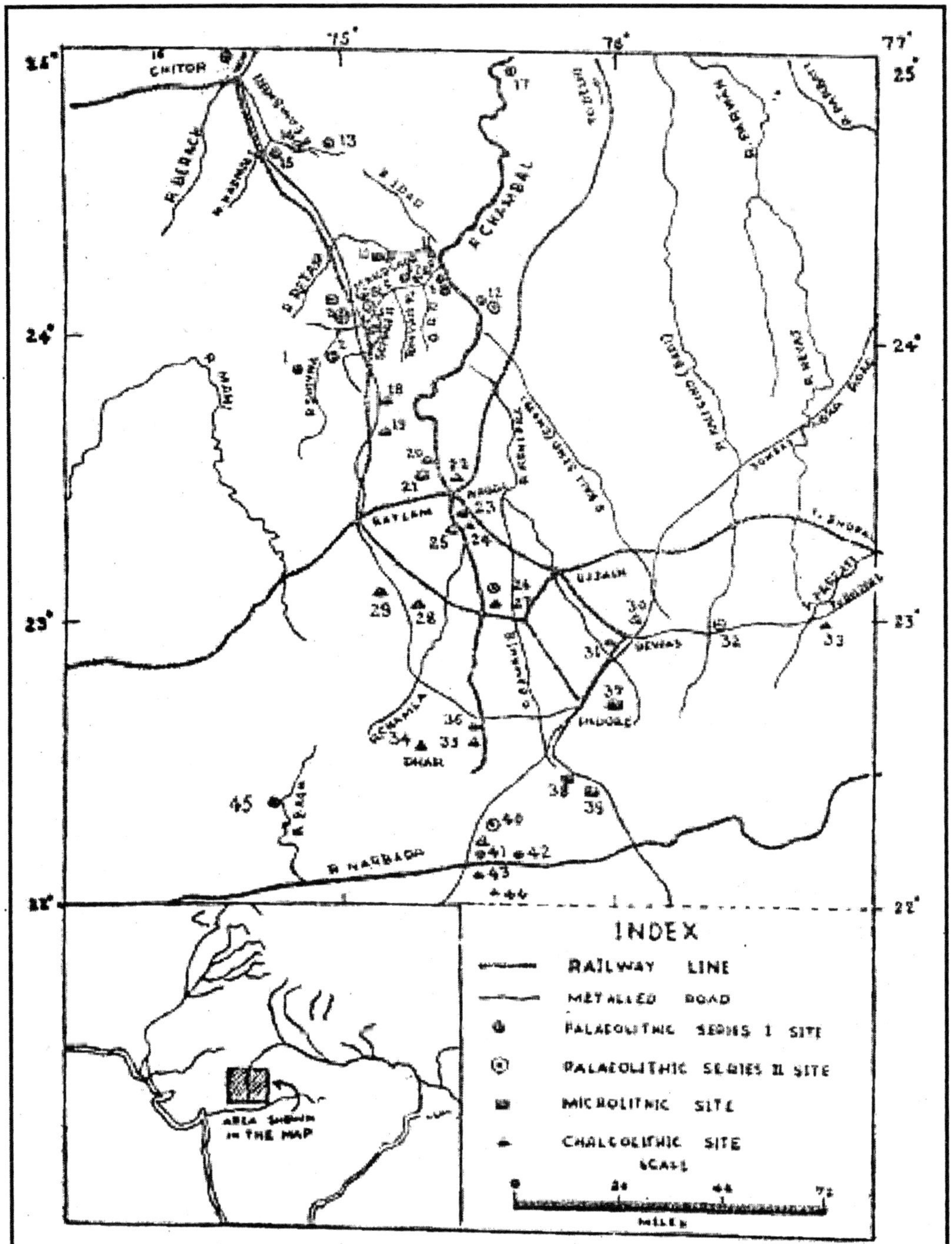

Source: H.D. Sankalia, 1974, *Prehistory and Protohistory of India and Pakistan.*

MAP 10: Prehistoric Sites of Malwa

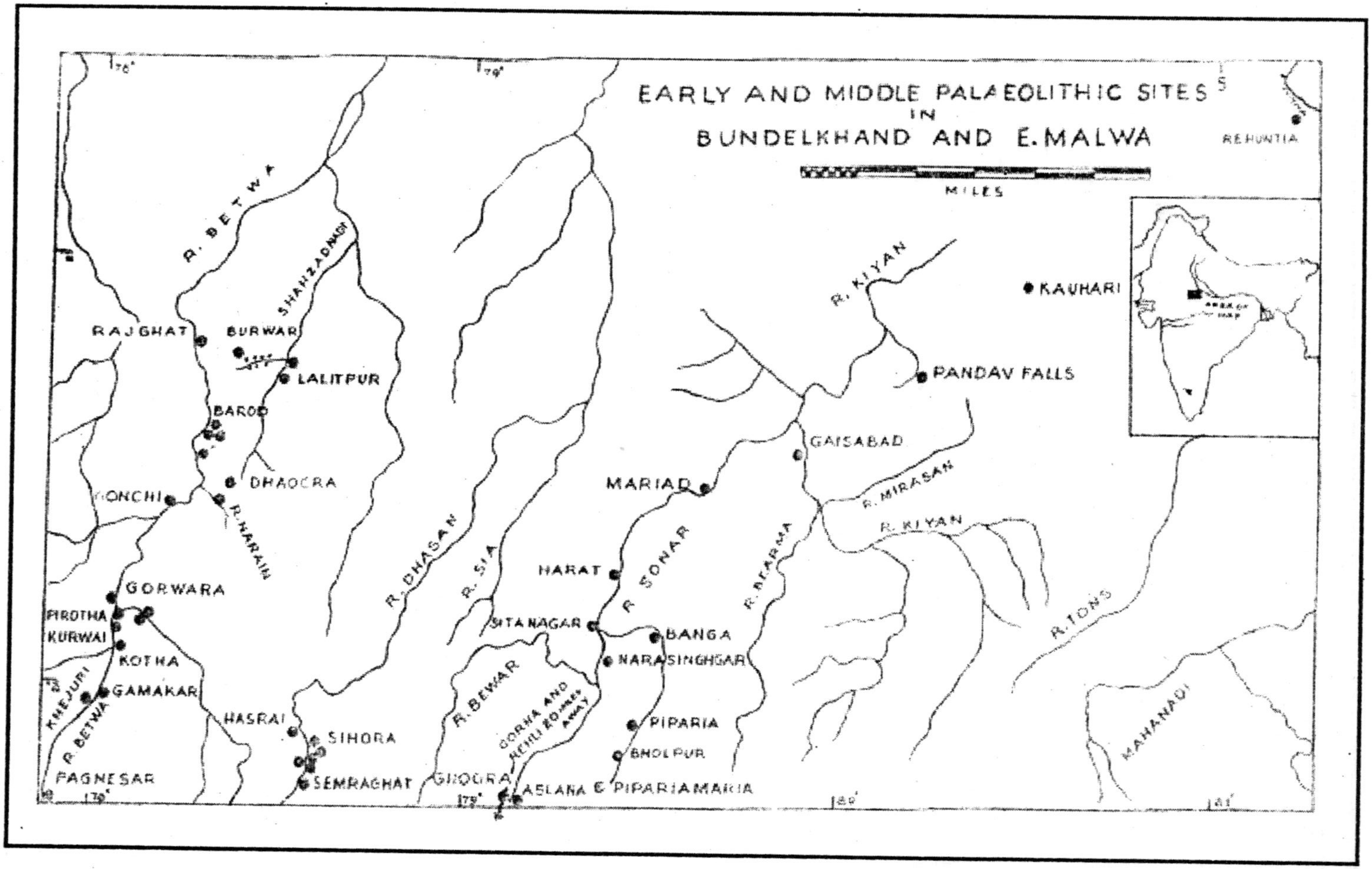

Source: H.D. Sankalia, 1974, *Prehistory and Protohistory of India and Pakistan.*

MAP 11: Early and Middle Palaeolithic Sites in Bundelkhand and East Malwa

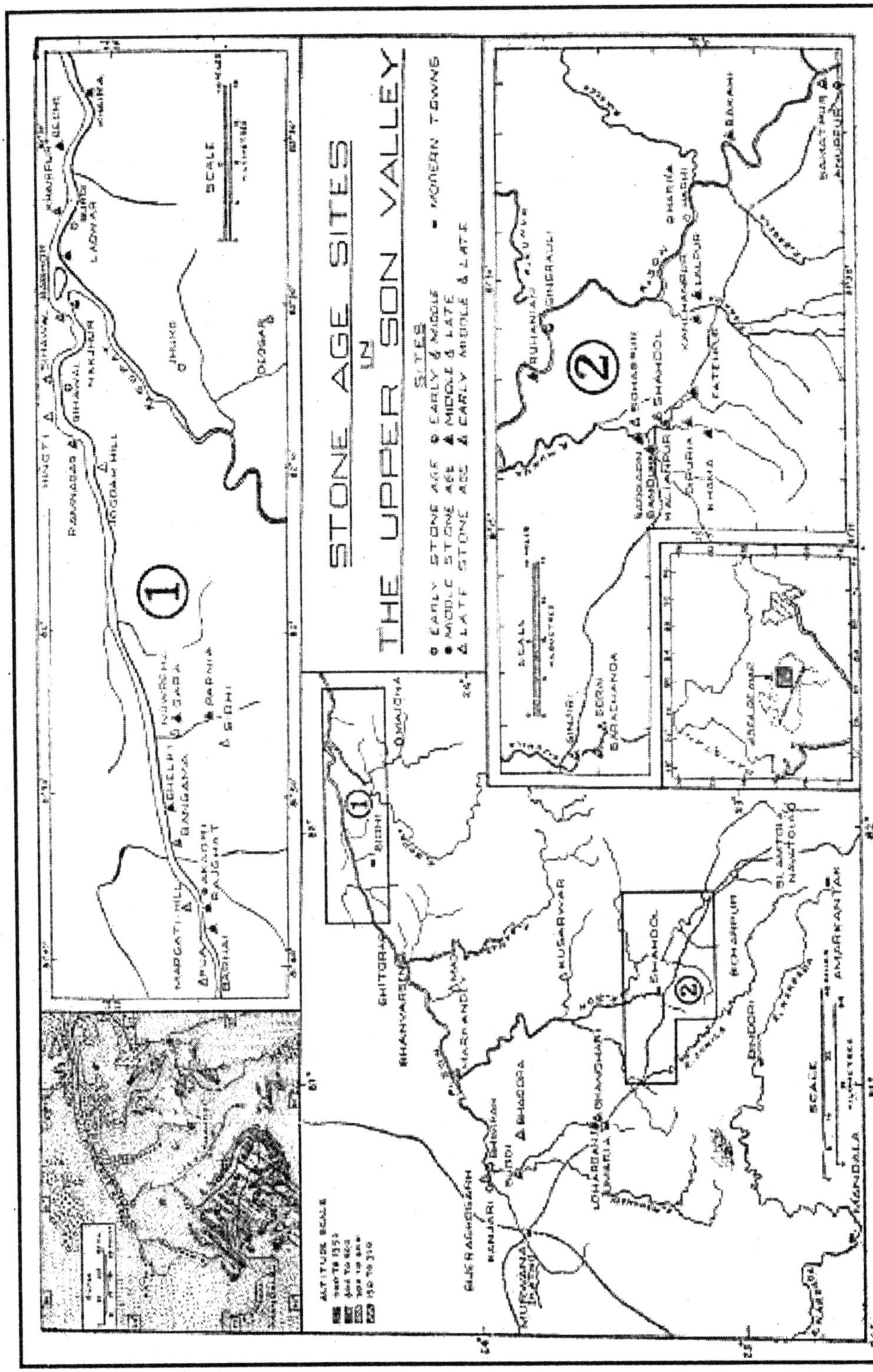

Source: H.D. Sankalia, 1974, *Prehistory and Protohistory of India and Pakistan.*

MAP 12: Stone Age Sites in Upper Son Valley

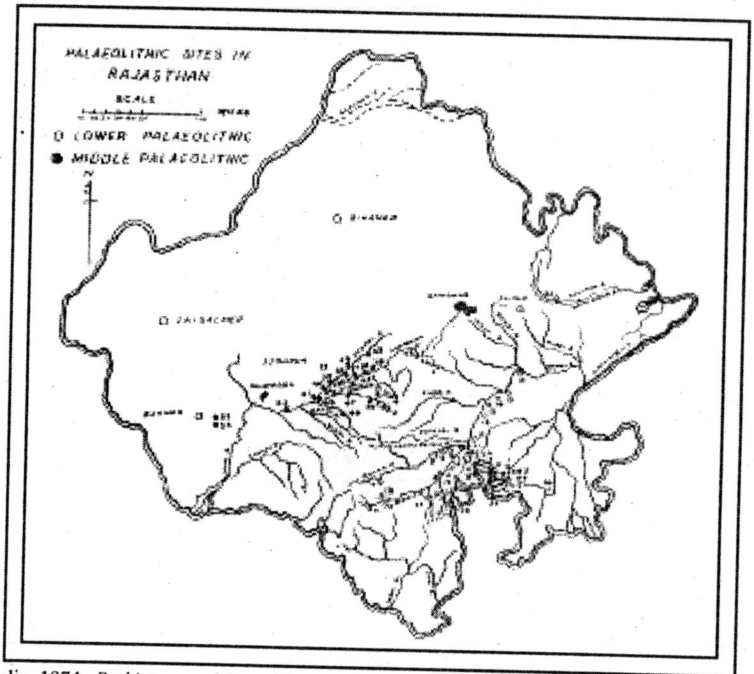

Source: H.D. Sankalia, 1974, *Prehistory and Protohistory of India and Pakistan.*

MAP 13: Palaeolithic Sites in Rajasthan

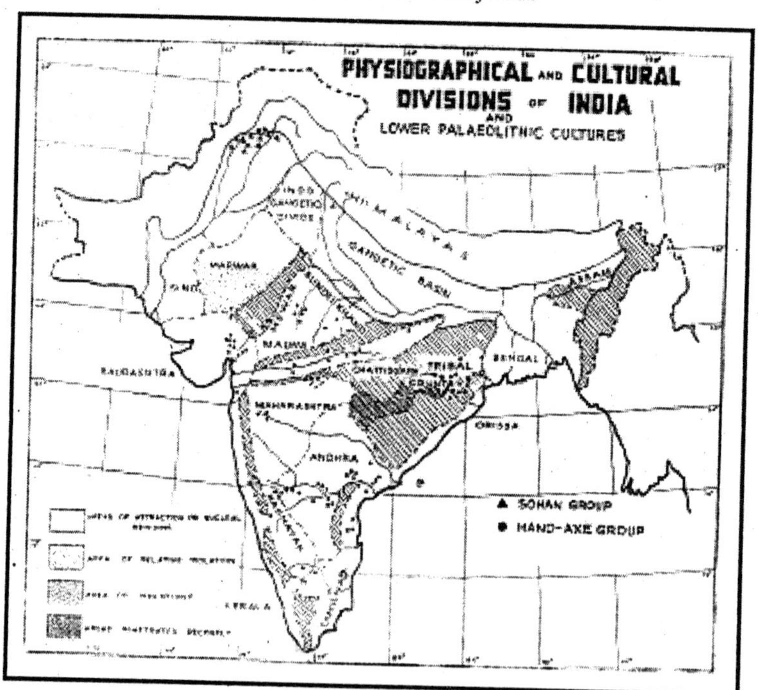

Source: H.D. Sankalia, 1974, *Prehistory and Protohistory of India and Pakistan.*

MAP 14: Physiographical and Cultural Division of India and Lower Palaeolithic Cultures

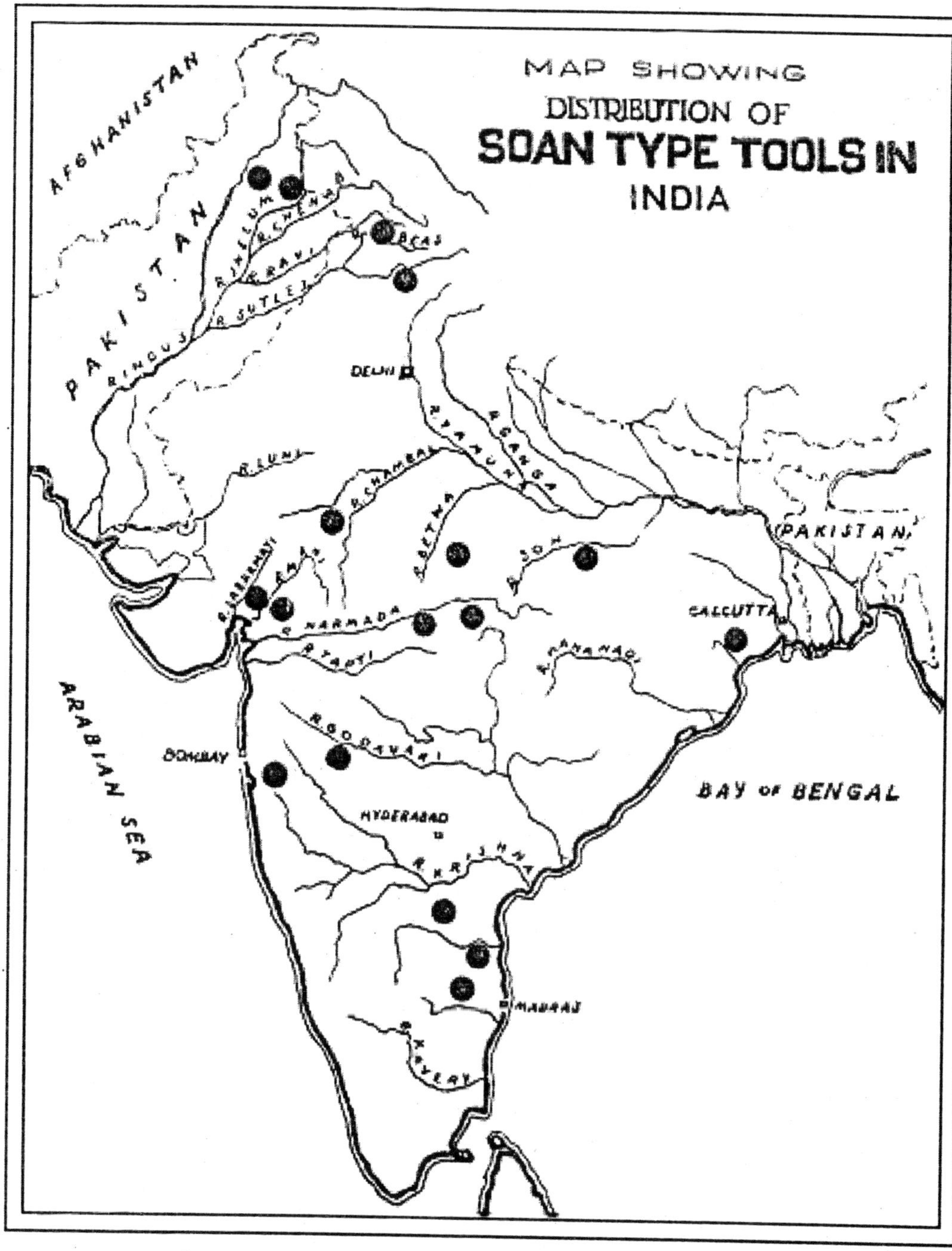

Source: H.D. Sankalia, 1974, *Prehistory and Protohistory of India and Pakistan.*

MAP 15: Soan Type Tools in India

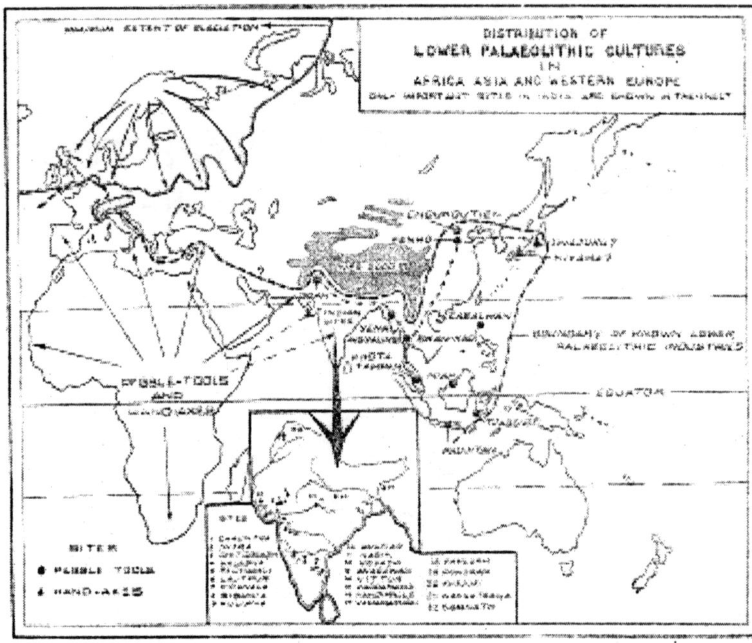

Source: H.D. Sankalia, 1974, *Prehistory and Protohistory of India and Pakistan.*

MAP 16: Lower Palaeolithic Cultures of Africa, Asia and Western Europe

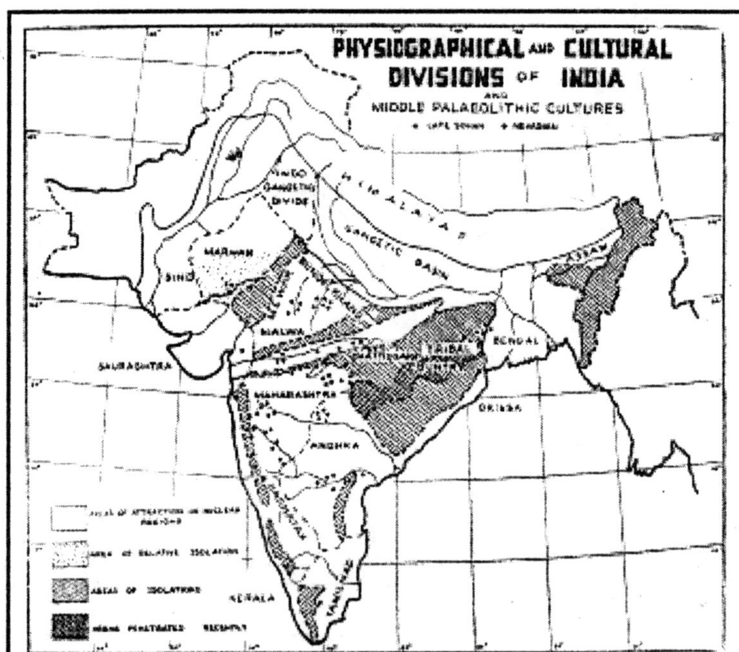

Source: H.D. Sankalia, 1974, *Prehistory and Protohistory of India and Pakistan.*

MAP 17: Physiographical and Cultural Divisions of India and Middle Palaeolithic Cultures

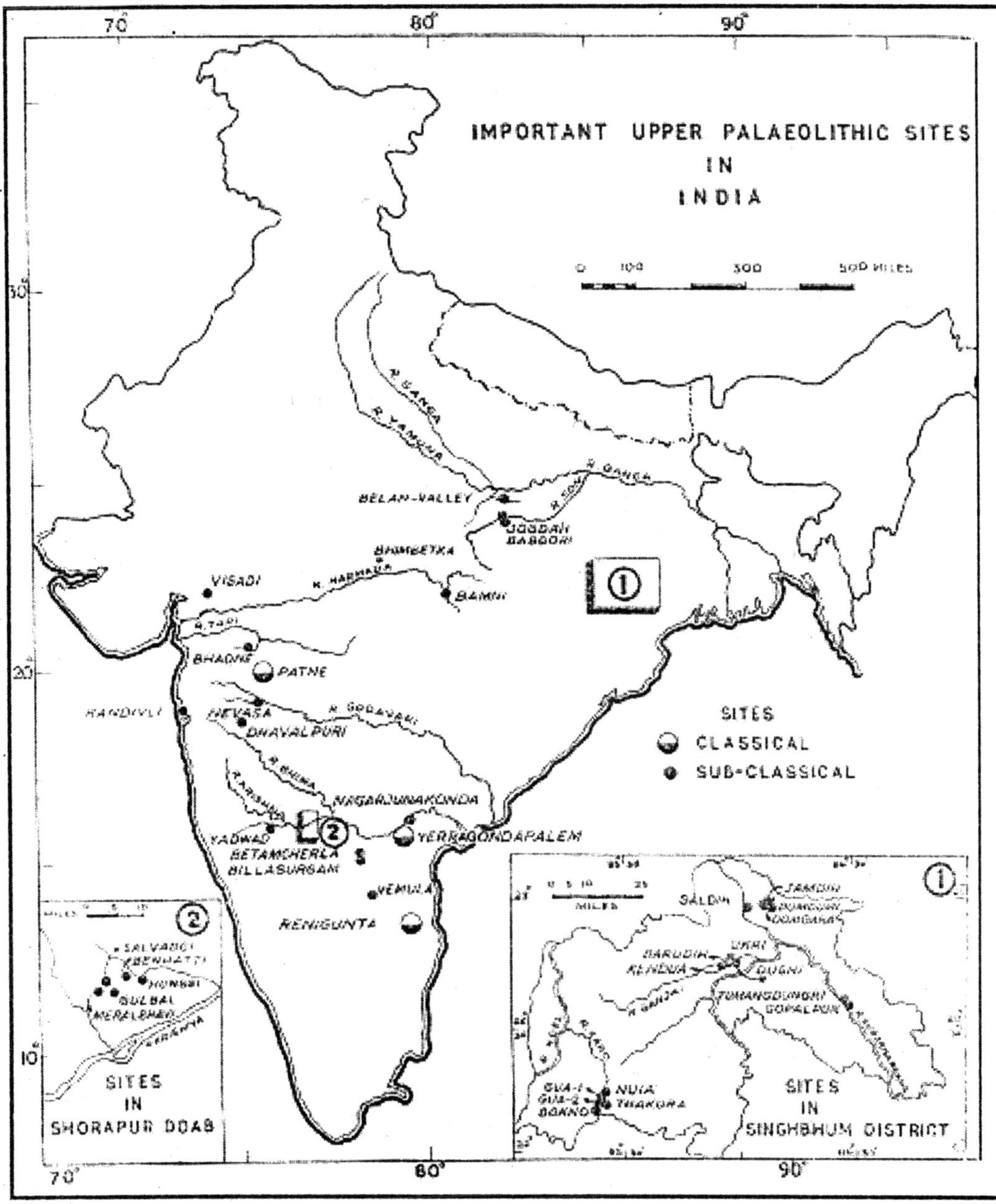

Source: H.D. Sankalia, 1974, *Prehistory and Protohistory of India and Pakistan.*

MAP 18: Important Upper Palaeolithic Sites in India

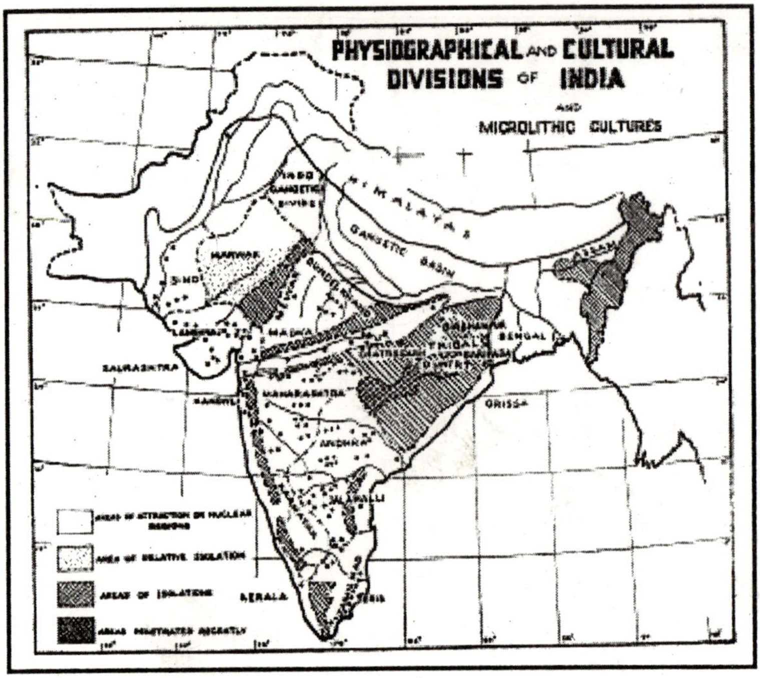

Source: H.D. Sankalia, 1974, *Prehistory and Protohistory of India and Pakistan*.

MAP 19: Physiographical and Cultural Divisions of India and Microlithic Cultures

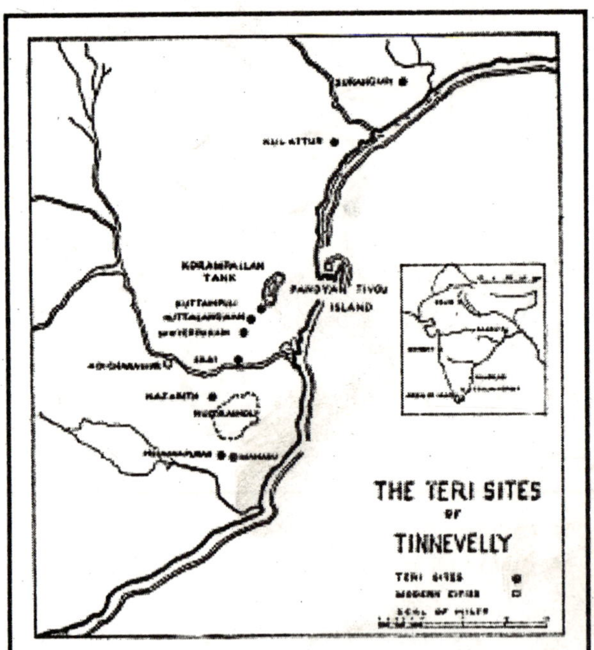

Source: H.D. Sankalia, 1974, *Prehistory and Protohistory of India and Pakistan.*

MAP 20: Teri Sites of Tinne Valley

Source: H.D. Sankalia, 1974, *Prehistory and Protohistory of India and Pakistan.*

MAP 21: Microlithic Sites in Rajasthan

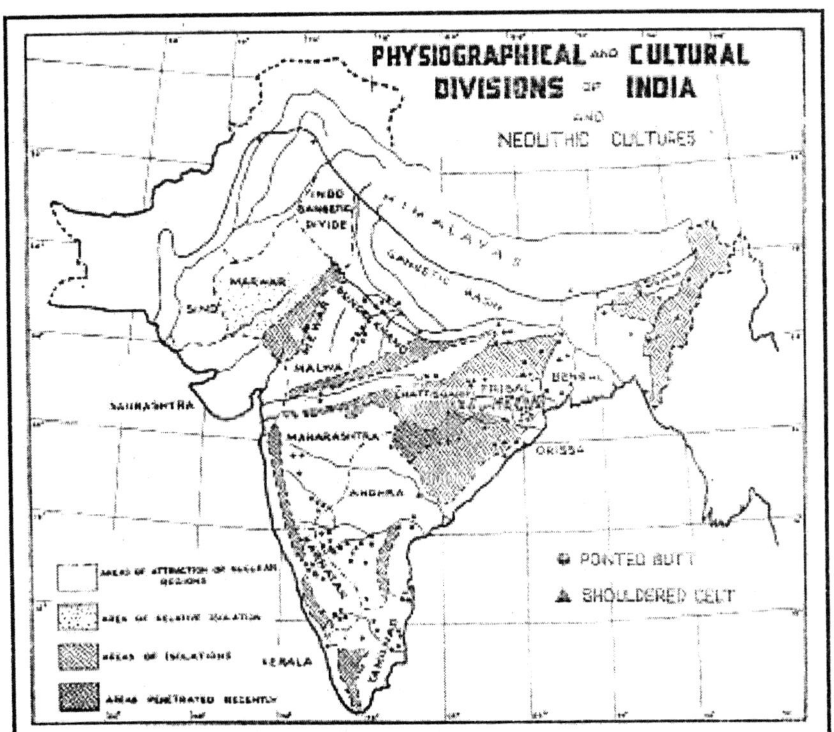

Source: H.D. Sankalia, 1974, *Prehistory and Protohistory of India and Pakistan.*

MAP 22: Physiographical and Cultural Divisions of India and Neolithic Cultures

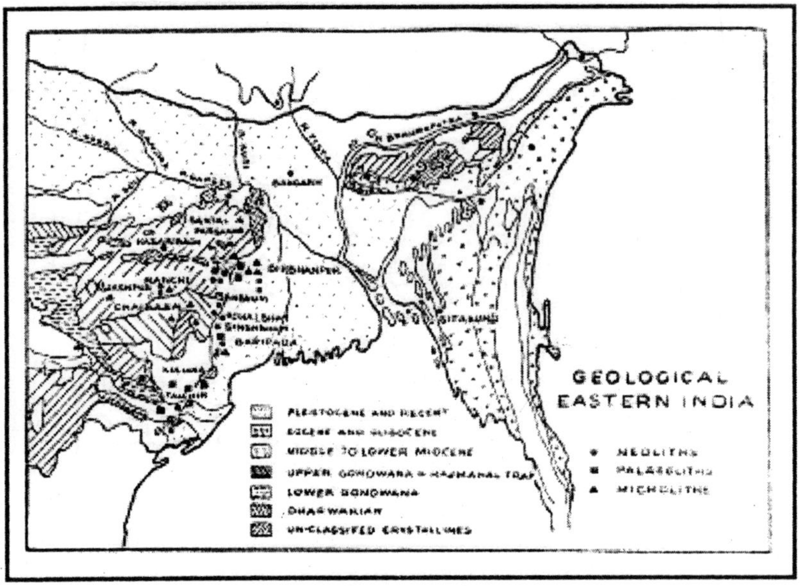

Source: H.D. Sankalia, 1974, *Prehistory and Protohistory of India and Pakistan.*

MAP 23: Geological Sites in Eastern India

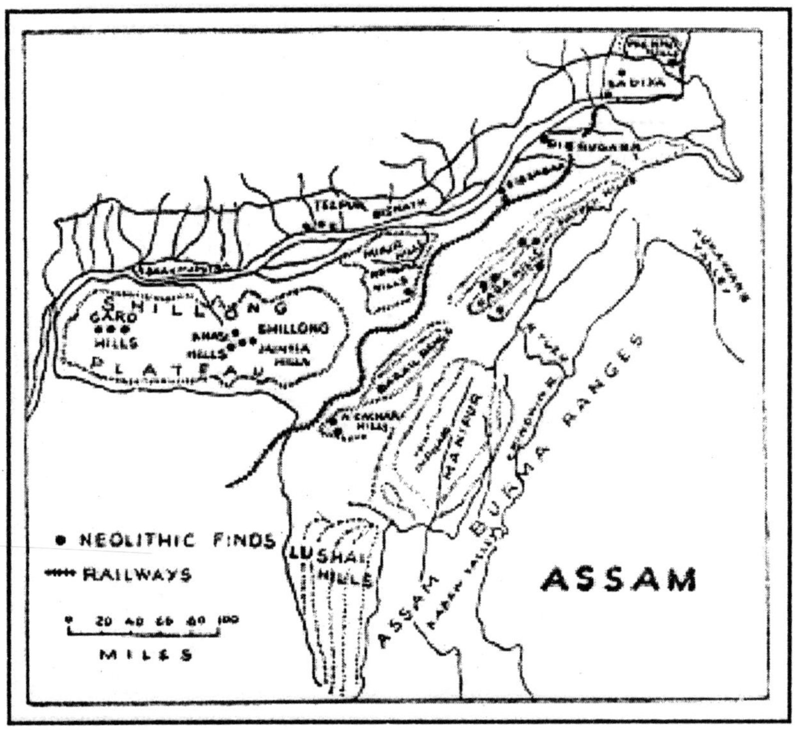

Source: H.D. Sankalia, 1974, *Prehistory and Protohistory of India and Pakistan.*

MAP 24: Neolithic Finds in Assam

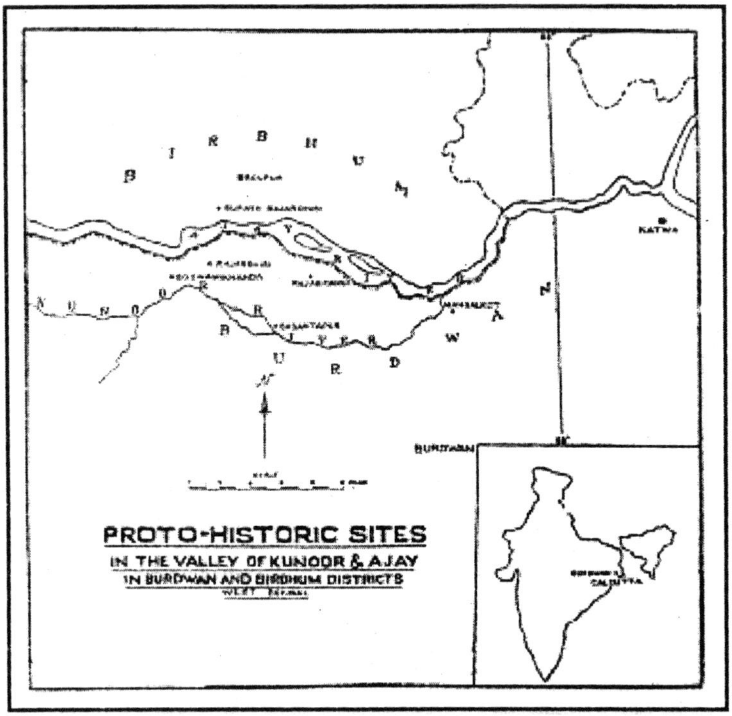

Source: H.D. Sankalia, 1974, *Prehistory and Protohistory of India and Pakistan.*

MAP 25: Protohistoric Sites in Burdwan and Birbhum District, West Bengal

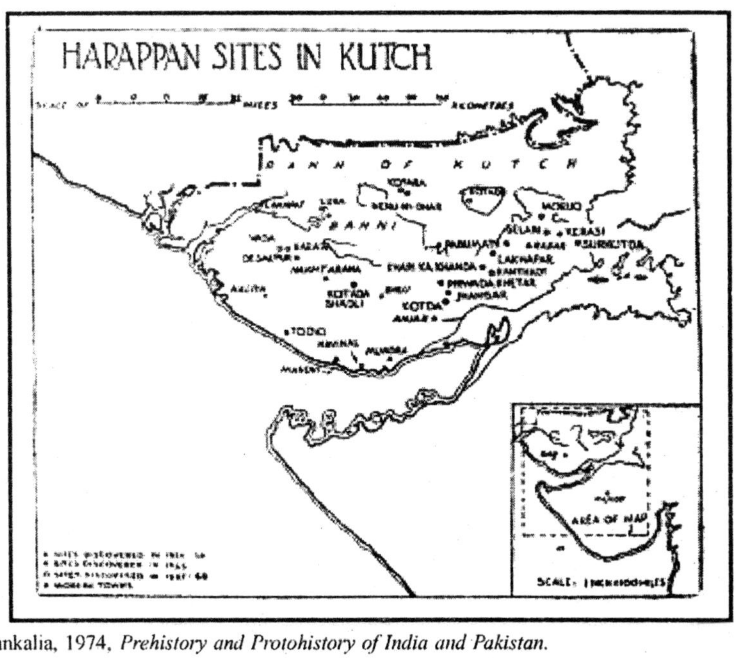

Source: H.D. Sankalia, 1974, *Prehistory and Protohistory of India and Pakistan.*

MAP 26: Harappan Sites in Kutch, Gujarat

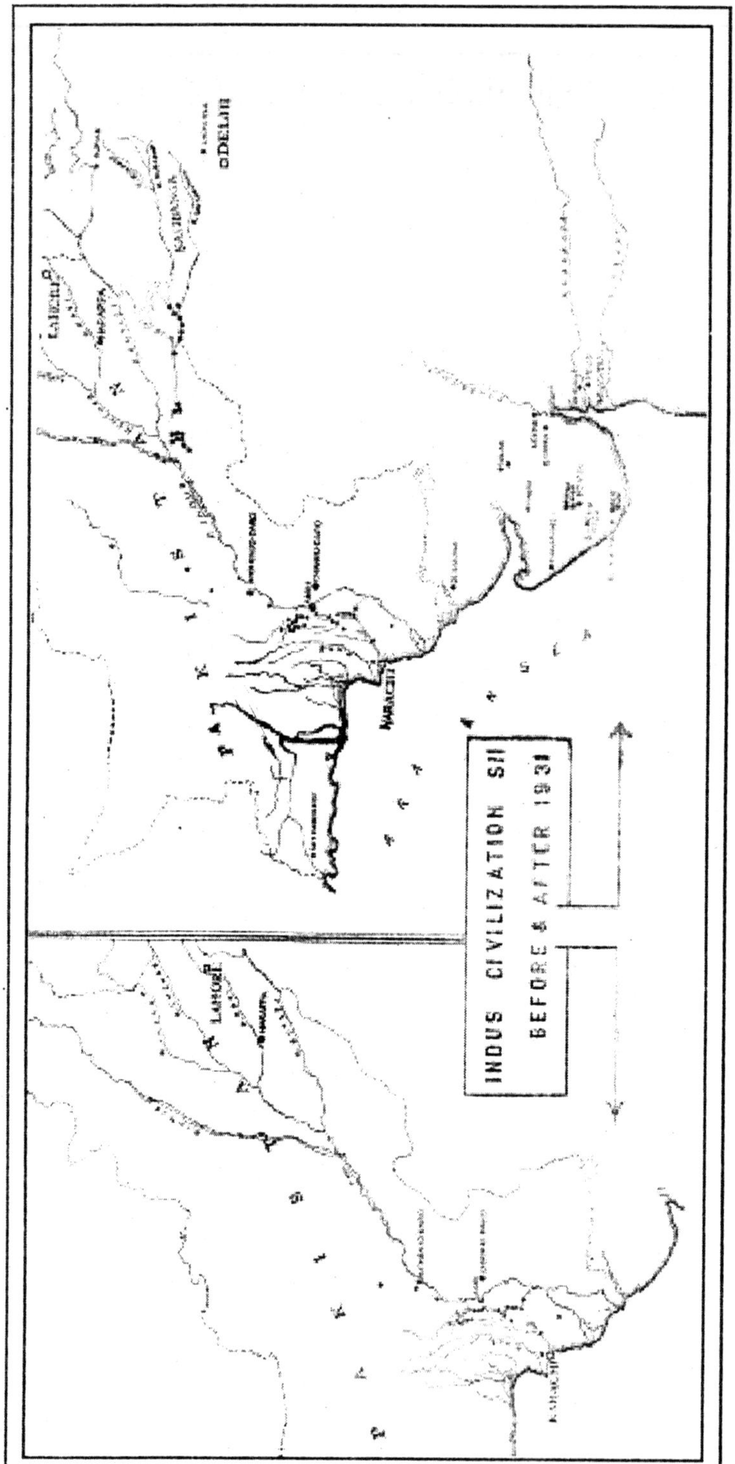

Source: H.D. Sankalia, 1974, *Prehistory and Protohistory of India and Pakistan.*

MAP 27: Indus Valley Civilization Sites

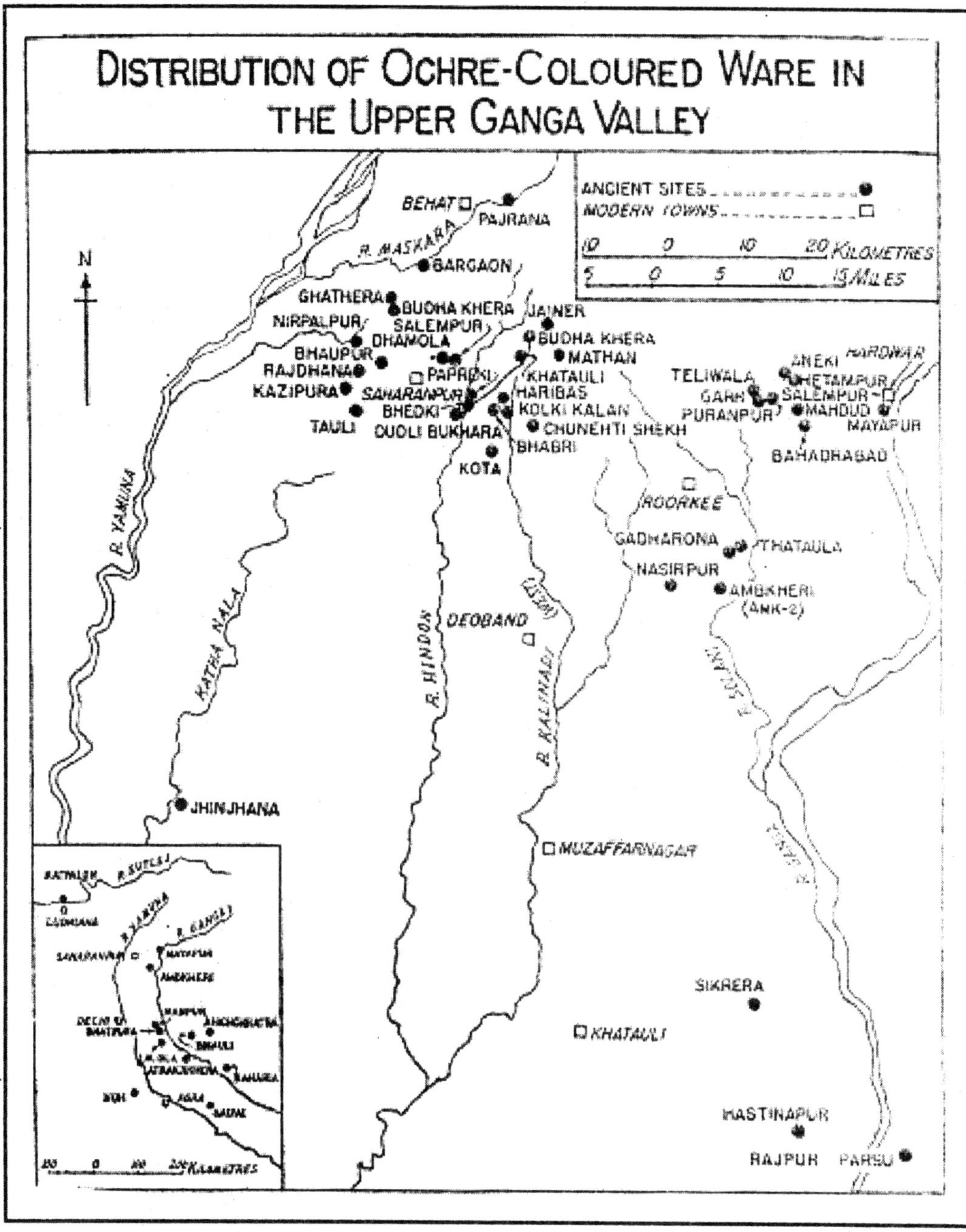

Source: H.D. Sankalia, 1974, *Prehistory and Protohistory of India and Pakistan.*

MAP 28: Distribution of Ochre-Coloured Ware in Upper Ganga Valley

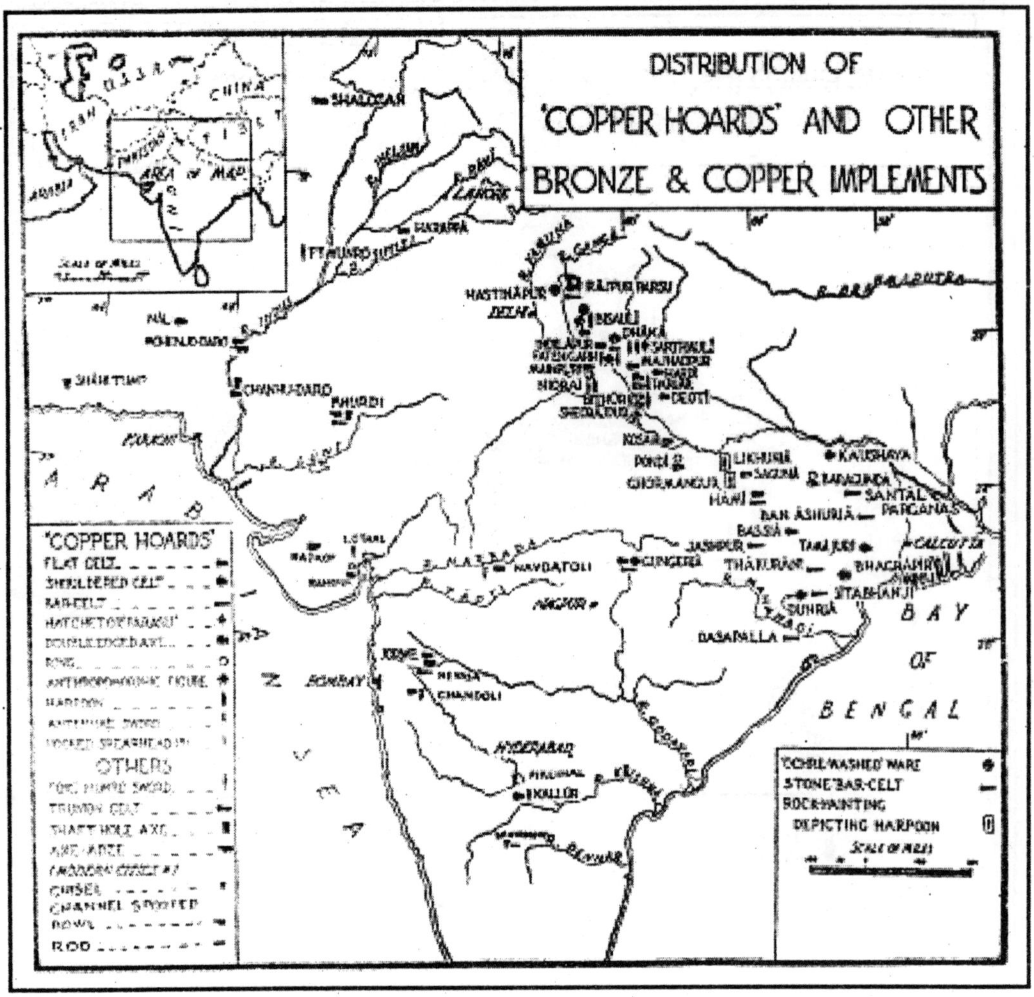

Source: H.D. Sankalia, 1974, *Prehistory and Protohistory of India and Pakistan.*

MAP 29: 'Copper Hoards' and Other Bronze & Copper Implements in India

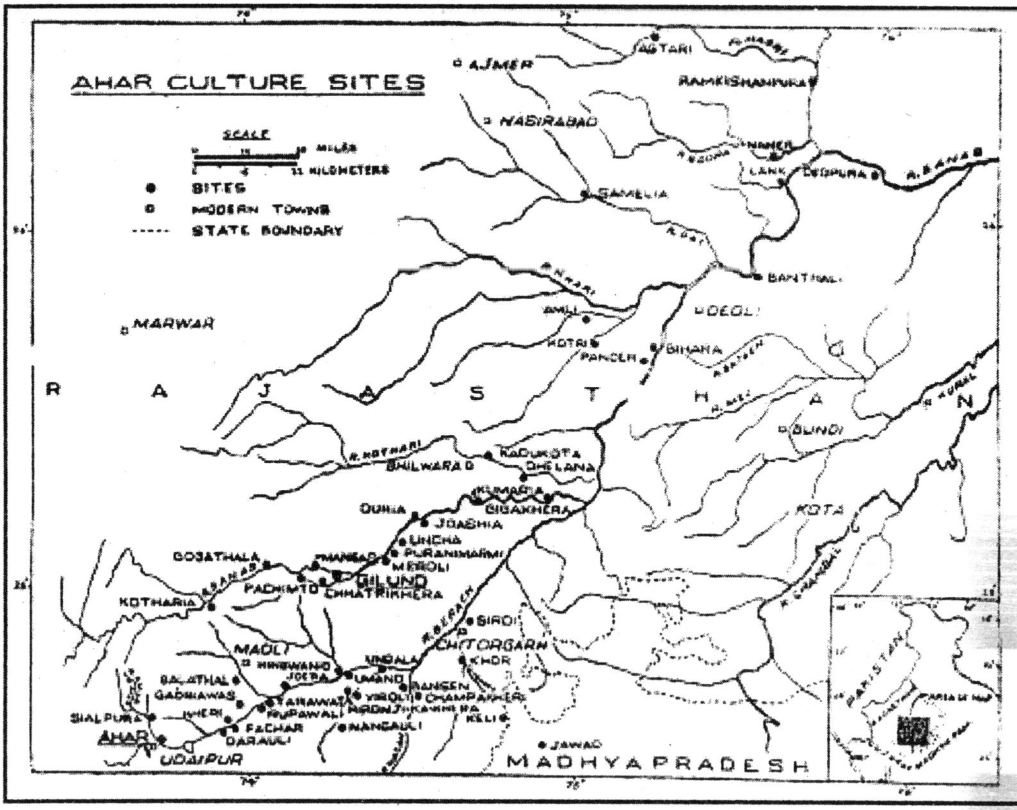

Source: H.D. Sankalia, 1974, *Prehistory and Protohistory of India and Pakistan.*

MAP 30: Ahar Culture Sites

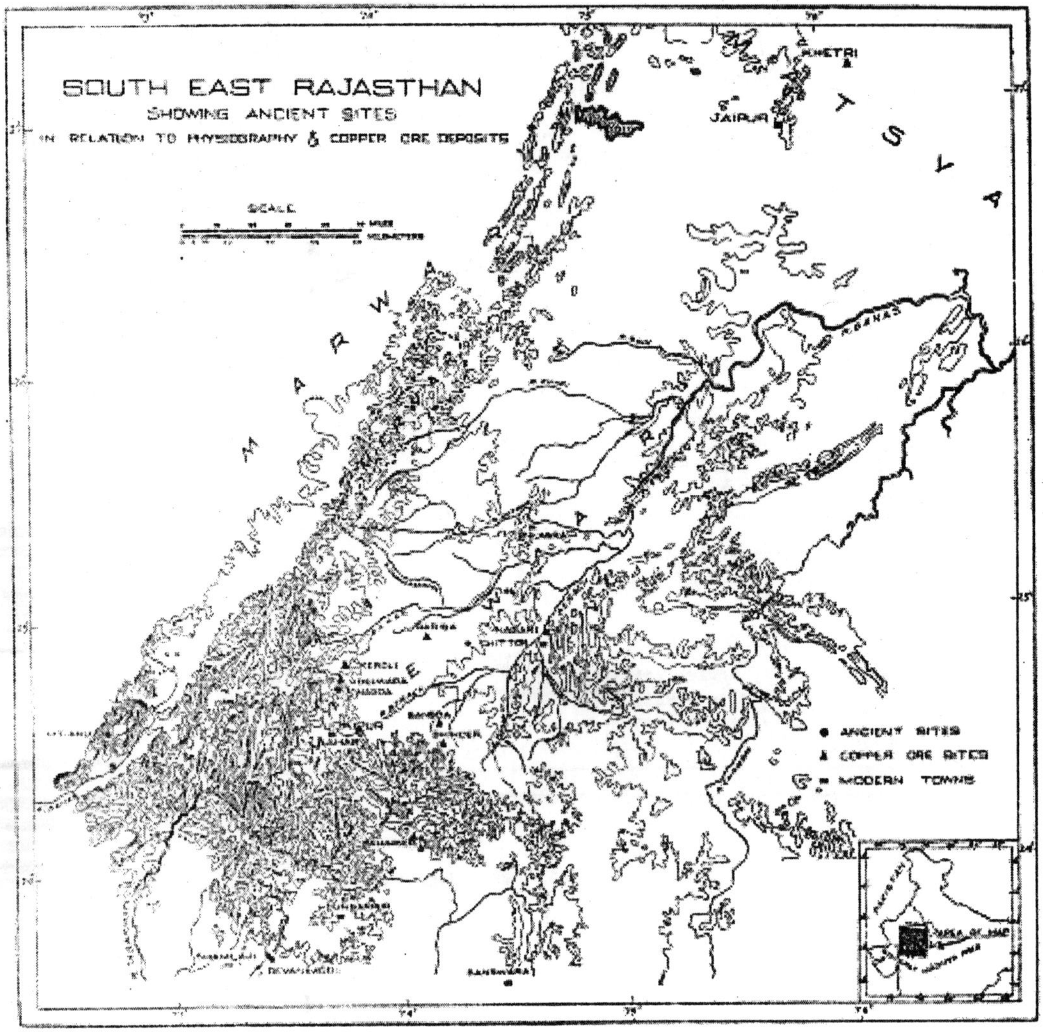

Source: H.D. Sankalia, 1974, *Prehistory and Protohistory of India and Pakistan.*

MAP 31: Ancient Sites in South-east Rajasthan in relation to Physiography and Copper Ore Deposits

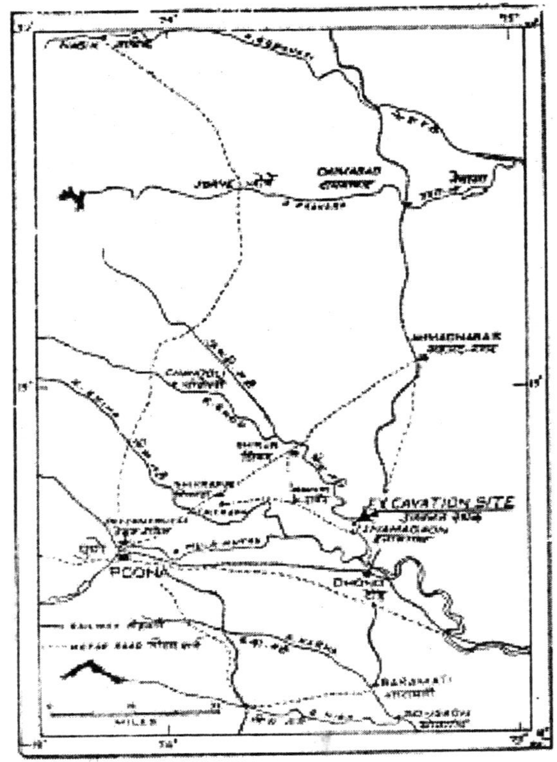

Source: H.D. Sankalia, 1974, *Prehistory and Protohistory of India and Pakistan*.

MAP 32: Important Excavation Sites in Western Maharashtra

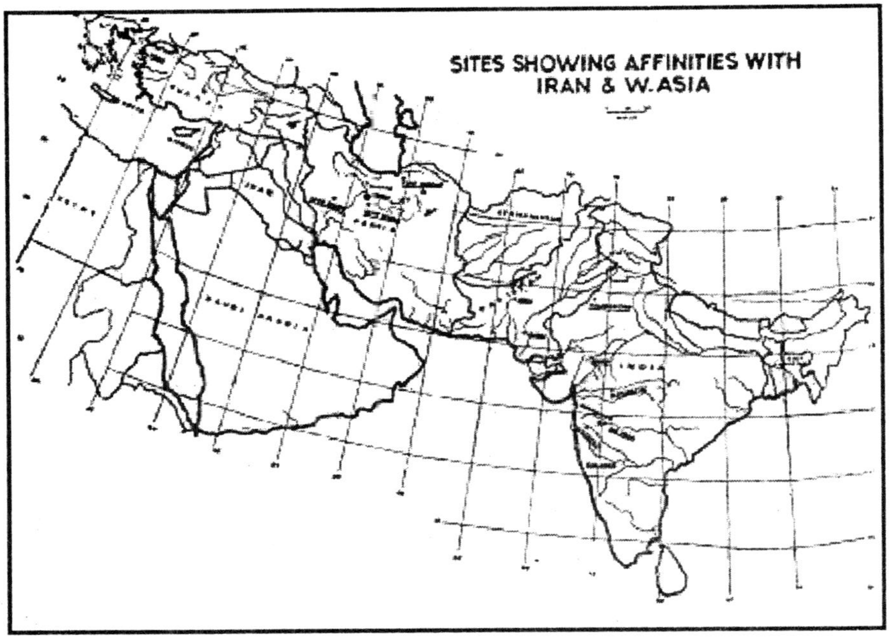

Source: H.D. Sankalia, 1974, *Prehistory and Protohistory of India and Pakistan*.

MAP 33: Sites Showing Affinities in Pottery Designs, Shapes, Terracotta Female Figurine with Iran and West Asia

APPENDIX-C

Figures of Tools, Potteries, House Types, and Urban Centres

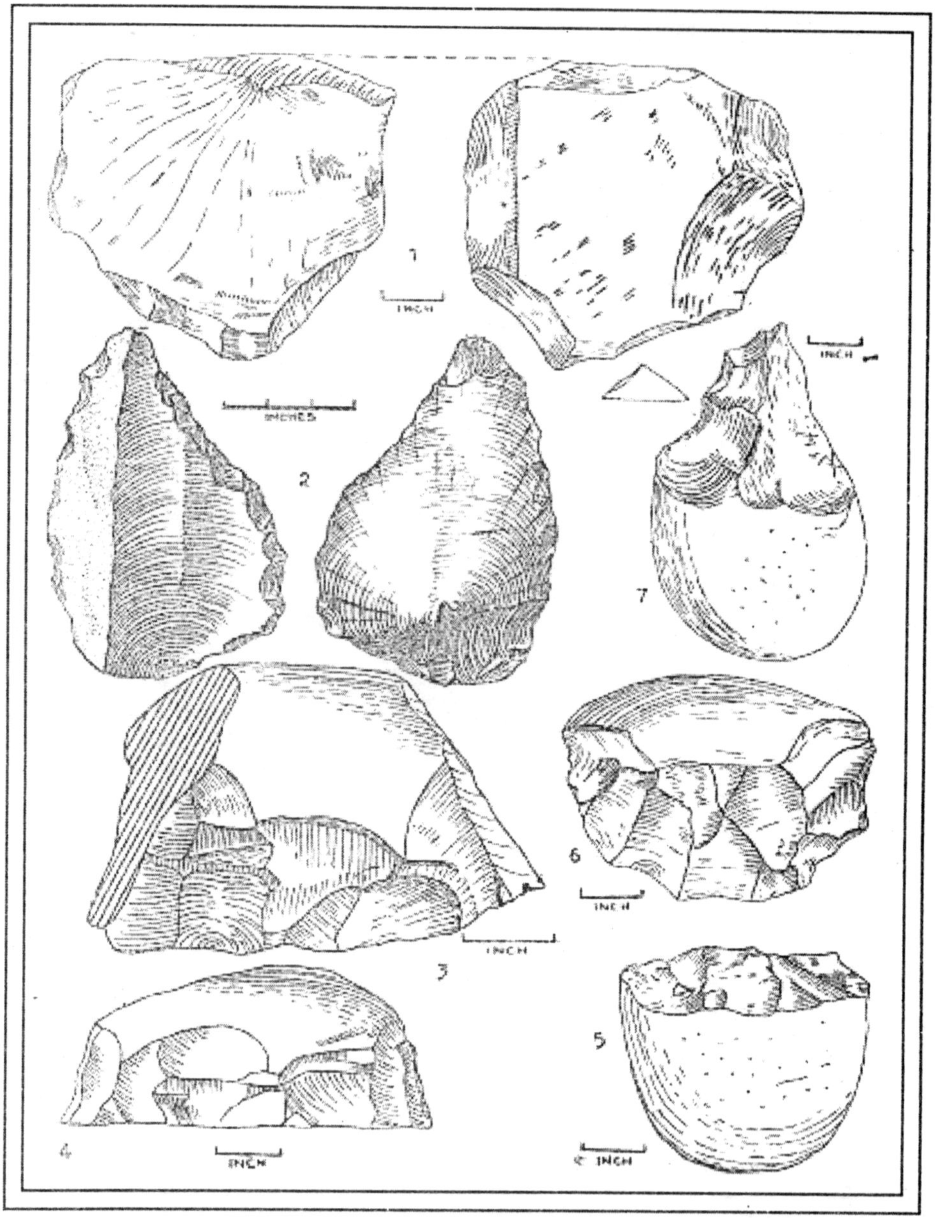

Source: H.D. Sankalia, 1974, *Prehistory and Protohistory of India and Pakistan.*

FIGURE 1: Pre Soan and Early Soan Type Tools

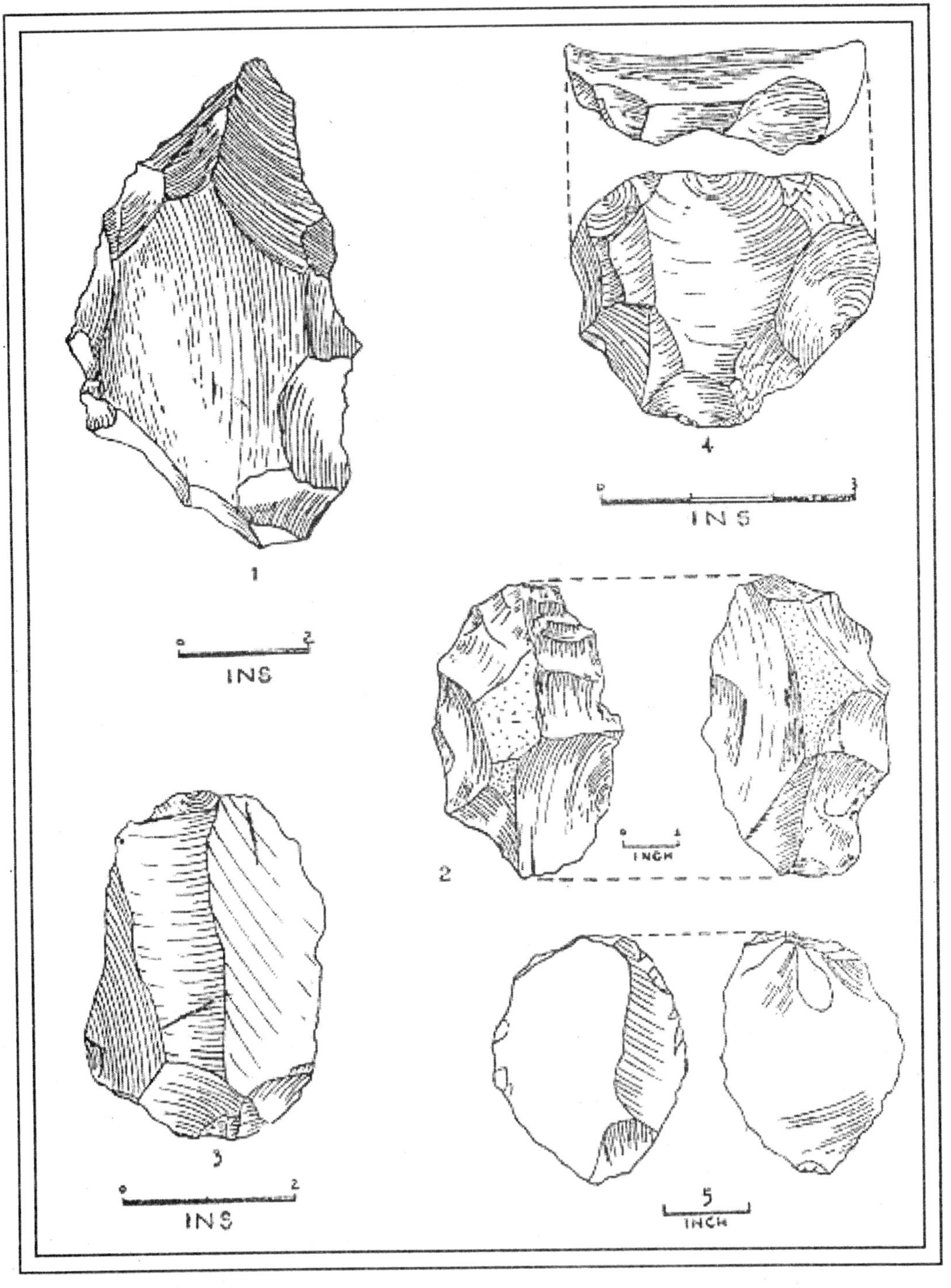

Source: H.D. Sankalia, 1974, *Prehistory and Protohistory of India and Pakistan.*

FIGURE 2: Early Soan Flakes and Cores

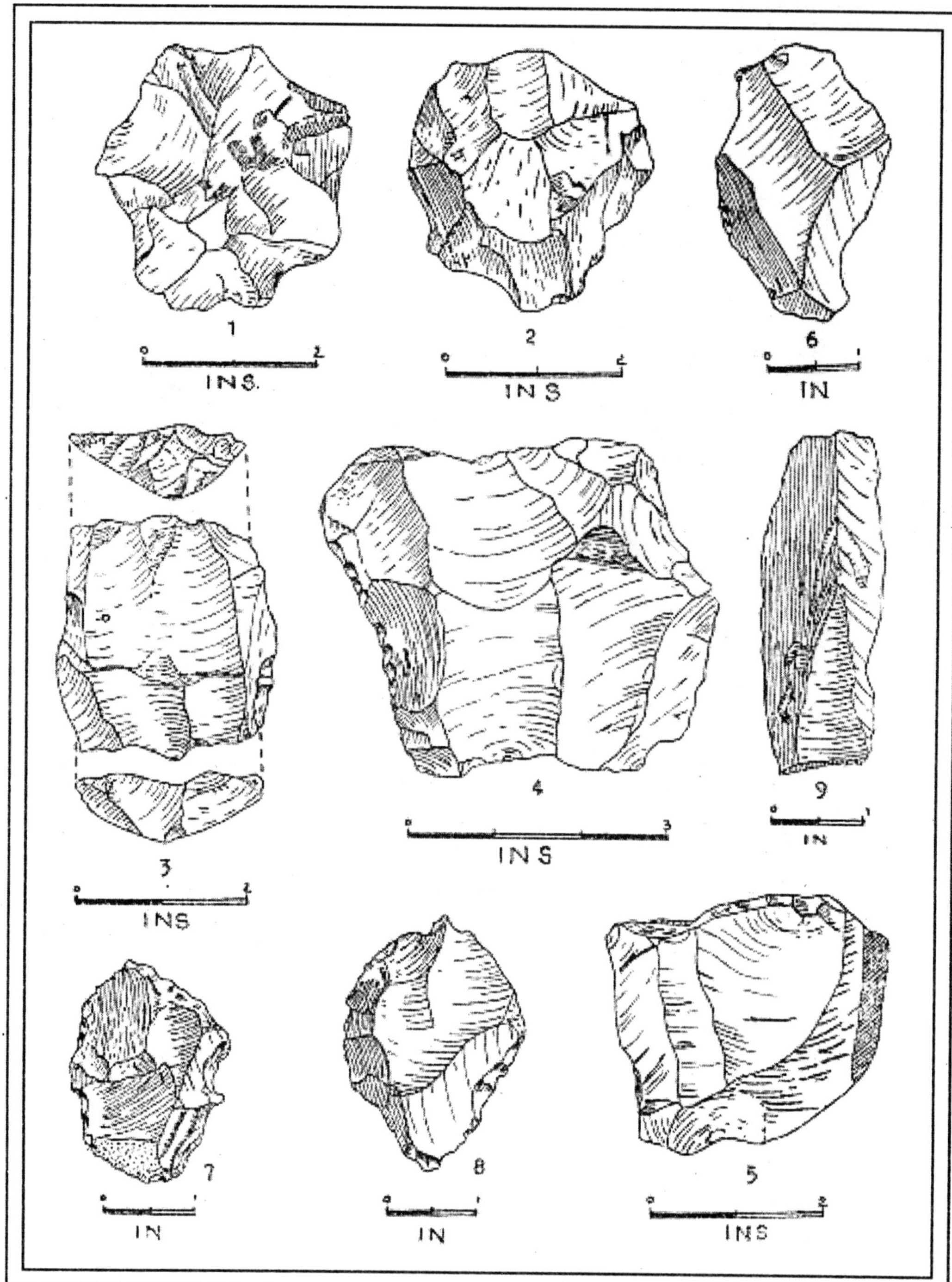

Source: H.D. Sankalia, 1974, *Prehistory and Protohistory of India and Pakistan.*

FIGURE 3: Late Soan Cores and Flakes

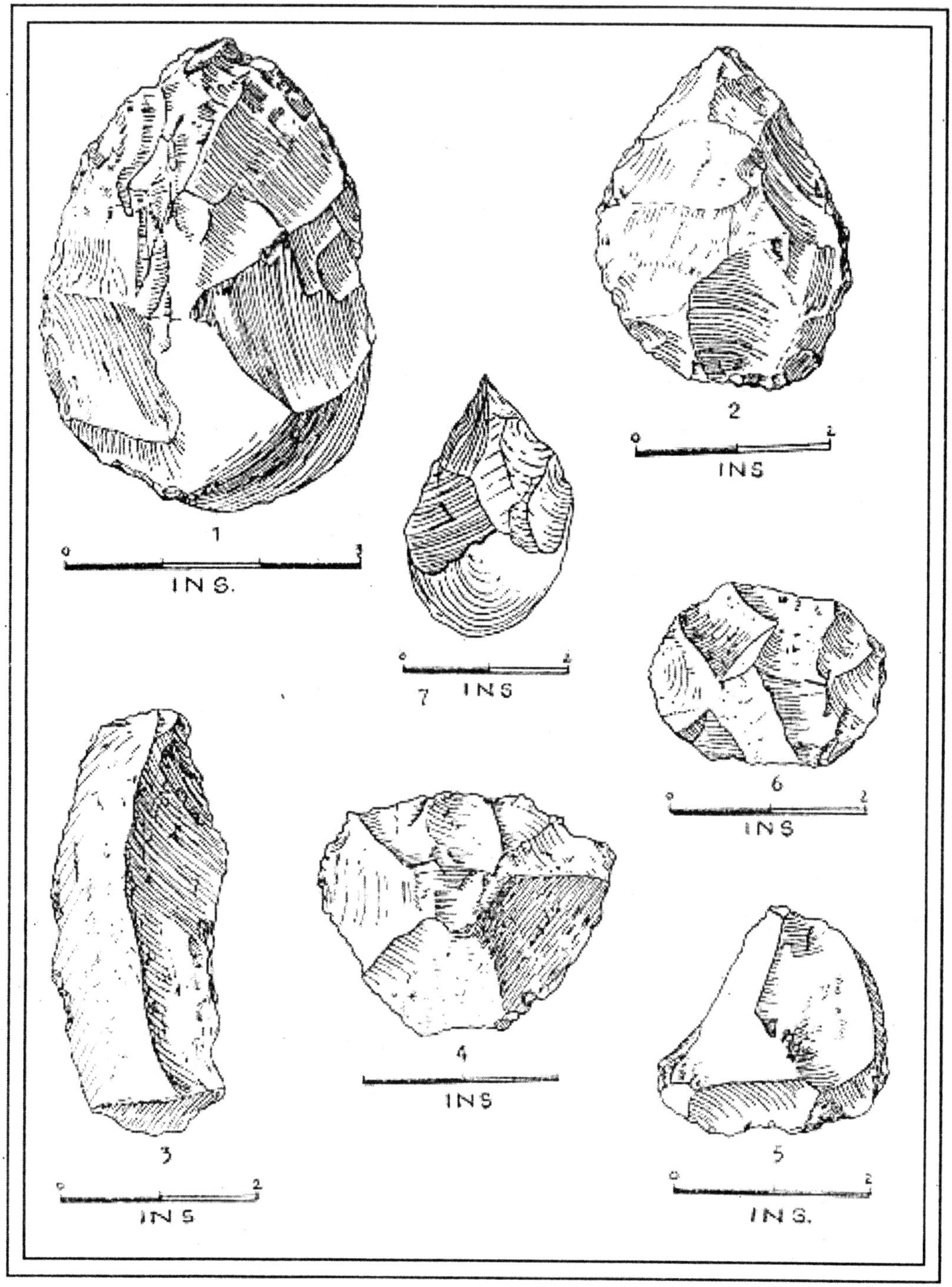

Source: H.D. Sankalia, 1974, *Prehistory and Protohistory of India and Pakistan.*

FIGURE 4: Chauntra and Evolved Soan Tools

Source: H.D. Sankalia, 1974, *Prehistory and Protohistory of India and Pakistan.*

FIGURE 5: Handaxe from Meghalaya

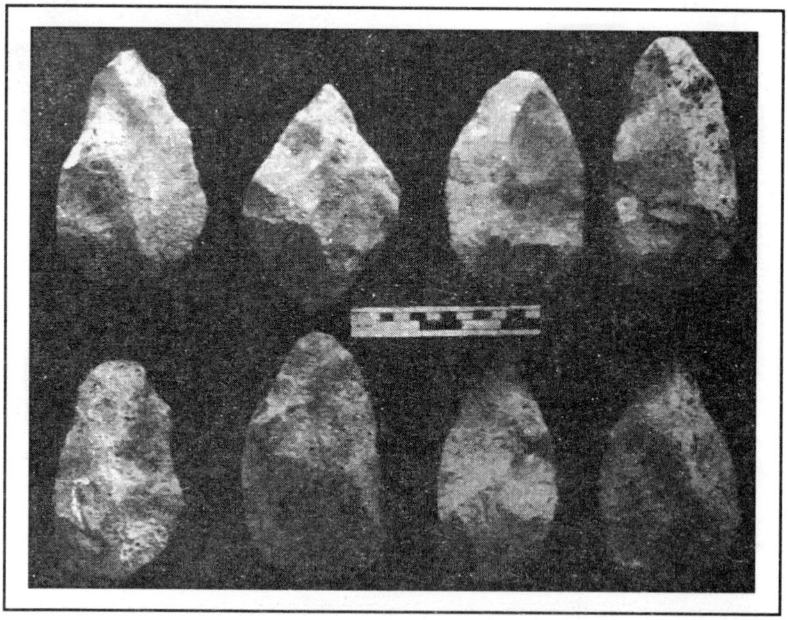

Source: H.D. Sankalia, 1974, *Prehistory and Protohistory of India and Pakistan.*

FIGURE 6: Cleavers from Meghalaya

Source: H.D. Sankalia, 1974, *Prehistory and Protohistory of India and Pakistan.*

FIGURE 7: Sections on Rongram River, Garo Hills, Meghalaya

Source: H.D. Sankalia, 1974, *Prehistory and Protohistory of India and Pakistan.*

FIGURE 8: Early Stone Age Tools from Bhimbandhi, District Monghyr, Bihar

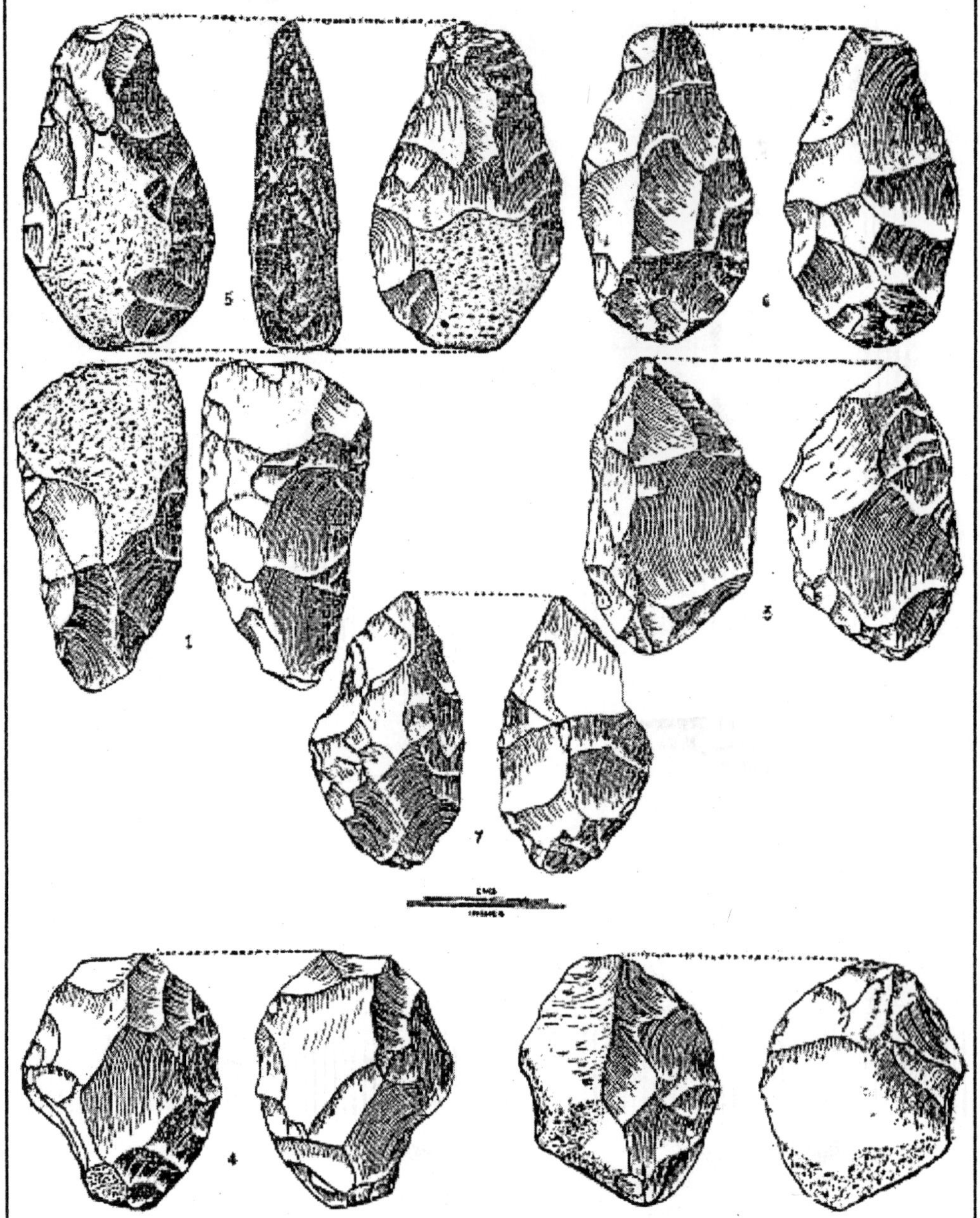

Source: H.D. Sankalia, 1974, *Prehistory and Protohistory of India and Pakistan.*

FIGURE 9: Early Stone Age Tools from Chittoor District, Andhra Pradesh

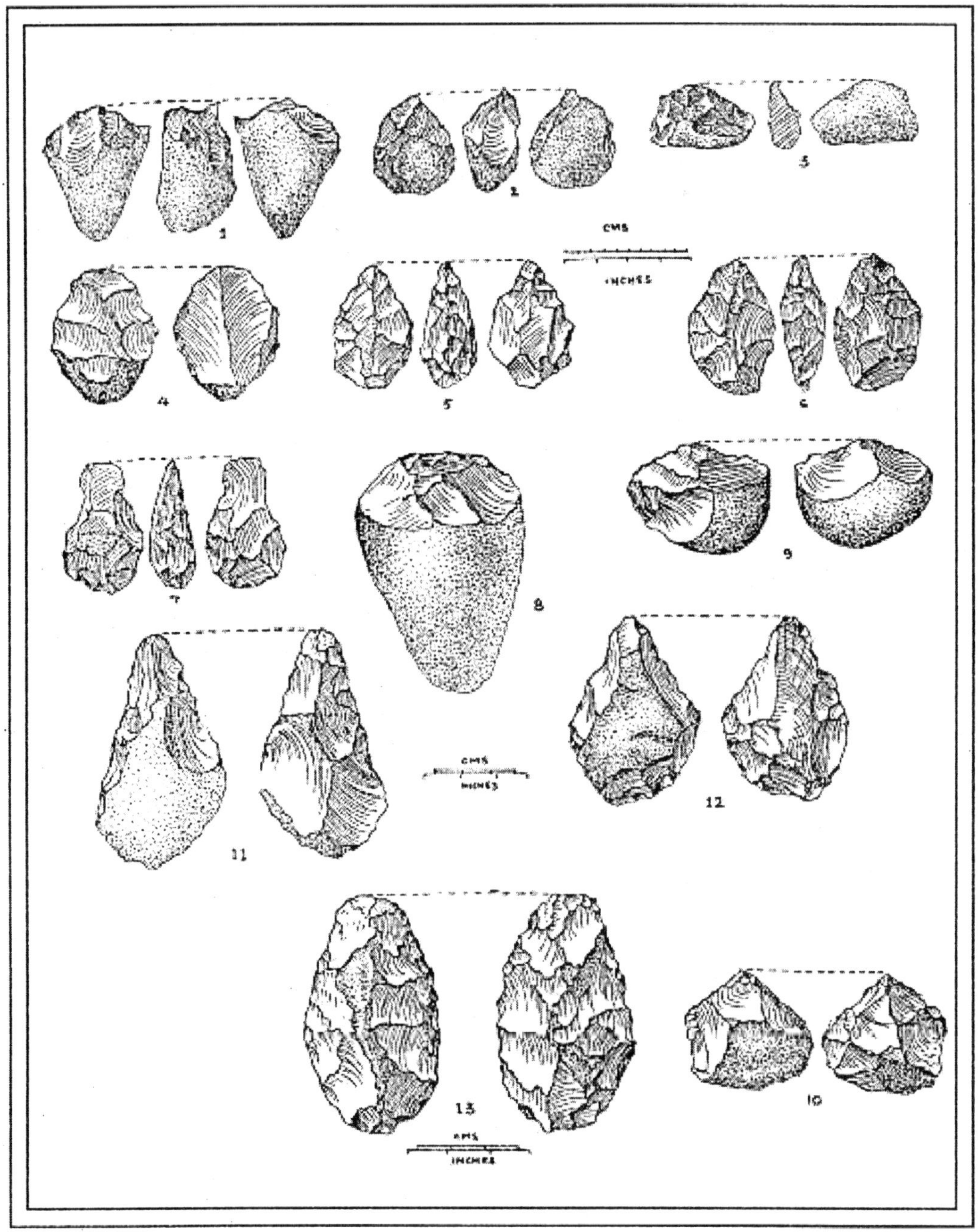

Source: H.D. Sankalia, 1974, *Prehistory and Protohistory of India and Pakistan.*

FIGURE 10: Lower Palaeolithic Tools from Andhra Pradesh
1-3, Pebble Tools from Nagarjunkonda; 4-7, Handaxes from Nagarjunkonda; 8-10, Pebble Tools from Nalgonda District; 11-13, Handaxes from Nalgonda Districts

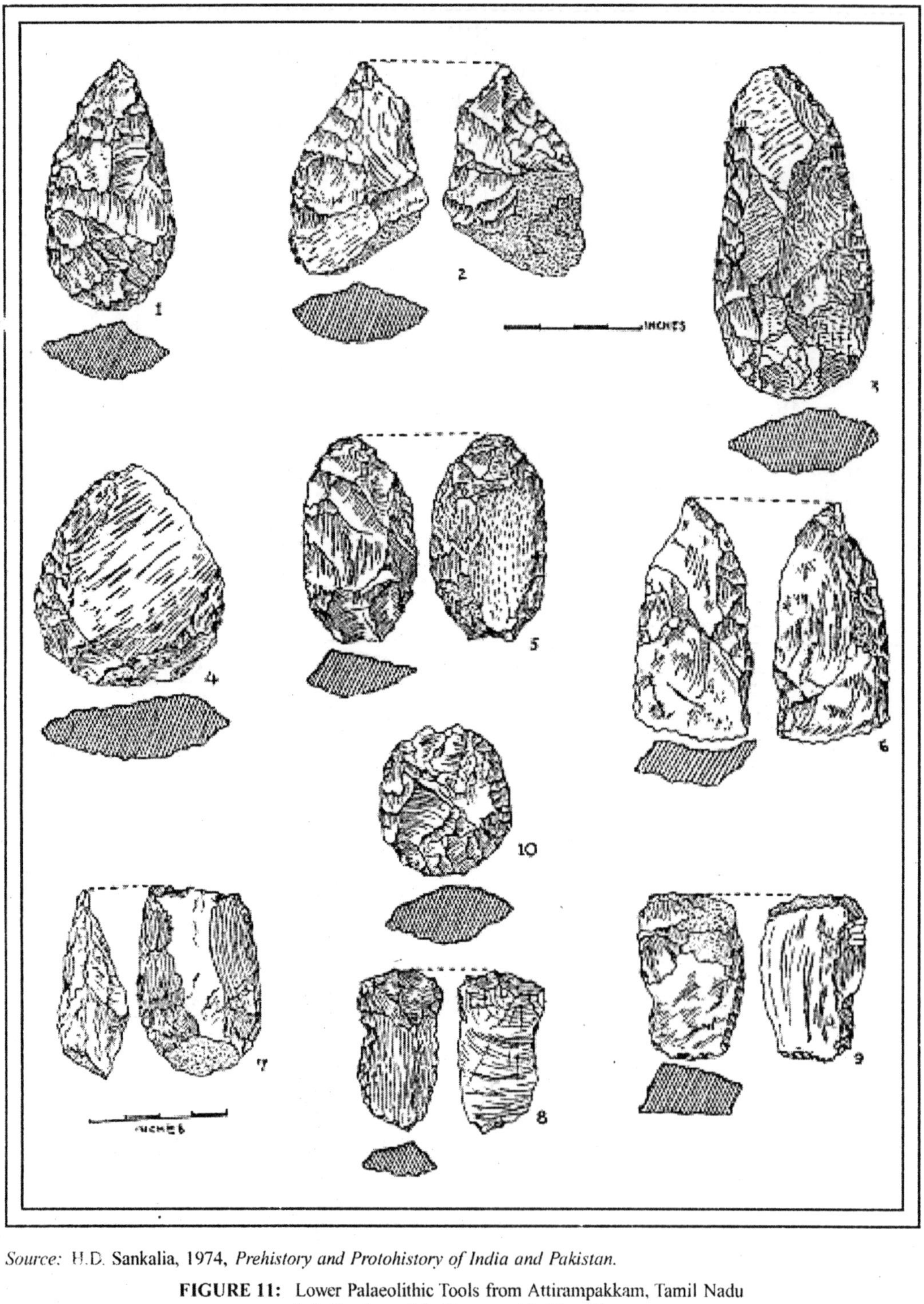

Source: H.D. Sankalia, 1974, *Prehistory and Protohistory of India and Pakistan.*

FIGURE 11: Lower Palaeolithic Tools from Attirampakkam, Tamil Nadu
1-5, Handaxe; 6-9, Cleavers; 10, Discoid

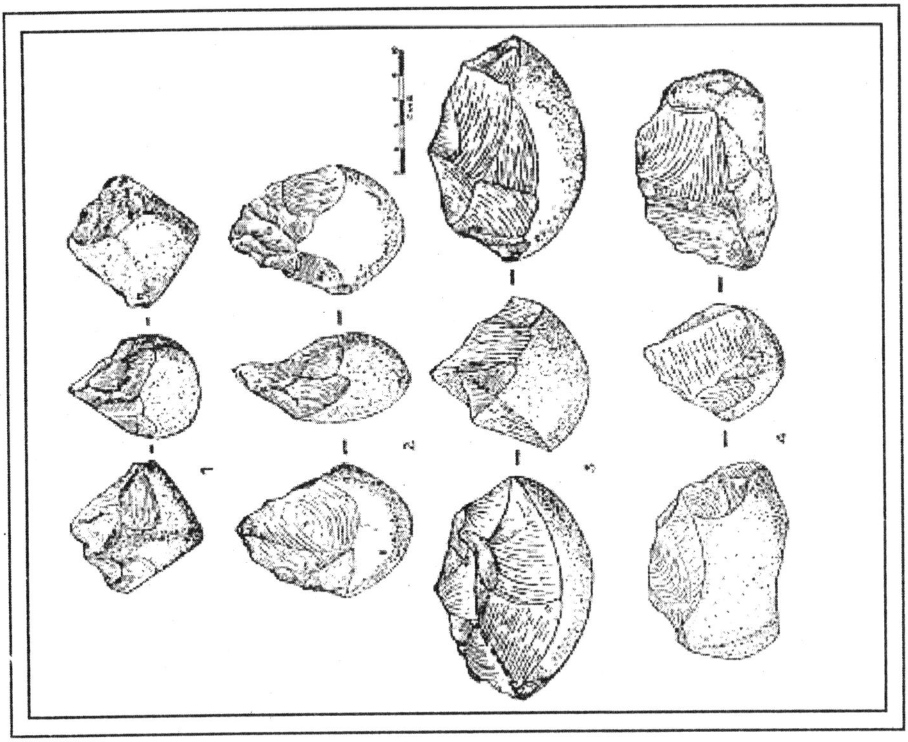

Source: H.D. Sankalia, 1974, *Prehistory and Protohistory of India and Pakistan.*

FIGURE 12: Pebble Tools from Papamiyatekdi, Chanda District, Maharashtra

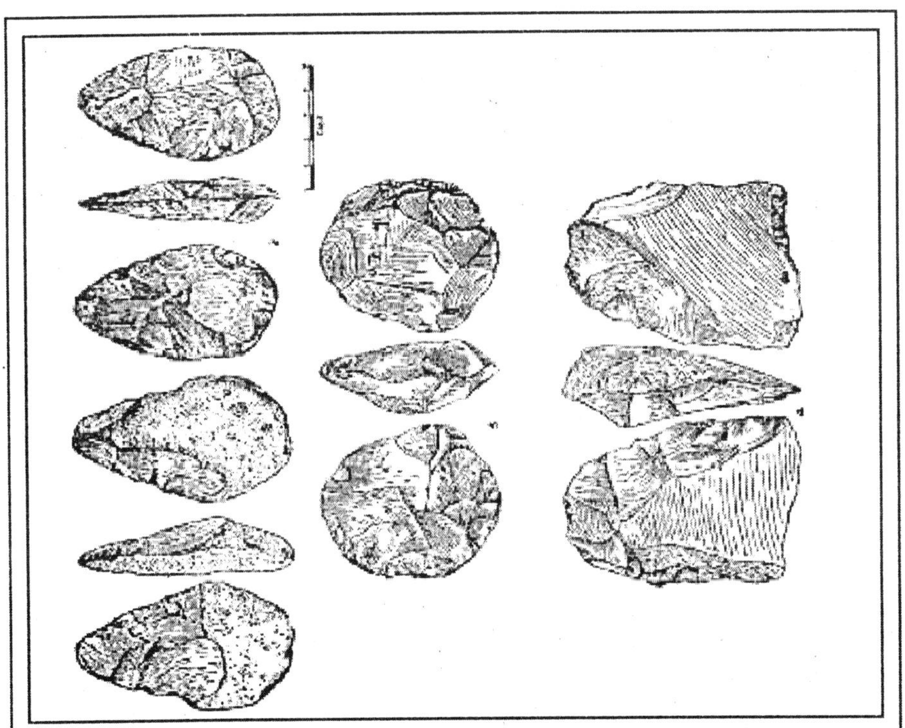

Source: H.D. Sankalia, 1974, *Prehistory and Protohistory of India and Pakistan.*

FIGURE 13: Cleavers and Handaxes from Papamiyatekdi, Chanda District, Maharashtra

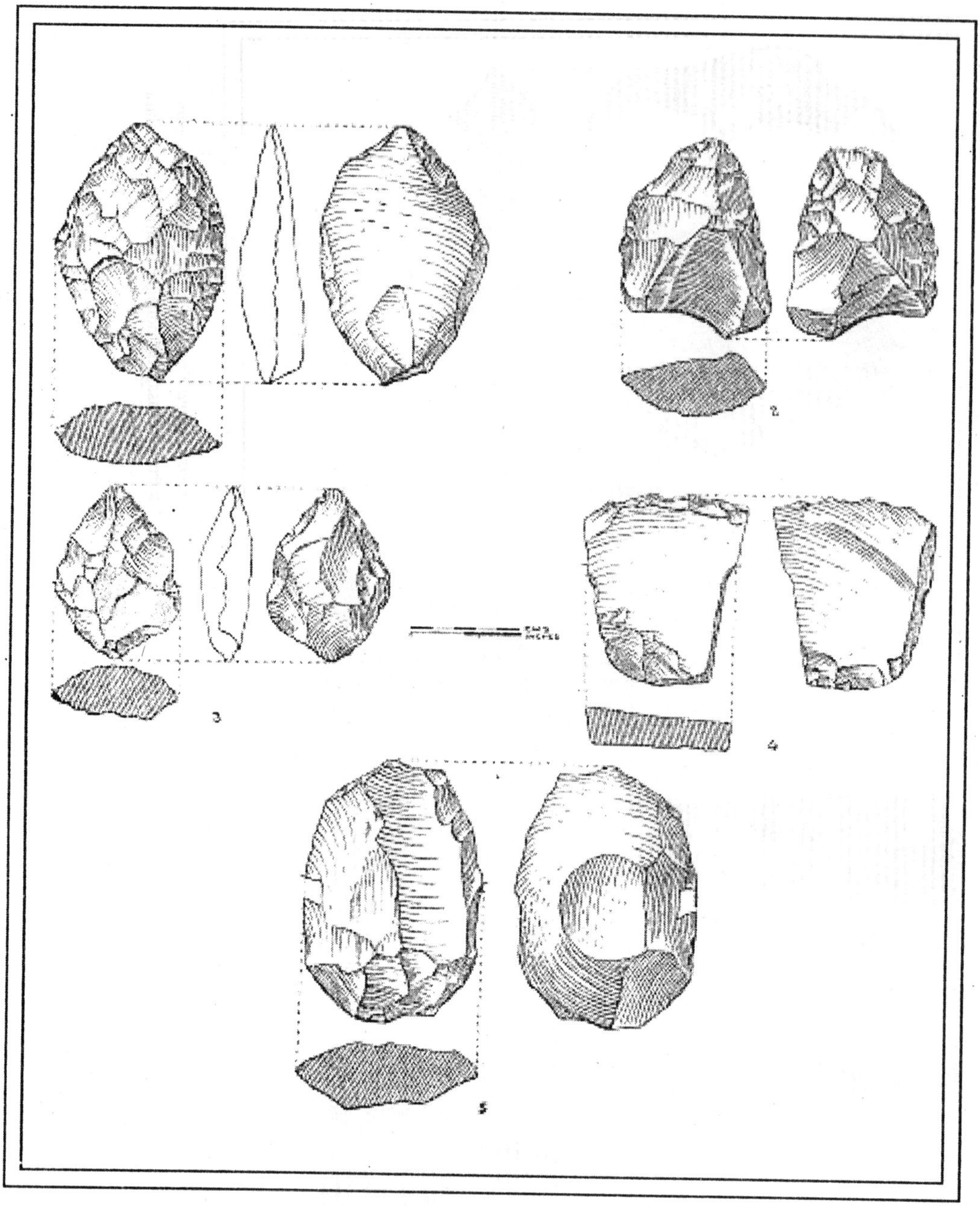

Source: H.D. Sankalia, 1974, *Prehistory and Protohistory of India and Pakistan.*

FIGURE 14: Early Stone Age Tools from Gangpur (Nasik) on Godavari River, Maharashtra

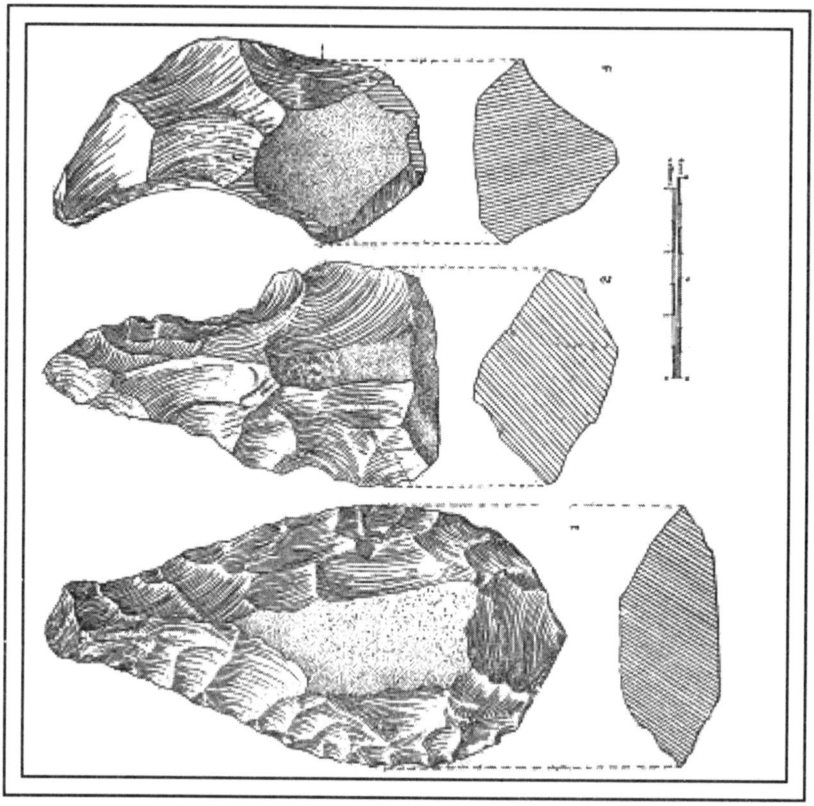

Source: H.D. Sankalia, 1974, *Prehistory and Protohistory of India and Pakistan.*

FIGURE 15: Handaxes from Nevasa, Ahmadnagar District, Maharashtra

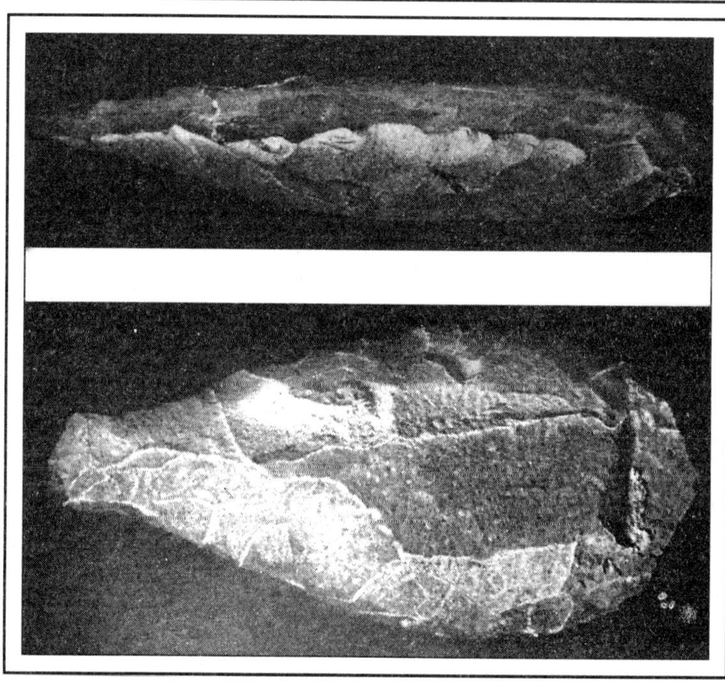

Source: H.D. Sankalia, 1974, *Prehistory and Protohistory of India and Pakistan.*

FIGURE 16: Handaxes from Nevasa, Maharashtra

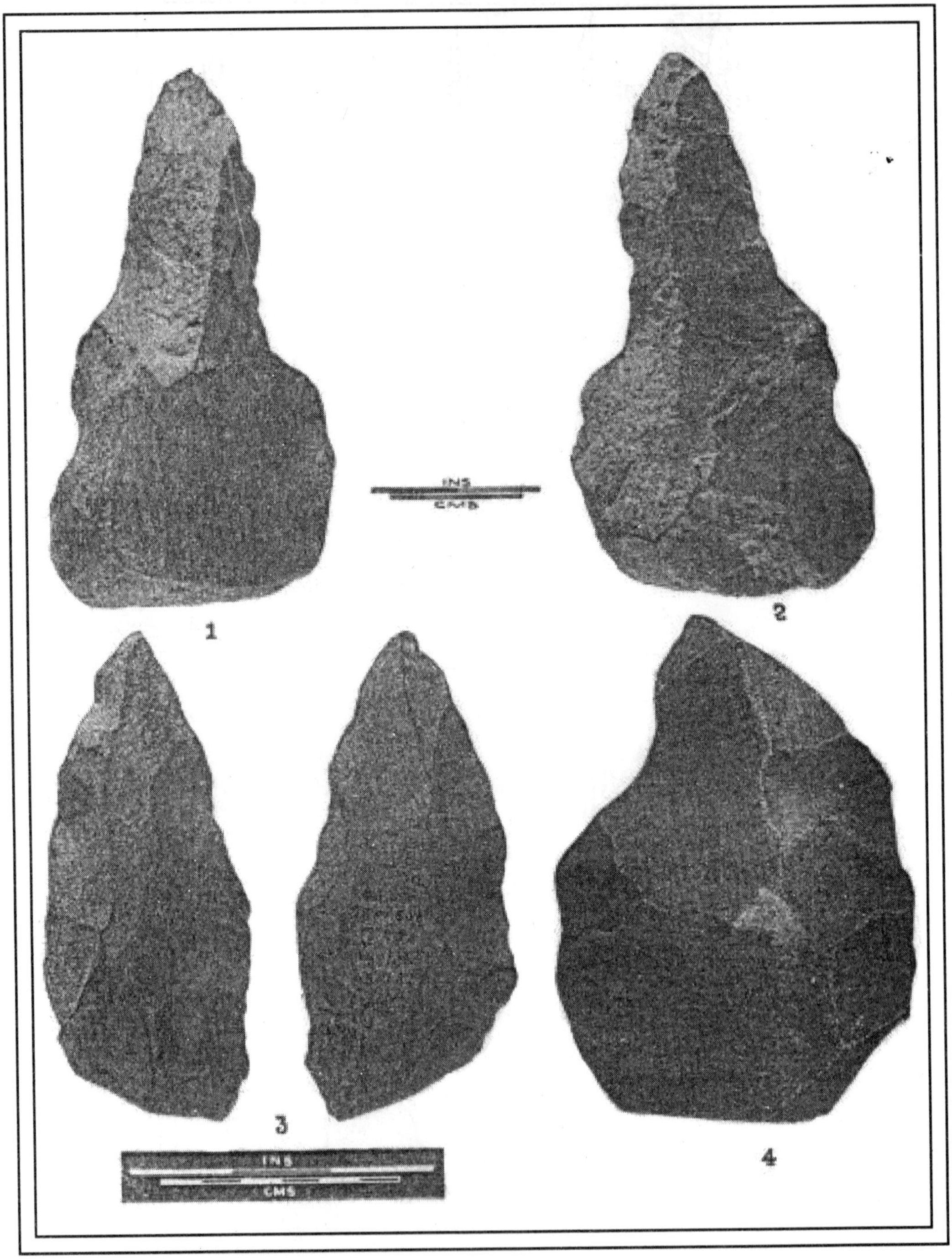

Source: H.D. Sankalia, 1974, *Prehistory and Protohistory of India and Pakistan.*

FIGURE 17: Handaxes from Nevasa, Maharashtra

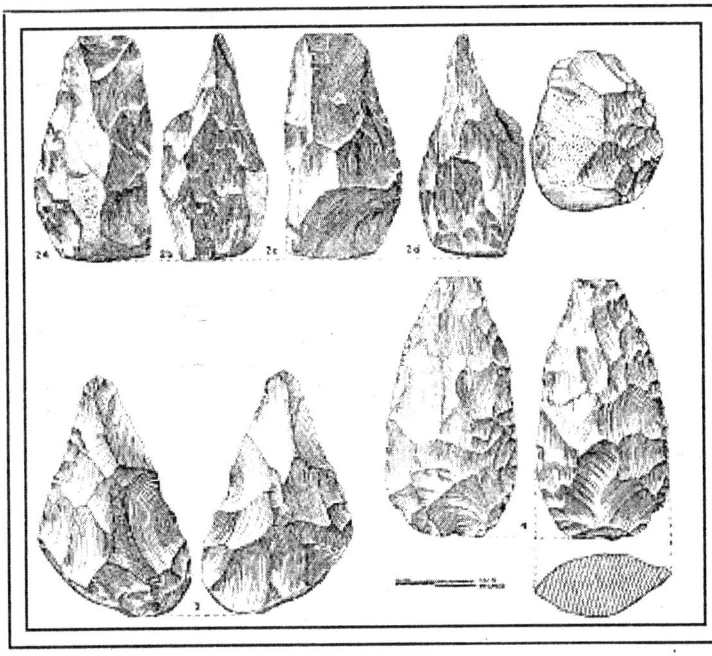

Source: H.D. Sankalia, 1974, *Prehistory and Protohistory of India and Pakistan.*

FIGURE 18: Early Stone Age Tools from Sabarmati River, Gujarat

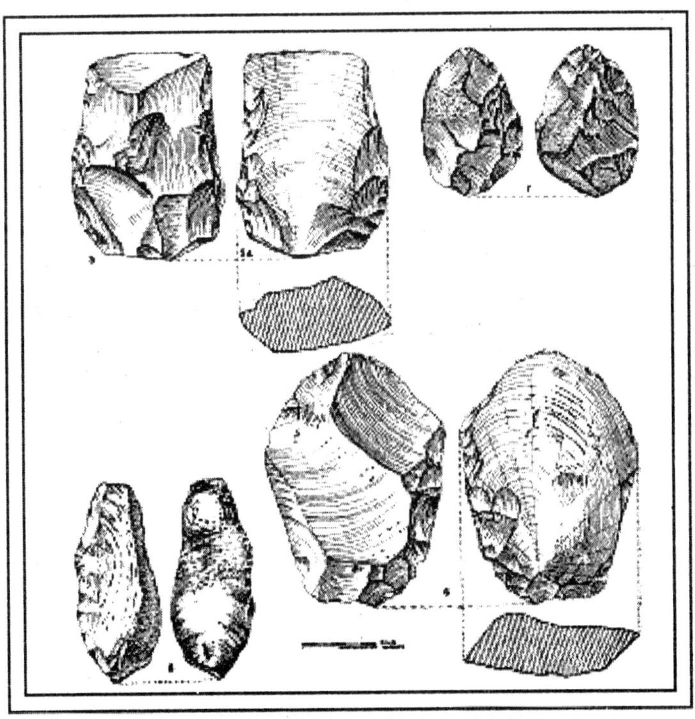

Source: H.D. Sankalia, 1974, *Prehistory and Protohistory of India and Pakistan.*

FIGURE 19: Early Stone Age Tools from Sabarmati-Arsang Rivers, Gujarat

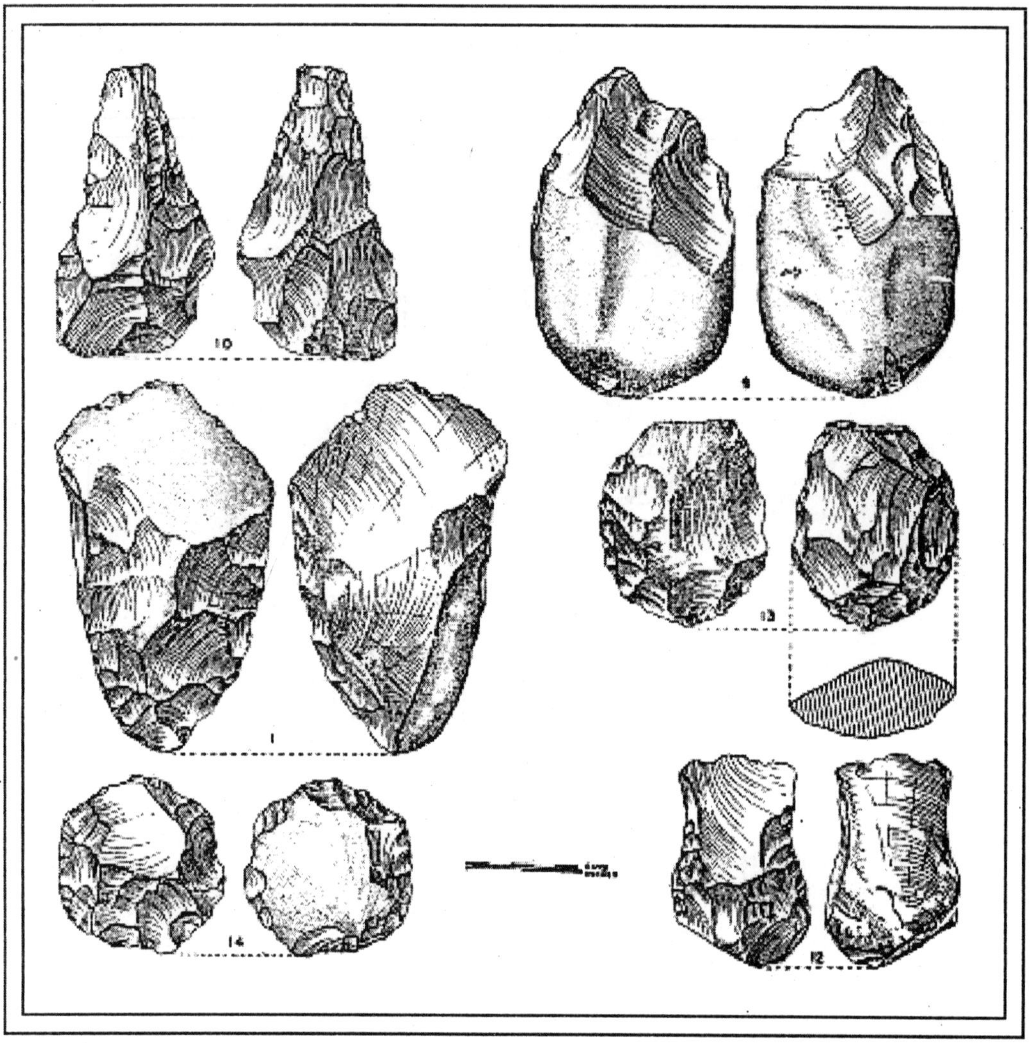

Source: H.D. Sankalia, 1974, *Prehistory and Protohistory of India and Pakistan.*

FIGURE 20: Early Stone Age Tools from Karjan River, Gujarat

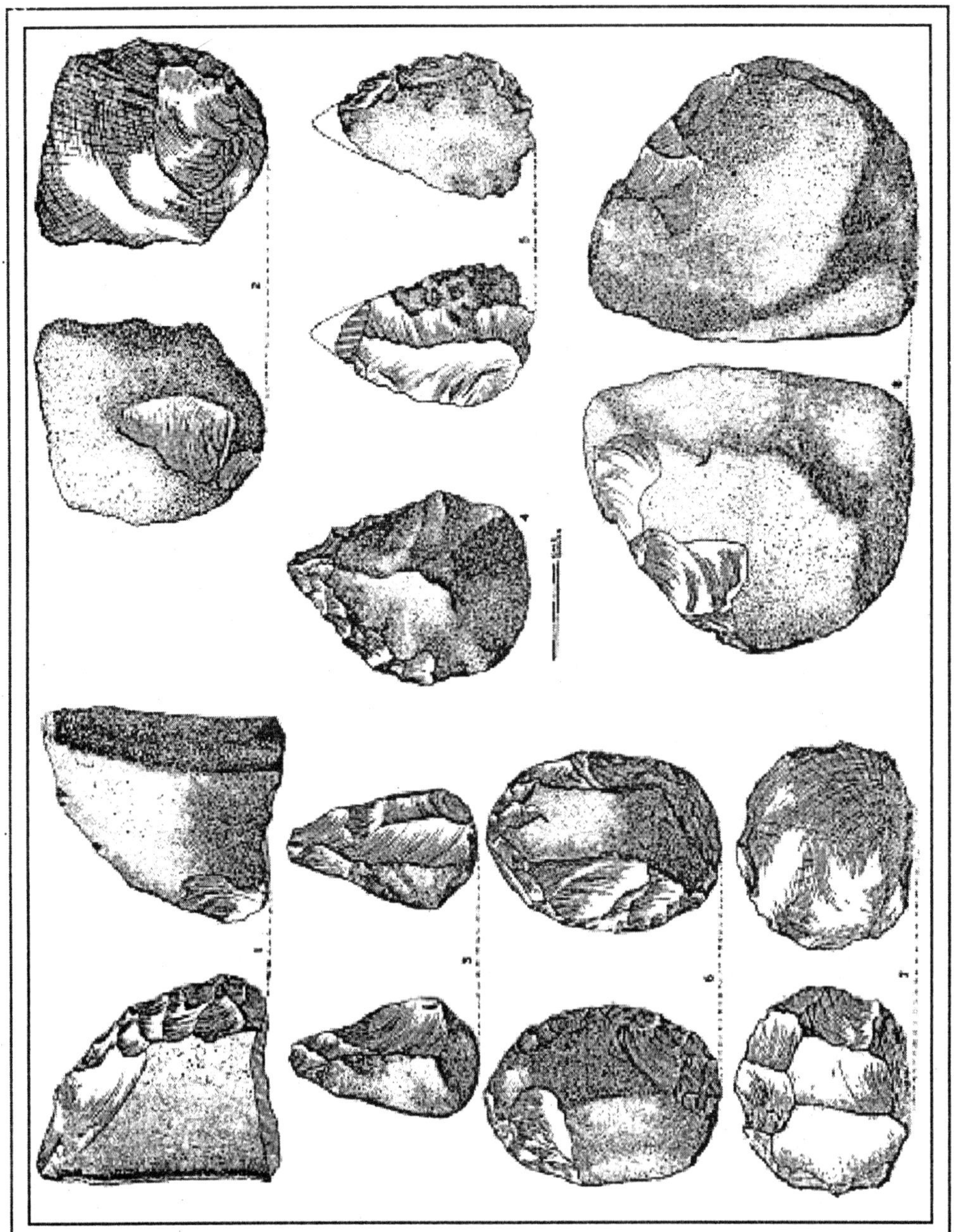

Source: H.D. Sankalia, 1974, *Prehistory and Protohistory of India and Pakistan.*

FIGURE 21: Early Stone Age Tools from Kutch, Gujarat

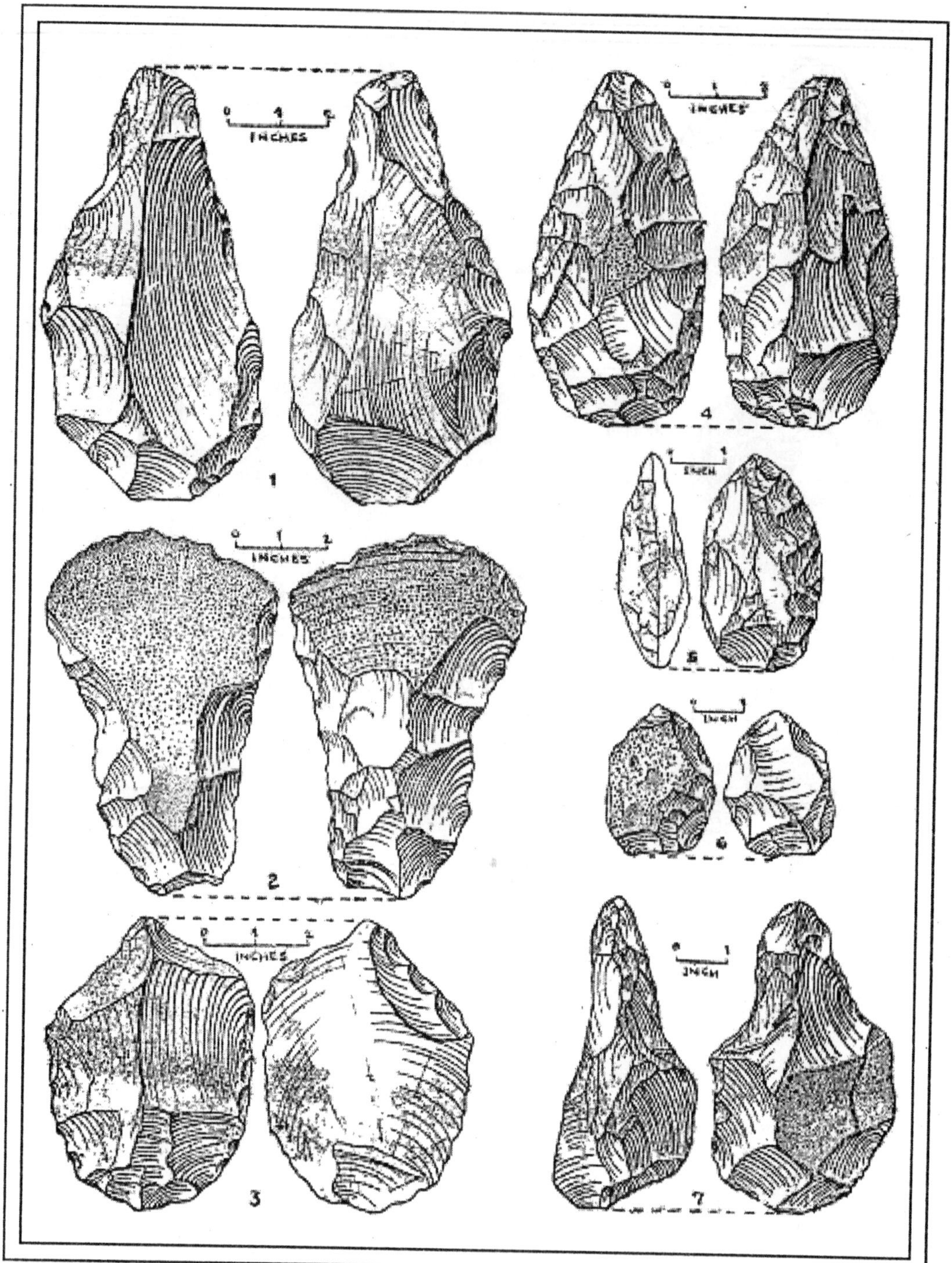

Source: H.D. Sankalia, 1974, *Prehistory and Protohistory of India and Pakistan.*

FIGURE 22: Early Stone Age Tools from Lalitpur on the Baina Nala, Jhansi District, Uttar Pradesh

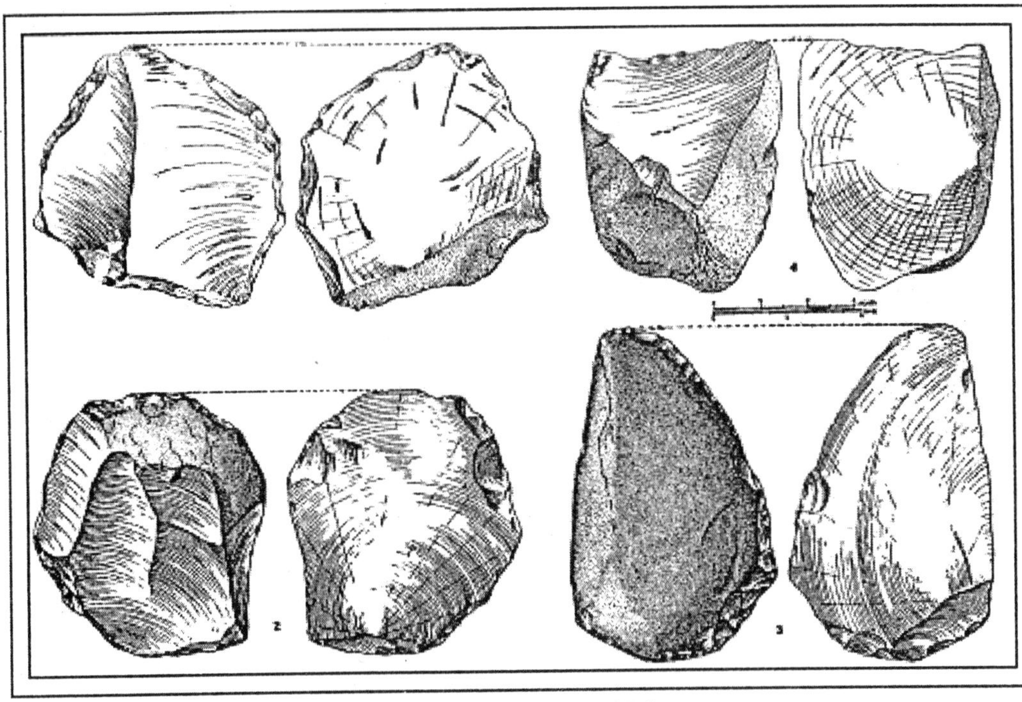

Source: H.D. Sankalia, 1974, *Prehistory and Protohistory of India and Pakistan.*

FIGURE 23: Early Stone Age Tools from Maheshwar on Narmada River, Madhya Pradesh

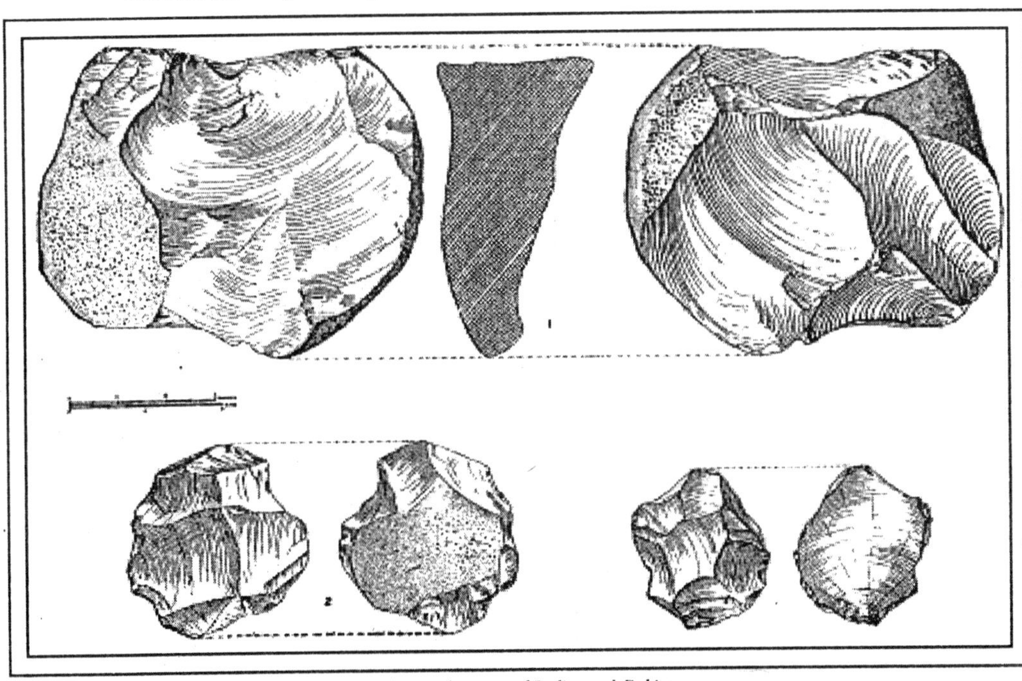

Source: H.D. Sankalia, 1974, *Prehistory and Protohistory of India and Pakistan.*

FIGURE 24: Early Stone Age Tools from Maheshwar on Narmada River, Madhya Pradesh

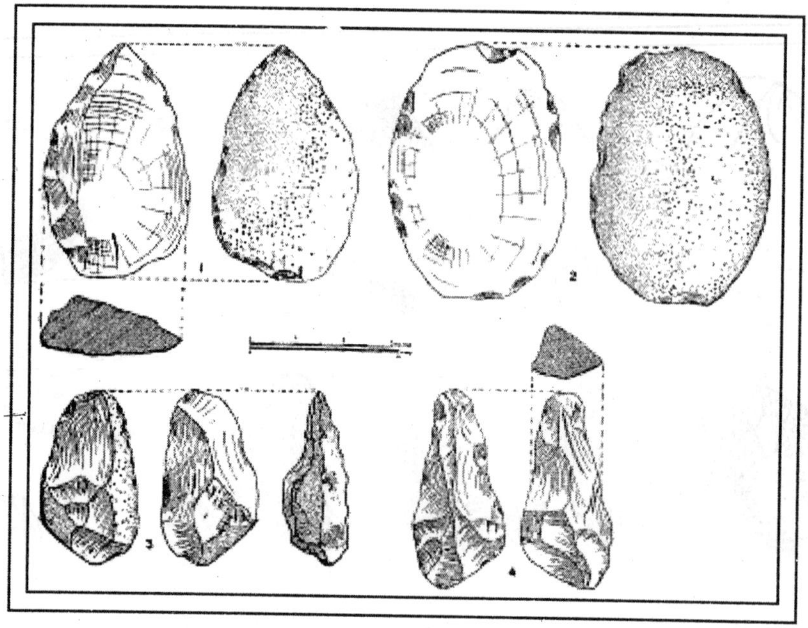

Source: H.D. Sankalia, 1974, *Prehistory and Protohistory of India and Pakistan.*

FIGURE 25: Early Stone Age Tools from Maheshwar on Narmada River, Madhya Pradesh

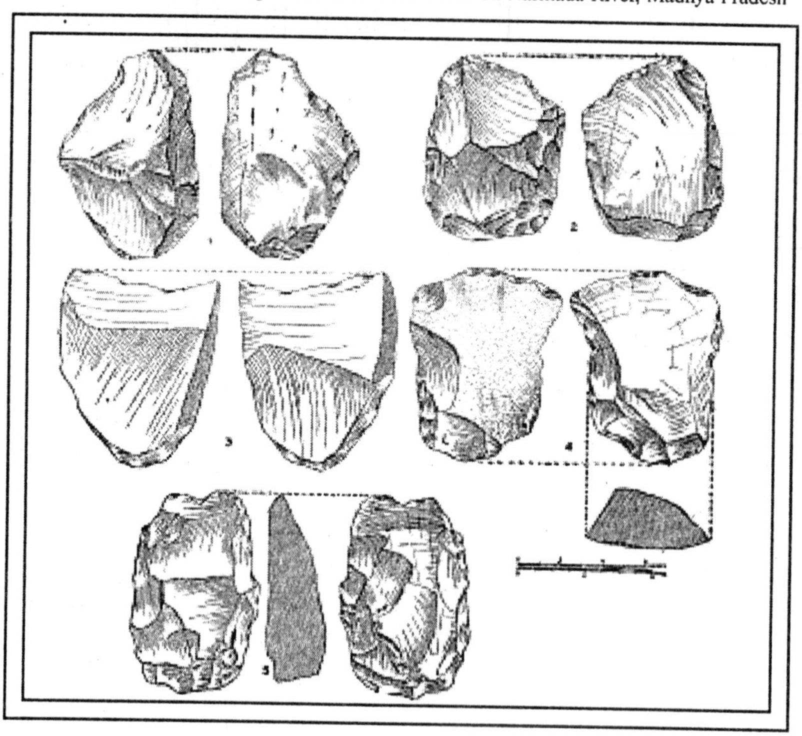

Source: H.D. Sankalia, 1974, *Prehistory and Protohistory of India and Pakistan.*

FIGURE 26: Cleavers from Maheshwar on Narmada River, Madhya Pradesh

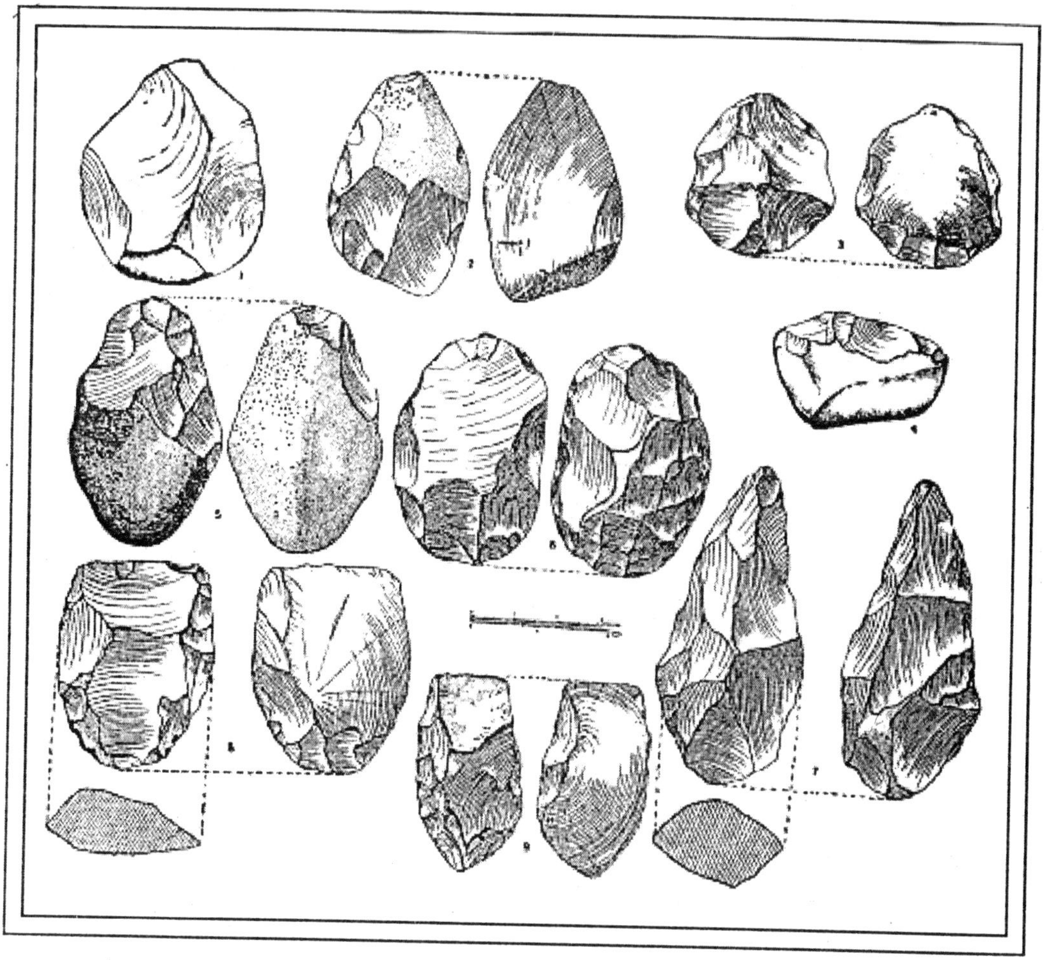

Source: H.D. Sankalia, 1974, *Prehistory and Protohistory of India and Pakistan.*

FIGURE 27: Early Stone Age Tools from South-East Rajasthan

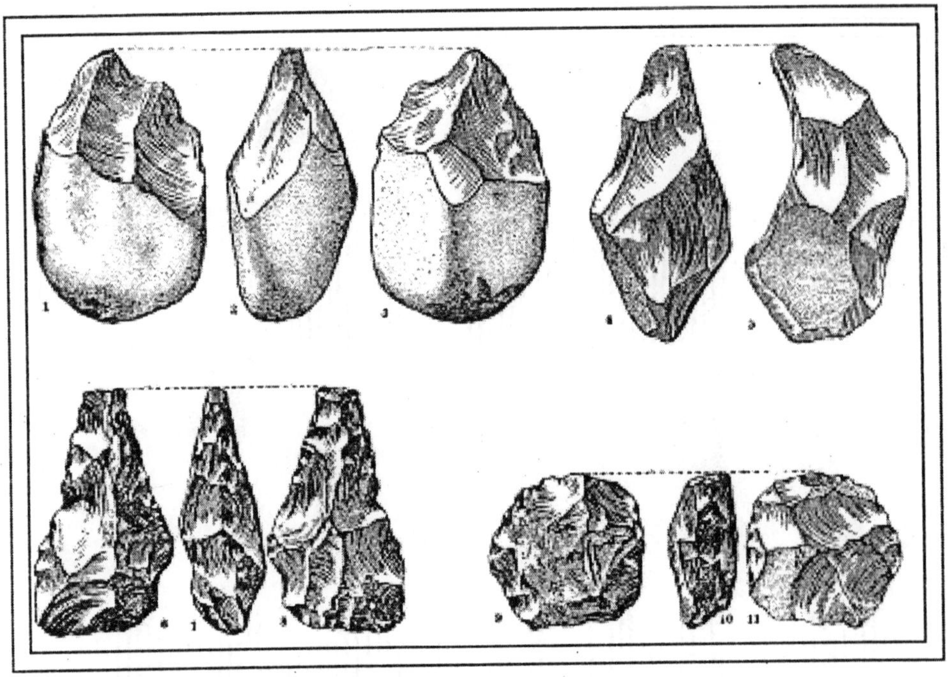

Source: H.D. Sankalia, 1974, *Prehistory and Protohistory of India and Pakistan.*

FIGURE 28: Pebble-butted Handaxe (1-3), Rostrocarinate (4-5), Abbevillian Handsxe (6-8), Discoid Scraper (9-11) (½)

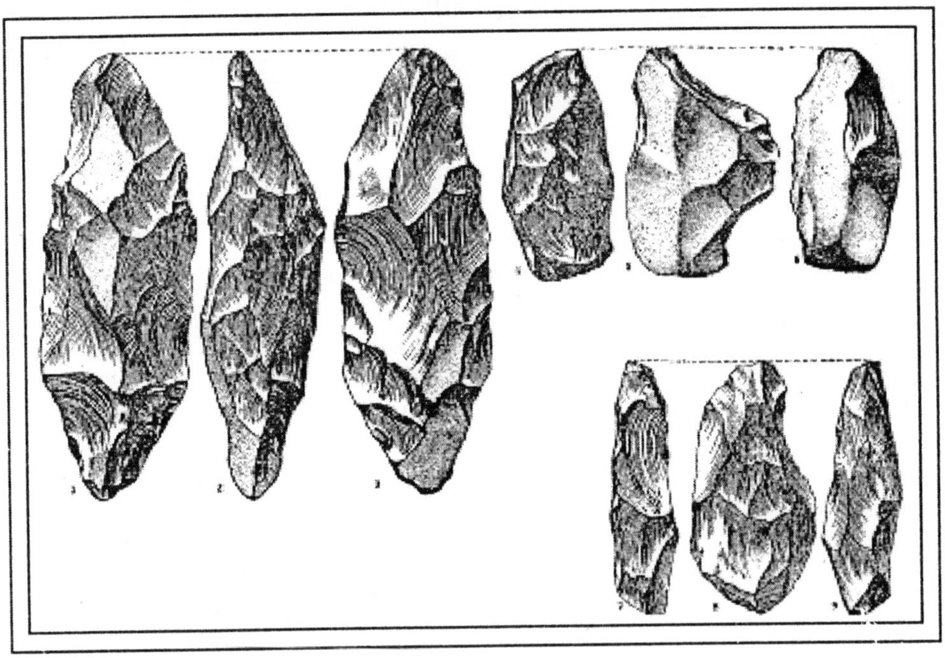

Source: H.D. Sankalia, 1974, *Prehistory and Protohistory of India and Pakistan.*

FIGURE 29: Double-pointed Handaxe (1-3), Hammer-*cum*-Chopper (4-6), Side-Scraper (7-9) (½)

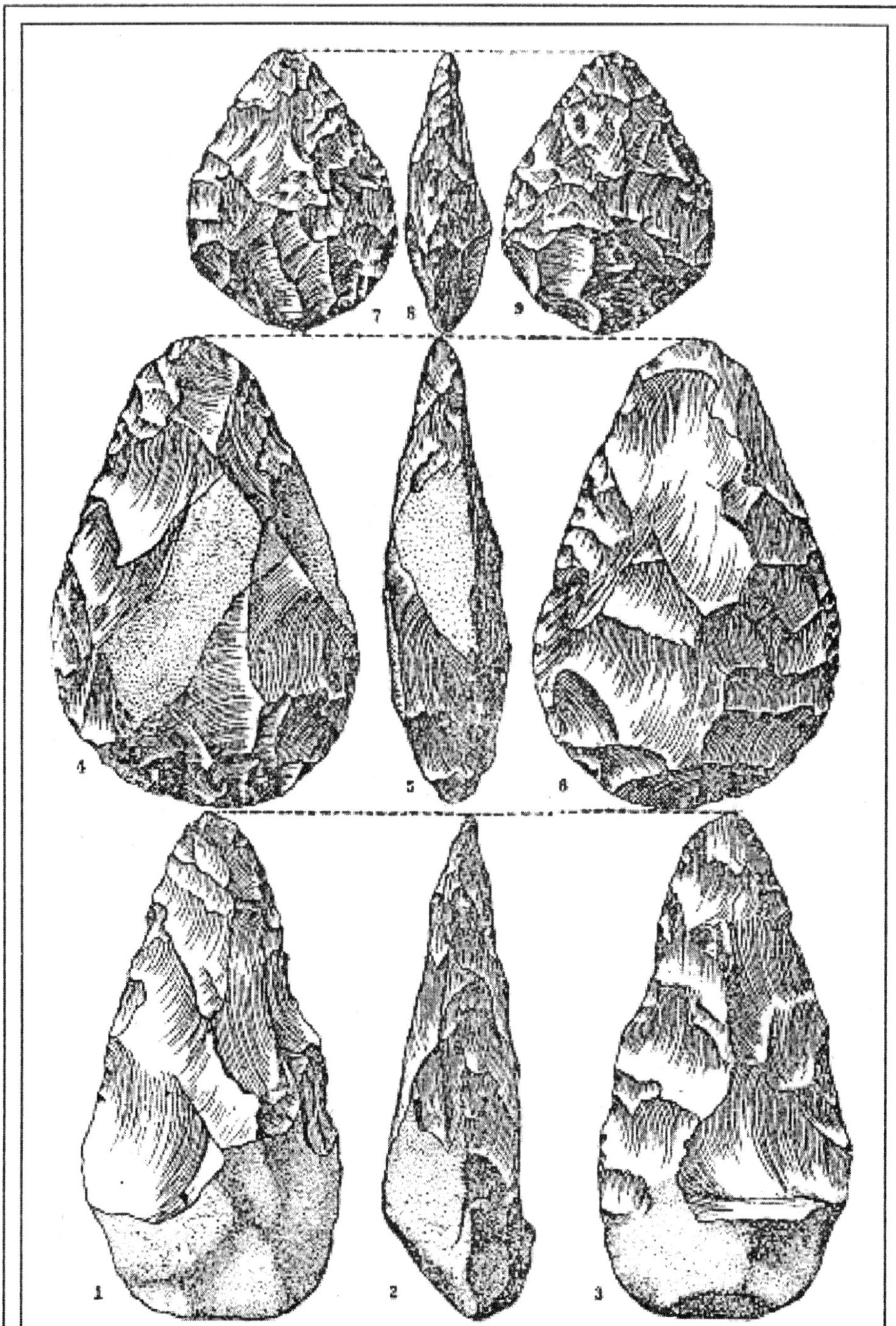

Source: H.D. Sankalia, 1974, *Prehistory and Protohistory of India and Pakistan.*

FIGURE 30: Acheulian Handaxes: Pear-Shaped (1-3), Ovate (4-6), Cordate (7-9) (½)

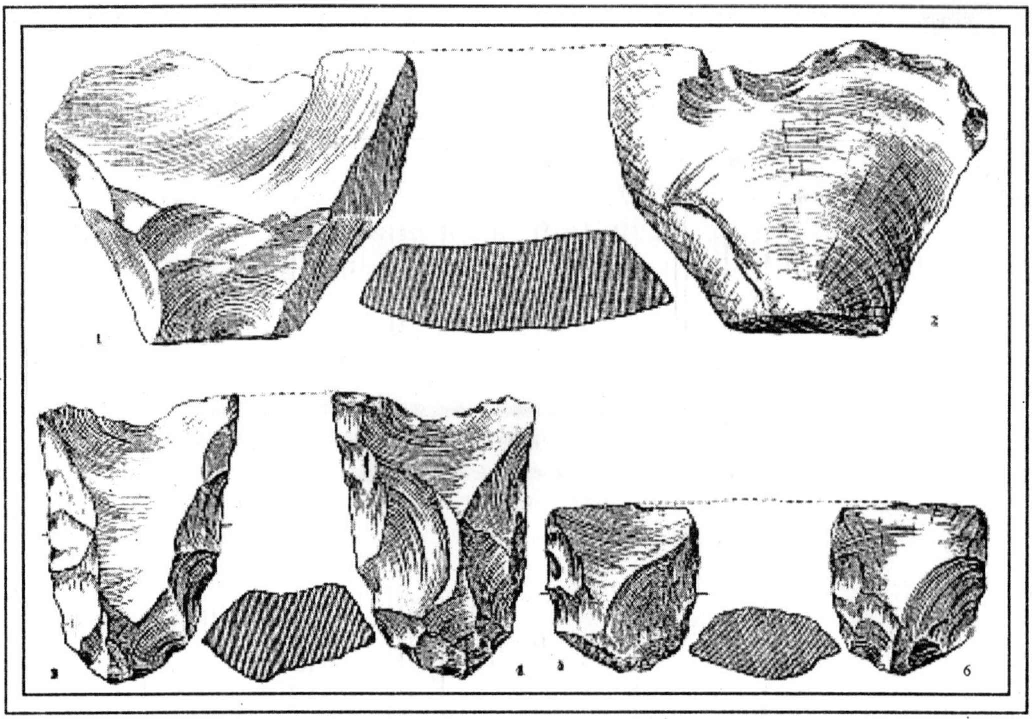

Source: H.D. Sankalia, 1974, *Prehistory and Protohistory of India and Pakistan.*

FIGURE 31: Cleavers: Concave-edge with Tapering or Point Butt (1-4), Straight-edge with U-Shaped Butt (5-6) (½)

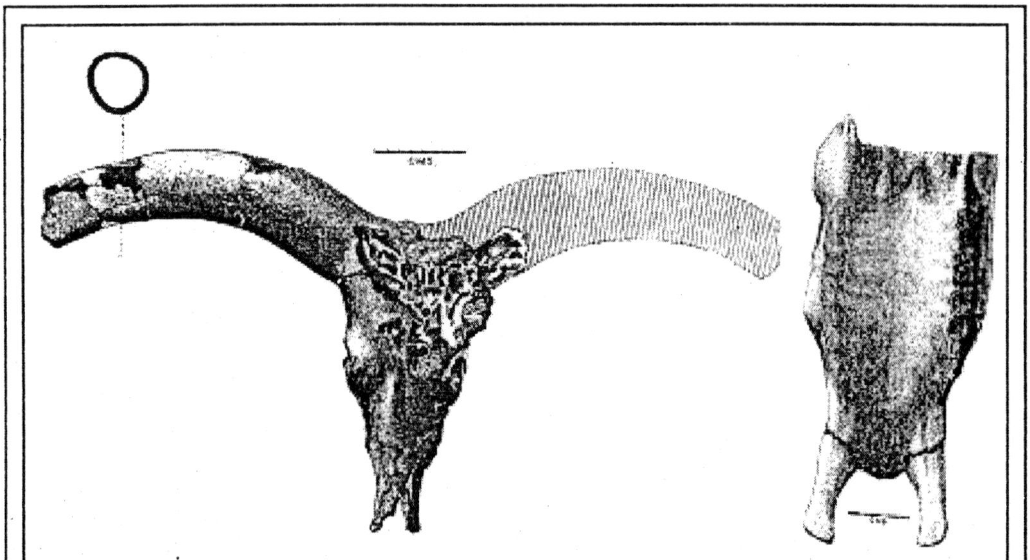

Source: H.D. Sankalia, 1974, *Prehistory and Protohistory of India and Pakistan.*

FIGURE 32: Skull with Horn of Bos Namadicus, Kalegaon

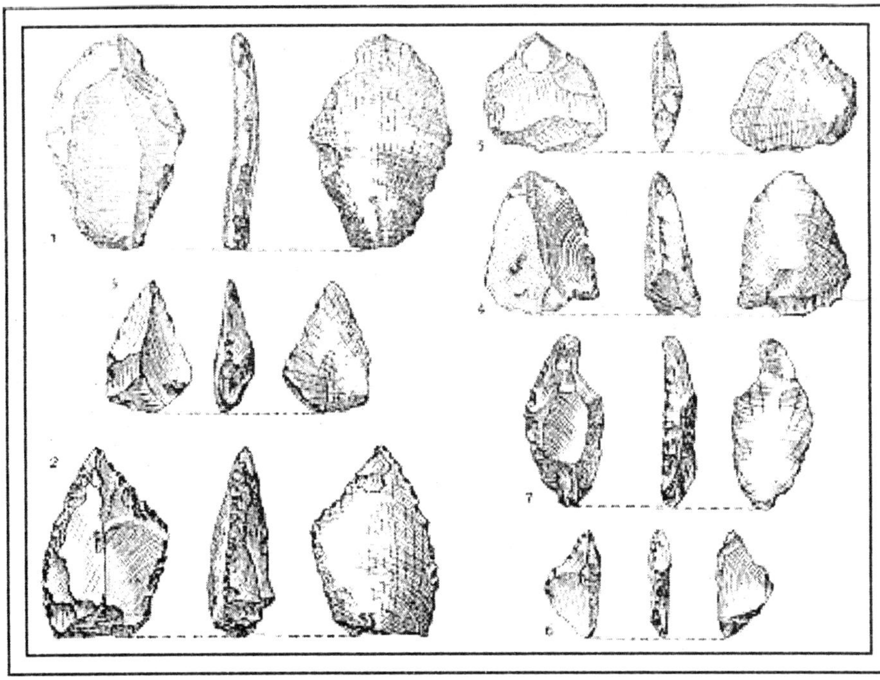

Source: H.D. Sankalia, 1974, *Prehistory and Protohistory of India and Pakistan.*

FIGURE 33: Points and Scrapers, Maharashtra

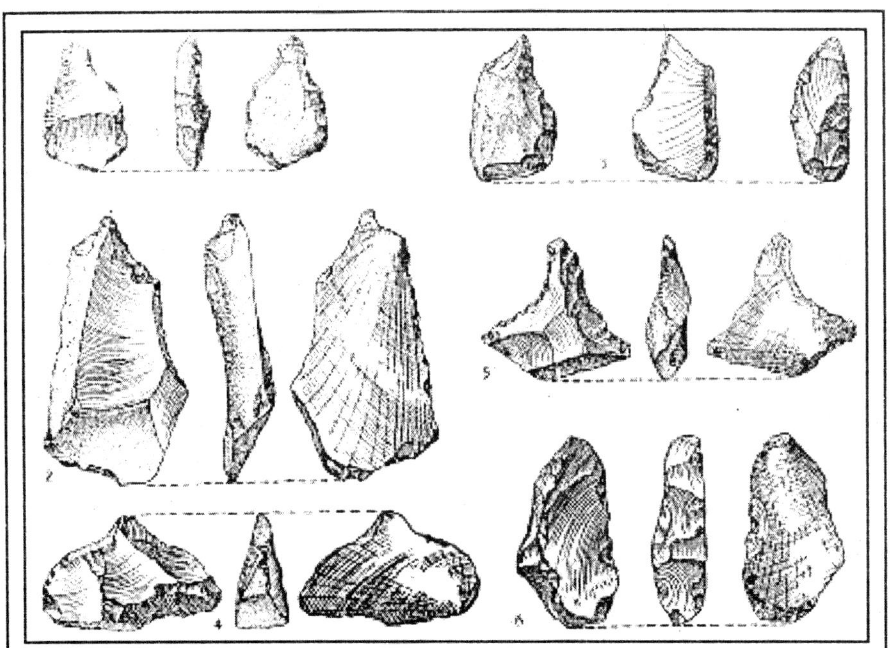

Source: H.D. Sankalia, 1974, *Prehistory and Protohistory of India and Pakistan.*

FIGURE 34: Borers and Scrapers, Maharashtra

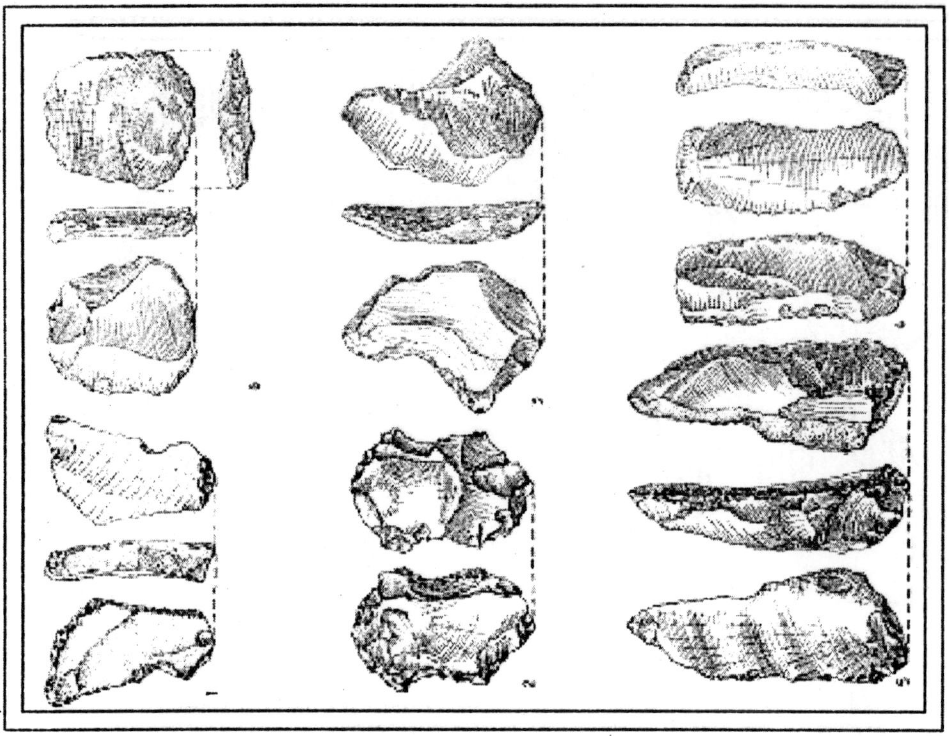

Source: H.D. Sankalia, 1974, *Prehistory and Protohistory of India and Pakistan.*

FIGURE 35: Scrapers, Maharashtra

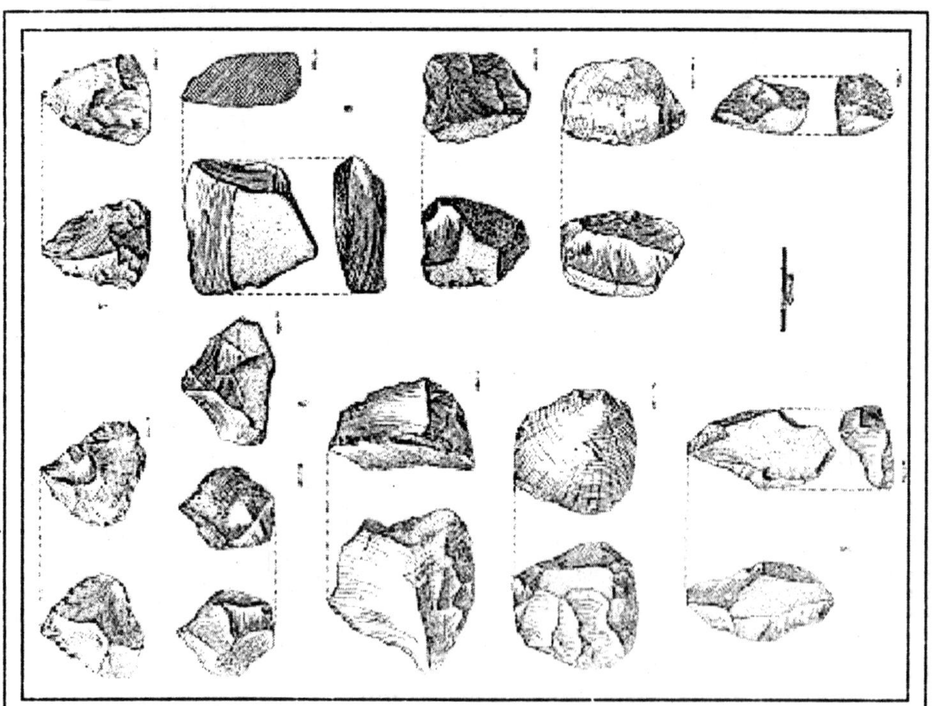

Source: H.D. Sankalia, 1974, *Prehistory and Protohistory of India and Pakistan.*

FIGURE 36: Middle Palaeolithic Tools from Kandivli (1-11)

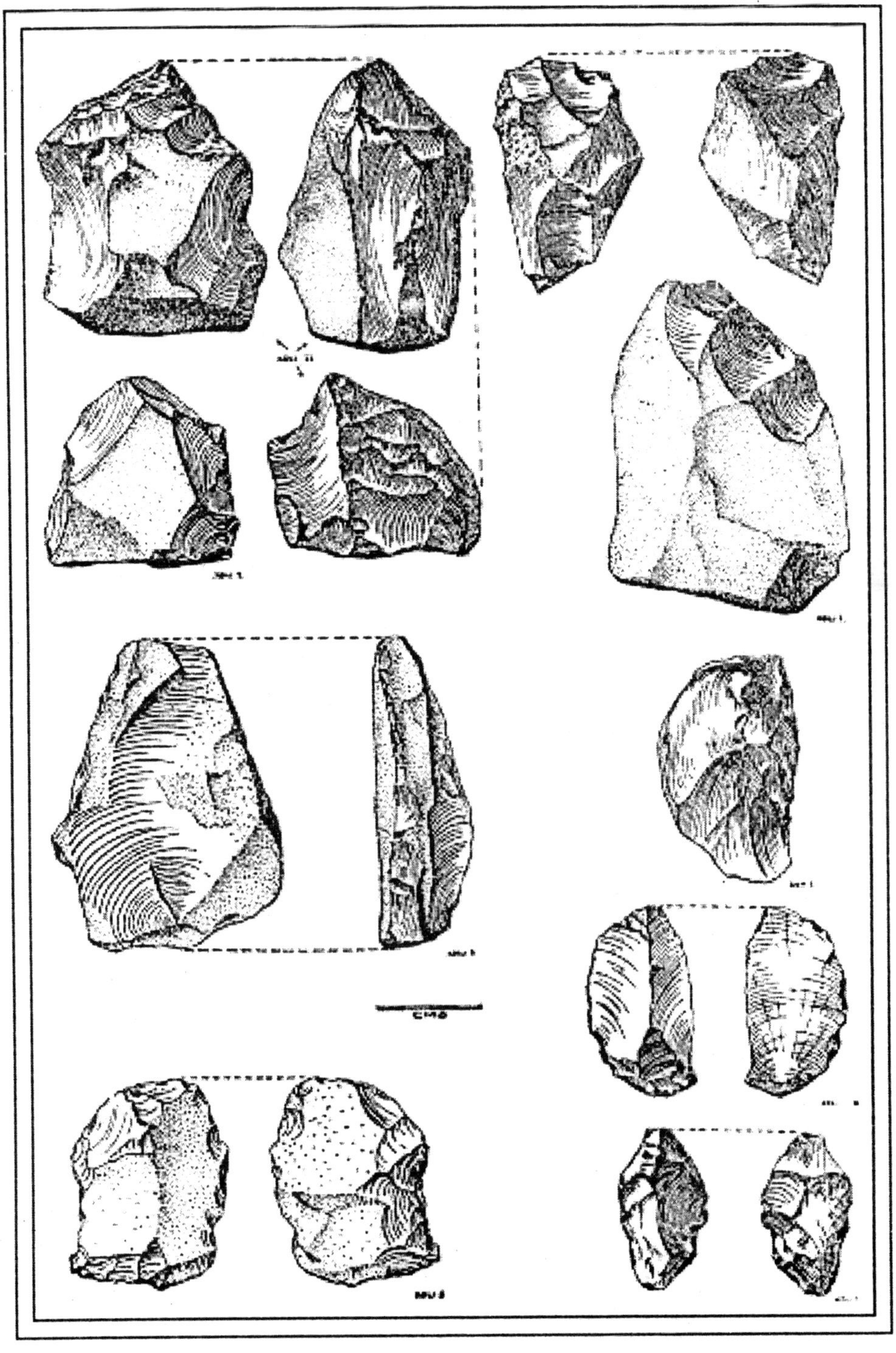

Source: H.D. Sankalia, 1974, *Prehistory and Protohistory of India and Pakistan.*

FIGURE 37: Middle Palaeolithic Tools from Kandivli (12-20)

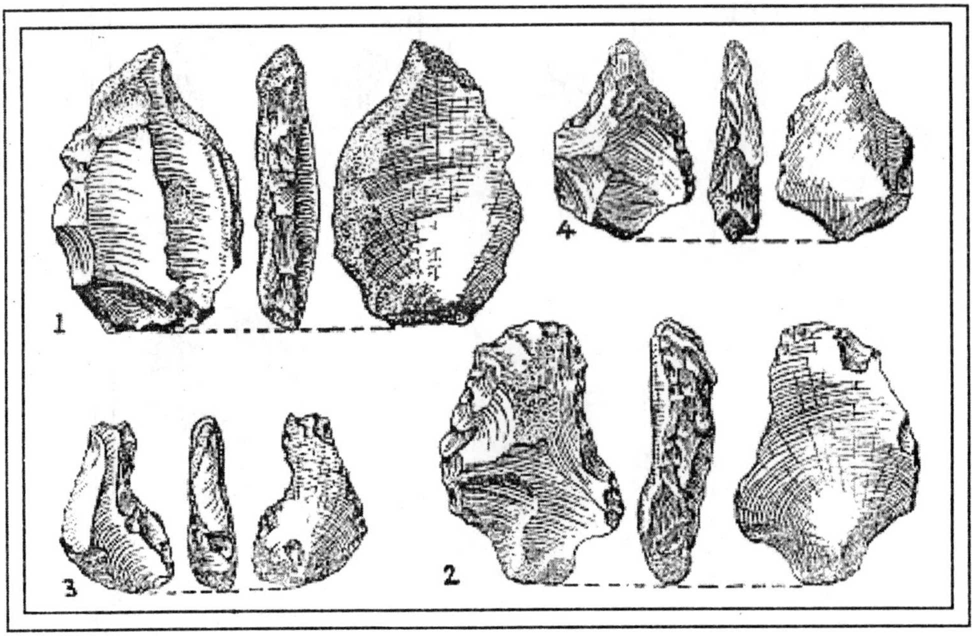

Source: H.D. Sankalia, 1974, *Prehistory and Protohistory of India and Pakistan.*

FIGURE 38: Points, Borer and Scraper, Karnataka

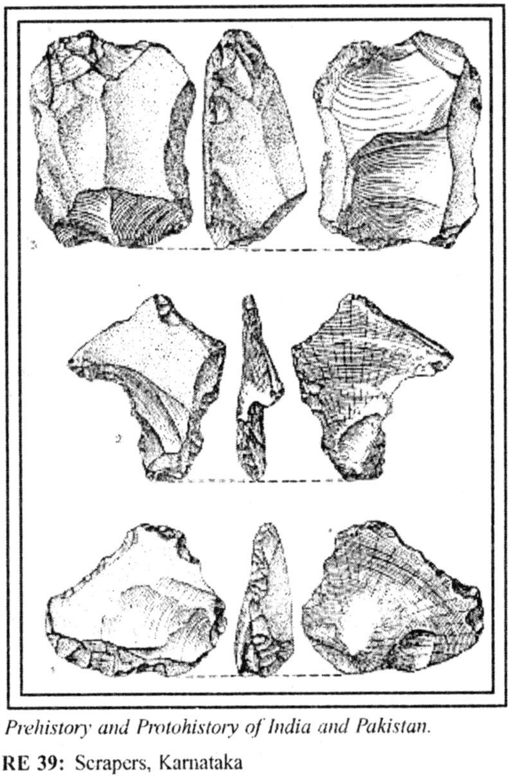

Source: H.D. Sankalia, 1974, *Prehistory and Protohistory of India and Pakistan.*

FIGURE 39: Scrapers, Karnataka

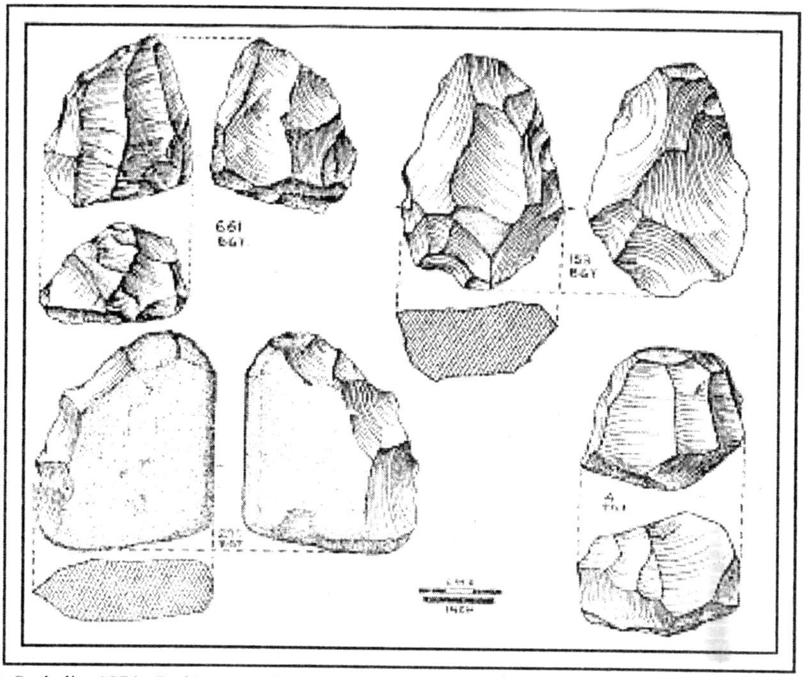

Source: H.D. Sankalia, 1974, *Prehistory and Protohistory of India and Pakistan.*

FIGURE 40: Pre-Mesolithic Industry in Painted Basalt from Bangaltota, Sangankallu, Bellary District, Karnataka

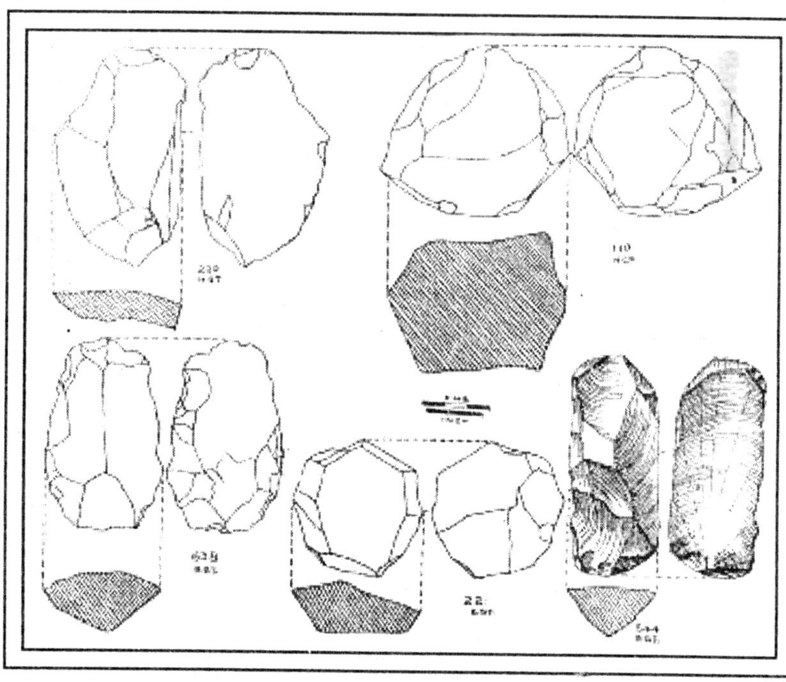

Source: H.D. Sankalia, 1974, *Prehistory and Protohistory of India and Pakistan.*

FIGURE 41: Pre-Mesolithic Industry from Bangaltota, Sanganakallu, Bellary District, Karnataka

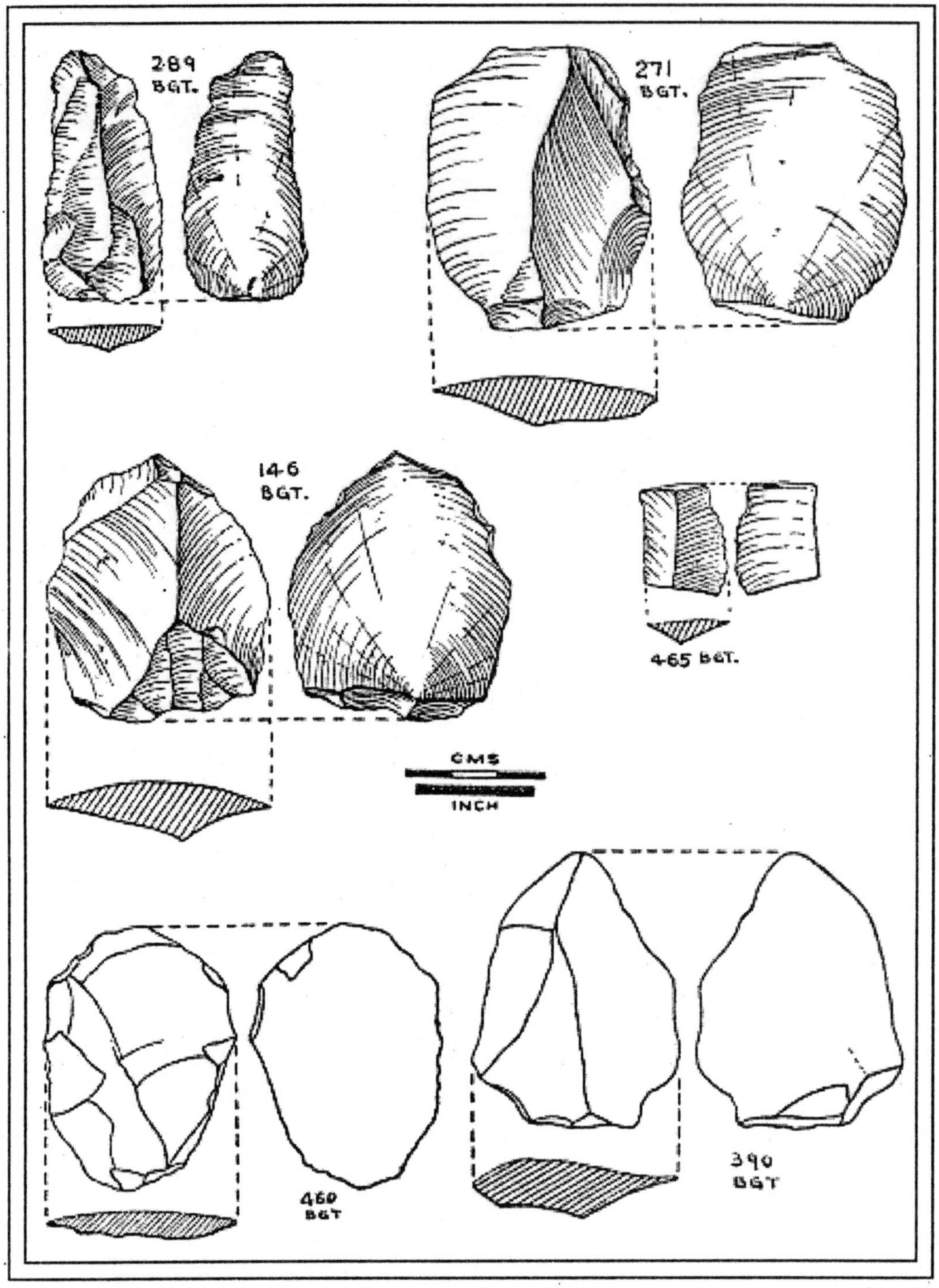

Source: H.D. Sankalia, 1974, *Prehistory and Protohistory of India and Pakistan.*

FIGURE 42: Pre-Mesolithic Industry from Bangaltota, Layer 2 (Murrum), Sanganakallu, Bellary District, Karnataka

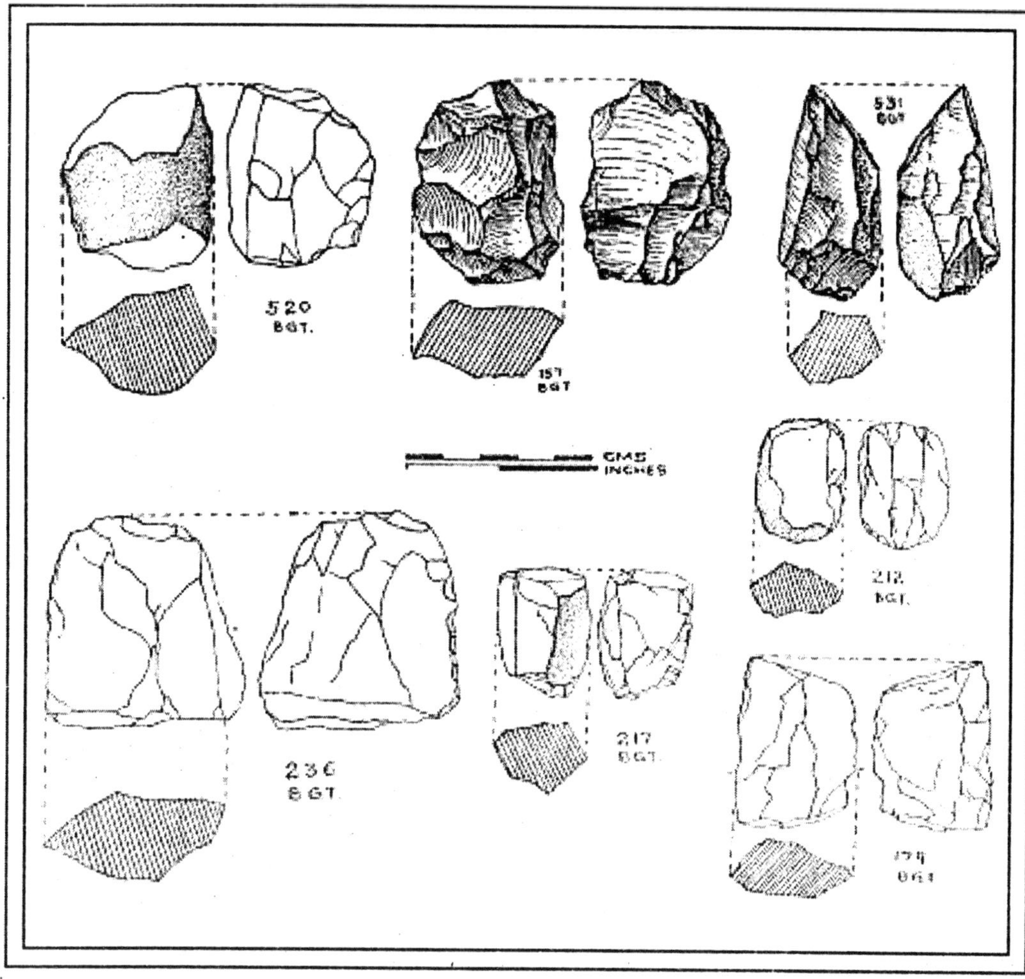

Source: H.D. Sankalia, 1974, *Prehistory and Protohistory of India and Pakistan.*

FIGURE 43: Pre-Mesolithic Industry in Quartz, Bangaltota, Layer 2 (Murrum), Sanganakallu, Bellary District, Karnataka

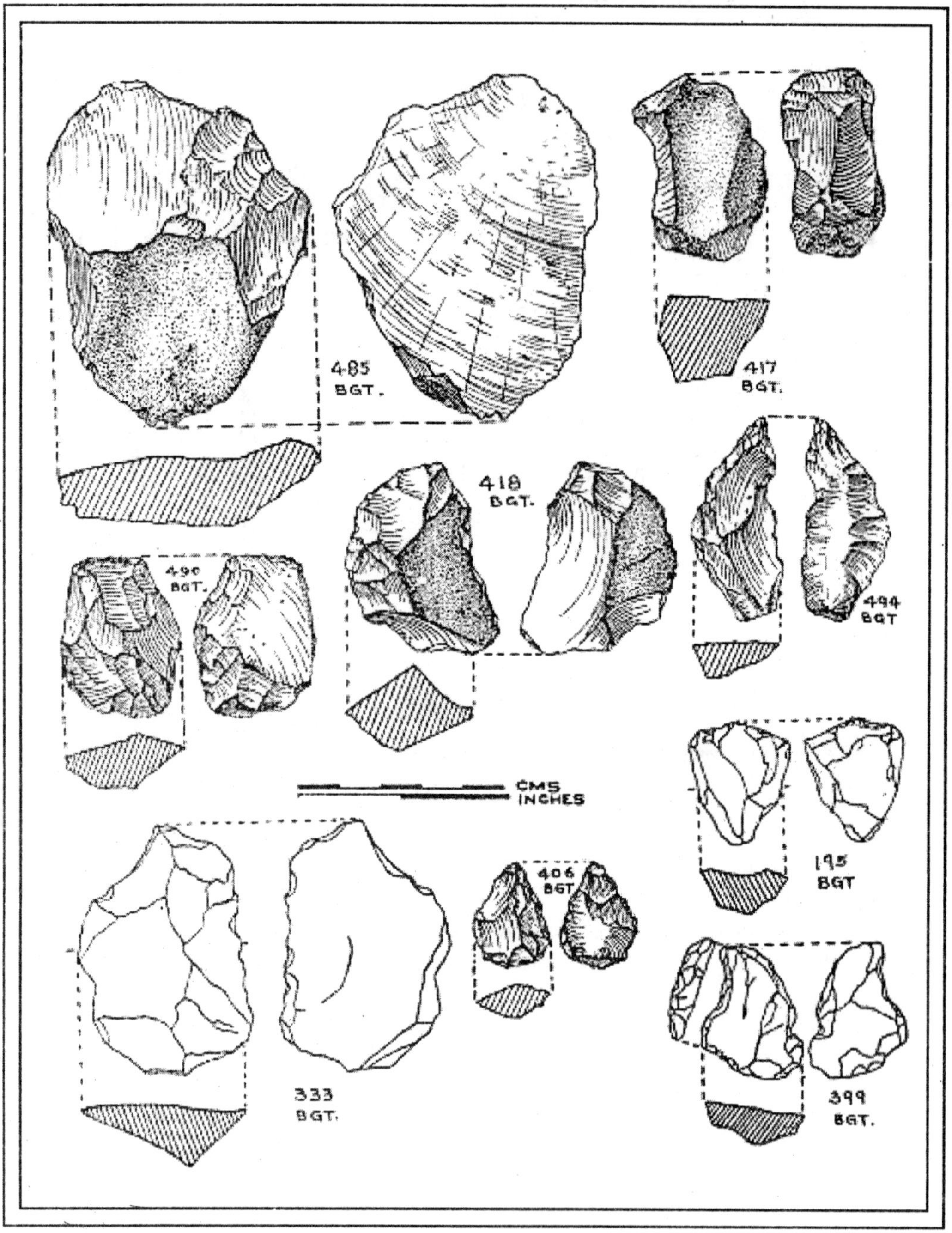

Source. H.D. Sankalia, 1974, *Prehistory and Protohistory of India and Pakistan.*

FIGURE 44: Pre-Mesolithic Industry, Bangaltota, Layer 2 (Murrum), Sanganakallu, Bellary District, Karnataka

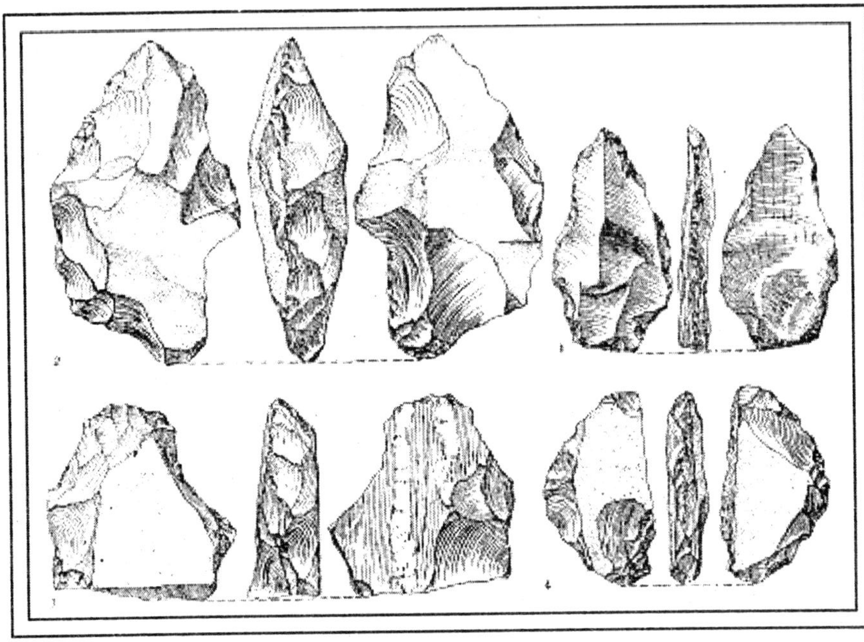

Source: H.D. Sankalia, 1974, *Prehistory and Protohistory of India and Pakistan.*

FIGURE 45: Points and Scrapers, Kurnool District, Andhra Pradesh

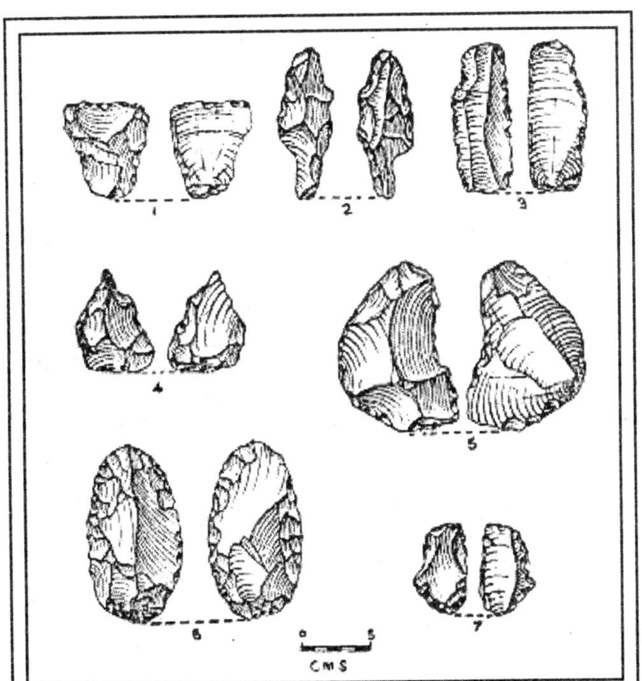

Source: H.D. Sankalia, 1974, *Prehistory and Protohistory of India and Pakistan.*

FIGURE 46: Middle Palaeolithic Tools from Renigunta, Chittoor District, Andhra Pradesh

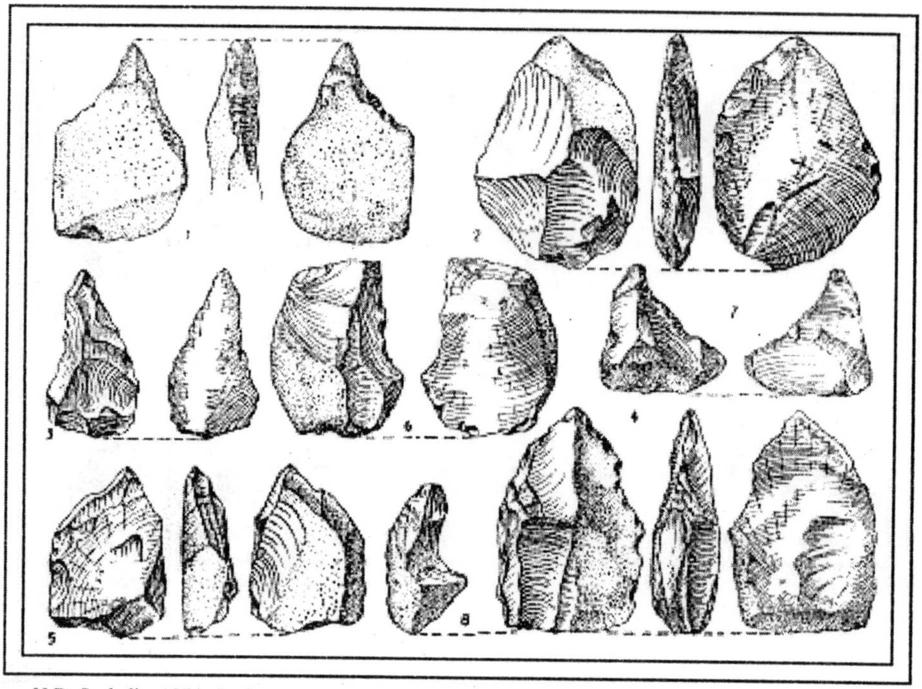

Source: H.D. Sankalia, 1974, *Prehistory and Protohistory of India and Pakistan.*

FIGURE 47: Points, Borers and Scrapers, Orissa

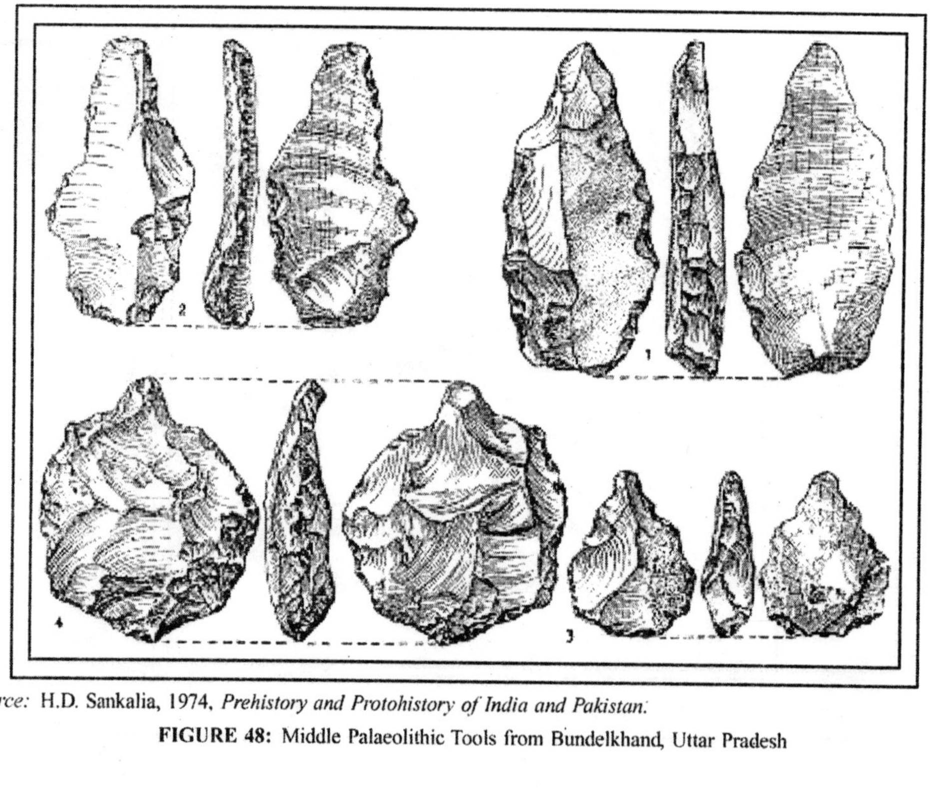

Source: H.D. Sankalia, 1974, *Prehistory and Protohistory of India and Pakistan.*

FIGURE 48: Middle Palaeolithic Tools from Bundelkhand, Uttar Pradesh

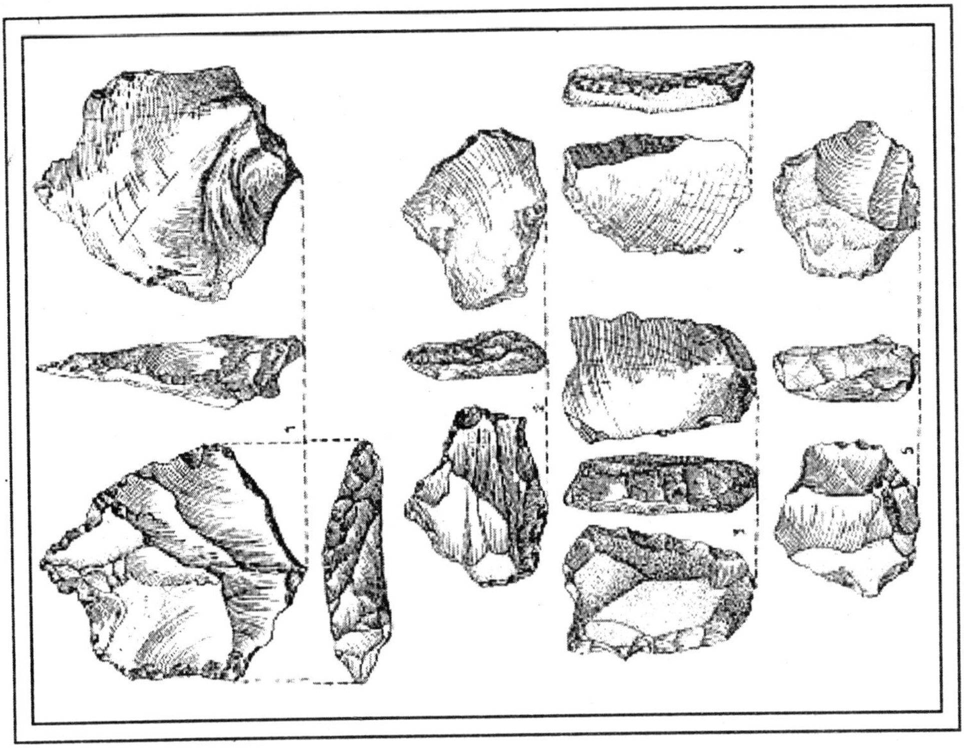

Source: H.D. Sankalia, 1974, *Prehistory and Protohistory of India and Pakistan*.

FIGURE 49: Middle Palaeolithic Tools from Bundelkhand, Uttar Pradesh

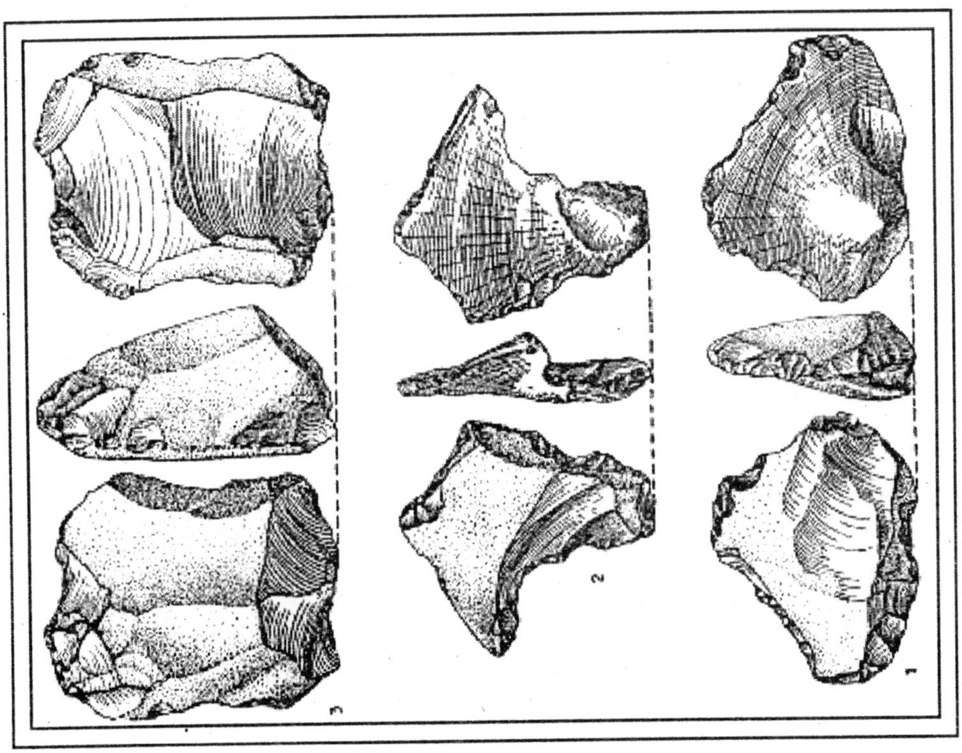

Source: H.D. Sankalia, 1974, *Prehistory and Protohistory of India and Pakistan*.

FIGURE 50: Scrapers, Malwa, Madhya Pradesh

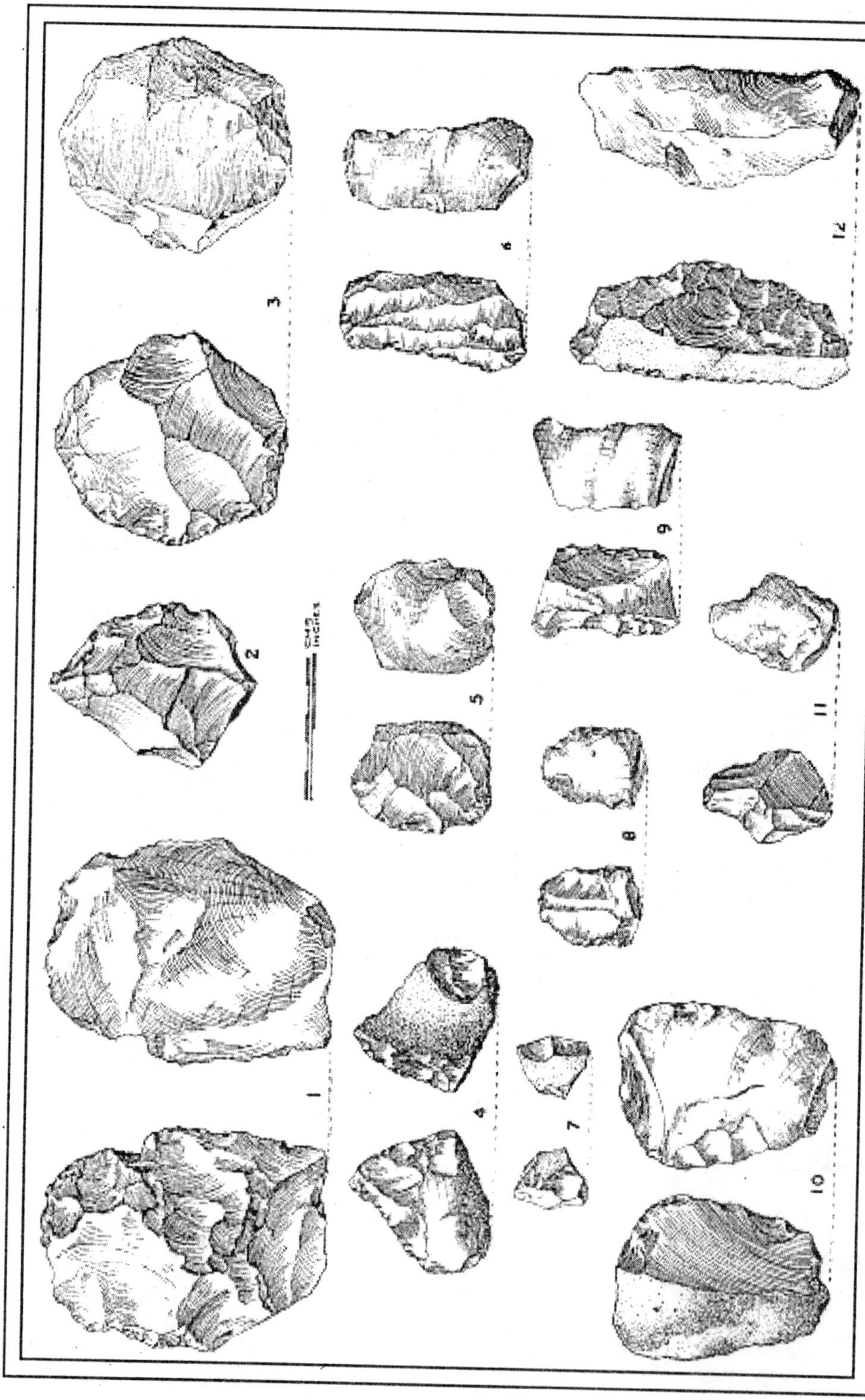

FIGURE 51: Middle Stone Age Tools, Kutch, Gujarat

Source: H.D. Sankalia, 1974, *Prehistory and Protohistory of India and Pakistan.*

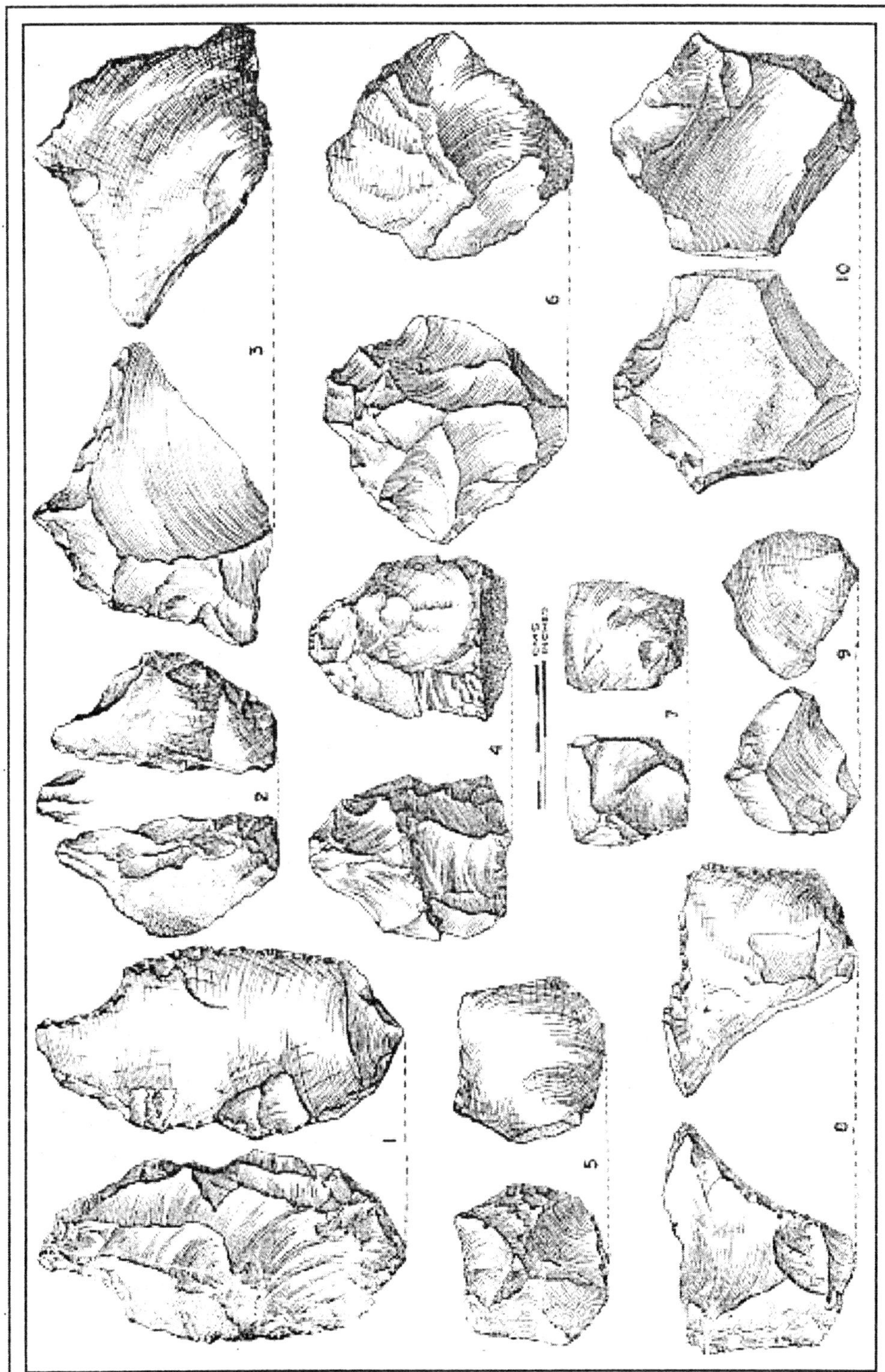

Source: H.D. Sankalia, 1974, *Prehistory and Protohistory of India and Pakistan*.

FIGURE 52: Middle Stone Age Tools, Kutch, Gujarat

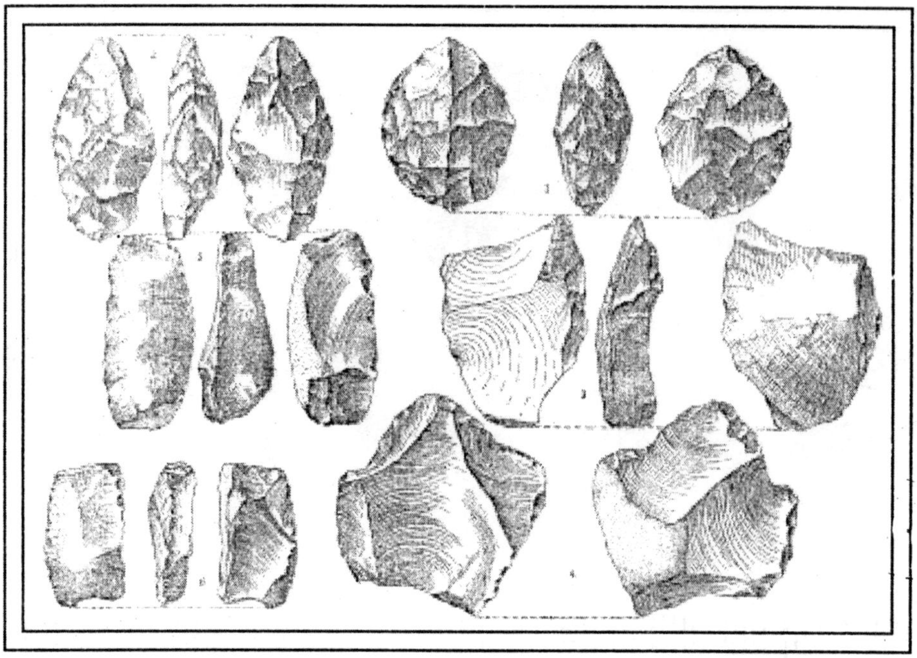

Source: H.D. Sankalia, 1974, *Prehistory and Protohistory of India and Pakistan.*

FIGURE 53: Small Handaxes, Cleavers, Flake Knives, and Tortoise Core, Rajasthan

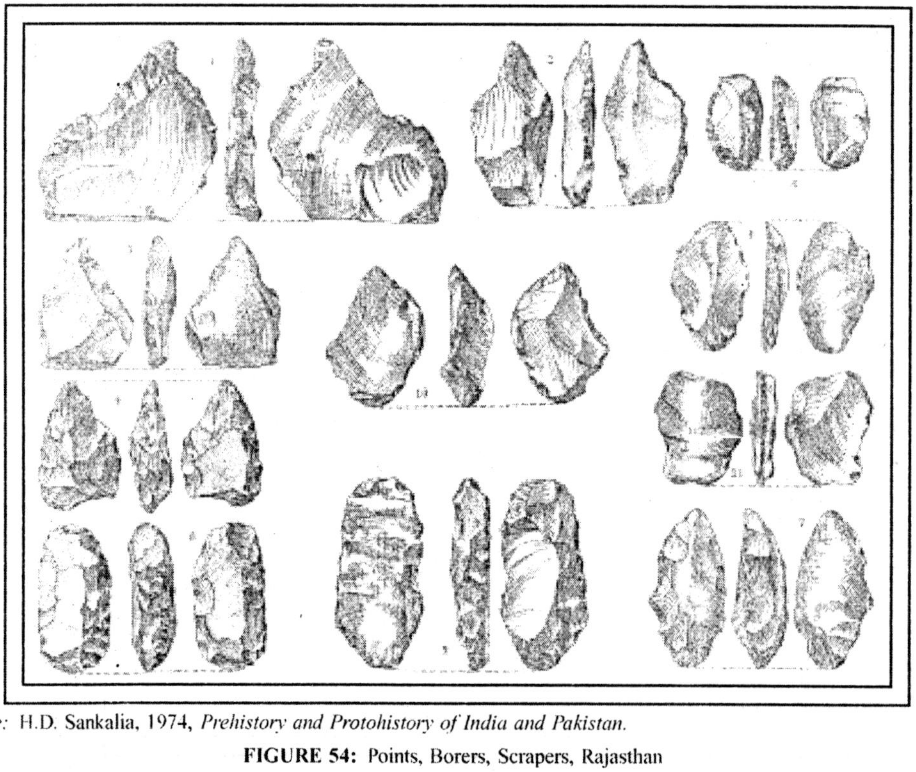

Source: H.D. Sankalia, 1974, *Prehistory and Protohistory of India and Pakistan.*

FIGURE 54: Points, Borers, Scrapers, Rajasthan

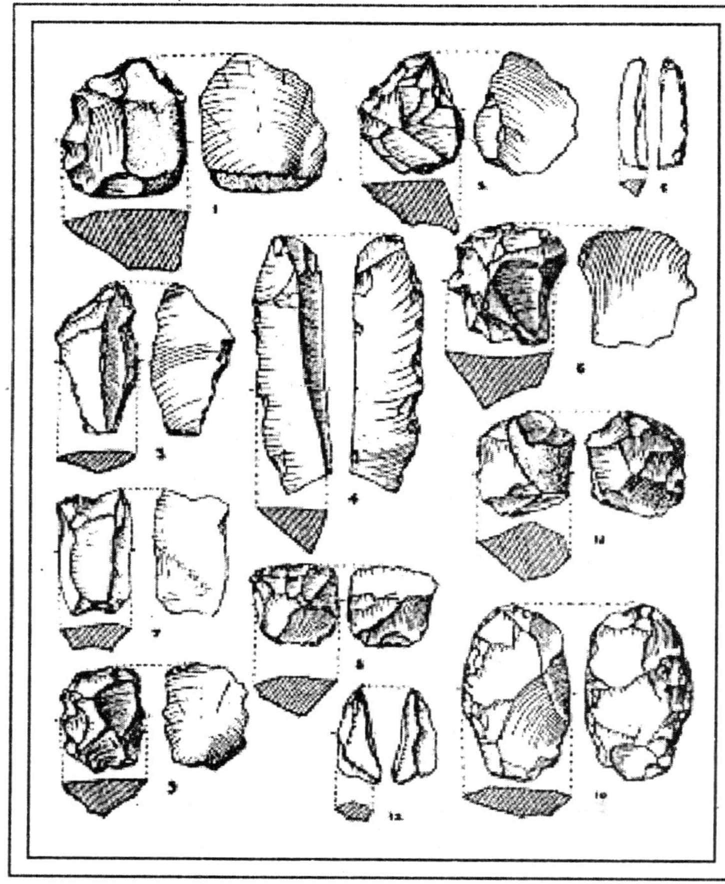

Source: H.D. Sankalia, 1974, *Prehistory and Protohistory of India and Pakistan.*

FIGURE 55: Upper Palaeolithic Tools from Renigunta
1, Chopper; 2-11, Scrapers; 12, Burin (central type) (less than half size)

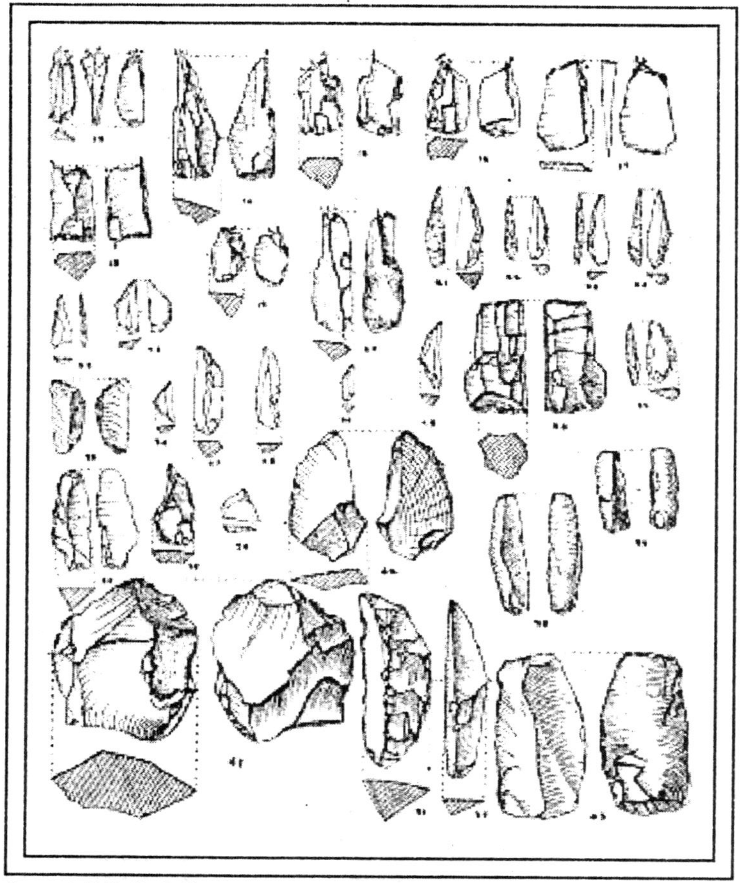

Source: H.D. Sankalia, 1974, *Prehistory and Protohistory of India and Pakistan.*

FIGURE 56: Upper Palaeolithic Tools from Renigunta
13, Burin (central type); 14-15, Burins (bevel type); 16-17, Burins (rectangular type); 18-19, Burins (concave); 20, Burin (unfinished); 21-34, Backed Blade Tools; 35-36, Awls; 37-40, Blades; 41, Primary Flake; 42, Flake; 43, Core Flake; 44, Core (less than half size)

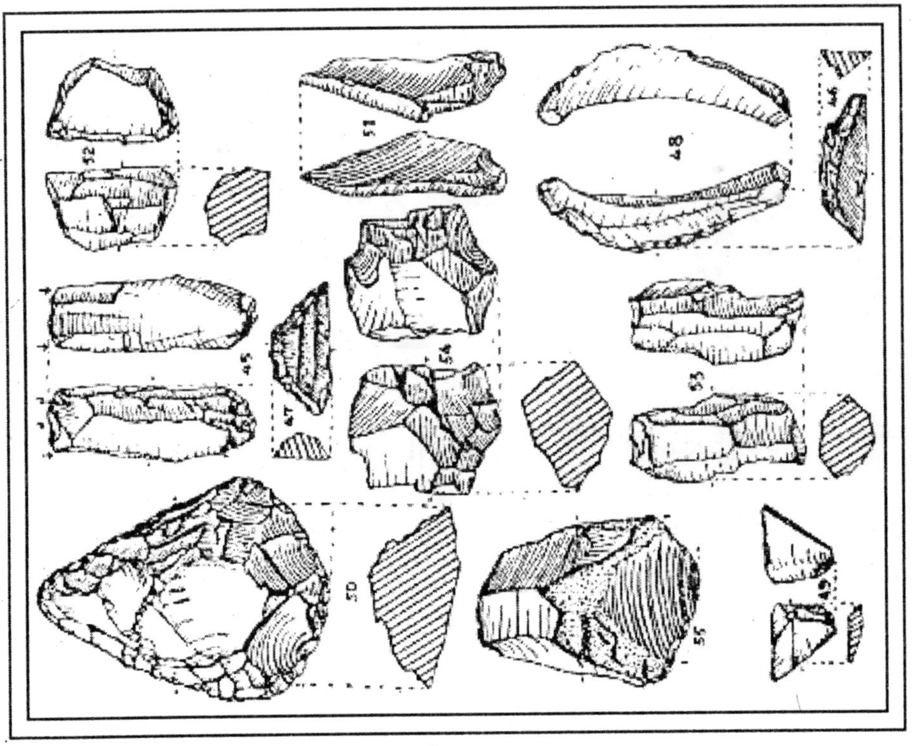

Source: H.D. Sankalia, 1974, *Prehistory and Protohistory of India and Pakistan.*

FIGURE 57: Upper Palaeolithic Tools from Renigunta
45, Burins (convex); 46-49, Backed Blade Tools; 50, Point; 51, Blade; 52-55, Cores (half size)

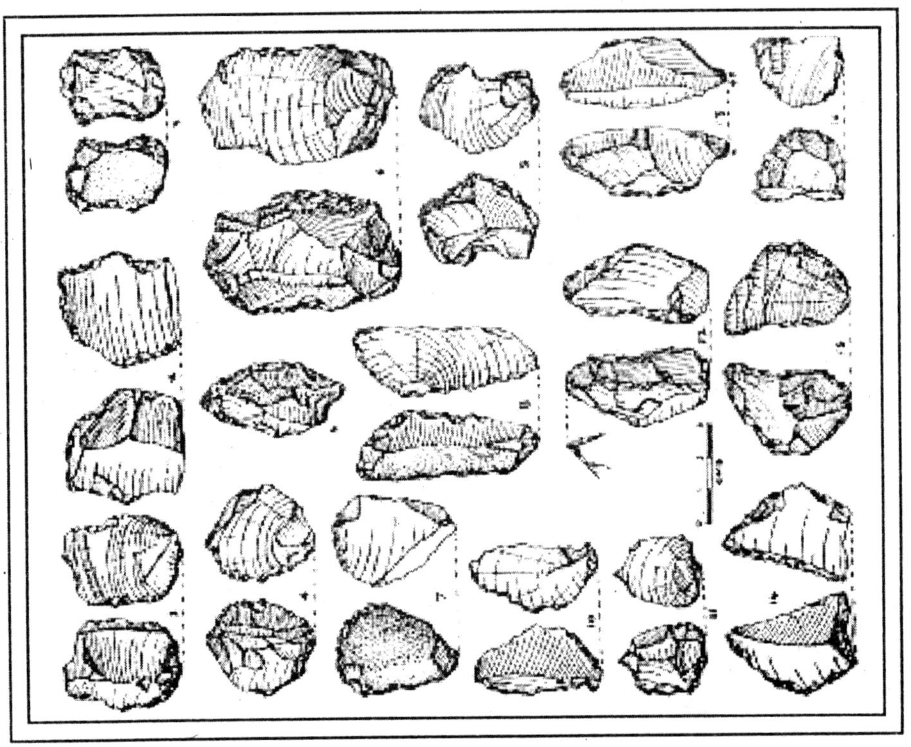

Source: H.D. Sankalia, 1974, *Prehistory and Protohistory of India and Pakistan.*

FIGURE 58: Vemula Industry
1-2, 4-5, 14-16, Tools on Flake; 3, 6, 8-9, Blade Flake; 10, Point; 11, Borer; 12-13, Burins

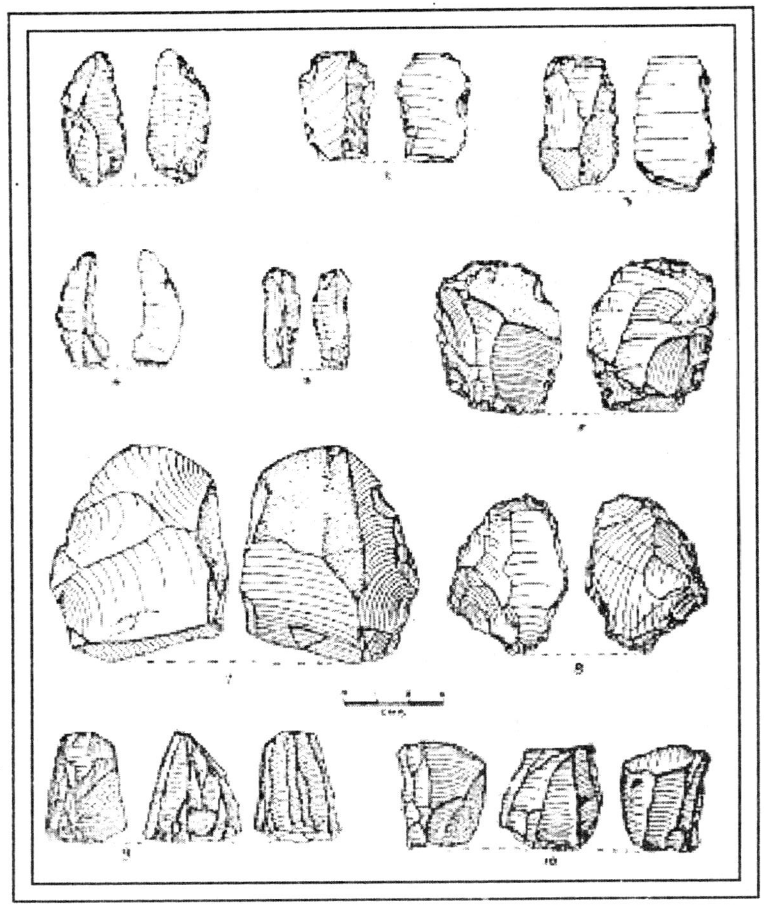

Source: H.D. Sankalia, 1974, *Prehistory and Protohistory of India and Pakistan.*

FIGURE 59: Vemula Industry
1-5, Retouched Blades; 6, 8, Retouched Flakes; 7, 9-10, Cores

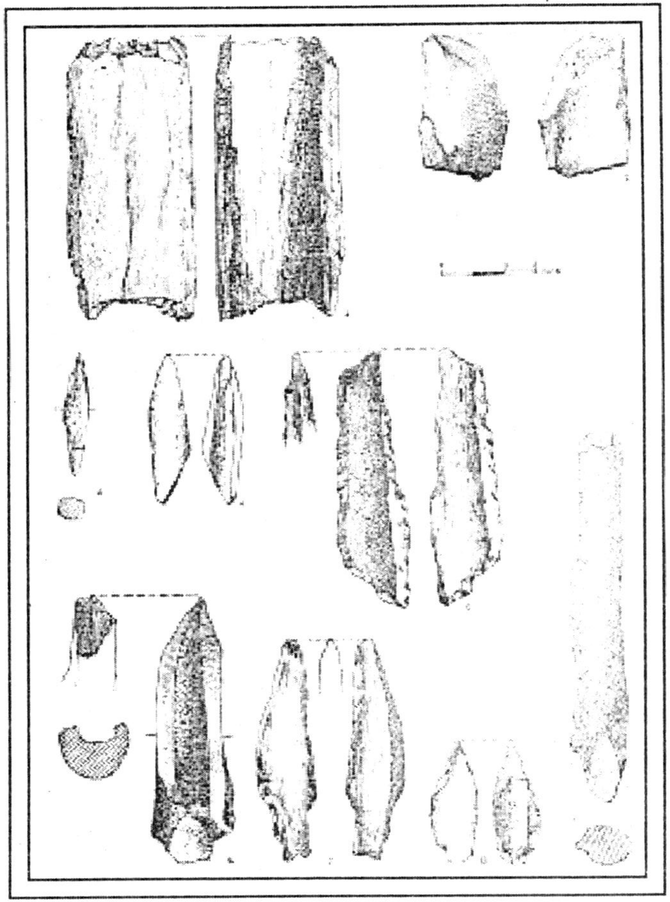

Source: H.D. Sankalia, 1974, *Prehistory and Protohistory of India and Pakistan.*

FIGURE 60: Upper Palaeolithic Bone Tools from Muchchatla Chintamanu Gavi (Andhra Pradesh) 1-2, Scrapers; 3-4, Perforators; 5-6, Chisels; 7, Tomged Point; 8, Barb; 9, Spatula

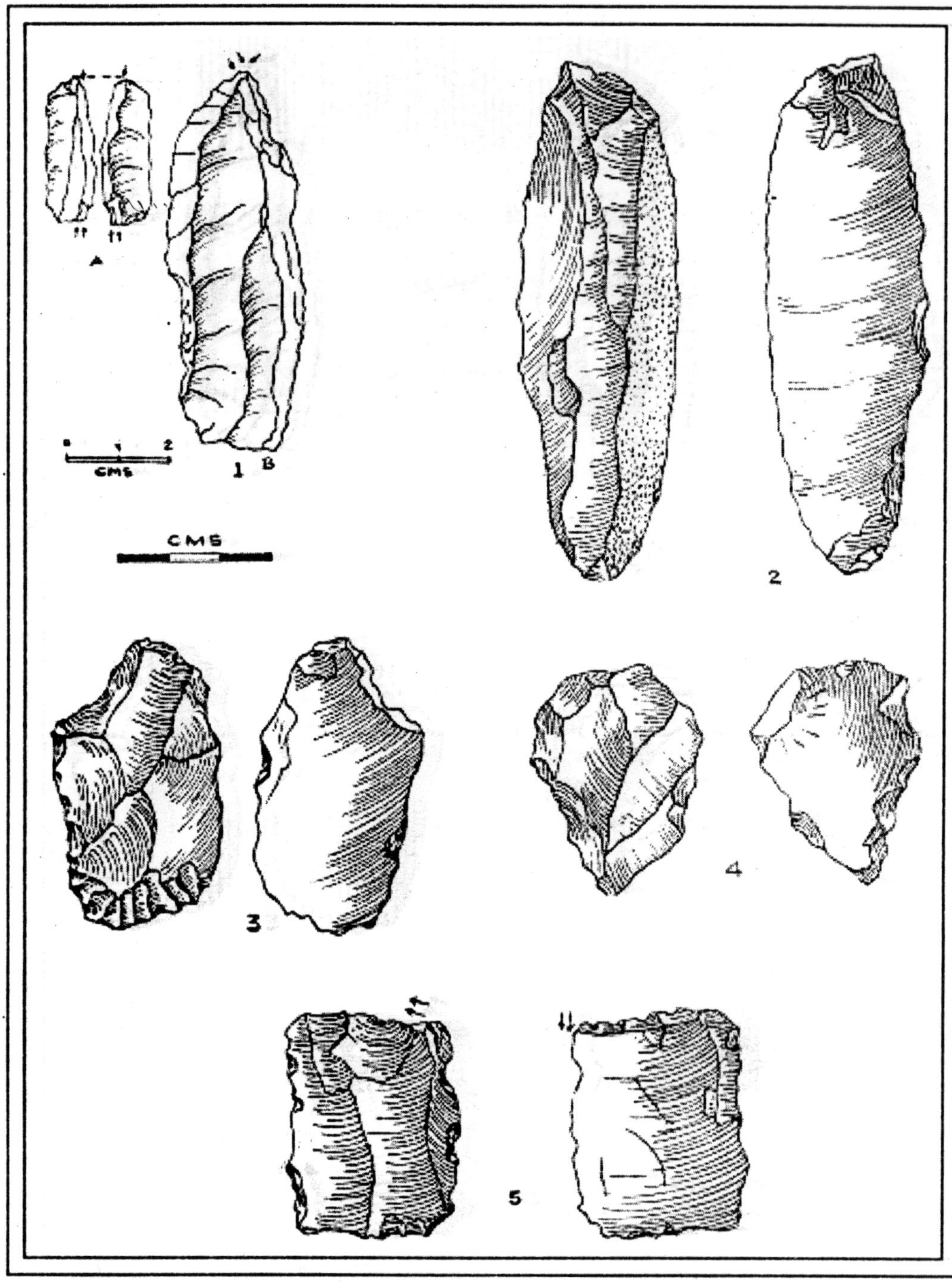

Source: H.D. Sankalia, 1974, *Prehistory and Protohistory of India and Pakistan.*

FIGURE 61: Upper Palaeolithic Tools, Karnool District, Andhra Pradesh
A & B, Burins from Gundla-Bhramhesvaram and Nandikanama Pass, Nagarjunkonda; 2, Blade; 3, Medium-to-Diminutive Scrapers; 4, Triangular Flake with Retouch; 5, Burin

Source: H.D. Sankalia, 1974, *Prehistory and Protohistory of India and Pakistan.*

FIGURE 62: Cliff Section at Salvadgi Showing Black, Brown Silt

Source: H.D. Sankalia, 1974, *Prehistory and Protohistory of India and Pakistan.*

FIGURE 63: Cliff Section at Hunsgi Showing Black, Brown Silt with Lenses of Pebbly and Granular Gravel

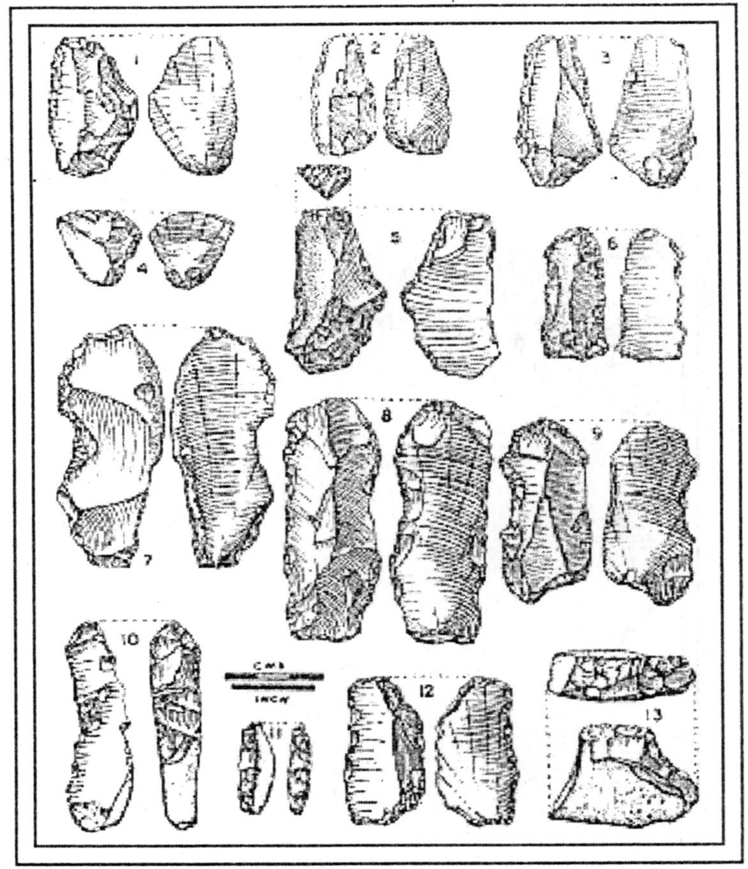

Source: H.D. Sankalia, 1974, *Prehistory and Protohistory of India and Pakistan.*

FIGURE 64: Upper Palaeolithic Tools from Sherapur Doab
1-3, Blades with Straight Edge; 4-5, Blades with Transverse Edge; 6, Blade with Lateral-*cum*-Transverse Edge; 7, Notched Blade; 8, Lateral-*cum*-Notched Blade; 9, Transverse-*cum*-Notched Blade; 10-12, Backed Blades; 13, Nosed Edged Tool

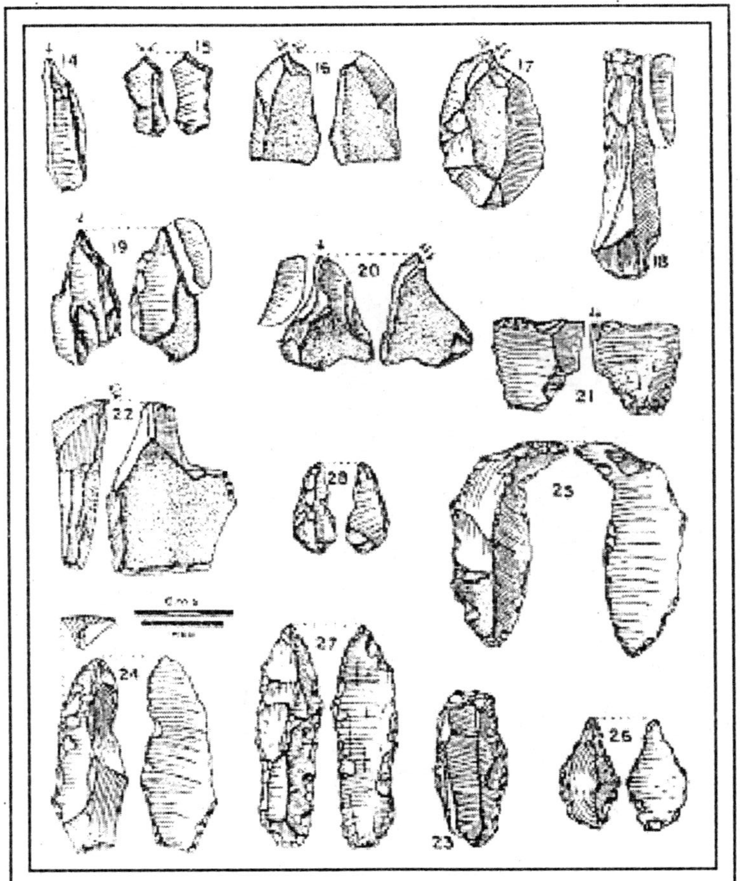

Source: H.D. Sankalia, 1974, *Prehistory and Protohistory of India and Pakistan.*

FIGURE 65: Upper Palaeolithic Tools from Sherapur Doab
14-22, Burins; 23, Scraper on Fluted Core; 24-28. Points

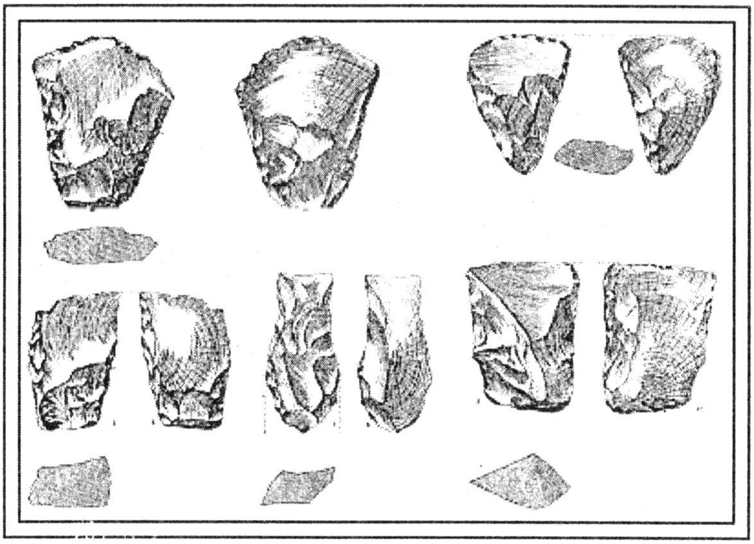

Source: H.D. Sankalia, 1974, *Prehistory and Protohistory of India and Pakistan.*

FIGURE 66: Cleavers of Various Types:
Convex-edged with Tapering Butt (1-4); Oblique or Straight-edged with Square or U-Shaped Butt (5-6), (9-10); Straight-edged with Pointed Butt (7-8)

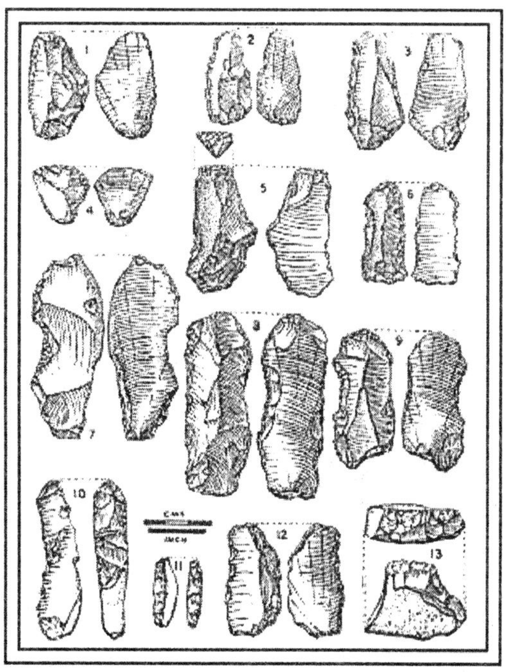

Source: H.D. Sankalia, 1974, *Prehistory and Protohistory of India and Pakistan.*

FIGURE 67: Upper Palaeolithic Tools from Shorapur Doab:
1-3, Blades with Straight-edge; 4-5, Blades with Transverse-edge; 6, Blade with Lateral-*cum*-Transverse-edge; 7, Notched Blade; 8, Lateral-cum-Notched Blade, 9, Transverse-cum-Notched Blade; 10-12, Backed Blades; 13, Nosed-edged Tool

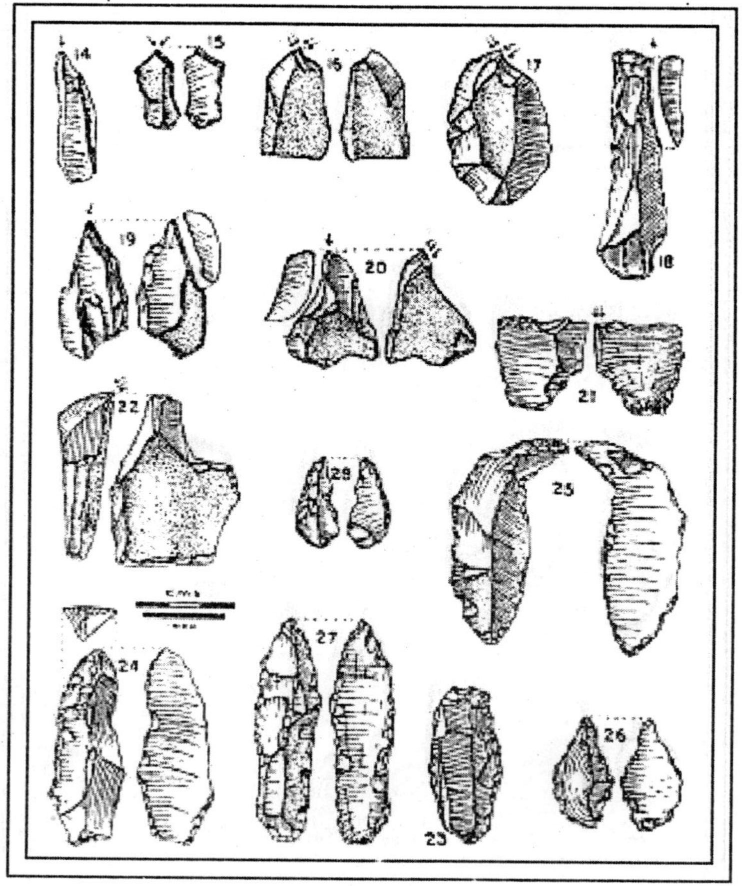

Source: H.D. Sankalia, 1974, *Prehistory and Protohistory of India and Pakistan.*

FIGURE 68: Upper Palaeolithic Tools from Sherapur Doab
14-22, Burins; 23, Scraper on Fluted Core; 24-28, Points

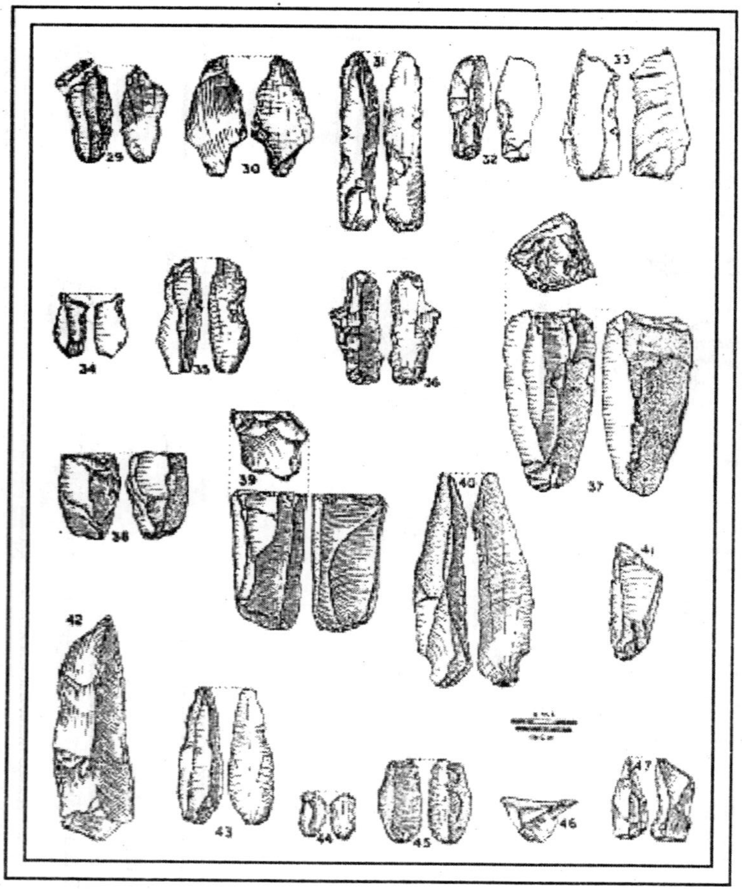

Source: H.D. Sankalia, 1974, *Prehistory and Protohistory of India and Pakistan.*

FIGURE 69: Upper Palaeolithic Tools from Sherapur Doab
29, Point; 30-32, Tanged Points; 33-34, Borers; 35-36, Multiple Tools; 37-39, Fluted Cores; 40-45, Unretouched Blades; 46-47, Crores Rejuyanation Flakes

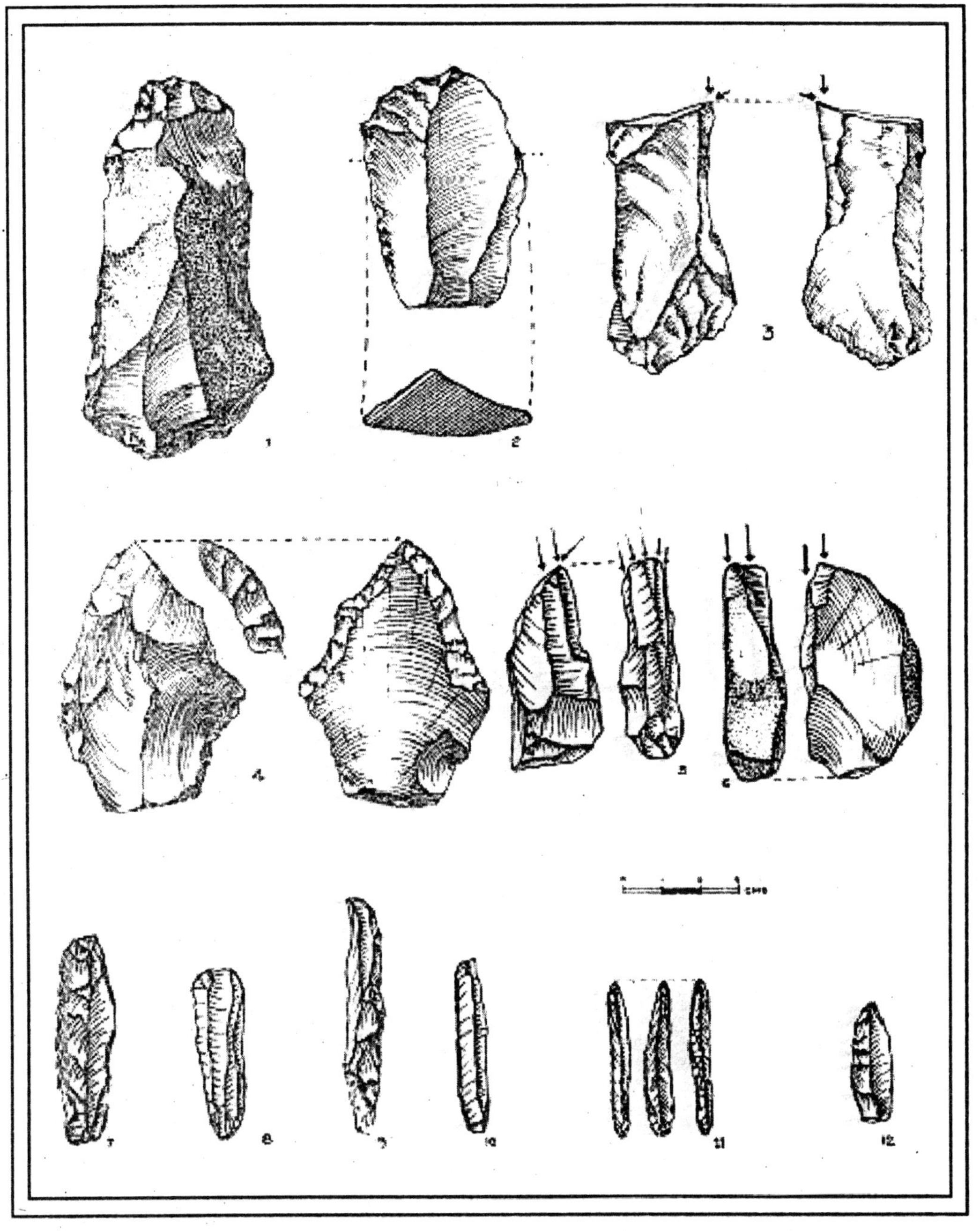

Source: H.D. Sankalia, 1974, *Prehistory and Protohistory of India and Pakistan.*

FIGURE 70: Upper Palaeolithic Tools, Bhimbetka
1-2, End Scrapers; 3, 6, Burins; 4, Point Patne; 5, Burin; 7-12, Black Tools

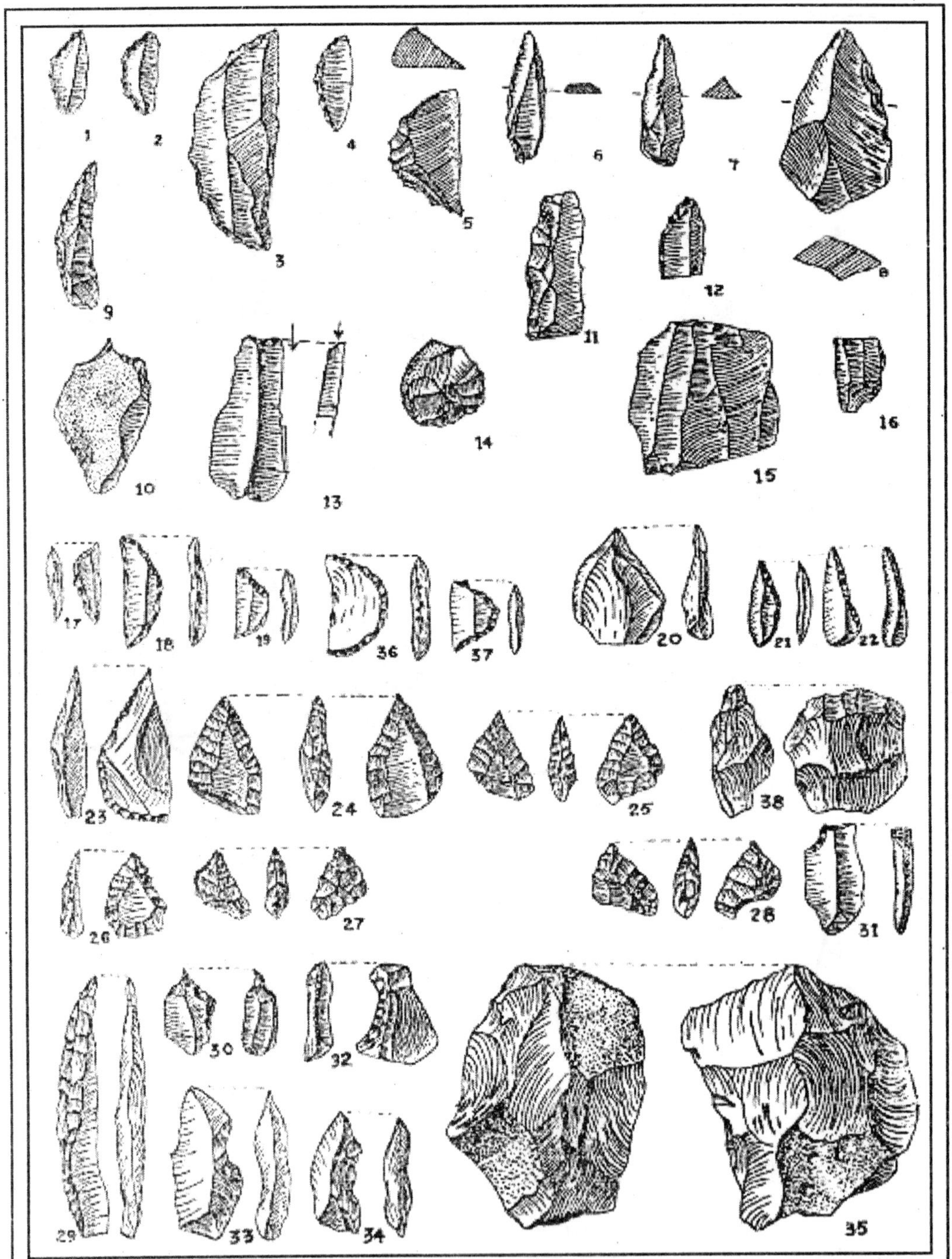

Source: H.D. Sankalia, 1974, *Prehistory and Protohistory of India and Pakistan.*

FIGURE 71: Mesolithic Artifacts from Birbhanpur (Nos. 1-16), West Bengal and Tinne Valley (Nos. 17-35), Tamil Nadu

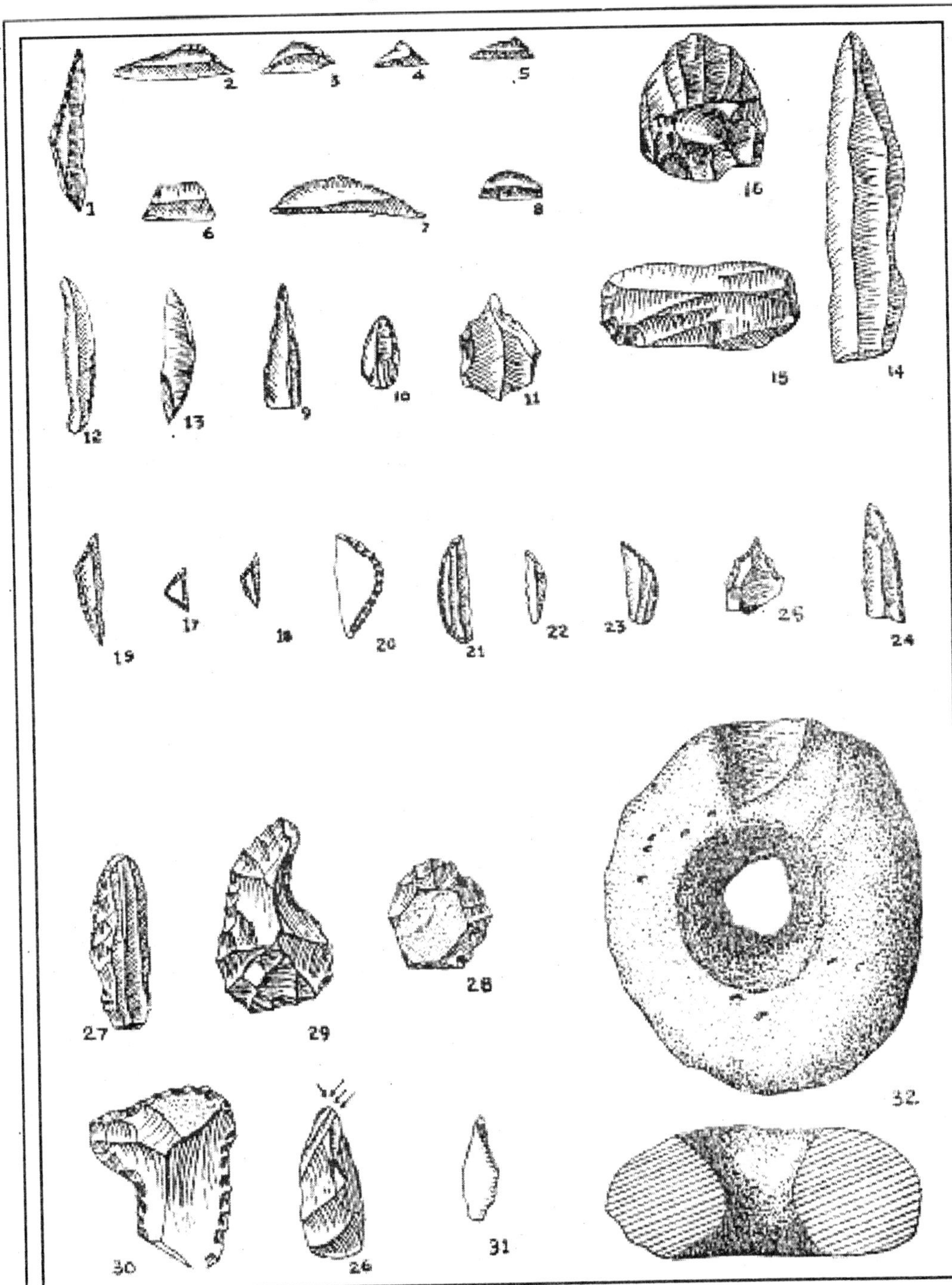

Source: H.D. Sankalia, 1974, *Prehistory and Protohistory of India and Pakistan.*

FIGURE 72: Artifacts of the Mesolithic Culture, Jabalpur (Nos. 1-16); and Bombay (Nos. 17-32) (After Gordon and Todd)

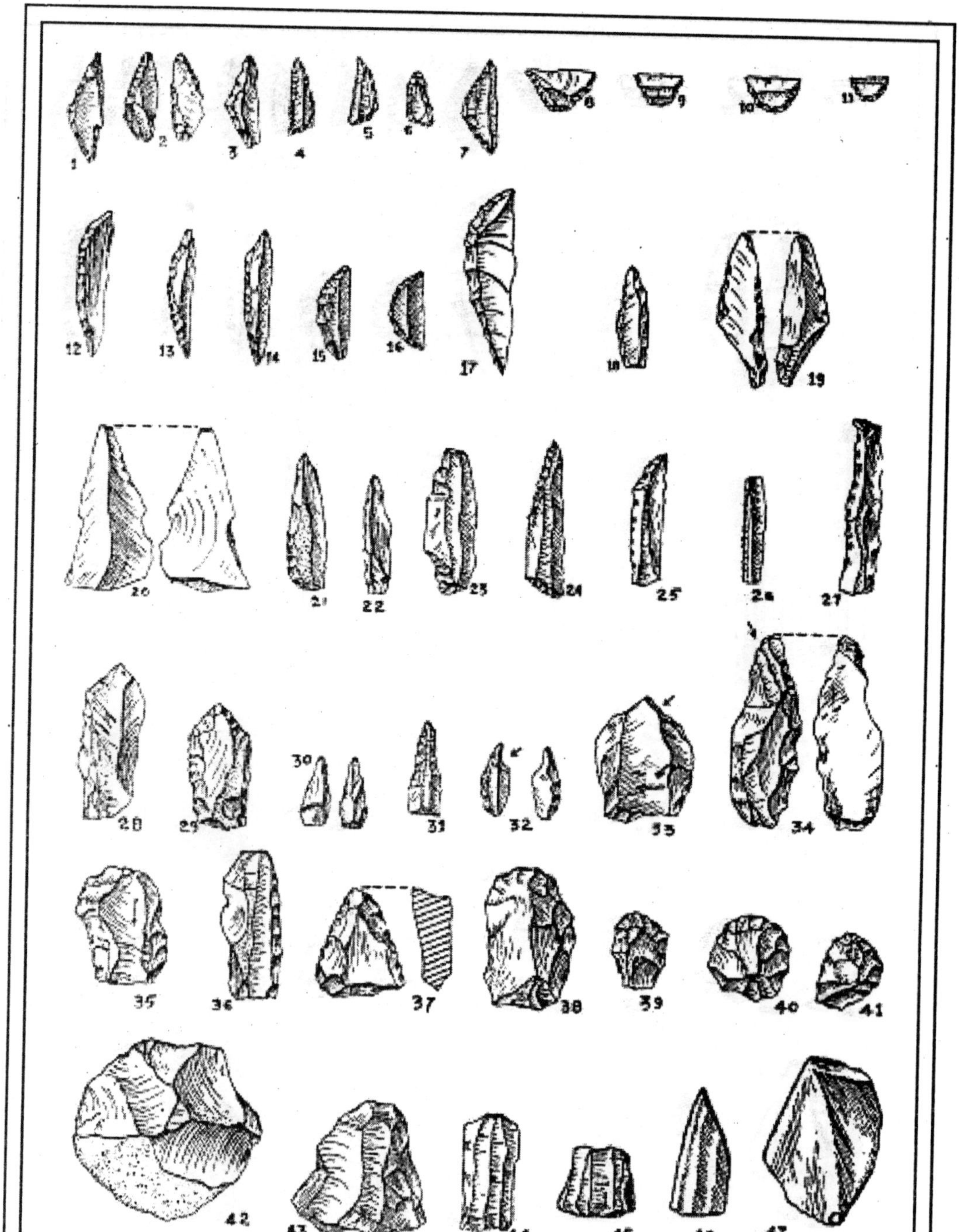

Source: H.D. Sankalia, 1974, *Prehistory and Protohistory of India and Pakistan.*

FIGURE 73: Microlithic Industry at Langhnaj, North Gujarat

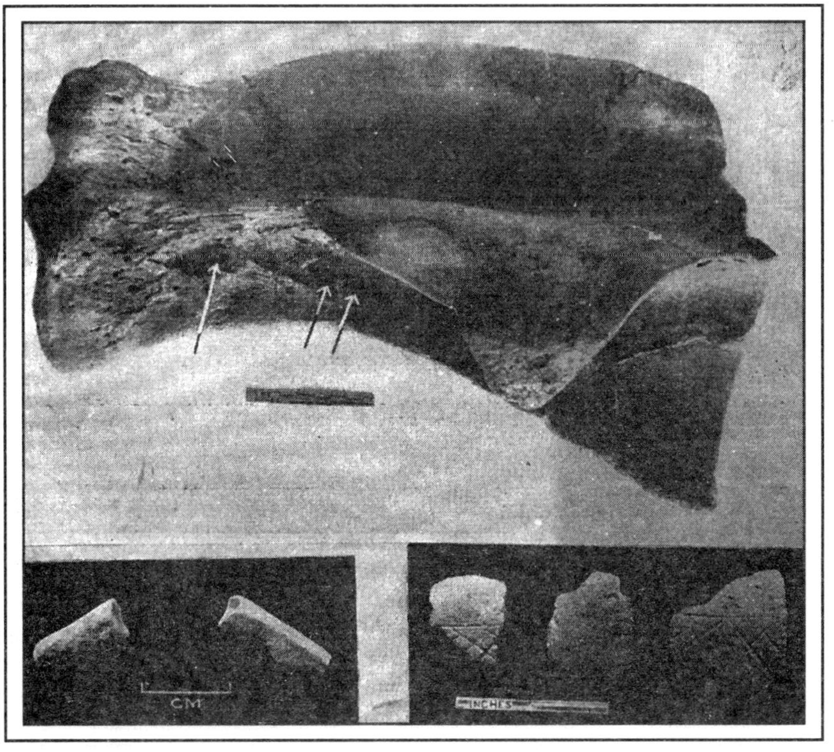

Source: H.D. Sankalia, 1974, *Prehistory and Protohistory of India and Pakistan.*

FIGURE 74: Rhinoceros, Shoulder Blade, Dentalium Shell Beads and Postsherds, Langhnaj, Northern Gujarat

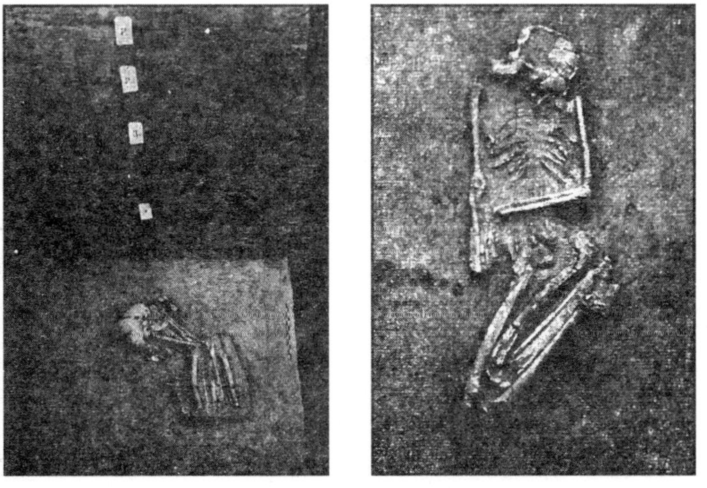

(i) (ii)

Source: H.D. Sankalia, 1974, *Prehistory and Protohistory of India and Pakistan.*

FIGURE 75: Human Skeleton from Langhnaj, Northern Gujarat

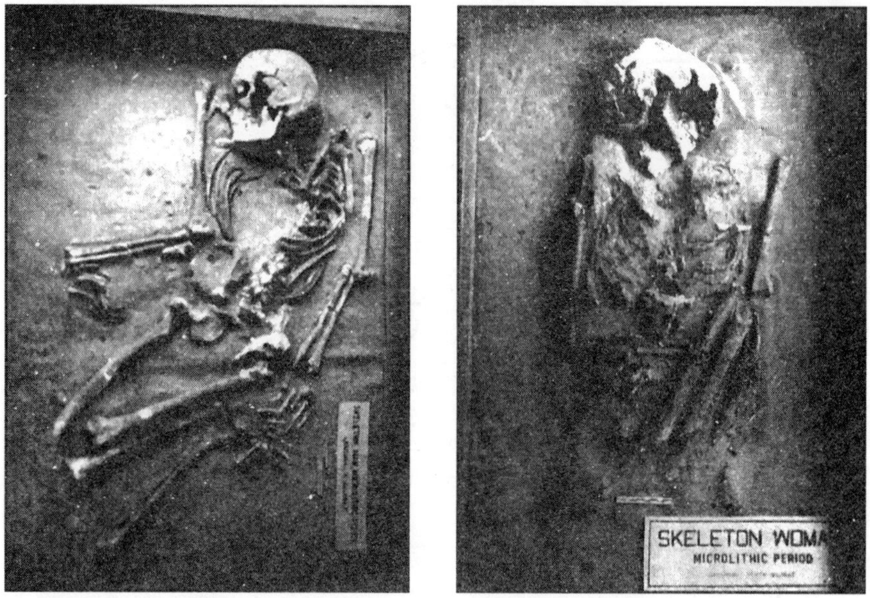

(i) (ii)

Source: H.D. Sankalia, 1974, *Prehistory and Protohistory of India and Pakistan.*

FIGURE 76: Skeletons of Man and Woman from Langhnaj, Northern Gujarat

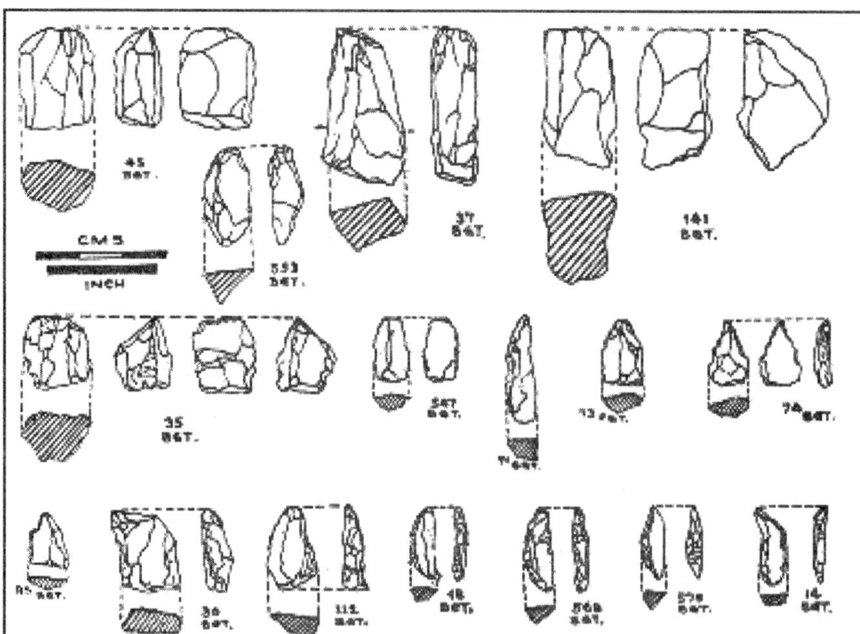

Source: H.D. Sankalia, 1974, *Prehistory and Protohistory of India and Pakistan.*

FIGURE 77: Microlithic Industry in Quartz from Layer 1, Bangaltota Locality (Sangankallu), Karnataka

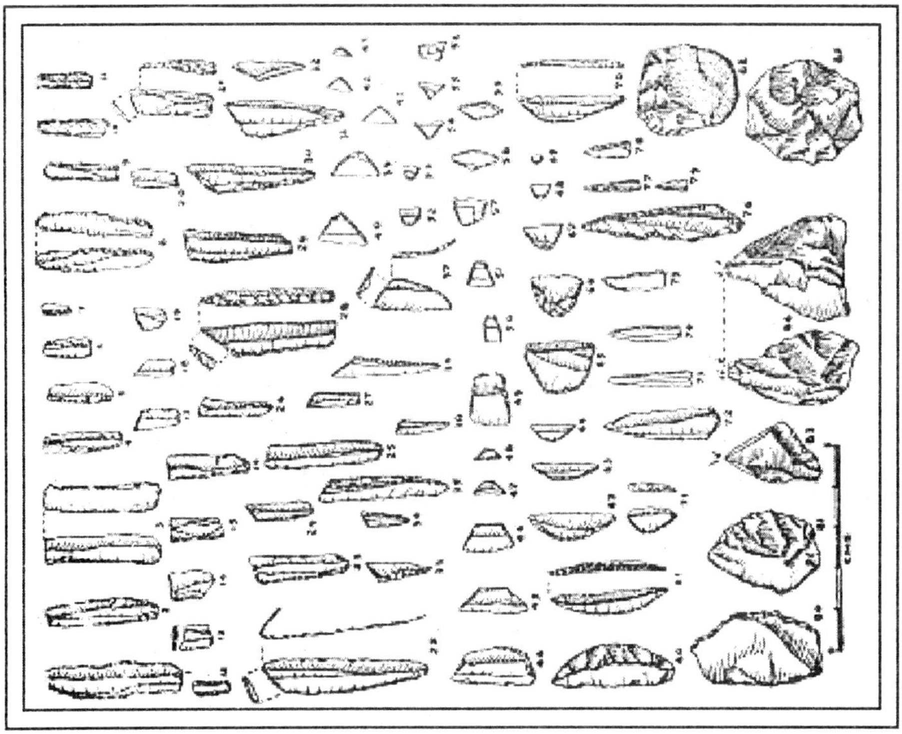

FIGURE 78: Microlithic Industry of Bagor, Rajasthan

Source: H.D. Sankalia, 1974, *Prehistory and Protohistory of India and Pakistan.*

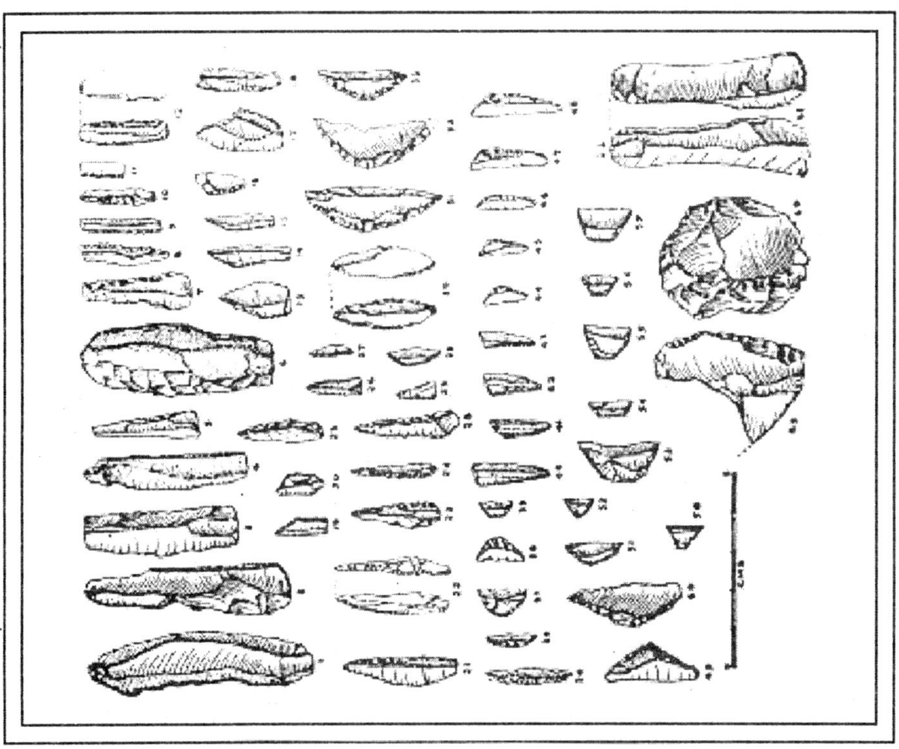

FIGURE 79: Microlithic Industry of Tilwara, Rajasthan

Source: H.D. Sankalia, 1974, *Prehistory and Protohistory of India and Pakistan.*

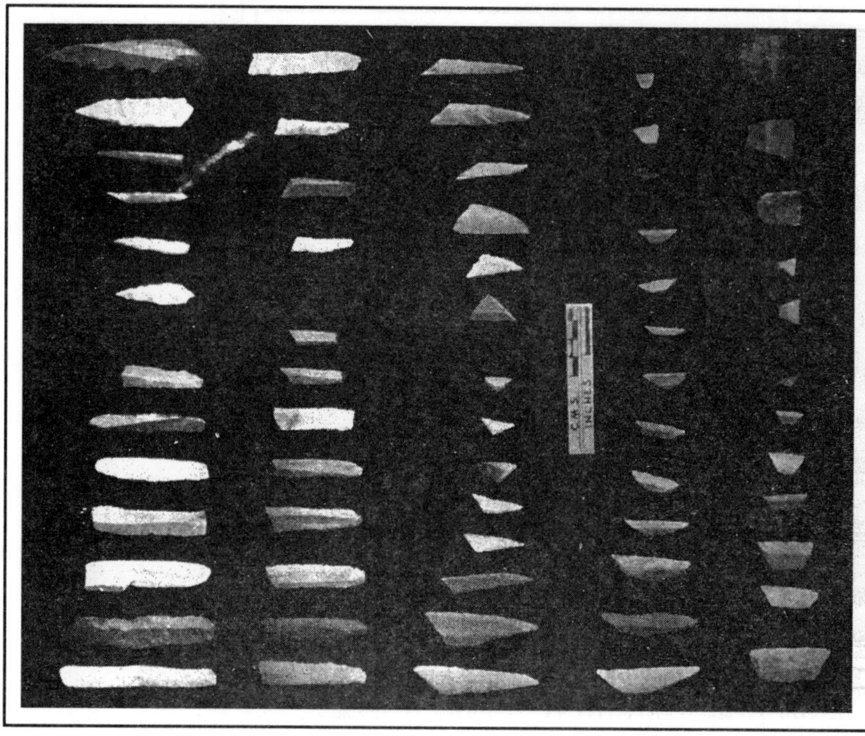

Source: H.D. Sankalia, 1974, *Prehistory and Protohistory of India and Pakistan.*

FIGURE 80: Microlithic Industry of Bagor, Rajasthan

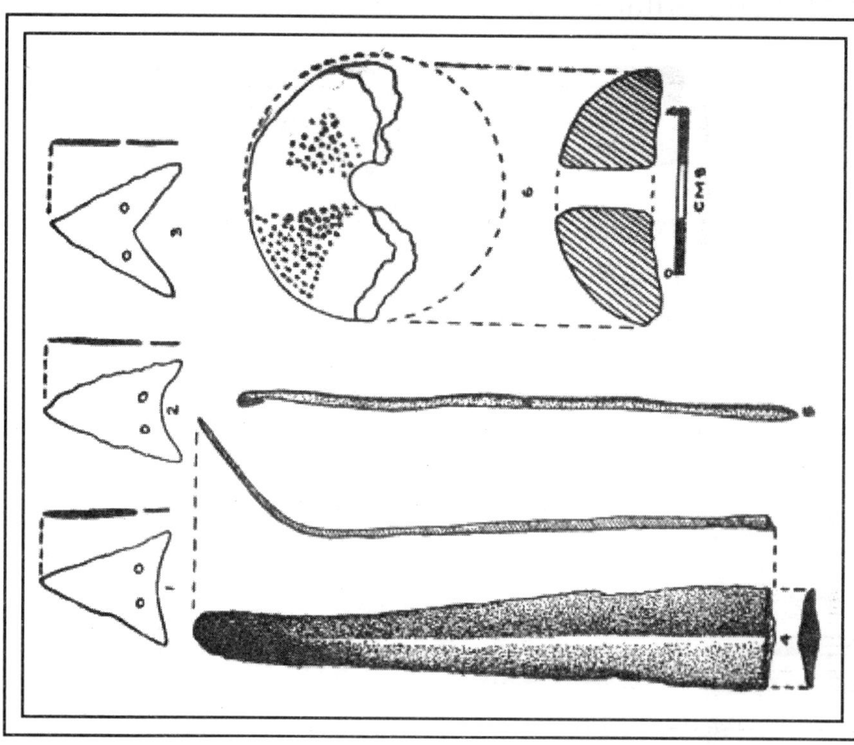

Source: H.D. Sankalia, 1974, *Prehistory and Protohistory of India and Pakistan.*

FIGURE 81: 1-5 Copper Objects, 6 Terracotta Spindle Whorl from Phase-II, Bagor, Rajasthan

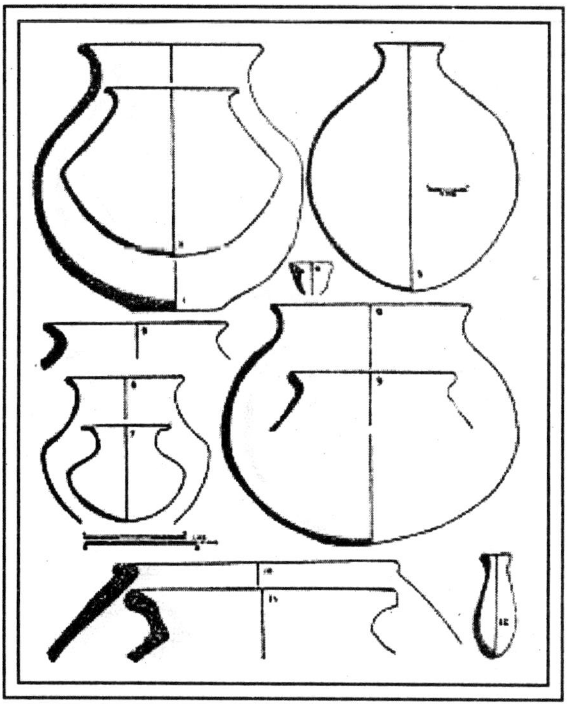

Source: H.D. Sankalia, 1974, *Prehistory and Protohistory of India and Pakistan.*

FIGURE 82: Pottery Types, Phase-II, Bagor, Rajasthan

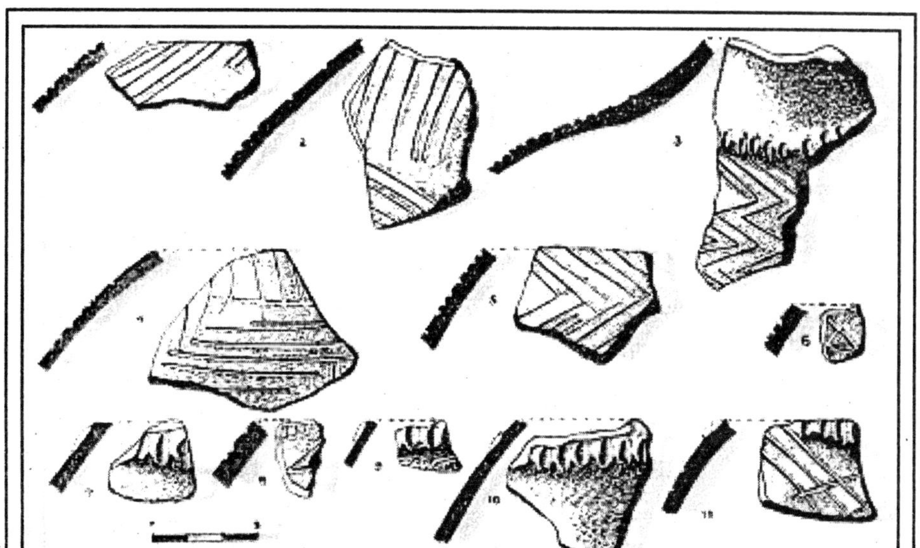

Source: H.D. Sankalia, 1974, *Prehistory and Protohistory of India and Pakistan.*

FIGURE 83: Pottery Designs, Phase-II, Bagor, Rajasthan

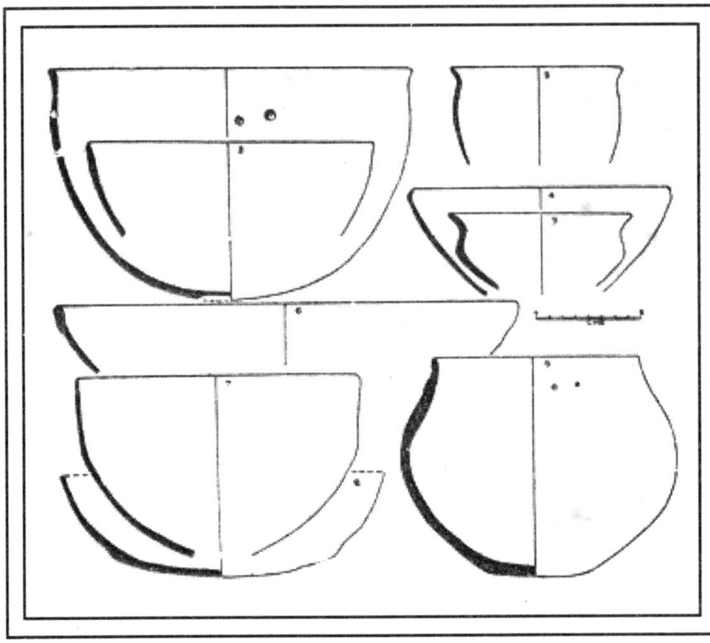

Source: H.D. Sankalia, 1974, *Prehistory and Protohistory of India and Pakistan.*

FIGURE 84: Pottery Types, Phase-II, Bagor, Rajasthan

Source: H.D. Sankalia, 1974, *Prehistory and Protohistory of India and Pakistan.*

FIGURE 85: Stone Paved Floor, Phase-I, Bagor, Rajasthan

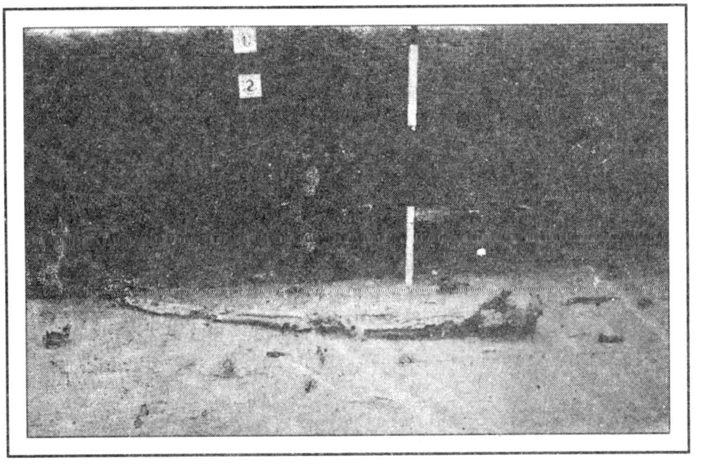

Source: H.D. Sankalia, 1974, *Prehistory and Protohistory of India and Pakistan.*

FIGURE 86: Extended Burial from Phase-I, Bagor, Rajasthan

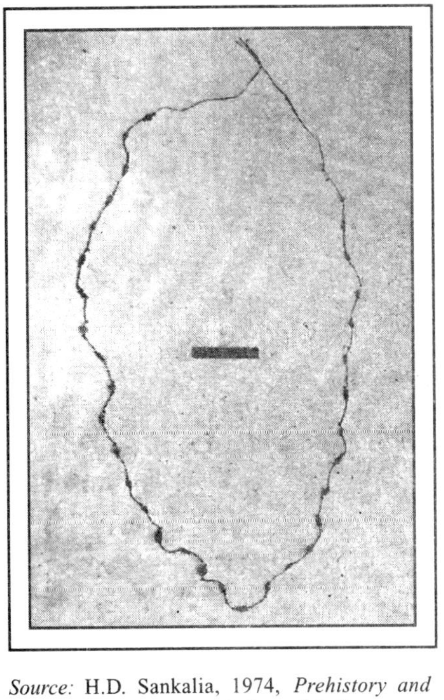

Source: H.D. Sankalia, 1974, *Prehistory and Protohistory of India and Pakistan.*

FIGURE 87: Stone and Bone Bead Necklace, Phase-II, Bagor, Rajasthan

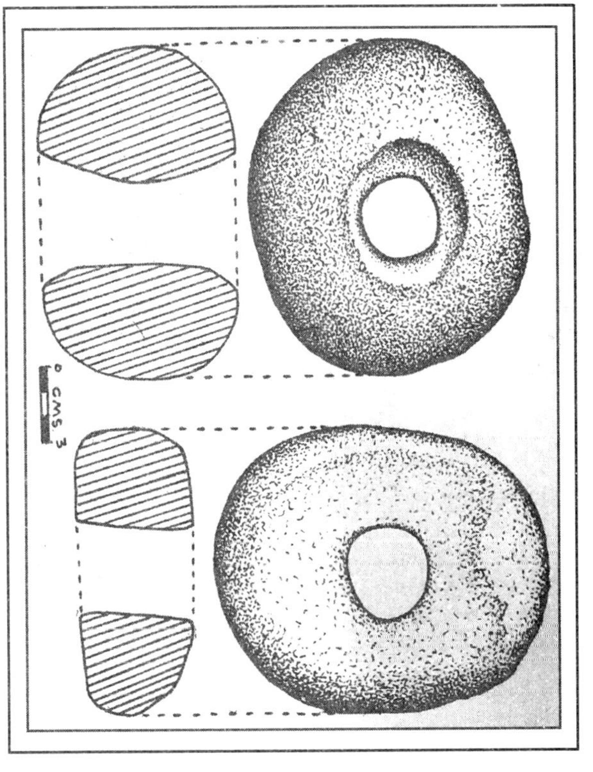

Source: H.D. Sankalia, 1974, *Prehistory and Protohistory of India and Pakistan.*

FIGURE 88: Bored Stones from Phase-II, Bagor, Rajasthan

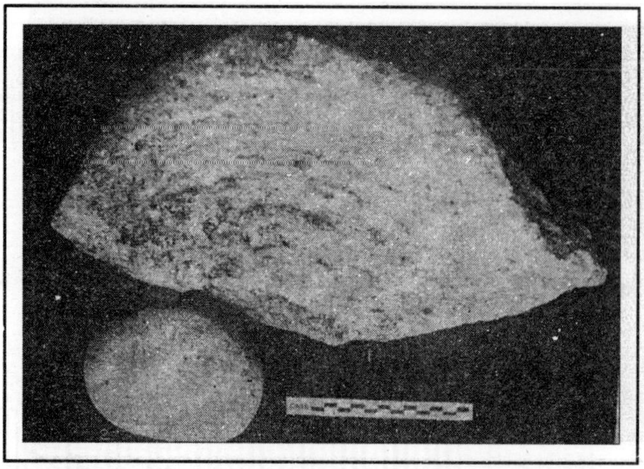

Source: H.D. Sankalia, 1974, *Prehistory and Protohistory of India and Pakistan.*

FIGURE 89: Stone Quern and Rubber from Phase-II, Bagor, Rajasthan

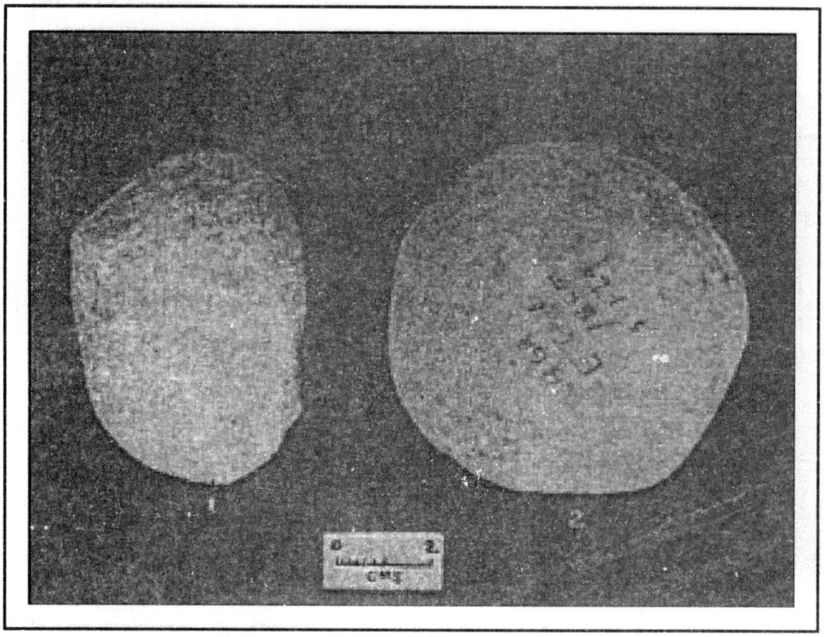

Source: H.D. Sankalia, 1974, *Prehistory and Protohistory of India and Pakistan.*

FIGURE 90: Sling Balls, Phase-II, Bagor, Rajasthan

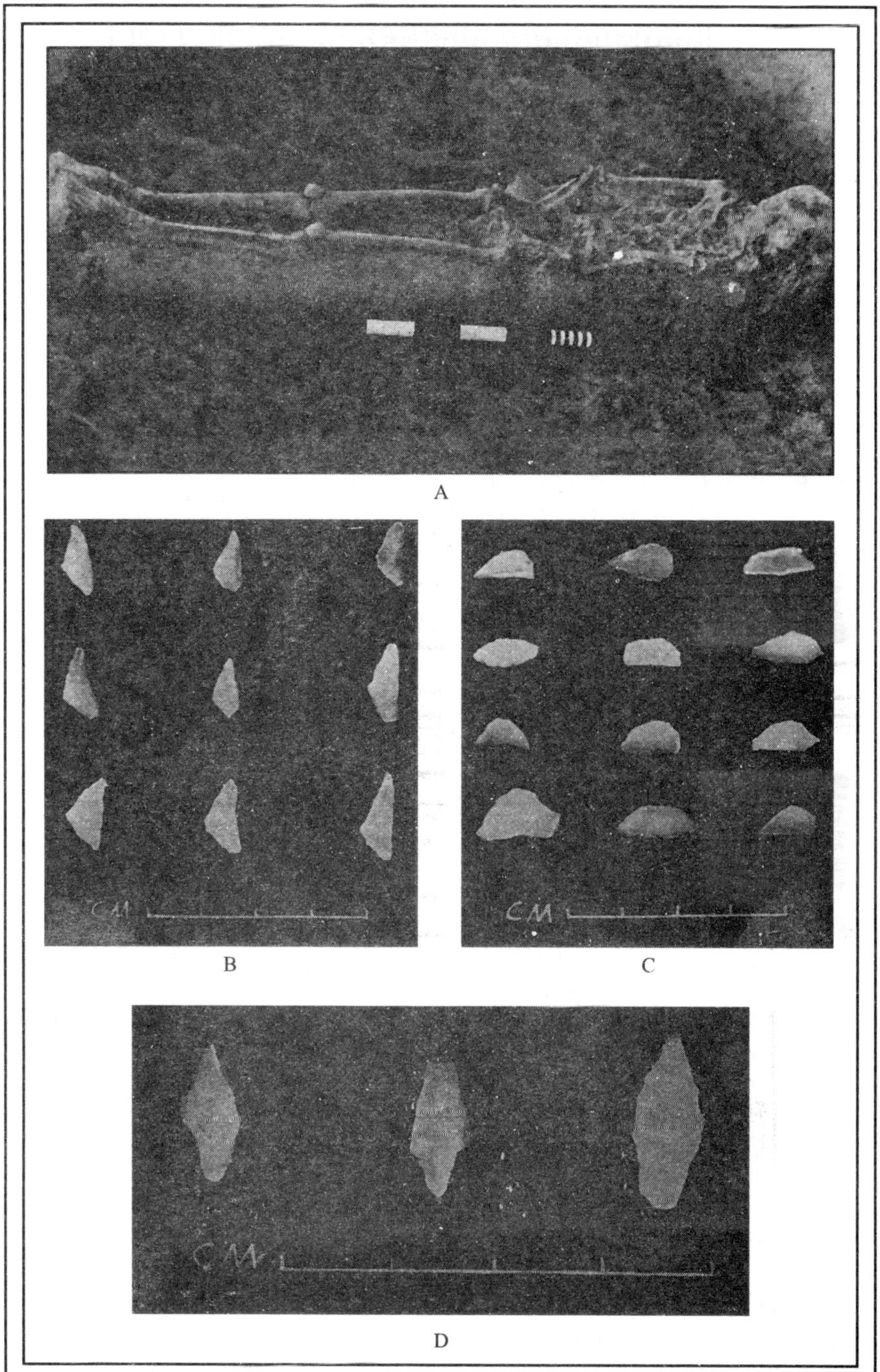

Source: H.D. Sankalia, 1974, *Prehistory and Protohistory of India and Pakistan.*

FIGURE 91: Burial (A) and Microliths (B-D) from Sarai Nahar Rai, Uttar Pradesh

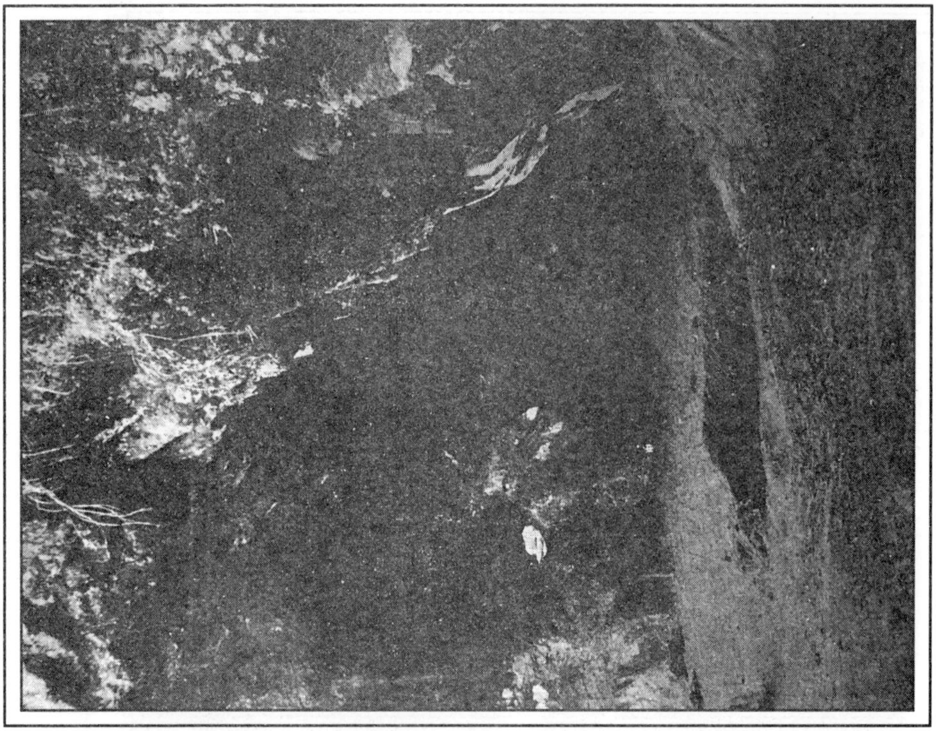

Source: H.D. Sankalia, 1974, *Prehistory and Protohistory of India and Pakistan.*

FIGURE 92: View of Natural Cave at Pachad, Maharashtra

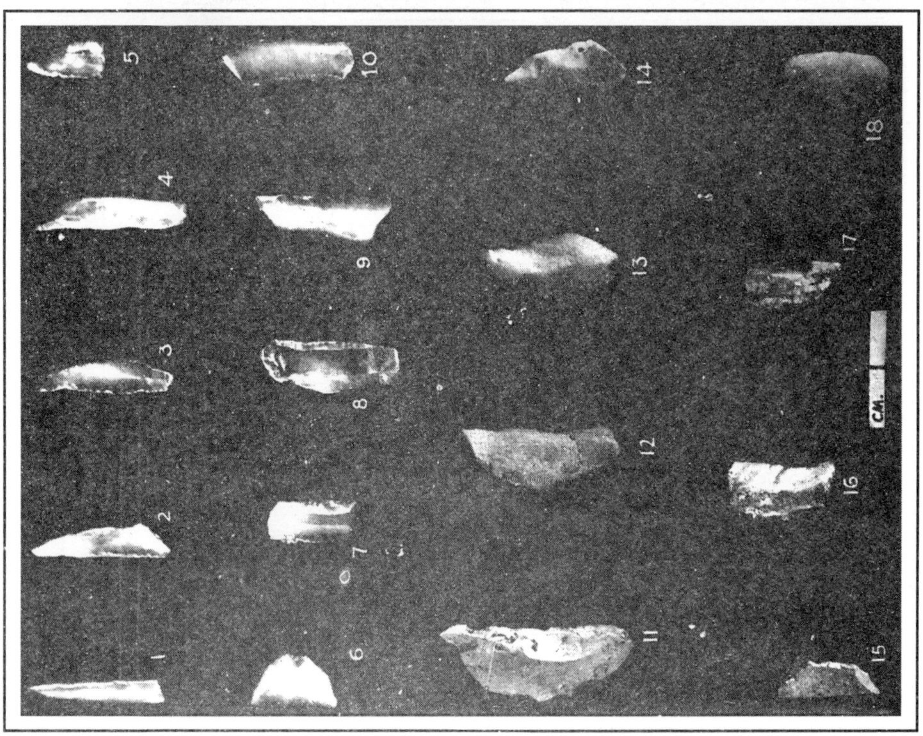

Source: H.D. Sankalia, 1974, *Prehistory and Protohistory of India and Pakistan.*

FIGURE 93: Mesolithic Artifacts from Pachad Cave, Maharashtra

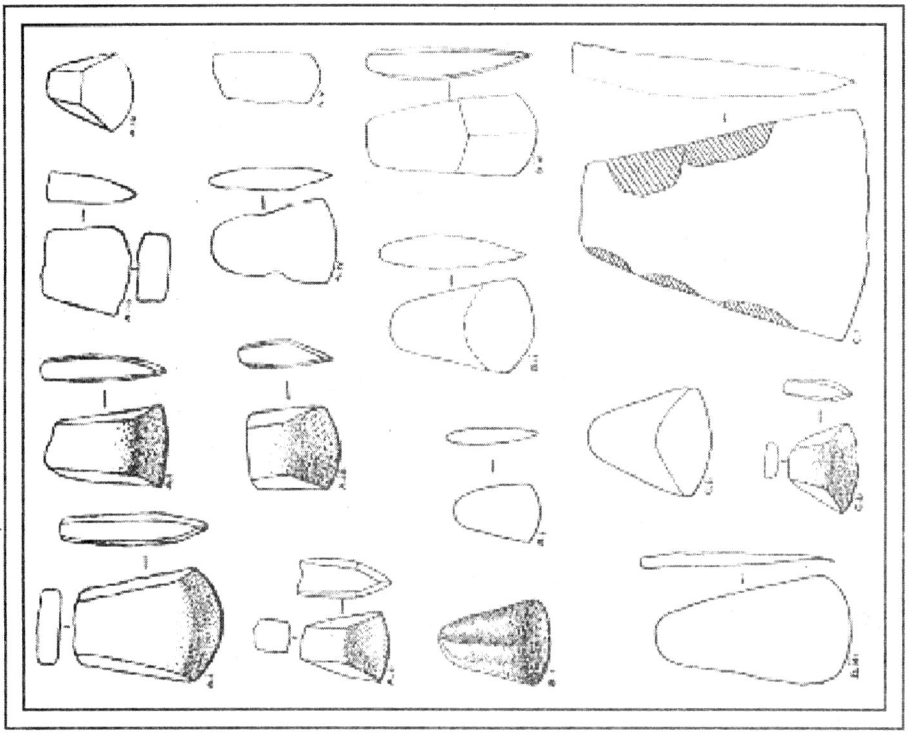

Source: H.D. Sankalia, 1974, *Prehistory and Protohistory of India and Pakistan.*

FIGURE 94: Neolithic Tools from Assam (Ai-Aii), Facetted Tools; (Bi-Biii), Round-Butted Axes; and (Ci-Cii), Axes with Broad Cutting-edge

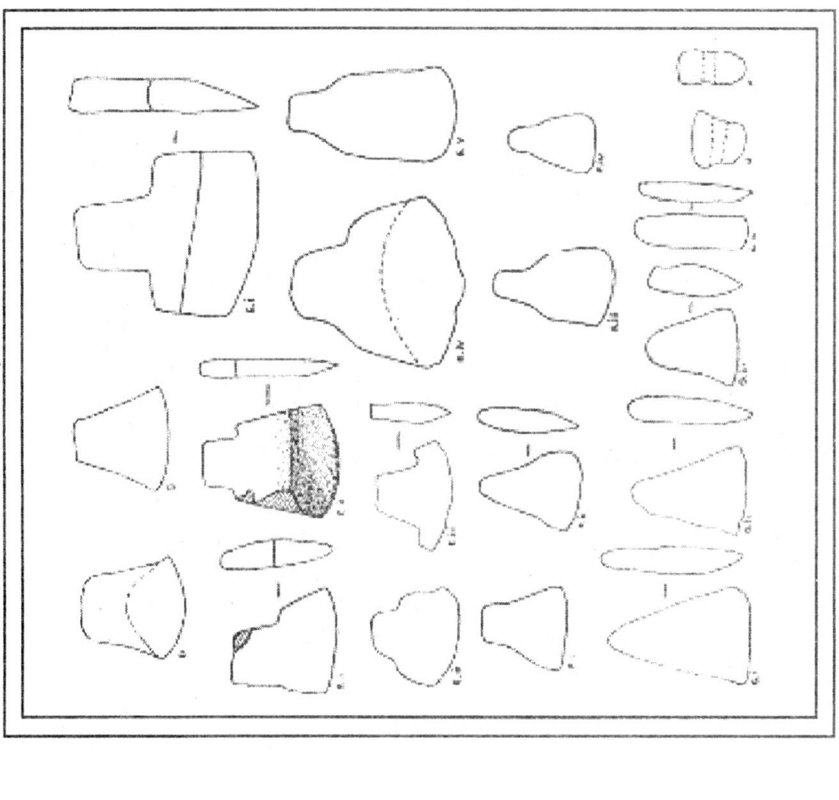

Source: H.D. Sankalia, 1974, *Prehistory and Protohistory of India and Pakistan.*

FIGURE 95: Neolithic Tools from Assam (D), Splayed Axes; (Ei-Eii), Shouldered Tools; (Fi-Fiv), Tanged Axes. (Gi-Giv), Wedge-Blades; and (H), Grooked Hammer Stones

Source: H.D. Sankalia, 1974, *Prehistory and Protohistory of India and Pakistan.*

FIGURE 96: Old and New Stone Age Tools, Lohit District, Assam

Source: H.D. Sankalia, 1974, *Prehistory and Protohistory of India and Pakistan.*

FIGURE 97: Old and New Stone Age Tools from Lohit District, Assam

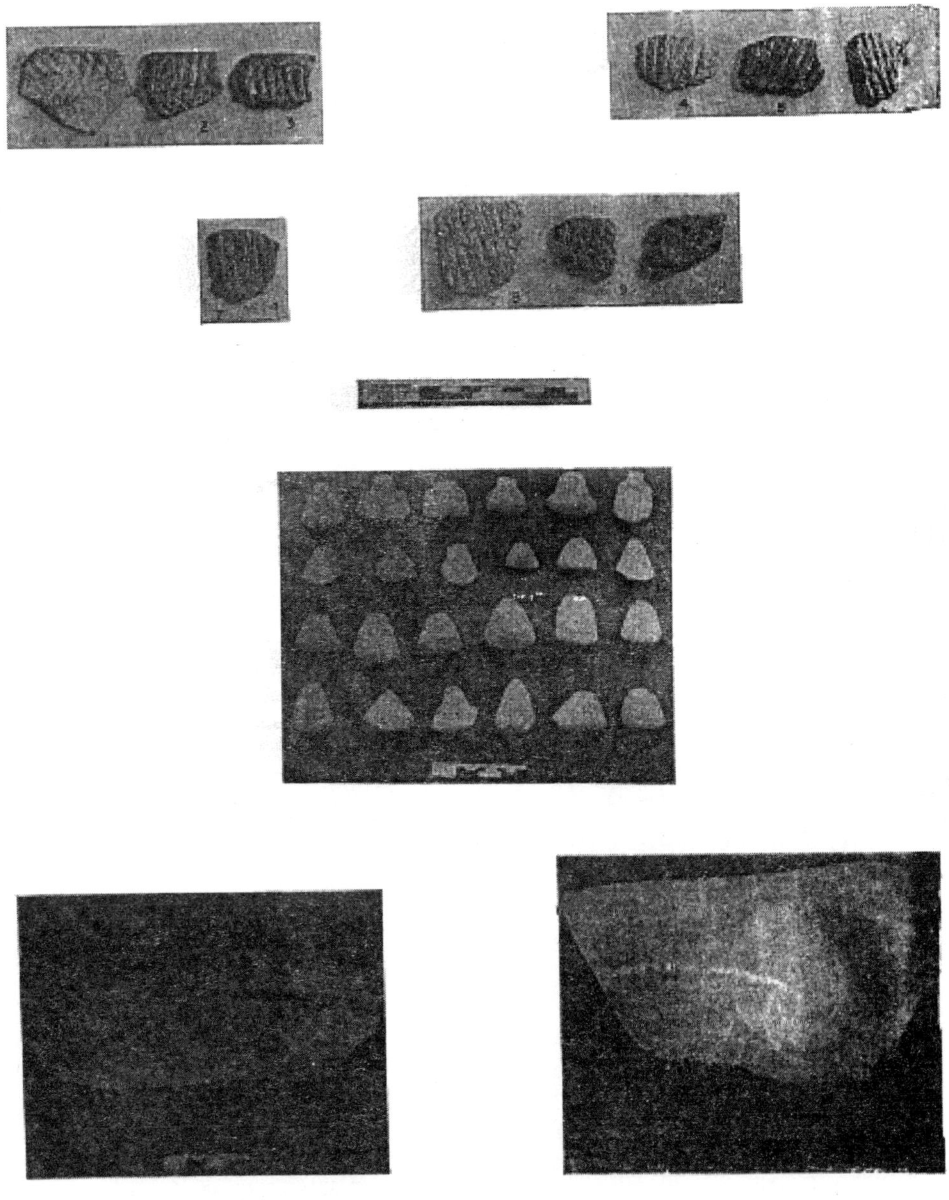

Source: H.D. Sankalia, 1974, *Prehistory and Protohistory of India and Pakistan.*

FIGURE 98: Pottery, Polished Stone Tools and Quern for Grinding and Polishing from the Excavation at Deojali Hading, Assam

Source: H.D. Sankalia, 1974, *Prehistory and Protohistory of India and Pakistan.*

FIGURE 99: Pit-Dwellings from Burzahome, Kashmir

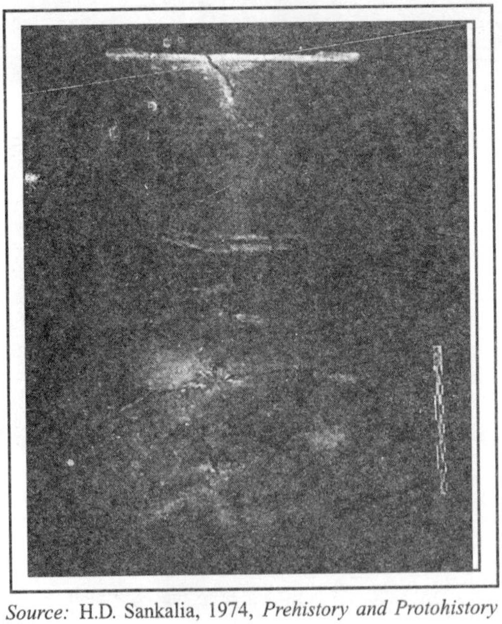

Source: H.D. Sankalia, 1974, *Prehistory and Protohistory of India and Pakistan.*

FIGURE 100: High Necked Vessel in Steel Grey Ware, Phase-I, Burzahome, Kashmir

Source: H.D. Sankalia, 1974, *Prehistory and Protohistory of India and Pakistan.*

FIGURE 101: Polished Stone Axes, Phase-II, Burzahome, Kashmir

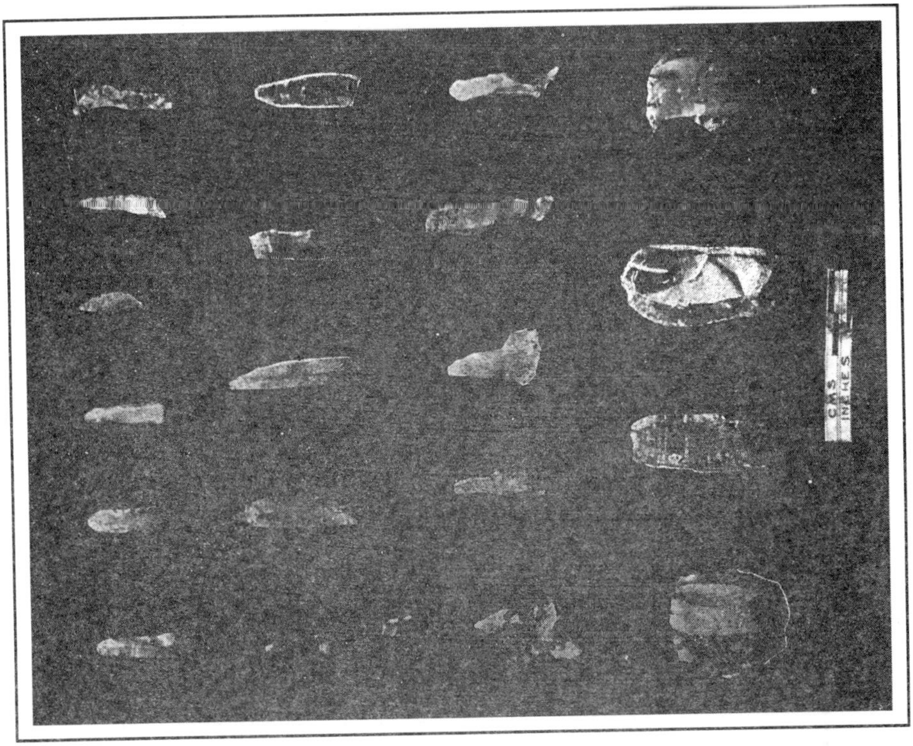

Source: H.D. Sankalia, 1974, *Prehistory and Protohistory of India and Pakistan.*

FIGURE 102: Articles of Lithic Blade Industry, Chirand, Bihar

Source: H.D. Sankalia, 1974, *Prehistory and Protohistory of India and Pakistan.*

FIGURE 103: Bones and Antler Tools from Chirand, Bihar

Source: H.D. Sankalia, 1974, *Prehistory and Protohistory of India and Pakistan.*

FIGURE 104: Pecked and Ground Stone Tool from Chirand, Bihar

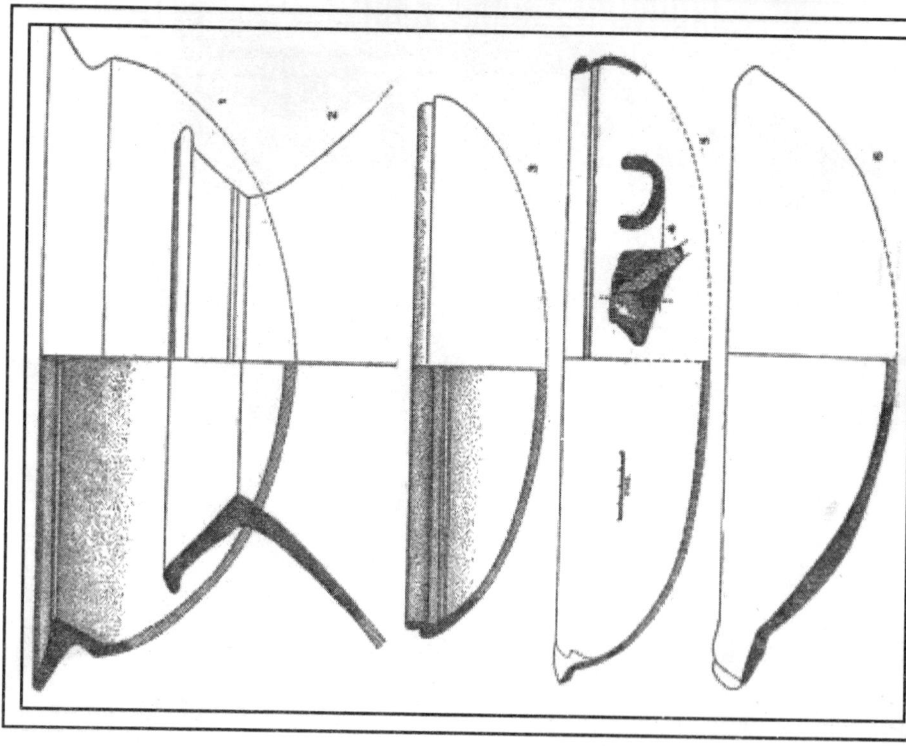

Source: H.D. Sankalia, 1974, *Prehistory and Protohistory of India and Pakistan.*

FIGURE 105: 1-3: Black and Red Ware from Ahar, Rajasthan, 4-6: Channel Spouted Bowls fromPandu Rajar, Dhibi, West Bengal

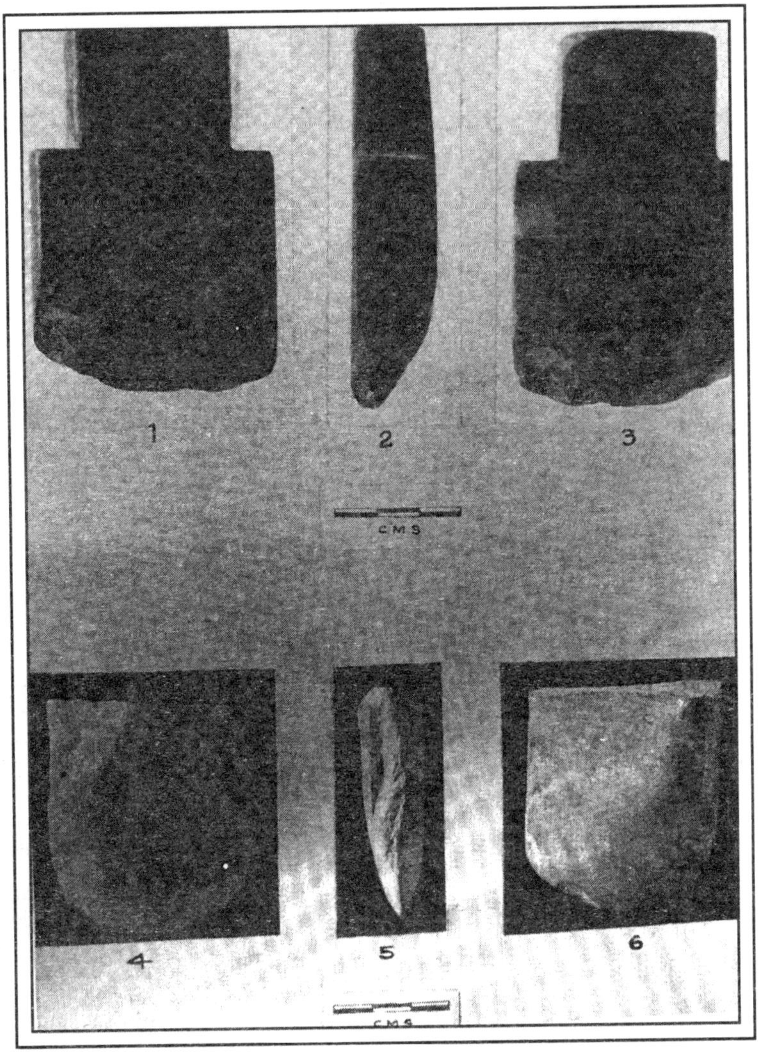

Source: H.D. Sankalia, 1974, *Prehistory and Protohistory of India and Pakistan.*

FIGURE 106: Polished Stone Axes, Orissa

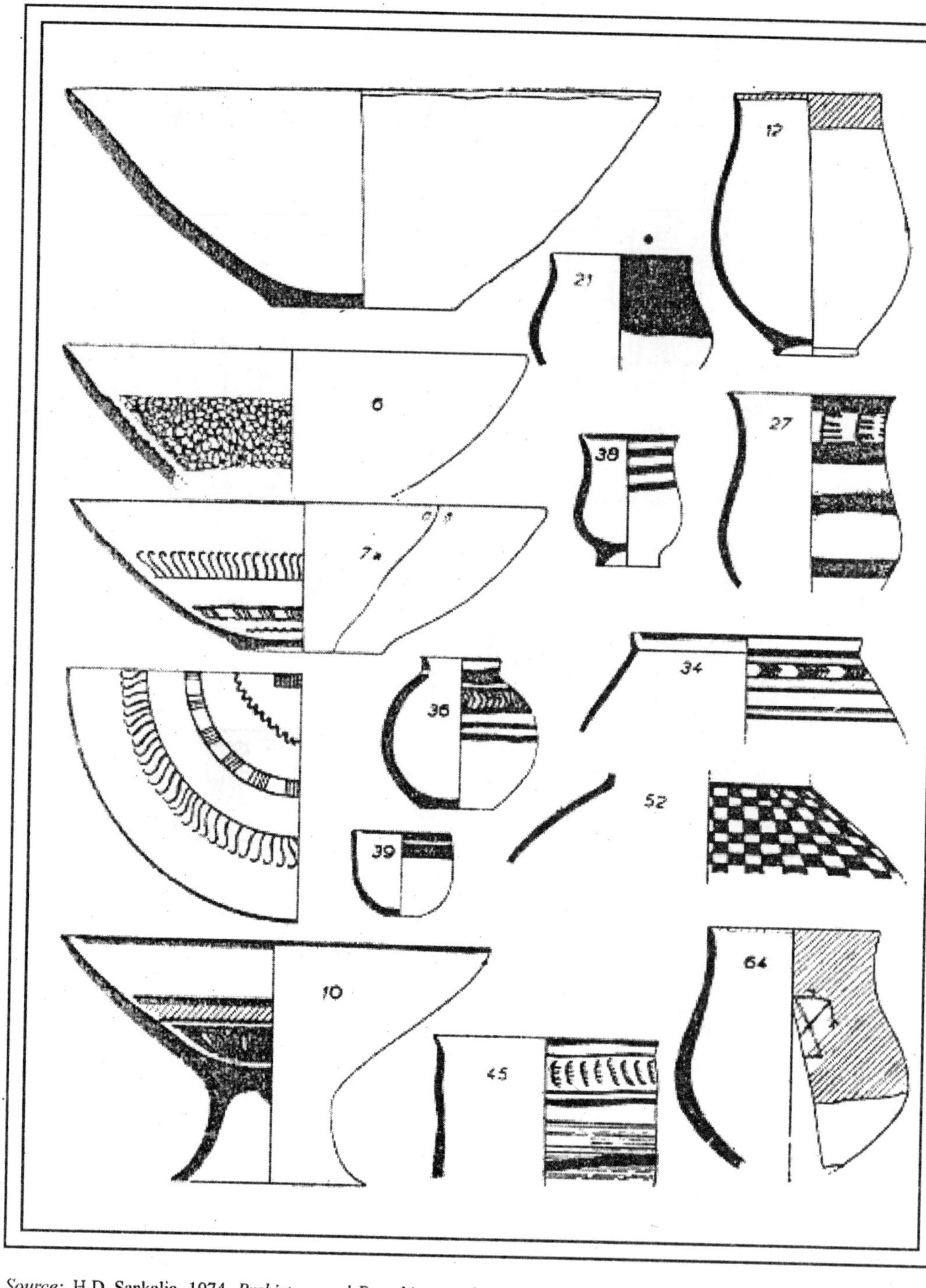

Source: H.D. Sankalia, 1974, *Prehistory and Protohistory of India and Pakistan.*

FIGURE 107: Pottery from Period IA, Amri, Pakistan

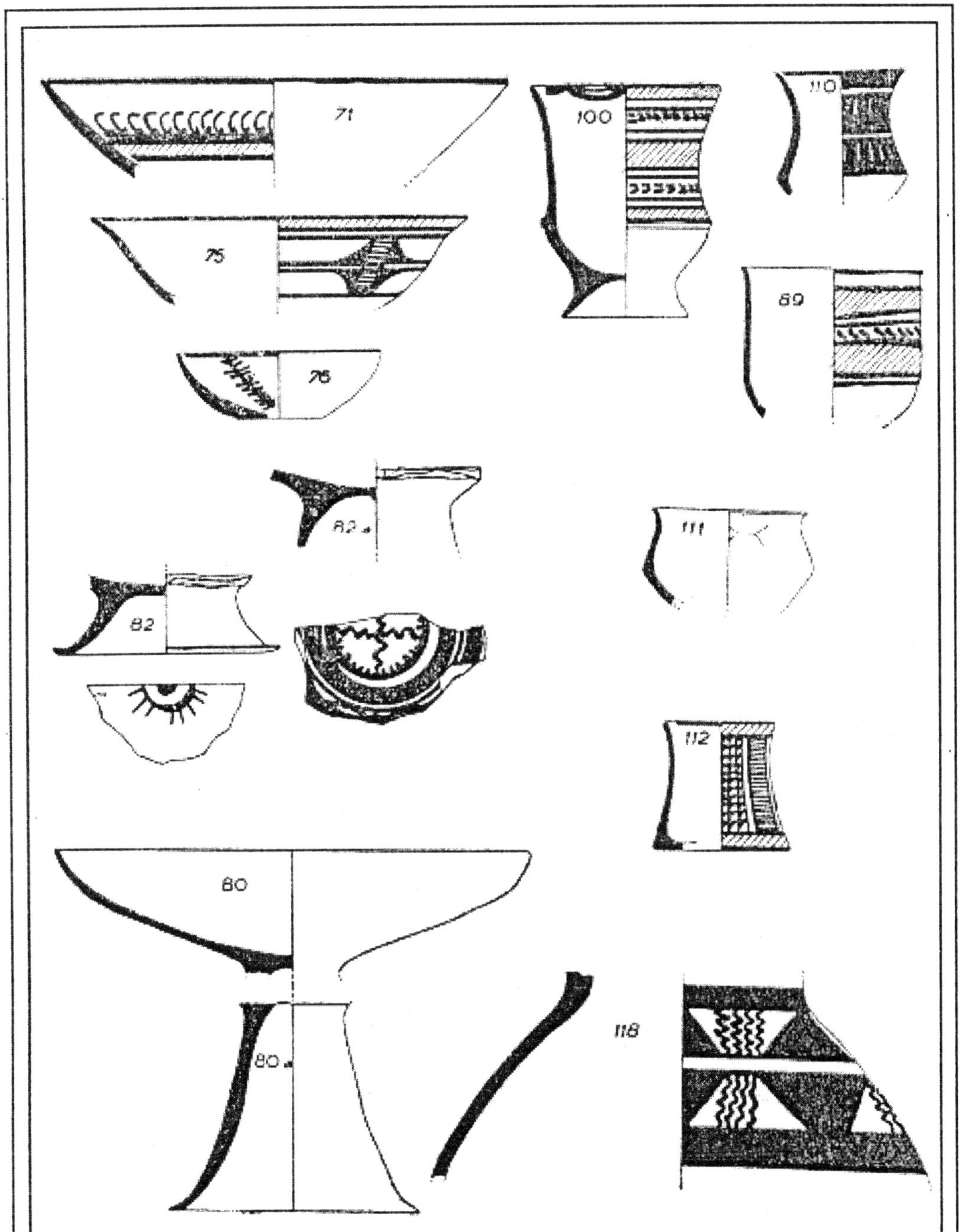

Source: H.D. Sankalia, 1974, *Prehistory and Protohistory of India and Pakistan.*

FIGURE 108: Pottery from Period IB, Amri, Pakistan

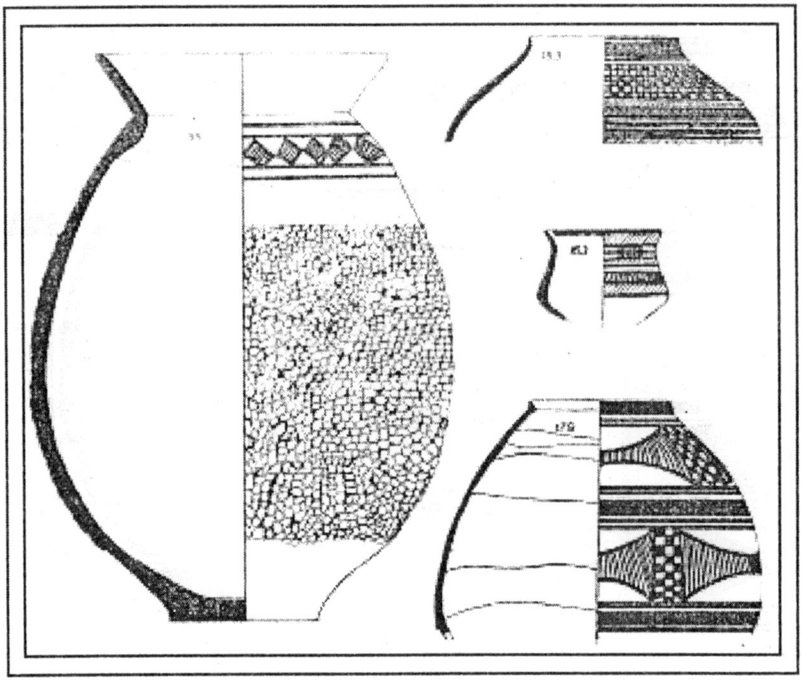

Source: H.D. Sankalia, 1974, *Prehistory and Protohistory of India and Pakistan.*

FIGURE 109: Pottery from Period IC, Amri, Pakistan

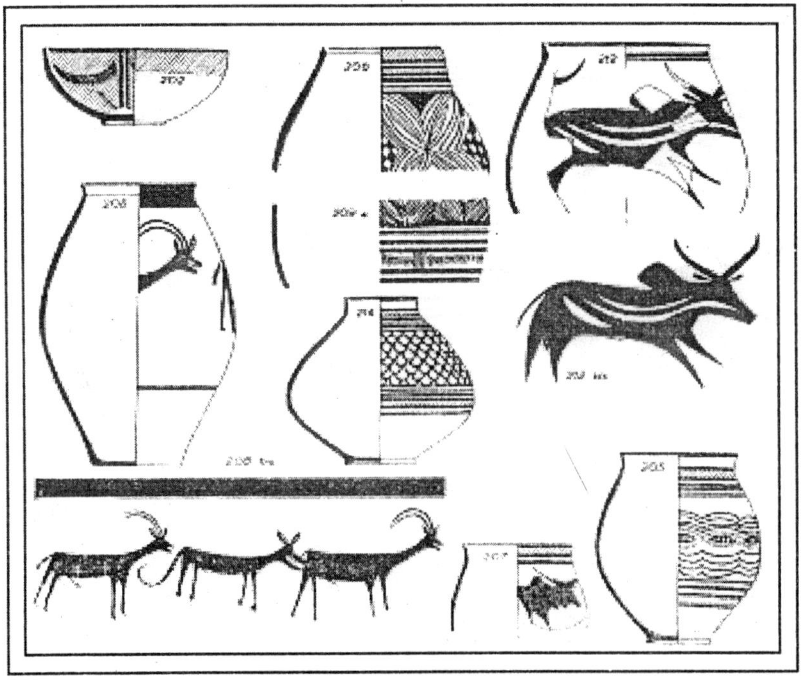

Source: H.D. Sankalia, 1974, *Prehistory and Protohistory of India and Pakistan.*

FIGURE 110: Pottery from Period ID, Amri, Pakistan

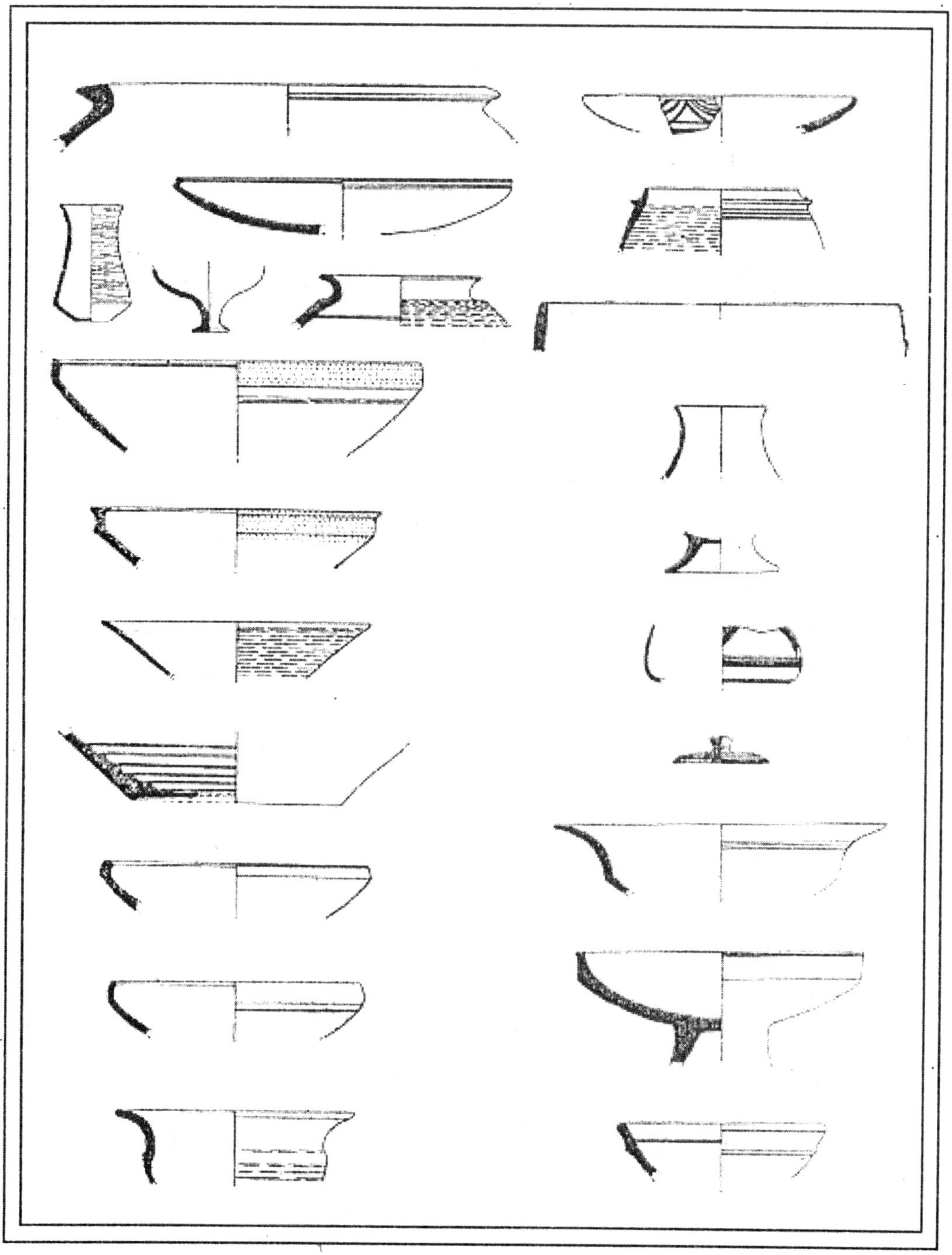

Source: H.D. Sankalia, 1974, *Prehistory and Protohistory of India and Pakistan.*

FIGURE 111: Pottery of the Middle and Middle-Late Phases of the Pre-Harappan Pottery (Kot Dijian) Culture, Kot Diji, Pakistan

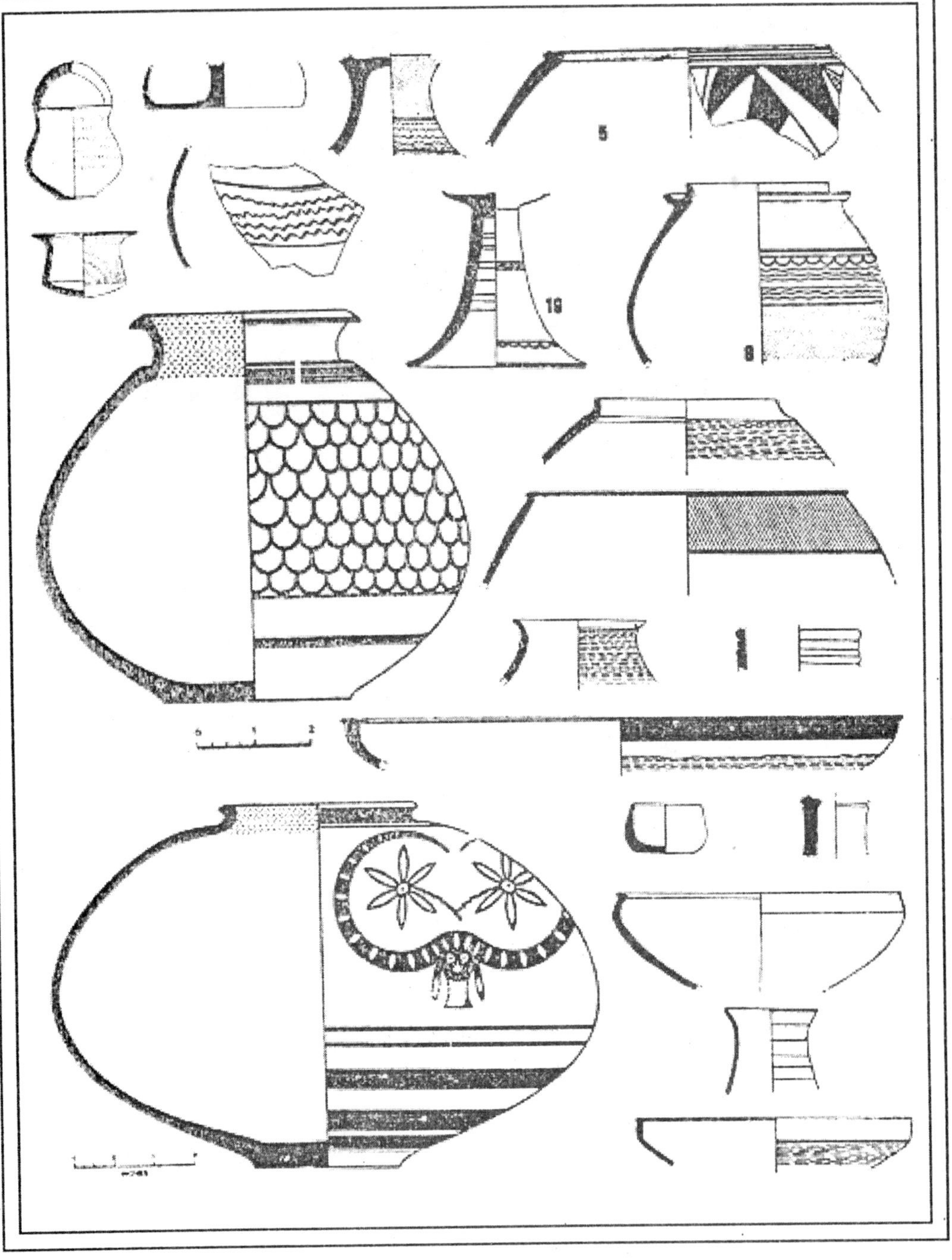

Source: H.D. Sankalia, 1974, *Prehistory and Protohistory of India and Pakistan.*

FIGURE 112: Pottery of the Harappan (1-3); Harappan-Kot Dijian (4-5); and Early and Middle Kot Dijian Periods (6-20) at Kot Diji, Pakistan

Source: H.D. Sankalia, 1974, *Prehistory and Protohistory of India and Pakistan.*

FIGURE 113: Pre-Harappan Structure, Kalibangan

Source: H.D. Sankalia, 1974, *Prehistory and Protohistory of India and Pakistan.*

FIGURE 114: Pre-Harappan Structure, Kalibangan

Source: H.D. Sankalia, 1974, *Prehistory and Protohistory of India and Pakistan.*

FIGURE 115: Oven in a Pre-Harappan House, Kalibangan

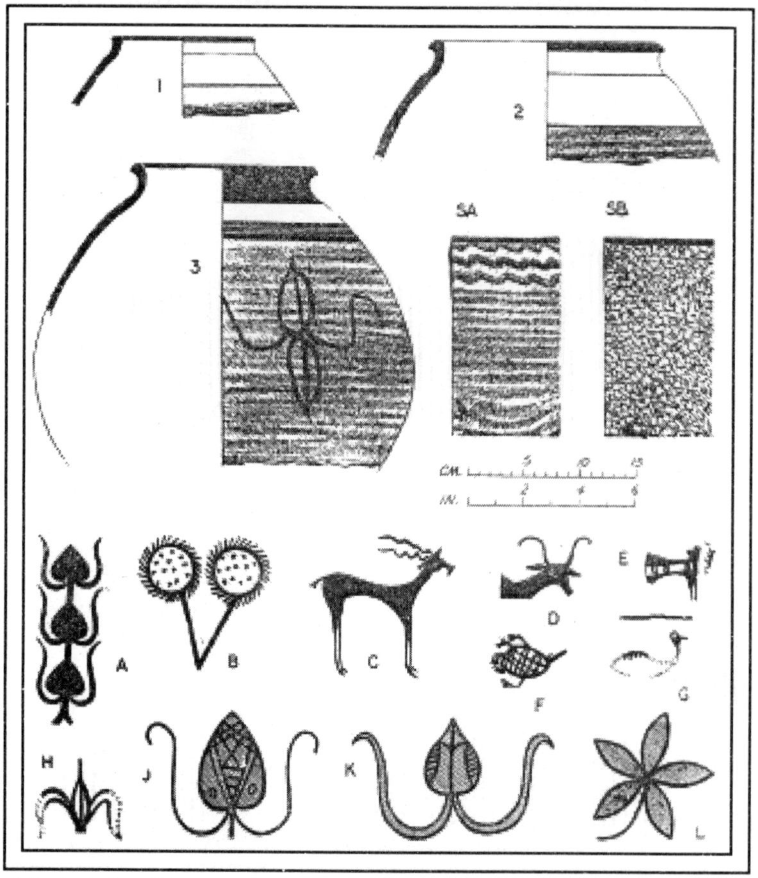

Source: H.D. Sankalia, 1974, *Prehistory and Protohistory of India and Pakistan.*

FIGURE 116: Pre-Harappan Pottery Types and Painted Designs, Kalibangan

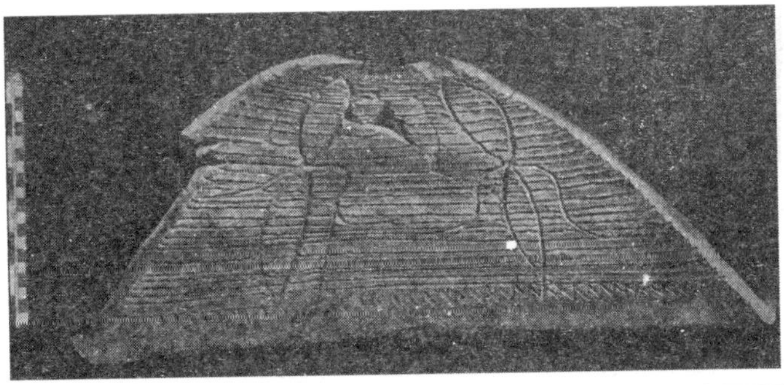

Source: H.D. Sankalia, 1974, *Prehistory and Protohistory of India and Pakistan.*

FIGURE 117: Pre-Harappan Pottery with Incised Decorations, Kalibangan

Source: H.D. Sankalia, 1974, *Prehistory and Protohistory of India and Pakistan.*

FIGURE 118: Arterial Thoroughfare, Harappan, Kalibangan

Source: H.D. Sankalia, 1974, *Prehistory and Protohistory of India and Pakistan.*

FIGURE 119: Fire Places, Kalibangan

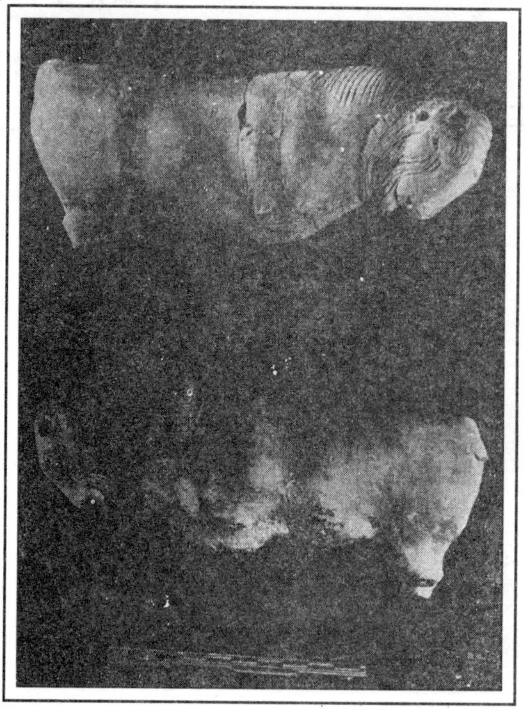

Source: H.D. Sankalia, 1974, *Prehistory and Protohistory of India and Pakistan.*

FIGURE 120: Terracotta Figurine of a Bull, Harappan, Kalibangan

Source: H.D. Sankalia, 1974, *Prehistory and Protohistory of India and Pakistan.*

FIGURE 122: Terracotta Cake with Incised Figures Obverse and Reverse, Kalibangan

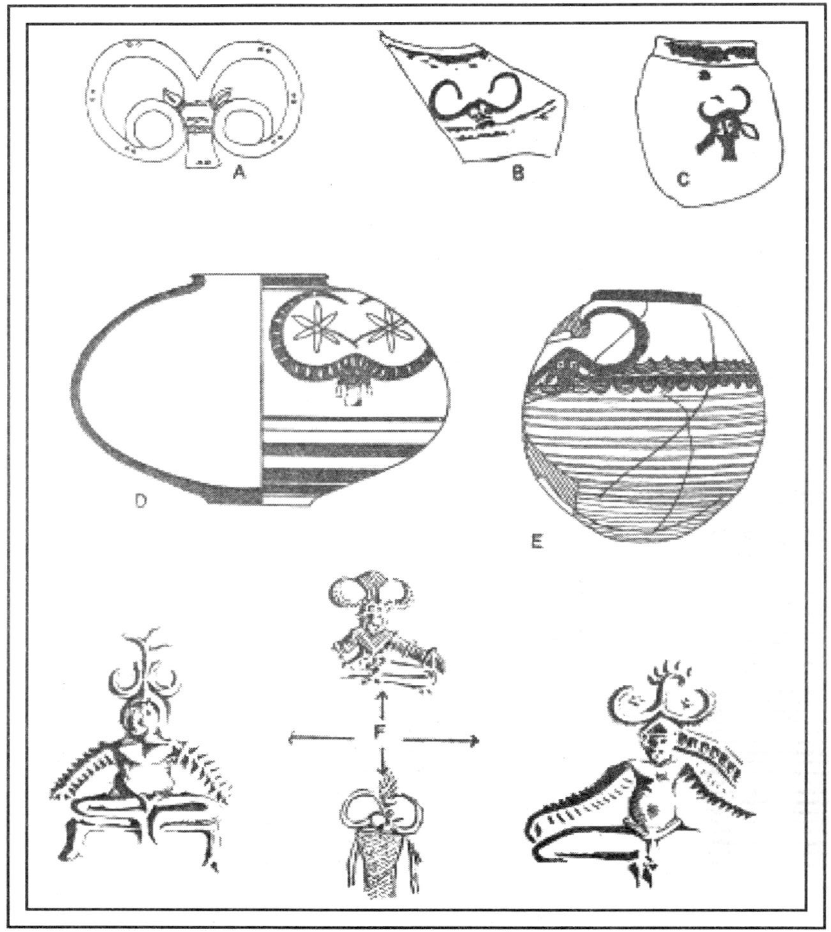

Source: H.D. Sankalia, 1974, *Prehistory and Protohistory of India and Pakistan.*

FIGURE 121: Horned Figures from (A) Hissar, (B-C) Gumla, (D) Kot Diji, (E) Burzahom, (F) Mohenjodaro, (G) Kalibangan

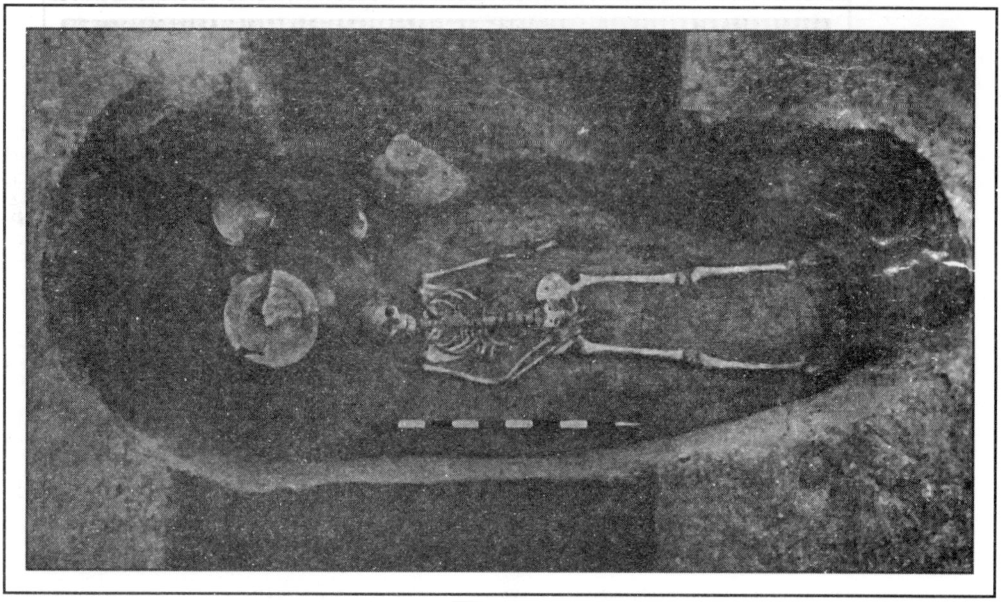

Source: H.D. Sankalia, 1974, *Prehistory and Protohistory of India and Pakistan.*

FIGURE 123: Extended Burial in Grave Pit, Kalibangan

Source: H.D. Sankalia, 1974, *Prehistory and Protohistory of India and Pakistan.*

FIGURE 124: Extended Burial with Burial Pottery, Kalibangan

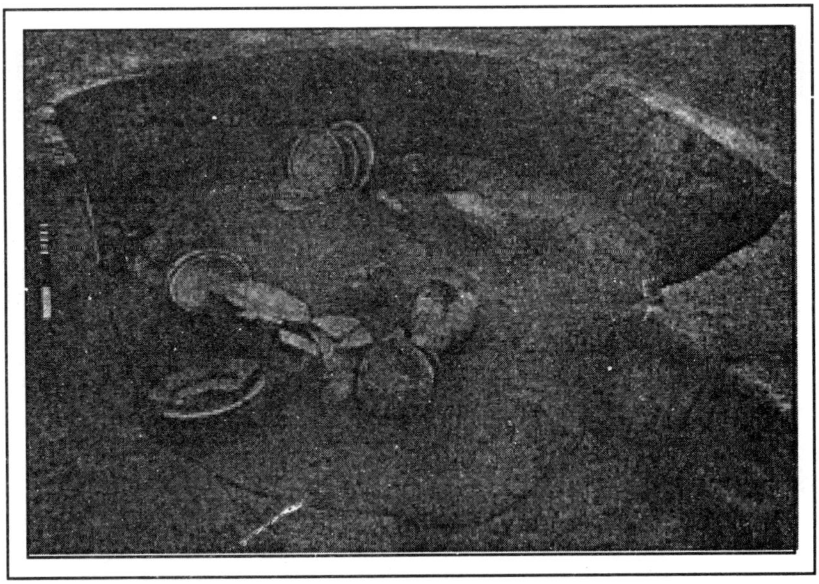

Source: H.D. Sankalia, 1974, *Prehistory and Protohistory of India and Pakistan.*

FIGURE 125: Grave Pit with Burial Pottery, Kalibangan

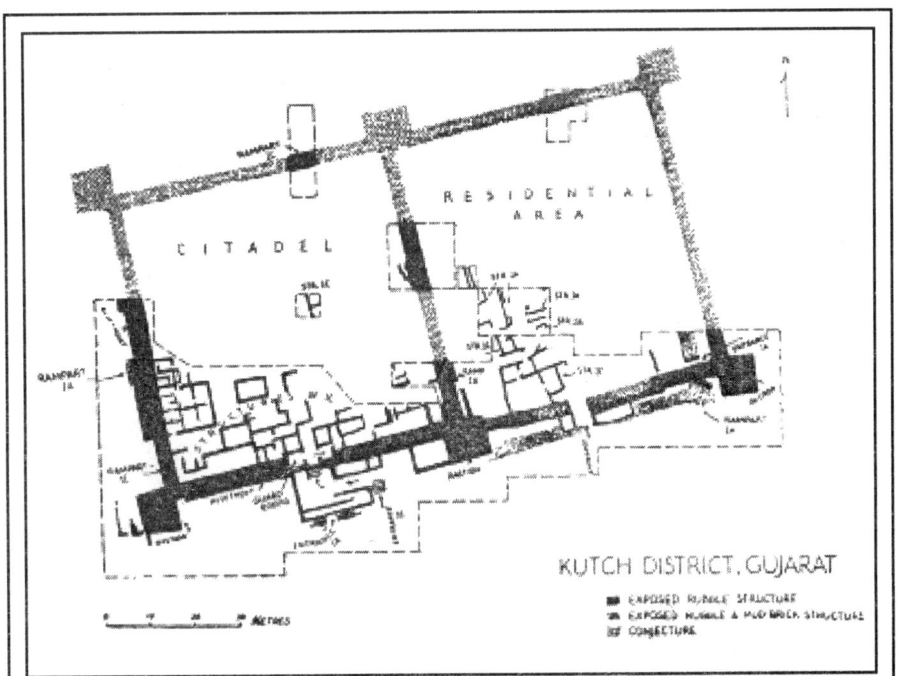

Source: H.D. Sankalia, 1974, *Prehistory and Protohistory of India and Pakistan.*

FIGURE 126: Residential Area, Surkotada, Gujarat

Source: H.D. Sankalia, 1974, *Prehistory and Protohistory of India and Pakistan.*

FIGURE 127: General View of the Site, Surkotada, Kutch, Gujarat

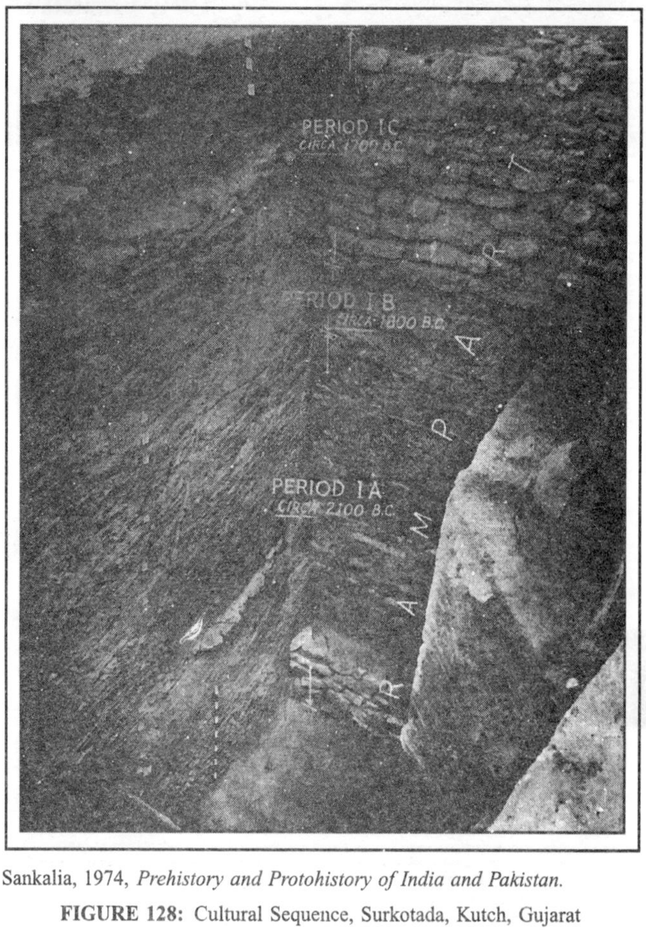

Source: H.D. Sankalia, 1974, *Prehistory and Protohistory of India and Pakistan.*

FIGURE 128: Cultural Sequence, Surkotada, Kutch, Gujarat

Source: H.D. Sankalia, 1974, *Prehistory and Protohistory of India and Pakistan.*

FIGURE 129: Drain IA, Surkotada, Gujarat

Source: H.D. Sankalia, 1974, *Prehistory and Protohistory of India and Pakistan.*

FIGURE 130: Harappan Pottery, Surkotada, Kutch, Gujarat

Source: H.D. Sankalia, 1974, *Prehistory and Protohistory of India and Pakistan.*

FIGURE 131: Harappan Script Painted on Potsherd, Surkotada, Kutch, Gujarat

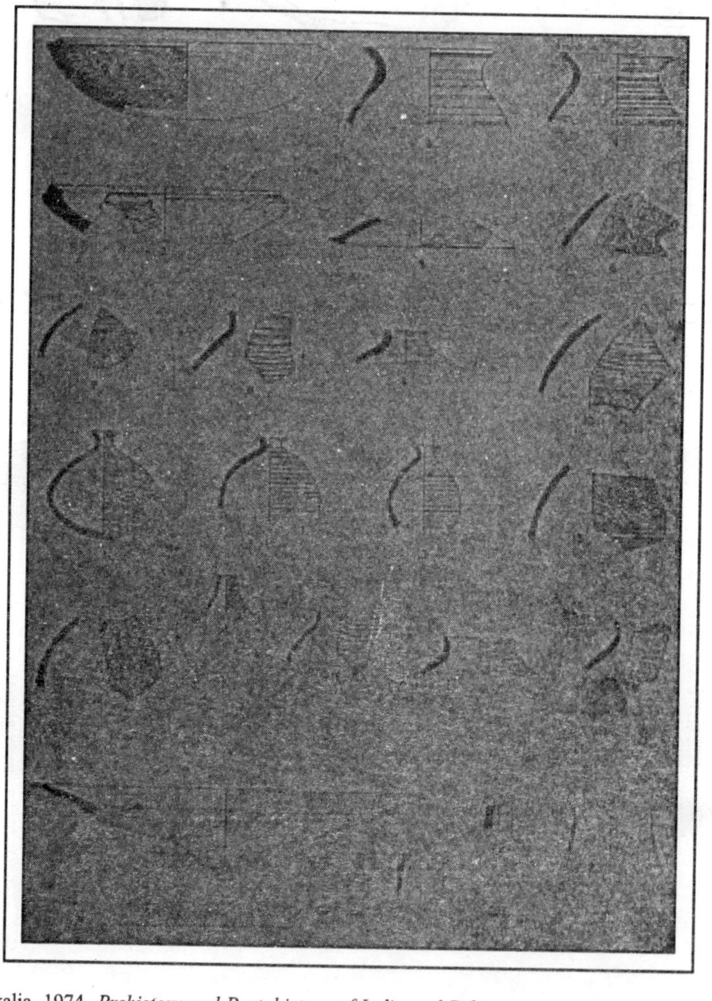

Source: H.D. Sankalia, 1974, *Prehistory and Protohistory of India and Pakistan.*

FIGURE 132: 1-19: Reversed Slip Ware, 20-23: Deep Red Slipped Ware of Waxy Touch, IA, Surkotada, Gujarat

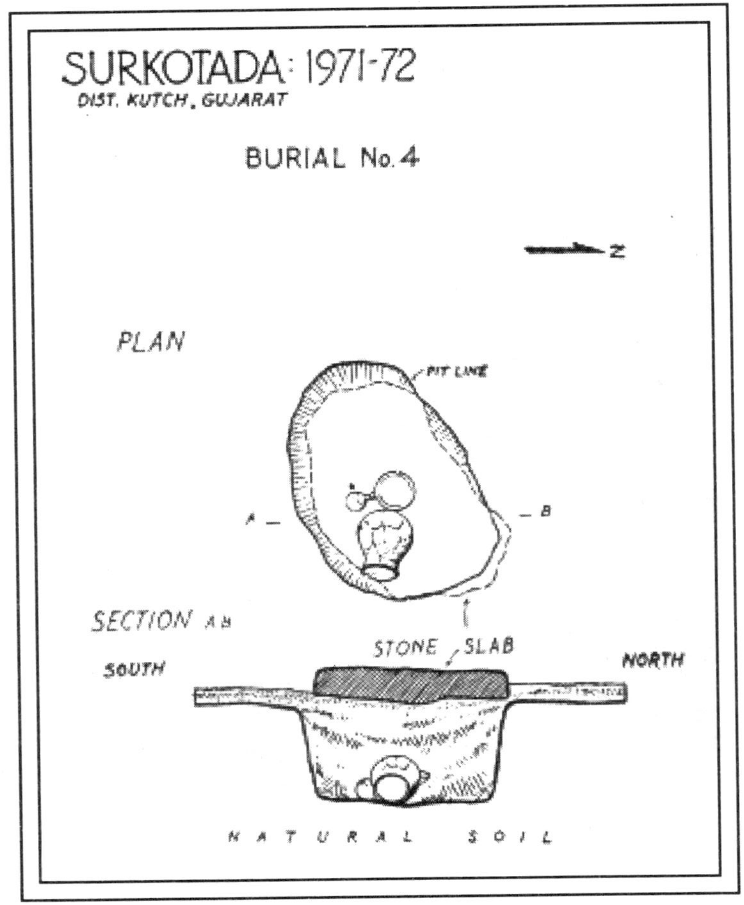

Source: H.D. Sankalia, 1974, *Prehistory and Protohistory of India and Pakistan.*

FIGURE 133: Pot Burials, IA, Surkotada, Gujarat

Source: H.D. Sankalia, 1974, *Prehistory and Protohistory of India and Pakistan.*

FIGURE 134: Polished Stone Axe, Jokha, S. Gujarat

Source: H.D. Sankalia, 1974, *Prehistory and Protohistory of India and Pakistan.*

FIGURE 135: Embankment of the Ditch, Malvan, S. Gujarat

Source: H.D. Sankalia, 1974, *Prehistory and Protohistory of India and Pakistan.*

FIGURE 136: Ditch with Animal Bones, Malvan, S. Gujarat

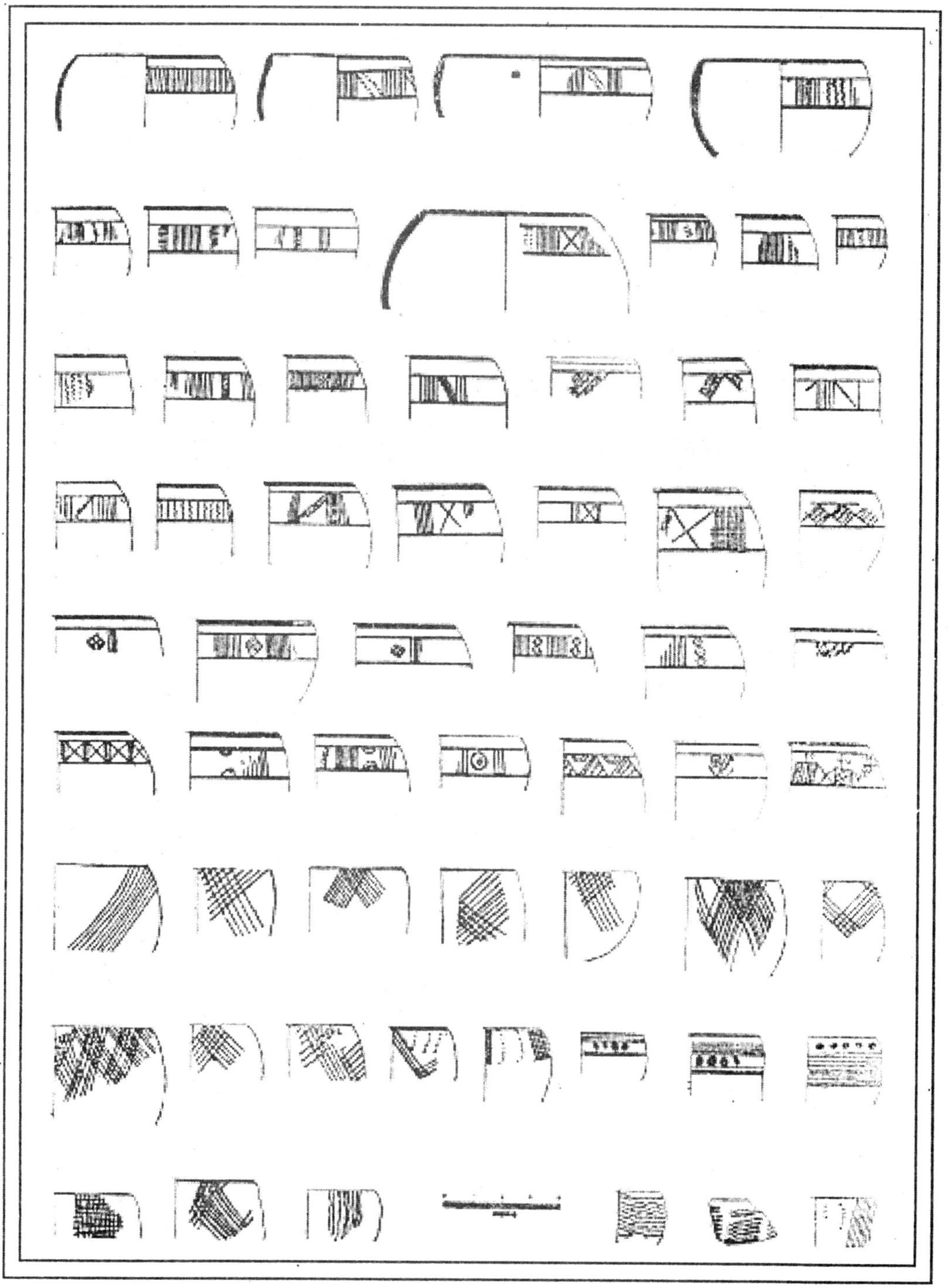

Source: H.D. Sankalia, 1974, *Prehistory and Protohistory of India and Pakistan.*

FIGURE 137: Prabhas Ware Bowls with Designs

Source: H.D. Sankalia, 1974, *Prehistory and Protohistory of India and Pakistan.*

FIGURE 138: The Dockyard, Lothal, Gujarat

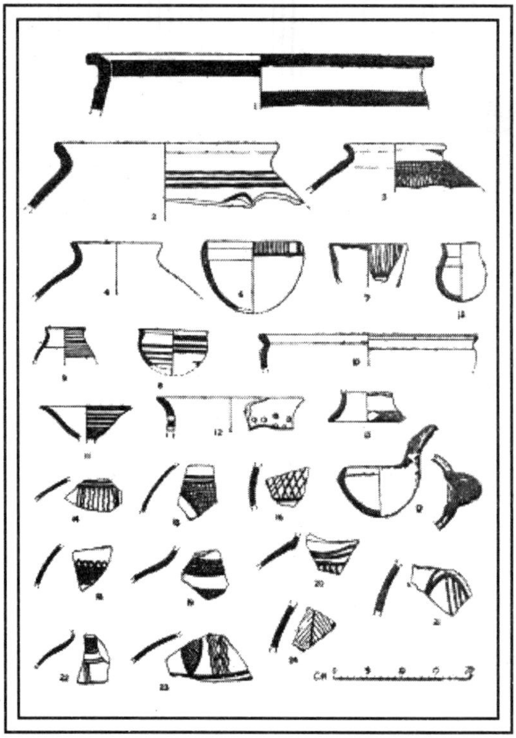

Source: H.D. Sankalia, 1974, *Prehistory and Protohistory of India and Pakistan.*

FIGURE 139: Coarse Red Ware, IB, Surkotada, Kutch, Gujarat

Source: H.D. Sankalia, 1974, *Prehistory and Protohistory of India and Pakistan.*

FIGURE 140: General View of Citadel, IC, Surkotada, Kutch, Gujarat

Source: H.D. Sankalia, 1974, *Prehistory and Protohistory of India and Pakistan.*

FIGURE 141: Bastion and Rampart Residential, Period IV, Surkotada, Kutch, Gujarat

Source: H.D. Sankalia, 1974, *Prehistory and Protohistory of India and Pakistan.*

FIGURE 142: Layout of a Residential House IC, Surkotada, Kutch, Gujarat

Source: H.D. Sankalia, 1974, *Prehistory and Protohistory of India and Pakistan.*

FIGURE 143: Bull (on wheel) Period IC, Surkotada, Kutch, Gujarat

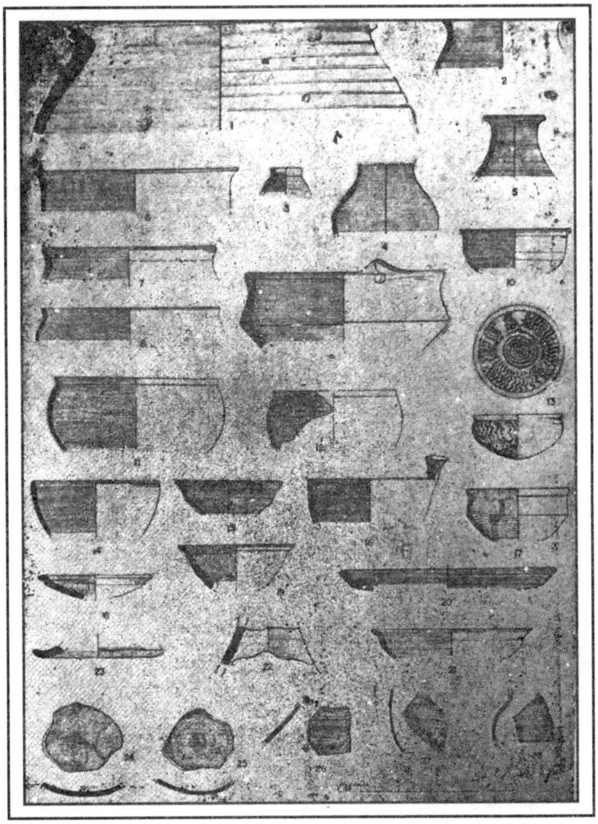

Source: H.D. Sankalia, 1974, *Prehistory and Protohistory of India and Pakistan.*

FIGURE 144: White Painted, Black and Red Ware, Period IC, Surkotada, Kutch, Gujarat

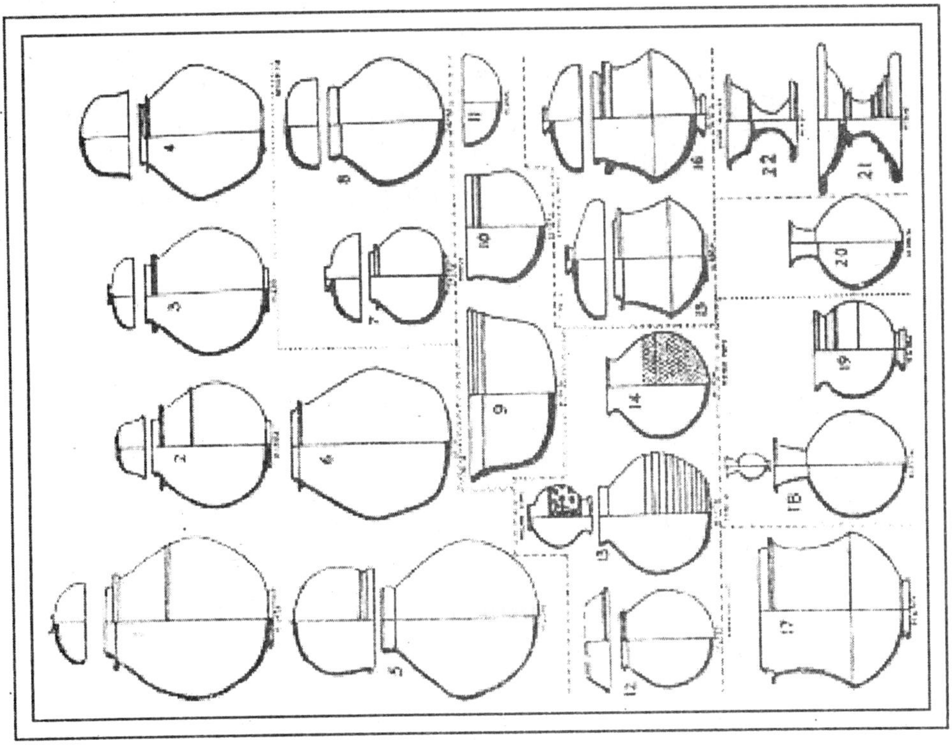

Source: H.D. Sankalia, 1974, *Prehistory and Protohistory of India and Pakistan.*

FIGURE 145: Pottery from Cemetery-H, Harappa

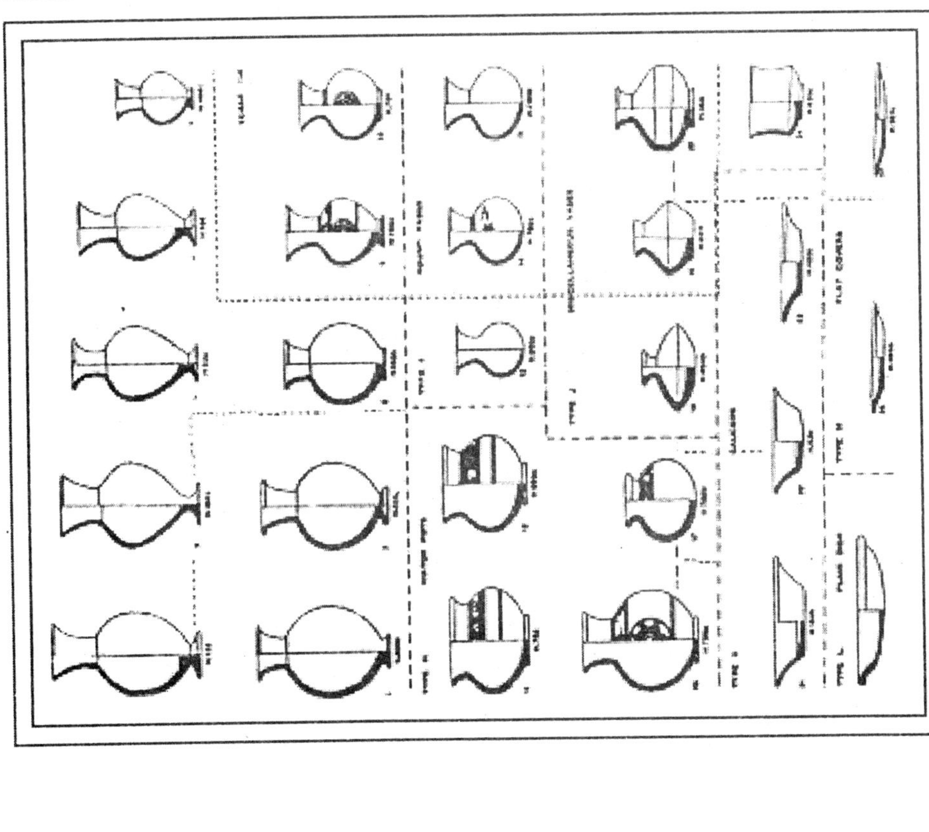

Source: H.D. Sankalia, 1974, *Prehistory and Protohistory of India and Pakistan.*

FIGURE 146: Pottery from Cemetery-H, Harappa

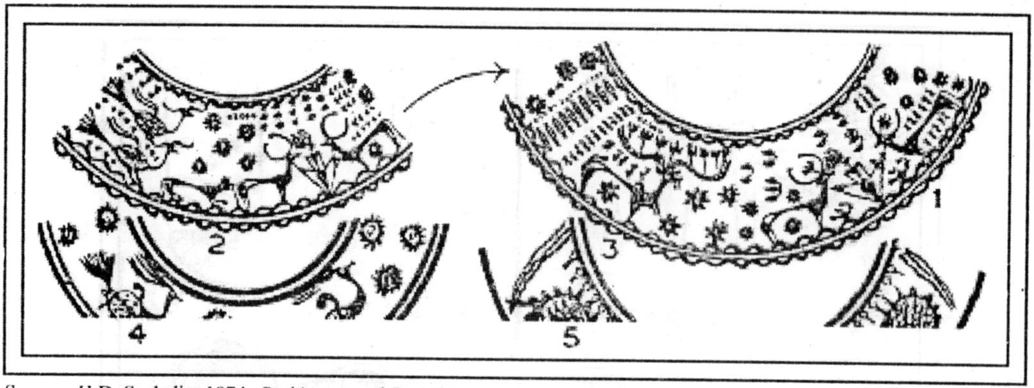

Source: H.D. Sankalia, 1974, *Prehistory and Protohistory of India and Pakistan.*

FIGURE 147: A Story-telling Painting on Pottery from Cemetery-H, Harappa

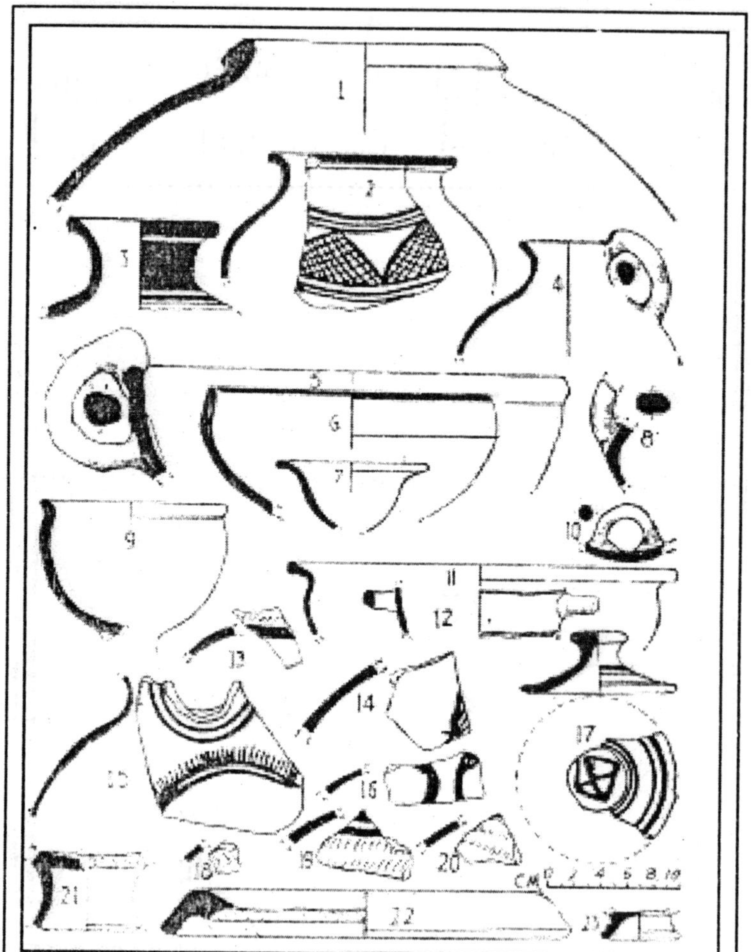

Source: H.D. Sankalia, 1974, *Prehistory and Protohistory of India and Pakistan.*

FIGURE 148: Ochre Coloured Pottery from Saiyal and Other Sites

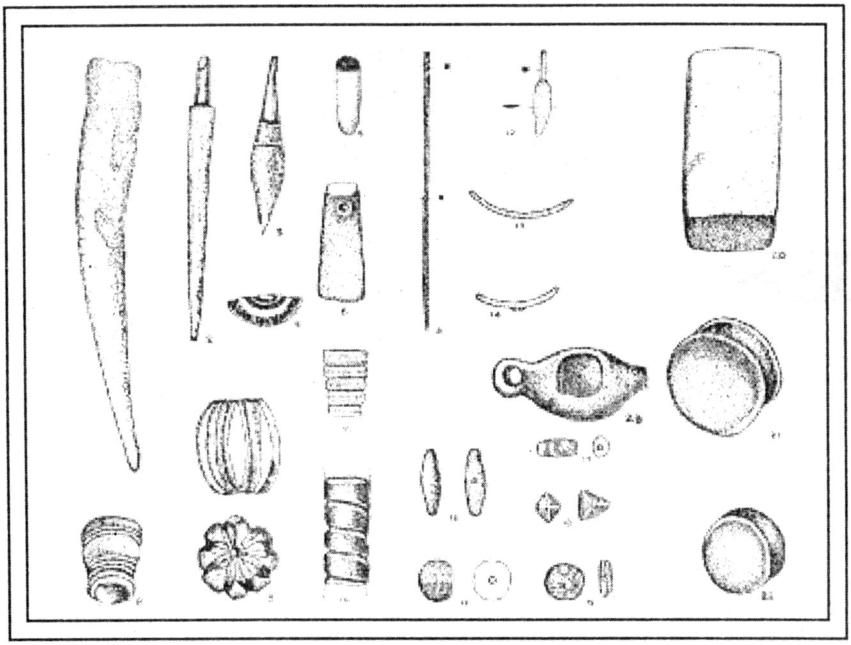

Source: H.D. Sankalia, 1974, *Prehistory and Protohistory of India and Pakistan.*

FIGURE 149: Objects of Bone, Terracotta, Chert and Jasper, Copper and Glass (Bangles) of Painted Grey Ware Culture

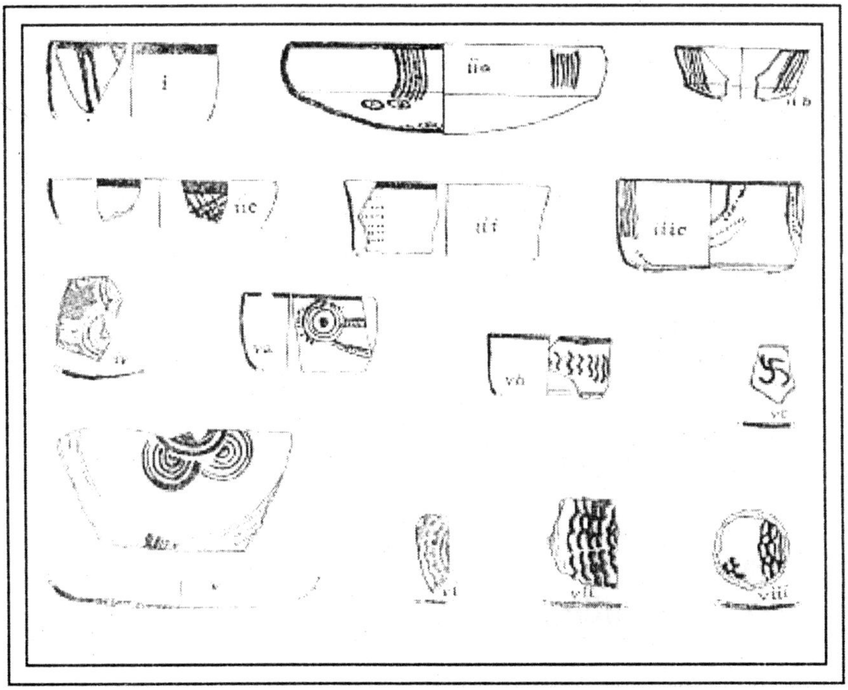

Source: H.D. Sankalia, 1974, *Prehistory and Protohistory of India and Pakistan.*

FIGURE 150: Designs on Painted Grey Ware Pottery

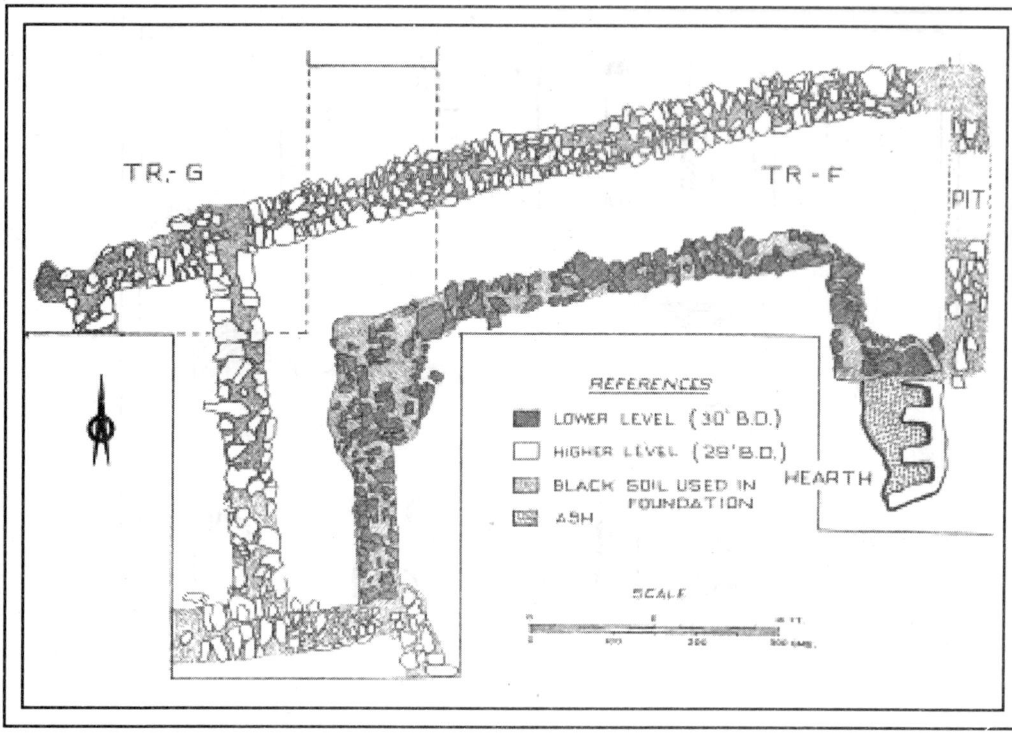

Source: H.D. Sankalia, 1974, *Prehistory and Protohistory of India and Pakistan.*

FIGURE 151: Plan of Longest (Exposed) House, Period Ia, Ib, Ahar, Rajasthan

Source: H.D. Sankalia, 1974, *Prehistory and Protohistory of India and Pakistan.*

FIGURE 152: A Row of *Chulha* (Hearths) and Saddle Quern (at the Left Hand Bottom), Ahar, Rajasthan

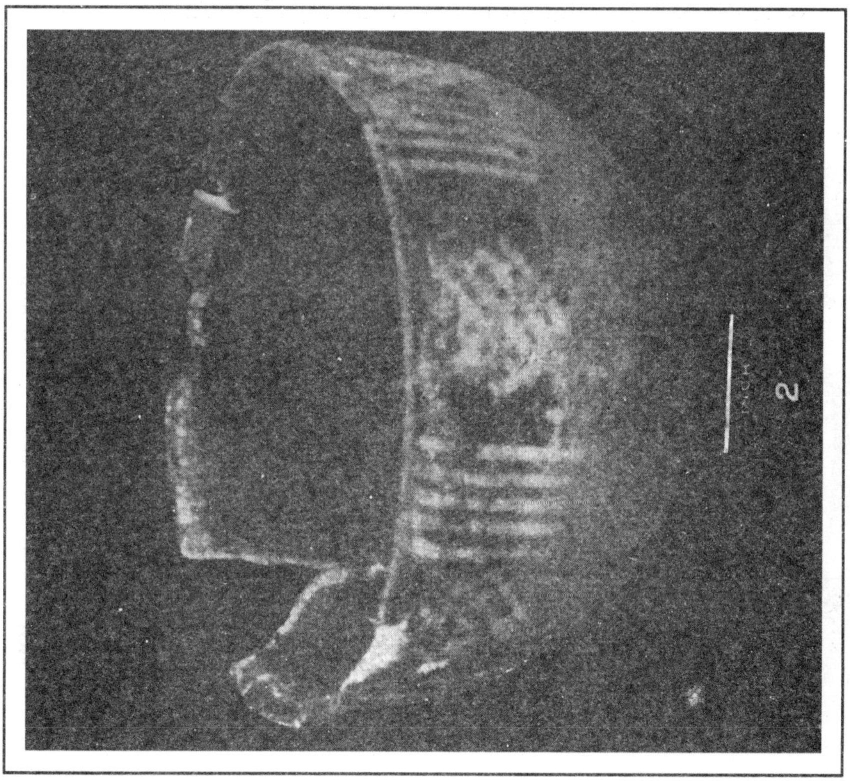

Source: H.D. Sankalia, 1974, *Prehistory and Protohistory of India and Pakistan.*

FIGURE 154: Bowl, White Painted Black and Red Ware, Ahar, Rajasthan

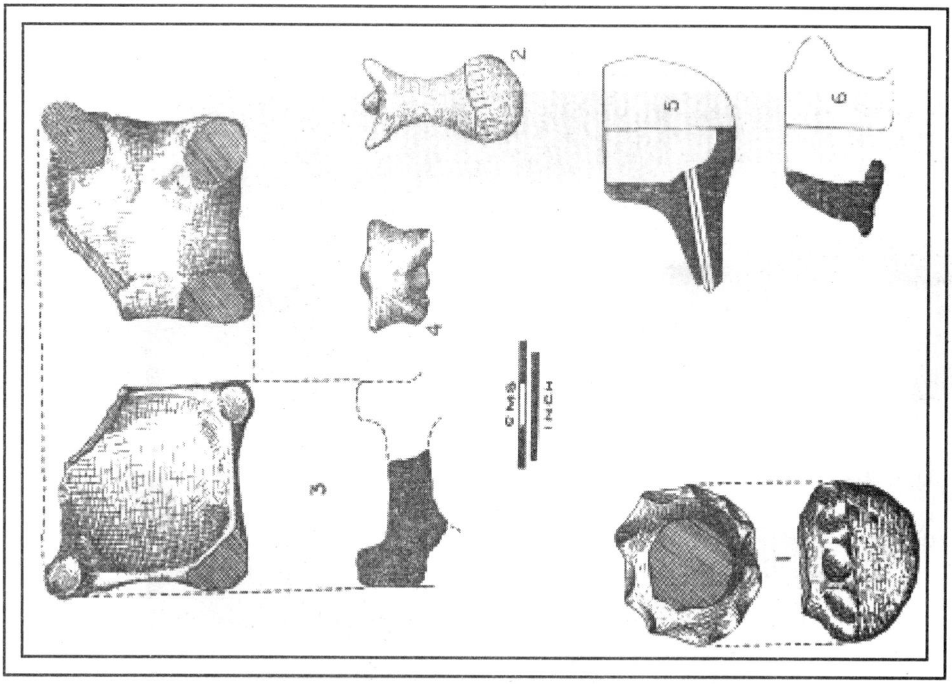

Source: H.D. Sankalia, 1974, *Prehistory and Protohistory of India and Pakistan.*

FIGURE 153: Stylized Bull and Other Unidentified Objects, Ahar, Rajasthan

Source: H.D. Sankalia, 1974, *Prehistory and Protohistory of India and Pakistan*.

FIGURE 155: *Lota*, Tan Ware, Aha:, Rajasthan

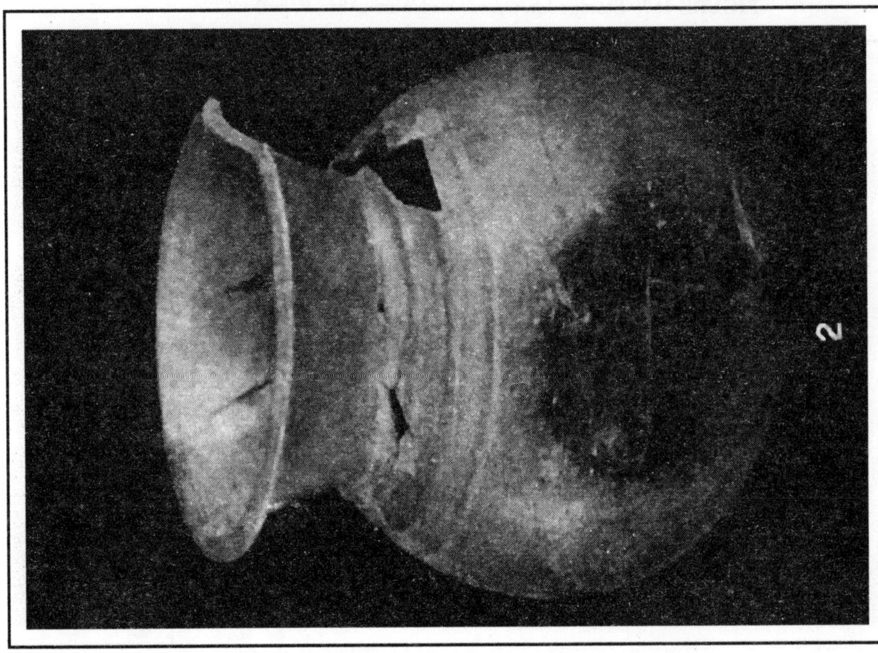

Source: H.D. Sankalia, 1974, *Prehistory and Protohistory of India and Pakistan*.

FIGURE 156: *Lota*, Tan Ware Phase-I, Ahar, Rajasthan

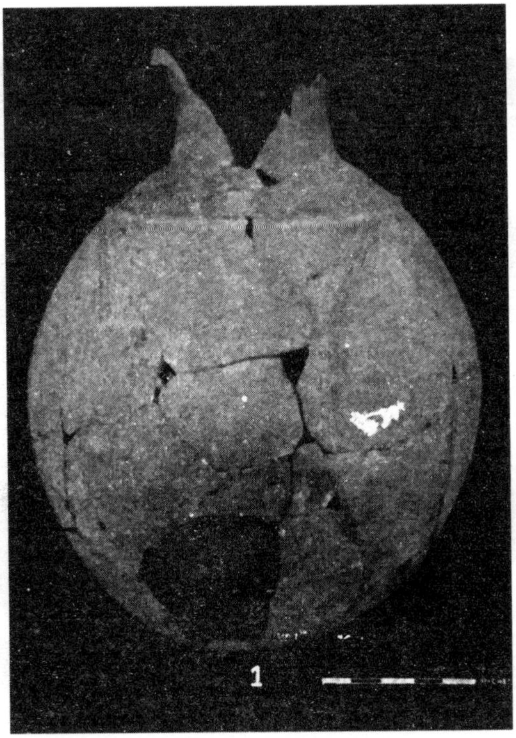

Source: H.D. Sankalia, 1974, *Prehistory and Protohistory of India and Pakistan.*

FIGURE 157: Storage Jar, Coarse Red Ware, Ahar, Rajasthan

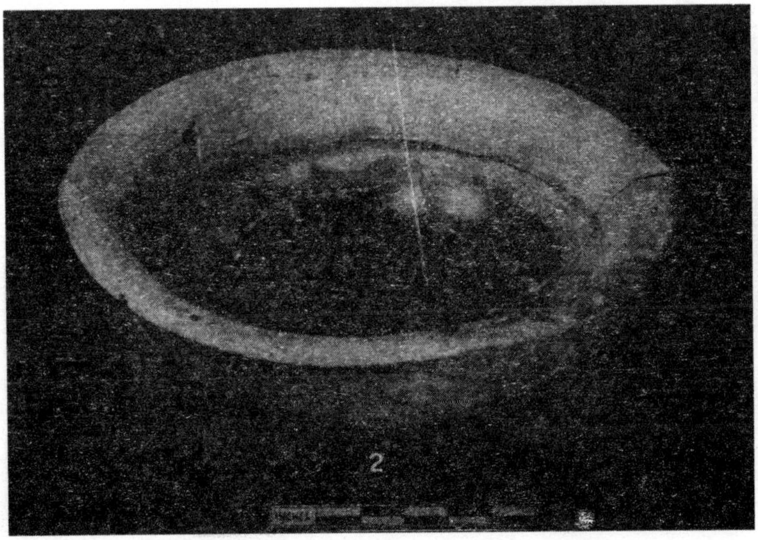

Source: H.D. Sankalia, 1974, *Prehistory and Protohistory of India and Pakistan.*

FIGURE 158: Basin, Tan Ware, Ahar, Rajasthan

Source: H.D. Sankalia, 1974, *Prehistory and Protohistory of India and Pakistan.*

FIGURE 159: Incised and Applique Decoration on a Large Globular Storage Jar, Ahar, Rajasthan

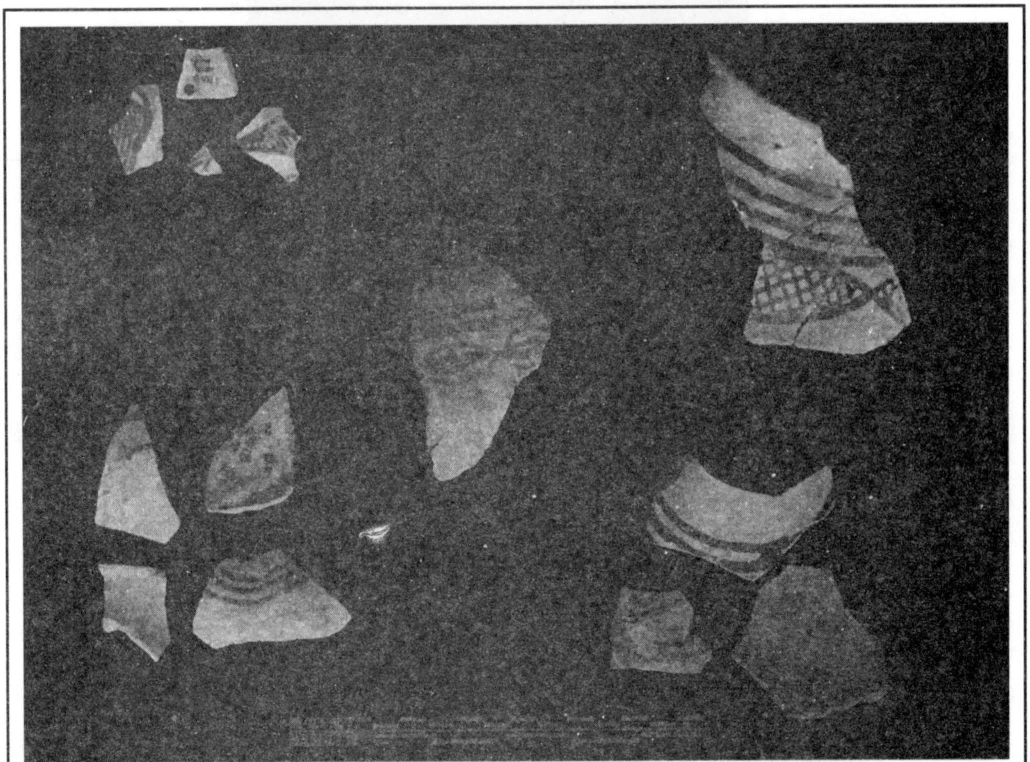

Source: H.D. Sankalia, 1974, *Prehistory and Protohistory of India and Pakistan.*

FIGURE 160: Buff and Buff-slipped Ware, Ahar, Rajasthan

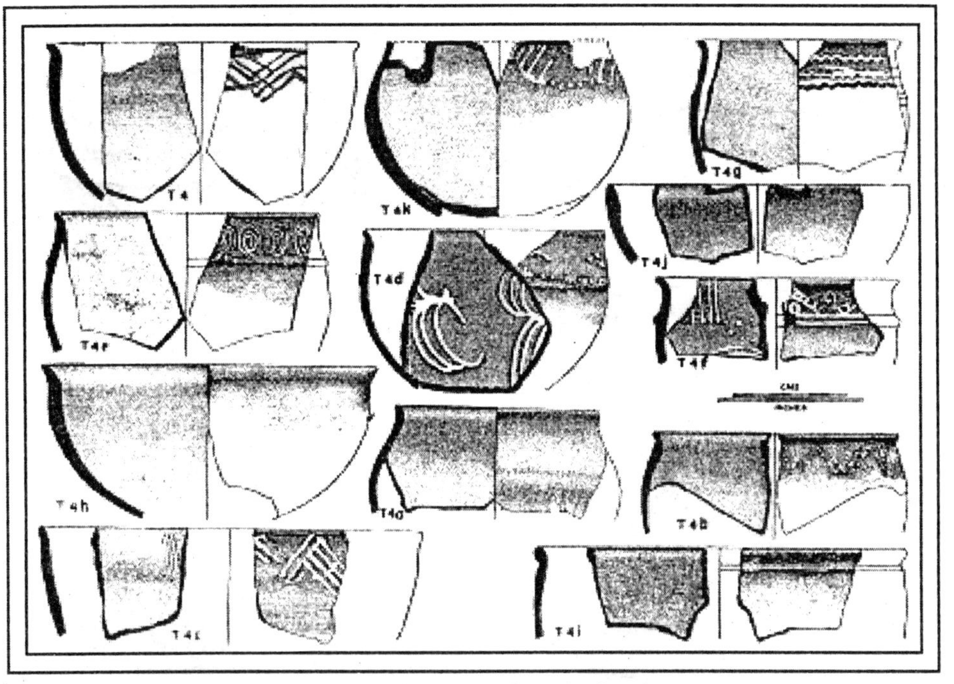

Source: H.D. Sankalia, 1974, *Prehistory and Protohistory of India and Pakistan.*

FIGURE 161: Bowls, White Painted Black and Red Ware, Period IA, Ahar, Rajasthan

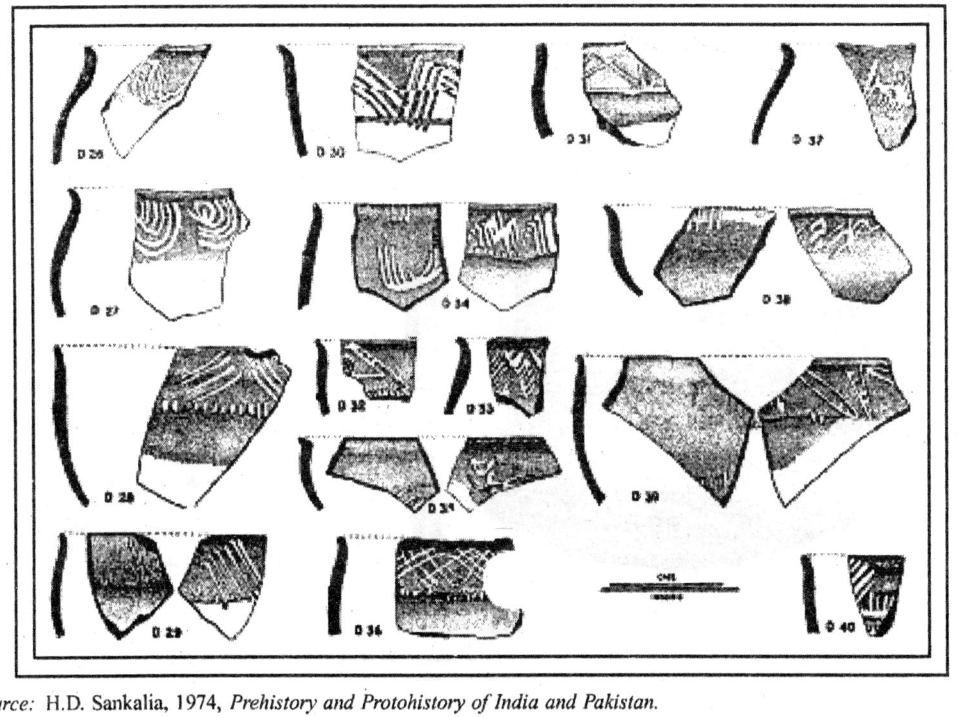

Source: H.D. Sankalia, 1974, *Prehistory and Protohistory of India and Pakistan.*

FIGURE 162: White Painted Black and Red Ware, Period IA, Ahar, Rajasthan

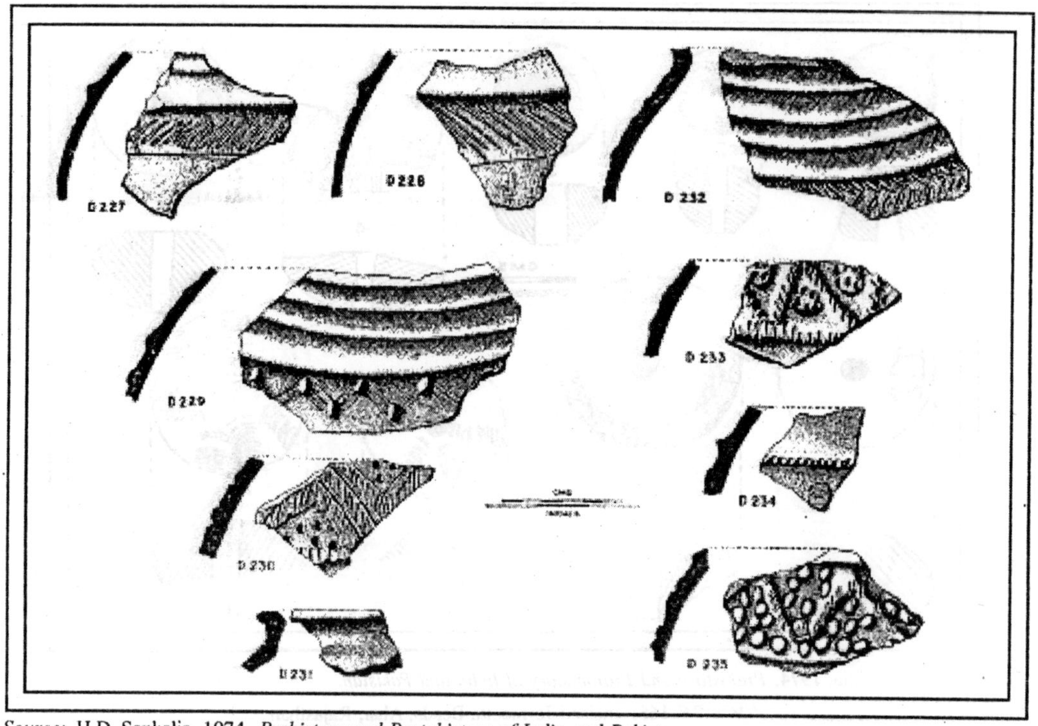

Source: H.D. Sankalia, 1974, *Prehistory and Protohistory of India and Pakistan.*

FIGURE 163: Grey Ware Incised Designs and Punctured Designs and Applique Designs, Ahar, Rajasthan

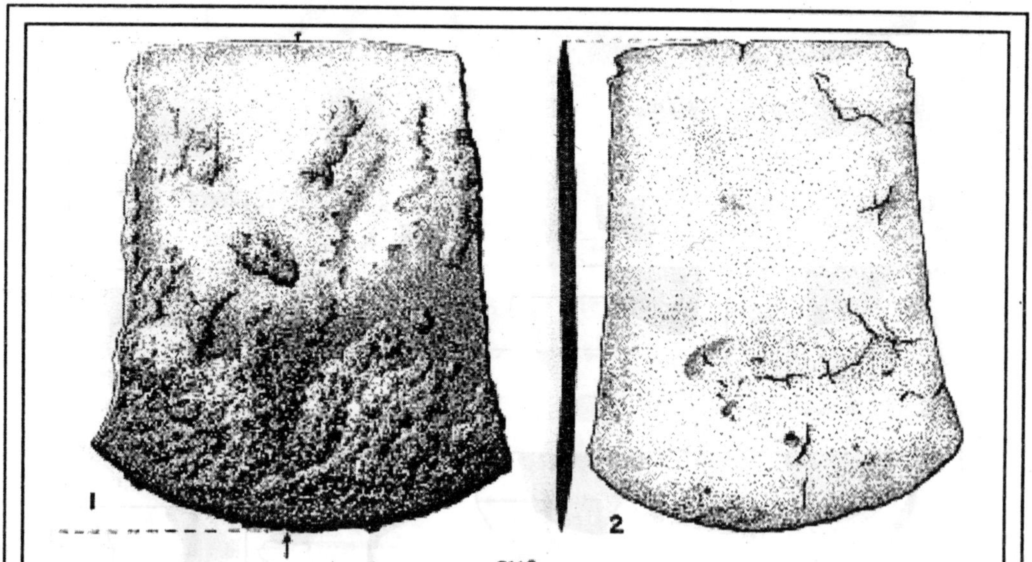

Source: H.D. Sankalia, 1974, *Prehistory and Protohistory of India and Pakistan.*

FIGURE 164: Copper Axe, Ahar, Rajasthan

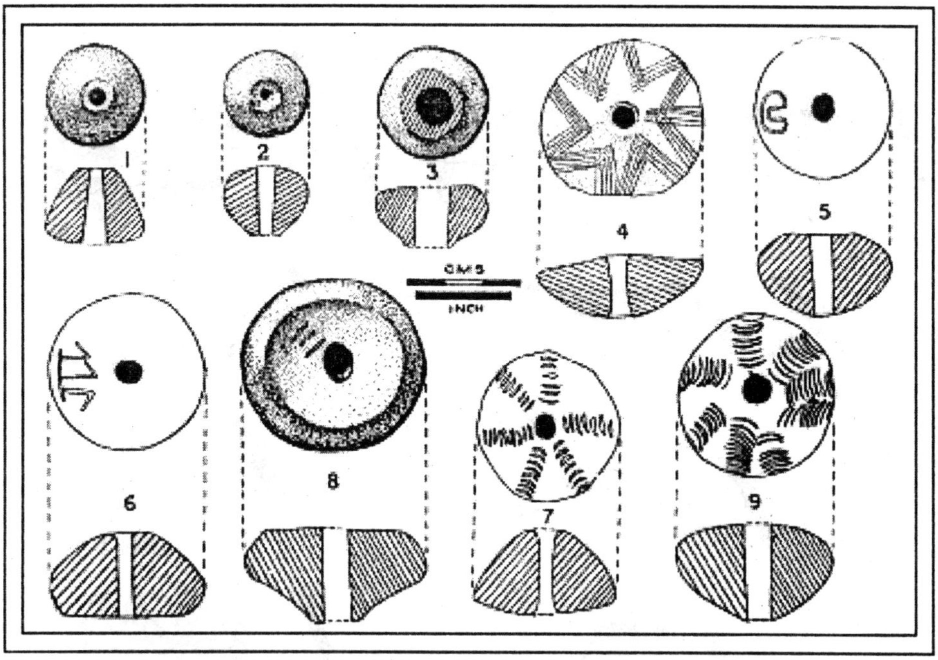

Source: H.D. Sankalia, 1974, *Prehistory and Protohistory of India and Pakistan.*

FIGURE 165: Incised Terracotta Beads, Ahar, Rajasthan

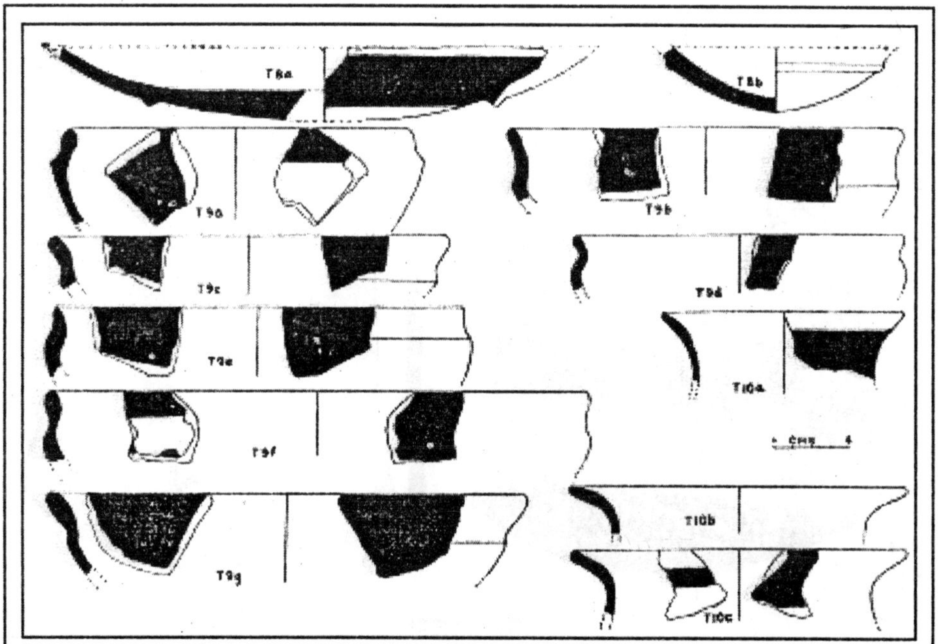

Source: H.D. Sankalia, 1974, *Prehistory and Protohistory of India and Pakistan.*

FIGURE 166: Thick and Thin Wares and Pots with Ring-base, Period I, Kayatha

FIGURE 167: Reconstruction of Prehistoric Towns, Ahar, Rajasthan

Source: H.D. Sankalia, 1974, *Prehistory and Protohistory of India and Pakistan.*

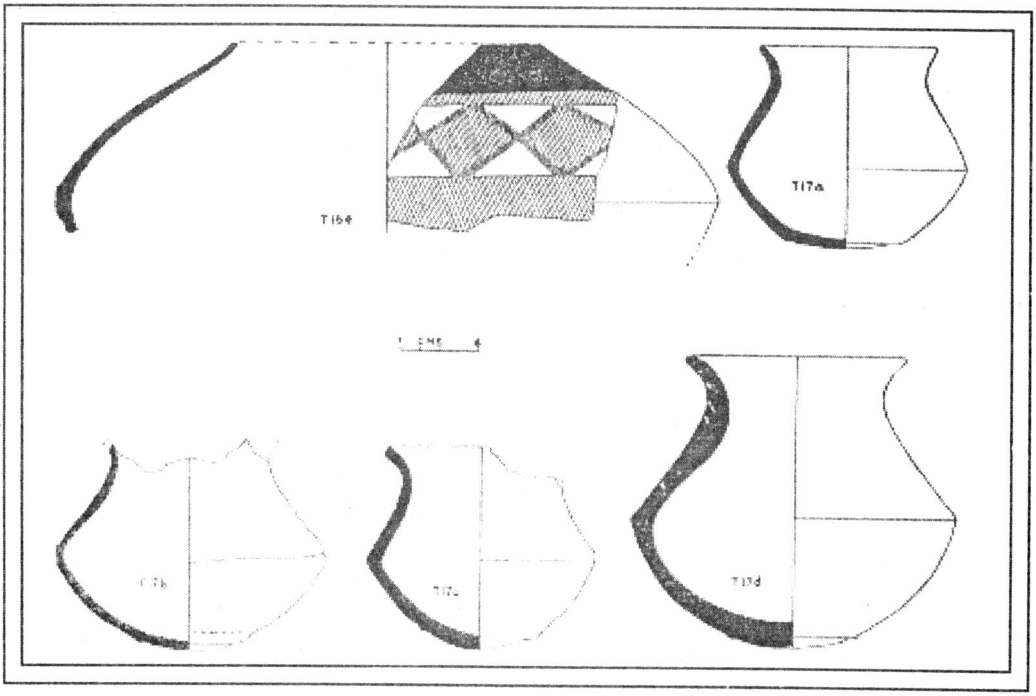

Source: H.D. Sankalia, 1974, *Prehistory and Protohistory of India and Pakistan.*

FIGURE 168: Red and Buff Ware Concave Necked Vessels, Period I, Kayatha

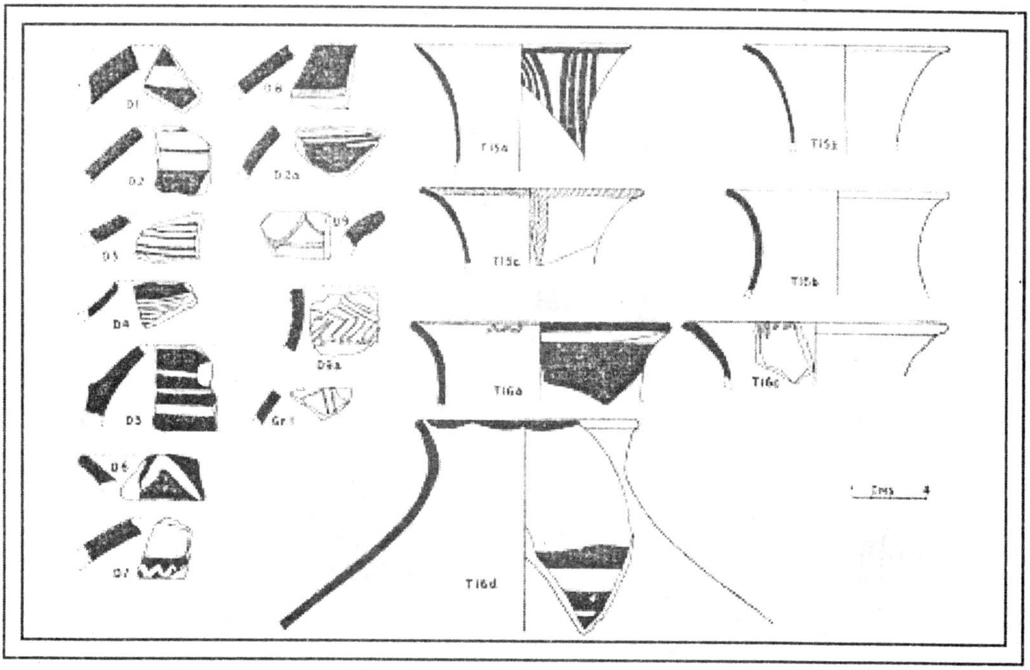

Source: H.D. Sankalia, 1974, *Prehistory and Protohistory of India and Pakistan.*

FIGURE 169: Designs on Thick and Thin Kayatha Ware, Red and Buff Ware, Period I, Kayatha

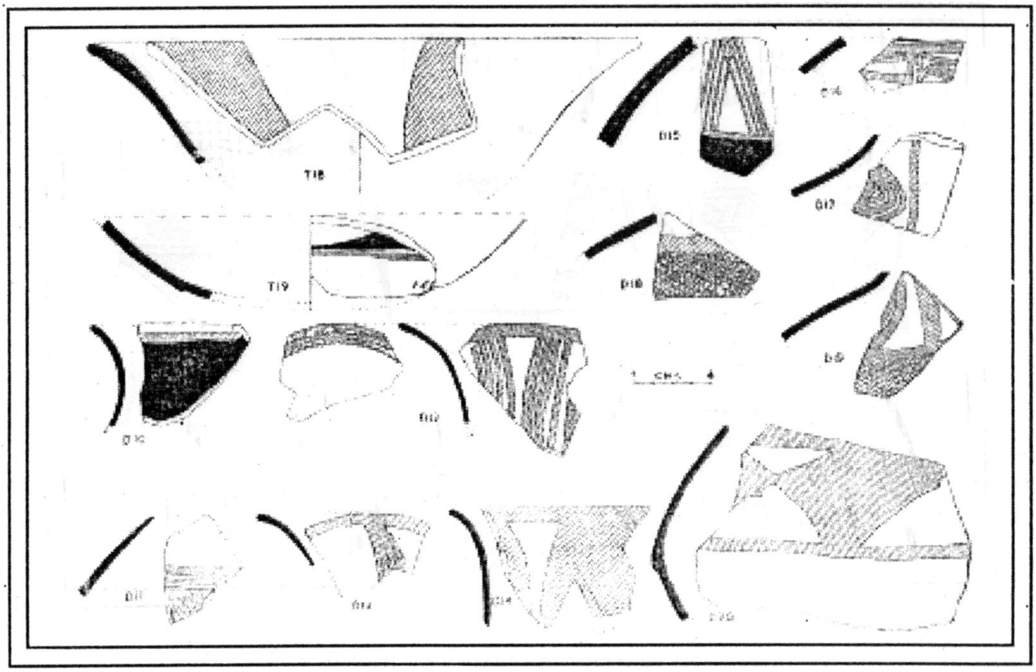

Source: H.D. Sankalia, 1974, *Prehistory and Protohistory of India and Pakistan.*

FIGURE 170: Red and Buff Ware, Basins, Bases and Designs, Period I, Kayatha

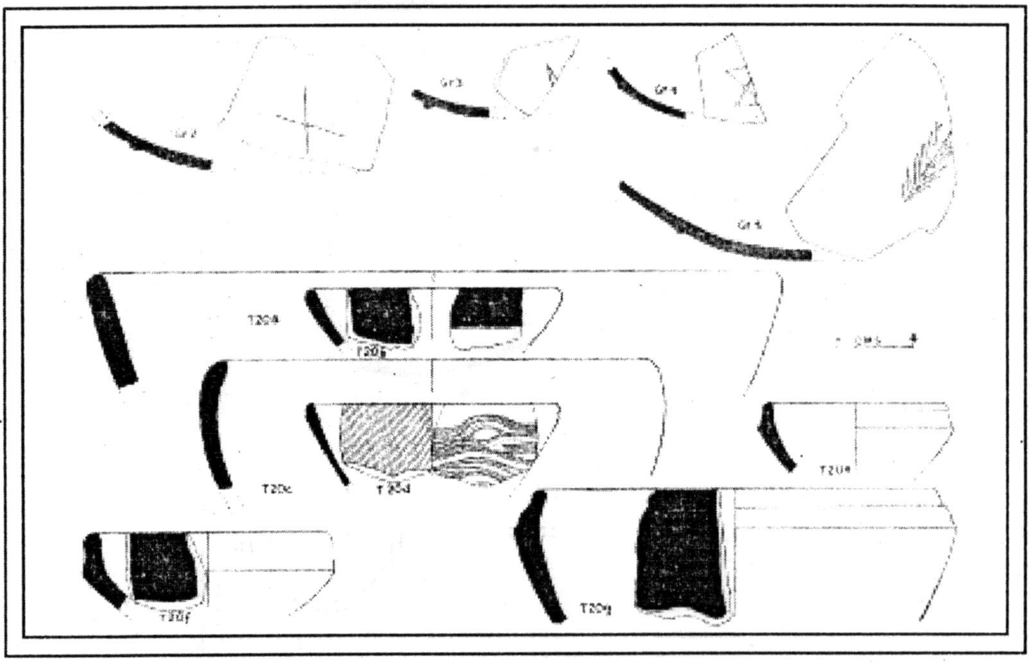

Source: H.D. Sankalia, 1974, *Prehistory and Protohistory of India and Pakistan.*

FIGURE 171: Graffiti and Combed Ware, Period I, Kayatha

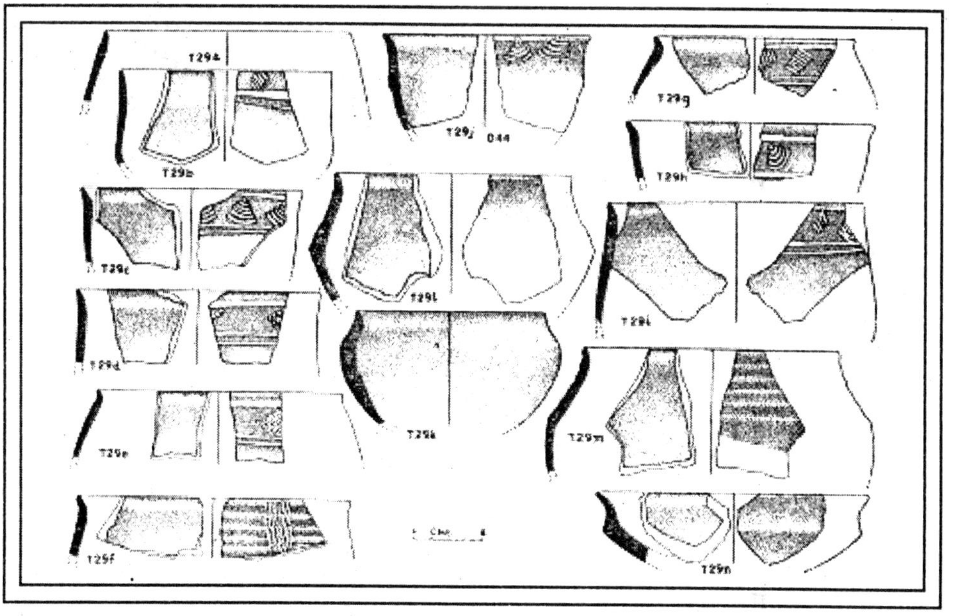

Source: H.D. Sankalia, 1974, *Prehistory and Protohistory of India and Pakistan.*

FIGURE 172: Bowls, Black and Red Pottery, Period II, Kayatha

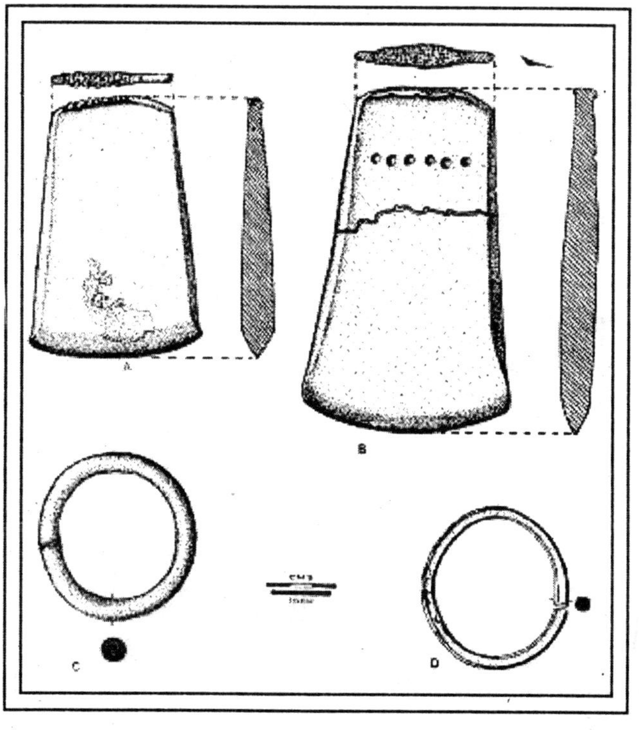

Source: H.D. Sankalia, 1974, *Prehistory and Protohistory of India and Pakistan.*

FIGURE 173: Copper Axes and Bangles, Period I, Kayatha

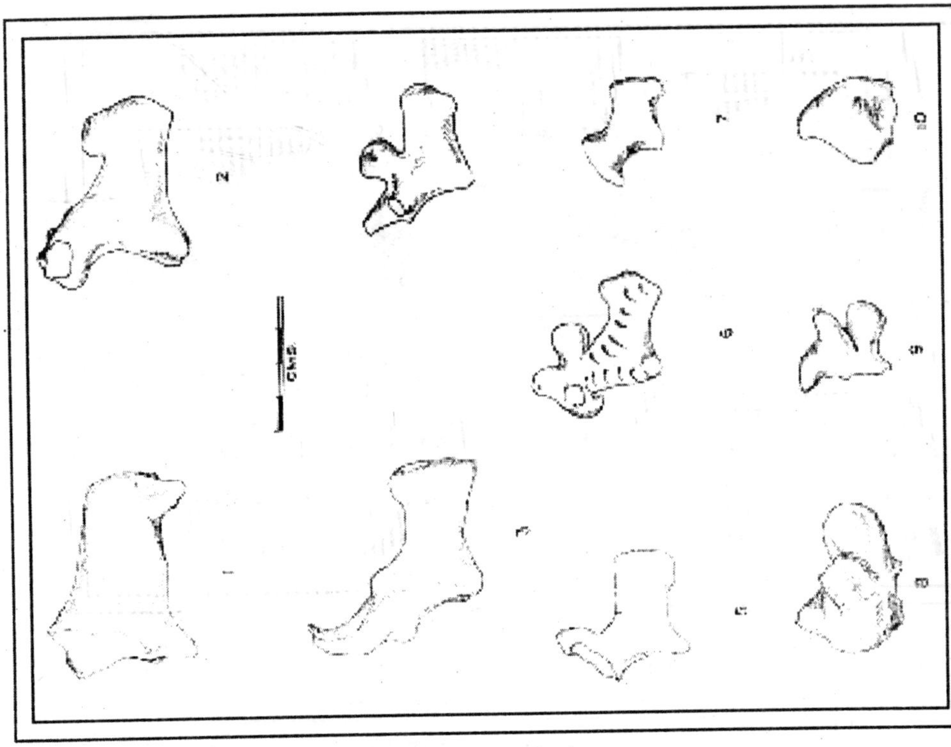

Source: H.D. Sankalia, 1974, *Prehistory and Protohistory of India and Pakistan.*

FIGURE 174: Stylized Terracotta, Bulls, Period II, Kayatha

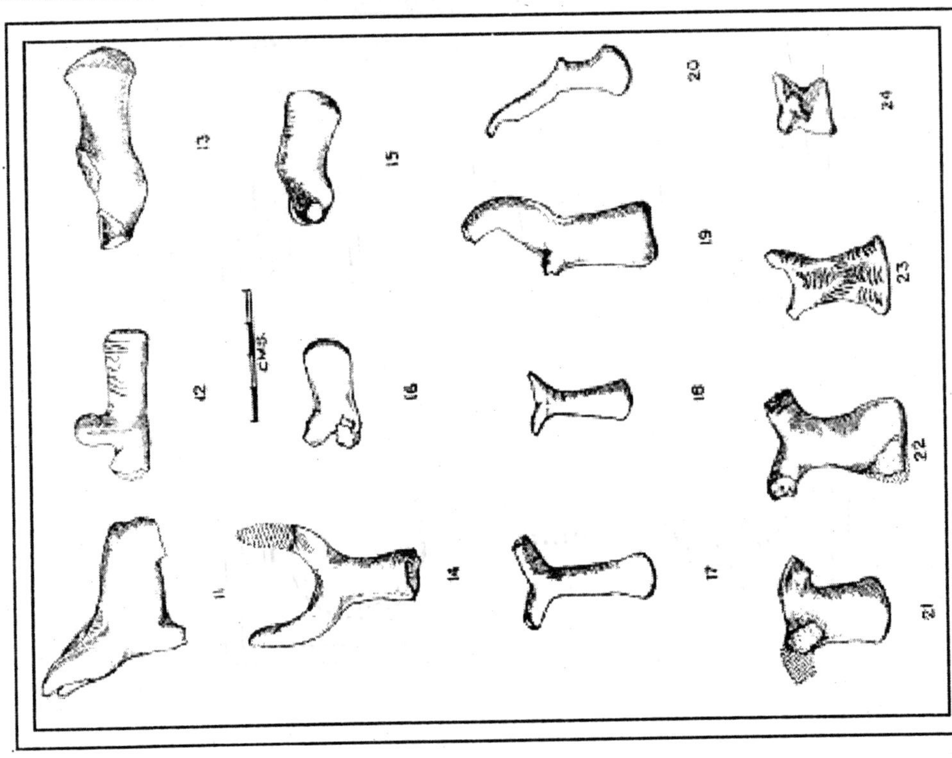

Source: H.D. Sankalia, 1974, *Prehistory and Protohistory of India and Pakistan.*

FIGURE 175: Stylized Terracotta, Bulls, Period II, Kayatha

Source: H.D. Sankalia, 1974, *Prehistory and Protohistory of India and Pakistan.*

FIGURE 176: General View of Maund IV, Navdatoli

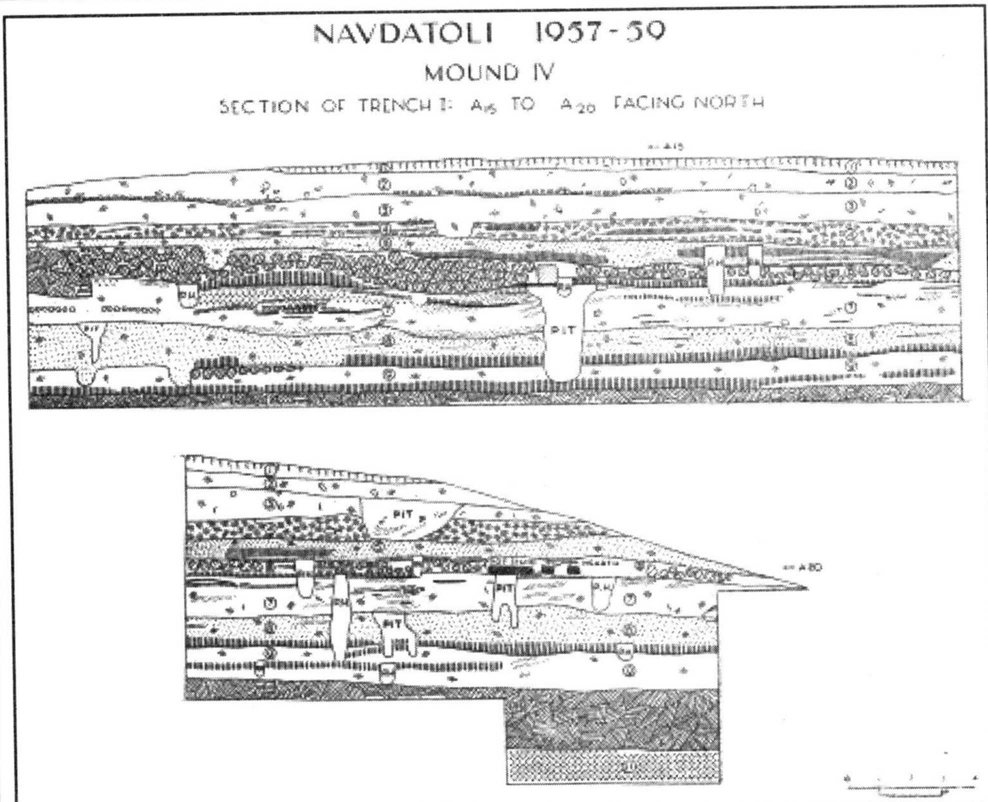

Source: H.D. Sankalia, 1974, *Prehistory and Protohistory of India and Pakistan.*

FIGURE 177: Section of Trench I: A-15 to A-20 Facing North, Navdatoli

Source: H.D. Sankalia, 1974, *Prehistory and Protohistory of India and Pakistan.*

FIGURE 178: General View of Mound IV with Pottery Yard in the Foreground, Navdatoli

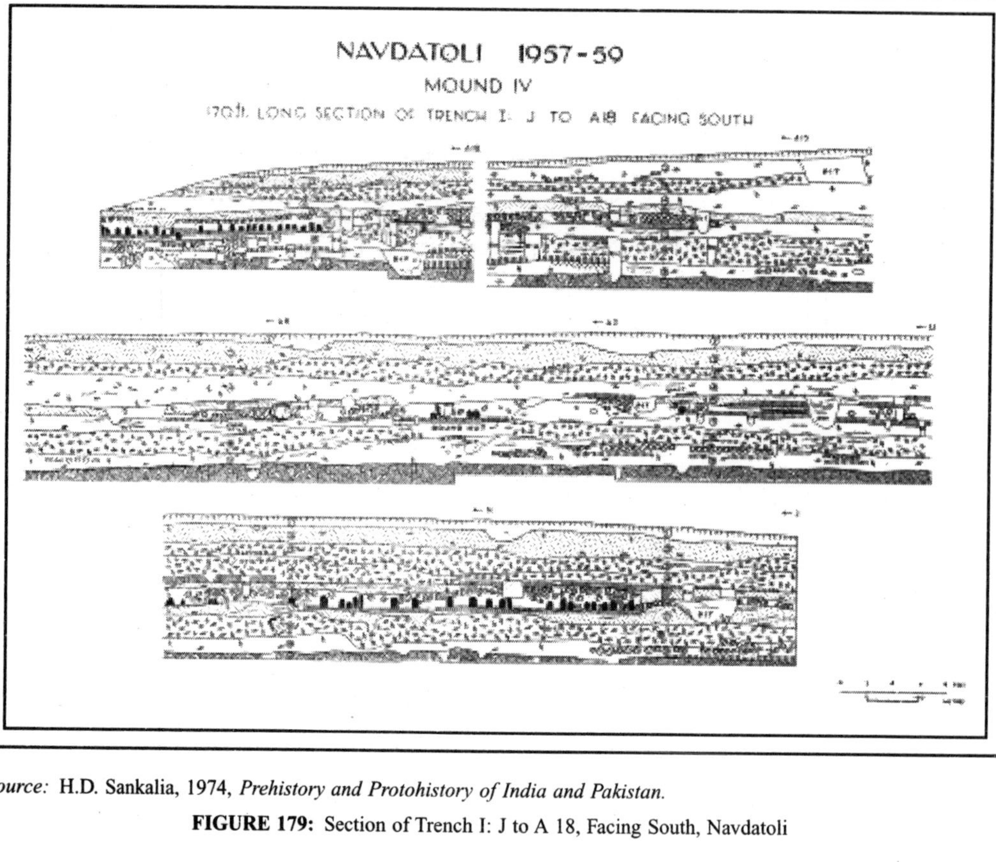

Source: H.D. Sankalia, 1974, *Prehistory and Protohistory of India and Pakistan.*

FIGURE 179: Section of Trench I: J to A 18, Facing South, Navdatoli

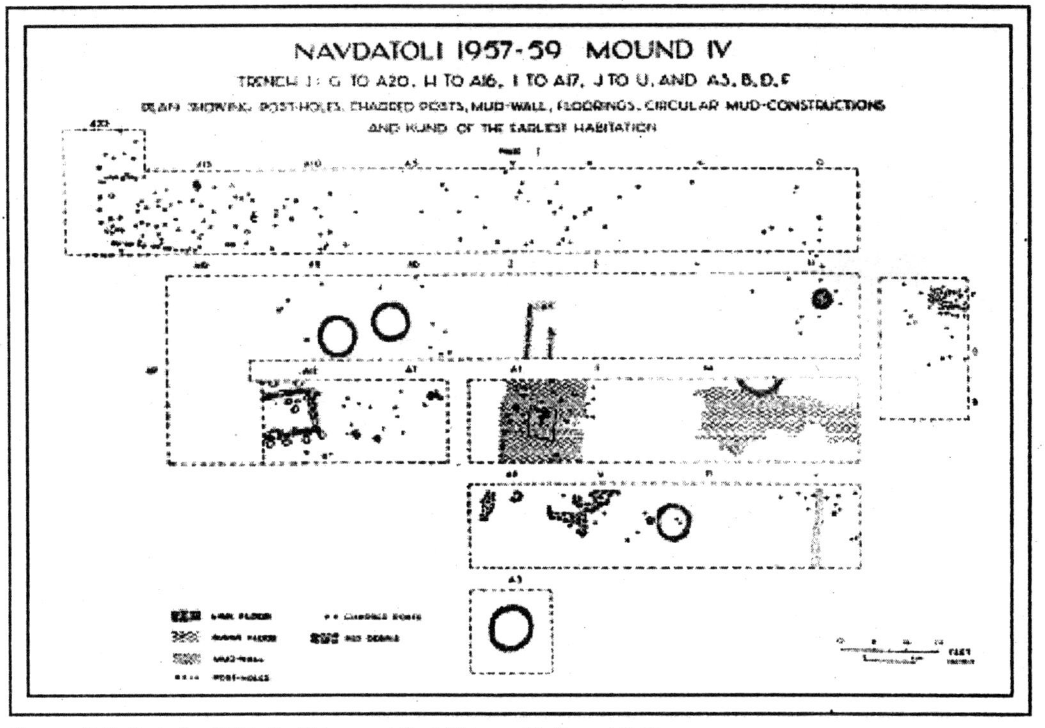

Source: H.D. Sankalia, 1974, *Prehistory and Protohistory of India and Pakistan.*

FIGURE 180: Plan Showing Post-Holes, Mud-Walls, etc., Phase-I, Navdatoli

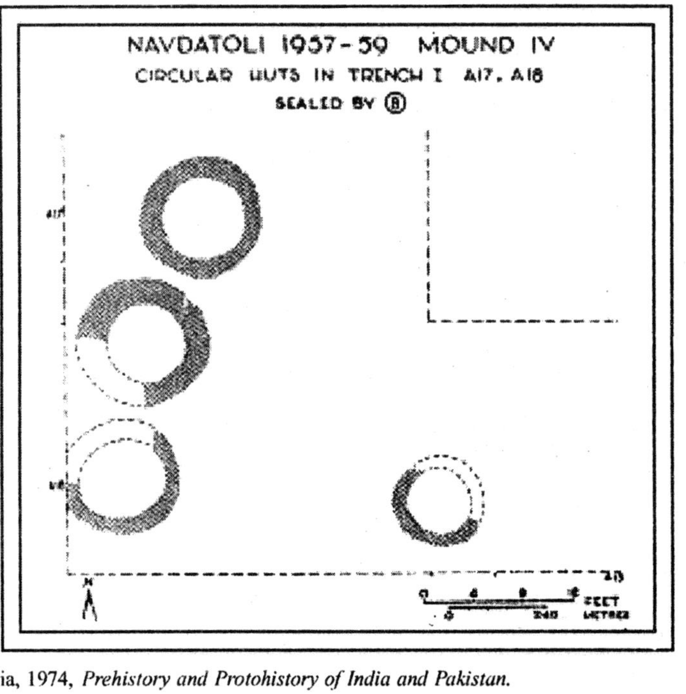

Source: H.D. Sankalia, 1974, *Prehistory and Protohistory of India and Pakistan.*

FIGURE 181: Plan of Circular Huts Trench I: A-17, A-18, Navdatoli

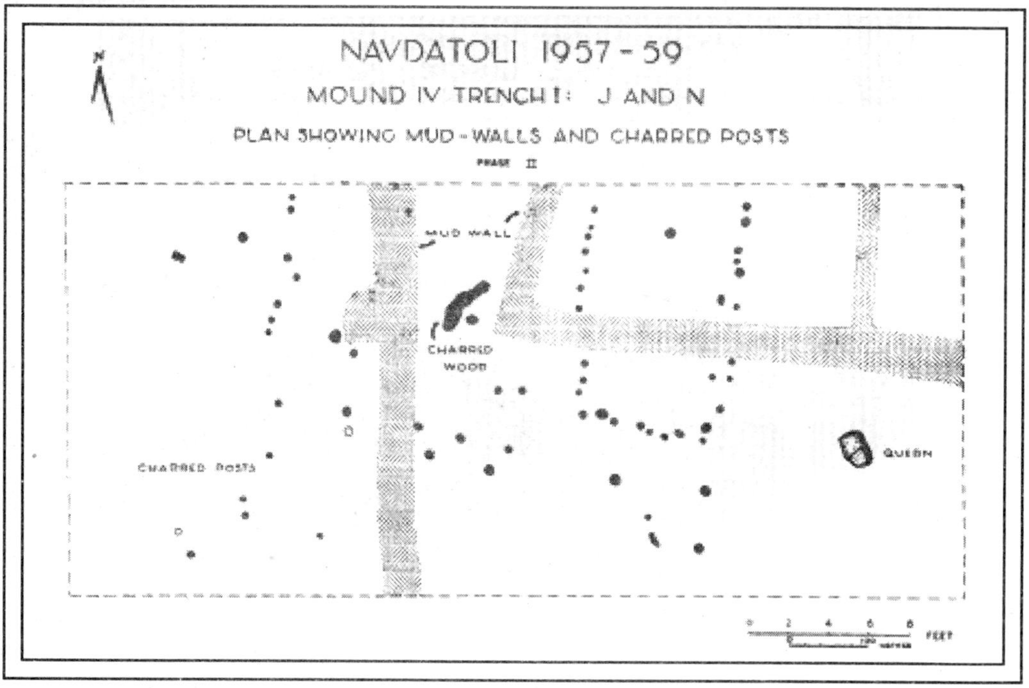

Source: H.D. Sankalia, 1974, *Prehistory and Protohistory of India and Pakistan.*

FIGURE 182: Plan Showing the Charred Pots of a Rectangular House, Trench I, Phase-II, Navdatoli

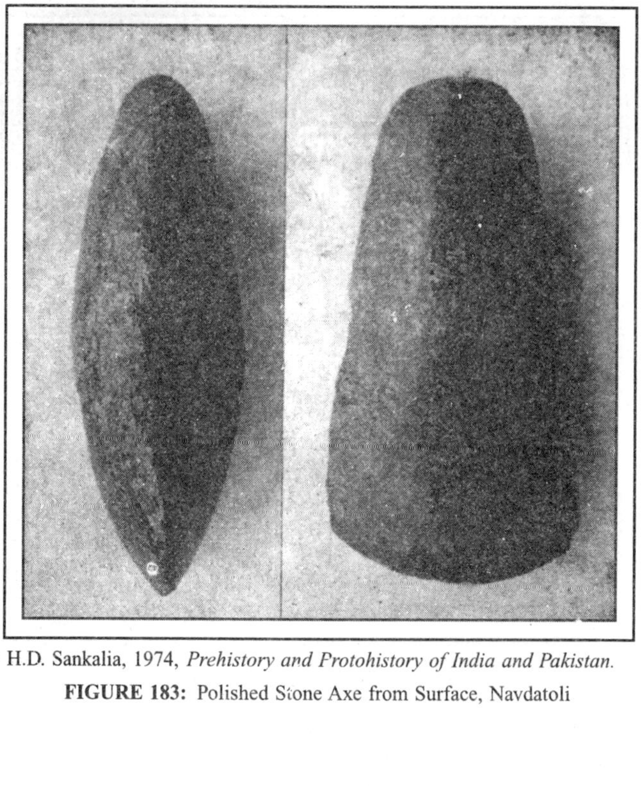

Source: H.D. Sankalia, 1974, *Prehistory and Protohistory of India and Pakistan.*

FIGURE 183: Polished Stone Axe from Surface, Navdatoli

Source: H.D. Sankalia, 1974, *Prehistory and Protohistory of India and Pakistan.*

FIGURE 184: A Piece of Mud-Wall with Lime Plaster and Impression in Mud of Split Bamboo Frame, Navdatoli

Source: H.D. Sankalia, 1974, *Prehistory and Protohistory of India and Pakistan.*

FIGURE 185: Remains of a House, Navdatoli

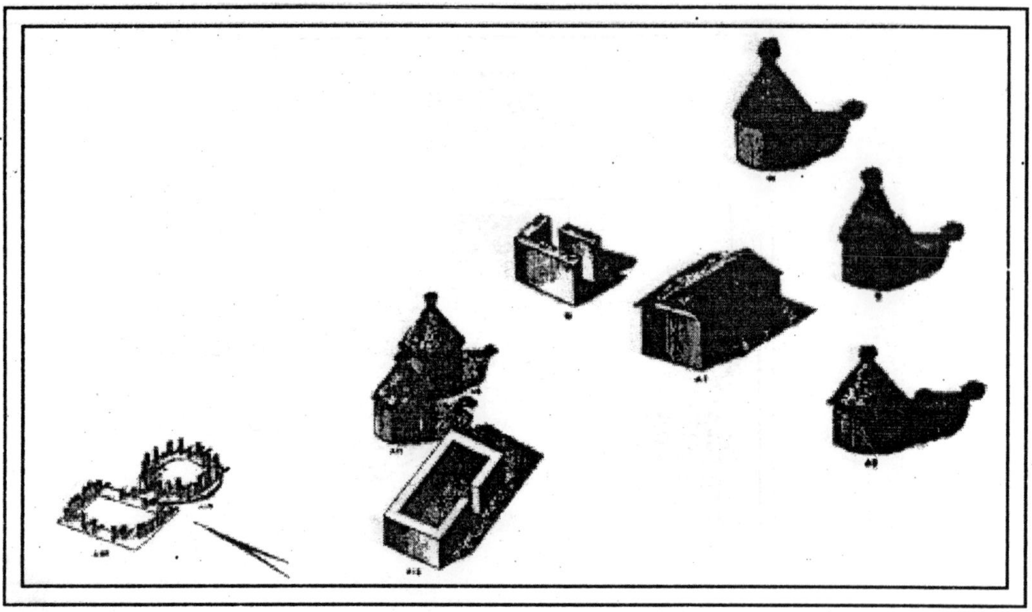

Source: H.D. Sankalia, 1974, *Prehistory and Protohistory of India and Pakistan.*

FIGURE 186: Isometric Reconstruction of some of the Houses, Navdatoli

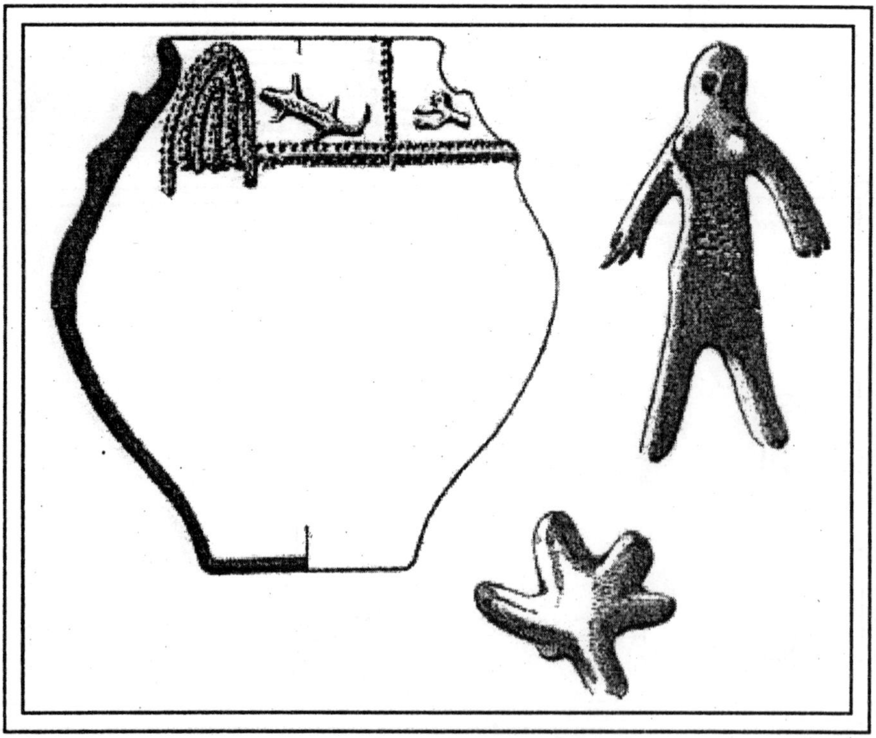

Source: H.D. Sankalia, 1974, *Prehistory and Protohistory of India and Pakistan.*

FIGURE 187: Applique Figures on Storage Jars, Phase-IV, Navdatoli

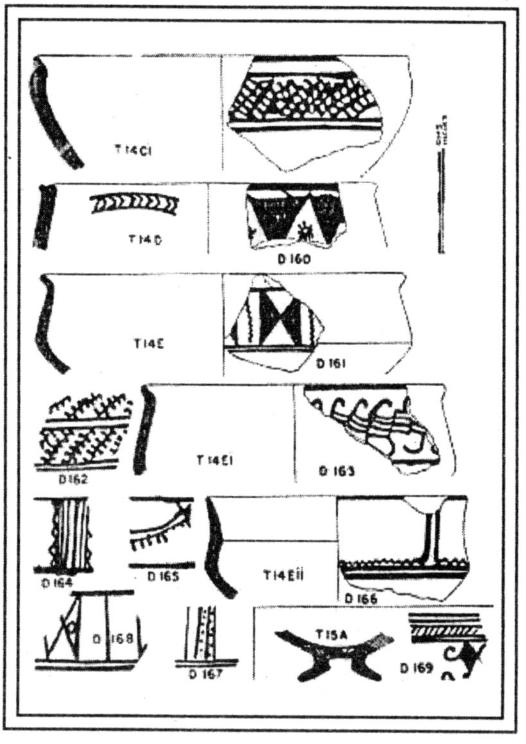

Source: H.D. Sankalia, 1974, *Prehistory and Protohistory of India and Pakistan.*

FIGURE 188: Bowls and Designs in Malwa Ware, Phase-I, Navdatoli

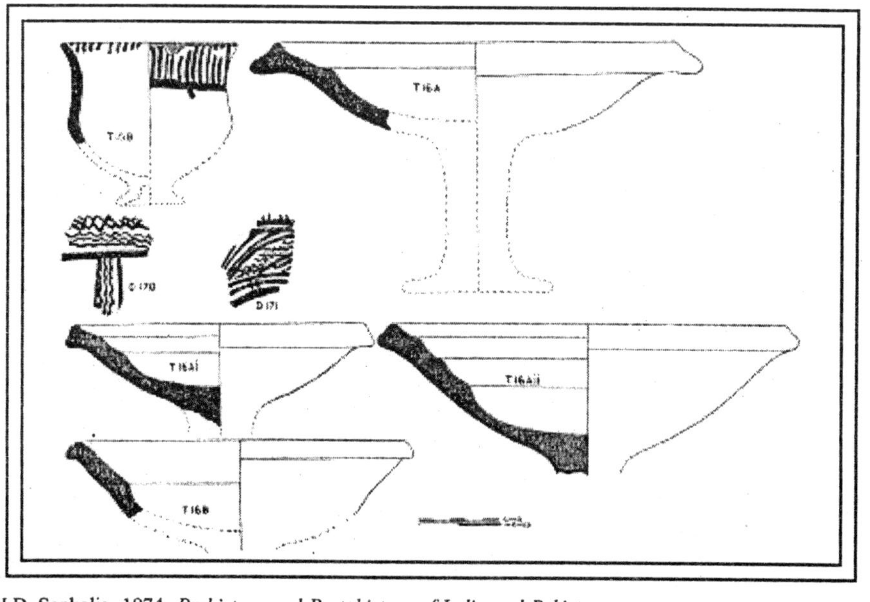

Source: H.D. Sankalia, 1974, *Prehistory and Protohistory of India and Pakistan.*

FIGURE 189: Goblets and Dishes-on-Stand, Phase-I, Navdatoli

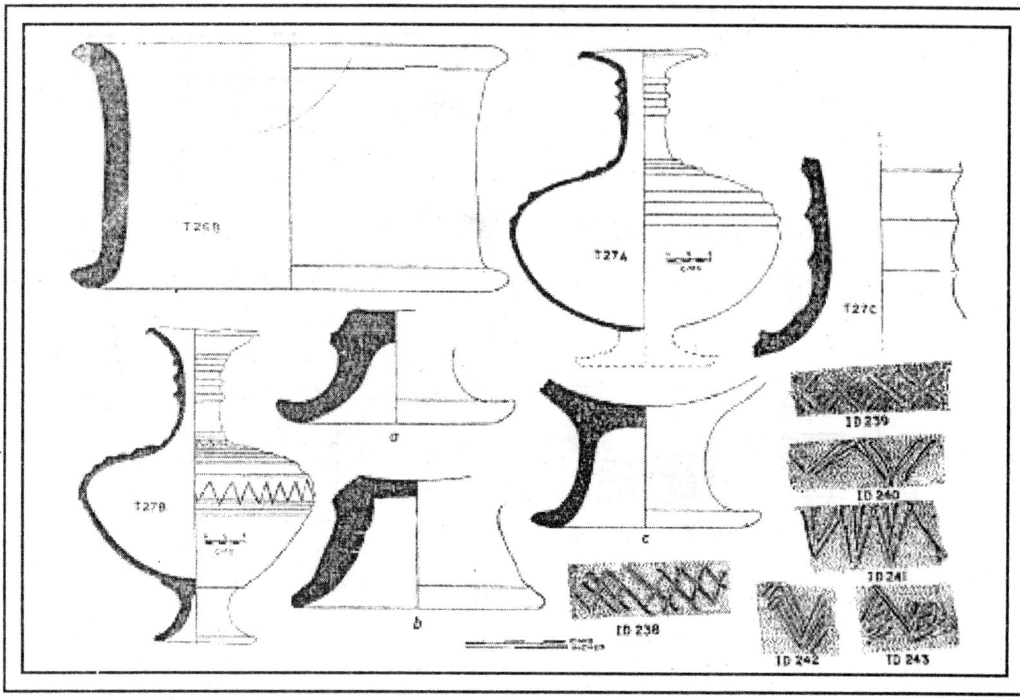

Source: H.D. Sankalia, 1974, *Prehistory and Protohistory of India and Pakistan.*

FIGURE 190: Ridged *Kujas* and Potrest, Navdatoli

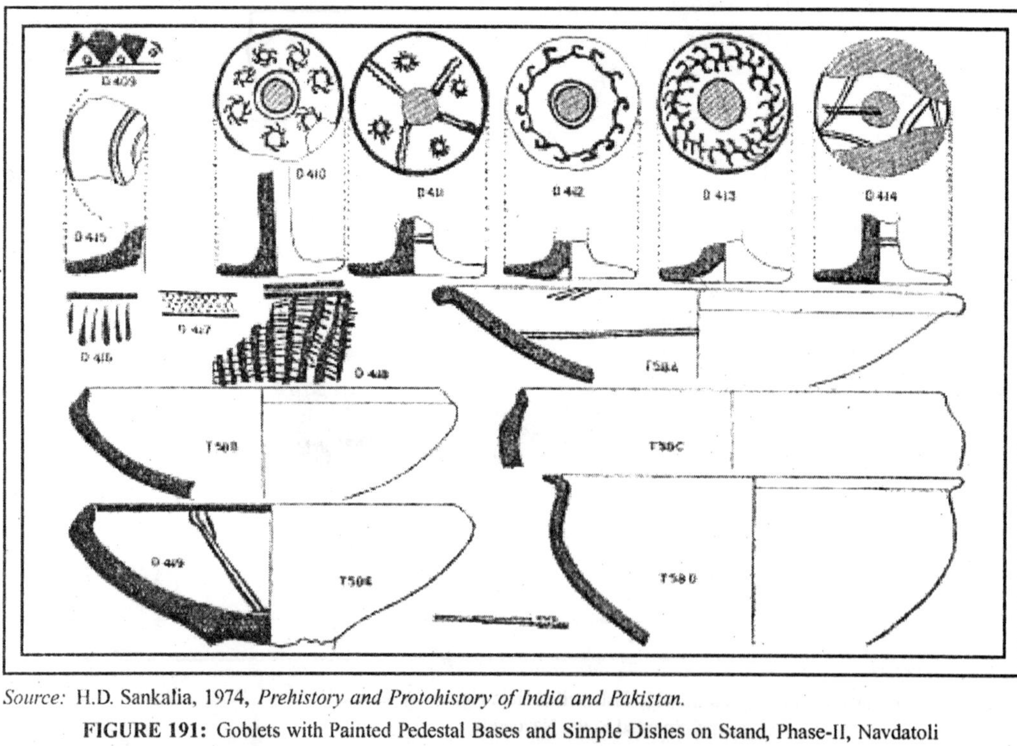

Source: H.D. Sankalia, 1974, *Prehistory and Protohistory of India and Pakistan.*

FIGURE 191: Goblets with Painted Pedestal Bases and Simple Dishes on Stand, Phase-II, Navdatoli

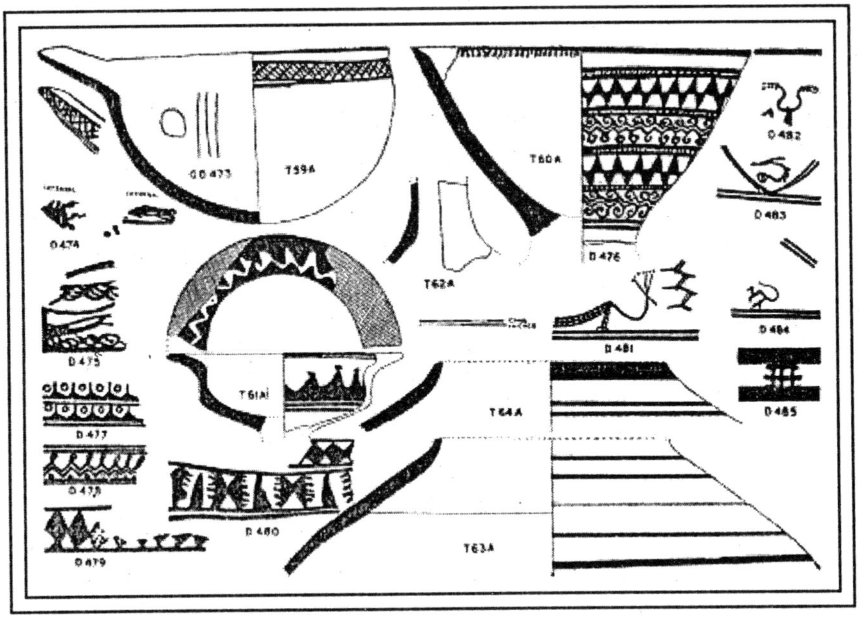

Source: H.D. Sankalia, 1974, *Prehistory and Protohistory of India and Pakistan.*

FIGURE 192: Some Rare Shapes in Malwa Ware, Channel-Spouted Bowl, Conoid, Fully Painted Bowl, Dish-on-Stand with Painting, Phase-II, Navdatoli

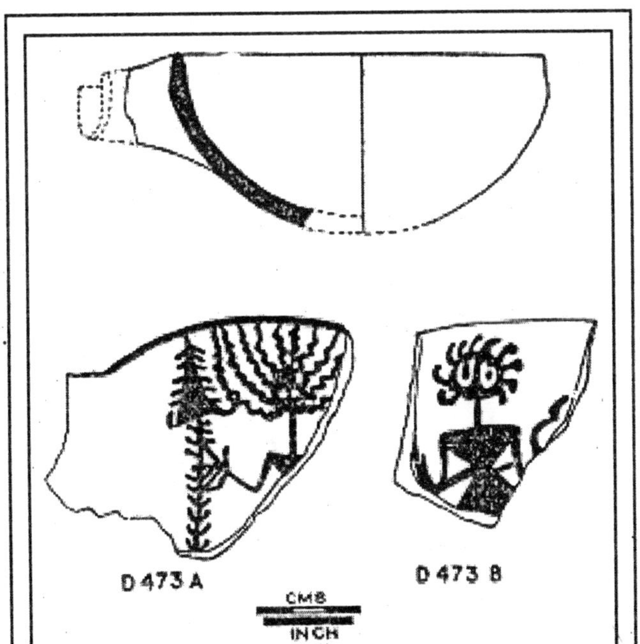

Source: H.D. Sankalia, 1974, *Prehistory and Protohistory of India and Pakistan.*

FIGURE 193: Painting of a Man with Dishevelled Hair, Narrow Waist and Holding a Pointed Object in his Right Hand inside a Channel-Spouted Bowl, Navdatoli.

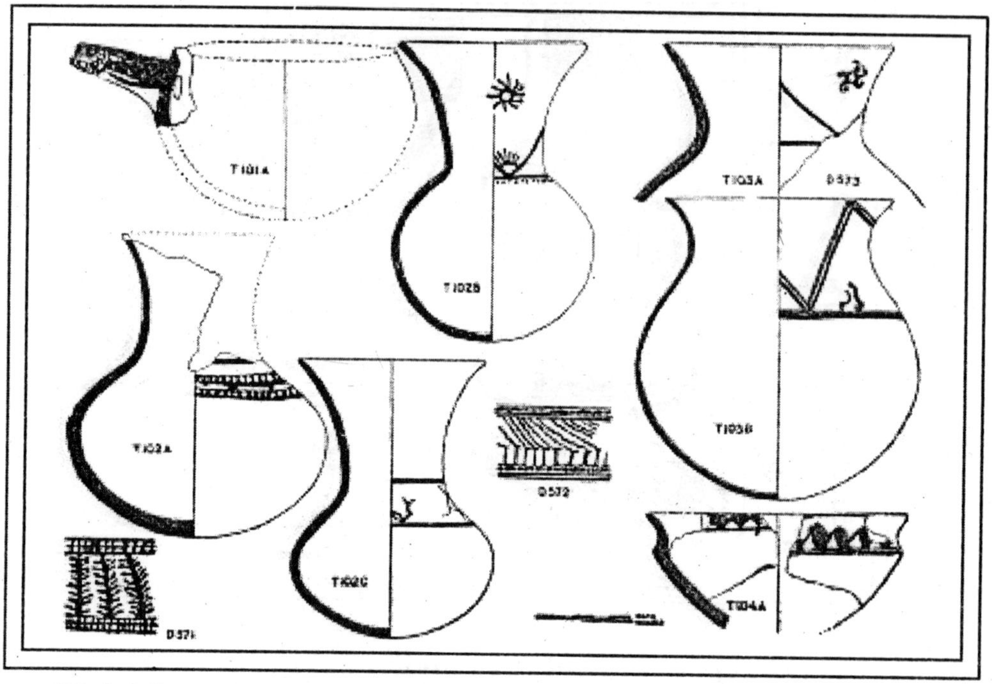

Source: H.D. Sankalia, 1974, *Prehistory and Protohistory of India and Pakistan.*

FIGURE 194: *Lota* (small water vessel), Malwa Ware, Phase-III, Navdatoli

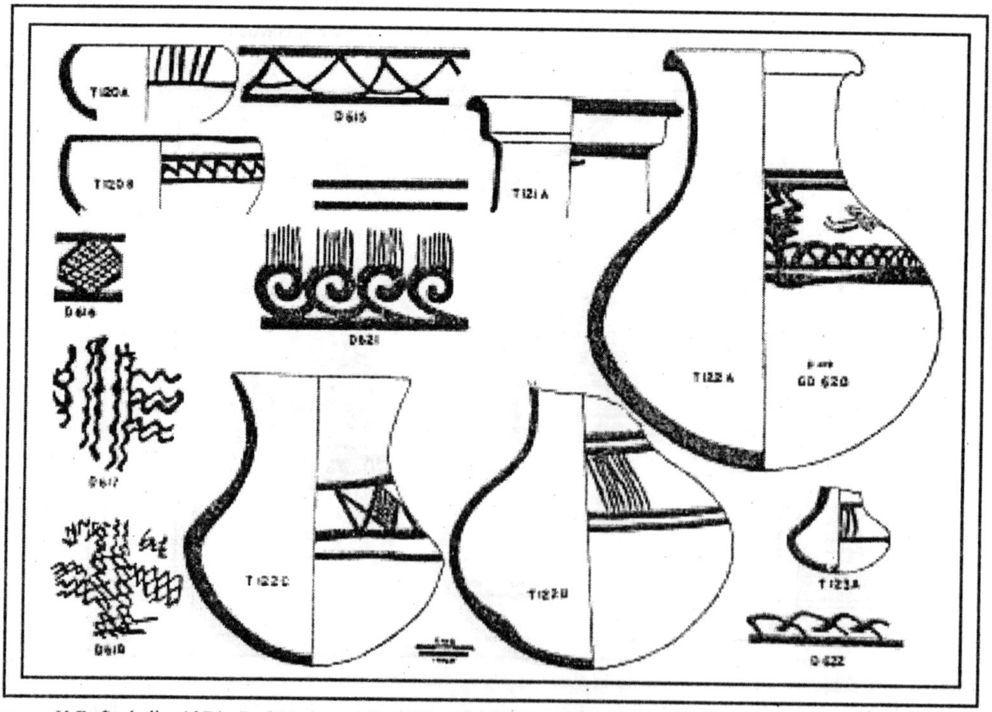

Source: H.D. Sankalia, 1974, *Prehistory and Protohistory of India and Pakistan.*

FIGURE 195: Shapes and Designs, Jorwe Ware, Navdatoli

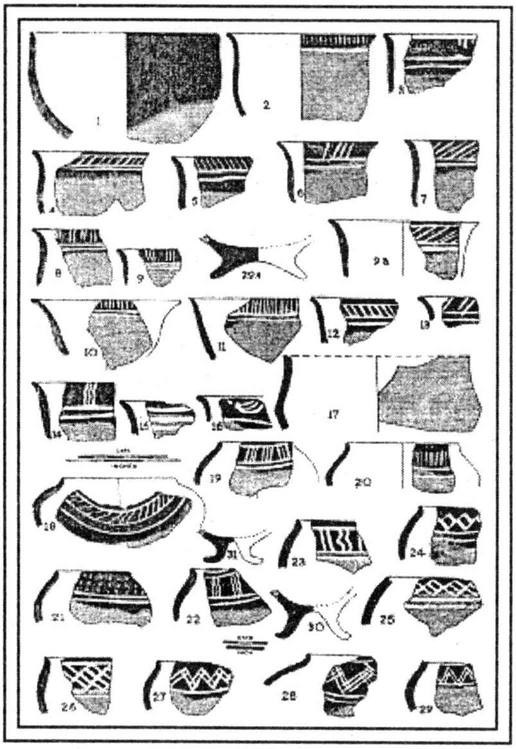

Source: H.D. Sankalia, 1974, *Prehistory and Protohistory of India and Pakistan.*

FIGURE 196: White Painted, Black and Red Ware, Phase-I, Navdatoli

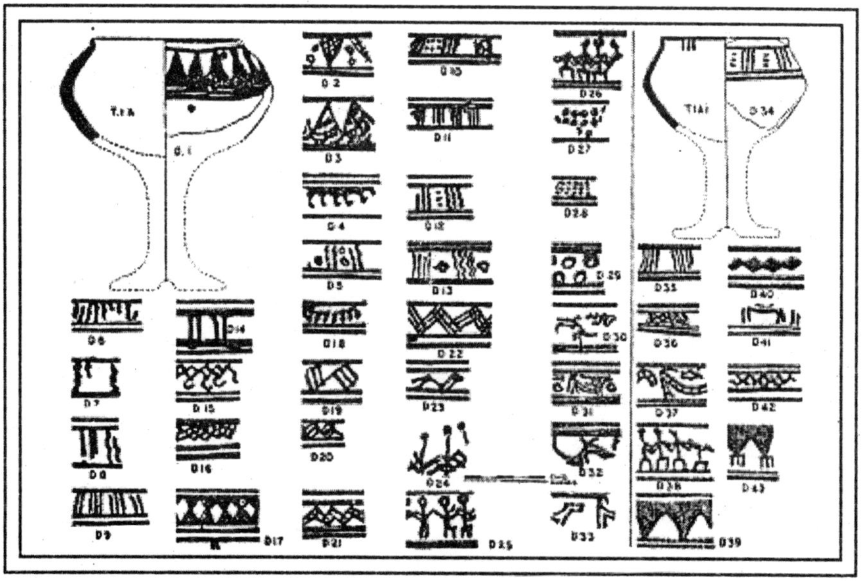

Source: H.D. Saṇkalia, 1974, *Prehistory and Protohistory of India and Pakistan.*

FIGURE 197: Goblets and Designs in Cream-Slipped Ware, Navdatoli

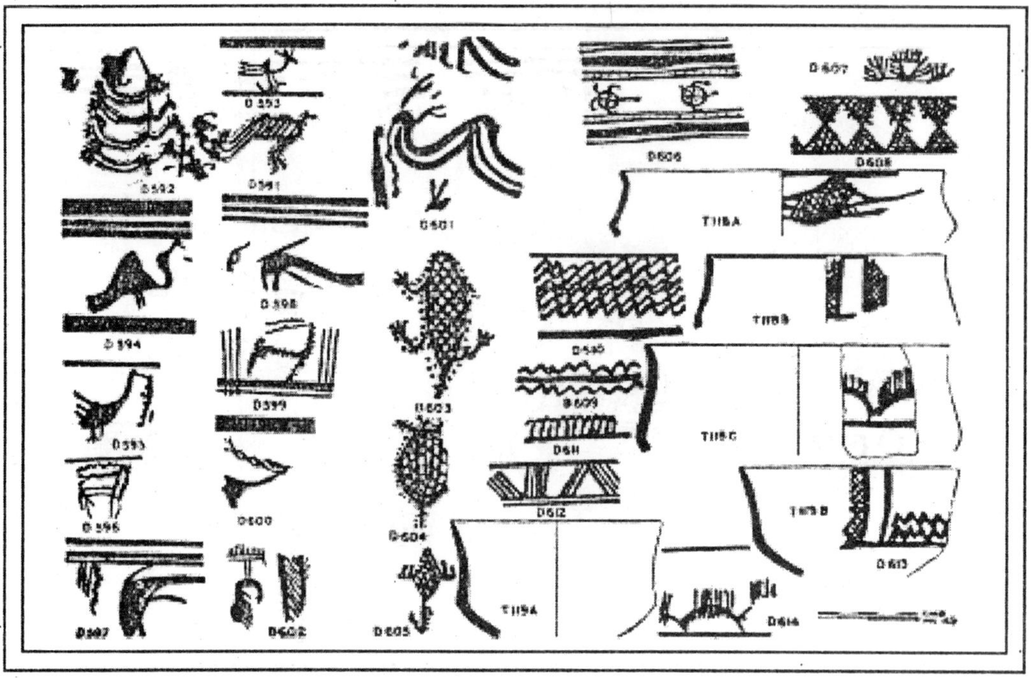

Source: H.D. Sankalia, 1974, *Prehistory and Protohistory of India and Pakistan.*

FIGURE 198: Designs, Malwa Ware, Navdatoli

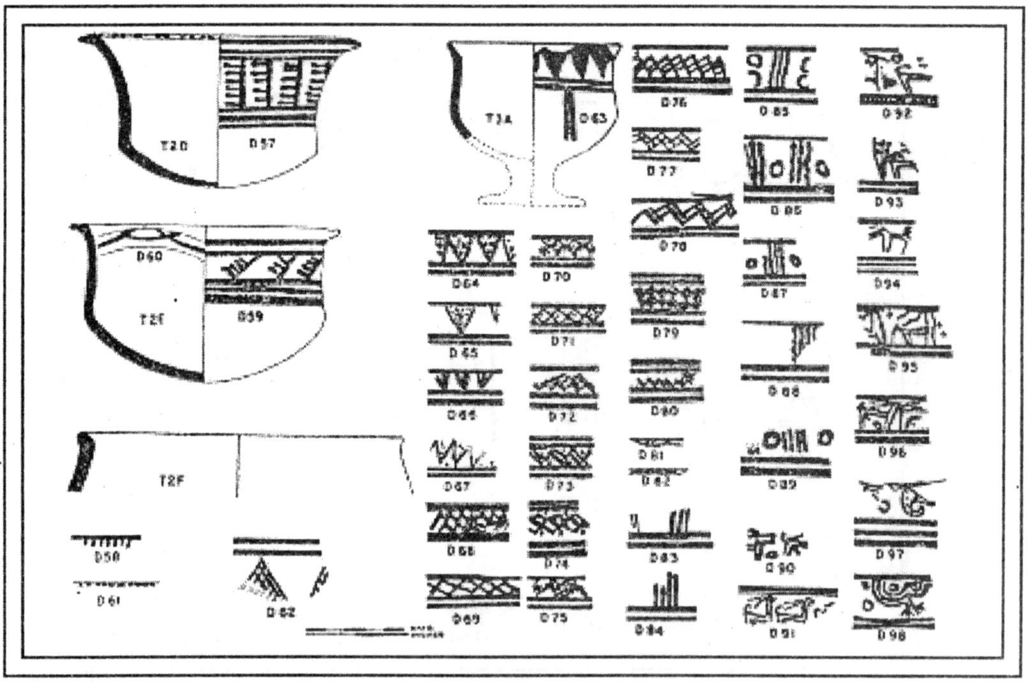

Source: H.D. Sankalia, 1974, *Prehistory and Protohistory of India and Pakistan.*

FIGURE 199: Bowls and Designs in Cream Slipped Ware, Navdatoli

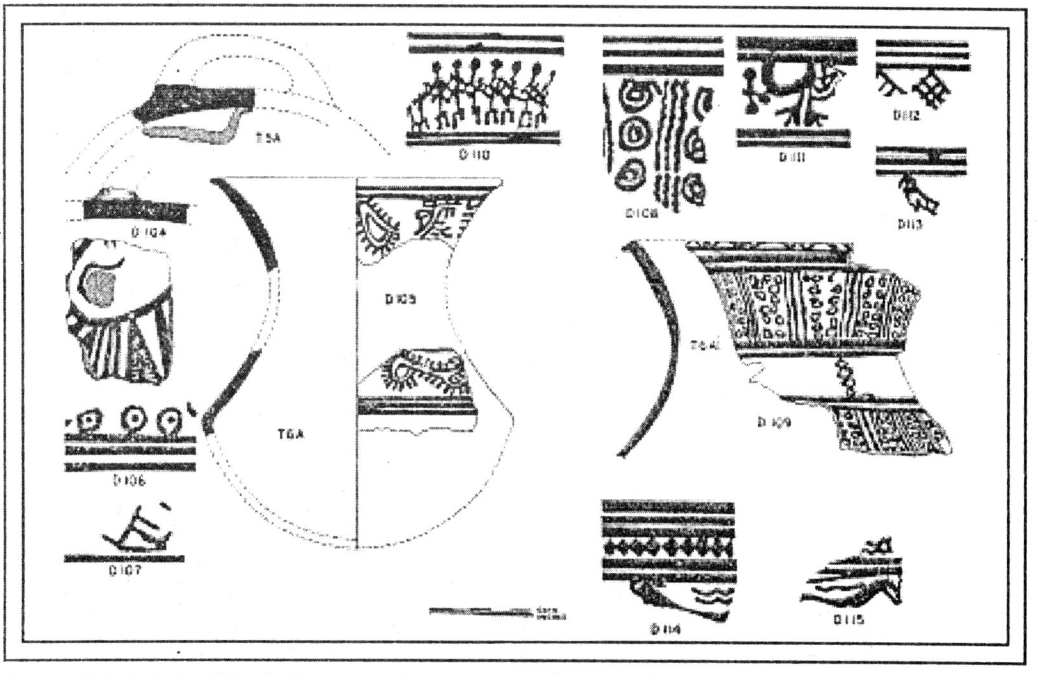

Source: H.D. Sankalia, 1974, *Prehistory and Protohistory of India and Pakistan.*

FIGURE 200: *Lota* and Vessel Types and Designs in Cream-Slipped Ware, Navdatoli

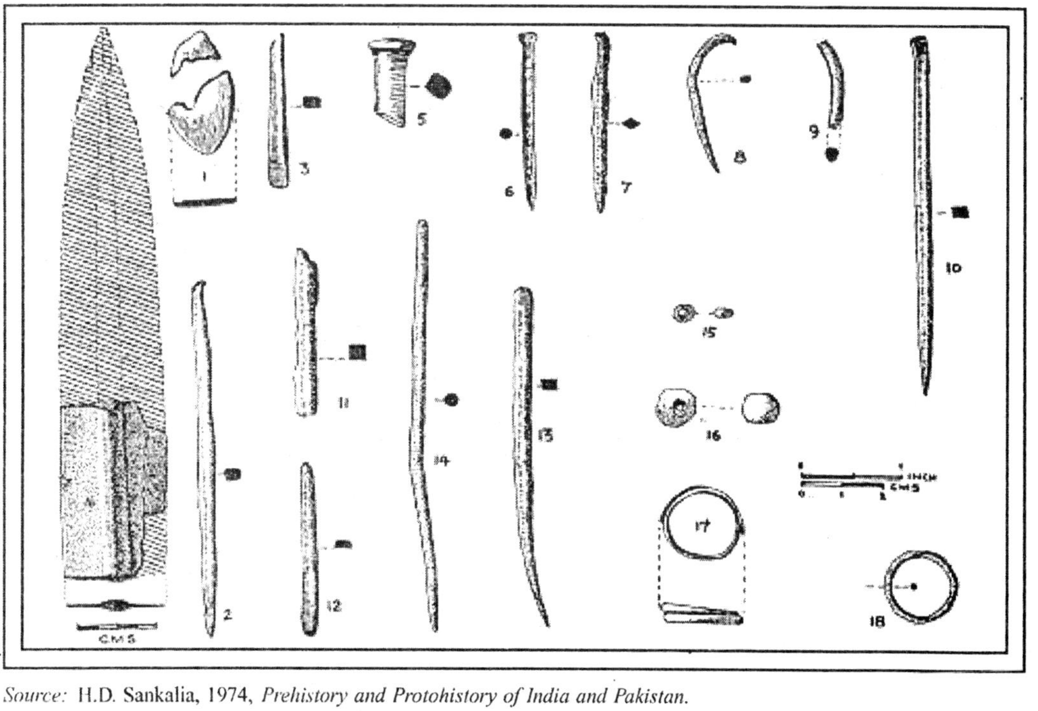

Source: H.D. Sankalia, 1974, *Prehistory and Protohistory of India and Pakistan.*

FIGURE 201: Copper Objects: Arrow Head 1, Chisels 2-3, Swordor Dagger Fragment 4, Nails 5-7, Fish-hooks 8-9, Point-*cum*-Engraver 10-13, Poker 14, Beads 15-16 and Rings 17-18, Navdatoli

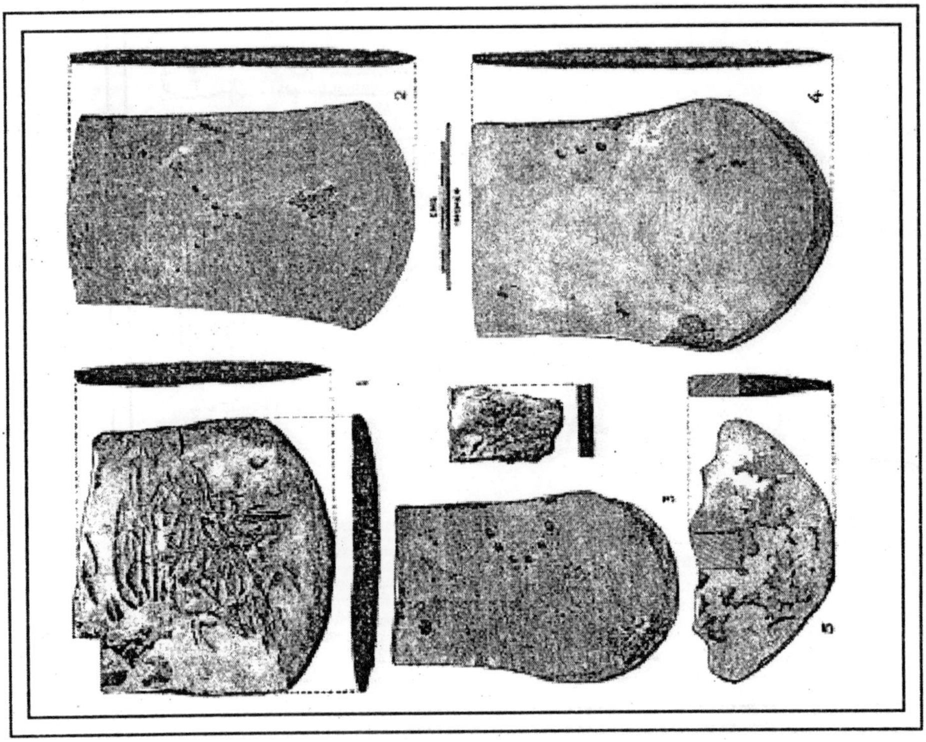

Source: H.D. Sankalia, 1974, *Prehistory and Protohistory of India and Pakistan.*

FIGURE 202: Copper Axes, Navdatoli

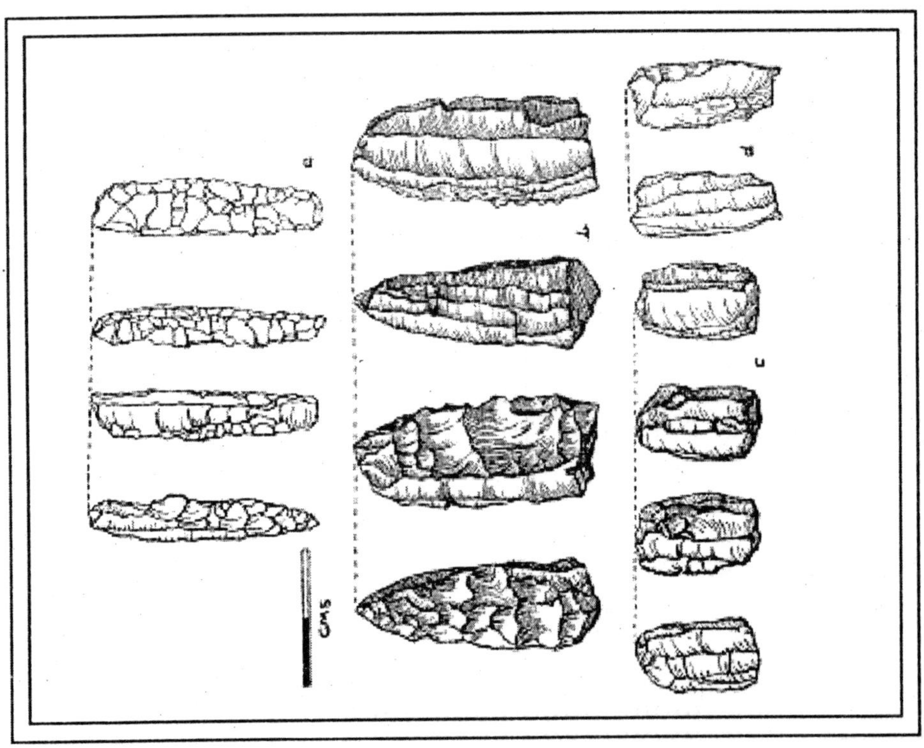

Source: H.D. Sankalia, 1974, *Prehistory and Protohistory of India and Pakistan.*

FIGURE 203: a. Flake with Crested Ridge; b. Conical Core; c-d. Trauncated Cores, Navdatoli

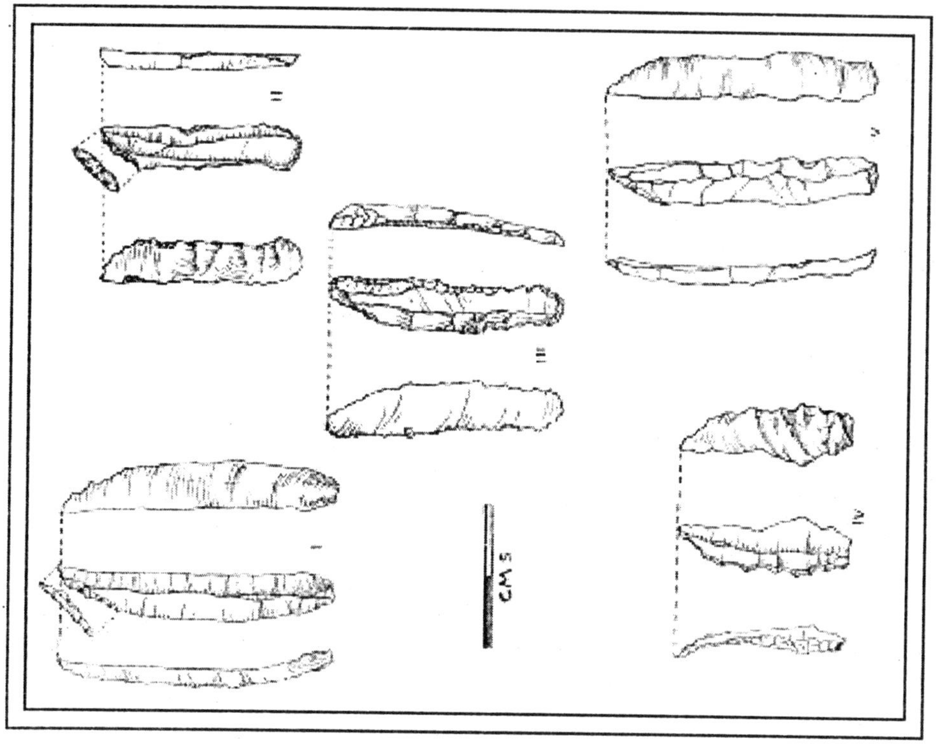

Source: H.D. Sankalia, 1974, *Prehistory and Protohistory of India and Pakistan.*

FIGURE 204: Penknife Blades, Navdatoli

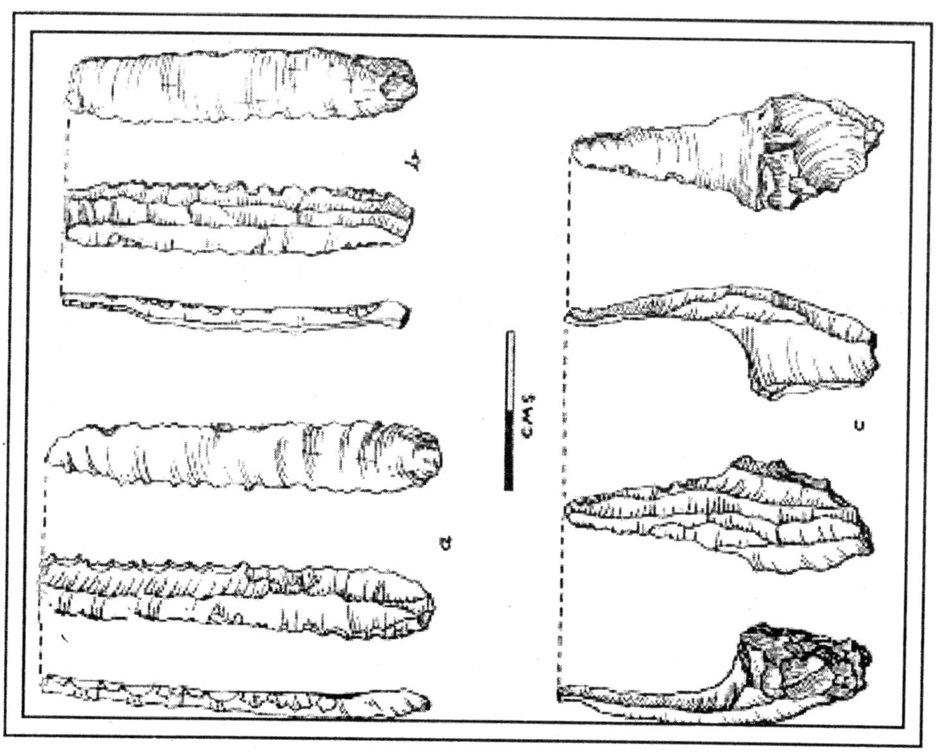

Source: H.D. Sankalia, 1974, *Prehistory and Protohistory of India and Pakistan.*

FIGURE 205: a and b. Serrated Blades, c. Plunging or Rejuvenating Flakes, Navdatoli

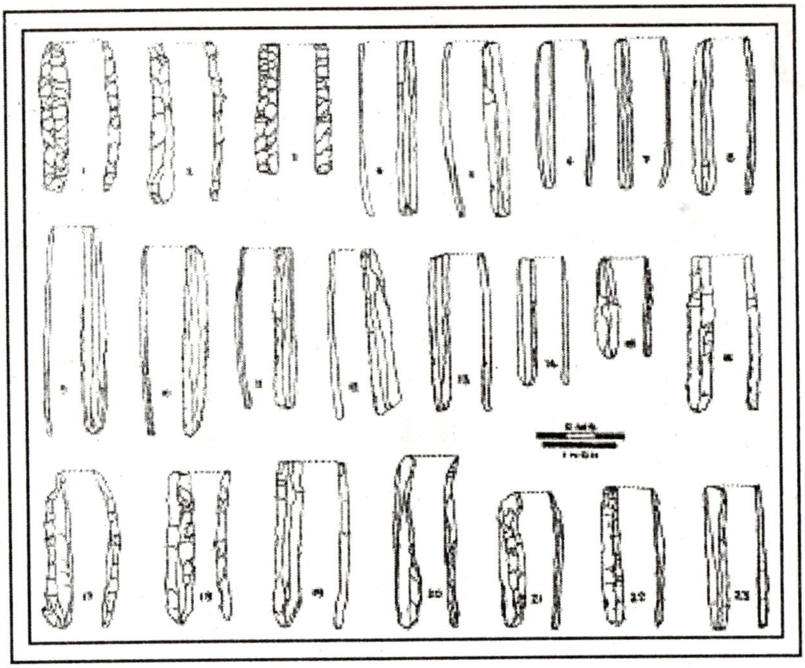

Source: H.D. Sankalia, 1974, *Prehistory and Protohistory of India and Pakistan.*

FIGURE 206: Crested Ridge Flakes (1-3); Parallel Sided Blades (4-23), Navdatoli

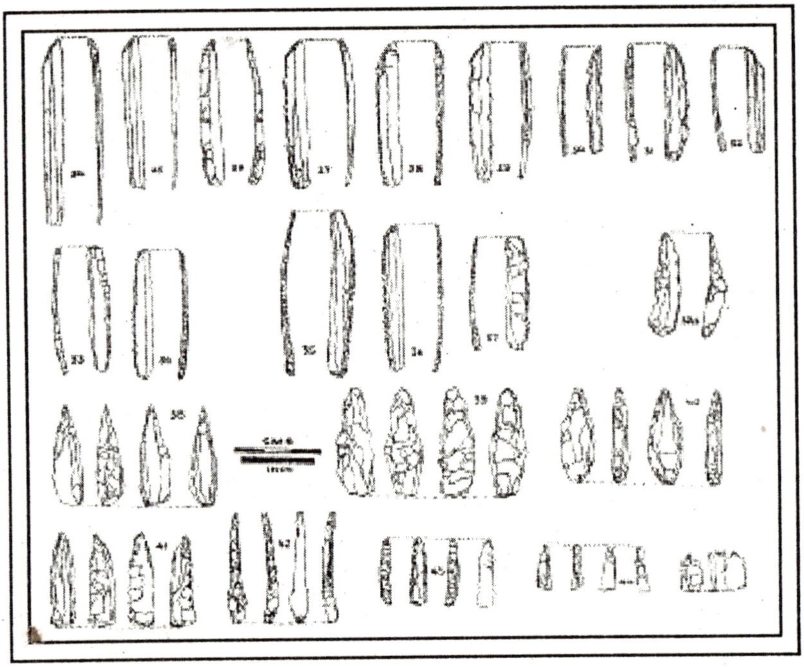

Source: H.D. Sankalia, 1974, *Prehistory and Protohistory of India and Pakistan.*

FIGURE 207: Penknife Blades (24-31); Blunted Back Blades (33-34); Saw (35-37); Asymmetrical Point (37a); Point (38); Borers (39-45), Navdatoli

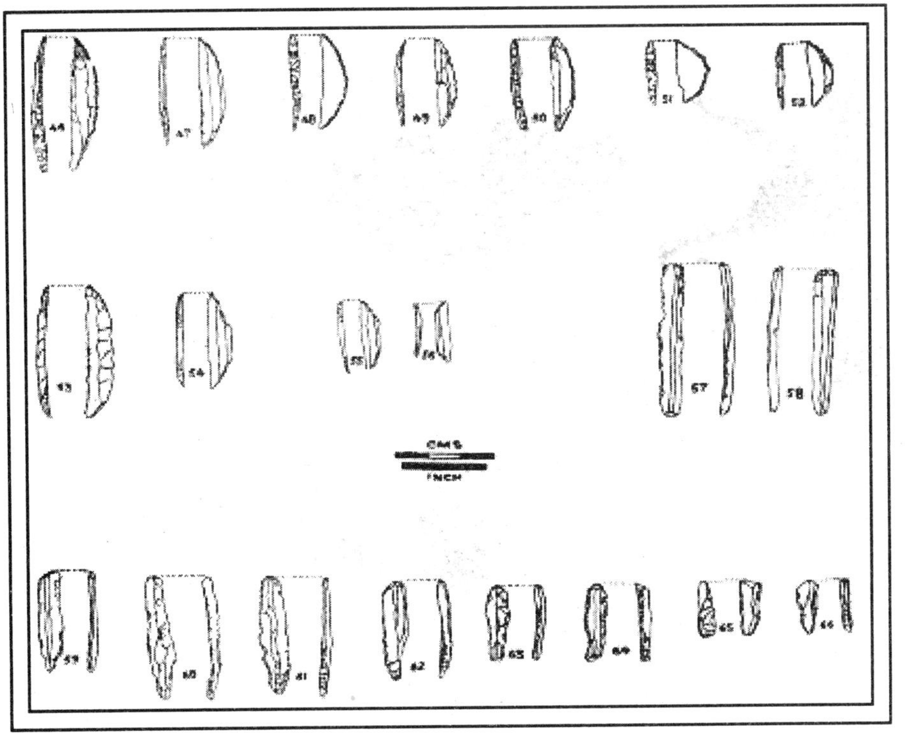

Source: H.D. Sankalia, 1974, *Prehistory and Protohistory of India and Pakistan.*

FIGURE 208: Lunates (46-53); Trapezes (54-56); Scrapers on Blade (57-58); Tanged or Notched Flakes (59-66), Navdatoli

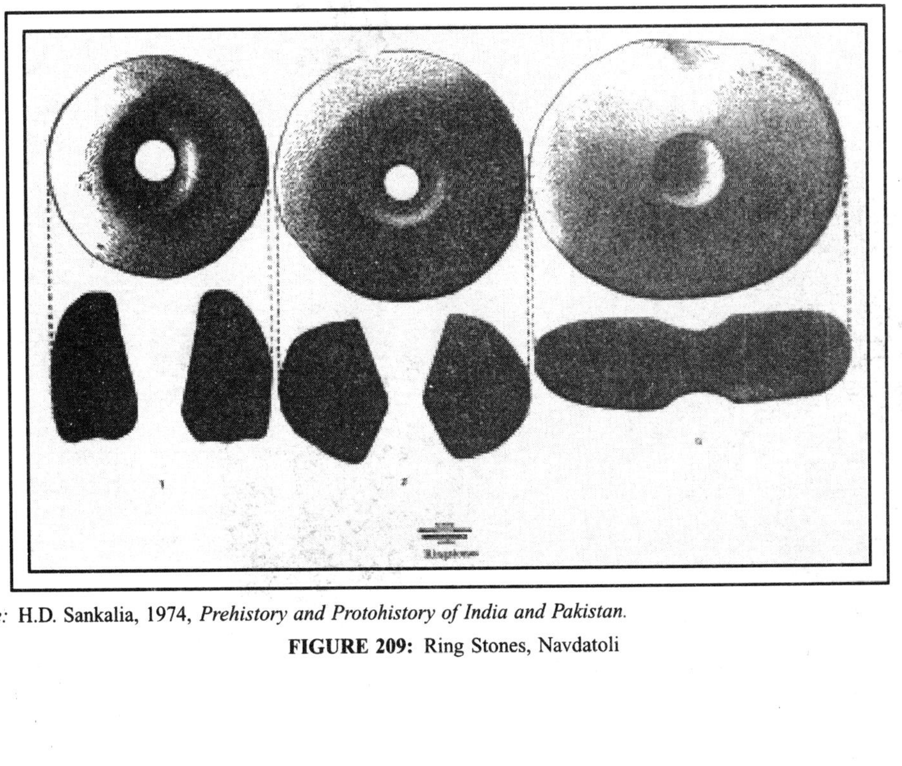

Source: H.D. Sankalia, 1974, *Prehistory and Protohistory of India and Pakistan.*

FIGURE 209: Ring Stones, Navdatoli

Source: H.D. Sankalia, 1974, *Prehistory and Protohistory of India and Pakistan.*

FIGURE 210: Sherds of Malwa Ware Animal Designs, Navdatoli

Source: H.D. Sankalia, 1974, *Prehistory and Protohistory of India and Pakistan.*

FIGURE 211: The Mounds with the Ghod River in Foreground, Inamgaon

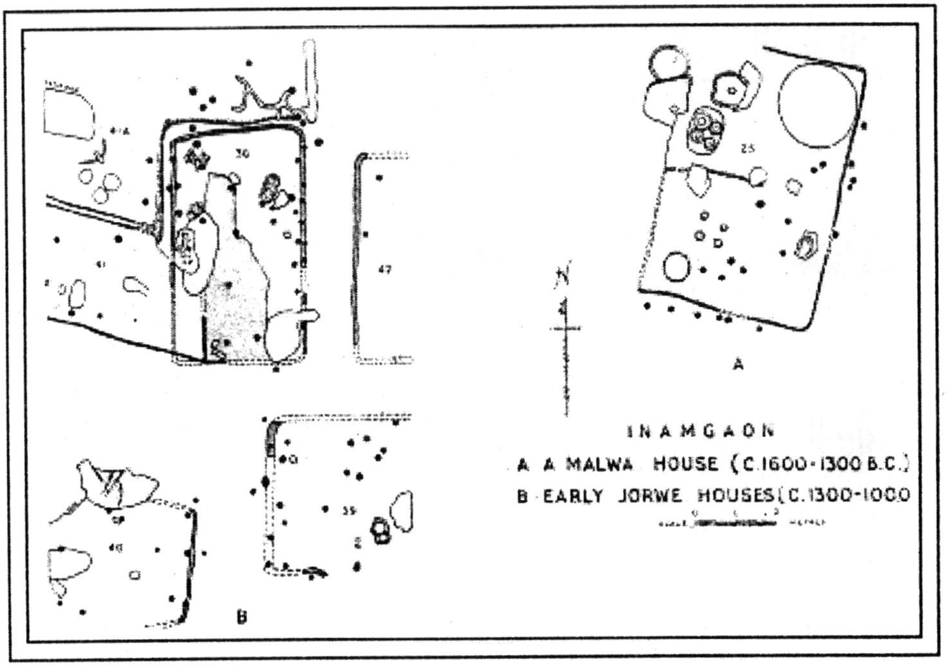

Source: H.D. Sankalia, 1974, *Prehistory and Protohistory of India and Pakistan.*

FIGURE 212: Malwa and Early Jorwe Houses, Inamgaon

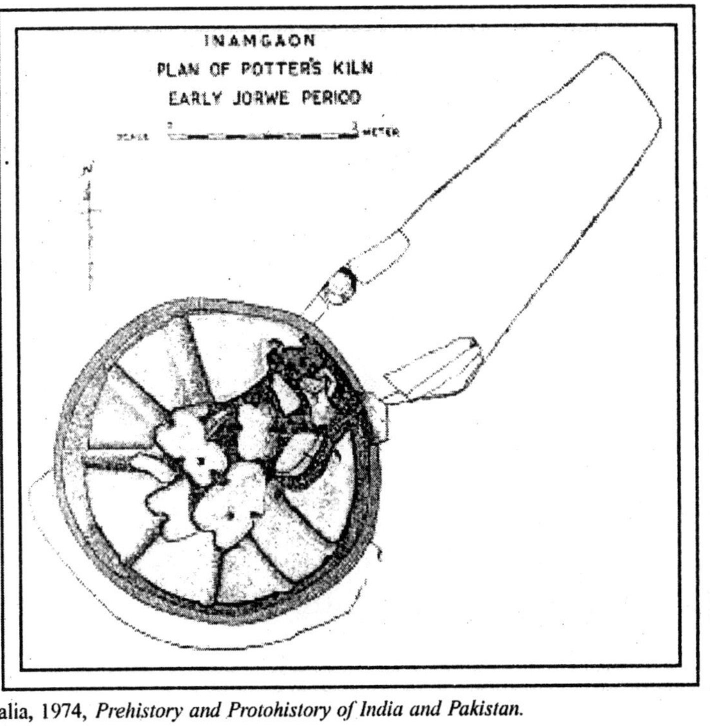

Source: H.D. Sankalia, 1974, *Prehistory and Protohistory of India and Pakistan.*

FIGURE 213: Potter's Kiln, Early Jorwe Period, Inamgaon

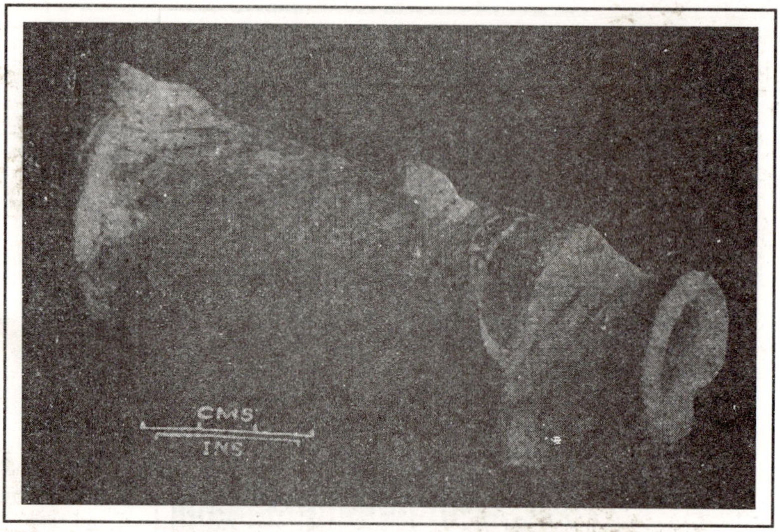

Source: H.D. Sankalia, 1974, *Prehistory and Protohistory of India and Pakistan.*

FIGURE 214: Anthropomorphic Bull in Jorwe Fabric

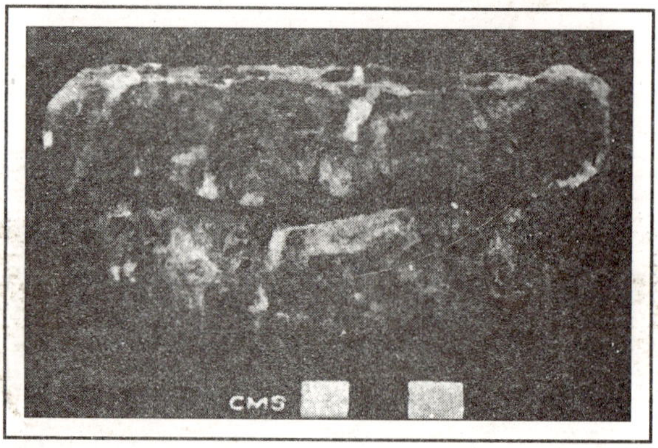

Source: H.D. Sankalia, 1974, *Prehistory and Protohistory of India and Pakistan.*

FIGURE 215: Clay Box with a Female Figurine within, Inamgaon

Source: H.D. Sankalia, 1974, *Prehistory and Protohistory of India and Pakistan.*

FIGURE 216: A Rectangular Wooden Box with Closely Fitting lid from Shrin VI-A, Catal Huyuk, Turkey

Source: H.D. Sankalia, 1974, *Prehistory and Protohistory of India and Pakistan.*

FIGURE 217: Headless Clay Female Figurine shown Standing on Back of a Bull, Inamgaon

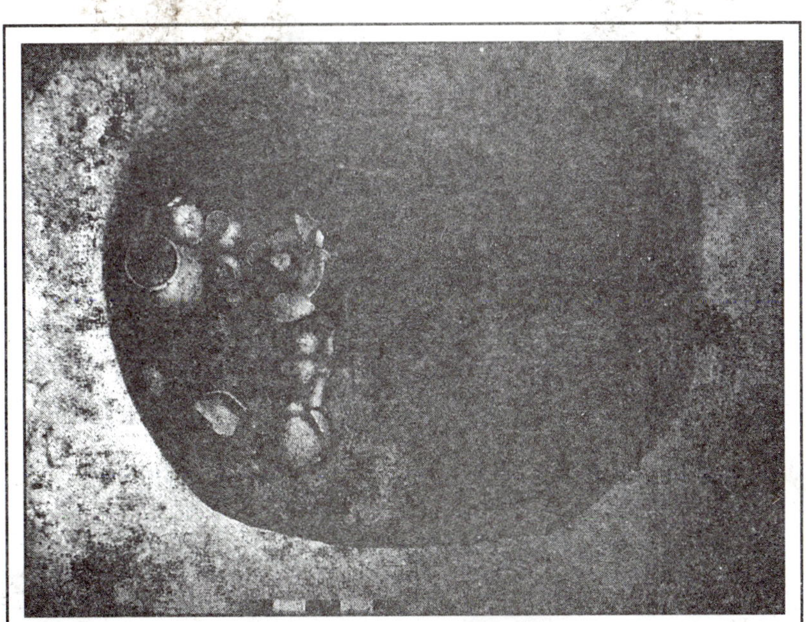

Source: H.D. Sankalia, 1974, *Prehistory and Protohistory of India and Pakistan.*

FIGURE 218: Burials, Inamgaon

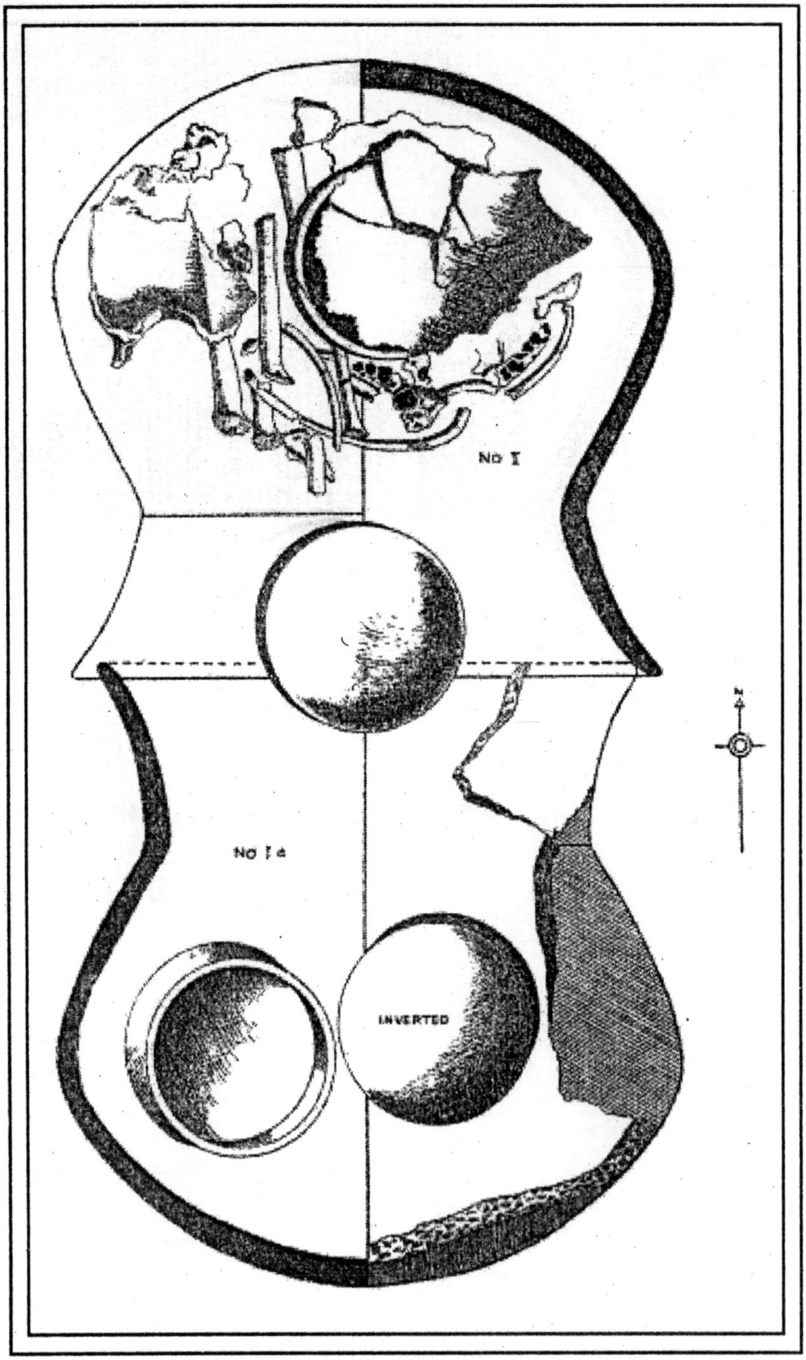

Source: H.D. Sankaḷia, 1974, *Prehistory and Protohistory of India and Pakistan.*

FIGURE 219: Burial No. 1, Tr. A. after Opening, Nevasa (1954-55)

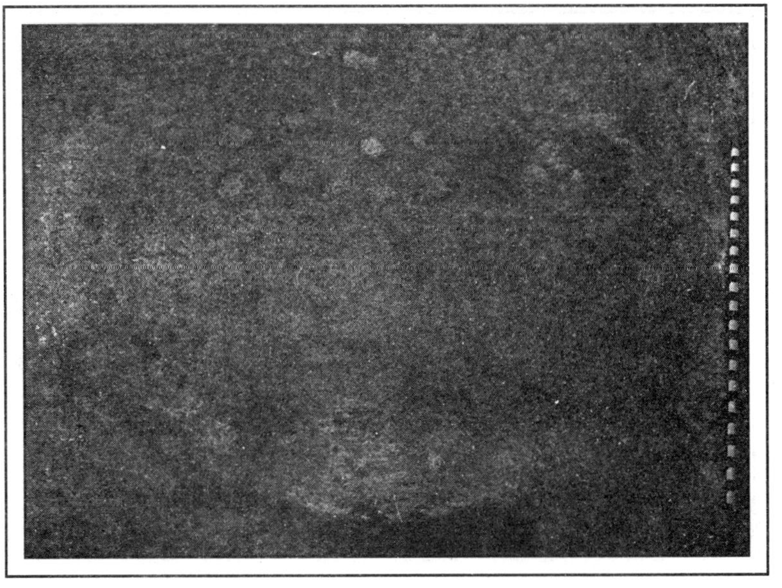

Source: H.D. Sankalia, 1974, *Prehistory and Protohistory of India and Pakistan.*

FIGURE 220: Lime Floor with a Group of Four Stones and Postholes of a Circular House, Inamgaon

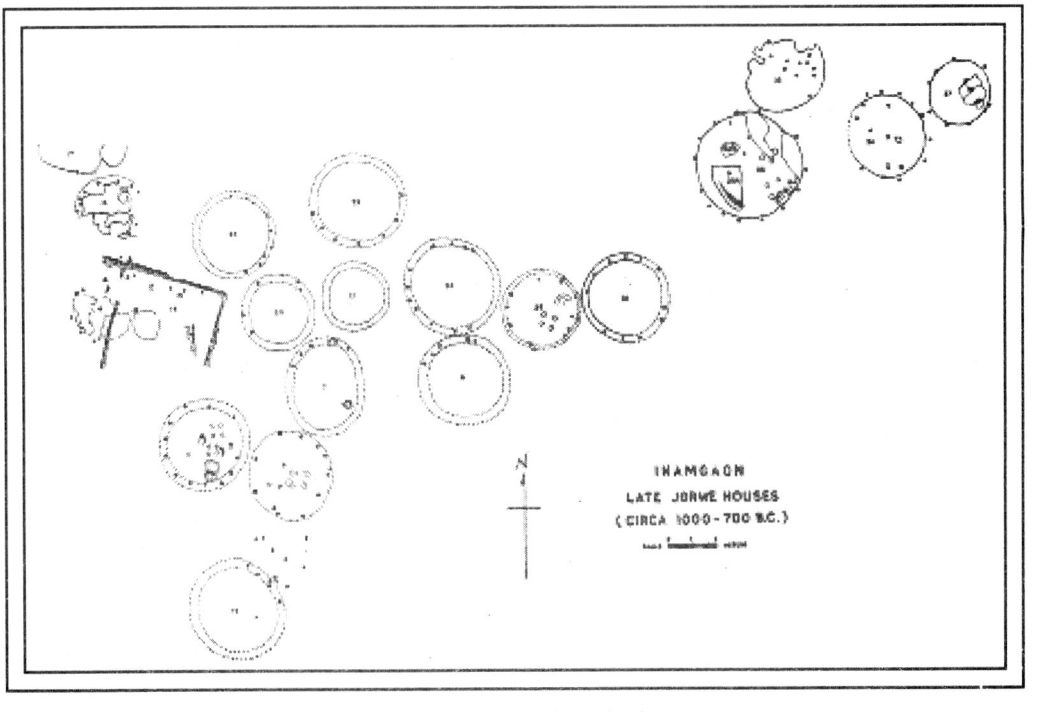

Source: H.D. Sankalia, 1974, *Prehistory and Protohistory of India and Pakistan.*

FIGURE 221: Settlement Pattern, Late Jorwe Period, Inamgaon

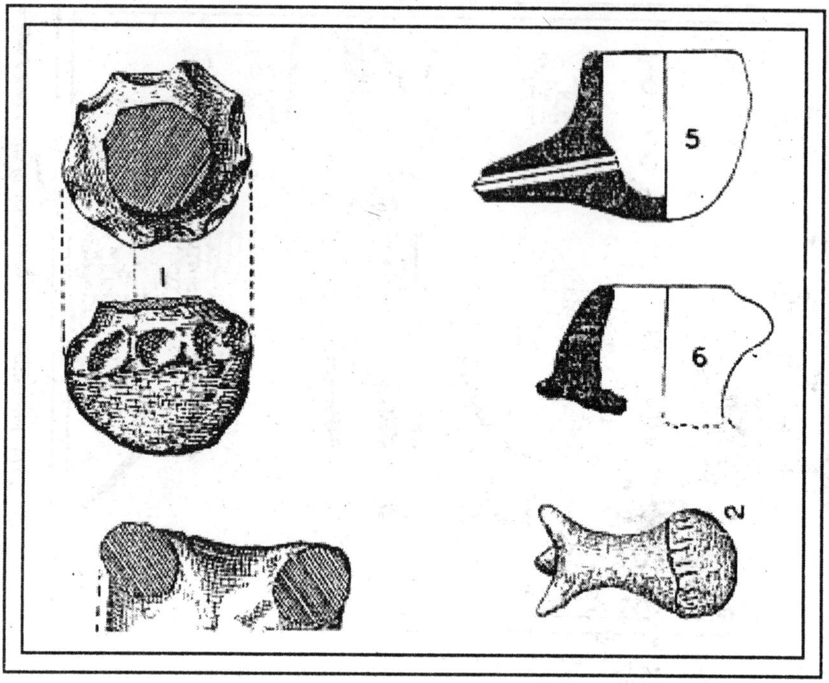

Source: H.D. Sankalia, 1974, *Prehistory and Protohistory of India and Pakistan.*

FIGURE 222: Stylized Bull (2) and Other Unidentified Objects, Ahar, Rajasthan

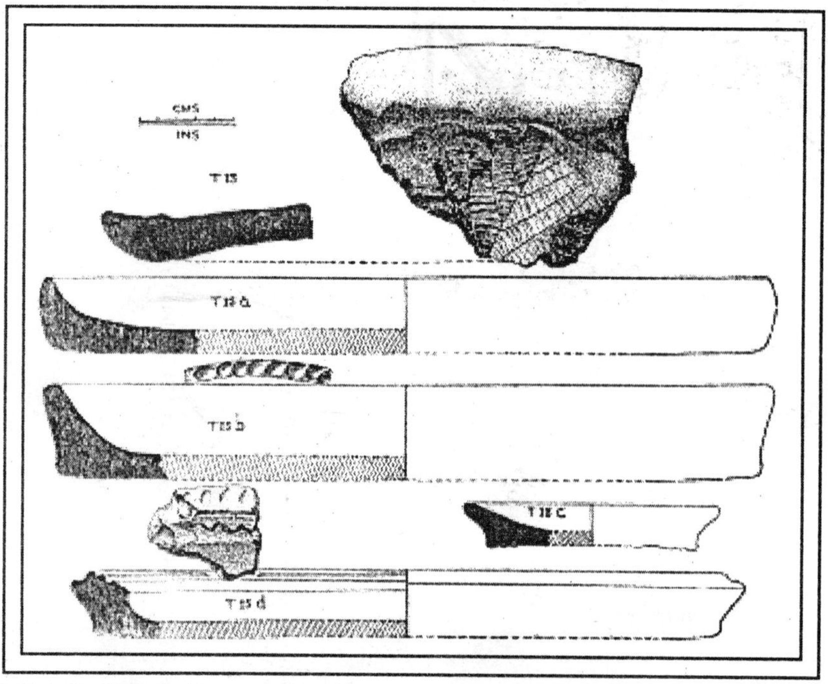

Source: H.D. Sankalia, 1974, *Prehistory and Protohistory of India and Pakistan.*

FIGURE 223: Coarse Red Ware, (d) Plates, Nevasa

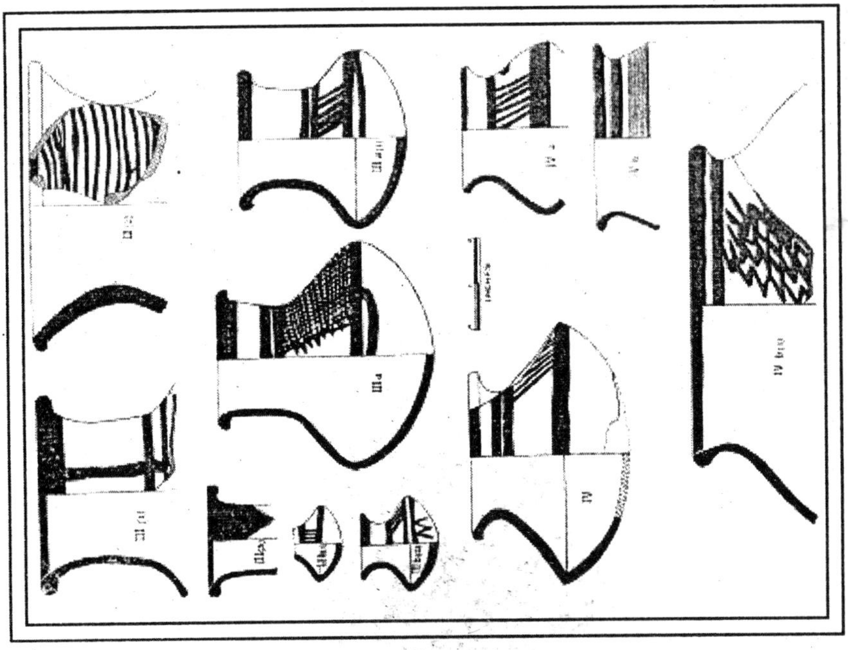

Source: H.D. Sankalia, 1974, *Prehistory and Protohistory of India and Pakistan.*

FIGURE 224: Miniature and Medium Type Vessels, Jorwe Fabric, Chandoli

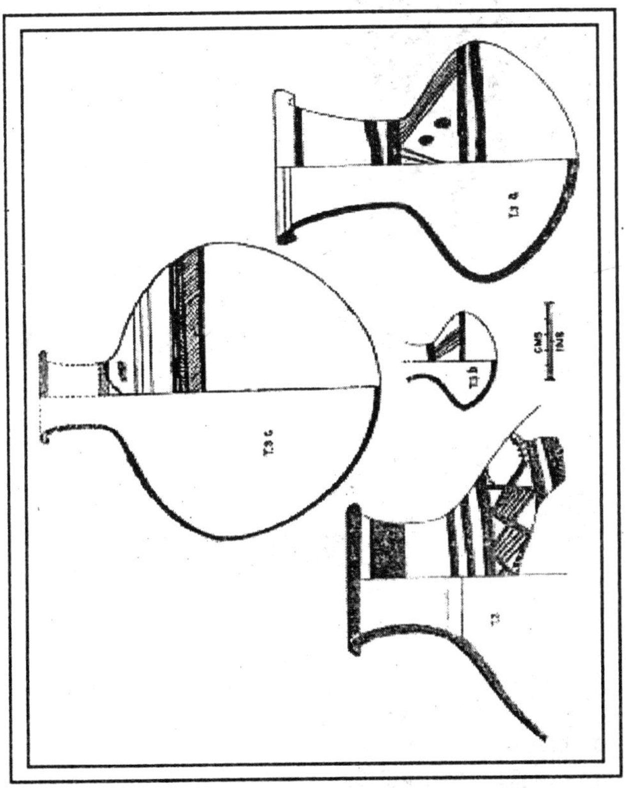

Source: H.D. Sankalia, 1974, *Prehistory and Protohistory of India and Pakistan.*

FIGURE 225: Vessels with High Neck, Globular Body and Sagered Base, Nevasa

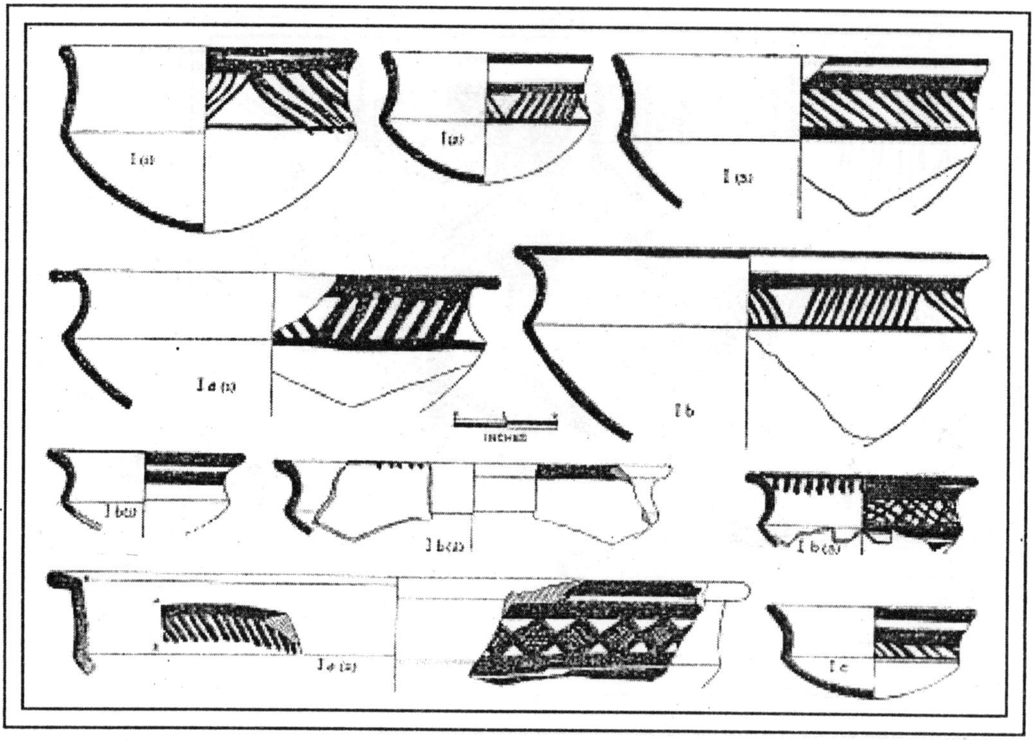

Source: H.D. Sankalia, 1974, *Prehistory and Protohistory of India and Pakistan.*

FIGURE 226: Carinated Bowls, Jorwe Fabric, Chandoli

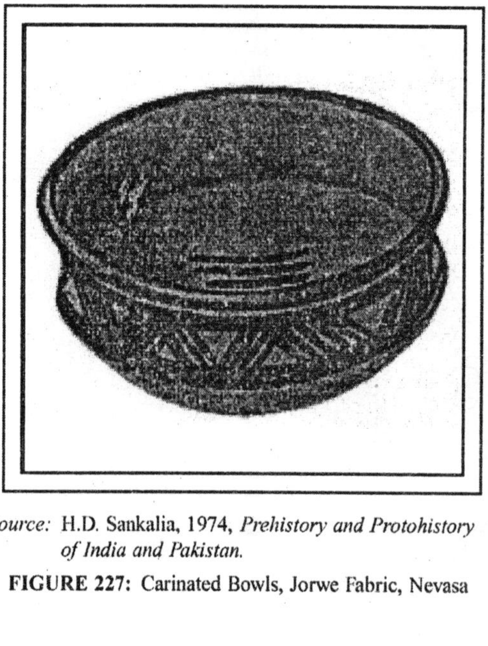

Source: H.D. Sankalia, 1974, *Prehistory and Protohistory of India and Pakistan.*

FIGURE 227: Carinated Bowls, Jorwe Fabric, Nevasa

Source: H.D. Sankalia, 1974, *Prehistory and Protohistory of India and Pakistan.*

FIGURE 228: Spouted Pot, Jorwe Fabric, Nevasa

Source: H.D. Sankaḷia, 1974, *Prehistory and Protohistory of India and Pakistan.*

FIGURE 229: Spouted Pot, Jorwe Fabric, Nevasa

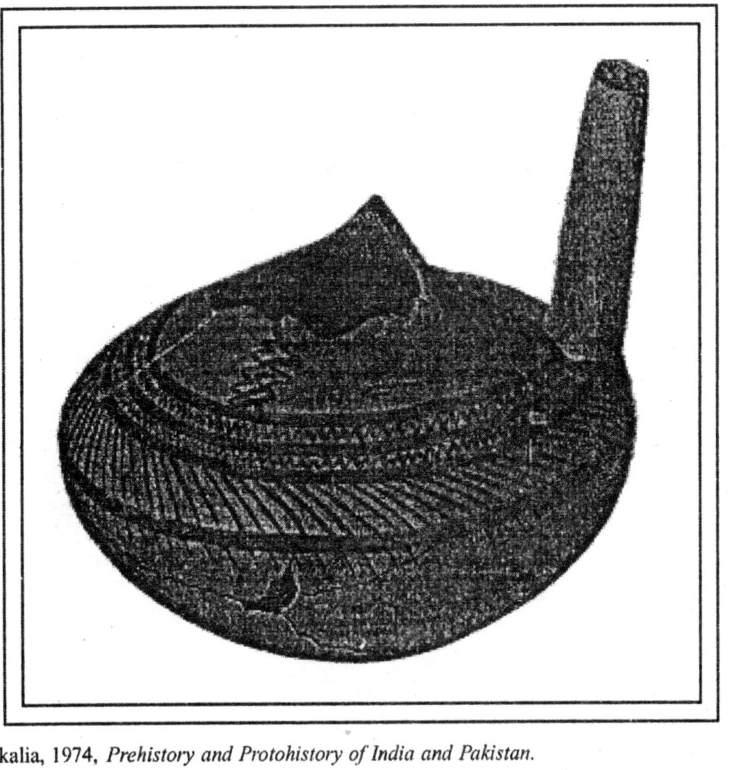

Source: H.D. Sankalia, 1974, *Prehistory and Protohistory of India and Pakistan.*

FIGURE 230: Spouted Pot, Jorwe Fabric, Nevasa

Source: H.D. Sankalia, 1974, *Prehistory and Protohistory of India and Pakistan.*

FIGURE 231: Channel Spouted Dish of Red Sand Stone from Shrine VIA.8, Catal Huyuk, Turkey

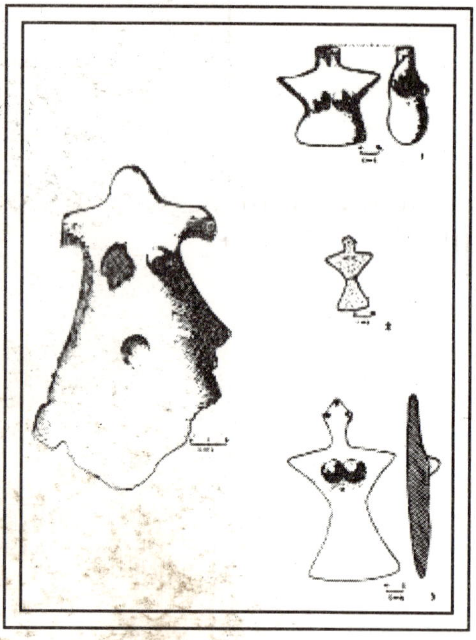

Source: H.D. Sankalia, 1974, *Prehistory and Protohistory of India and Pakistan.*

FIGURE 232: Human (female) Effigy or Mother Goddess from Hissar (1-3) and Nevasa (4)

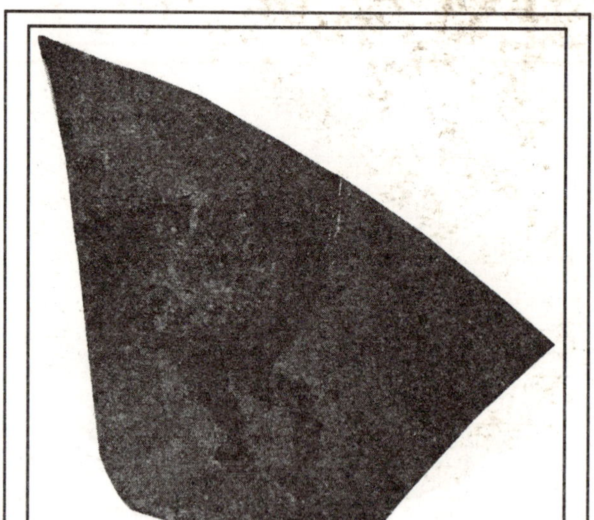

Source: H.D. Sankalia, 1974, *Prehistory and Protohistory of India and Pakistan.*

FIGURE 233: Dog or Dog-like Animal Painted in Black on Red Slipped Jorwe Pottery, Nevasa

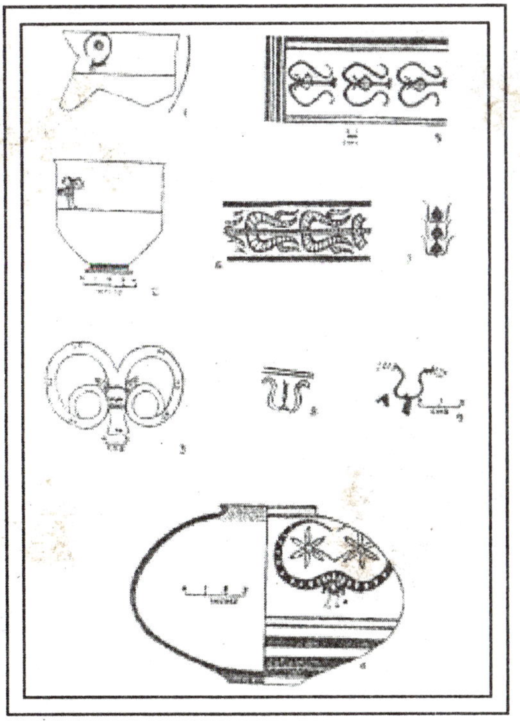

Source: H.D. Sankalia, 1974, *Prehistory and Protohistory of India and Pakistan.*

FIGURE 234: The Buccranian (Bull or Wild Sheep Horn), Motif: 1-3, 5-9: Iran and W. Asia; 4. Kot Diji

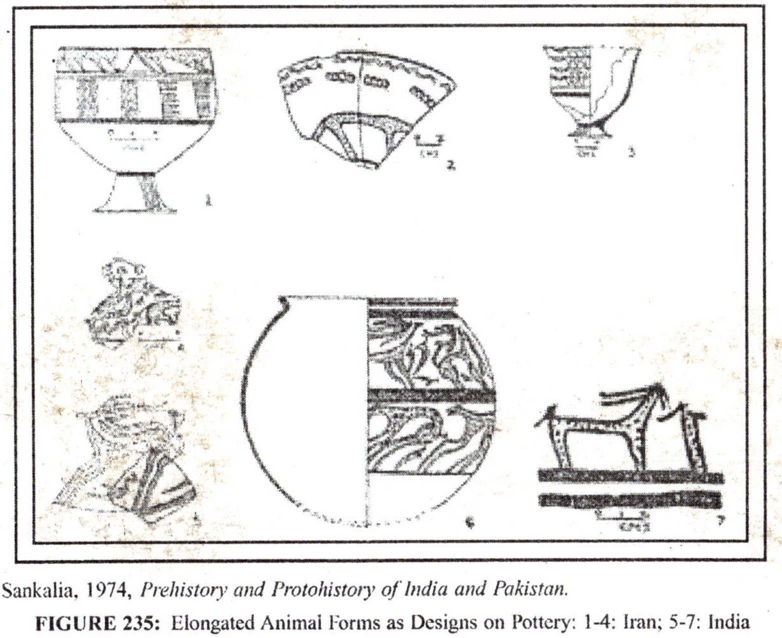

Source: H.D. Sankalia, 1974, *Prehistory and Protohistory of India and Pakistan.*

FIGURE 235: Elongated Animal Forms as Designs on Pottery: 1-4: Iran; 5-7: India

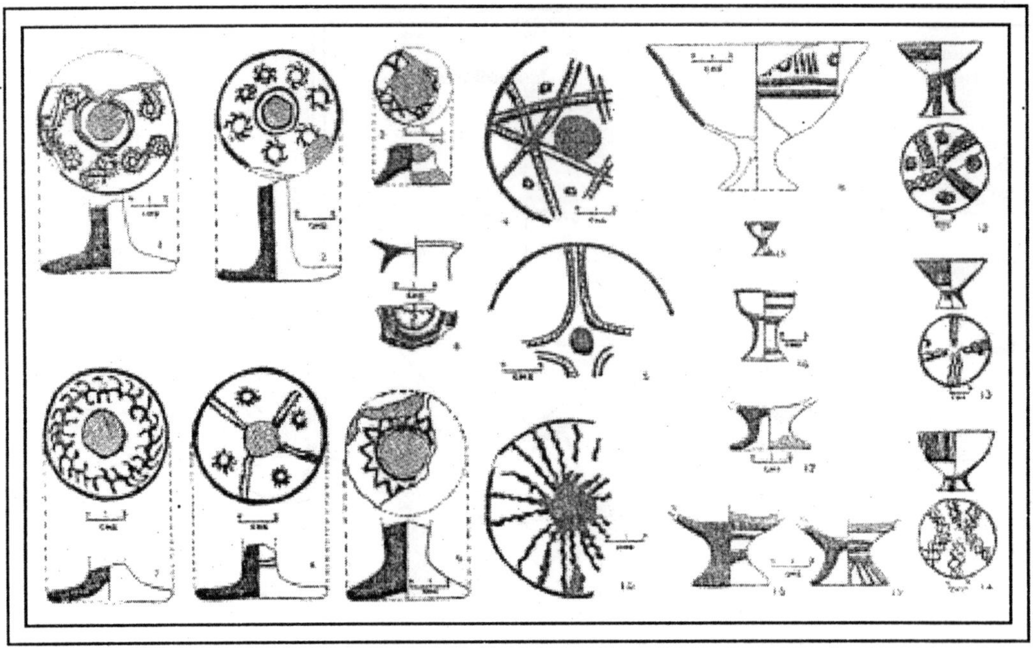

Source: H.D. Sankalia, 1974, *Prehistory and Protohistory of India and Pakistan.*

FIGURE 236: Painting of Wavy Lines on the Base of Footed Cups of Goblets, Navdatoli

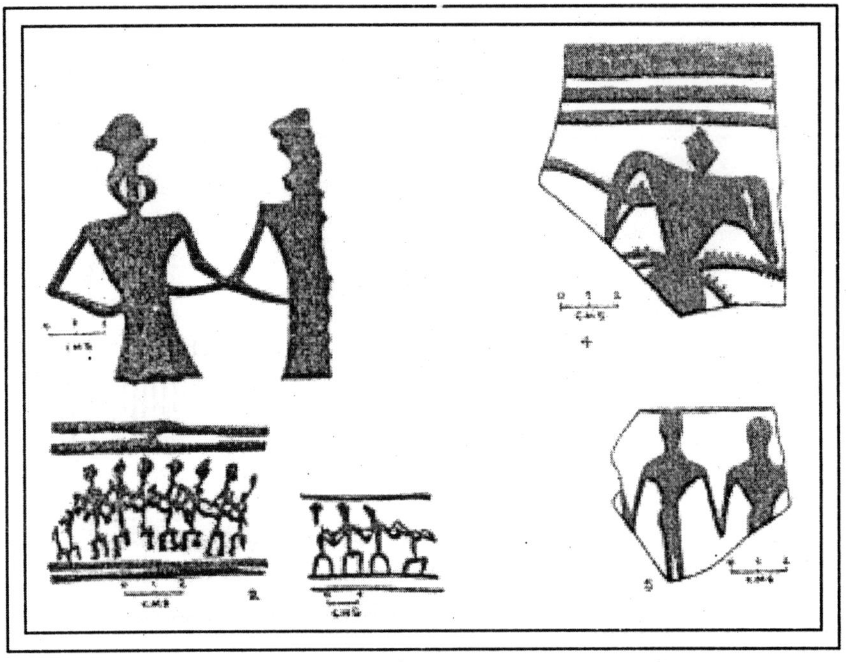

Source: H.D. Sankalia, 1974, *Prehistory and Protohistory of India and Pakistan.*

FIGURE 237: Dancing Human Figures or Human Figures standing with hands clasped or seemingly holding some Object in the Hand or on the Head: 1-4: Navdatoli; 5: Sialk

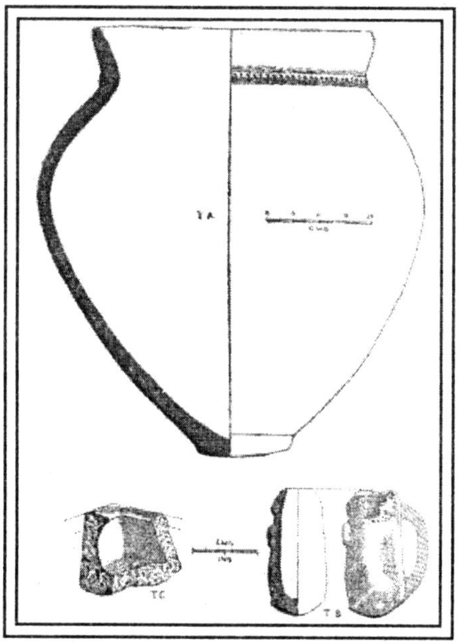

Source: H.D. Sankalia, 1974, *Prehistory and Protohistory of India and Pakistan.*

FIGURE 238: Storage Jar, Anthropomorphic Bul! (broken); (Its suggested 'handle'should now be deleted) and a Squarish Pot, Nevasa

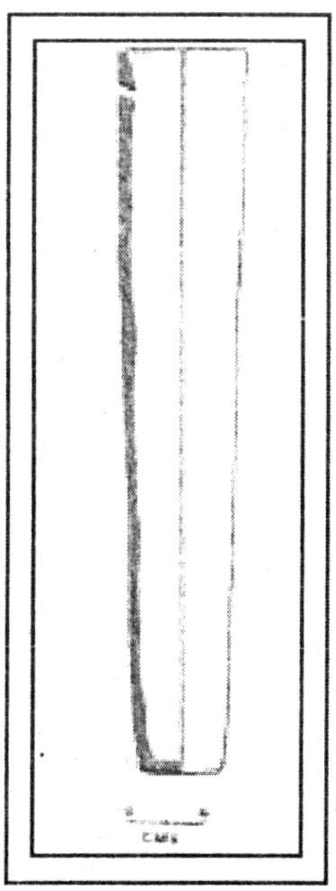

Source: H.D. Sankalia, 1974, *Prehistory and Protohistory of India and Pakistan.*

FIGURE 239: Exceptionally Tall, Cylindrical Vessel, Inamgaon

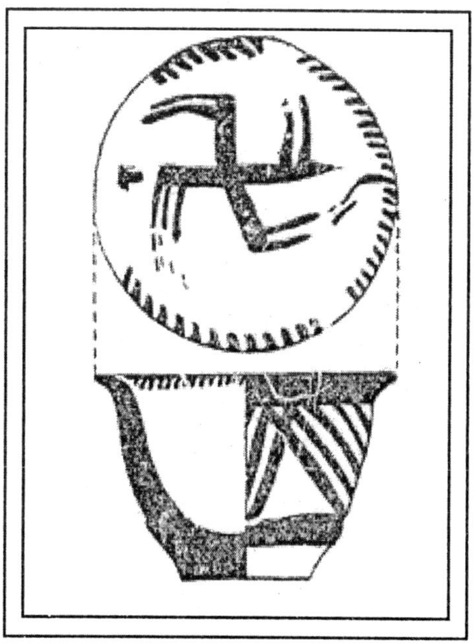

Source: H.D. Sankalia, 1974, *Prehistory and Protohistory of India and Pakistan.*

FIGURE 240: Unique Bowl, Jorwe Fabric with Swastic Design, Inamgaon

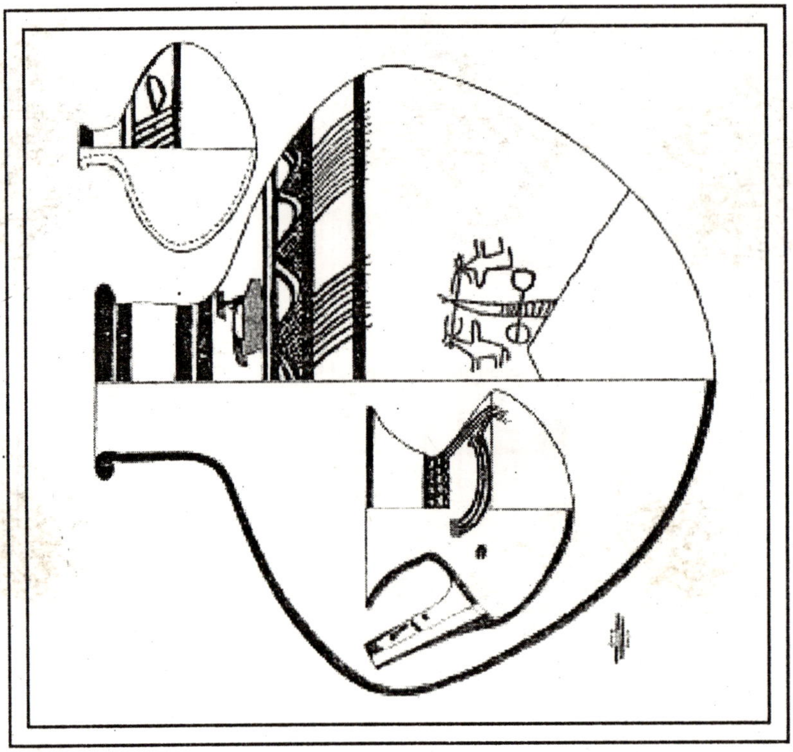

Source: H.D. Sankalia, 1974, *Prehistory and Protohistory of India and Pakistan.*

FIGURE 241: Three New Characteristic Vessels in Jorwe Fabric, Inamgaon. The large pot has an engraving of a cart drawn by two humped bulls. To its left, the spouted pot has a painting of a boat. Top right shows a very narrow mouthed vessel.

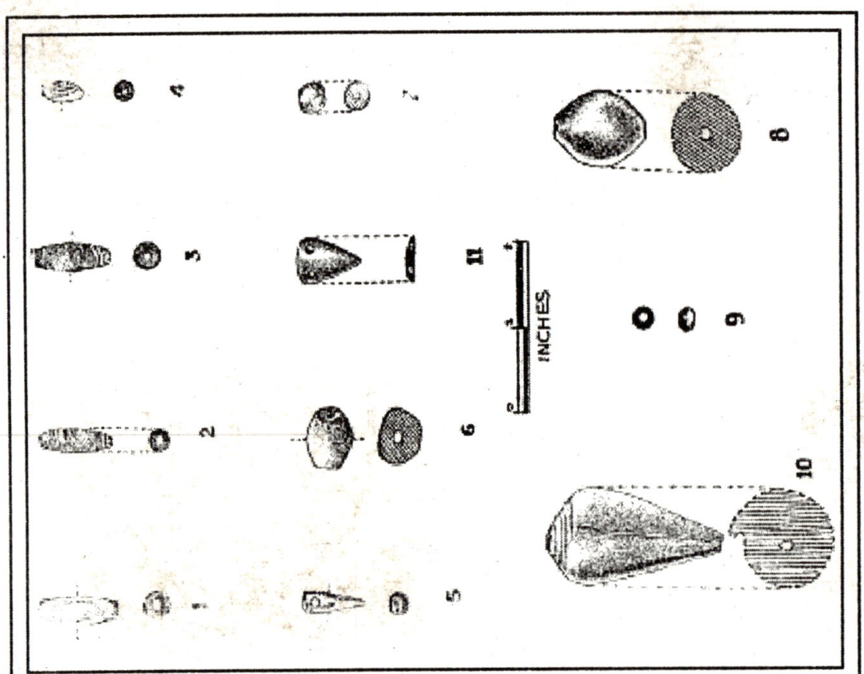

Source: H.D. Sankalia, 1974, *Prehistory and Protohistory of India and Pakistan.*

FIGURE 242: Various Types of Beads, Agate 1-3; Carnelian 4-5; Shell 6-11, Chandoli

Source: H.D. Sankalia, 1974, *Prehistory and Protohistory of India and Pakistan.*

FIGURE 243: Main Types of Chalcedony Blades, Parallel-sided Flakes (1), Lunate (2), Borer (3), Obliquely Blunted Point (4), Penknife Blade (5), Tanged Point (6), Backed Blade (7), Serrated Blade (8), Point (9), Chandoli

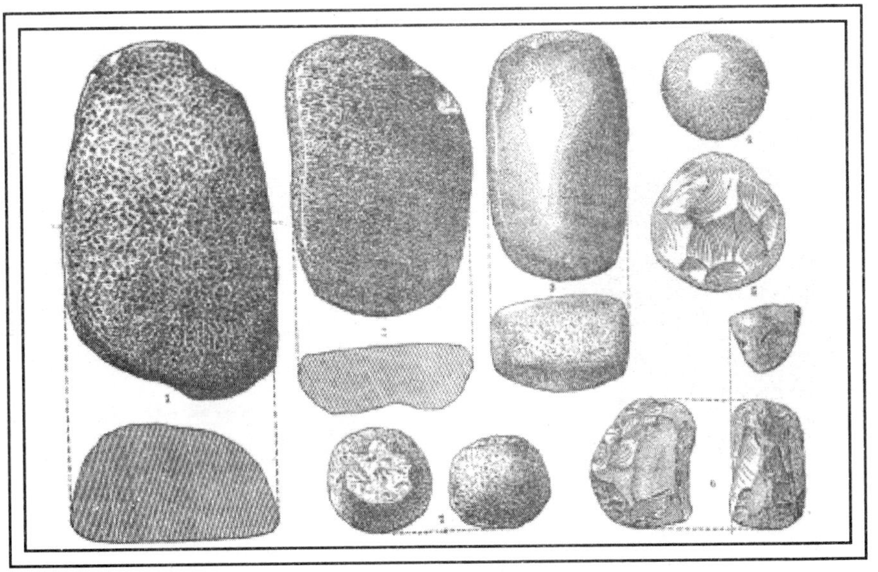

Source: H.D. Sankalia, 1974, *Prehistory and Protohistory of India and Pakistan.*

FIGURE 244: Anvils (1-2), Mutter (3), Stone Balls (4), Hammer Stones (5-7), Nevasa

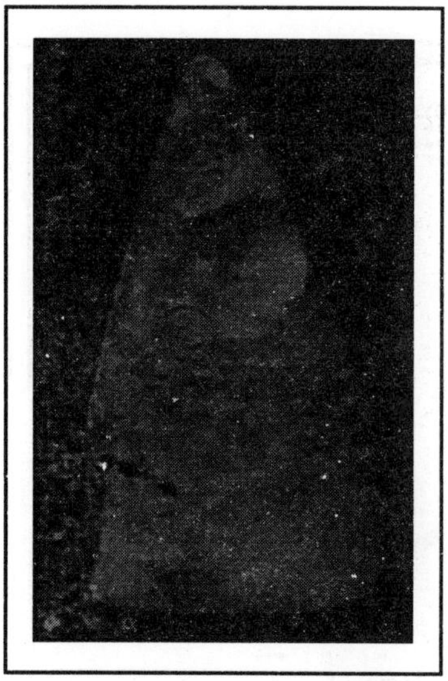

Source: H.D. Sankalia, 1974, *Prehistory and Protohistory of India and Pakistan.*

FIGURE 245: Stone Adze, Nevasa

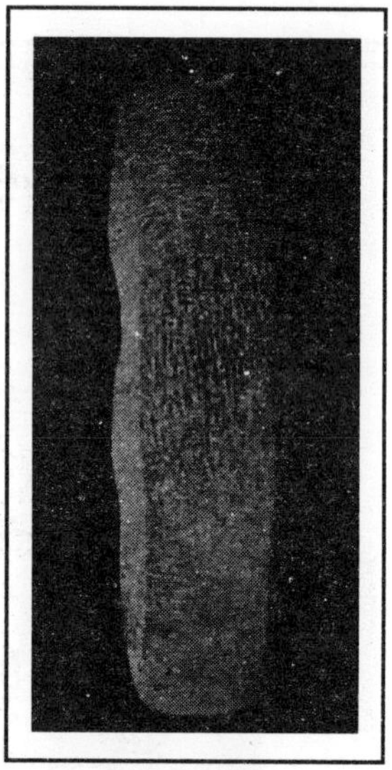

Source: H.D. Sankalia, 1974, *Prehistory and Protohistory of India and Pakistan.*

FIGURE 246: Stone Chisel, Nevasa

Source: H.D. Sankalia, 1974, *Prehistory and Protohistory of India and Pakistan.*

FIGURE 247: Fully Polished Stone Axe, Nevasa

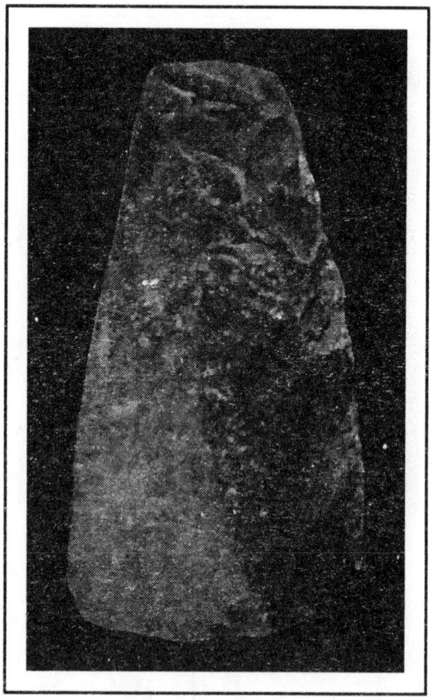

Source: H.D. Sankalia, 1974, *Prehistory and Protohistory of India and Pakistan.*

FIGURE 248: Partly Polished and Partly Unfinished Stone Axe, Nevasa

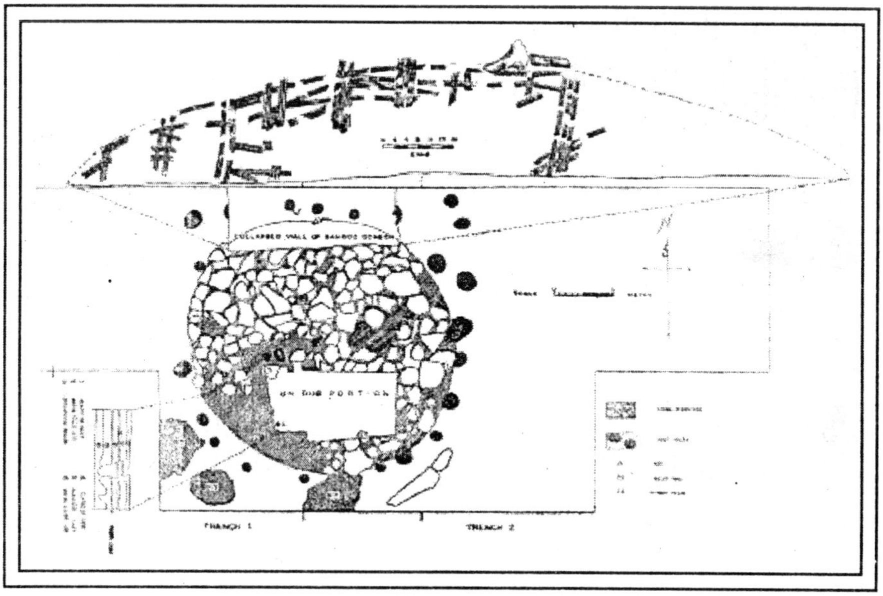

Source: H.D. Sankalia, 1974, *Prehistory and Protohistory of India and Pakistan.*

FIGURE 249: Plan of a Circular Structure, Early Neolithic, Sanganakallu

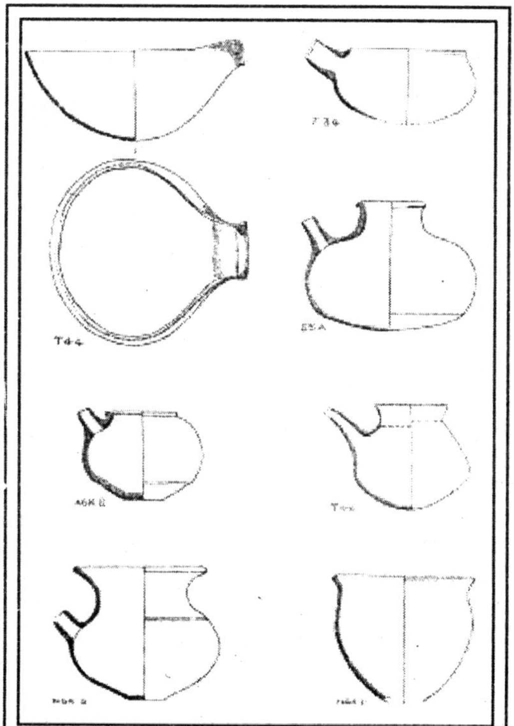

Source: H.D. Sankalia, 1974, *Prehistory and Protohistory of India and Pakistan.*

FIGURE 250: Pottery Types from Piklihal, Brahmagiri and Nagarjunakonda

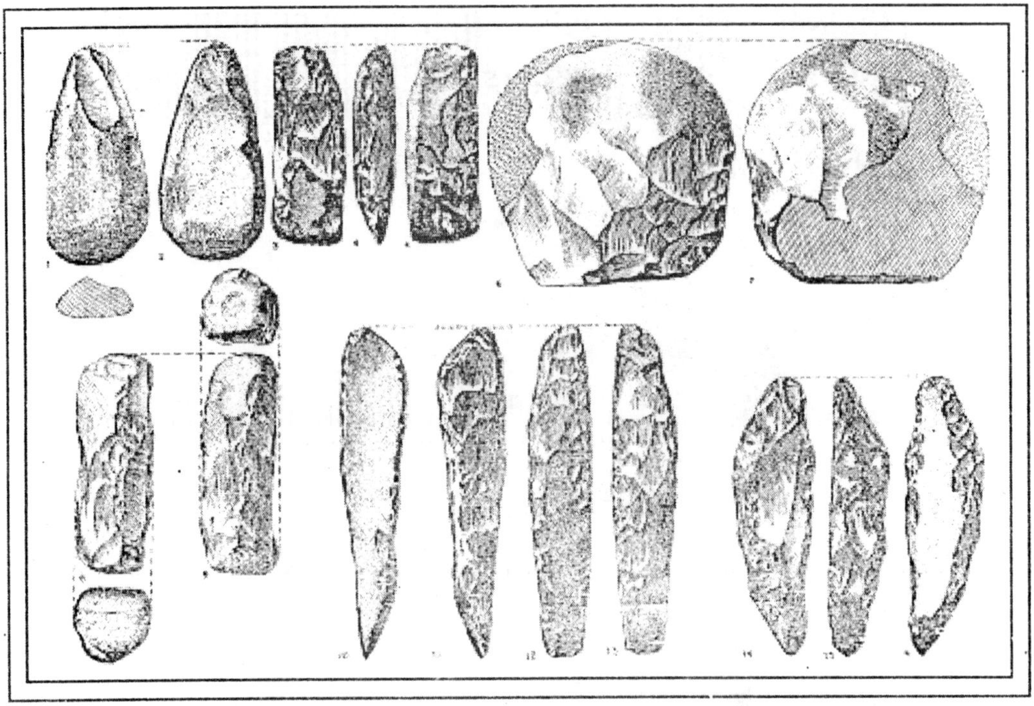

Source: H.D. Sankalia, 1974, *Prehistory and Protohistory of India and Pakistan.*

FIGURE 251: "Shoe-last" Celt, Fabricators and Chisels, Sanganakallu

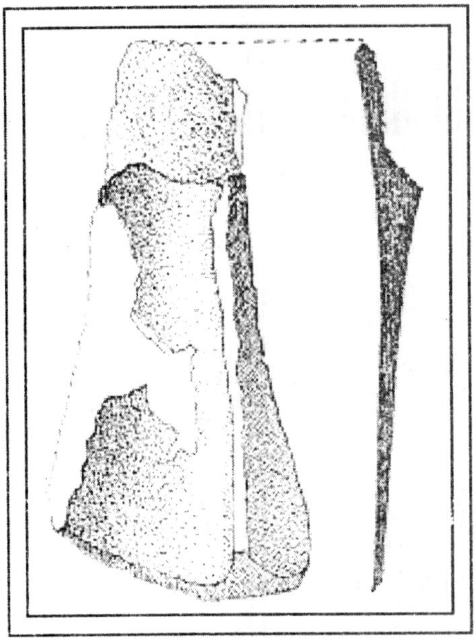

Source: H.D. Sankalia, 1974, *Prehistory and Protohistory of India and Pakistan.*

FIGURE 252: Bone Axe from Palavoy

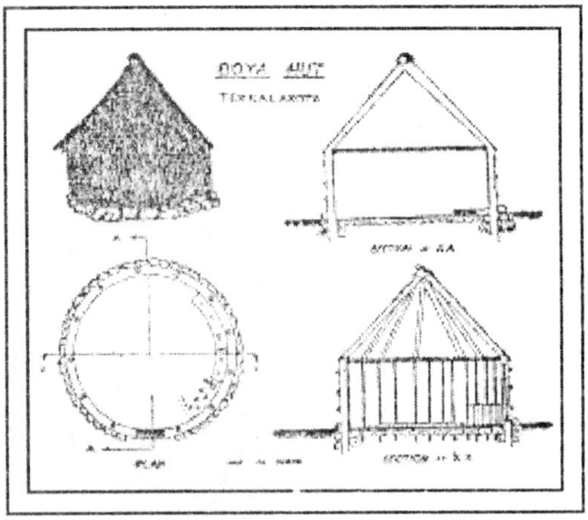

Source: H.D. Sankalia, 1974, *Prehistory and Protohistory of India and Pakistan.*

FIGURE 253: Plaso and Elevation of Boya Huts, Tekkalakota

Source: H.D. Sankalia, 1974, *Prehistory and Protohistory of India and Pakistan.*

FIGURE 254: Boya Huts, Tekkalakota

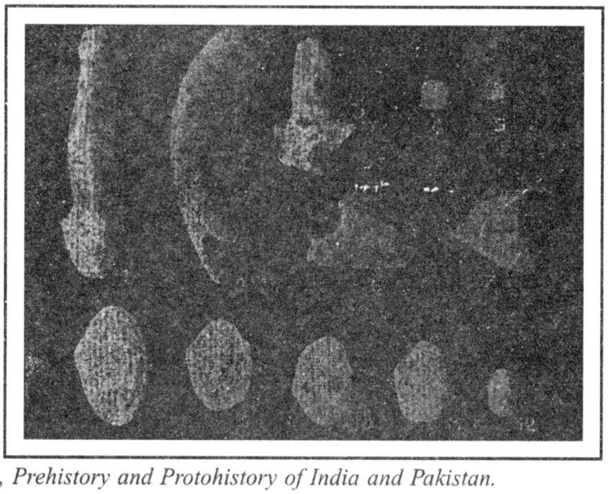

Source: H.D. Sankalia, 1974, *Prehistory and Protohistory of India and Pakistan.*

FIGURE 255: Bone and Shell Objects, Tekkalakota

Source: H.D. Sankalia, 1974, *Prehistory and Protohistory of India and Pakistan.*

FIGURE 256: Bone Tools, Tekkalakota

Source: H.D. Sankalia, 1974, *Prehistory and Protohistory of India and Pakistan.*

FIGURE 257: A Lid of Grey Ware with Punctured Decoration, depicting a Bull (top centre), a Cobra (right), and an Antelope (left), Tekkalakota

Source: H.D. Sankalia, 1974, *Prehistory and Protohistory of India and Pakistan.*

FIGURE 258: Copper Axe, Tekkalakota

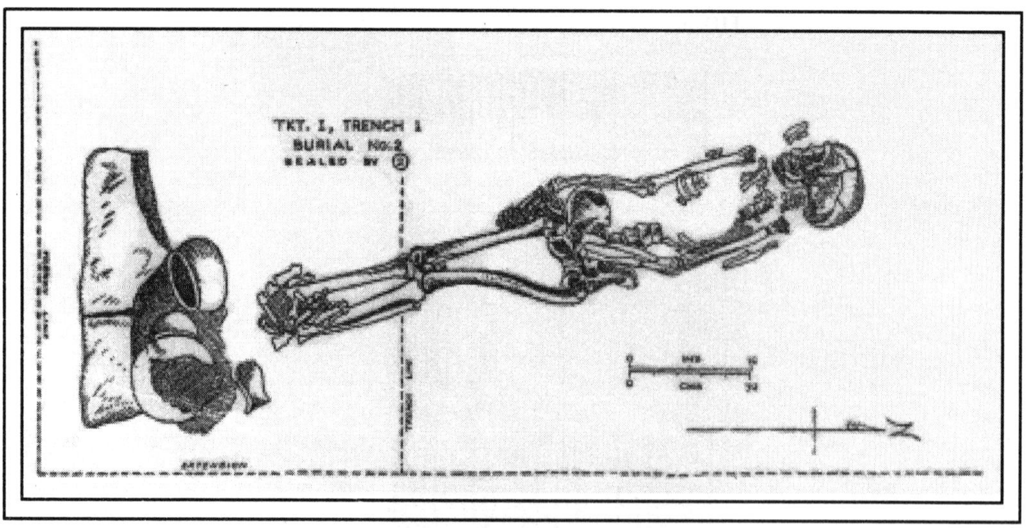

Source: H.D. Sankalia, 1974, *Prehistory and Protohistory of India and Pakistan.*

FIGURE 259: Skeleton, Adult Woman with 7 Funerary Vessels at a Little distance to the south of the feet

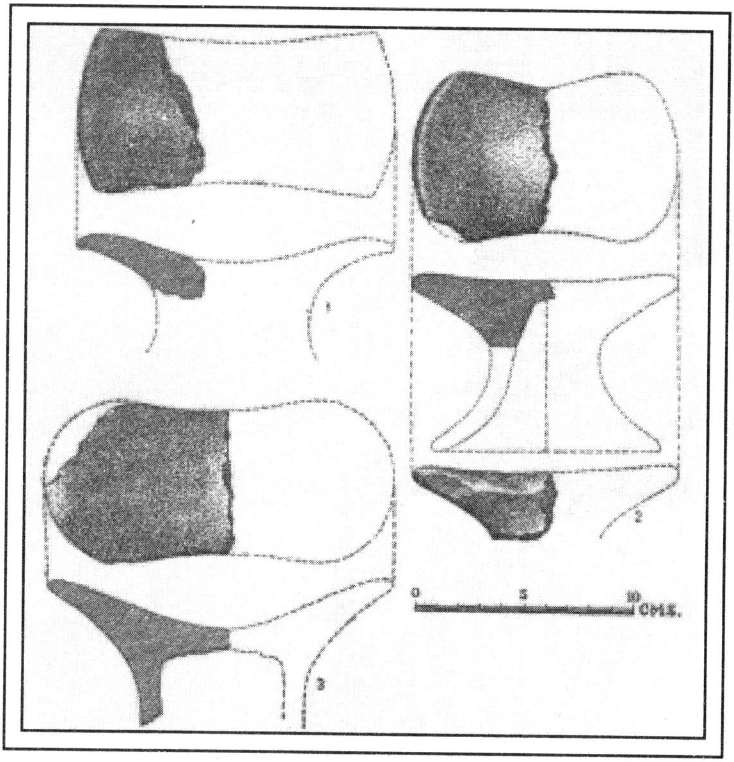

Source: H.D. Sankalia, 1974, *Prehistory and Protohistory of India and Pakistan.*

FIGURE 260: Fragments of Head Rest, Hallur

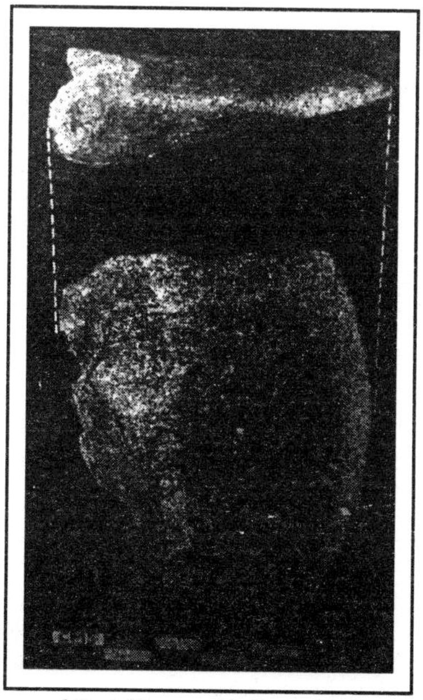

Source: H.D. Sankalia, 1974, *Prehistory and Protohistory of India and Pakistan.*

FIGURE 261: Pottery Head Rest, Hallur

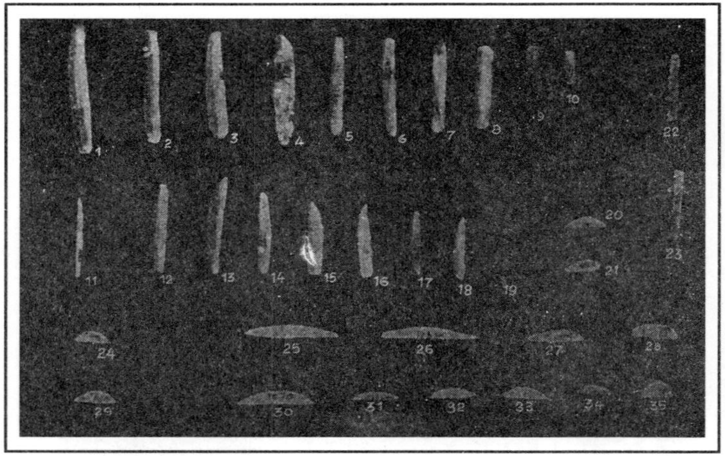

Source: H.D. Sankalia, 1974, *Prehistory and Protohistory of India and Pakistan.*

FIGURE 263: Parallel Sided Blades, Penknife, Blades and Lunates, Tekkalakota

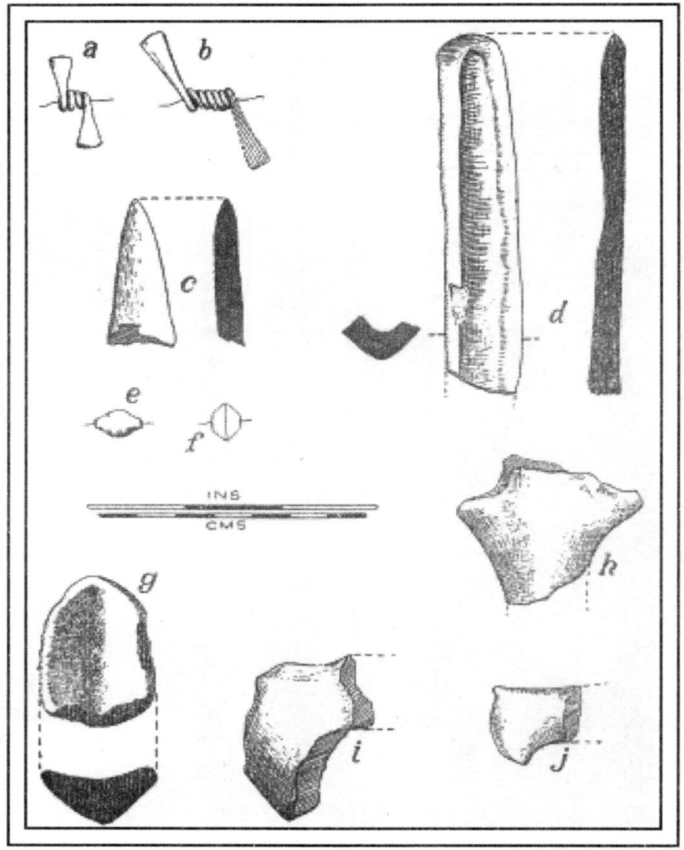

Source: H.D. Sankalia, 1974, *Prehistory and Protohistory of India and Pakistan.*

FIGURE 262: a-b: Gold Ornaments, c: Bone Points, d: Bone Chisel, e-f: Beads, g: Terracotta Lamp (broken), h: Terracotta Torso of a figurine, and i-j: Broken Terracotta Bulls, Tekkalakota

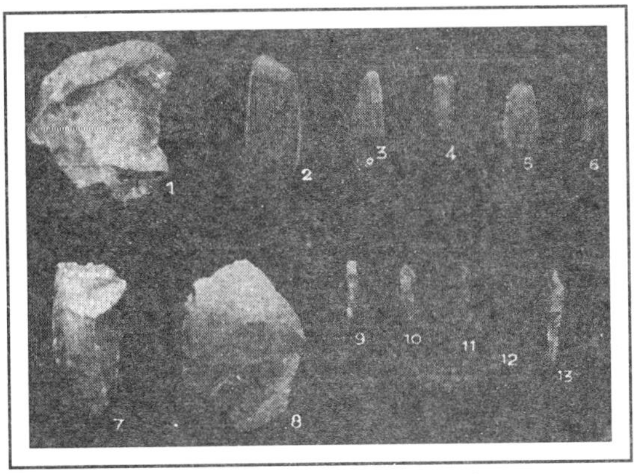

Source: H.D. Sankalia, 1974, *Prehistory and Protohistory of India and Pakistan.*

FIGURE 264: Cores, Scrapers and Crested Ridge Flake, Tekkalakota

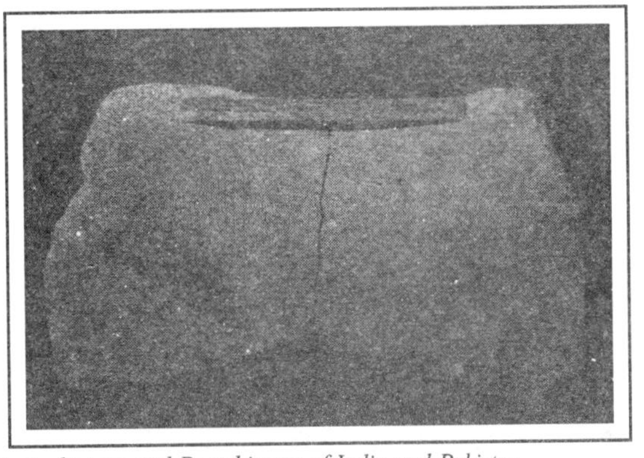

Source: H.D. Sankalia, 1974, *Prehistory and Protohistory of India and Pakistan.*

FIGURE 265: Saddle Quern, Tekkalakota

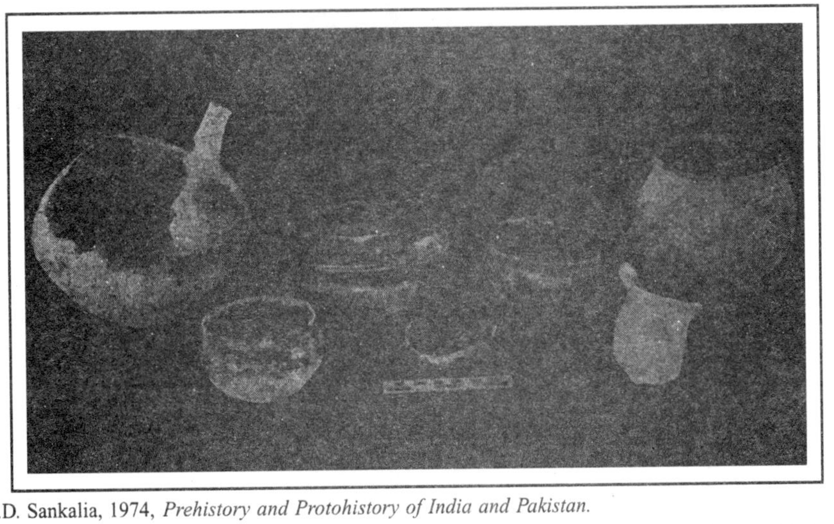

Source: H.D. Sankalia, 1974, *Prehistory and Protohistory of India and Pakistan.*

FIGURE 266: Funerary Vessels (found at a little distance away from the feet of Burial 2, an adult female), Tekkalakota

Source: H.D. Sankalia, 1974, *Prehistory and Protohistory of India and Pakistan.*

FIGURE 267: A Carinated Bowl with Pedestal, Tekkalakota

Source: H.D. Sankalia, 1974, *Prehistory and Protohistory of India and Pakistan.*

FIGURE 268: Tea-Kettle like Pot in Grey Ware, Tekkalakota

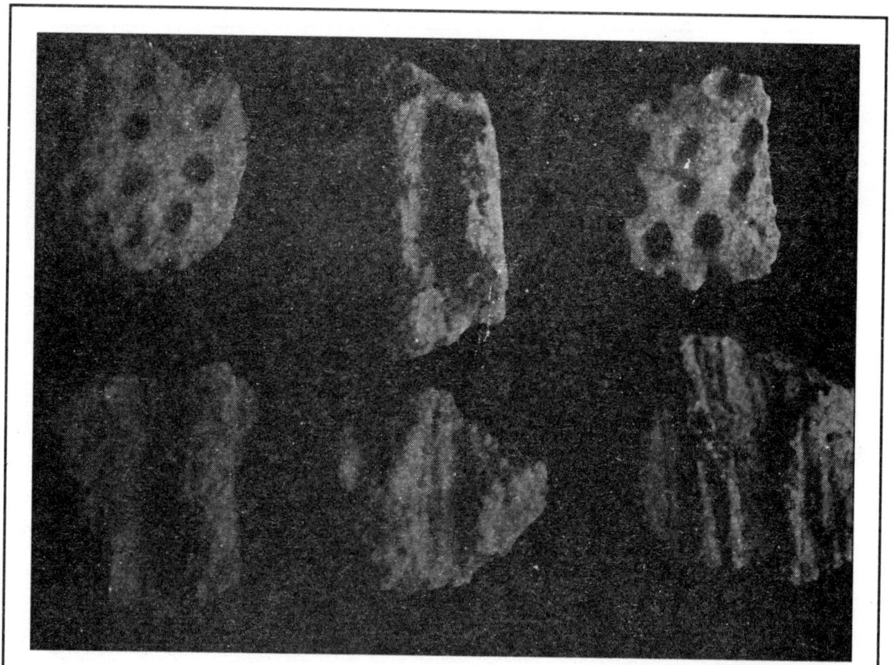

Source: H.D. Sankalia, 1974, *Prehistory and Protohistory of India and Pakistan.*

FIGURE 269: Burnt Clay Clods with Bamboo Impression, Tekkalakota

Source: H.D. Sankalia, 1974, *Prehistory and Protohistory of India and Pakistan.*

FIGURE 270: A Roughly Circular Structure without Postholes (its outlines defined by natural boulders, Tekkalakota. On the right centre is an used saddle quern belonging to Phase II), Tekkalakota

Source: H.D. Sankalia, 1974, *Prehistory and Protohistory of India and Pakistan.*

FIGURE 271: A View of the Horizontal Excavations on Terrace 2, Tekkalakota

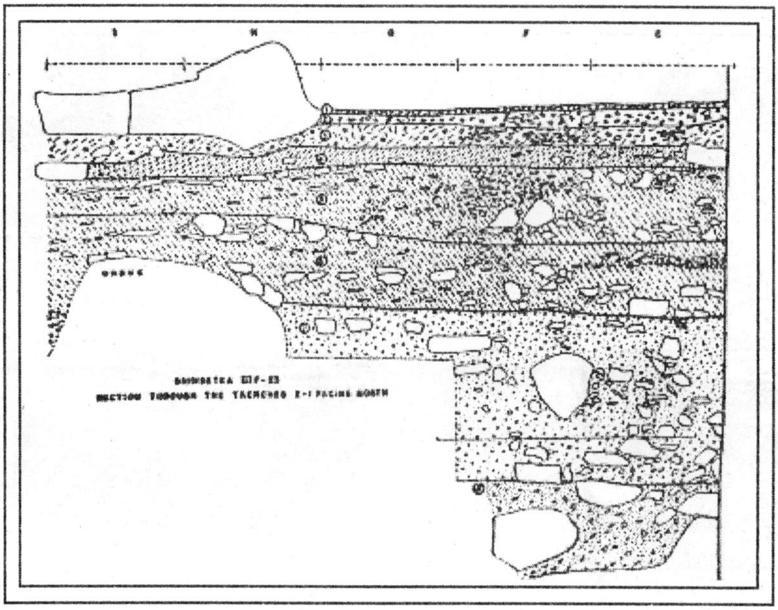

Source: V.N. Mishra, Yashodhara Math Pal and Malti Nagar, 1971, *Bhimbetka: Prehistoric Man and His Arts in Central India.*

FIGURE 272: Bhimbetka III F-23, Section through the Trenches E-I Facing North, Bhimbetka

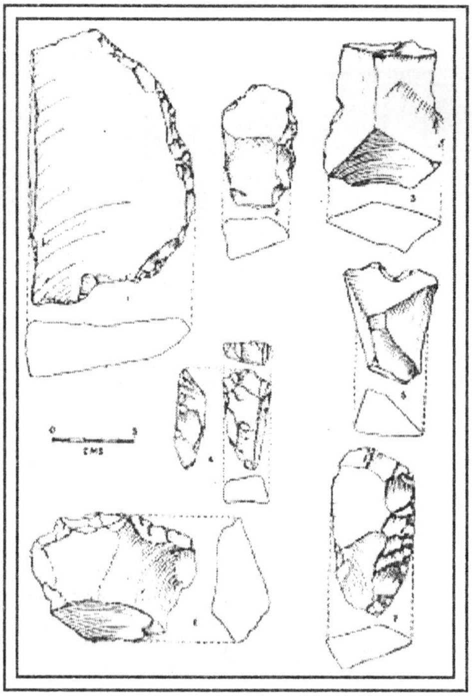

Source: V.N. Mishra, Yashodhara Math Pal and Malti Nagar, 1971, *Bhimbetka: Prehistoric Man and His Arts in Central India.*

FIGURE 273: Acheulian Scrapers, Bhimbetka

Source: V.N. Mishra, Yashodhara Math Pal and Malti Nagar, 1971, *Bhimbetka: Prehistoric Man and His Arts in Central India.*

FIGURE 274: Pandapur Water Hole, Bhimbetka

Source: V.N. Mishra, Yashodhara Math Pal and Malti Nagar, 1971, *Bhimbetka: Prehistoric Man and His Arts in Central India.*

FIGURE 275: A View of the Excavation, Bhimbetka

Source: V.N. Mishra, Yashodhara Math Pal and Malti Nagar, 1971, *Bhimbetka: Prehistoric Man and His Arts in Central India.*

FIGURE 276: Food Gatherers, Bhimbetka

Source: V.N. Mishra, Yashodhara Math Pal and Malti Nagar, 1971, *Bhimbetka: Prehistoric Man and His Arts in Central India.*

FIGURE 277: Tubers Eaten by Local People, Bhimbetka

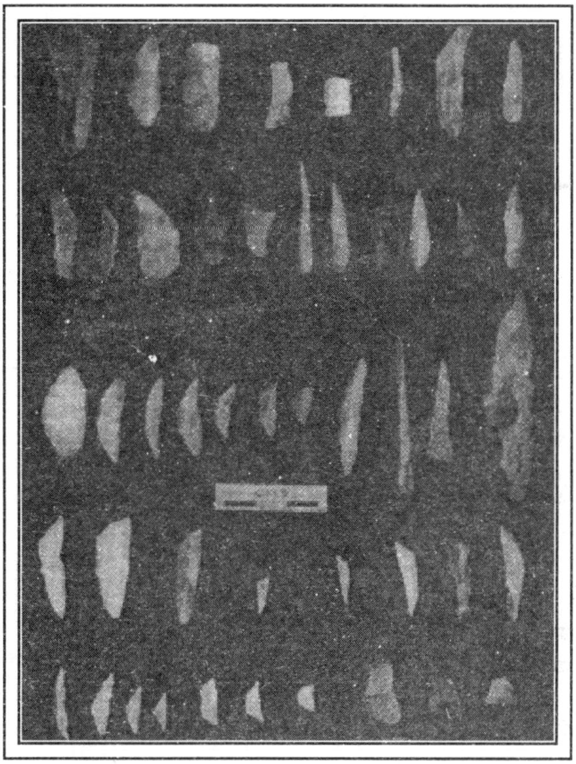

Source: V.N. Mishra, Yashodhara Math Pal and Malti Nagar, 1971, *Bhimbetka: Prehistoric Man and His Arts in Central India.*

FIGURE 278: Mesolithic Tools, Bhimbetka

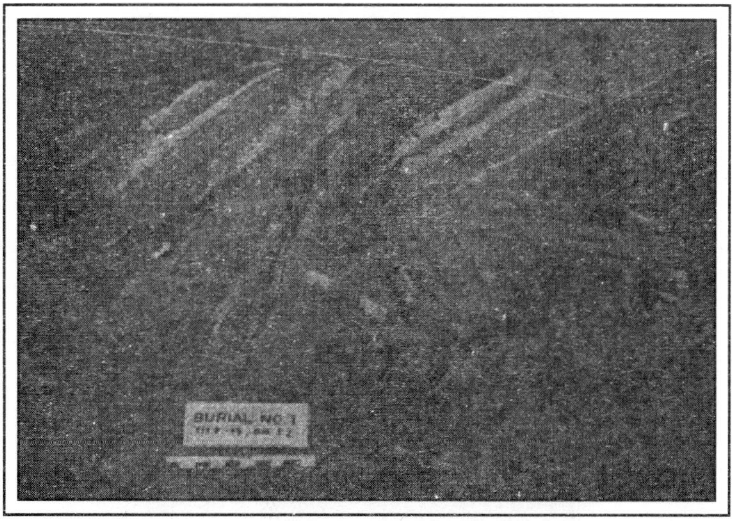

Source: V.N. Mishra, Yashodhara Math Pal and Malti Nagar, 1971, *Bhimbetka: Prehistoric Man and His Arts in Central India.*

FIGURE 279: Mesolithic Human Burial, Bhimbetka

Source: V.N. Mishra, Yashodhara Math Pal and Malti Nagar, 1971, *Bhimbetka: Prehistoric Man and His Arts in Central India.*

FIGURE 280: Prehistoric Drawings Overlapped by Historic Figures, Bhimbetka

Source: V.N. Mishra, Yashodhara Math Pal and Malti Nagar, 1971, *Bhimbetka: Prehistoric Man and His Arts in Central India.*

FIGURE 281: Bewildered Buffaloes, Bhimbetka

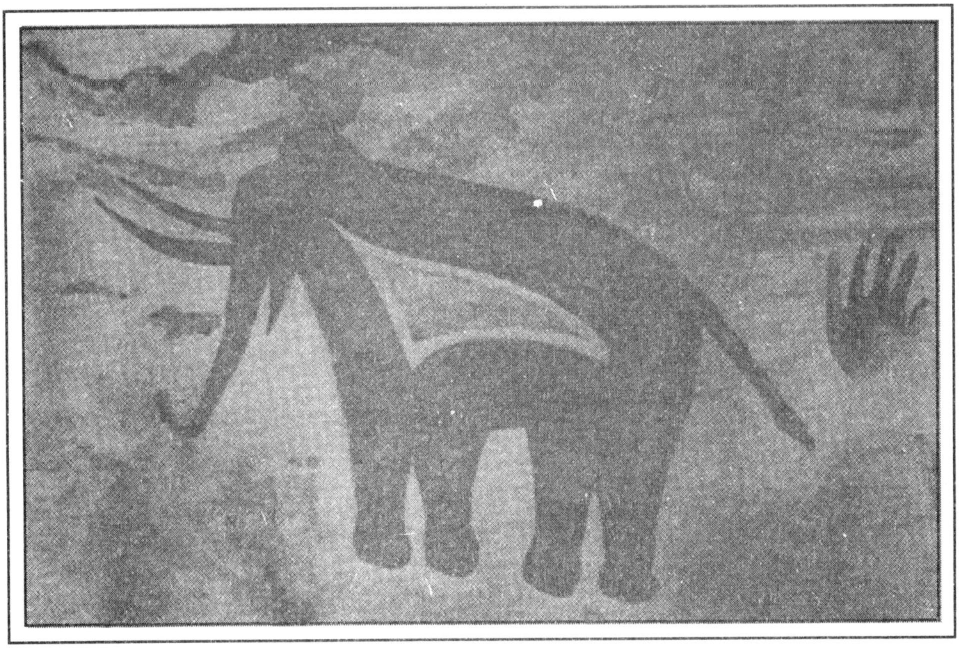

Source: V.N. Mishra, Yashodhara Math Pal and Malti Nagar, 1971, *Bhimbetka: Prehistoric Man and His Arts in Central India.*

FIGURE 282: His Majesty the Elephant, Bhimbetka

Source: V.N. Mishra, Yashodhara Math Pal and Malti Nagar, 1971, *Bhimbetka: Prehistoric Man and His Arts in Central India.*

FIGURE 283: The Mythical Boar, Bhimbetka

Source: V.N. Mishra, Yashodhara Math Pal and Malti Nagar, 1971, *Bhimbetka: Prehistoric Man and His Arts in Central India.*

FIGURE 284: Marching Soldiers, Bhimbetka

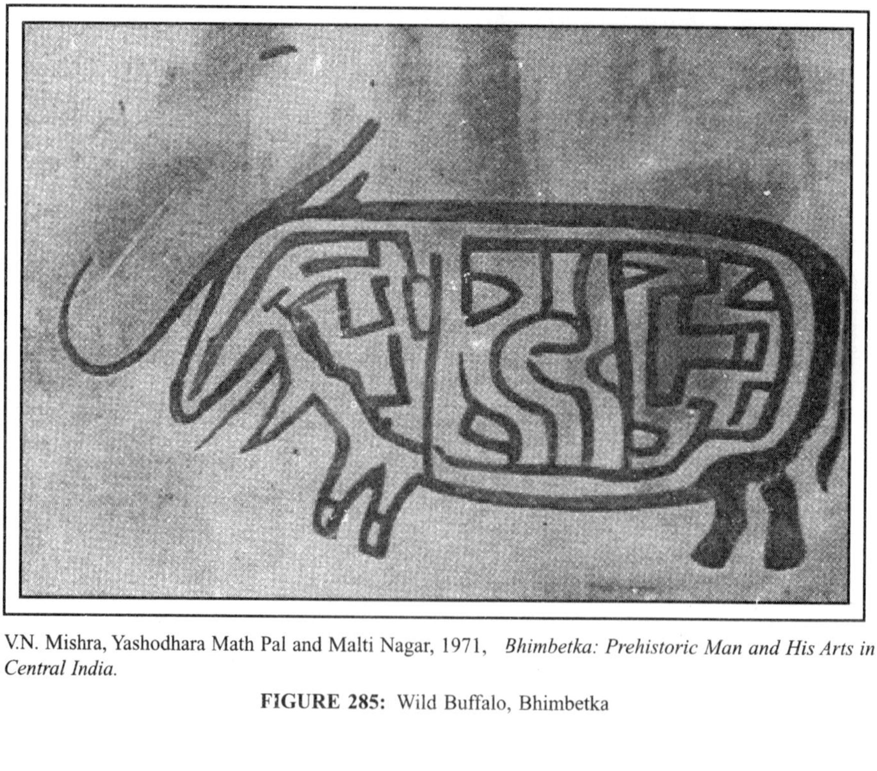

Source: V.N. Mishra, Yashodhara Math Pal and Malti Nagar, 1971, *Bhimbetka: Prehistoric Man and His Arts in Central India.*

FIGURE 285: Wild Buffalo, Bhimbetka

Source: V.N. Mishra, Yashodhara Math Pal and Malti Nagar, 1971, *Bhimbetka: Prehistoric Man and His Arts in Central India.*

FIGURE 286: Hunters in Fight, Bhimbetka

Source: V.N. Mishra, Yashodhara Math Pal and Malti Nagar, 1971, *Bhimbetka: Prehistoric Man and His Arts in Central India.*

FIGURE 287: Dancers, Bhimbetka

Source: V.N. Mishra, Yashodhara Math Pal and Malti Nagar, 1971, *Bhimbetka: Prehistoric Man and His Arts in Central India.*

FIGURE 288: Soldiers on a Campaign, Bhimbetka

Source: V.N. Mishra, Yashodhara Math Pal and Malti Nagar, 1971, *Bhimbetka: Prehistoric Man and His Arts in Central India.*

FIGURE 289: Falling Deer, Bhimbetka

Source: V.N. Mishra, Yashodhara Math Pal and Malti Nagar, 1971, *Bhimbetka: Prehistoric Man and His Arts in Central India.*

FIGURE 290: Ready for March, Bhimbetka

Source: V.N. Mishra, Yashodhara Math Pal and Malti Nagar, 1971, *Bhimbetka: Prehistoric Man and His Arts in Central India.*

FIGURE 291: Wild Cattle and Other Animals, Bhimbetka

Source: V.N. Mishra, Yashodhara Math Pal and Malti Nagar, 1971, *Bhimbetka: Prehistoric Man and His Arts in Central India.*

FIGURE 292: Hunters and their Game, Bhimbetka

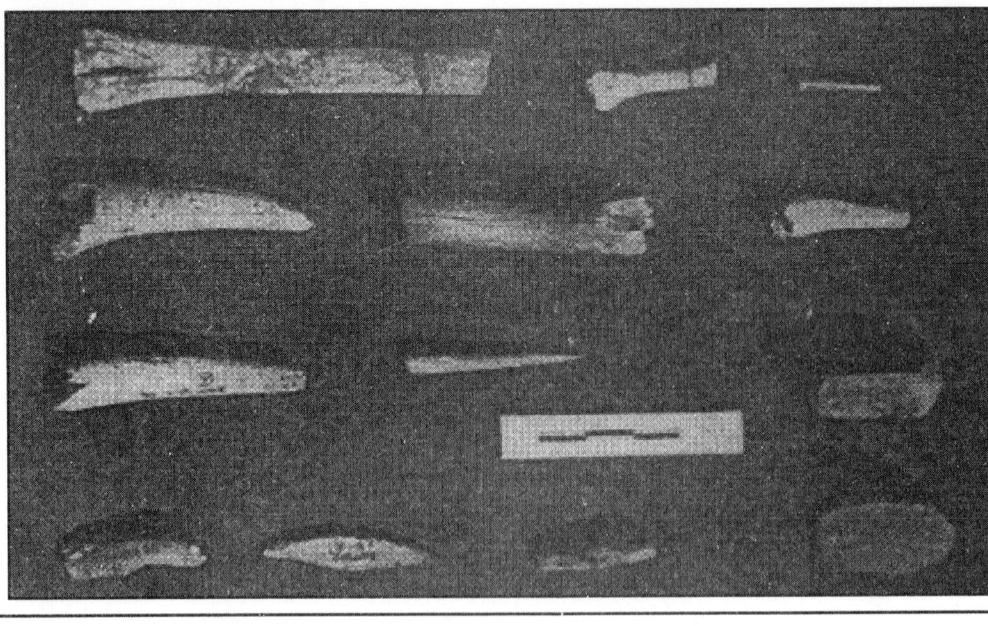

Source: V.N. Mishra, Yashodhara Math Pal and Malti Nagar, 1971, *Bhimbetka: Prehistoric Man and His Arts in Central India.*

FIGURE 293: Bone Tools and Ornaments, Bhimbetka

Source: V.N. Mishra, Yashodhara Math Pal and Malti Nagar, 1971, *Bhimbetka: Prehistoric Man and His Arts in Central India.*

FIGURE 294: Sequence of Cave Painting Styles in Central India, Bhimbetka

Source: V.N. Mishra, Yashodhara Math Pal and Malti Nagar, 1971, *Bhimbetka: Prehistoric Man and His Arts in Central India.*

FIGURE 295: Gond Shrine, Bhimbetka

Source: V.N. Mishra, Yashodhara Math Pal and Malti Nagar, 1971, *Bhimbetka: Prehistoric Man and His Arts in Central India.*

FIGURE 296: Memorial Stones of the Gonds, Bhimbetka

Source: V.N. Mishra, Yashodhara Math Pal and Malti Nagar, 1971, *Bhimbetka: Prehistoric Man and His Arts in Central India.*

FIGURE 297: Acheulian Floor, Bhimbetka

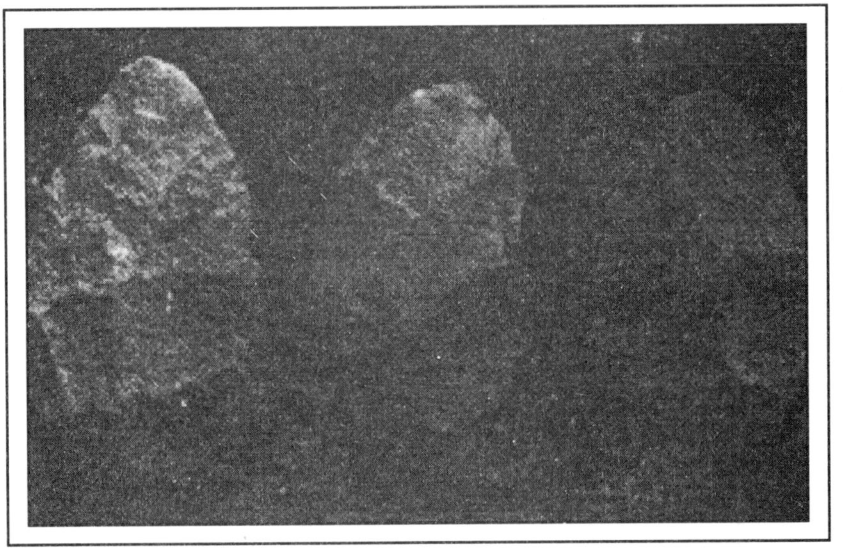

Source: V.N. Mishra, Yashodhara Math Pal and Malti Nagar, 1971, *Bhimbetka: Prehistoric Man and His Arts in Central India.*

FIGURE 298: Acheulian Handaxes, Bhimbetka

Source: V.N. Mishra, Yashodhara Math Pal and Malti Nagar, 1971, *Bhimbetka: Prehistoric Man and His Arts in Central India.*

FIGURE 299: Acheulian Cleavers, Bhimbetka

Bibliography

Agrawal, D.P. (1971): *The Copper Bronze Age in India*, New Delhi: Select Book Services Syndicate.

Agrawal, D.P. (1974): *Prehistoric Chronology and Radio Carbon Dating in India*, New Delhi: Select Book Services Syndicate.

Agrawal, D.P. (1984): *Archaeology of India*, New Delhi: Select Book Services Syndicate.

Ahmad, N. (1966): *Stone Age Cultures of the Upper Son Valley*, Unpublished Ph.D. Thesis, Pune: Deccan College.

Alchin, B. (1959): *The Indian Stone Age: Some New Sites in Central and Southern India and Their Implications*, Bulletin of Archaeology.

Alchin, B. and F.R. Alchin (1968): *The Birth of Indian Civilization*, London: Harmonds Worth.

Alchin, B. and K. Hegde (1978): *The Prehistory and Palaeography of the Great Indian Desert*, London: Academic Press.

Alchin, F.R. and D.K. Chakravarty (1979): *The Source of Indian Archaeology*, Vol. 1, New Delhi: Munshiram Manoharlal.

Ansari, J.D. (1970): "Pebble Tools From Nellur", *Indian Antiquity Series,* Vol. 4, Nos. 1-4, pp. 1-7.

Ansari, J.D. (1970-72): *Stone Age in Kuchchha*, Vol. 31, Poone: Bulletin of Deccan Research Institute.

Banerjee, K.G. (1957): *Middle Palaeolithic Industries of Deccan*, Unpublished Ph.D. Thesis, Pune: Deccan College.

Barnett, A. (1957): *The Human Species: A Biology of Man,* London: Harmonds Worth: Penguin Books.

Bhattacharya, D.K. (1972), *Prehistoric Archaeology*, Delhi: Hindustan Publishing Corporation.

Bhattacharya, D.K. (1989): *An Outline of Indian Prehistory*, New Delhi: Palka Prakashan.

Bose, N.K. and Dharni Sen (1948): *Excavations in Mayurbhanj*, Kolkata: Calcutta University Press.

Bose, N.K. and Dharni Sen (1958): "Geological and Cultural Evidences of Stone Age in Mayurbhanj", *Man in India*, Vol. 38, No. 1.

Bose, N.K., Paril Gupta and Arvinda Bose (1960): "Palaeolithic From Munger District Bihar", *Man in India*, Vol. 40.

Burkitt, M.C. and Cammiade, L.A. (1930): "Fresh Light on the Stone Age in South India", *Indian Antiquity*, Vol. 4.

Burkitt, M.C., Cammiade, L.A. and Richards, F.I. (1931): "Climatic Change in South-East India during early Pleistocene", *Geological Magazine*, No. LXIX.

Cammiade, L.A. and Burkitt, M.C. (1919): "Fresh Light on the Stone Age in South-East India", *Indian Antiquary*, Vol. 4.

Carvinus, Gudrun (1970): *The Acheulian Workshop at Chiraki, the Pravara River*, Maharashtra.

Chard, C.S. (1969): *Man in Prehistory*, London: McGraw Hills & Company.

Charlesworth, J.K. (1966): *The Quarternary Era*, Vol. 4, London: Watts.

Childe, V. Gordon (1956): *New Light on the Most Ancient East*, London: Harmonds Worth.

Childe, V. Gordon, (1925): *The Dawn of European Civilization*, London: Harmonds Worth.

Clark, Grahme (1961): *World Prehistory: An Outline*, Cambridge: Cambridge University Press.

Clark, Grahme (1960): *Archaeology and Society*, London: Methuen University.

Clark, J.D. (1959): *The Prehistory of Southern Africa,* London: Harmonds Worth: Penguin Books.

Daini, A.H. (1960): *Prehistory and Protohistory of Eastern India*, Kolkata: Firma K.L.M.

DeTerra, H. (1939): "The Quarternary Terrace System of Southern Asia and the Age of Man", *Geographical Review*, No. 4.

DeTerra, H. and I.P. Paterson (1939): *Study of Ice Age in India and Associated Human Culture*, Washington: Carnegie Institution.

Deniel, Glyn (1950): *Hundred Years of Archaeology*, London: MacMillan.

Deniel, Glyn (1967a): *The Idea of Prehistory*, London: MacMillan.

Deniel, Glyn (1967b): *The Origin and Growth of Archaeology*, London: MacMillan.

Foote, Robbert Bruce (1886): "On the Occurrence of Stone Age Implements on the Various Parts of Madras and North Arcot District", *Journal of Ancient Society*, Series-III, and Part-II.

Foote, Robbert Bruce (1901): *Catalogue of the Prehistoric Antiquity*, Chennai: Collection of Government Museum.

Foote, Robbert Bruce (1914): *The Foote Collection of Indian Prehistoric and Protohistoric Antiquities: Notes on Their Ages and Distribution*, Chennai: Government Museum.

Ghosh, A.K. (1961): "A Neolithic Site in Mandala District", *Indian Antiquery*, Vol. XIV, No. 3.

Ghosh, A.K. (1964): *Studies on the Palaeolithic Culture of Singhbhum*, Unpublished Ph.D. Thesis, Kolkata: Calcutta University.

Ghosh, A.K. (1970): *Palaeolithic Industries of Eastern India in the Light of Recent Discovery*, Academic Institute of Archaeology, Published by SAV.

Goyal, Sri Ram (1961): *Pragaitihasik Manav Aur Sanskritiyan*, Gorakhpur: Gorakphur University Press.

Hunter, G.R. (1936): "Final Excavations in the Mahadeo Hills", *Ancient Antiquery*, No. 2.

Issac, N. (1970): *Stone Age Cultures of Karnool*, Unpublished Ph.D. Thesis, Pune: Deccan College.

Jain, K.C. (1979): *Prehistory and Protohistory of India*, Delhi: Agamkala Prakashan.

Jaiswal, Vindula (1982): *Chopper-Chopping Components of Palaeolithic India*, Delhi: Agamkala Prakashan.

Jaiswal, Vindula (2006): *Palaeolithic Culture of India*, Delhi: Agamkala Prakashan.

Jaiswal, Vindula (2006): *Mesolithic Culture of India*, Delhi: Agamkala Prakashan.

Jaiswal, Vindula (2006): *Neolithic Culture of India*, Delhi: Agamkala Prakashan.

Khatri, A.P. (1957): *Stone Age Culture of Malda*, Unpublished Ph.D. Thesis, Pune: Deccan College.

Khatri, A.P. (1966): "Origin and Evolution of Hand Axe Culture in Narmada Valley", *Studies in Prehistory* (Ed.) by Sen and Ghosh.

Kosambi, D.D. (1965): *Culture and Civilization of Ancient India*, London: Routledge and Kegan Paul.

Krishna Swamy, B.D. (1938): "Changes of the Prehistoric Man Near Madras", *Journal of Madras Association*, Vol. XIII.

Krishna Swamy, B.D. (1962): "Neolithic Pattern in India", *Ancient India*, Vol. 14.

Lal, B.B. (1956): "Palaeoliths from the Van and Vyas Valleys, Punjab", *Ancient India*, No. 12.

Lal, B.B. and K.B. Nautiyal (1974): *Lower and Middle Palaeolithic Industries*, Seminar, 1974.

MacBanne, C.B.M. (1960): *The Stone Age of Northern Africa*, London: Thames and Hudson.

Mahadevan, I. (1977): *The Indus Script*, Delhi: Archaeological Survey of India.

Makay, E.J.H. (1943): "Chanhudaro Excavation", *A.O.S.*, Vol. 20, pp. 1-338.

Makay, E.J.H. (1948): *Early Indus Civilization*, 2nd Edition, London: MacMillan.
Mallic, S.C. (1959): *Stone Age Industries of Bombay and Santara District*, Pune: Deccan College.
Marshal, John (1931): *Mohenjodaro and Its Civilization*, in three volumes, London: MacMillan.
Math Pal, Yashodhara (1984): *Prehistoric Arts of India*, Delhi: Agamkala Prakashan.
Mishra, V.N. (1961): *The Stone Age Cultures of Rajputana*, Unpublished Ph.D. Thesis, Pune: Deccan College.
Mishra, V.N. (1963): *Palaeolithic Cultures of Western Rajputana*, Pune: Deccan College.
Mishra, V.N. (1967): *Pre and Protohistory of Berach Basin, South Rajputana*, Pune: Deccan College.
Mishra, V.N. (1971): "Microlithic Sites in Rajasthan", *Indian Antiquery*, Vol. 23.
Mishra, V.N. (1974): *The Acheulian Industry of Rockshelter*, Pune: Deccan College.
Mishra, V.N. and M.S. Mathe (ed.) (1965): *Indian Prehistory*, Pune: Deccan College.
Mishra, V.N., Math Pal Yashodhara and Malti Nagar (1971): *Bhimbetka: Prehistoric Man and His Arts in Central India*, Pune: Deccan College.
Mohpatra, G.C. (1962): *The Stone Age Cultures of Orissa*, Pune: Deccan College.
Mohpatra, G.C., S.B. Bhatia and B.K. Sahu: "The Discovery of a Stone Age Site in Indian Desert, Punjab", *University Research Bulletin*, Vol. 14, Part III.
Movius, H.A.L. (1938): "The Lower Palaeolithic Cultures of Southern and Eastern India", *American Philosophical Society*, Vol. 30.
Movius, H.A.L. (1944): *Early Man and Pleistocene Stratigraphy in Southern and Eastern Asia*, Cambridge: Massachusetts.
Movius, H.A.L. (1957): "Pebble Tool Terminology in India and Pakistan", *Man in India*, Vol. 37.
Murray, M.L.K. (1966): *Stone Age Culture of Chittur District*, Unpublished Ph.D. Thesis, Pune: Deccan College.
Murray, M.L.K. (1968): "Blade and Burin Stone Age Industry near Renigunta", *PPS*, Vol. 28, pp. 83-101.
Murray, M.L.K. (1970): "Blade-Burin and Late Stone Age Industries Around Chittur District", *Indian Antiquery*, Vol. 4, Nos. 1-4, pp. 106-128.
Nagar, Malti (1966): *Ahar Culture: An Archaeological and Ethnographic Study*, Unpublished Ph.D. Thesis, Pune: Deccan College.
Nagaraja Rao, M.S. (1971): *Prehistoric Culture of Tungbhadra Valley, Dharwar*, Pune: Deccan College.
Nagaraja Rao, M.S. and K.C. Malhotra (1974): *The Stone Age Hill Dwellers of Tekkalkota*, Pune: Deccan College.
Narain, Lala Aditya (1970): "The Neolithic Settlement of Chirand", *JBRS*, Vol. 66, pp. 1-35.
Noon, V.U. "A Classification of Flint, Burin and Gravers", *Journal of Royal Anthropological Society*, Vol. 64.
Okaley, K.P. (1956): *Man the Tool Maker*, London: Trustees of the British Museum.
Paddayya, K. (1968): *Pre and Protohistoric Investigation in Sherapur Doab*, Unpublished Ph.D. Thesis, Poona: Deccan College.
Paddayya, K. (1970): "The Blade Tool Industry of Sherapur Doab", *I.A.*, Vol. 4, Nos. 1-4, pp. 165-190.
Pandey, Gaya (2010): *Bio-Cultural Evolution*, New Delhi: Concept Publishing Company Pvt. Ltd.
Pandey, Gaya (2012): "Prehistoric Culture of Jharkhand, Ranchi", *Anusandhanika*, Vol. 11, No. 1-2.
Pandey, Gaya (2014): *Bharatiya Pragaitihasik-Puratatvik Manavshastra*, New Delhi: Concept Publishing Company Pvt. Ltd.

Pandey, R.V. (1952): "Indian Palaeography", *I.A.*, Vol. 1, No. 1, pp. 1-10.
Pant, P.C. (1982): *The Prehistoric Uttar Pradesh*, Delhi: Agamkala Prakashan.
Pappu, R.S., *Pleistocene Studies in the Upper Krishna Basin*, Poona: Deccan College.
Rajguru, S.N. (1969): *Study in Late Pleistocene of Mullar Mutha Valley*, Pune: Deccan College.
Reddy, K.T. (1968): *Prehistoric Culture of Kuddupa District*, Poona: Deccan College.
Reddy, V. Rammy (1987): *Elements of Prehistory*, New Delhi: Mittal Publication.
Roy, S.N. (1966): *The Stone Age Culture of Nalgonda District*, Poona: Deccan College.
Sali, S.A. (1970): "Quarternary Stratigraphy in Deccan Basin", *J.A.C.*, Vol. 30-40, pp. 157-167.
Sali, S.A. (1975): "Upper Palaeolithic Research Since Independence", *Bulletin of Deccan College*, Poona.
Sankalia, H.D. (1956): "Animal Fossils and Palaeolithic Industries from the Pravara Basin and Nevasa", *A.E.*, No. 12.
Sankalia, H.D. (1961): "New Evidences for Early Man in Kashmir", *Current Anthropology*, Vols. 4-5.
Sankalia, H.D. (1962): *Indian Archaeology Today*, Poona: Deccan College.
Sankalia, H.D. (1964): *Stone Age Tools*, Pune: Deccan College.
Sankalia, H.D. (1974): *Prehistory and Protohistory of India and Pakistan*, Pune: Deccan College.
Saundarrajan, K.B. (1951): "The Little Tool Industries of Singrauli Basin", *Ancient India*, No. 7.
Saundarrajan, K.B. (1952): "Stone Age Industries Near Giddalur Karnool District", *Ancient India*, No. 8.
Saundarrajan, K.B. (1958): "Study in the Stone Age of Nagarjun Konda and Its Neigbourhood", *Ancient India*, No. 14.
Saundarrajan, K.B. (1961): "Quarternary Pebble Core and Flake Tool Culture of India: An Appraisal", *Ancient India*, No. 18.
Sen, D. (1958): "Nalgarh Palaeolithic Cultures", *Man in India*, Vol. 35.
Sen, D. and A.K. Ghosh (1960): "On the Occurrence of Palaeolithic", *Man in India*, Vol. 40.
Sen, D., A.K. Ghosh and M. Chatterjee (1963): "Palaeolithic Industries of Bankura", *Man in India*.
Sharma, G.R. (1973): "Mesolithic Flake Cultures in Ganga Valley", *PPS*, Vol. 39, pp. 129-146.
Sharma, G.R. (1975): *Seasonal Migrants and Mesolithic Lake Cultures in Ganges Valley*, Allahabad: Allahabad University.
Sharma, T.C. and H.C. Sharma (1974): *Stone Age Cultures of Garo Hills*, Seminar, Indian Prehistory, Poona: Deccan College.
Singh, M.M. (1961): *Puratatwa Ki Rup-Rekha*, Patna: Param Jyoti Prakashan.
Singh, R. (1965): *Palaeolithic Industries of Northern Bundelkhand*, Unpublished Ph.D. Thesis, Poona: Deccan College.
Smith, V.A. (1906): "Pigmy Flints", *Indian Antiquery*, Vol. 35.
Soundar Rajan, K.V. (1952): "Stone Age Industry Near Giddalur", *A.I.*, No. 8, pp. 64-92.
Soundar Rajan, K.V. (1958): "Studies in Stone Age of Nagarjunkonda", *A.I.*, No. 14, pp. 49-113.
Soundar Rajan, K.V. (1960): "Middle Stone Age in Gujarat", *JOI*, Vol. 10, pp. 166-179.
Subba Rao, B. (1948): *Stone Age Culture of Bellary*, Poona: Deccan College.
Subba Rao, B. (1958): *Personality of India*, 2nd Edition, Baroda: M.S. University.
Supekar, S.G. (1968): *Pleistocene Stratigraphy and Prehistoric Archaeology of Central Narmada Basin*, Unpublished Ph.D. Thesis, Poona: Deccan College.
Supekar, S.G. (1974): *A Reappraisal of Pleistocene Stratigraphy and Prehistory of Central Narmada Basin*, Unpublished Ph.D. Thesis, Poona: Deccan College.

Triger, Bush G. (1968): *Beyond History: The Method of Prehistory*, London: John Murray.

Tripathi, Vibha (1976): *The Painted Grey Ware: An Iron Iage Culture of North India*, New Delhi: Concept Publishing Company.

Todd, K.R.U. (1939): *Studies of Ice Age in India and Associated Human Cultures.*

Tylor, E.B. (1871): *Primitive Culture*, London: John Murray.

Verma, R.K. (1969): *Problems of Terminology in Prehistory: In the Light of New Evidences*, Varanasi: Proceedings of Indian Prehistory Congress.

Verma, R.K. (1970): *Bharatiya Pragaitihasa*, Allahabad: Param Jyoti Prakashan.

Verma, R.K. (1974): *Upper Palaeolithic Industries of Belan Valley*, Seminar, Poona: Deccan College.

Verma, R.K. (1977): *Bharatiya Pragaitihasika Sanskritiyan*, Allahabad: Param Jyoti Prakashan.

Wheeler, R.E.M. (1959): *Archaeology from the Earth*, London: Pelicon Book.

Wheeler, R.E.M. (1959): *Early India and Pakistan*, London: MacMillan.

Wheeler, R.E.M. (1965): *Civilization of Indus Valley and Beyond*, London: MacMillan.

Wheeler, R.E.M. (1968): *The Indus Civilization*, 3rd Edition, Cambridge: Supplementary Volume to Cambridge History of India.

Zeuner, F.E. (1950): *Stone Age Chronology in Gujarat*, Pune: Deccan College.

Zeuner, F.E. (1952): *Microlithic Industries of Langhnaj*, Pune: Deccan College.

Zeuner, F.E. (1958): *Dating the Past*, London: John Murray.

Zeuner, F.E. (1959): *Pleistocene Period*, 3rd Edition, London: John Murray.

Zeuner, F.E. (1961): *Environment of Early Man with Special Reference to Tropical Regions*, Baroda: M.S. University.

Zeuner, F.E. and B. Alchin (1956): "Microlithic Sites of Tinne Valley, Madras", *Ancient India*, No. 12, pp. 4-30.

INDEX